Please send S.A.S.E. when writing Bud Hastin for encyclopedia information.

This book is updated and the latest information on Avon collecting is released to the public every two years. Send your name and address to Bud Hastin to be first to know when the next book will be released. Be sure to include the edition of the book you last purchased.

Bud Hastin's

Avon & C.P.C. Collector's Encyclopedia™

The official Guide For Avon Bottle Collectors

15th Edition

Published, Written, Photographed and Researched by Bud Hastin
P.O. Box 9868, Kansas City, MO 64134

The Bud Hastin's Avon & C.P.C. Collectors Encyclopedia™ is recognized by Avon Collectors and Avon Representatives as the official and only complete collector's guide in print.

AVON COLLECTING FOR THE MILLENNIUM

Dear Avon Collectors,

Certain Avon Items Have Been Removed From This Book. Avon collecting has changed many times since 1967 when collectors first started saving Avon Decanters. Many Avon items and even complete categories of items that were once very popular can not be given away today. You will find this true with almost anything in life.

Remember, if its a household kitchen or decorator item and not marked Avon on the product we do not feel it is a true Avon Collectible. **It must be marked Avon on the product.** We have removed all Christmas Tree ornaments and hanging ornaments, that do not have the Avon name or logo or the year or date on each item. **Collect only ornaments that can be identified as Avon.**

Avon Plates are still very popular, but most collectors only want porcelain, ceramic or glass plates. Pewter plates are not desirable and most collectors will not want them.

Candles are popular in Glass, Ceramic or in Wax, only in Figural type design. The wax candles must have Avon on them. Do not collect taper candles of any kind, they are not marked Avon and will not stand and display on their own. All taper candles have been removed from this book. We have included all candles made by Avon that are now collectible.

Soaps of all kinds are very popular in the Avon line. **Soaps must not be damaged in any way. If they are, we suggest not buying them. All Soaps must be in New Mint Boxed Condition.**

We have used the Inflation Index method to reprice many older Men's and Women's Decanters, Candles and Plates. The new products now issued by Avon are much higher in original issue cost. They cost more than similar, much older items we had priced in past books. We feel if you will pay the price to get a new item from your Avon Representative that is plentiful, you should be willing to pay the same price for older and much harder to find Avon Collectibles in Mint Condition.

Avon Representative Awards and Gifts are still very popular with many collectors. We have removed some items in the Award section. Many Paper items, Purses & Bags, Clothing, Scarfs and Award Plaques that are not national level awards, and trophies have been removed. **All awards should be marked Avon on the award or an Avon trademark.**

We have weeded out many items in each of these categories and left many in. Most of this type of item is becoming less popular over the years. **If you have any of these items and they are not pictured in this book, just use a item in this book that is similar to get a price for the current value.**

Most of the avid Award collectors tell me they are now only interested in Awards that are given on a National level. They must fit on a shelf or hang on a wall and display well. If they don't fit this description, they will not appeal to the next collector when you decide to sell your collection.

A word of warning! I know how excited many collectors get to get a new item or award and pay a big price to get it, then find it much lower in price in a few months. This is particularly true with the Albee Figurine Awards. I have seen this happen on every Albee Award to date. Have patience. Wait a few months and you will save a lot.

National Association of Avon Clubs are no longer issuing Club Bottles, Plates or Convention Bells. There will be no new items of this type in the future in NAAC collectibles.

I hope this information helps guide you in your Avon Collecting.

Bud Hastin

NOTE: Bud Hastin lives in Ft. Lauderdale, Florida but all book orders are processed in Kansas City, Mo.

When writing to Bud Hastin, Box 9868, Kansas City, MO 64134 for information of any kind please send a (SASE) self addressed stamped envelope.

A Short History Of Bud Hastin's Life _____

Wilbur H. "Bud" Hastin was born April 24, in Butler, Missouri, a small farm town south of Kansas City, MO. His father was an automobile dealer and taught Bud many of the things he would need in his life.

The most important thing was to always be honest and be self-reliant. Bud grew up with a burning desire to achieve success in everything he did, and see and learn as much about this wonderful world as he could. Bud opened his first bank savings account at age 9 and it continued to grow through his childhood business ventures. For years, Bud picked up every pop and beer bottle within 3 miles of Butler. He then moved on to his own bicycle repair shop. By the time he got to high school and at age 14 he was cutting grass. At age 17 Bud was cutting 55 yards a week and making more money than most men in Butler.

After finishing high school he joined the U.S. Air Force and became a fireman. His first day on the flight line in Denver, Colorado, he witnessed a jet crash and watched 2 pilots burn to death. He knew then how precious life was and to live to its fullest from that day on. After a year in Denver and 2 years on the Japanese island of Okinawa, Bud returned to Butler, Mo. to work for his father at "Hastin Glass Company." Bud spent more of his time running a used car lot and making 40' grain trailer truck tarps for all the local truckers than he did working for his father. After 18 months of this, Wilbur, Sr., fired Wilbur, Jr. He told Bud he would be better off working for himself. They laughed years later and said it was the best thing that ever happened to Bud.

Bud went to Ft. Lauderdale, Florida in 1963 for 1 year working in the auto glass business before returning to Kansas City. He went to work for an auto glass company which lasted for 3 months. The owners were always fighting and Bud decided he had worked for others long enough. This was to be his last job. With a young wife and 2 baby girls, "Roxanne and Stephanie", Bud bought an old 1949 van truck for $75.00. He put his tools in the truck (which had no heater for the cold Kansas City winters), had $50.00 to his name and started down the street in Kansas City stopping at every auto dealership asking for glass business. He knew no one but had a burning desire to succeed. He says he made more money the first day on his own than he ever made working for someone else. He knew then he would never work for anyone else again.

Bud says his career in auto glass peaked when he made $504.00 profit in one day. His worse day was after he had shot himself in the right kneecap while hunting with his 11 year old nephew in Butler a week before Christmas in 1970. The very next day, it was 15 degrees and Bud had to put in 10 wind-shields outside in the cold. He said his leg was killing him but he always put business first. He was so busy that by the third day, he had forgotten about the pain and didn't even know he had been shot. He says that when you are busy, you don't have time to think about your problems.

By June of 1971, Bud had already published his first 3 books on Avon collecting and the book business was getting much bigger than the auto glass business. He decided to go full-time into the publishing business. This business exploded on Bud and up to now with this 15th edition on Avon Collecting, Bud has written, photographed, researched and published 763,300 books on Avon collecting. In 1971, when Avon collecting really started to take-off, he started the "Bud Hastin Avon Collectors Club." He said, "If we have a book about collecting Avons, then we need a source to buy, sell or trade

Avons on a national scale." Within one year, Bud had over 1,000 members subscribing to the monthly newsletter, He would build his club to over 6,500 members. The club name was later changed to "Avon Times" as it is today. Bud sold "Avon Times" to Dwight and Vera Young in 1982, the present owners and publishers.

Bud decided in early 1971 to organize all the smaller local clubs around the country into one organization under the name of "National Association of Avon Collectors." This organization thrived and grew to over 200 clubs.

In 1972, at the first N.A.A.C. convention in Kansas City, Bud had created and sold the idea of a "National Avon Collector's Club bottle series." The first club bottle was sold to all club members for $10.95 and the resale price rose to $250.00 over the years. Bud continued to create and produce these limited edition club bottles and club bells until 1986. Bud served as founder and chairman of the board of the N.A.A.C. until he retired in 1986.

Back in 1970, Bud thought if Avon and others could sell bottles, "Why couldn't he?" He then started out with a series of cologne filled bird and animal bottles under the name of "Collector's Art." This is when he started doing business in Japan making fine detailed hand-painted limited edition porcelain bottles. He then branched out his collectors art line to include whiskey bottles. All of these series were filled and distributed by McCormick distilling company in Western, Mo. under Bud's personal whiskey label, "Collector's Art." The bottle business ran out of steam in 1985 for Bud but not before over 100 different collector bottles were created and distributed in all 50 states.

In 1972, Bud took his first trip out of the U.S., since he came back from Okinawa in 1960. From 1972 to 1998, Bud has traveled to 134 different foreign countries. It is this love of travel that has taught Bud about every corner of this planet and all the differences of the people. Traveling is Bud's personal hobby and he hopes to travel to at least 250 countries before he can't go anymore. Bud also wrote a book on "Travel by Eurail to 24 Countries of Europe." He sold this book in 1990 to a European publisher.

He likes to keep up on world events. Bud left Kansas City as his home in 1979 and moved to Ft. Lauderdale, Florida. In 1981 he moved to Las Vegas, Nevada and returned to Ft. Lauderdale, Florida in 1988 where he and his wife Sondra Hitchcock Hastin now reside.

Besides publishing, Bud invented a shower head water saver valve in 1975 and sold it all over the world wherever there was a shortage of water. In 1979, Bud produced a full length motion picture called, "Scream for Vengeance," which was sold and distributed worldwide but never in the U.S. theaters. It was sold in the U.S. video stores.

In 1991, Bud bought an old waterfront home in Ft. Lauderdale. He designed most of it and contracted it himself and tore most of the old house down. Nine months later it was done and won first place for the best new designed and landscaped home in the beach area of northeast Ft. Lauderdale. Bud said he always wanted to be a contractor and wanted to see if he could do it. "I knew I was working hard 16 hour days 7 days a week, but never expected to win an award for my first house." He lives in the only area of Ft. Lauderdale where you can water ski in your backyard. He says it reminds him of the 15 years he spent going to the Lake of the Ozarks when he lived in Missouri. Bud's major regret is his father, who died of cancer in 1990, never got a chance to see him build his house since his father was also a builder. Bud has always believed that hard work brings good benefits no matter what it is you do in life. There is no success without effort. "I believe you can do anything you want in life if you have the desire to do it and the willingness to do what is necessary to achieve that success."

Bud's lifelong idol is Ray Kroc, the founder of McDonalds. Mr. Kroc was 55 years old when he changes careers and started McDonalds as a poor man. Before he died he had built one of the most successful companies in the world and one of the biggest personal fortunes for himself. Bud says, "If Ray Kroc can do it, so can we, at whatever we want in life."

"Avon Calling" is a registered trade mark of Avon Products

The phrase "Avon Calling" rings 'round the world' as the signature of a firm devoted to the manufacture and sales of high quality cosmetic and toiletry items for all members of the family.

From its start in 1886 as the California Perfume Company, Avon has grown steadily, expanding its operation throughout the world. Today fourteen manufacturing laboratories and twenty-five distribution branches, all using the most modern and efficient equipment and all staffed by well trained and experienced employees, produce a vast variety of ever changing, imaginative products.

The Avon representative, focal point of the company, employs the oldest method of distribution in the world . . . direct-to-the-home selling. This means she brings the latest news in beauty and grooming, the finest products, and the most personal kind of service directly to her customers in their homes.

Avon's growth from a one room laboratory in down town New York to the current world wide network of manufacturing laboratories and distribution branches is a success story based on quality... quality of product, quality of service, quality of relationships with people.

Avon is the worlds largest manufacturer and distributor of cosmetics, fragrances and costume jewelry. Its products are sold by more than 1,600,000 active Representatives to customers in the home in the United States and other countries. Plus their products are sold in almost every country in the world.

1969

1970

1971

1971

1972

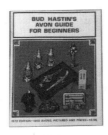

1972

1974

1976

1979

1981

1982

1984

Avon Collecting:
One of Today's Best Hobbies

Bud Hastin's father was responsible for getting him interested in the bottle hobby when someone gave him some fancy cut glass bottles and Bud liked them so much that he started collecting.

The Avon hobby as a whole, covers a tremendous volume of material. There is far too much to collect for the average person to work on all categories. **No.1 Rule in Avon Collecting:** "Set a goal for your hobby and collect only what you want to collect." You rule the hobby, it doesn't rule you. Decide what part of the overall hobby appeals to you, set your goal and work hard toward that goal. Ask yourself some questions. How much room do I have? How much can I spend each month? What do I enjoy most about Avon Collecting? Base your goal on the answer.

Since 1969 Bud has sold over 763,300 copies of his Avon Collectors book. This book is the 15th book on Avon collecting by Bud Hastin. The first, being sold in 1969, was the Avon Collectors Guide, Vol. 1, then followed the 1970 Avon Collectors Guide Vol. II, The Avon Collectors Encyclopedia, the 1971 Avon Collectors Guide for Beginners, the 1972 Avons Collectors Encyclopedia, the 1972 Avon Beginners Guide, the 1974 Avon Collectors Encyclopedia, and the Avon Collectors Encyclopedia special hardbound edition for collectors. Only 1,000 were printed and each was signed by Bud.

Bud Hastin, Author / Publisher

The 1976-77 Avon Collectors Encyclopedia - There were 500 hardbound copies of the 1976 Avon Collectors Encyclopedia - There were 350 special hardbound collectors editions of the 1979 Encyclopedia, 1982-83 Encyclopedia, 1984 Encyclopedia, 1987 Encyclopedia, 1991 Avon Price Guide, 1995 and 1998 Encyclopedia. Many people are starting to collect the older Avon books published by Bud.

Bud's personal views on collecting are: "I think the Avon collecting hobby is the best hobby around today. It is one of the few hobbies that you will probably never find all of them and that's what collecting is all about, the challenge to find something you don't have. The thrill is finding a high priced Avon bottle in a flea market or garage sale for a low price. You see very few Avon collections the same and this always makes the challenge greater to find the one that your friend has. Avon collecting is one of the biggest hobbies in the U.S. I wonder how many of the old and rare C.P.C. and Avon bottles are lying around in somebodies attic and cellars just waiting to be discovered by some informed collector ? Garage sales, rummage sales, etc. are the gold fields and it is almost as big a thrill to find a $100.00 C.P.C. as it was for the treasure hunters of old to find gold. Avon collecting is for all ages, both young and old. It's a hobby for the entire family.

1987

1991

National Association Of Avon Collectors

Bud was the founder of the National Association of Avon Collectors Clubs in 1971 and served as Chairman of its Board of Directors until 1986. The N.A.A.C. is not a club, but an organization to help promote Avon collecting world wide. The N.A.A.C. is run by an elected Board of Directors. The N.A.A.C. is ready to help anyone start a new Avon collectors club in your area. For information on starting a new Avon Collectors Club, write to N.A.A.C. in care of Bud Hastin and we will assure all N.A.A.C. material is sent to you. At present there are over 60 active Avon Collectors Clubs in the N.A.A.C. A National Convention is held each year along with a National Avon Bottle Show. Each year it is held in a different section of the U.S. The N.A.A.C. is a non-profit organization. See the N.A.A.C. section of this book for N.A.A.C. Club Bottles. These club bottles are very limited editions.

New Products 1984 and Newer:
How They Are Priced & What Is Truly Collectable

Avon collecting has matured and is in for some adjustment and a little regulation. Avon Products has expanded their product lines to include many products that do not seem to fit into an Avon collection. They are making a number of household products, decorator items, and etc., that are not marked Avon or have an Avon trademark on them or labels. We suggest that this type of product be purchased for the purpose it was intended and not as a collectable. If we include everything in the book that Avon is mass producing, this book would be 1000 pages thick and most of it with little or no value as a collectable.

I, along with many others I have talked to in the last couple of years, agree that unless it is marked Avon on the product, don't collect it to put in an Avon collection. It will never have any real value. We have also found little or no interest in cosmetic fragrance lines newer than 1975. This applies both to men's and women's products. For this reason we have taken out all fragrance lines 1975 or newer. The only products in these lines to collect are soaps, sets, and awards after 1975. These products are produced in the millions of pieces. There will never be a resale market for this type of product in our lifetime.

We want Avon Collecting to be as exciting as possible but for the prices to be fair to all concerned.

What Is Hot And What Is Not In Avon Collecting

For the absolute best advise in Avon collecting, nothing can beat something old and in new condition. This of course is the California Perfume Company products. This is the original Avon Product's name from the late 1800's to 1939 when the name was changed to Avon Products Inc. as it remains today. Almost anything in mint condition with the CPC label will sell quickly and usually bring a good price. **It's like any other collectable, the older the better.** DECANTERS, FIGURINES, both men's and women's, SOAPS, KID'S TOYS, SETS, AVON REPRESENTATIVE AWARDS, OLD FRAGRANCE LINES both men's and women's, PERFECTION PRODUCTS, OLD MISC. BOTTLES 1935 or older. These are the collectables that are hot if they are older and in mint condition.

What Not To Collect For Future Resale

We have removed from this book all items listed because they are mass produced in the millions of pieces and may never have a value for resale. We have left only the older items in each category that is truly rare or harder to find for a collection. Any new items will not be included in this book in the future as collectors just do not want them. We suggest you dispose of them.

Items not to collect are all tubes, tin cans, misc. bottles, stuffed animals or non porcelain head dolls, any plastic bottle unless it is part of a set or a children's toy unless it is listed in this book. This goes both for American and Canada and Foreign products. All fragrance lines from 1975 up should be avoided as there is little or no resale market for them. **Any Avon item may be collectible after a period of 30 to 50 years. Otherwise when they become a antique. People will buy anything old.**

Collect only what you truly enjoy for yourself. You may collect any of the things I have listed as not collectable as long as you understand that there is not much of a resale market for them. Otherwise when you are done with them, dispose of them. Happy collecting.

Helpful Hints And Meaning Of Terms In Book

The Avon Collectors Encyclopedia has been compiled by Bud Hastin. **To best understand this book and its contents, please read this before starting through the book.**

All items from 1929 to 1984 will give the first year and the last year date that the items were sold by the Avon Company. Dates will read, for instance, 1930-36. This means this item was introduced sometime in 1930 and was discontinued for the last time in 1936. Dates like 1970-71 mean the item sold in both years, but is very possible it sold for less than one year selling time. An item dated for three years like 1958-60 means it sold in all three years, but could have only been on the market for a period of about two years total time. All items dated 1886 to 1928 mean the first and last year sold. All dates from 1929 to 1983 with only one year given, means this item was sold during that one year only and usually for a very short period. These items are usually considered a short-issue and hard to find. 1984 and up gives only the issue date.

O.S.P. means Original Selling Price. This is the full value price Avon puts on an item. It does not represent a special selling price which is from 20% to 50% off the O.S.P.

C.M.V. means Current Market Value that most collectors are willing to pay for that particular item. Many items priced in this book are priced both item only and item in box. Items in the original box need not be full. The collectors price is for an empty bottle. If it is current and full, and in the box, then you can expect to pay full retail price or the special selling price that Avon sells this item for. Only after Avon stops selling the and demand for that item rises, will it be considered as a Collectors item and the value may start to increase.

B.O. means bottle only mint, no box. M.B. means mint and boxed in perfect condition.

All Avon tubes priced in this book are for full mint condition tubes. If a tooth paste tube or other type tube has been used then it would not be mint. Tubes and soaps are the only items in this book that have to be full to be mint condition. Most all other items are priced empty unless otherwise stated. In most cases all older items will bring as much empty as they would full.

This book has been compiled from original CPC and Avon Catalogs. Original California Perfume Company catalogs used in the Avon Collectors Encyclopedia have been copied completely and all items pictured in these original catalogs are pictured in this book. The CPC was used from the years 1896 to 1929. From 1916 to 1929 the CPC sales catalogs were black leather type covers. 1916 to 1923 these books were hard bound. 1924 to 1929 the same size books were soft cover bound. January, 1929, was the introduction of Avon Products with the Avon name first appearing on a number of CPC products.

The CPC sales catalogs 1896 to 1906 were smaller booklet type with soft covers measuring 6 5/8" x 4 3/4". The 1915 book is dated and measures 4" x 7 1/8". 1930 through 1935 the Avon sales catalogs had CPC/Avon Products in them in a 6 3/4" x 10" dark blue soft cover book. 1936 through 1957 the sales catalogs are the same size only with a green cover.

An entire set of Avon sales catalogs from 1930 to present were used to compile the Avon Collectors Encyclopedia. A complete set of Avon Sales Outlook or Avon Calling from 1905 to 1993 were also used. Special Christmas sales catalogs from 1934 to present were also used showing many special sets sold only at Christmas time each year.

Grading Condition of Avons

People have asked me **WHAT A BOTTLE IS WORTH WITHOUT A LABEL.** If it's an old bottle where the label is the main thing that identifies the bottle and it is missing, then it's worth whatever you can get, which is usually not too much. If it is a new figural bottle, then it will usually take a few dollars off the price.

MINT CONDITION means items must be in new condition as originally sold, with all labels bright and correct, and cap and/or stopper. Items need not be full or boxed, but will bring a higher price in most cases if they are in the box. All items in the book are priced empty in mint condition only with the right cap and all labels. Bottles with no cap or label are of little or no value.

IF ANY AVON IS DAMAGED IN ANY WAY - I WOULD NOT BUY IT.
Collect only mint Avons
and throw away the less than mint ones in the Avon Line.

IF ANYTHING IS TOO BADLY DAMAGED,
DON'T BUY IT OR SELL IT!

CPC bottles may have the same shape but with different labels. Be sure to check labels and boxes to get the right date on your bottles.

All items are dated in this book from actual old Avon catalogs. They did not change the bottles for many years in the early days of CPC. 1896 was the first year a CPC catalog was printed.

TO BUY AND SELL AVONS. Garage sales, flea markets, antique shops, bottle shops are the best places to buy and sell Avon bottles locally. To sell Avons in your own town, place a small ad in your local paper and say Avon bottles for sale with your address or phone number. Have a garage sale and put Avon bottles on your sign. People will come to you. If you have no luck locally, **The Avon Times is the number one spot in the U.S. to sell those extra Avons.** The Avon Times is the largest in the world and Avon ads get the best result anywhere. Write **Avon Times, P.O. Box 9868, Kansas City, MO 64134, for a sample copy of this club magazine. Send $3.00 for sample copy.**

"Don't Pay Too Much":
Pricing "Current Market Value"

All pricing in this book for CMV has been set by several qualified Avon bottle dealers and collectors across the United States. The prices reflected are what the item is actually selling for in their respective areas. While many items have increased in value, some have been lowered, only slightly. This in no way reflects a fall out in the market of Avon collecting. It is stronger today than ever and we are trying to reflect the approximate true collector's value; or what a collector will actually pay for the item in Mint condition. All items are priced empty unless otherwise stated. There are several reasons for pricing all items empty. After Shave bottles are known to explode in sun light or heat. Full bottles sitting on glass shelves increase the chance of the shelves breaking. After a few years, the contents become spoiled or unsafe to skin and dangerous in the hands of children. I feel if you buy the item new, use the contents and you will still have the pretty bottles. On the pricing of new Avon products dated 1978 to 1995, the CMV is usually the same as the Special Selling Price Avon sold it for, or it is priced a little under the SSP. The future CMV on these products may very well fall somewhat in future issues of this book to reflect the true collector's value. <u>Remember, the price paid to the Avon Representative is not a collector's price, but a new product price. You are paying for the contents. After you use the product, the price usually goes down and it becomes a collectable.</u> It takes some time for the item to become scarce on the collector's market before you see a true collector's price. **It could take up to twenty years or more for an intem to increase in value over the original selling price from Avon.**

What Is CMV?

Current Market Value - Definition: A willing buyer and a willing seller with neither under duress to make the transaction.

What makes an Avon valuable? Shape, color, unusual design, scarcity and how well it will display:

a. Too big - takes too much room
b. Too small - gets lost in collection
c. Odd shapes - doesn't fit shelves, also takes too much room

Condition: Refer to coin collectors. **Mint means perfect condition, unused, exceptional and undamaged.** Mint commands top dollar:

a. Boxes were made to protect the container, keeping it clean and brilliant. Boxes advertise the product and instruct the user. Boxes tell a story. When you say original condition, that was with a box. Boxes (especially men's) were usually thrown away immediately. A good clean, crisp box will help make the item bring a premium.
b. Grading and condition become even more important for an item with a CMV over $25.00.
c. Example: 1966-67 Tall Pony Post. The box is probably the hardest to find of the modern figurals. Box should have a premium price.

Sets - The bug-a-boo of Avon grading!! Many sets have a premium value because they display so well. They are packaged in unusual ways and are much harder to find with perfect box and superior contents. I agree with the statement: Poor box - poor set, subtract 50% to 75% of listed value.

A mint box is at least twice as hard to obtain as the mint bottle that came in it. As good as Avon is in packing - order 10 items of the same thing and only 4 will be truly mint boxes and containers. That is: creased or crushed box, corner of label not securely glued.

Several people ask about **INSURANCE ON BOTTLE COLLECTIONS.** Bottle insurance is available through your home owners policy. Check with your local agent.

Bottles will differ in color shades due to various dates in manufacture. It is difficult to get exactly the same color each time. Unless a bottle comes out in a completely different color, it will be of the same value. **THE SILVER METAL SALT & PEPPER SHAKERS WITH AVON PAT.DATE 1926-28,** are not Avon Cosmetic Co. items. **THE AVON NAME WAS NOT USED UNTIL 1929.** The name Avon has been used by several companies and still is. Only the name Avon Products Incorporated is copyrighted.

Rules For Collecting

"The hunger to find a tin toy for $30.00, rather than a good night's sleep drives a painter to wake up at three in the morning in his Brooklyn home. He's rushing to Renneger's flea market in Pennsylvania by the time the rosy fingers of dawn peak over the tents." Does this sound familiar? Of course it does, if you're an Avon collector. How many foolish things have you ever done while seeking that hoped-for bargain or very much sought after item? People are doing this kind of thing in every part of America - and they are doing it for almost anything you could name; be it a tin toy or a campaign button. In today's market, anything is collectible if it has aesthetic value, if it's pleasing to the eye and to the senses. However, we are interested in Avon and California Perfume. . . and Avon collecting is now a big collecting field. For the new collectors and to refresh seasoned collectors - we have found collecting, like other investments, has rules to follow for the best results:

- If you don't like an item, don't buy it no matter how much of a bargain it seems to be. The only good investments are those that are enjoyed.

- The old goes up in value, or at least retains its resale value. New items take longer to increase in value and stay around longer. Of course, we all know, there are more collectors today.

- Buy it when you see it. Avons don't stay put . . .some don't have a very long shelf life.

- If you don't know your dealers, be sure you know your Avons. Fakes can be convincing (don't we all know that!).

- It is acceptable to haggle - it cannot hurt to ask if there is a lower price. Often in a booth or flea market there will be a better price available - don't be timid.

- Start small and learn the market. Browse, study the guides and learn all you can before you start buying.

- Measure your space - don't be the collector who buys a lot of items only to bring them home with no place to put them (ha, ha).

- Don't change your item in any way - don't paint it, add lettering, etc. . .this may destroy the value.

The above rules are good ones to keep in mind - the advice I've found most helpful is to have FUN while collecting . . .whether it be at a flea market, garage sale or convention.

A HISTORY OF THE
CALIFORNIA PERFUME CO.
NOW AVON PRODUCTS INCORPORATED

Written by the Founder, D. H. McConnell, Sr., in 1903

To give you a sketch or history of the birth and growth of the *California Perfume Company is, in a measure, like writing an autobiography. Our lives have become so identical and so interwoven that it seems almost impossible to separate us, even in history. I will ask you, therefore, to pardon whatever personal reference I may make of myself in describing to you how the California Perfume Company has become the largest of its kind, not only in the United States, but I believe, in the entire world.

In 1878, when but a mere lad, I left my father's farm located near Oswego City, New York State. Here I spent my boyhood days, and through hard work and proper training developed a good, strong, hardy, rugged constitution. When I started out in the world "to make my fortune", I had this positive advantage over many who were less favored.

My first experience in the business world was as a book agent. I took this up during my school vacation, and developed quite a faculty for talking, which I have since learned is quite essential, and has stood me well in hand many times.

My success in canvassing was such as to invite me into the same field the following year, and after two years hard work in the canvass, I was promoted from local canvasser to that of General Traveling Agent. As General Agent I traveled in nearly every state east of the Rocky Mountains; this gave me a valuable knowledge regarding the country. And my experience, both as canvasser and as General Agent, gave me a good insight into human nature.

It is uninteresting to you to follow me through the different work from Chicago to New York and from New York to Atlanta, Georgia, and back to Chicago, and finally back to New York. During all these years I represented in different ways the same publishing company with which I originally started as a canvasser; canvassing, appointing and drilling agents; starting and drilling General Agents, and corresponding with both after they once entered the field. My work as a canvasser and on the road taught me not to enter right into the everyday work of the canvasser and advise and encourage, so as to obtain the best results. If I learned to be anything, I learned to be practical.

The book business was not congenial to me, although I was, in every sense, successful in it, but there were many things that were not pleasant.

On my return from Chicago, I purchased the entire business from my employer and managed it myself for sometime. During this time the one thing I learned successfully was how to sell goods to the customer.

My ambition was to manufacture a line of goods that would be consumed, used up, and to sell it through canvassing agents, direct from the factory to the consumer.

The starting of the perfume business was the result of most careful and thorough investigation, guided by the experience of several years successful operation in the book business. That is, in selling goods direct to the consumer or purchaser. I learned during this time that the proper and most advantageous way of selling goods was to be able to submit the goods themselves to the people. In investigating this matter nearly every line of business was gone over, and it seemed to me, then, as it has since been proved, that the perfume business in its different branches afforded the very best possible opportunity to build up a permanent and well established trade. Having once decided that the perfume business was the business, the question naturally presented itself, "By what name are these perfumes to be known: by what name is this company to be called?" The gentleman who took me from the farm as a boy became in the past years, not only my employer but my personal friend, and after buying him out he moved to California, and while there wrote me glowing accounts of the country, and to him belongs the idea of the name California, as associated with this business.

I started the perfume business in a space scarcely larger than an ordinary kitchen pantry. At first I manufactured but five odors: Violet, White Rose, Heliotrope, Lily-of-the-Valley, and Hyacinth. I did much experimental work in making these odors, and the selling price to the first batch of perfumes I made did not cover one-half the actual cost of the goods, but experience is a great teacher, and I applied myself to the task of making perfumes with the same vim and energy that I had in selling books and after a short time, I fancied that I could produce as fine an odor as some of the old and tried perfumes. At least my perfumes pleased my customers; they were the natural perfumes of the flower, made in the most natural way and by the process employed by the large French perfumers.

I soon found it necessary to increase the odors, and to add to the line other articles for the toilet. Among those first put out were: Shampoo Cream, Witch Hazel Cream, Almond Cream Balm, Tooth Paste, which afterwards was made into the Tooth Tablet, Toilet Waters, etc.
As the business increased the laboratory must, of necessity grow, so that at the end of two years I was occupying one entire floor in this building for manufacturing purposes alone.

It is perhaps unfair to note the progress of one side of the business without carrying with it the natural development on the other.

My ambition was to manufacture a line of goods superior to any other, to be moneyed value into the goods themselves, and just enough money in the package to make them respectable, and as stated above, take these goods through canvassing agents direct from the laboratory to the consumer.

While in the book business I had in my employ as *General Traveling Agent, a Mrs. P.F.E. Albee, of Winchester, NH. Mrs. Albee was one of the most successful General Agents

**Mrs. P.F.E. Albee
1st CPC-Avon Sales Lady**

I had in the book work, and it was in her hands I placed the first sample case, or outfit, in the perfume business. Mrs. Albee was the only General Agent employed for the first six months of the business. During that time she secured a number of good workers, some of whom are with us today. It is, therefore, only befitting that we give her the honorary title of Mother of the California Perfume Company. For the system that we now use for distributing our goods is the system that was put in practical operation by Mrs. Albee.

As the business grew, through the work of our agents, we were forced from time to time to increase our laboratory space, and in 1895 we built our own laboratory in Suffern, New York, 32 miles out on the main line of the Erie Railroad. This building has been enlarged and remodeled three different times, until today we have a building 120 feet long, main building 50 feet wide and the wing 30 feet, all three stories and basement giving us four working floors, each floor having 4,800 square feet of floor space, or a total floor capacity of 17,200 feet. This building is equipped with the best possible machinery, the latest devices for bottling goods and so on, until I feel we can truthfully say that there is not a plant of our kind in the country so large and so well fitted for our business, as the laboratory of the California Perfume Company.

As well directed efforts and hard work must eventually win their way to the front, so the manufacturing end of the California Perfume Company grew out of my hands; that is to say, I found that it was almost impossible for me to manufacture, to give the personal attention to both manufacturing and correspondence which the merits of each required. Therefore, in 1896, I secured the services of the best perfumer I could find, a gentleman who had been in the perfume business himself for 25 years and had the reputation in New York and vicinity for making the finest perfumes on the American market. In order to secure his services I was obliged to buy out his business and close up his laboratory, and he now has full charge of the manufacturing of every ounce of goods we put out.

My object in locating the laboratory at Suffern was that as Suffern is my home I can give much more personal attention and supervision to the affairs of the laboratory than if it was located in New York. So that every day in the year, unless when I am out on one of my trips, visiting agents and general agents, I am at the laboratory every morning, and spend an hour with our chemist, going over his work and see that every ounce of goods, every package in every department is made and put up in the best possible shape.

Contrast, if you please, the appearance of our office today with that of when Mrs. Albee first started out with the California Perfume Company's goods. Then, I had one stenographer, and I myself filled the position of correspondent, cashier, bookkeeper, shipping clerk, office boy, and manufacturing chemist. Today we have on our weekly payroll over 125 employees. Mrs. Albee for the first six months was the only general agent on the road. Today we have 48 general agents traveling over this country and selecting and drilling agents for this work. The first six months we had perhaps 100 agents in the field, today we have over 10,000 good, honest, industrious and energetic Depot Managers. All of you have your own customers, so that it is difficult to accurately estimate today the vast number of families that are using our goods. If each of you have 100 customers, or sell goods to only one different family, we are supporting goods to at least one million families in the United States. This will give you an idea of the magnitude of our business. The growth of the California Perfume Company only emphasizes what energy and fair dealing with everyone can accomplish. We propose first to be fair to our customers - your customers - by giving them the very best goods that can be made for the money. We propose to be fair and just, even liberal, with you who form the bone and sinew of our business.

Avon Representatives in the early days of the California Perfume Company were called Agents or Depot Managers.

Gallery Originals by Avon are not considered a collectors item. Only Avon Products are considered collectibles by most Avon Collectors.

David Hall McConnell

Founder
CPC –Avon Products

David Hall McConnell, manufacturer, was born in Oswego, NY, July 18, 1858, son of James and Isabel (Hall) McConnell, who came from Calvin County, Ireland, in 1845 and settled in Oswego, where James McConnell became a farmer and brick manufacturer. Brought up on a farm, David Hall McConnell attended a district school and the Oswego State Normal School and was planning to become a mathematics teacher, but instead entered business life in 1879 as a salesman for a New York book selling agency. In 1880 he joined the Union Publishing Co. of Chicago and three years later was placed in charge of the southern territory, making his home in Atlanta, GA. He decided that, if books could be sold house-to-house, perfumes could also. Out of this conception grew his California Perfume Co. At first he manufactured his own perfumes at home and went out during the day selling them along with books until the enterprise grew and he had to discontinue his book selling and establish a perfume laboratory in Suffern, NY. Other toiletries and cosmetics were soon added to his line of products which he sold under the name of CPC, standing for California Perfume Co. Later the company also began to manufacture flavoring extracts and other household articles sold under the brand name, Perfection. From the onset McConnell effected distribution of his products through housewives and other women who could devote only a portion of their time to the work. The years brought steadily increasing success and at the time of his death his sales force had grown to over 30,000 agents and the volume of sales was measured in the millions. The California Perfume Co. was incorporated in January 1916, and through subsequent changes in name it became Allied Products, Inc., and later Avon Allied Products, Inc., with the following subsidiaries: Avon Products, Inc., distributors of Avon cosmetics and toiletries , the trade name Avon having been adopted in 1929 because of the similarity of the landscape surrounding the laboratories in Suffern, NY to that of Avon, England; Perfection Household Products; Avon Products of Canada, Ltd., incorporated in 1924, being an outgrowth of the California Perfume Company of Canada, Ltd., which was started in 1906; Hinz Ambrosia, Inc., and Technical Laboratories, Inc. McConnell was president, chairman of the board and principal owner of Avon Allied Products, Inc., and its affiliated companies until his death. He was also treasurer of G.W. Carnrick & Co., manufacturers of pharmaceutical supplies in Newark, NJ, and a director of the Holly Hill Fruit Products, Inc., a large orange grove and canning enterprise of Davenport, FL. He was one of the founders of the Suffern National Bank of which he became vice president in 1901, president in 1922 and chairman of the board in 1927. He was again elected chairman of the board and president in 1933 and continued in one or the other office until his death. For varying periods he was superintendent of schools in Suffern; president of the Suffern Board of Education, and treasurer of the Rockland County Republican committee. During the First World War he was chairman of the Rockland County selective service board. A Presbyterian in religion, he was instrumental in starting and played a major part in building the Suffern Presbyterian Church and for many years was superintendent of its Sunday school. He was a Mason and a member of the Union League Club of New York City, the Ormond Beach Club of Florida, the Arcola, NY Country Club and Houvenkoph Country Club of Suffern, NY. Fishing, golf and horseback riding were his recreations. He was married in Chicago, March 31, 1885, to Lucy Emma, daughter of Ward Hays of Le Porte, IN and had three children: Edna Bertha, who married William Van Allen Clark; Doris Hall, who married Edward Hall Faile; and David Hall McConnell, Jr. His death occurred in Suffern, NY, January 20, 1937.

Avon Miscellanea

EARLY DAYS

The company's name suggests a likely California beginning, but it has no such meaning; the manufacturing, shipping, and office work in the beginning was done at 126 Chambers St., New York City. The name followed a suggestion made by a friend of Mr. McConnell's who had just visited California and returned to New York greatly enthused over the gorgeous flowers he had seen there. Since only perfumes were being sold, he suggested that the name of the company be "The California Perfume Company".

A LARGE LINE

By 1915 we had a large line. Our products were well and favorably known among our customers but were not known to the public at large. No advertising was done. The customers told their friends about these splendid products and the CPC Representatives' service. From the beginning all products were sold under the CPC trademark. All were offered to customers by Representatives (our products have never been sold through stores) and, always the products were unconditionally guaranteed. This was most unusual in the early days.

THE PANAMA PACIFIC EXPOSITION

We were invited to exhibit at the Panama Pacific Exposition in San Francisco in 1914-1915. This was a World's Fair, and prizes were given for the best articles exhibited in various classifications. Our entire line of perfumes, toilet articles and household products was entered in competition with like products from all over the world, and were awarded the Gold Medal, both for the quality of the products, and the beauty of the packages. This Gold Medal appeared on all packages until it was replaced by the seal that is recognized and followed throughout the world as a consumer's guide to the highest quality of merchandise - The Good Housekeeping Seal of Approval.

NEW NAMES - NEW PACKAGES

Through the years, our chemists were following every avenue of research, improving products wherever possible, and discovering new ones that in every way measured up to the standards of the first one. Manufacturing methods were improved to the point that every product was the sum of perfection as to blending and handling. Then in 1929, the chemist suggested an entirely new line of cosmetics. They had it ready, the managers agreed, and the Avon line was presented to Representatives and customers. The household line was named "Perfection" and given its own trademark.

GOOD HOUSEKEEPING'S SEAL OF APPROVAL

In 1931, the first group of Avon Cosmetics were approved by Good Housekeeping, and from that time on, other groups were sent, tested, approved, and the Seal added to our packages. By 1936, our 50th Anniversary year, Good Housekeeping completed their tests and approved all Avon and Perfection products which came within their scope. All products added since that time bear the Seal of Approval.

A NEW POLICY - NATIONAL ADVERTISING

Steadily increasing business over a period of years without any advertising was a remarkable record, but with the celebration of a Golden Jubilee we changed our policy and began to advertise. All during 1936 and 1937, our advertisements appeared in Good Housekeeping. They are appearing now, telling the public that Avon products are unconditionally guaranteed and that our Representatives give the Avon service. We tell readers how convenient shopping the "Avon Way" is for them.

Calendar of Events

Late 1800's
David McConnell starts the California Perfume Company, at the age of 28, in a room in downtown Manhattan. He and his wife, Lucy, create and manufacture the first products. It is sold by the first Representative, Mrs. P.F.E. Albee, who recruits others to sell at the same time.

1894
Mr. McConnell expands to four floors in the Manhattan building.

1896
The first catalog is issued on Nobember 2. Text only (no pictures).

1897
The first laboratory is built, a three story wooden structure in Suffern.

1902
10,000 Representatives are now selling the company's products.

1903
The first branch is opened in Kansas City, Missouri.

1905
The first Outlook is published, with news and selling tips for Representatives.

1906
The first company advertisement appears. The product: Roses perfume. The magazine: Good Housekeeping.

1912
Over 5,000,000 products are sold during this year.

1914
A Canadian office is opened in Montreal.

1915
The company wins the Panama-Pacific International Exposition gold medal for quality and packaging.

1920
Sales reach the $1,000,000 mark.

1928
A line of new products, called "Avon" is introduced. It includes a toothbrush, cleaner and talc.

1932
Three week selling campaigns begin in August. Up to this time, Representatives have been asked to send in orders every month. As a result of the change, sales increase by over 70% during America's bleak Depression years. The first Specials also appear with products sold at less than regular prices.

1935
The company sponsors a national radio program, called "Friends", a twice weekly show of music and chatter.

1936
An important step is taken to reach customers in urban and suburban areas. Site of this experiment is the Midwest, where several cities, Kansas City, Wichita and Oklahoma City, are divided into territories. Each Territory is to be covered by a Representative with a manager in charge. Later, after the war, this is to become the universal Avon sales structure.

1937
The home office moves to 30 Rockefeller Plaza in New York City. David McConnell dies at age 79.

1939
On October 6, the California Perfume Company changes its name to Avon Products, Inc.

1942-45
The company joins the war effort, with over 50% of the Suffern plant converted to production for the Armed Forces. Among the items manufactured are insect repellent, pharmaceuticals, paratrooper kits and gas mask canisters.

1949
Avon now has 2,500 employees. 1,175 shareholders, 65,000 Representatives and $25 million in sales. The company has facilities in New York City, Suffern, Kansas City, Middletown, Chicago and Pasadena.

1951
The Atlanta distribution branch opens.

1952
The Newark distribution branch opens.

1954
On TV advertising, the "Ding-Dong, Avon Calling" bell is heard for the first time. Avon goes international with its entry into Puerto Rico and Venezuela.

1955
Sales brochures are introduced to support campaign selling.

1956
The Morton Grove shipping facilities opens.

1959
Monrovia shipping and warehousing facilities open.

1960
The Rye branch opens.

1964
On April 2, the New York Stock Exchange starts trading Avon stock. The "advance call-back" brochure selling plan is adopted, with Representatives leaving mini-brochures at customers homes, then returning for the orders.

1965
The Springdale laboratory distribution facilities open. A new research and development laboratory is completed in Suffern.

1968
Two week selling is introduced in the U.S. The first car decanter appears, launching our most successful decanter series.

1970
The Glenview distribution branch opens.

1971
Jewelry is first introduced in the U.S.

1972 to Present
Avon moves into new world headquarters in New York City. Sales top the billion dollar mark. Sales continue to climb worldwide. Avon continues to open new operations around the world each year.

Avon Products, Inc.

Pictured here are two contrasting buildings that have housed Avon through the years. On the left is the 1900 California Perfume Factory and on the right is the present Avon World Headquarters (50 stories) at 9 West 57th St., New York, NY.

1890s - TRADEMARKS OF QUALITY - 1995

It is interesting to see the changes that have been made over the years in the Avon trademark. As you may know, in the early days your Company was called the California Perfume Company. The founder, Mr. D. H. McConnell, selected this name for his flourishing perfume business because he had heard so many glowing accounts of the great beauty and abundance of flowers in the state of California. This name, however, was changed in the early 1930s to Avon . . .a name that today is known and respected in all parts of the world.

These labels and trademarks are given as reference only. Some dates may vary. Some early CPC products also have Chicago on the label. This label is very rare.

1888-1904

1904-1911

1911-1930

1929

1930-1936

1936-53

AVON

1940's

Avon

1953

1976

1978. . .

1991

16

TOOTH TABLETS

TOOTH TABLET 1934-36
Aluminum lid on white glass bottom.
OSP 36c, **CMV $60., $80. MB.**

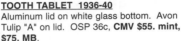

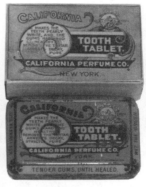

TOOTH TABLET 1936-40
Aluminum lid on white glass bottom. Avon
Tulip "A" on lid. OSP 36c, **CMV $55. mint,
$75. MB.**

TOOTH TABLET 1921-23
(Left) Aluminum lid & clear glass bottom.
OSP 25c, **CMV $60. mint.**
TOOTH TABLET 1923-24
(Right) Aluminum lid with white glass bottom.
OSP 36c, **CMV $55. mint.** Both have same
lid, different bottoms. Add $30. each in MB.

TOOTH TABLET 1906-1921
Painted metal top with clear glass bottom
embossed with Calif. Tooth Tablet in glass. 2
different boxes. 1906 to 1921 lid is painted
just under New York with Food & Drug Act
1906. OSP 25c, **CMV $70. mint, $100. MB
each.**

CALIFORNIA TOOTH TABLET 1896-1905
Blue and white painted metal lid. Clear glass
bottom has embossed California Tooth Tablet,
Most Perfect Dentifrice. OSP 25c, **CMV $100.
mint, $135.00 MB.**

FRAGRANCE JARS

**AMERICAN BEAUTY FRAGRANCE JAR
1923-33**
(Far Left) - Clear glass jar & lid. Red ribbon
around neck. OSP, $2.95, **CMV, $75.**
LAVENDER FRAGRANCE JAR 1914-23
3 different sizes. Left - 5 1/2" high, 3" wide
base. Center - 5 7/8" high, 3" wide base.

Right - 7" high, 3 9/16" wide base. OSP $2.50
each, **CMV $90. each size.** One on far right is
1st issue. Add $25. MB each.

AMERICAN BEAUTY FRAGRANCE JAR 1934-43
6 oz. glass jar and stopper. Red tassel around neck.
OSP $2.75, **CMV $25. jar only mint, with tassel
$40. MB.**

FRAGRANCE JAR 1946
Made of pink ceramic, white flower on pink lid. Very short issue. Does not say "Avon" on it. Also came with white, blue and green flowers on lid. OSP $2.75, **CMV $60., MB. Jar only mint $40.** Also came with white flowers on white lid.

AMERICAN BEAUTY FRAGRANCE JAR CUBES 1923
4 oz. can. OSP 48c, **CMV $50. mint.** Front and back view shown.

FRAGRANCE JAR CUBES 1943-49
3 oz. jar. OSP 85c, **CMV $25., $35. MB.**

ROSE FRAGRANCE JAR 1948-57
6 oz. 1st issue came out with clear rose shaped glass stopper. 1949 issue had frosted rose glass stopper. Both had red silk neck ribbon. OSP $3.50, **CMV $20.** clear stopper, $15. with stopper. Add $20. MB. each.

FRAGRANCE JAR LIQUID 1921
(Left) 4 oz. cork stopper, brown label. OSP 96c, **CMV $100., $115. MB.**
AMERICAN BEAUTY FRAGRANCE JAR LIQUID 1925
4 oz. bottle, brown label, metal cap. OSP 96c - **CMV $85. MB, $75. BO.**

FRAGRANCE JAR LIQUID 1934-36
6 oz. bottle, aluminum cap. Silver and blue label. OSP $1.75, **CMV $45. mint, $50. MB**
FRAGRANCE JAR LIQUID 1955-57
7 oz. white cap, gray label. OSP $1.39. **CMV $15, $20. MB.**

ROSE FRAGRANCE JAR TEST 1948
Dark amber glass. Was not sold. Test bottle at factory. **CMV $100.**

AMERICAN IDEAL

ROSE FRAGRANCE JAR SET 1948-57
Box contains one 6 oz. fragrance jar liquid. One 3 oz. fragrance jar cubes. One 8 oz. empty fragrance jar. **CMV $90. set MB.**

AMERICAN IDEAL PERFUMES 1911
Introductory size glass stoppered bottle with green neck ribbon and pink paper label with ladies face, in green box. OSP 60c, **CMV $160. MB, $120. BO mint.**

AMERICAN IDEAL INTRODUCTION LETTER 1914
Given to customers on trial size bottle of perfume. **CMV $20.**

AMERICAN IDEAL

AMERICAN IDEAL PERFUME "INTRODUC-TORY SIZE" 1910
Glass stopper in round screw on wood box, gold label. OSP 75c, **CMV $120. BO.** Bottle in wood box, **$225. mint.**

AMERICAN IDEAL PERFUME 1913 only
(Right) Introductory size octagonal shaped glass stoppered bottle fits in wood box with screw on wood lid, paper label with ladies face. OSP 75c, **CMV $120. mint, $225. MB.** Both came with neck ribbons.

AMERICAN IDEAL PERFUME 1911
1 and 2 oz. size bottles, glass stopper. Ladies face on paper label in green box. OSP $2.50 and $4.75. **CMV $165. MB, $125. BO mint each.**

AMERICAN IDEAL PERFUME 1941
1/8 oz. clear glass bottle, gold cap. Gold and blue label. OSP 75c. **CMV $35. BO, $55. MB.**

AMERICAN IDEAL PERFUME 1908
Glass Stoppered bottle came in 1 and 2 oz. size. Velvet lined wood box. Neck ribbon on bottle, gold front and neck label. OSP $2. and $3.75. **CMV $200. MB, $150. BO.**

AMERICAN IDEAL PERFUME 1917
Glass stoppered bottle came in green box. 1 and 2 oz. size, gold neck and front label. Green neck ribbon. OSP $2.50 and $4.75. **CMV $180. MB, $140. BO.**

AMERICAN IDEAL PERFUME 1917
1/2 oz. glass stoppered bottle, green box, gold label on front and neck. Green neck ribbon. OSP 75c, **CMV $125. MB, $100. BO mint.**

AMERICAN IDEAL PERFUME 1919
1 oz. with frosted flower embossed glass stopper. Green label. OSP $2.40. **CMV $125., $150. MB.**

AMERICAN IDEAL PERFUME 1925
1 oz. bottle with wide flat glass stopper. Green neck ribbon and gold and green label. OSP $2.40. **CMV $150. MB, $125. BO mint.**

AMERICAN IDEAL PERFUME 1910
Wood case with dark velvet lining holds 1 oz. glass stoppered bottle with green and gold label with ladies face. Neck ribbon matches inside of box. OSP $2., **CMV $200. MB, $150. BO mint.**

AMERICAN IDEAL PERFUME 1930-33
1 oz. clear glass bottle with frosted glass stopper. In silver box. Label on top of bottle. OSP $2.40. **CMV $145. MB., $110. BO.**

AMERICAN IDEAL PERFUME 1925
Flaconette size embossed bottle with brass cap over long dabber glass stopper. OSP $1.10. **CMV $90. BO, $110. MB.**

AMERICAN IDEAL SACHET 1910
Box holds ribbed sided bottle with brass cap and ladies face on green and gold label. OSP 50c. **CMV $125. MB, $100. BO mint.**

AMERICAN IDEAL TALCUM   1911
Pink can with gold top. OSP 35c. **CMV $100.
$130. MB.**

AMERICAN IDEAL PERFUME 1941 only
3 dram glass stopper, paper neck tag. Name
was changed to Apple Blossom in 1941. OSP
$2.25. **CMV $120. ʃø with tag, $150. MB.**
AMERICAN IDEAL POWDER SACHET 1923
(Right) Glass bottle, brass cap, green label.
OSP $1.20. **CMV $120. BO mint - $115. MB.**

AMERICAN IDEAL SACHET 1908
Glass bottle with metal cap. 2 piece gold
label. OSP 50c. **CMV $105. BO mint, $125.
MB.**

AMERICAN IDEAL COMPACT 1920
Contains face powder or rouge. Brass
container with mirror on lid. OSP 59c. **CMV
$75. MB. compact only $60. mint.**

AMERICAN IDEAL TOILET SOAP 1911
Pink and gold metal can holds 1 bar of soap
wrapped in same design as can. OSP 50c.
**CMV can only $60., with wrapped soap
$100 mint.**
AMERICAN IDEAL POWDER SACHET 1911
Large size sachet bottle with brass cap and
lady on paper label. OSP $1. **CMV $65. BO
Mint $85. MB.**

AMERICAN IDEAL TALCUM POWDER 1917
3 1/2 oz. glass jar, gold metal lid and gold
label. OSP 75c. **CMV $90. BO, $115. MB.**

AMERICAN IDEAL FACE POWDER 1923
Green and gold box with green and gold label.
OSP 96c. **CMV $65. MB, $55. powder box
only mint.**
AMERICAN IDEAL SOAP 1923
One bar toilet soap in white paper with gold
label. OSP 48c. **CMV $60. mint.**

**AMERICAN IDEAL DOUBLE COMPACT
1921**
Contains face powder and rouge. Made of
solid brass. OSP $1.17. **CMV $85. MB.
Compact only $70. mint.**

AMERICAN IDEAL TALCUM 1923-28
3 1/2 oz. glass jar, brass cap, gold and green
label. OSP 72c. **CMV $90. BO mint, $115.
MB.**

AMERICAN IDEAL FACE POWDER 1915
Green and gold box. OSP 75c. **CMV $80.
MB,** powder box only $65. mint.

AMERICAN IDEAL FACE POWDER 1922
Green box holds green and gold paper
container. OSP 96c. **CMV $60., $75. MB.**

AMERICAN IDEAL TALCUM 1928
Frosted glass bottle with brass lid, gold &
green label. OSP 75c. **CMV $75. MB - $70.
BO.**
AMERICAN IDEAL FACE POWDER 1925
Green & gold box. OSP 96c. **CMV $50. mint,
$65. MB.**

AMERICAN IDEAL CREAM DELUXE 1923
White glass jar with CPC on metal lid. Gold &
green label. OSP 96c. **CMV $55. MB - $40.**
jar only mint.
AMERICAN IDEAL PERFUME 1929
1 oz. glass stoppered bottle in green satin
lined box. Paper label on top of bottle. OSP
$2.20. **CMV $150. MB - $110. BO mint.**

AMERICAN IDEAL TOILET SOAP 1920
White box, green label. OSP 48c. **CMV $75.
MB.**

AMERICAN IDEAL TOILET SOAP 1925
Green box holds 2 bars. OSP 96c. **CMV $90.
MB.**

(Left to Right)
AMERICAN IDEAL PERFUME 1919
1 & 2 oz. glass bottle with glass stopper, green
& gold label, green box, green neck ribbon.
OSP $2.40 $ $4.65. **CMV $150. MB - $125.
BO.**
AMERICAN IDEAL PERFUME 1923
Introductory size bottle. Glass bottle &
stopper. Green label & neck ribbon. OSP
75c. **CMV in green box $135. $110. BO. mint.**

Also came with octagonal glass stopper set in
cork with long dabber. Same CMV.
AMERICAN IDEAL SACHET POWDER 1919
Glass bottle with brass cap, green label. OSP
$1.20. **CMV $80. BO - $110. MB.**
AMERICAN IDEAL TOILET WATER 1923
2 & 4 oz. glass stoppered bottle with green
front & neck label & neck ribbon. Green box.
OSP $1.50 & $2.85. **CMV $140. MB - $115.
BO mint.**

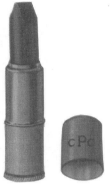

AMERICAN IDEAL LIPSTICK 1929
CPC on green metal tube. OSP $1. **CMV $40. tube only, $60. MB.**

AMERICAN IDEAL SET 1919
Green silk lined box holds 1 oz. glass stoppered American Ideal perfume, powder sachet, bottle of talcum powder & toilet soap. All have green labels. OSP set $5.50. **CMV $450. MB.**

AMERICAN IDEAL BOX C SET 1911
Flip top box holds glass stoppered perfume & powder sachet. OSP 50c. **CMV $300. MB.**

AMERICAN IDEAL FOURSOME SET 1925
Green box holds 1 oz. bottle with glass stopper of perfume, glass bottle of talcum, green box of face powder & white jar of vanishing cream. OSP $6.50. **CMV $400. MB.**

AMERICAN IDEAL SET 1911
Large fancy box with green lining holds American Ideal talcum powder, powder sachet, 1 oz. glass stoppered perfume & bar of toilet soap in pink soap can. OSP $4. **CMV $500. MB.**

AMERICAN IDEAL THREESOME 1923
Green box contains 2 oz. toilet water, bottle of sachet & glass bottle of talc. Green & gold label. OSP $3.95. **CMV $350. MB.**

AMERICAN IDEAL POWDER SACHET 1917
2 piece label on front. Rare with this label. Metal cap. **CMV $125. Mint.**

AMERICAN IDEAL PERFUMES
Shown for the different sizes of bottles, glass stoppers. **CMV same as bottles listed with the same labels.**

AMERICAN IDEAL PERFUME "INTRODUCTORY SIZES" 1913
2 different size glass stopper bottles & labels are different size. **CMV $120. each Mint.**

ARIEL

ARIEL PERFUME "RIBBED" 1933-36
(Left) 1/2 oz. ribbed glass bottle with black octagonal cap & gold label. Came in Gold Box Set. **CMV $45. mint.**
ARIEL PERFUME 1933-36
(Right) Small six sided octagonal shaped bottle with black octagonal cap. Came in Little Folks set and Handkerchief set. Has silver label. **CMV $45. mint.**

ARIEL BATH SALTS 1933-37
8 1/2 oz. ribbed glass, navy blue cap. Silver & blue label. OSP 63c. **CMV $60. MB - $40. BO mint.**
ARIEL BATH SALTS 1929-30
10 oz. clear glass with chrome cap, silver & blue label. **CMV $60. BO - $75. MB.**

ARIEL THREESOME 1932-33
Blue & silver compact, blue & silver Avon face powder & Ariel flaconette with brass cap. In silver & blue box. OSP $3.12. **CMV $145. MB.**

ARIEL PERFUME 1930
(Right) 1 oz. glass stoppered bottle with small silver label. Silver box. OSP $2.50. **CMV $120. BO - $150. MB.**
ARIEL PERFUME FLACONETTE 1930
(Left) Brass cap over glass stoppered embossed bottle. OSP 84c. **CMV $90. BO mint - $115. MB.**

ARIEL BATH SALTS SAMPLE 1933-37
Small ribbed glass bottle with dark blue or black octagonal shaped cap. Silver label. **CMV $60. mint.**
ARIEL TOILET WATER 1930-35
2 oz. glass stoppered bottle, small label on top of bottle. Came in silver & blue box. OSP $1.75. **CMV $110. B) - $135. MB.**

ARIEL POWDER SACHET 1932-36
(Left) 1 1/4" oz. ribbed glass. Dark blue cap. OSP 78c. **CMV $28. - $33. MB.**
ARIEL SACHET 1930-32
(Right) Metal cap, silver & blue label. OSP 78c. **CMV $60. mint - $75. MB.**

ARIEL PERFUME 1930
1 oz. glass stoppered bottle, large silver & blue label. Came in silver box. OSP $2.50. **CMV $105. BO mint - $135. MB.**

ARIEL FACE POWDER 1930-36
Silver & blue round box in special issue 1935 red Christmas box. OSP 78c. **CMV $12. container only mint - $16. MB as shown in Christmas box - or $13. In regular issue box on left.**

ARIEL SET NO.2 1931-33
(Right) Silver & blue round box in special issue 1935 red Christmas box. OSP 78c. **CMV $12. container only mint - $16. MB as shown in Christmas box - or $13. in regular issue box on left.**

24

DAPHNE

DAPHNE TALCUM 1931-36
Silver and blue can with blue cap. OSP 35c.
CMV $20., $30. MB. Same can in gold color.
CMV $35. Silver and blue can in large 1 Lb.
family size. OSP $1. **CMV $30. can only.
$40. MB.**

DAPHNE TALCUM CHRISTMAS BOX 1943
Pale blue and pink outer box issued only at
Christmas 1943 with cardboard large size talc
with top & bottom cover caps. OSP 98c. **CMV
$40. MB as shown.** Talc only $30. mint.

DAPHNE TALCUM 1936-43 THEN 1946-50
(Right) 2.75 oz. turquoise & white can,
turquoise cap. OSP 37c. **CMV $8., MB $10.**
DAPHNE TALCUM 1936-43 THEN 1946-50
(Left) 14.5 Turquoise and white can, turquoise
cap. OSP $1.19. **CMV $20. MB $25.**

DAPHNE TALCUM
Silver can in 2 special boxes. 49 Year box on
left 1935 & 50th Year box on right 1936. OSP
20c. **CMV mint & boxed only in either box
$50. each.** Also came in gold can in 50th year
box. **CMV $60. MB.**

**DAPHNE TALCUM CHRISTMAS PACKAGE
1940-41**
Outer sleeve fits over short issue blue
Christmas box with white Christmas tree.
Holds large size 14.5 oz. metal talc turquoise
and white can of Daphne Talcum. Can only
sold 1936-50. OSP 89c. **CMV $40. MB as
shown.**

DAPHNE PERFUME 1925
1 and 2 oz. glass bottle with flat glass stopper.
Bottle and top of stopper have embossed
flowers. Came in green and gold box, gold
label and green neck ribbons. OSP $1.95 and
$3.45. **CMV $135. BO $175. MB.**

DAPHNE TALCUM 1933-36
(Left) Metal can came in sets only. **CMV $35.
mint.**
DAPHNE TALCUM 1943-46
(Right) Turquoise & white paper box. No top
cover, bottom cover, cap only. Family size.
OSP $1.19. **CMV $30. MB.**

**DAPHNE TALC 52nd ANNIVERSARY 1938
only**
Turquoise & white can in special box sold for
10c during 52nd anniversary campaign. **CMV
$32.50 in box shown.**

**DAPHNE TALCUM 1937 only - 51st
ANNIVERSARY**
Special box was given to Avon customers with
any purchase. **CMV $25. MB as shown.**

DAPHNE

DAPHNE TALC MAY POLE BOX 1940 ONLY
Yellow box with dancing girls around May Pole holds regular issue 2.75 oz. Daphne Talc. can. Sold in May 1940 for 10c with regular order from Avon lady. **CMV $30. MB as shown.**

DAPHNE POWDER SACHET 1922
Brass cap, green and gold square label. OSP 96c. **CMV $90. BO mint, $115. MB.**
DAPHNE PERFUME 1925-30
Clear glass, brass cap, box is brown, yellow & green. Came in Jack & Jill Jungle Jinks Set. **CMV $60. MB.**

DAPHNE GLYCERINE SOAP 1925
Green box & wrapping with gold labels. Two bars of soap. OSP 72c. **CMV $90. MB.**

DAPHNE FACE POWDER VANITY COMPACT 1917
Green box, came in white, pink & brunette tints. OSP 75c. **CMV $50. MB.** Same box also came in Daphne Rouge. **Same CMV, $35. compact only mint.**

DAPHNE PERFUME 1916
1 & 2 oz. bottles shown with frosted glass stoppers. Also came in 1/2 oz. size. Each came in green box. OSP $1., $1.90 & $3.50. **CMV $120. BO, $145. MB.**

DAPHNE TOILET WATER 1923
Green box holds 2 or 4 oz. size bottle with frosted glass stopper, gold front & neck label, green neck ribbon. OSP $1.20 & $2.25. **CMV $105. BO, $135. MB.** Came with 2 different glass stoppers set in cork as pictured & outer box. **CMV for both boxes $140. MB.**

DAPHNE DOUBLE VANITY COMPACT 1917
Contained face powder & rouge. Green compact with mirror on lid. OSP $1. **CMV $70., $45. compact only mint.**
DAPHNE VANITY COMPACT 1917
Face powder, came in white, pink & brunette. Green compact with mirror on lid. OSP 50c. **CMV $55. MB, $45. compact only mint.**

DAPHNE DERMA CREAM 1925
White glass jar 1/2" thick green lid. Came in Septette Gift box. **CMV $40. mint.**
DAPHNE CERATE 1925
1/2" thick white glass jar, green lid. Came in Septette gift box. **CMV $40. mint.** Also came in large size jar.

DAPHNE POWDER SACHET 1920
Brass cap & gold label. OSP 96c. **CMV $80. mint, $100. MB.**

<u>OSP</u> means Original Selling Price.
<u>CMV</u> means Current Market Value in Mint Condition.
<u>BO.</u> means Bottle Only Mint.

DAPHNE PERFUME 1922
1/4 oz. vial given to customers for each $5.
order in March 1922. **CMV $155. MB, $130.
BO mint.**

DAPHNE TALCUM POWDER 1923
4 oz. green can, brass cap. OSP 48c. **CMV
$75, MB, $65. can only.**
**DAPHNE ROLLING MASSAGE CREAM
1923**
White glass jar with CPC on metal lid, gold
label. OSP 69c. **CMV $50., $60. MB.**

DAPHNE CERATE 1923
White glass jar with CPC on metal lid, gold
label. Small & large size jars. OSP 72c &
$1.35. **CMV $50., $60. MB.**
DAPHNE DUPLEX COMPACT 1923
Green compact & puffs, mirror on lid. OSP
98c. **CMV $55., $65. MB.**

DAPHNE CERATE 1926
1/2" thick white glass jar, solid green lid says
Daphne CPC Cerate on top. Also came in
Daphne Derma Cream. Came in Septette gift
box set. **CMV $35. each mint.**

DAPHNE LIPSTICK 1919
Metal case. Daphne on case. OSP 50c.
CMV $55. mint - $65. MB.

DAPHNE THREESOME 1923
Green box contains 2 oz. toilet water, bottle of
sachet & can of talc. OSP $3.20. **CMV $325.
MB.**

DAPHNE CREAMS 1929
Square white glass jars with ribbed sides & CPC on
aluminum lids & gold labels. Came in Daphne Cerate,
Daphne Derma Cream & Daphne Rolling Massage
Cream. OSP 75c. **CMV $50. each MB, $40. jar only.**
DAPHNE BATH SALTS 1925
Ribbed glass jar with brass lid, gold label. OSP 98c.
CMV $65. MB, $50. BO.

DAPHNE/MISSION GARDEN

DAPHNE SET 1918
Green box holds Daphne Perfume in 1 oz. glass stoppered bottle, green box of Daphne Face Powder & green box of Daphne rouge. OSP $3.50. **CMV $210. MB.**

DAPHNE LIPSTICK 1925
2-1/8" metal lipstick has embossed name & CPC on side. OSP 39c. **CMV $35. mint, $50 MB.**

DAPHNE CREAMS 1926
Large & small size glass jars with gold and green labels and green lids. Came in Daphne Derma Cream & Daphne Rolling Massage Cream. Came in large size jars only. OSp 72c. **CMV $50. each MB, $45. jar only.**

DAPHNE EYEBROW PENCIL 1925
Metal tube in box. **CMV $30. mint, $45. MB.**

DAPHNE POWDER SACHET 1915
Brass cap, brown flower label. Flower box. **CMV $90. BO, $115. MB.**

DAPHNE TALCUM 1944-46
Turquoise and white paper container. Plastic cap. OSP 39c. **CMV $20. mint.**

MISSION GARDEN

DAPHNE SEPTETTE GIFT BOX 1925
Green box holds jar of Derma Cream, jar of Cerate, green box of face powder, rouge compact, can of talcum, 1 oz. bottle of toilet water & flaconette of perfume. All in Daphne fragrance. OSP $2.95. **CMV $500. MB.**

MISSION GARDEN PERFUME 1922-25
1 1/2 oz. bohemian glass bottle with frosted sides & frosted glass stopper. Satin lined tan box. OSP $4.95. **CMV $200. MB, $150. BO mint.**

MISSION GARDEN TOILET WATER 1922
2 & 4 oz. glass bottle with frosted glass stopper. Gold label on front & neck. OSP $2.25 and $4.35. **CMV $135. BO, $165. MB.**

MISSION GARDEN DOUBLE COMPACT 1922
Contains face powder & rouge. Made of solid brass. OSP $1.45. **CMV $45., $60. MB.**

MISSION GARDEN PERFUME 1925
Flaconette size, gold box, embossed glass bottle with glass stopper. Brass cap over stopper. OSP $1.20. **CMV $95. BO, $115. MB.**

MISSION GARDEN PERFUME 1925
1 oz. glass bottle, flat embossed glass stopper. Satin lined gold box. OSP $2.85. **CMV $110. BO, $140. MB.** Also came in 2 oz. size. **$150. MB.**

MISSION GARDEN COMPACT 1925
Mission Garden CPC on edge of compact. Embossed brass case in single or double compact. OSP 98c and $1.48. **CMV $65. each MB, $50. compact only mint.**

MISSION GARDEN FLACONETTE 1926
Glass tube of perfume in brass case. Sold at Easter time. OSP 98c. **CMV $100. MB. Tube in case only $85.**

MISSION GARDEN TALC 1925
4 oz. red & gold can, brass cap. Came in Mission Garden Threesome Set only. **CMV $90. mint.**

MISSION GARDEN SACHET POWDER 1922
Glass bottle with brass cap & gold label. OSP $1.75. **CMV $90. BO, $110. MB.**

MISSION GARDEN FLACONETTE 1922
Brass tubes and cap with gold label on the tube. Holds clear glass vial with blue stripes and steel cap, glass stopper. OSP 98c. **CMV $100. mint as shown. Metal case only $60. mint.**

MISSION GARDEN TALC SET 1923
2 cans of Mission Garden Talc was a gift set to CPC employees. Red and gold silk lined box. **CMV $235. MB.**

NARCISSUS

MISSION GARDEN THREESOME 1925
Satin lined gold box holds 1 oz. Mission Garden Perfume, Talc & gold compact. OSP $7. **CMV $325. MB.**

NATOMA - NATOMA ROSE

NARCISSUS PERFUME 1925
1 oz. glass bottle with frosted embossed glass stopper. Bottle in blue & gold box, blue label & neck ribbon. OSP $2.19. **CMV $120. BO mint, $175. MB.**

NARCISSUS PERFUME 1929-30
1 oz. glass stoppered bottle. Came in silver, blue & gold box. Blue label on top of bottle. OSP $2.20. **CMV $110. BO, $175. MB.**

NATOMA ROSE PERFUME 1914-15
1/2 oz. glass stoppered bottle with front & neck label. Green ribbon, green snap shut box. OSP 40c. **CMV $175. MB, $140. BO.**

NARCISSUS PERFUME 1931-34
(Left) 1 oz. glass stoppered bottle came in silver & blue box, label on top of bottle. Same as 1929 perfume only box is changed. OSP $2.25. **CMV $115. BO, $150. MB.**
NARCISSUS PERFUME FLACONETTE 1925
(Right) Embossed bottle with glass stopper with long glass dobber under brass cap. OSP 84c. **CMV $95. BO mint, $115. MB.**

NATOMA ROSE PERFUME 1915
1 oz. glass stopper bottle, green front and neck label. Green neck ribbon in green felt box. OSP 40c. **CMV $140. BO mint, $175. MB.**

NATOMA ROLLING MASSAGE CREAM 1918-21
Metal screw on lid, green paper label. OSP 75c. **CMV $145., $170. MB.**

NATOMA MASSAGE CREAM 1911
1st issue glass jar, cork lid stopper. Side, neck & lid labels. OSP 75c. **CMV $155., $180. MB.**

NATOMA ROSE ART OF MASSAGE BOOKLET 1913
10 page booklet on giving a massage with Natoma Massage. **CMV $20.**

NATOMA ROSE PERFUME 1915
1 oz. bottle, glass stoppered, front and neck label. OSP 60c. **CMV $140. BO mint$165.MB.**

NATOMA ROSE PERFUME 1916
(Left) 1/2 oz. glass stoppered bottle, green riibbon on neck, green neck & front label. Green box. OSP 40c. **CMV $140. BO mint, $175. MB.**

NATOMA ROSE PERFUME 1914-21
(Right) 1 oz. clear glass, glass stopper, green label. OSP $1.40. **CMV $175. MB, $140. BO mint.**

NATOMA ROSE PERFUME 1914-21
Green box , holds 1,2 or 4 oz. size glass stoppered bottle with green front & neck label with green neck ribbon. OSP $1.40, $2.75 & $5.25. **CMV $175. MB, $150. BO.**

NATOMA TALCUM POWDER
(Left) 2" tall Brass top. Came in Juvenile Set only. **CMV $300.** came 3 1/2 oz. regular size on ri **CMV $300. mint.**

NATOMA TALCUM POWDER 1911
3 1/2 oz. metal can. Brass cap. Label an cap a little different from 1915 issue. OSP 25c. **CMV $350. MB as shown. Can onl mint, $300.**

NATOMA ROSE TALCUM 1914-21
brass cap. 3 4 oz. green can with pink ros one brass cap different. 1 has green sifter top on top of can and and one has flowers paint brass cap. OSP 25c. **CMV $200. Mint, $250. MB**

NATOMA ROLLING MASSAGE CREAM 1914-17
Glass stoppered jar with front & neck label. OSP 50c. **CMV $165. mint, $190. MB.**

NATOMA LEATHER TABLE COVER 1913
Full size sheep skin leather cover with Natoma Indian head or male Indian head in center. Laid out like a baseball field. Given to Reps for meeting sales goals. **CMV $350.**

TRAILING ARBUTUS

TRAILING ARBUTUS PERFUME 1940-42
3/8 oz. bottle, gold octagonal cap. Gold speckled box. OSP $1.50. **CMV $60. BO mint, $85. MB.**

TRAILING ARBUTUS PERFUME 1928-29
Came in 1 & 2 oz. glass stoppered bottle with blue label. Blue box. OSP $1.20 & $2.10. **CMV $160., MB $120. BO.**

TRAILING ARBUTUS TOILET WATER 1933-34
2 oz. ribbed glass, black cap. Silver label. OSP 75c. **CMV $50. BO mint. $60 MB.**
TRAILING ARBUTUS TOILET WATER 1915
2 oz. clear glass bottle with blue & gold front & neck label. Metal crown stopper set in cork. OSP 35c. **CMV $140. BO mint, $155. MB.**

TRAILING ARBUTUS PERFUME 1915
Fancy embossed box holds glass stoppered bottle with front & neck label. Came in 1, 2 & 4 oz. size. OSP $1.10, $2.10 & $4. **CMV $175. MB $140. BO mint.**

TRAILING ARBUTUS VEGETABLE OIL SOAP SAMPLE 1925
Small 2" X 1 1/8" size sample bar. **CMV $50. mint.**

NATOMA ROLLING MASSAGE CREAM 1912
Green front label, white label on back side. Aluminum lid. Label does not say NATOMA, only Indian Head & CPC. 5 oz. white glass jar. Rare. **CMV $150. mint.**

NATOMA ROSE SAMPLE
1 oz. bottle with atomizer. Green Natoma labels. Back label says bottle is a free sample. Rare. **CMV $175. mint.**

TRAILING ARBUTUS PERFUME 1923
(Left) 2 oz. glass stoppered bottle. Basket design front label and neck label. OSP $2.10. **CMV $125. BO mint. $150. MB.**
TRAILING ARBUTUS PERFUME 1933-36
(Right) Small 6 sided octagonal bottle and black cap came in Little Folks Set and Handkerchief set. Silver label. Came with CPC or CPC Avon Products, Inc. division label. **CMV $45. mint.**

TRAILING ARBUTUS PERFUME FLACON 1926
Frosted ribbed glass with long glass stopper under CPC embossed brass cap. Front paper label. OSP 59c. **CMV $90. mint with brass cap and label, $110. MB.**
TRAILING ARBUTUS TALCUM REFILL CAN 1918
1 lb. metal can with brass finish. Front paper label. **CMV $75. mint in new condition.**

TRAILING ARBUTUS PERFUME 1923 ONLY
1 oz. travelers bottle, gold labels. Metal cap over glass stopper. Short issue. OSP 78c. **CMV $150., $175. MB.**

TRAILING ARBUTUS PERFUME 1930
1/2 oz. bottle with frosted glass stopper, silver label. **CMV $95. mint.**

TRAILING ARBUTUS PERFUME 1941-45
1/8 oz. bottle, white paper label, brass cap. OSP $1. **CMV $35. BO mint., $40. MB.**

TRAILING ARBUTUS COLD CREAM SAMPLE 1925
Small sample tube in box marked sample. Came with CPC instruction sheet. **CMV $65. MB $40. tube only mint.**

TRAILING ARBUTUS SACHET 1915
Brass cap, flowered label, clear glass, 2 different labels. OSP 60c. **CMV $90. BO mint each, $115. MB.**

TRAILING ARBUTUS ROUGE 1928-29
Blue box. OSP 40c. **CMV $35. in box. Rouge only $30. mint.**

TRAILING ARBUTUS FACE POWDER 1928-29
Blue & pink box. OSP 35c. **CMV $45. in box. $35. powder box only mint.**

TRAILING ARBUTUS FACE POWDER 1925
Blue box. OSP 33c. **CMV $55. MB., $40. powder box only mint.**

TRAILING ARBUTUS BATH POWDER 1920
Blue 1 lb. size can with brass cap. This label says only "Trailing Arbutus Bath Powder". OSP 89c. **CMV $95. MB, $80. can only mint.**

TRAILING ARBUTUS TALCUM POWDER 1920
16 oz. Blue can, brass cap. OSP 89c. **CMV $85. MB, $70. can only mint.**

TRAILING ARBUTUS VEGETABLE OIL SOAP 1925
Blue box holds 3 embossed soap bars. OSP 39c. **CMV $110. MB.**

TRAILING ARBUTUS COLD CREAM CAN 1925-30
Came in Jack & Jill Jungle Set, gold can with blue and pink lid. Box is brown, yellow and green. Also came in plain brown CPC box. **CMV $40. MB.**

TRAILING ARBUTUS

TRAILING ARBUTUS TALCUM POWDER 1914

4 oz. blue can. 1914-17 can had brass sifter cap with grooved edge. **CMV $85. MB, $70. can only.** 1917-29 can came with removable brass cap. OSP 33c. **CMV $70. MB, $45. can only.** Both came with "The Story of Italian Talc" in box. 2 different labels on can. With the top section of can all gold, rare - $110.

TRAILING ARBUTUS TALCUM POWDER SAMPLE 1914

Small blue sample can, gold cap. Front of box in English and back side in French. **CMV $85. mint, $105. MB.**

TRAILING ARBUTUS CREAMS 1928-29

Large & small round white glass jars with CPC on blue lids. Came in cold cream & vanishing cream. OSP 33c & 59c. **CMV $55. MB, jar only $45. each.**

BRILLANTINE 1923

A hair dressing with Trailing Arbutus perfume scent. Glass bottle with frosted glass stopper. Blue front & neck label. OSP 39c. **CMV $125. BO mint, $150. MB.**

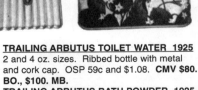

TRAILING ARBUTUS PERFUME 1925

1 and 2 oz. sizes. Ribbed bottle with glass stopper. Came in blue box. Front and neck lael. OSP $1.17 and $2.10. **CMV $115. BO, $140. MB.**

TRAILING ARBUTUS POWDER SACHET 1925

Brass cap and blue & green label with pink flowers. Rare label is all pink with black border. Same CMV. OSP 72c. **CMV $90. BO mint, $110. MB.**

TRAILING ARBUTUS TOILET WATER 1925

2 and 4 oz. sizes. Ribbed bottle with metal and cork cap. OSP 59c and $1.08. **CMV $80. BO., $100. MB.**

TRAILING ARBUTUS BATH POWDER 1925-29

4 3/4 oz. blue can and cap. OSP 35c. **CMV $80. MB, $65. can only mint.**

TRAILING ARBUTUS BATH POWDER 1925-29

1 lb. size blue can with brass cap. OSP 89c, 2 different labels on front and top of can. This can says only "Bath Powder". **CMV $100. MB, $80. can only mint.**

TRAILING ARBUTUS SEXTETTE BOX 1925

Box only showing label in center of box. **CMV box only $40. mint.**

TRAILING ARBUTUS SEXTETTE GIFT BOX 1928-29
Blue box holds 2 bars Vegetable Oil Soap, Cold Cream jar & Vanishing Cream jar, box of Face Powder & can of Talcum Powder. All are trimmed in blue & have Trailing Arbutus labels. OSP $1.60. **CMV $350. MB.**

TRAILING ARBUTUS CREAMS 1925
(left) Large and small white glass jars of Cold Cream and Vanishing Cream. CPC on blue or plain aluminum metal lids. OSP 33c and 59c. **CMV $55. each MB, jar only $45. mint.**

TRAILING ARBUTUS COLD CREAM TUBE 1925
(Above) Large and small size. Blue tubes. OSP 23c and 45c. **CMV $45. MB, tube only**

VERNAFLEUR
All CPC'S MUST BE NEW MINT CONDITION FOR CMV

ATOMIZER PERFUME 1928
2 oz., 5 3/4" tall. Green frosted bottle with gold plated top. Came in Vernafleur Perfume. Is not marked Avon or CPC. OSP $2.50. **CMV $80. BO. mint, 110. MB.**

VERNAFLEUR TOILET WATER 1928
4 oz. Ribbed glass - CPC brass crown top, front & neck label. OSP $1.35. **CMV $90. BO. mint, $110. MB.**

TRAILING ARBUTUS THREESOME 1923
Blue box contains 2 oz. bottle of toilet water, 4 oz. can of talcum & bottle of sachet powder. OSP $1.85. **CMV $325. MB.**

TRAILING ARBUTUS GIFT BOX 1915
Red, green & pink box contains Trailing Arbutus talcum can, powder sachet & 4 oz. toilet water. OSP $1.25. **CMV $350.**

TRAILING ARBUTUS SEXTETTE SET 1925
(Right) Large blue box holds white glass jar of Trailing Arbutus Cold Cream & Vanishing Cream. Both have blue lids. Blue can of Talcum Powder, blue box of Face Powder & 2 bars of Vegetable Oil Soap. OSP $1.59. **CMV $400. MB.**

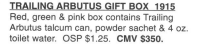

VERNAFLEUR PERFUME 1931-33
1 oz. bottle with plastic sealed cork stopper, silver and blue label. Silver box. **CMV $70. BO. mint, $100. MB.**

VERNAFLEUR

VERNAFLEUR PERFUME FLACON 1925
(Left) Brass cap over glass stopper with long glass dabber. OSP 69c. **CMV $90. - $110. MB.**

VERNAFLEUR PERFUME 1933-36
(Right) 2 1/4" tall - six sided bottle with black octagonal cap. Silver label. Came in sets only. **CMV $45. mint.**

VERNAFLEUR PERFUME 1928
1 oz. ribbed clear glass bottle, frosted glass stopper, front label, neck ribbon. OSP $1.17. **CMV $110. BO. mint, $135. MB.**

VERNAFLEUR SAMPLES 1923
3 different small glass vials with cork stoppers. one is 1 1/2" the other is 2" high & the fat one is 1 3/4" high. Not for sale on label. **CMV $75. each mint.**

VERNAFLEUR BATH SALTS 1927-29
Clear glass, brass cap. Sent to Representatives to give to each customer that orders $2. worth of merchandise. Representative must attain $45. in customer sales on January 1927 order. Offer expired Jan. 31, 1927. (Not a sample) Rare. **CMV $150. mint. $175. MB as shown with paper.**

VERNAFLEUR TOILET SOAP 1936-39
Turquoise & white box & wrapping holds 3 violet colored bars. OSP 77c. **CMV $60. MB.**

VERNAFLEUR BATH SALTS 1946
9 oz. jar, turquoise lid. Short issue. Special blu& white label. OSP 63c. **CMV $40. - $55. MB.** See Bath Salts Misc. section for regular issue.

VERNAFLEUR TOILET SOAP 1925-28
Gray box & wrapping holds 3 bars. OSP 69c. **CMV $110. MB.**

CHRISTMAS CHEER 1929
Red, white & blue boxes of Vernafleur Sachet Powder. Came in sets of 4 boxes. OSP $1.20. **CMV $50. each box.**

ATOMIZER GIFT SET 1933
Blue box with green & red holly leaves holds 1 oz. bottle of Vernafleur perfume with small silver label & 1 oz. red glass bottle with spray atomizer. OSP $2.86. **CMV $185. MB.**

VERNAFLEUR TOILET SOAP 1931-36
Lavender in color, in white wrapper. Box of 3 bars. OSP 75c. **CMV $60. MB.**

VERNAFLEUR FACE POWDER SAMPLE 1928
Adherent Powder sample. Came several in a box. OSP 48c per box of samples. **CMV $25. per box.**

VERNAFLEUR PERFUME EXTRACT 1923
1/4 oz. glass bottle with glass stopper. Neck label & ribbon. OSP 48c. **CMV $100. MB., $80. BO.**

VERNAFLEUR ADHERENT POWDER 1923
Gray metal can. OSP 48c. **CMV $45. MB., $35. can only.**

VERNAFLEUR PERFUME 1923
Gray box holds 1 oz. ribbed glass bottle with frosted glass stopper. Front & neck label. Green ribbon on neck. OSP 1 oz. size $1.44., 2 oz. size $2.70. **CMV $110. BO., $135. MB.**

VERNAFLEUR TOILET WATER 1923
2 & 4 oz. glass bottle with metal & cork shaker cap. OSP 74c & $1.35. **CMV $110. MB., $90. BO. mint.**

VERNAFLEUR TOILET WATER 1925
2 & 4 oz. Ribbed glass bottle with metal & cork cap. OSP 74c & $1.35. **CMV $85. BO., $100. MB.**

VERNATALC 1922
4 oz. can of Talc Powder. Gray. OSP 30c. **CMV $75. MB. Can only $60. mint**

VERNAFLEUR TISSUE CREAM 1923
White glass jar with ribs on sides. CPC on metal lid. Large & small size jars. OSP 48c & 89c. **CMV $50. MB. Jar only $40.**

VERNAFLEUR NUTRI CREAM 1923
Large & small white glass jar with ribs on sides. CPC on metal lid. OSP 48c & 89c. **CMV $50. MB, $40. Jar only.**

VERNAFLEUR BATH SALTS 1925
10 oz. glass bottle with brass lid, ribbed glass sides. OSP 75c. **CMV $85. MB, $70. jar only mint.**

VERNAFLEUR PERFUME FLACON 1925
Flaconette size frosted ribbed bottle with glass stopper, brass cap over stopper. Small front label. CPC on cap. Comes in yellow & green box. OSP 70c. **CMV $90. with cap, $110. MB.**

VERNAFLEUR TISSUE CREAM 1928
Small & Large size white glass jar with ribbed sides. Came with or without CPC on aluminum lid. OSP 50c & 90c. **CMV $55. MB, $40. jar only.**

VERNAFLEUR PERFUME 1928
1 oz. glass stoppered bottle, blue, yellow & black box. OSP $1.45. **CMV $150. MB, $110. BO. mint.**

VERNAFLEUR COMPACT 1928
Silver compact with Vernafleur on lid. Single & double compact. OSP $1. & $1.50. **CMV $55. MB, $40. compact only mint.**

VERNAFLEUR THREESOME GIFT BOX 1928
Gray box holds 2 oz. bottle of Vernafleur Toilet Water, jar of Vanishing Cream & can of Face Powder. OSP $2.10. **CMV $225. MB.**

VERNA TALC 1928
4 oz. multi-colored can, brass cap. OSP $1.15. **CMV $75. mint, $90. MB.**
VERNAFLEUR NUTRI CREME 1928
Large & small white glass jar with ribbed sides. CPC on aluminum lid. OSP 50c & 90c. **CMV $50. MB, $40. jar only mint.**
VERNAFLEUR TOILET SOAP 1928-31
Box holds 3 bars of soap in blue paper. OSP 75c. **CMV $90.**
VERNAFLEUR FACE POWDER 1925
Blue, yellow & black metal can. OSP 48c. **CMV $30. MB, $20. can only mint.** This was also called Vernafleur Adherent Powder.

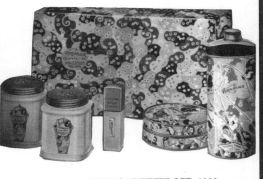

VERNAFLEUR QUINTETTE SET 1929
Blue, black & gold box holds Vernafleur Tissue Cream & Nutri-Cream, Face Powder, Talc & Flaconette of Perfume. OSP $2.25. **CMV $350. MB.**

VERNAFLEUR BATH SET 1929
Black & gold box holds bottle of Vernafleur Bath Salts, Dusting powder in gold & black striped can & 1 bar of Vegetable Oil Soap. OSP $3.50. **CMV $250. MB.**

VIOLET

SEE MISCELLANEOUS CPC JARS
FOR OTHER VIOLET PRODUCTS.

VERNAFLEUR NUTRI-CREME SAMPLE 1925
(Top) Multi-colored tube, says on back side "not for Sale Sample." **CMV $50. MB, $40. tube.**
VERNAFLEUR FACE POWDER SAMPLE 1925
(Bottom) 1 1/2" small paper box used as sample. **CMV $50. mint.**

VIOLET ALMOND MEAL 1912
(Right) Glass jar with metal shaker lid. Came in 3 1/2 oz. & 3 3/4 oz. size. Two different labels. OSP 50c. **CMV $110., $130. MB.**

VIOLET ALMOND MEAL 1893
8 oz. glass jar with metal lid. OSP 50c. **CMV $145. MB, $125. jar only mint.**

VIOLET TOILET WATER 1915
(Left) 2 oz. bottle, metal crown stopper in cork, front & neck label. OSP 35c. **CMV $100. BO. mint, $125. MB.**

VIOLET TOILET WATER 1915
(Center) 1/4 oz. clear glass, cork stopper. Came only in 1915 Juvenile Set. Rare. **CMV $125. mint.**

VIOLET PERFUME 1915
(Right) Front & neck label, glass crown stopper in cork. OSP 50c. **CMV $175. mint.**

VIOLET WATER 1908
8 oz. glass bottle, glass stopper. Eureka Trade Mark label in color. Neck ribbon. **CMV $150.**

VIOLET TALCUM POWDER 1912
Blue paper sides, metal shaker top & metal bottom. Eureka Trade Mark label. **CMV $75. mint.**

VIOLET ALMOND MEAL 1908
(Left) 8 oz. Glass jar with metal lid. OSP 50c. **CMV $115. jar only mint, $135. MB.** 1910 issue same only Eureka Trade Mark in place of CP at top of label.

VIOLET PERFUME 1915
1 oz. size, cork stopper. Used with spray atomizer. Came in 1915 Violet Gift Box H set only. **CMV $100. mint.**

VIOLET TALCUM 1923
(Left) 3-1/3" oz. Violet & green colored can, brass cap. OSP 23c. **CMV $75. mint, $90. MB.**

VIOLET TOILET WATER 1916
(Right) 2 oz. bottle with metal crown pour cap in cork. Colorful front and neck label. OSP 35c. **CMV $100. BO. mint, $125. MB.**

VIOLET NUTRI-CREME 1912
(Left) Small & large size white glass jars with aluminum lid. OSP 50c & 90c. **CMV $55. each MB. $45. jar only mint.**

VIOLET NUTRI-CREME 1923
(Right) Large & small white glass jars with CPC on metal lid. OSP 49c & 89c. **CMV $45. each, $55. MB.**

VIOLET PERFUME 1896
New York label. Eureka trade mark. Round glass stopper. Colored flower box. **CMV $175. BO., $200. MB.**

VIOLET GIFT SET H 1915
Green, white & purple box contains botle of Violet Talcum, 1 oz. Perfume bottle with cork stopper & Atomizer, Violet Powder Sachet. OSP $1.35. **CMV $435. MB.**

VIOLET/BABY ITEMS - CPC

VIOLET ALMOND MEAL 1923
4 oz. sifter top metal can. 2 different labels. OSP 48c.
CMV $60., $75. MB.

VIOLET ALMOND MEAL 1907
8 oz. Clear glass - metal shaker top. OSP
50c. **CMV $110. jar only mint, $140. MB.**

VIOLET THREESOME SET 1923
Contains 2 oz. bottle of Toilet Water, 3 & 1/3
oz. can of Talcum & bottle of Sachet Powder in
violet colored box. OSP $1.40. **CMV $325.
MB.**

VIOLET NUTRI-CREME 1910
White glass jar, aluminum lid. Paper label all
around jar. Bottom pat. Dec. 9, 1890. OSP
50c. **CMV $55. mint, $65. MB.**

BABY ITEMS - CPC

VIOLET TALCUM POWDER 1915
(Left) 3 1/2 oz. Glass jar, OSP 25c. **CMV
$110. MB, $90. BO.**
VIOLET TALCUM POWDER 1908
(Right) 3 1/2 oz. Glass jar with metal cap has
2 variations of labels. OSP 25c. **CMV $110.
Jar only mint $135. MB.**

BABY SET 1923
Yellow box contains 2 oz. bottle of Toilet
Water, bar of Baby Soap & can of Baby
Powder. OSP 99c. **CMV $350. MB. - CMV
Toilet water only $125. mint.**

BABY SET 1910
Box with kids playing on lid holds 1905 Baby
Powder can, 2 oz. bottle of Violet Toilet Water
and box of Baby Soap. OSP 75c. **CMV $325.
MB.**

CALIFORNIA BABY SOAP 1902
Box of one bar. OSP 15c. **CMV $75. mint.**

BABY POWDER 1898
Metal can. Eureka Trade Mark on label. OSP
25c. **CMV $120. mint, $145. MB.**

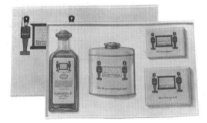

BABY POWDER 1905
(Left) Metal can lift off cap 1905. 1906 cap
has sifter top, CP in center of Trade Mark.
1910 same can sifter cap a little different and
Eureka trade mark in place of CP. **CMV $115.,
$135. MB.**
BABY POWDER 1912-16
(Right) Metal can. OSP 25c. **CMV $110.
mint, $130. MB.**

BABY POWDER 1916
(Top) Blue & pink can. OSP 25c. **CMV $120.
MB, $100. can only, mint.**
BABY SET 1916
(Bottom) Baby set box holds can of baby
Powder as pictured above, without box, bar of
Baby Soap & 2 oz. bottle of Violet Toilet Water.
OSP 75c. **CMV $350. MB.**

BABY SET 1925
Yellow box holds 4 oz. bottle of Supreme Olive
Oil, 4 oz. yellow can of Baby Powder, yellow
box of Boric Acid $ 5 oz. yellow cake of
genuine imported Castile Soap. OSP $1.78.
CMV $350. MB.
SUPREME OLIVE OIL FOR BABY'S 1925
4 oz. bottle with yellow label & cork stopper.
Came in Baby Set only. **CMV $100. mint.**
CASTILE SOAP FOR BABY'S 1925
5 oz. cake wrapped in yellow paper. Came in
Baby Set only. **CMV $75. mint.**
BORIC ACID FOR BABY 1925
Yellow Box with soldiers on top. OSP 33c.
CMV $50.
BABY POWDER 1923
4 oz. Yellow can. OSP 29c. **CMV $95. MB,
can only $80.**

ALSO SEE AVON BAY RUM SECTION.

BAY RUM - CPC

ALL BOTTLES PRICED MINT.

BAY RUM 1898
4 oz. clear glass square bottle. Glass stopper.
colored label. OSP 40c. **CMV $190., $220.
MB.**

CALIFORNIA BABY SOAP 1905
4 oz. white embossed bar in wrapping. OSP
15c. **CMV $75. MB., $50. soap only.**

BAY RUM 1896
(Left) 4 oz. glass stoppered bottle. OSP
40c. **CMV $150.** Also came in 8 & 16 oz.
size with glass stoppers. OSP 75c & $1.25.
CMV $150. each BO $200. MB.
BAY RUM 1905
(Right) 16 oz. size glass stopper. OSP
$1.25. **CMV $150. mint, BO $200. MB.**

BAY RUM 1930-36
(Right) 8 oz. clear glass bottle, black cap,
green & black label. OSP 89c. **CMV $40.
BO mint, $50. MB.**

BAY RUM

BAY RUM 1908
(Left) 4 oz. glass stoppered bottle. OSP 40c.
CMV $135., BO $160. MB. Also came in 8 &
16 oz. size glass stoppered bottles. **CMV
$140. each mint., $165. MB.**
BAY RUM 1912
(Right) 4 oz. glass stoppered bottle. Also
came in 8 & 16 oz. size glass stoppered
bottles. OSP 40c. **CMV $140. each mint,
$165. MB.**

BAY RUM 1927
4 oz. metal & cork CPC embossed stopper.
Front & neck label. Also came in 8 "shown on
right" & 16 oz. size with cork stopper. OSP
50c. **CMV $100. BO 4 oz., $120. 8 & 16 oz.
Add $25. for box, mint.**

BAY RUM 1929
(Left) 16 oz. size with metal cap. OSP $1.44.
CMV $95. BO, $110. MB.
BAY RUM 1923
(Right) 4 oz. bottle, metal shaker cap in cork.
OSP 47c. **CMV $95. MB, $85. BO.** Also
came in 8 oz. OSP 84c, 32 oz. $2.40. **CMV
$95. BO each, $110. MB.**

LEFT TO RIGHT
BAY RUM 1915
4 oz. with crown metal & cork stopper. OSP
25c. **CMV $125. mint. $150. MB.**
BAY RUM 1921
4 oz. front & neck label. Cork stopper. OSP
47c. **CMV $175. MB, $125. BO.**
BAY RUM 1898
4 oz. cork stopper. 126 Chambers St. on label
where CPC started. Very rare. **CMV $200. -
$240. MB.**

BAY RUM 1920
4 oz. clear glass botle, glass stopper. **CMV
$110. mint, $135. MB.**
BAY RUM 1912
16 oz. clear glass, cork stopper. RARE. **CMV
$150., $175. MB.**

BAY RUM 1915
(Left) 4 oz. glass stopper. CPC logo label.
CMV $125. mint.
BAY RUM SUPERIOR 1898
4 oz. botle, 126 Chambers St., New York
address on label. Chrome crown stopper in
cork. **CMV $175. mint.**

BAY RUM 1930-36
4 oz. Ribbed glass bottle with black cap &
green label. OSP 50c. **CMV $50. MB, $45.
BO.** Also came in 16 oz. size OSP 89c. **CMV
$50. BO $60. MB.**

BAY RUM 1905
4 oz. glass stopper. **CMV $140. mint.**

BAY RUM 1936
4 oz. bottle sold 1930-36. Yellow label, Black
cap. Shown with red & green Christmas box.
Good House Keeping on label. **CMV $50. BO,
$65. MB as shown.**

CPC BOTTLES - MISC.

LAIT VIRGINAL 1900
2 oz., cork stopper. OSP 60c. **CMV $115. - $140. MB.**

BENZOIN LOTION 1915
(Left) 2 oz. size, metal crown stopper in cork. Flowered label. OSP 75c. Also came in 4 oz. size $1.50. **CMV $100. each mint - $125. MB.**
BENZOIN LOTION 1923
(Right) 2 oz. bottle with metal & cork stopper. OSP 59c. **CMV $75. - $100. MB.**

FACE LOTION 1896
(Left) Glass bottle with cork stopper. OSP $1. **CMV $110. - $135. MB.**
FACE LOTION 1908
(Right) Glass bottle, cork stopper, front & neck label. OSP $1. **CMV $110. - $135. MB.**

LIQUID SHAMPOO 1923
6 oz. front & neck label. Metal shaker cap in cork. OSP 48c. **CMV $90., $110. MB.**

BENZOIN LOTION 1925
(Left) 2 oz. ribbed glass bottle with metal & cork stopper, blue & gold label. OSP 59c. **CMV $75. BO, $90. MB.**
LAIT VIRGINAL 1896
(Right) 2 oz. size, ribbed glass bottle has ribbed glass stopper set in cork. OSP 65c. **CMV $150. mint, $175. MB.**

FACE LOTION 1912
(Left) 6 oz. clear glass botle, cork stopper. Front & neck label. Came in white & pink shades. OSP $1. **CMV $100. BO, $125. MB.**
LIQUID SHAMPOO 1914
(Right) 6 oz. glass bottle with metal cap. OSP 35c. **CMV $95. BO, $120. MB.**

FACE LOTION 1918
(Left) 6 oz. glass bottle has cork stopper, green front & neck label. Came with small sponge tied to neck. OSP $1. **CMV $80, $100. MB.**
FACE LOTION 1923
(Right) 6 oz. glass bottle, blue label, cork stopper. OSP 97c. **CMV $80, $100. MB.**

EAU DE QUININE HAIR TONIC 1905
Glass stopper in cork. Eureka Trade Mark on neck label. OSP 65c. **CMV $125. - $150. MB.**

CUTICLE REMOVER OR SOFTENER 1929-30
(Left) 1/2 oz. bottle with brown label & cork stopper with glass dabber. Also came in Boudoir Set. OSP 35c. **CMV $70. BO, $85. MB.**

CUTRANE 1924
(Center) Glass·bottle with cork stopper with camel hair brush on stopper. Gold & black label. OSP 30c. **CMV $70. BO mint, $85. MB.**

LIQUID FACE POWDER 1920
(Right) 6 oz. clear glass, cork stopper. Has green front & neck label. OSP 97c. **CMV $80. mint BO, $100. MB.**

LAIT VIRGINAL 1910
(Right) 2 oz. shown, metal crown in cork stopper. ALso came in 4 and 8 oz. size. Front and neck labels. OSP 65c, $1.25 and $2. **CMV $100. mint, $125. MB.**

WITCH HAZEL 1923
16 oz bottle, cork stopper.
CMV $85.00 mint

EAU DE QUININE 1915
(Left) 6 oz. glass bottle with metal crown & cork cap. OSP 65c. **CMV $100. BO, $125. MB.**

EAU DE QUININE 1923
(Right) 6 oz. glass bottle, metal shaker cap in cork. OSP 69c. **CMV $90. BO, $110. MB.**

EAU DE QUININE 1900
(Left) 6 oz. bottle with sprinkler top. OSP 65c. **CMV $125. - $150. MB.**

EAU DE QUININE 1908
(Right) Glass bottle has cork stopper with metal cap. Label has Eureka CP Trade Mark. OSP 65c. **CMV $125. - $150. MB.**

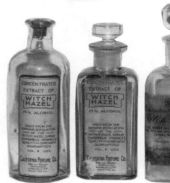

WITCH HAZEL 1924
Both bottles on left 8 oz. size, same label. Left is cork stopper and right is glass stopper. **CMV $85. cork stopper round bottle. $110. for glass stopper & square bottle.** Bottle on right is 1910, 8 oz. size glass stopper. **CMV $125. mint.**

WITCH HAZEL 1910
16 oz. clear glass, glass stopper. OSP 75c. **CMV $150. - $175. MB.**

WITCH HAZEL 1896

(Left) 4 & 8 oz. bottles came with sprinkler top. OSP 25c & 45c. **CMV $100.** Pint bottle came with glass stopper. OSP 75c. **CMV $150. mint, $200. MB.**

WITCH HAZEL 1905

(Right) 16 oz. size, glass stopper. OSP 75c. **CMV $150. mint, $200. MB.**

WITCH HAZEL 1915

(Left) 4 oz. glass bottle with cork stopper. OSP 25c. **CMV $90.** 8 & 16 oz. size with glass stopper. OSp 45c & 75c. **CMV $125. each mint, $145. MB.**

WITCH HAZEL 1924

(Center & Right) 4 oz. clear glass bottle, cork stopper. Front & neck label. 3 different labels. 2 shown. OSP 39c. **CMV $75. BO mint, $90. MB.**

ROSE WATER GLYCERINE AND BENZOIN 1930

4 oz. ribbed glass, black screw on cap. color label. **CMV $75.**

WITCH HAZEL 1908

(Left) 16 oz. size glass stopper. OSP 75c. **CMV $150. mint, $200. MB.**

WITCH HAZEL 1908

(Right) Came in 4, 8 & 16 oz. bottles with glass stopper. Eureka Trade Mark on label. OSP 25c, 45c & 75c. **CMV $150. mint, $200. MB.**

WITCH HAZEL 1920

(Left) 16 oz. clear glass, cork stopper. Front label. Rare. OSP 75c. **CMV $135. mint, $160. MB.** Also came in 8 oz. size with metal crown & cork stopper. OSP 45c. **CMV $100. Mint, $125. MB.**

WITCH HAZEL 1930

(Right) 4 oz. ribbed glass bottle, black cap, green label. Rare. **CMV $80. - $90. MB.**

ROSE WATER GLYCERINE AND BENZOIN SAMPLE 1925

Small sample bottle on 1st introduction of this product in January 1925. Rare. **CMV $75., $85. MB.**

WITCH HAZEL 1923

(Left) 4 oz. bottle with cork stopper, green front & neck label. OSP 39c. **CMV $75.** Also came in 8, 16 & 32 oz. size. OSP 69c, $1.20 & $2.25. **CMV each, $75. mint, add $25. MB each.**

WITCH HAZEL 1925

(Right) 4 oz. bottle with cork stopper, green label on front & neck. OSP 39c. **CMV each $75. mint, add $25. MB each.**

TOOTH WASH 1921

(Left) 2 oz. glass bottle, brass & cork stopper. OSP 25c. **CMV $100., $125. MB.**

TOOTH WASH 1923

(Right) 2 oz. glass bottle, metal and cork cap. Front & neck label. OSP 33c. **CMV $85., $110. MB.**

TOOTH WASH 1908
(Left) Glass bottle has cork stopper with metal crown top. Eureka Trade Mark on neck label. OSP 25c. **CMV $140. MB - $115. MB.**
TOOTH WASH 1915
(Right) Glass bottle with metal & cork cap. Back side of bottle is embossed California Tooth Wash. OSP 25c. **CMV $105. with label mint. Embossed bottle only $25. - $130. MB.**

ROSE WATER GLYCERINE & BENZOIN 1923
(Left) 6 oz. clear glass bottle. Glass stopper set in cork. Print front & neck label. OSP 60c. **CMV $100. - $125. MB.**
ROSE WATER GLYCERINE & BENZOIN 1924-25
(Right) 6 oz. bottle with cork stopper. Front & neck label. This was a very short issue bottle. OSP 60c. **CMV $100. BO, $125. MB.**

LOTUS CREAM 1917
12 oz. bottle has glass stopper. OSP $1.23. **CMV $160.** 4 oz. bottle has cork stopper. OSP 48c. **CMV $120. Add $25. MB. each.** Both have front & neck labels. Also came in 1 quart, 1/2 & 1 gallon size.

ROSE WATER GLYCERINE & BENZOIN SAMPLE 1924
Glass bottle, cork stopper. **CMV $75. MB, $60. BO mint.**

CALIFORNIA NAIL BLEACH 1900
Eureka Trade Mark New York label. Glass stopper. 1 oz. size. **CMV $135.**

ROSE WATER GLYCERINE & BENZOIN 1929 ONLY
(Left) 4 oz. clear glass ribbed bottle with black cap. Bottle came from Avon with small sample pink label marked not for resale. Bottle with this label rare. **CMV $100. mint BO.**
ROSE WATER GLYCERINE & BENZOIN 1926
(Right) 4 oz. ribbed bottle with cork stopper, front & neck label. OSP 50c. **CMV $75. mint, $90. MB.**

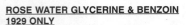

LOTUS CREAM SAMPLE 1917
Blue and white box holds 1/2 oz. sample bottle with cork stopper. Blue label. **CMV $80. MB, $65. BO. mint.**

EYE BROW PENCIL 1915
Wood box holds metal pencil. Has CPC label & Tax Stamp. **CMV $50. Mint.**

NAIL BLEACH 1914
2 oz. round bottle with glass stopper, front paper label. 2 different labels shown. OSP 25c. **CMV $90. BO, $110. MB. each.**

LOTUS CREAM 1925
4 oz. ribbed bottle with cork stopper, front & neck label. OSP 48c. **CMV $85. BO mint, $100. MB.**

HAIR TONIC EAU DE QUININE 1931-36
(Left) Ribbed glass bottle with black cap & silver label. OSP 90c. **CMV $40. bottle only, $45. in box.** Also came in 16 oz. size. OSP $1.75. **CMV $50. BO mint, $55. MB.**
NULODOR 1928
(Right) Bottle has clear stopper, front & neck label. OSP 35c. **CMV $120. mint. Rare.**

NAIL BLEACH 1916
2 oz. glass stopper, square bottle. Rare. OSP 25c. **CMV $125. BO, $150. MB.**

GERTRUDE RECORDON'S PEACH LOTION 1929 ONLY
Clear glass. Box states "This merchandise sent free for demonstration purposes or personal use. It must not be sold." **CMV $100. MB., $85. BO.**

NAIL BLEACH - 1 OZ. 1912
(Left) 1 oz. bottle, cork stopper. OSP 25c. **CMV $100. - $115. MB.**
DEPLIATORY 1915
(Right) 1 oz. bottle with cork stopper. OSP 50c. **CMV $100. - $120. MB.**

ROUGE 1908
Rouge powder can. **CMV $50., $70. MB.**
LIQUID ROUGE
Bottle. **CMV $100., $125. MB.** OSP each 25c. Eureka trademark on both labels and CP in center of early label instead of Eureka.

BRILLIANTINE 1930 ONLY
(Left) 2 oz. bottle with frosted glass stopper in cork. Silver label. OSP 50c. **CMV $75. mint, $95. MB.**
DEODORANT 1930 ONLY
(Right) 2 oz. bottle with corked frosted glass stopper. OSP 50c. **CMV $80. - $100. MB.**

ROSE POMADE 1914
(Left) White glass jar. Top & side label. OSP 25c. **CMV $65.**
NAIL BLEACH - 2 OZ. 1912
(Right) 2 oz. clear glass round bottle, cork stopper, front & neck label. OSP 25c. **CMV $95. BO, $110. MB.**

ROUGE 1916
(Left) Rough. OSP 25c. **CMV $45., $60. MB.**
LIQUID ROUGE 1916
(Right) Glass bottle, cork stopper. OSP 25c. **CMV $80. BO, $100. MB.**

SHAVING SOAP 1905
(Left) 1 bar of soap. OSP 20c. **CMV $70. in wrapper, mint.**
BAYBERRY SHAVING STICK 1923
(Right) Three piece nickel metal container holds shaving soap. OSP 33c. **CMV $55. mint.**

SHAVING CREAM STICK 1915
Gold or silvertone metal can. Came with soap stick, CPC on lid. OSP 25c. **CMV $55. MB., $30. can only mint.**

CPC JARS

AUTOMASSAGE SHAVING BRUSH 1915
Automassage on handle. Rubber center of brush as shown. This was not made for CPC but sold by CPC on a special offer with CPC shaving powder. OSP 25c. **CMV $50. MB, $30. brush only.**

LAVENDER SALTS 1890s
(Left) Teal green glass, octagonal shaped bottle. Ground glass stopper. Rare. OSP 35c. **CMV $275. - $300. MB.**
LAVENDER SALTS - METAL TOP 1890s
(Right) Emerald green glass, glass stopper with screw on metal top. Rare. OSP 35c. **CMV $275. - $300. MB.**

LAVENDER SALTS 1893
(Left) Emerald green glass bottle with green glass stopper with leather liner. OSP 35c. **CMV $200. mint, $225. MB.**
LAVENDER SALTS 1915
(Right) Glass stoppered bottle. OSP 35c. **CMV $115. mint, $140. MB.**

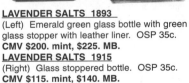

LAVENDER SALTS 1923
Glass stoppered bottle, front & neck label. OSP 49c. **CMV $110. mint, $135. MB.**

LAVENDER SALTS 1910
Emerald green glass. Same label only 1 bottle is 1/8" bigger than the other. Green glass stoppers set in rubber. OSP 35c. **CMV $200. each mint, $225. MB.**

MASSAGE CREAM 1896
Glass jar with glass stopper. OSP 75c. **CMV $150. mint, $175. MB.**

LAVENDER SALTS 1912
(Left) Glass stoppered bottle. OSP 35c.
CMV $110. - $135. MB.
LAVENDER SALTS 1908
(Right) Green glass bottle has green glass stopper with rubber base. OSP 35c. **CMV $160. mint, $185. MB.**

MASSAGE CREAM 1916
Glass jar has glass stopper, green ribbon on neck. OSP 50c. **CMV $125. mint, $145. MB.**

TOOTH POWDER 1908
White glass bottle with metal cap. OSP 25c.
CMV $110. mint, $130. MB.

LEMONOL CLEANSING CREAM 1926-30
Frosted glass jar with brass lid. OSP 50c.
CMV $75. MB, $65. jar only.

SHAMPOO CREAM 1896
4 oz. white glass jar, metal lid. OSP 35c.
CMV $90., $110. MB.

DERMOL MASSAGE CREAM 1920-23
Glass jar with metal screw on lid. OSP 96c.
CMV $75. mint, $90. MB.

DERMOL MASSAGE CREAM 1923
(Left) White glass jar with ribbed sides. CPC on metal lid. OSP 96c. **CMV $50. - $60. MB.**
VIOLET NUTRI-CREME 1926
(Right) White glass jar with flowered label. OSP 89c. **CMV $50. - $60. MB.**

SHAMPOO CREAM 1905
4 oz. white glass jar. OSP 35c. **CMV $85. jar only mint, $105. MB.**

SHAMPOO CREAM 1896
4 oz. glass jar. Man's picture, washing his hair on lid. Rare. OSP 35c. **CMV $125. - $150. MB.**

SHAMPOO CREAM 1908
4 oz. white glass jar with metal lid. OSP 35c.
CMV $75. jar only, $95. MB.

SHAMPOO CREAM 1912
4 oz. white glass jar, metal lid, with or without CPC on lid. Early issue 1912 has Eureka trademark on box - 1915 one does not. OSP 35c. **CMV $80. jar only $95. MB for Eureka trademark, $10. less without it.**

BANDOLINE HAIR DRESSING 1923-30
Tall 4 oz. clear glass with cork stopper. Comes with neck label to be mint. OSP 45c. **CMV $75. BO mint, $90. MB.**

BANDOLINE 1908
2 oz. glass bottle, cork stopper. OSP 25c. **CMV $110. MB, $90. BO.**

SHAMPOO CREAM SAMPLE 1915
Small 1"size aluminum round bottom container. Rare. **CMV $50. mint.**

COLD CREAMS 1915
Large & small white glass jars with CPC on metal lid. OSP 25c & 45c. **CMV $75. MB. each, $60. jar only, mint.**

BANDOLINE HAIR DRESSING 1923-30
(Left) 2 oz. yellow label & cork stopper, clear glass jar. OSP 24c. **CMV $60. mint, $75. MB.**
BANDOLINE HAIR DRESSING 1923-30
(Right) 4 oz. size. Glass bottle, cork stopper, front & neck label. OSP 45c. **CMV $65. BO, $80. MB.**

COLD CREAM 1896
White glass jar with metal lid. Eureka trademark on label. OSP 25c. **CMV $90. mint, $110. MB.**

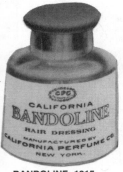

CALIFORNIA COLD CREAM 1908
2 oz. white glass jar with metal lid. OSP 25c. **CMV $95. MB, $80. jar only mint.**

BANDOLINE 1915
(Left) Glass bottle with cork stopper. OSP 25c. **CMV $75. mint, $90. MB.**
BANDOLINE 1930-35
(Right) Frosted glass or clear glass bottle with blue wrapped cork stopper. OSP 37c. **CMV $60. BO, $70. MB.**

COLD CREAM 1926
(Left) White glas jar with CPC on aluminum lid. OSP 63c. **CMV $50. mint, $65. MB.**

CPC PERFUMES - MISC.

CPC COLD CREAM 1912
Large white glass jar with metal lid. OSP 45c.
CMV $60. jar only, $75. MB.

ROSE POMADE 1900
(Left) Eureka Trademark. Same in CPC sets.
1914 on right. Both white glass, top & side
paper labels. **CMV $55. each mint.**

TRAVELERS PERFUME 1 OZ. 1917
1 oz. octagonal shaped bottle with glass
stopper & screw on nickel lid. OSP 90c.
CMV $135. BO mint, $160. MB.

CALIFORNIA SHAMPOO CREAM 1900
Both 4 oz. glass jars, metal lids are different
sizes. 1 plain - 1 with man washing his hair &
CPC. Both has plain paper flower design front
labels. **CMV $125. with man's head lid,
$100. for plain lid.**

DERMOL MASSAGE CREAM 1923
1 lb. white glass jar. Aluminum lid, colored
front label. Very rare. 4 1/4" high. **CMV $100.
mint** SHown next to 1915 Cold Cream jar
regular size, for size comparison.

TRAVELER'S PERFUME 1900-1923
1/2 oz. size. Metal cap over glass stopper.
Gold label. Bottle is octagonally shaped.
Came in all fragrances of 1896-1908. Red
flowered box. OSP 50c. **CMV $125. BO
mint, $150. MB.** Also came in 1 oz. size on
left. RARE. **CMV $150. - $175. MB.**

PERFUME FLACONETTE 1923
Octagonal shaped bottle with long glass
stopper, neck label. Came with & without
brass cap with CPC on cap. Came in Daphne,
Crab Apple, Vernafleur, Trailing Arbutus, White
Rose, Carnation, Violet, White Lilac,
Heliotrope, Roses, Lily of the Valley, Mission
Garden. OSP 49c. **CMV with brass cap
$90., without cap $75. - $110. MB.**

PERFUME FLACONETTE 1930-35
(Left) Embossed clear glass stopper, brass
cap over glass stopper. Avon on cap. Came
in all perfumes of 1930-35. OSP $1.10. **CMV
$90. each mint, $110. MB.**
ROSE PERFUME SAMPLE 1900
(Right) 1/2 oz. size, cork stopper. Came in all
fragrances of 1900. **CMV $125. mint.**

PERFUME FLACONETTE 1925
Flaconette size embossed glass bottle with
glass stopper. Brass cap over stopper. Came
in Mission Garden, American Ideal, Narcissus,
Daphne, Jardin D' Amour. OSP $1.10. **CMV
$90. BO, mint with brass cap. $120. MB.**
The cap has fragrance on it.

1896 TO 1914 PERFUMES

The following list of perfumes were sold by CPC from 1896 to 1914. Use this list to identify misc. perfumes.

The regular line of CP Floral extracts consists of thirty odors, in the following range of prices and sizes:

1915 TO 1921 PERFUMES

The very extensive CPC line gives a wide range of selection, and among the 27 different odors there is sure to be one or more to satisfy the most fastidious and exacting.

The prices are according to the cost of production and the value of the goods offered. All perfumes are in attractive bottles, put up in beautiful lithographed boxes, as illustrated.

Concentrated Floral Odors Triple Extracts

Roses		
Lily of the Valley		
White Rose		
Violet		
White Lilac		
Sweet Peas		
Hyacinth		
Heliotrope	1 ounce bottle	$ .60
Carnation	2 ounce bottle	1.10
Bouquet Marie	4 ounce bottle	2.00
New Mown Hay		
Marie Stewart	1/2 pint bottle	3.75
Rose Geranium	1 pint bottle	7.00
Stephanotis		
Ylang Ylang		
Jack Rose		
Tube Rose		
Treffle		
California Bouquet		

Crab Apple Blossom	1 ounce bottle	$ .75
Trailing Arbutus	2 ounce bottle	1.40
Frangipanni	4 ounce bottle	2.75
May Blossom	1/2 pint bottle	5.25
Jockey Club	1 pint bottle	10.00
White Heliotrope		

Lou Lillie	1 ounce bottle	$ .50
Musk	2 ounce bottle	.90
Golf Club	4 ounce bottle	1.75
Venetian Carnation	1/2 pint bottle	3.25
Golf Violet	1 pint bottle	6.00

Violet		
White Rose		
Carnation		
Heliotrope		
Lily of the Valley	1 ounce bottle	$ .50
White Lilac	2 ounce bottle	.90
Hyacinth	4 ounce bottle	1.75
California Bouquet	1/2 pint bottle	3.25
Roses	1 pint bottle	6.00
New Mown Hay		
Sweet Pea		
Treffle		
Rose Geranium		
Jack Rose		

Quadruple Extracts

Crab Apple Blossom	1 ounce bottle	$ .60
Trailing Arbutus	2 ounce bottle	1.10
Jockey Club	4 ounce bottle	2.00
Honeysuckle	1/2 pint bottle	3.75
White Heliotrope	1 pint bottle	7.00

Extra Concentrated Odors

Natoma Rose	1 ounce bottle	$.75
Venetian Carnation	2 ounce bottle	1.40
Golf Violet	4 ounce bottle	2.75
Musk	1/2 pint bottle	5.25
	1 pint bottle	10.00

PERFUME SPRAY ATOMIZER 1928
1 is green opaque over clear glass & 1 is green painted over clear, gold plated top. **CMV $90. each.**

PERFUME 1918
1/2 oz. bottle with crown glass stopper set in cork. Front & neck label. Came in all fragrances of 1918. OSP 50c. **CMV $100. BO mint, $125. MB.**

CPC PERFUME 1918
(Left) 1/2 oz. glass & cork stopper. Came in 1918 Gift Box A Set. **CMV $110. mint.**
1/2 OZ. PERFUME 1919
(Right) 1/2 oz. glass crowned shaped stopper in cork. Came in all 1919 fragrances. OSP 75c. **CMV $100. mint, $125. MB.**

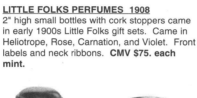

WHITE ROSE PERFUME 1918
2 oz. size, RARE, cork stopper. Front & neck label with neck ribbon. OSP $1. **CMV $125. mint.**

LITTLE FOLKS PERFUMES 1908
2" high small bottles with cork stoppers came in early 1900s Little Folks gift sets. Came in Heliotrope, Rose, Carnation, and Violet. Front labels and neck ribbons. **CMV $75. each mint.**

LITTLE FOLKS PERFUME 1915
(Left) Small gem size bottle with front label & ribbon on neck. Cork stopper. Came in 1915 Little Folks Set only. Came in Carnation, Violet, White Rose, Heliotrope. **CMV $75. each mint.**
LITTLE FOLKS PERFUME 1910
(Right) 2" high, cork stopper. Came in Little Folks Set only from 1910 to 1915. Both bottles pictured came in same fragrances. **CMV $75. mint.**

PERFUME FLACONETTE 1926
Frosted ribbed glass bottle with long glass stopper. Small paper label on front. Came with brass cap with CPC on cap. Came in Crab Apple, Daphne, Trailing Arbutus, Vernafleur, American Ideal, Carnation, Heliotrope, White Rose, Violet, Lily of the Valley. OSP 59c. **CMV with brass cap $90., $70. BO, $110. MB.**

LITTLE FOLKS PERFUME 1925-32
(Left) 1/2 oz. bottle with brass screw on cap. Came in 1925 Little Folks Set only. Came in Violet, Carnation, Heliotrope, White Lilac, Daphne, Vernafleur, Trailing Arbutus. **CMV $65. each mint.**
LITTLE FOLKS PERFUME 1896
(Right) 2" high. Came in 1896 & 1906 Little Folks Set only in Rose, or White Rose, Heliotrope, Violet, & Carnation. Cork stopper. **CMV $75. each mint.**

PERFUMES 1906

1 oz. round bottles came in Atomizer Perfume Set with cork stopper. Came in all fragrances of 1908. **CMV $110. each mint.**

PERFUME 1/2 oz 1915

(Left) 1/2 oz. bottle with glass stopper set in cork. Front and neck label. Came in Violet, White Rose, Carnation, White Lilac, Heliotrope, Lily of the Valley. Two different stoppers as shown on left. OSP 25c. **CMV $110., $135. MB.**

1 OZ. EXTRA CONCENTRATED PERFUMES

(Right) 1 oz. size, front and neck label. Came in Golf Violet, Musk, Crab Apple Blossom, Natoma, Rose, Venetian Carnation. OSP 75c. **CMV $175. MB, $135. BO.**

FRENCH PERFUMES 1900

(Left) Trial size 1/4 oz. on left. 2 oz. size on right. Cork stoppers. **CMV $125. BO trial size mint, CMV $200. 2 oz. size mint, add $25. MB.**

FRENCH PERFUMES 1916

(Right) 2 different embossed glass bottles. Cork stoppers. Trial size. OSP 25c. **CMV $150. BO mint, $175. MB.**

PERFUME 1896

1 oz. octagonal shaped bottle, front & neck label with Eureka Trade Mark. Came in Atomizer Perfume Set with cork stopper. Came in all fragrances of 1896. **CMV $165. mint.**

EXTRACT ROSE GERANIUM PERFUME 1896

1 oz. glass stopper, paper label. OSP 40c. **CMV $200. mint.**

PERFUMES 1923

1/2 oz. bottle with crown glass stopper set in cork. Front & neck label. Crab Apple, Blossom, White Rose, Trailing Arbutus, Rose Carnation, Heliotrope, Violet, White Lilac & Lily of the Valley. Came in red box, 2 different bottles as shown. OSP 59c. **CMV $110. BO, $135. MB.**

FRENCH PERFUMES 1900

(Left) 1/4 oz. bottle with glass stopper. Came in Le Perfume Des Roses, L' Odeur de Violette, Peau d'Espagne. OSP 25c. **CMV $125. BO, $150. MB.**

FRENCH PERFUMES 1896

(Right) 1/4 oz. glass bottle, cork stopper. Came in Le Perfume Des Roses, L'Odeur de Violette, Peau d'Espagne. OSP 25c. **CMV $125. BO mint, $150. MB.**

ATOMIZER PERFUME 1908

(Left) 1 oz. 6 sided bottle with cork stopper. Green neck & front label. Came in all fragrances of 1908. Came only in CPC Atomizer Sets. Used with Spray Atomizer. OSP 50c. **CMV $100. mint.**

ATOMIZER PERFUME 1914

(Right) 1 oz. bottle with green & gold front & neck label, cork stopper. Came in 1918 Atomizer Box Set only. Used with Spray Atomizer. Came in all 1918 perfumes. OSP 50c. **CMV $100. BO mint.**

JOCKEY CLUB PERFUME 1908
Green front and neck label and green neck ribbon. OSP 50c. **CMV $100. mint, $130. MB.**

PEAU D'ESPAGNE PERFUME 1896
(Left) 4" high flaconette size, cork stopper. CPC French perfume. OSP 25c. **CMV $160. mint, $180. MB.**

CRAB APPLE BLOSSOM PERFUME 1910
(Center) 1 oz. glass stopper, front & neck label. CPC on label. **CMV $110. mint, $135. MB.**

WHITE ROSE PERFUME 1896
(Right) 1 oz. glass stopper. Bottom part of label is missing on bottle shown. OSP 40c. **CMV $150. BO, $200. MB.**

PERFUME 1908
(Left) 1 oz. glass stopper, gold label. Eureka Trade Mark on label. Came in all fragrances of 1908. **CMV $180. MB, $150. BO. mint.** Also came in several different glass stoppers. 2 different shown on left.

PERFUME 1906-1918
(Right) 4 oz. glass stoppered bottle, gold embossed front and neck label. Came in all perfumes of the period. See list on front of this section. OSP $2.75. **CMV $150. BO, $200. MB.**

CPC PERFUME 1906
1 oz. perfume, gold front & neck label. Came in all 1908 perfumes. **CMV $200. MB, $150. BO.**

VIOLET PERFUME 1900
Eureka Trade Mark. Neck ribbon, neck label is plain. **CMV $165. BO mint.**

CHRISTMAS BOX NO. 5 PERFUME 1906
(Left) White leather covered box holds 3 oz. glass stoppered perfume. OSP $1.50. **CMV $175. BO mint, $225. MB.**

MUSK PERFUME 1896
(Right) 1 oz. size, glass stoppered. Came in all fragrances, with Chicago label. RARE. **CMV $125. mint, $150. MB.**

CUT GLASS PERFUME 1915-20
2 oz. bottle with cut glass stopper. 2 different labels in embossed gold. White leatherette box. Came in Trailing Arbutus & Crab Apple Blossom. OSP $2.25. **CMV $225., $265. MB.** Octagonal label on bottom is 1911 issue. Same CMV.

PERFUME & ATOMIZER 1918
1 oz. bottle with atomizer came in black box. Bottle has cork stopper & green front & neck label. Came in all fragrances of 1918, including American Ideal & Daphne. OSP $1.50. **CMV $150. MB with atomizer. $100. BO mint.**

CHRISTMAS PERFUME 1905
2 oz. glass stopper perfume. OSP 75c. **CMV $150. BO, $200. MB.**

EXTRACT PERFUMES 1905
1 oz. glass stopper, white paper label. Came in all fragrances of 1896. OSP 50c. **CMV $215. MB, $175. BO mint.**

EXTRACT PERFUMES 1896
(Left) 2 oz. round glass stopper. New York, Chicago, San Francisco on label. Came in all fragrances in 1908. OSP 90c to $1.40. **CMV $150. BO, $200. MB.**
FRENCH PERFUME 1896-1908
(Right) 1/2 oz. bottle with glass stopper. Eureka Trade Mark in center of label. Came in Le Perfume des Roses, Peau d'Espagne, L'Odeur de Violette. OSP 55c. **CMV $150. BO, $200. MB.**

PERFUME "FLORAL EXTRACTS" 1908
1 oz. glass stoppered bottle with Eureka CP Trade Mark on label. Came in all 1908 perfumes. OSP 50c. **CMV $150. BO, $200. MB.** Also came in 2, 4, 8 & 16 oz. bottles. **CMV same as 1 oz. size.**

CPC PERFUME 1916
3 different glass stoppers shown. 1 & 2 oz. sizes. OSP 50c. **CMV $135. BO mint, $175. MB.**

WHITE ROSE PERFUME 1908
2 oz. Extract of White Rose perfume. Neck ribbon & glass stopper. OSP 90c. **CMV $150. BO mint, $200. MB.**

1 OZ. PERFUMES 1908
1 oz. glass stoppered bottle. Eureka Trade Mark on label. In gray flowered box. Came in all fragrances of 1908. OSP 50c to 75c. **CMV each $200. MB, $150. BO.** Each fragrance came with different flower on label. Heliotrope on left and Crab Apple Blossom on right.

PERFUME 1915
(Left) 1 oz. clear glass bottle with glass stopper. Came in all 1915 fragrances. OSP 75c. **CMV $150. mint, $175. MB.**
CRAB APPLE BLOSSOM 1905
(Right) 1 oz. clear glass bottle, glass stopper, label has CPC Eureka Trade Mark. Came in all 1908 fragrances. Bottle came with different shaped stopper also. OSP 50c - 75c. **CMV $150. BO, $200. MB.**

FRENCH PERFUME 1905
Glass stoppered bottle came in 1/2, 1, 2 & 4 oz. sizes in these fragrances: Le Perfume des Roses, L'Odeur de Violette & Peau d'Espagne. 1 oz. size pictured. OSP 25c to $3.75. **CMV $165. BO, $215. MB.**

CPC PERFUME SAMPLE SET 1922
Black carrying case with "California Perfume Co." on front. 4 glass flaconette with gold cap & fits into gold case. **CMV $350. MB, $75. each flaconette.**

2 OZ. PERFUME 1916
2 oz. glass stopper either faceted or round. Front & neck label. Came in all fragrances of 1915. OSP $1.10. **CMV $200. MB, $150. BO.**

PERFUMES 1923
1 & 2 oz. bottle in same shape & design with glass stopper. Front & neck label with gold basket design. Beige box. Came in Carnation, Roses, Heliotrope, Violet, White Lilac, Lily of the Valley, Crab Apple Blossom, Trailing Arbutus, White Rose. OSP $1.17 & $2.10. **CMV $135. BO, $170. MB.** Also came in 4 oz. size.

PERFUMES 8 OZ. 1905
(Left) 8 oz. glass stoppered bottle. Came in California Bouquet, shown. Violet, White Rose, Carnation, Heliotrope, Lily of the Valley, White Lilac, Hyacinth, Roses, New Mown Hay, Sweet Pea, Treffle, Rose Geranium, Jack Rose, front paper label and also came with neck label. OSP $3.25 each. **CMV $175. each BO, $225. MB.**
PERFUME 1923
(Right) 1 oz. glass stoppered bottle is ribbed. Came in Carnation, Crab Apple Blossom, Heliotrope, Lily of the Valley, Violet & White Rose. Front & neck label. OSP $1.17. **CMV $135. BO, $160. MB.**

PERFUMES 1915
2 oz. on left & 1 oz. on right, different labels & diamond cut shaped glass stoppers. **CMV $125. each mint.**

TRIAL SIZE PERFUMES
Shown for different size glass stoppers, bottles & labels. **CMV $120.00 ea. mint**

WHITE ROSE PERFUME 1896
1 oz., round glass stopper, long neck. Square round shoulder bottle.
SWEET PEA PERFUME 1896
1 oz. only has cork stopper. Bottle is shorter than one on left. **CMV $150. each mint.**

WHITE ROSE PERFUME 1930
Silver & blue box holds 2 oz. bottle with flat glass stopper, pink neck ribbon & red paper rose label. RARE. **CMV $150. MB, $115. BO mint.**
WHITE ROSE PERFUME FLACONETTE 1926
CPC brass cap over glass stopper ribbed bottle. Red paper rose label. **CMV $90. mint.**

CARNATION PERFUME 1890s
(Left) 1 oz, glass stopper. Plain paper label. **CMV $150.**
FRENCH PERFUME ROSES 1897
(Right) 1/4 oz. bottle, cork stopper. **CMV $140. mint.**

PERFUMES 1908
The 6 glass stoppered 1 oz. bottles shown on left came in California Bouquet, Carnation, Heliotrope, Hyacinth, Lily of the Valley, New Mown Hay, Rose Geranium, Sweet Pea, Treffle, Violet, White Lilac & White Rose. OSP 50c. **CMV $150. BO, $195. MB.**

PERFUME SAMPLE SET 1931
Four 3 dram ribbed & frosted glass bottles with clear ribbed stoppers. Black carrying case. Came in Daphne, Trailing Arbutus, Vernafleur, American Ideal, Crab Apple, Carnation, Heliotrope, White Rose, Violet & Lily of the Valley. **CMV set $315. mint.** Came with card on proper way to demonstrate perfumes. **Add $10. for card.**

PERFUME SAMPLE SET - SILVER LABELS 1931
Same CPC black case & bottles, only has very rare silver & blue labels on bottles. **CMV $400. set, mint.**

CPC PERFUME SAMPLE SET 1923
Black box holds 4 glass stoppered perfume samples. Box has California Perfume Co. on front, 3 dram size. Each has neck labels. Labels read Daphne, Vernafleur, American Ideal, Trailing Arbutus or Roses. **CMV $75. each bottle, $335. set MB.**

APPLE BLOSSOM PERFUME 1908
(Left) 1 oz. glass stopper. Special Christmas box. OSP 70c. **CMV $225. MB.**
HELIOTROPE PERFUME 1908
(Right) 1 oz. glass stopper. Special Christmas box. OSP 70c. **CMV $225. MB.**

FRENCH PERFUMES 1910
(Left) Bottle on left is 1 oz., center is 1/4 oz. trial size, right is 1/2 oz. size. Each has glass stopper. Came in L'Odeur De Violette, Le Perfume Des Roses & Peau de'Espagne. Also came in 2 & 4 oz size. OSP 25c, 55c, $1., $1.90 & $3.75. **CMV bottle 1/2 oz. size to 4 oz. $150. BO each 1/4 oz. size $125. BO., $175. MB.**

PERFUME CHRISTMAS BOX 8 OZ. 1905
Embossed paper box, satin lined. Holds 8 oz. glass stoppered bottle with neck ribbon. OSP $3.50. **CMV $200. - $275. MB.**

PERFUME CHRISTMAS BOX 4 OZ. 1905
Fancy flowered box holds 4 oz. glass stoppered bottle. Front & neck label. OSP $1.50. **CMV $175. - $225. MB.**

PERFUME CHRISTMAS BOX 4 OZ. 1905
(Left) Embossed paper box, satin lined. Holds 4 oz. glass stoppered bottle with neck ribbon. OSP $2. **CMV $175. - $250. MB.**

CPC TOILET WATERS

WHITE ROSE WATER 1910
(Right) 4 oz. clear glass stopper. Eureka trademark on label. OSP 35c. **CMV $150. mint, $190. MB.**

FLORIDA WATER 1905
(Left) 1 1/2 oz. size, glass crown & cork stopper. OSP 35c. **CMV $175. mint, $200. MB.**

EAU DE COLOGNE FOR THE TOILET 1896
(Right) 2 oz. ribbed glass bottle. Front & neck label with Eureka trademark. Glass stopper in cork. OSP 35c. **CMV $175. BO mint, $210. MB.**

CPC TOILET WATERS

TOILET WATER 1906

(Left) 2 oz. clear ribbed glass bottle & glass corked stopper. Pure food act 1906 on label. Came in Violet Water, White Rose, Lavender Water, Florida Water, California Sweet Cologne & Eau de Cologne. OSP 35c. **CMV $175. mint, $210. MB.**

TOILET WATERS 1896

(Right) 2 oz. ribbed glass bottle, glass stopper in cork. Front & neck label has Eureka trademark. Came in California Sweet Cologne, Violet Water, White Rose, Lavender Water & Florida Water. OSP 35c. **CMV $175. BO, $210. MB.**

TOILET WATERS 1908

(Left) 2, 4, 8 & 16 oz. sizes. Glass stoppered bottle. Came in Violet, White Rose, Lavender, Florida, California Sweet Cologne & Eau De Cologne. Bottle shown in 2 oz. size. OSP 35c, 65c, $1.25 & $2. **CMV each $150. BO, $200. MB.**

LAVENDER WATER 1910

(Right) 2 oz. glass stoppered bottle with Eureka trademark on label. Also came in Violet, White Rose, Florida Water, California Sweet Cologne & Eau De Cologne. Also came in 4 & 8 oz. & 1 pint sizes with glass stopper. OSP 35c. **CMV $150. BO mint, $190. MB.**

TOILET WATER 1916

4 oz. bottle with metal & cork stopper. Came in red & gold box. Came in California Sweet Cologne, Carnation, Eau De Cologne, Florida Water, Lavender Water, Trailing Arbutus, Violet, White Lilac, White Rose & Crab Apple Blossom. OSP 65c. **CMV $120. BO, $150. MB.**

TOILET WATERS 1922-25

Came in 2, 4 & 8 oz. sizes in Violet, Vernafleur, Lavender, White Lilac, Lily of the Valley, Carnation, White Rose, Trailing Arbutus, Crab Apple Blossom & Eau De Cologne. 2 & 4 oz. size same as pictured. Front & neck labels. Metal crown stopper in cork. OSP 59c, $1.08 & $1.95. **CMV $90. BO, $115. MB.**

TRIPLE EXTRACT TOILET WATER 1896

(Left) 4 oz. & 8 oz. size glass stopper, label has Eureka trademark. Came in Violet Water, White Rose, Lavender Water, Florida Water, Eau De Cologne, California Sweet Cologne. OSP each 65c. **CMV $200. MB, $150. BO mint.**

FLORIDA WATER 1900

(Right) 2 oz. botle, glass stopper. OSP 35c. **CMV $175. mint, $210. MB.**

TOILET WATER 1910

8 oz. bottle with glass stopper. Front & neck label. Came in all fragrances of 1916 in Toilet Waters. OSP $1.25. **CMV $175. BO mint, $225. MB.**

TOILET WATER 1910

(Right) 2 oz. bottle with metal pour cap in cork, 1916 up. California Sweet Cologne, Lait Virginal, Eau De Cologne, Trailing Arbutus, White Rose, Violet, White Lilac, Lavender Water, Florida Water, Crab Apple Blossom & Carnation. Front & neck label in 2 styles. OSP 35c. **CMV $115. BO, mint, $140. MB.** Also came with brass crown and cork stopper in 1910.

TREFFLE PERFUME 1905
1 oz. with glass stopper.
Eureka Trademark label. **CMV
$150. BO. Mint.$200.00 MB.**

TOILET WATER 1910
2 oz. size with metal crown cork stopper. Came in either of 2 labels shown in Carnation, Florida Water, Trailing Arbutus, White Lilac, White Rose, Violet, Lavender Water, Eau De Cologne, California Sweet Cologne. OSP 35c. **CMV $115. each Bo, $140. MB.**

LILAC VEGETAL 1928-29
(Left) 2 oz. ribbed glass bottle with crown metal top in cork. Pink front & neck label. This bottle with CPC on front label came in Humidor Shaving Set only. **CMV $80. - $100. MB.**
LILAC VEGETAL 1925-30
(Right) 2 oz. ribbed glass bottle with metal stopper in cork. Pink front & neck label. OSP $1.08. **CMV $80. BO, $100. MB.**

CPC POWDERS

WHITE LILAC TALCUM 1917
2 sizes, both 4 oz. 2 different metal shaker tops. Both lavender paper sides. **CMV $75. each, $90. MB.**

TOOTH POWDER 1915 ONLY
(Left) Small metal can came in 1915 Juvenile Set. **CMV $75. mint.**
TOOTH POWDER 1908
(Right) Metal can. OSP 25c. **CMV $85. MB, $70. can only mint.**

TOILET WATER 1923-29
(Left) 2 or 4 oz. metal crown cork stopper, ribbed bottle, front & neck label. Came in Lily of the Valley, Violet, White Rose, Carnation, Crab Apple Blossom. OSP 59c. **CMV $80. each mint, $125. MB.**
BABY TOILET WATER 1923
(Right) 2 & 4 oz. size bottles. Red soldier on front label, blue neck label. Brass & cork stopper. OSP 48c & 89c. **CMV $125. BO, $145. MB.**

PYROX TOOTH POWDER 1925
(Left) Blue metal can. OSP 24c. **CMV $75. MB, $60. can only mint.**
CALIFORNIA ROSE TALCUM 1923
(Right) 4 oz. pink can with brass cap. OSP 33c. **CMV $90., $110. MB.**

ELITE POWDER 1915
Glass jar, metal sifter lid in CPC box. OSP 25c. **CMV $80. BO mint, $95. MB.**

ELITE POWDER 1923
1 lb. blue can with English & French label. 2 different brass caps & narrow & wide blue band around top. OSP 89c. **CMV $85. each, $95. MB.**

ROSE TALCUM POWDER ANTISEPTIC 1907
Metal can with brass sifter cap. OSP 25c. **CMV $100. mint, $120. MB.**

SWEET SIXTEEN FACE POWDER 1916
(Left) Yellow, pink & green box. OSP 25c. **CMV $50. mint.**
CALIFORNIA NAIL POWDER 1916
(Right) Paper sides. Came bright green or beige in color. OSP 25c. **CMV $45. mint.**

ELITE FOOT POWDER 1919
Paper side round container. Sold for 25c each after WWI from the Army & Navy kits. RARE. **CMV $85. - $100. MB.**

CALIFORNIA ROSE TALCUM 1921
3 1/2 oz. glass jar with brass cap. OSP 33c. **CMV $85. jar only, $105. MB.**

ELITE POWDER 1911
(Left) Glass jar with aluminum lid. OSP 25c. **CMV $80. mint, $100. MB. Brown glass jar $150.**
ELITE POWDER 1923
(Right) Blue metal can with sifter cap. OSP 24c. **CMV $50. MB, $35. can only mint.** Came in 2 different sifter caps & 2 variations in labels. **Same CMV.**

WHITE LILAC TALCUM 1919
(Left) 4 oz. blue metal can, blue sifter cap. OSP 24c. **CMV $75. mint, $90. MB.**
WHITE LILAC TALCUM 1917
(Right) 4 oz. paper box, purple in color. OSP 25c. **CMV $70. mint, $90. MB.**

WHITE LILAC TALCUM 1920
4 oz. blue metal can with brass take off cap.
Box came with paper on the Story of Italian
Talc. OSP 24c. **CMV $75. can only mint,
$90. MB as shown.**

RADIANT NAIL POWDER 1924-29
(Left) Small gold & black can. All 3 pieces
came in 1924 Manicure Set. **CMV $35.**
CUTI CREME OR NAIL CREAM 1924-29
(Center) Small gold & black can. **CMV $15.-
$30.**
NAIL WHITE 1924-29
(Center Top) Small gold & black can. **CMV
$15. - $30. MB.**

DEPILATORY 1914
A metal can of hair remover. OSP 50c. **CMV
$90. MB, $75. mint.** Came with brass lift off
cap.

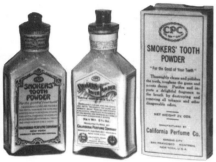

SMOKERS TOOTH POWDER 1918
(Left) 2 3/4 oz. bottle with metal & cork
stopper also comes with metal crown stopper.
OSP 50c. **CMV $105. BO, $130. MB.**
SMOKERS TOOTH POWDER 1920
(Right) 2 3/4 oz. metal & cork stopper. OSP
50c. **CMV $105. BO, $130. MB.**

CALIFORNIA BATH POWDER 1910
Gold, white & green can. Came with sifter cap
& take off cap. OSP 25c. **CMV $65. - $85.
MB.**

HYGIENE FACE POWDER 1906
Leatherette box trimmed in gold. OSP 50c.
CMV $90. mint.

 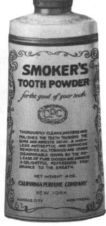

SMOKERS TOOTH POWDER 1925-33
4 oz. cream colored can. Label in French &
English. OSP 50c. **CMV $80. MB, $60. can
only mint.**

HYGIENE FACE POWDER 1918
Green, gold & red powder box. OSP 50c.
CMV $125. mint.

RADIANT NAIL POWDER 1923
(Left) Blue & pink can. 2 different labels.
OSP 24c. **CMV $65. mint each, $80. MB.**
SHAVING POWDER 1915
(Right) 2 oz. metal can. OSP 25c. **CMV $70.
mint, $85. MB.**

SACHET POWDER 1890s
Small envelope of powder. "CPC Eastern Agency - 7 Summer St., Bradford, Mass." on envelope. RARE. **CMV $50. mint.**
AMERICAN IDEAL CARD 1915
(Right) Small white card. **CMV $10.**

SWEET SIXTEEN FACE POWDER 1905
Paper box with outer box. OSP 25c. **CMV $55. - $75. MB.**

SACHET POWDER ENVELOPE 1910
Paper packet of sachet in Violet, White Rose or Heliotrope. OSP 25c. **CMV $50. mint.**

CPC BODY POWDER 1928-29
Yellow, black & maroon colored metal can. CPC New York, Montreal on bottom. Came in Trailing Arbutus, Daphne & Baby Powder. OSP $1.19. **CMV $50. mint, $65. MB.**

CALIFORNIA NAIL POWDER 1916 (LEFT), 1900 (RIGHT)
2 different labels & 1 has paper lift off top or metal sifter top. 1 only comes with paper top. OSP 25c each. **CMV $45. mint each.**

POWDER CAN REFILL 1920
1 lb. gold tone can. Came in several fragrances as a refill. **CMV $75. in new condition.**

HYGIENE FACE POWDER 1915
(Right) Green paper box. OSP 50c. **CMV $60. mint.**

CPC POWDER SACHETS MISC.

ALL CPC'S MUST BE IN NEW MINT CONDITION FOR CMV

POWDER SACHET 1923
(Left) Brass cap, dark flowered label. **CMV $95. BO, $110, MB.**
HELIOTROPE POWDER SACHET 1919
(Right) Clear glass bottle, gold cap, label yellow with lavender flowers and green leaves. Came in other fragrances. Rare. **CMV $110. BO, $125. MB.** Both bottles cam ein Carnation, Heliotrope, White Rose, Violet, White Lilac.

POWDER SACHET 1922-25
Large & small bottles with brass caps. Came in Carnation, Heliotrope, Violet, White Rose & Trailing Arbutus. OSP 49c & 72c. **CMV $100. BO, $115. MB each size.**

SACHET POWDER 1890s
Eureka Trade Mark on label. Maroon Box contins powder in Violet, White Rose, Heliotrope. OSP 25c. **CMV $75. per box, mint.**

POWDER SACHET 1905
(Left) Round glass bottle, aluminum lid. Came in Violet, Lilac, Rose, White Rose & Heliotrope. Came in sets only. **CMV $100. BO mint.**
POWDER SACHET 1890s-1912
(Right) Clear glass, gold cap, front label. Came in French Odors of Le Parfume de Roses, L'Odour de Violette, Peau D'Espagne. OSP 25c. **CMV $110. MB, $90. BO mint.**

SACHET POWDER 1890s
Heliotrope violet or white rose sachet in box. Metal cap. OSP 25c. **CMV $110. MB, $90. BO mint.**

SACHET POWDER BOXED 1908
In Violet, White Rose & Heliotrope. Box holds matching envelope. OSP 25c. **CMV $75. MB.**

POWDER SACHET 1890s-1912
Silver or gold cap on glass bottle with front label. Came in Lilac, Rose, White Rose, Violet, Heliotrope. OSP 25c. **CMV $110. MB, $90. BO mint.** Each one has different label.

FACE POWDER LEAVES 1916
Small book of 72 sheets of scented paper. Came in Rose, White, Rachel. OSP 20c. **CMV $50. mint.**

CPC SAMPLE CASES

IF YOU LOVE TO LAUGH, GO TO THE BACK PAGE FOR INFO ON BUD HASTIN'S NEW JOKE BOOK AND HOW TO GET IT. LAUGH MORE AND LIVE LONGER.

EARLY 1900s SAMPLE CASE
Plain wood box with brass handle. **CMV $100. mint with CPC price list.** Case was used by CPC Reps to sell products.

POWDER SACHET 1915
Gold cap, paper label on glass bottle. Came in Carnation, White Rose, Violet, White Lilac & Heliotrope. 2 different - Boxes 7 labels as shown. OSP 25c. **CMV $65. mint BO, $85. MB.**

CPC SALES CASE 1920
Black case with red velvet lining. California Perfume Co. on chrome handle. Used by Reps to show products. Case measures 14 1/2" long X 8" wide, 3 1/2" high. **CMV $100. mint.**

EARLY 1900s SAMPLE CASE
Plain wood box with leather handle. Red felt lining, printed paper price list inside lid. **CMV $75. mint with list.**

CPC SAMPLE CASE 1915
Straw basket weave case & leather handle & trim. Measures 11 X 17. The large CPC black catalogs fit inside perfectly. A CPC label is inside lid stating all contents that came in sample case. **CMV $100. with CPC label.**

CPC SAMPLE CASE 1890s
Small wood case, 6 1/2" X 12 1/2". Red felt lining. List of CPC products inside of lid. **CMV $100. mint.**

SAMPLE CASE 1900
Black leather covered case with leather strap. Case came with CPC list of all products glued inside lid of case. Case was carried by CPC Reps to show products. **CMV Case mint full of products, $1,500. Case only mint $100. with list.**

CPC SETS

WARNING!! Grading condition is paramount on sets. CMV can vary up to 90% on grade.

CALIFORNIA IDEAL HAIR TREATMENT SET 1915
Box holds 4 oz. glass stoppered Bay Rum White Jar of Shampoo Cream, 6 oz. Eau De Quinine. All products in set came in separate boxes in set with pamphlet on the 3 products. OSP $1.35. **CMV $500. MB as shown.**

ATOMIZER BOX SET 1908
Three 1 oz. bottles with cork stoppers & atomizer. Came in all fragrances of 1915. Green box. Each bottle has green front & neck labels. OSP $1.50. **CMV $350. MB complete set.**

ATOMIZER SET 1906
Box holds three 1 oz. bottles of perfume with cork stoppers & atomizer. Came in all fragrances of 1908. OSP $1.50. **CMV $400. MB.**

ATOMIZER SET 1896
Box holds atomizer & three 1 oz. bottles with cork stoppers. 2 bottles are round & center bottle is octagonal shape. Each has front & neck labels. OSP $1.35. **CMV $450. MB, completed set.** Came in all fragrances of 1896.

JUVENILE SET 1915 ONLY
Box holds miniature size cans of Natoma Talcum Powder, Tooth Powder, small bottle of Violet Water with cork stopper & small cake of Savona Bouquet Soap. Each item is about 2" high. OSP 50c. **CMV $450. MB.**

JACK & JILL JUNGLE JINKS SET 1925-30
Brown decorated box holds 1 can Superite Trailing Arbutus Talcum, 1 bottle of Daphne Perfume, 1 cake of Apple Blossom soap, 1 can Trailing Arbutus Cold Cream, 1 tube Sen-Den-Tal Cream, 1 imported juvenile size tooth brush. OSP $1.50. **CMV $335. MB metal box only $75. mint.**

MANICURE SET 1900
Box holds bottle of Nail Bleach with glass stopper. **CMV $100.** White jar of Rose Pomade. **CMV $70.** & paper box of Nail Powder, **CMV $50.** OSP each 25c. OSP complete set 65c, CP on center of labels. Replaced with Eureka Trade mark in 1910. **CMV set $250. MB.**

CPC SETS

MANICURE SET 1912
Gray box contains buffer, scissors, file, Nail Bleach, Nail Powder & Rose Pomade. OSP $3. **CMV $265. MB.**

MANICURE SET 1916
(Left) Box holds glass stoppered bottle of Nail Bleach, jar of Rose Pomade and paper container of Nail Powder. OSP 65c. **CMV complete set $250.**

MANICURE SET 1920
CPC box holds Rose Pomade jar, 1 oz. bottle of Nail Bleach, cork stopper & can of Radiant Nail Powder. OSP 65c. **CMV $250. MB.**

MANICURE SET 1923
White box holds can of Radiant Nail Powder, bottle of Nail Bleach with glass stopper, orange wood stick & jar of Rose Pomade. OSP 72c. **CMV $250. MB.**

CPC ATOMIZER SET 1929
Black box with green liner & gold tone lid holds green glass, lift off lid jar & 2 oz. green glass spray atomizer bottle. Both have gold tone lide. Does not say CPC on it or box. **CMV $150. MB,**

GIFT BOX A 1915
Same pattern as Holly Pattern set. Green & red holly box. Two 1/2 oz. glass stoppered perfumes in choice of Violet, White Rose, Carnation, hite Lilac, Heliotrope & Lily of the Valley. OSP 50c. **CMV $300. MB.**

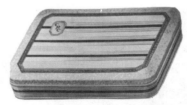

BOX A SET 1909
Holly green, red & gold box holds two 1/2 oz. perfumes with glass stoppers. OSP 50c. **CMV $325. MB.**

MANICURE SET BOX 1924-30
Gold and black stripped metal can. **CMV $25., metal box only, mint.**

LOVELY HANDS BOOKLET 1924-30
Came in Manicure Set shown. **CMV $10. booklet mint only.**

GERTRUDE RECORDON'S FACIAL TREATMENT SET 1929 ONLY
4 oz. bottle of astringent with cork stopper, **$85.** 4 oz. bottle of peach lotion with cork stopper, **$85.** Ribbed white glass jar with CPC on metal lid each in cleansing cream & skin food. **Each jar $60.** OSP $4. **CMV complete set $350. MB.**

MANICURE SET 1924-28
(Left) Gold & black striped metal can holds gold & black can of Radiant Nail Powder, 1 can each of Nail White & Cuti-cream & nottle of Cutrain with cork stopper. OSP $1.20. **CMV $165. MB.**

BOUDOIR MANICURE SET 1929-30
Same set as 1924 Manicure Set with name changed and has bottle of Cuticle Softener or Cuticle Remover, & small can of Nail Cream, Nail White & Radiant Nail Powder. All in same design. OSP $1.20 **CMV $175. MB.** Set came with Lovely Hands Booklet.

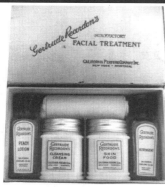

GERTRUDE RECORDON'S INTRODUCTORY FACIAL TREATMENT SET 1928-29
Box holds white jars of Gertrude Recordon's cleansing cream & skin food. **CMV each jar $60.** 2 bottles with cork stoppers of peach lotion & astringent. **CMV each bottle $60. & roll of facial tissues. CMV set mint $300. MB.**

HOLLY PATTERN BOX A 1921
Set has two 1/2 oz. glass & cork stoppered perfume bottles. Came in Carnation, Lily of the Valley, Violet, White Rose, White Lilac & Heliotrope. OSP 50c. **CMV $300. set MB.**

GIFT BOX NO. 3 1918
Box holds 2 half ounce bottles of perfume. Crown glass stopper set in cork. Came in all fragrances of 1917-18 period. **CMV $300. MB.**

HOLLY SET 1910
Holly design holds 2 half ounce bottles with glass & cork stoppers. Gold front & neck labels. Choice of Violet, White Rose, White Lilac, Carnation, Heliotrope, Lily of the Valley perfume. OSP 50c. **CMV $325. MB.**

HOLLY SET 1912
Holly pattern design box holds 2 - 1/2 oz. size glass & cork stopper bottles. OSP 50c. **CMV $300. MB.**

CHRISTMAS BOX SET NO. 4 1906
Box holds Hygiene Face Powder, Savona soap & glass stoppered perfume. Box is 6 3/4" square. OSP $1. **CMV $300. MB.**

CHRISTMAS BOX SET NO. 3 1906
Roses on box, 2 perfumes, glass stoppered. Gold labels. Box is 5 1/4 X 4 3/4 inches. OSP 65c. **CMV $335. MB.**

MEMORIES THAT LINGER SET 1913
3 glass stoppered perfumes in book shaped box. Box is 8 X 5 1/2 inches. Violet, White Rose & Carnation Perfume. OSP $2. **CMV $450. MB.**

CHRISTMAS BOX SET NO. 2 1906
Babies on box, 2 glass stoppered perfumes. Gold labels. OSP 50c. **CMV $335. MB.**

DRESSING TABLE VANITY SET 1926-30
Orange & gold two-section box has brass lipstick & eyebrow pencil & rouge compact in top half of box & bottom half is full of Jardin D'Amour or Ariel Face Powder. OSP $2.25. **CMV $150. MB.**

CPC SETS / LITTLE FOLK SETS

GIFT BOX NO. 2 1915
Box holds 1/2 oz. perfume with glass & cork stopper & powder sachet in Carnation, White Lilac, Heliotrope, Violet & White Rose. OSP 50c. **CMV $275. MB.**

CHRISTMAS SET NO. 4 1905
Fancy box holds 1 oz. glass stoppered of perfume. Round bottle of Powder Sachet, screw on cap & 1 wrapped bar of Savona Bouquet soap. OSP $1. **CMV $425.**

PERFUME SET NO. 2 1905
Lithographed box holds 2 crown sahped glass stoppered in cork bottles. Front & neck labels. OSP 50c. **CMV $350. MB.**

GIFT BOX NO. 2 1922
1/2 oz. bottle of perfume & bottle of sachet. Came in Violet, White Rose, Carnation, Heliotrope & White Lilac. OSP 97c. **CMV $250. MB.**

PERFUME SET NO. 5 1905
Holly Christmas Box holds two 1 oz. glass stoppered bottles. OSP $1. **CMV $350.**

GIFT BOX NO. 2 1915
Yellow & purple box holds 1/2 oz. perfume & powder sachet. Choice of Carnation, Heliotrope, White Lilac, Violet & White Rose. OSP 50c per set. **CMV set $275. MB.**

LITTLE FOLKS SET

LITTLE FOLKS SET 1912
Same box as 1906 set only different labels. Birds & kids on lid. OSP 40c. **CMV $350. MB.**

LITTLE FOLKS SET 1905
Boy & girl with dog inside lid of box. Four gem sized perfume bottles of Violet, Carnation, White Rose & Heliotrope. Bottles had cork stoppers & ribbons on neck. Flower on labels. Box size is 5 1/2" X 3 1/4". OSP 40c. **CMV $400. for set, mint, $75. each bottle.**

LITTLE FOLKS SET 1908
Four gem sized bottles of perfume came in Violet, Carnation, Rose & Heliotrope. Cork stoppers. Same bottles & labels as 1905 Little Folks s=Set. OSP 50c. **CMV $75. each bottle, $350. for set, mint.**

LITTLE FOLKS SET 1906
(Left) 4 small bottles of Violet, Carnation, White Rose or Rose & Heliotrope perfume. Birds & kids on lid & edge of box. OSP 40c. **CMV $350. MB.**

LITTLE FOLKS SET 1937-39
Fancy box has four bottles of perfume in Gardenia, Cotillion, Narcissus & Trailing Arbutus. 2 dram size. OSP 94c. **CMV $165. MB, each bottle $25.**

LITTLE FOLKS SET 1915-23
Contains 4 gem bottles of perfume with Violet, Carnation, White Rose & Heliotrope. OSP 50c. **CMV $75. each bottle, $350. set, MB.**

LITTLE FOLKS SET 1932 ONLY
Same box as 1923-32 Little Folks Set. Holds 4 octagonal shaped bottles. Silver labels, black caps. Came in Ariel, Bolero, Gardenia & Trailing Arbutus. OSP 90c. **CMV $275. set MB.**

Little Folks Set 1913
(Left) This set has 4 small bottles of Heliotrope Carnation, & 2 bottles of Violet Perfume, or White Rose. Cork stoppers have paper covers with green ribbons. Box has girl picking flowers on the top & inside of lid. **CMV $400. MB.**

LITTLE FOLKS SET 1904
Small red border box & 4 small cork stopper perfumes. Sleeping boy with red hat on lid. Sleeping girl in bed on inside lid. **CMV $400. mint.**

Little Folks Set II 1903
(Left) Same set as 1903 set only. Boy on top of lid is different. **CMV $400.**

LITTLE FOLKS SET 1932-36
Four small bottles, choice of Ariel, Vernafleur, Gardenia or Bolero, 391 & Trailing Arbutus perfume with black caps, silver labels. OSP 90c. **CMV $200. MB, $225. MB with outer turquoise box as shown.**

LITTLE FOLKS SET 1923-32
Blue box contains four gem size bottles of Floral perfumes in Daphne, Vernafleur, Trailing Arbutus & Carnation, Violet, Heliotrope or White Lilac. All have brass caps. OSP 69c. **CMV $300. for set, mint, $65. each bottle.**

LITTLE FOLKS SET 1910
Same box as 1908 set, same bottles & labels as 1912 set. OSP 50c. **CMV $350. MB.**

LITTLE FOLKS SET 1903
Blue flowers & farm house on inside lid. Boy in 1700 style clothes in blue coat holding white flowers on outside lid. 4 gem size perfumes: Violet, Rose, Carnation, Heliotrope. VERY RARE. Light blue box. **CMV $400.**

CPC MEN'S SETS

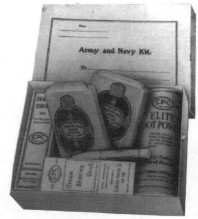

HUMIDOR SHAVING SET 1928-29
Gold & black metal box holds 4 oz. bottle Bay Rum, 2 oz. bottle Lilac Vegetal, styptic pencil, green tube Menthol Witch Hazel cream, green tube Bayberry shave cream & can of either White Lilac talcum or Avon Talc for Men. OSP $2.25. **CMV $350. complete set MB.**

HUMIDOR SHAVING SET BOX 1928-30
Metal gold striped box only. Measures 9 1/4" wide X 5 3/4" X 3" deep. Does not say CPC pn box. Picture of ship on lid. **CMV box only mint $40.**

HUMIDOR SHAVING SET 1925-28
Wood grained box trimmed in gold & black holds 2 oz. bottle of Lilac Vegetal, 4 oz. bottle of Bay Rum, blue can of White Lilac talcum, Trailing Arbutus cold cream, tube of Menthol Witch Hazel cream, Bayberry shave cream tube & styptic pencil. OSP $1.95. **CMV $360. MB.**

HUMIDOR SHAVING SET 1930-32
Gold & black metal box holds 4 oz. ribbed bottle of Bay Rum, 2 oz. bottle of Lilac Vegetal with crown cork stopper, styptic pencil, green tubes of Menthol Witch Hazel cream & Bayberry shaving cream & green can of Talc for Men. OSP $2.50. **CMV $300. MB.**

HUMIDOR SHAVING SET BOX 1925-29
Maroon & gold metal box only. Measures 9 1/4" wide X 5 3/4" X 3" deep. Bottom says Metal Packaging Corp. of New York. **CMV box only mint $40.**

ARMY & NAVY KIT 1918
Heavy cardboard box holds 2 bars of peroxide toilet soap, styptic pencil, Elite foot powder, cream shaving stick, dental cream. OSP $1.25. **CMV $275. MB.**

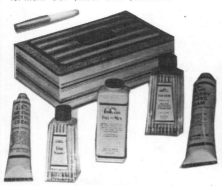

HUMIDOR SHAVING SET 1930-33
Gold & black metal box holds 4 oz. ribbed glass Bay Rum, 2 oz. ribbed glass Lilac Vegetal (black cap), styptic pencil, green tubes of Bayberry shaving cream & green can Talc for Men. OSP $2.50. **CMV $265. MB.**

SHAVING SET BOX 1914
Black cardboard box. CPC label inside lid. Contents list on lid.. **CMV $20. Box only.**

GENTLEMEN'S SHAVING SET 1923
Box contains Bayberry shave cream tube, White Lilac talcum, White Lilac toilet water, styrtic pencil, Bay Rum, Menthol Witch Hazel & shaving pad. OSP $1.95. **CMV $375. MB.**

GENTLEMEN'S SHAVING SET 1917
Brown box holds cream shaving stick, Menthol Witch Hazel cream tube, 50 sheet shaving pad, 2 oz. bottle of White Lilac toilet water, styptic pencil, 4 oz. bottle of genuine Bay Rum with glass stopper & box of White Lilac talcum or jar of Violet talcum. OSP $1.50. **CMV $450. MB complete set.**

GENTLEMEN'S SHAVING SET 1919
Box contains blue can of White Lilac talcum, green tube of Menthol Witch Hazel cream, can of cream shaving stick, 4 oz. Bay Rum with cork stopper, styptic pencil, 2 oz. bottle of White Lilac toilet water & 50 sheet shaving pad. OSP $2.25. **CMV $450. MB.**

GENTLEMEN'S SHAVING SET 1915
Box holds glass bottle of Violet talcum powder, can of cream shaving stick, tube of Menthol Witch Hazel cream, styptic pencil, 4 oz. glass stoppered bottle of Bay Rum, 2 oz. White Lilac toilet water & 50 sheet shaving pad. OSP $1.50. **CMV $460. MB.**

WHAT'S HOT AND WHAT'S NOT IN WOMEN'S FRA-GRANCE LINES

IMPORTANT - READ THIS

We suggest you do not collect any women's fragrance lines 1975 or newer as there is little to no collector demand. Only Soaps, Sets and Avon Representative awards are collectable. All fragrance line awards will be found in the Award section of this book. Mass production and way over supply means there may be no resale demand to collectors for fragrance lines in the future. Some children's fragrance lines might be added because of the cuteness of the product and some collector's interest in this type of product. We suggest you buy the newer fragrance products, use them and dispose of them. They will have no future value. **The older fragrance lines are very collectable. The older the better for resale, just like any collectable.** All fragrance line products 1975 or newer have been removed because of no value to most collectors. **The following fragrance lines have been removed from this book as of 1987 and no new fragrance lines will be added in the future.**

FRAGRANCE LINES DROPPED

Ariane
Avonshire Blue
Candid
Come Summer
Country Breeze
Delicate Daisies
Emprise
Foxfire
Lemon Velvet
Mineral Spring
Odyssey
Patchwork
Private World
Queens Gold
Raining Violets
Sea Garden
Sportif
Sun Blossom
Sweet Honesty
Tasha
Tempo
Tender Blossoms
Timeless
Toccara
Tracy
Unspoken
Zany

APPLE BLOSSOM

APPLE BLOSSOM PERFUME 1941-42
1/8 oz. gold cap. **CMV in box $45., $27.50 BO.** This bottle has two different gold labels and round or flat top caps.

APPLE BLOSSOM BEAUTY DUST 1946
Special short issue box holds regular issue beauty dust. **CMV $25. MB as shown.**

BLUE BIRD SET WITH PERFUME 1941
Blue satin lined box holds Apple Blossom Perfume and Apple Blossom Body Powder. **CMV $90. MB.**

APPLE BLOSSOM TOILET WATER 1941-42
2 oz. pink, white and blue. **CMV $30. BO, $40. MB.**

COLONIAL SET 1941-42
Satin lined box holds Apple Blossom Perfume with gold cap and blue feather box of Face Powder. **CMV $80. MB.** Also came with perfume on right side of box.

BLUE BIRD SET WITH LIPSTICK 1941
Satin lined box holds Apple Blossom, Body Powder, blue feather box of Face Powder and turquoise and gold lipstick.. **CMV $80. MB.**

APPLE BLOSSOM PERFUME 1941-43
Box holds 1/8 oz. bottle with gold cap and label. **CMV $27.50 BO mint, $40. MB as shown.**

APPLE BLOSSOM MOTHERS DAY BEAUTY DUST 1942-43
Special issue blue, pink and white lace design box. Holds feather design Apple Blossom beauty dust..Sold at Mothers Day only in this special box. **CMV $30. MB as shown.**

APPLE BLOSSOM COLOGNE 1941-43
6 oz. bubble sided bottle with pink cap. **CMV $45. BO, $60. MB.**

APPLE BLOSSOM COMPLEXION SOAP 1925
Yellow and pink wrapping on 3 bars of soap. **CMV $85. MB.**

APPLE BLOSSOM BEAUTY DUST 1941-48
6 oz. blue and white paper box. **CMV $20. MB, $15. for Beauty Dust only mint.**

ATTENTION

APPLE BLOSSOM BODY POWDER 1941-44
Blue feather design, flat sifter top container in special issue box as shown. **CMV $25. MB as shown. Can only $22.50 mint.**

PETAL OF BEAUTY SET 1943-44
Blue flowered box, pink satin lining, holds 6 oz. Apple Blossom cologne, pink cap and blue feathered Apple Blossom Beauty Dust. **CMV $100. MB.**

ATTENTION TOILET WATER 1942 ONLY
Special issue Christmas box holds 2 oz. Attention Toilet Water with purple cap and label. **CMV $45. MB as shown, $30. BO.**

APPLE BLOSSOM BEAUTY DUST 1941-48
6 oz. size blue and white feather design paper container. **CMV $18. mint.** The Feather Plume outer box shown was issued Christmas 1942 only. **Add $7. for this box.**

FLOWERTIME SET 1943-45
Box holds 6 oz. Attention cologne and Attention Body Powder. OSP $1.65, 1943 set is green satin lined box with flower carts on lid. **CMV $90. MB.** 1944 set in plain box with flower design on lid. **CMV $90. MB.** 1945 set in white box with boy and girl in 1700 style dress under a tree. **CMV $90.**

APPLE BLOSSOM BEAUTY DUST 1943-45
Blue and white feather design paper box. **CMV $35. mint, $40. MB.** Outer box pictured in 1943 Christmas issue only. This is rare. **CMV $45. MB as shown.**

SCENTIMENTS SET 1945 ONLY
Box holds 6 oz. Attention Cologne and 2 satin sachet pillows. **CMV $90. MB.**

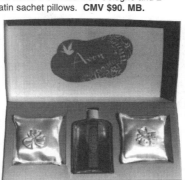

FLOWERTIME SET 1944
Box with flowers on lid holds 6 oz. Attention cologne and Attention body powder. **CMV $85. MB.**

SCENTIMENTS SET 1943 ONLY
2 oz. clear bottle toilet water, gold foil label, white cap or gold cap. White and pink or pink and blue satin sachet pillows. **CMV $75. MB.**

FLOWERTIME SET 1943
(Left) Green satin lined box with flower carts on lid. Holds 6 oz. Apple Blossom cologne and Apple Blossom Body Powder. **CMV $90.**

ATTENTION TOILET WATER 1942 ONLY
(Left) 2 oz. purple cap. **CMV $40. BO, $45. MB.**

ATTENTION TOILET WATER 1943-46
(Right) 2 oz. bottle, came with gold ribbed cap or plastic cap. **CMV $25. BO mint, $35. MB.**

ATTENTION SACHET CHRISTMAS BOX 1942
1 1/4 oz. bottle with turquoise cap sold 1942-48. Regular issue box in Misc. Powder Sachet section. The box pictured here is special issue for Christmas. **CMV $18. MB as shown. $12. BO mint.**

ATTENTION BODY POWDER 1941-43
Pink box, flat sifter top on paper container. **CMV $25. MB, can only $20. mint.**

ATTENTION COLOGNE 1943-47
6 oz. bubble sided bottle with pink tall or short cap. **CMV $50. BO, $65. MB.**

ATTENTION SACHET 1942
Special 1st issue blue box as shown. 1 1/4 oz. bottle, turquoise cap. **CMV $20. MB as shown in this box.** See Misc. Powder Sachet section for further details on regular issue bottles and box.

ATTENTION SACHET 57th ANNIVERSARY BOX 1943
Special issue purple and pink box with flowers. Holds regular issue Attention powder sachet. Sold for 25c, to celebrate Avons 57th Anniversary. **CMV $20. as shown ,MB.**

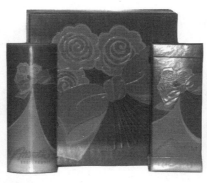

ATTENTION BATH SALTS 1943-44, THEN 46-48
Tulip "A" box holds 9 oz. or 8 1/2 oz. glass jar with turquoise lid. **CMV $25. MB, $15. BO mint.**

PINK RIBBON SET 1943-45
Blue and pink box holds blue and pink can of Attention Body Powder and paper box of Attention Bath Salts. **CMV $75. for set in box.**

ATTENTION BODY POWDER 1943-45
Blue and pink cardboard container. Came in Pink Ribbon set only. **CMV $30.**

ATTENTION BATH SALTS 1943-45
9 oz. blue and pink cardboard container. Came in Pink Ribbon set only. **CMV $30.**

ATTENTION BODY POWDER 1943-47
Blue and white carboard with feather design. **CMV $25. MB, container only $20. mint.**

AVON COLOGNE

AVON COLOGNE 1941
6 oz. flat sided bottle. Soon after Avon Cologne was introduced, the name was changed to Orchard Blossoms Cologne. **CMV $50. BO, $65. MB.**

AVON COLOGNE REPRESENTATIVE GIFT 1943
6 oz. clear bottle, maroon and gold label, blue cap. Bottom label reads "This is a gift to our representatives and must not be offered for sale." Came in blue and pink box, pink ribbon on box and bottle. 57th Anniversary Campaign card. **CMV bottle only $100. mint, $150. MB as shown.**

AVONSHIRE BLUE SOAP DISH & SOAP 1972
6" long blue dish trimmed in white with white bar of soap. Came with oval soap and round soap. **CMV $8. oval, $23. round soap MB.**

BABY PRODUCTS

Baby products 1975 or newer are not collectable except soaps & sets.

BABY CREAM 1961-64
2 oz. blue and white tube. **CMV $4.**
BABY SOAP 1961-64
Blue and white wrapper. OSP 39c. **CMV $8.**
TOT 'N TYKE BABY SHAMPOO 1959-64
6 oz. cwhite plastic bottle, blue cap. **CMV $6. BO, $7. MB.**
BABY LOTION 1958-64
6 oz. white plastic bottle, blue cap. **CMV $5.**
BABY OIL 1960-64
6 oz. white plastic bottle, blue cap. **CMV $6.**
BABY POWDER 1955-64
9 oz. blue and white can. **CMV $10.**

BABY TALC 1951-55
Blue and white box and can. **CMV $18. in box, $13. can only.**
LANOLIN BABY SOAP 1951-55
Blue and white box and wrapping, holds 2 bars. **CMV $25. in box.**
BABY LOTION 1951-55
4 oz. white plastic bottle, blue cap. **CMV $12. MB, $8. BO.**

BABY POWDER 1954-56
2 oz. pink can and cap with paper label around can. Came in Little Lamb set. RARE. **CMV $25.**
BABY POWDER 1954-56
2 oz. blue, white and pink can, pink cap. Came in Little Lamb set. **CMV $20.**

BABY OIL 1955-60
8 oz. bottle with indented sides, white cap. **CMV $15.**

AVONSHIRE BLUE

AVONSHIRE BLUE PRODUCTS 1971-74
Wedgewood blue and white over clear glass.
COLOGNE DECANTER
6 oz. Comes in Field Flowers, Brocade, Elusive, Charisma. **CMV $6. MB, $3. BO.**
PERFUME CANDLE
Holds Patchwork, Sonnet, Moonwind, Bird of Paradise, Charisma, Wassail, Roses Roses, Bayberry, Frankincense & Myrrh. **CMV $8. MB, $6. CO.**
BATH OIL DECANTER
6 oz. holds Skin So Soft or Field Flowers, Bird of Paradise. **CMV $6. MB, $4. BO.**
SOAP
3 bars, 2 oz. blue soap. **CMV $6. MB**

BABY LOTION 1955-57
8 oz. bottle with indented sides, white cap.
CMV $12.50 BO, $15. MB.

BABY & ME SET 1957-58
Clear glass bottle baby lotion, white cap and
Cotillion Toilet Water gold cap, pink paper
around neck. Box white, blue and pink. **CMV
$45. MB.**

TOT 'N TYKE BABY SHAMPOO 1959-64
Special issue box as shown. **CMV $12. MB
as shown.**

BABY PRODUCTS 1968-75
SHAMPOO 1969-74
Blue, white and pink, 6 oz. plastic bottle. **CMV
$1.**
NURSERY FRESH ROOM SPRAY 1968-79
6 oz. blue, white and pink can. **CMV $1.50.**
Also came with upside-down label. **CMV $8.**
BABY POWDER 1969-72
9 oz. blue, white and pink plastic bottle. **CMV
$2.**
BABY CREAM 1969-75
2 oz. tube, blue, pink and white. **CMV $1.**
BABY SOAP 1969-75
3 oz. bar wrapped in blue, pink and white
paper. **CMV $2.**
BABY LOTION 1969-75
6 oz. blue, white and pink plastic bottle. **CMV
$1.**

BABY SHAMPOO 1964-68
6 oz. white plastic bottle with blue cap. **CMV
$5.**
BABY LOTION 1964-68
6 oz. white plastic bottle with blue cap. **CMV
$5.**
BABY CREAM 1964-68
2 oz. blue and white tube with blue cap. **CMV
$3.**
BABY POWDER 1964-68
9 oz. white plastic bottle, blue cap. **CMV $5.**
BABY OIL 1964-66
6 oz. white plastic bottle with blue cap. **CMV
$6.**
TOT 'N TYKE BABY SOAP 1964-68
Blue and white wrapper, white cake of baby
soap. **CMV $7.**

C.P.C. BABY BOOK 1915
CMV $30. mint.

SWEETEST ONE BABY SET 1962-64
Pink and white box holds 1 bar Baby Soap,
Baby Powder and Lotion or Oil. Bar of soap
came with blue ends, white center and white
ends with blue center. **CMV $40. MB.**

TREE TOTS SET 1966
Box holds white plastic hair brush, 3 oz. plastic
tube Non-Tear Gel Shampoo, 3 oz. Baby Soap
with Lanolin and 6 oz. Nursery Fresh Room
Spray. **CMV $20. MB.**

LANOLIN BABY SOAP 1946-50
Pink box holds 2 wrapped bars. **CMV $45.
MB, $20. each bar.**

BALLAD

BALLAD AWARD PERFUME 1945
Avon label on bottom, Ballad label across top, glass stopper. **CMV $375. mint box.**

BALLAD PERFUME 1939-45
3 dram glass stoppered bottle with gold neck cord and gold label at base of bottle. Front of box lays down. **CMV $130. in box. Bottle only $90.** See misc. perfume for 1 dram Ballad Perfume.

BABY SOAP 1955-61
Blue and white box holds Castile & Lanolin white cake baby soap. **CMV $12. MB.** Also came with "Castile with Lanolin" on box and printed on soap horizontally. **Same CMV.**

BALLAD PERFUME 1945-53
Gold and white box holds 3 dram glass stoppered bottle with gold neck cord and gold label at base of bottle. **CMV $130. in box, $90. bottle only.**

BALLAD PERFUME 1945 ONLY
3 dram, clear glass with gold neck cord and label, box gray, white and gold. **CMV $135. in this box, $90. bottle only.**

BABY SOAP 1962-64
White ends and blue center line. **CMV $8. mint.**

BIRD OF PARADISE

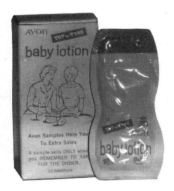

BIRD OF PARADISE PERFUME ROLLETTE 1970-76
1/3 oz. bottle with gold cap, turquoise and green box. OSP $3. **CMV $1. MB.**

BABY LOTION SAMPLES 1964-68
White foil with pink and blue design. Came 10 to a box. **CMV $6. box or 50c per sample.**

BIRD OF PARADISE BATH BRUSH & SOAP 1970-71
Blue box holds blue plastic bath brush and blue soap. **CMV $8. MB.**

BATH OIL EMOLLIENT 1969-75
6 oz. gold cap and neck tag. **CMV $1.**

COLOGNE 1969-72
4 oz. gold cap & neck tag. **CMV $2.**

BEAUTY DUST 1969-74
6 oz. turquoise and gold paper box. **CMV $3., $5. MB.**

COLOGNE MIST 1970-76
3 oz. blue plastic coated bottle with gold cap and neck tag. **CMV $1.**

CREAM SACHET 1969-75
.66 oz. blue glass with gold lid. **CMV 50c.**

SOAP 1970-76
3 oz. bars blue soap in blue & turquoise box. 1st issue no flower on soap. 1972 soap had flower. **CMV $. MB, no flowers $6. MB.**

BIRD OF PARADISE PERFUMED SKIN SOFTENER 1973-76
5 oz. blue plastic jar, gold and blue lid. **CMV 25c.**

SOAP 1975
3 oz. blue bar with blue wrapper and floral center. **CMV $1. mint.**

SOAP 1976-78
3 oz. blue bar with blue wrapper. **CMV $1. mint.**

BIRD OF PARADISE PERFUME GLACE RING 1970-72
(Left) Gold ring with turquoise top. Perfume glace inside. **CMV $7.**

COLOGNE 1970-72
(Right) 1/2 oz. bottle with gold cap. **CMV $2. MB.**

BIRD OF PARADISE PERFUMED TALC 1971-78
2 different labels. Left and center same labels but top is turquoise on one and dark blue on the other. One on right is dark blue label and top. Each is 3 1/4 oz. size. **CMV 50c.** Also came with upside down label. **CMV $4.**

BRISTOL BLUE

BIRD OF PARADISE PERFUMED SKIN SOFTENER 1971-73
(Left) 5 oz. blue glass jar with blue & gold lid. **CMV $1.**

COLOGNE FLUFF 1969-72
(Center) 3 oz. blue plastic coated bottle with gold top. Blue & gold neck tag. **CMV $1.**

PERFUMED POWDER MIST 1971-77
(Right) 7 oz. blue and gold can, gold cap. **CMV $1.**

BIRD OF PARADISE SCENTED HAIR SPRAY 1971-72
(Left) 7 oz. blue can & lid. **CMV $3.**

FOAMING BATH OIL 1971-74
(Right) 6 oz. blue plastic bottle with gold cap and blue & gold neck tag. **CMV $1.**

BRISTOL BLUE COLOGNE 1975
5 oz. translucent blue glass filled with Moonwind, Sonnet or Imperial Garden Cologne. **CMV $4. BO, $5. MB.**

BATH OIL 1975-76
5 oz. blue opaline glass decanter with plastic inner bottle that holds Skin So Soft bath oil. **CMV $4. BO, $5. MB.**

SOAP DISH & SOAP 1975-76
Translucent blue opaline glass dish with Moonwind, Sonnet or Imperial Garden soap. **CMV $10. MB.**

BLUE LOTUS

BRIGHT NIGHT

BLUE LOTUS AFTER BATH FRESHENER 1967-72
6 oz. glass bottle with blue cap. **CMV $2.**
CREAM SACHET 1968-72
.66 oz. blue frosted glass with blue cap. **CMV $1.50.**
FOAMING BATH OIL 1970-73
6 oz. plastic bottle with blue cap. **CMV $1.50.**
CREAM LOTION 1969-72
5 oz. plastic bottle with blue cap. **CMV $1.50.**
DEMI STICK 1969-73
.19 oz. white plastic with blue and green center. **CMV $1.**

BLUE LOTUS PERFUME SOAP 1967-71
3 oz. blue, white and purple wrapper. OSP 75c. **CMV $2.**
PERFUMED TALC 1967-71
3 1/2 oz. cardboard container with plastic shaker top. OSP $1.10. **CMV $2.**

BRIGHT NIGHT BEAUTY DUST 1959-61
White plastic box with gold stars on lid. **CMV $8. CO, $12. MB.**

BRIGHT NIGHT COLOGNE 1954-61
4 oz. gold speckled cap with gold neck cord and white paper label. **CMV $20. MB, $14. BO mint.**
BRIGHT NIGHT TOILET WATER 1955-61
2 oz. gold speckled cap with white paper label on gold neck cord. **CMV $20. MB, $14. BO.**

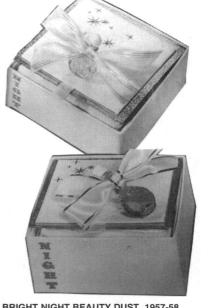

BRIGHT NIGHT BEAUTY DUST 1957-58
(Top) White cardboard box trimmed in gold. Came at Christmas with 5/8 dram Snowflake Perfume bottle with white ribbon and cap. **CMV $30. MB.**
BRIGHT NIGHT BEAUTY DUST 1956
(Bottom) Same as above. Came at Christmas 1956 with long neck perfume bottle with white cap and ribbon. **CMV $30. MB.**
BRIGHT NIGHT BEAUTY DUST 1954-59
Same powder box without perfume. **CMV $18. mint.**

BRIGHT NIGHT PERFUME 1954-59
Gold and white box holds 1/2 oz. glass stoppered bottle with white label on gold neck cord. **CMV $120. MB., $75. BO.** Also came with 1 dram perfume in felt wrapper on top of lid. Add $15. for 1 dram perfume with ribbon around box.

BRIGHT NIGHT COLOGNE MIST 1958-61
3 oz. white plastic coated over clear glass. Gold speckled cap, gold neck cord with white paper label. Came with 2 different caps. **CMV$20. MB, $14. BO.**

BRIGHT NIGHT GEMS 1957
Gold & white flip open box holds Bright Night 2 oz. toilet water in top & cream sachet in pull-out drawer in bottom. **CMV $45. mint.**

BROCADE

BRIGHT NIGHT POWDER SACHET 1955-61
(Left) .9 oz., 1 1/4, 1 1/2 oz. white glass jar with stars on white lid. Front paper label. **CMV $8. bo, $12. MB.** 1 1/2 oz. rare. **CMV $20. MB, $16. BO.**

BRIGHT NIGHT CREAM SACHET 1954-61
(Right) White glass jar with stars on white lid. **CMV $6. MB, $8.**

MELODY SET 1955-56
Gold & white box holds Bright Night 1 dram perfume, cream sachet, 4 oz. cologne & beauty dust. **CMV $85.**

BROCADE PERFUME GLACE 1967-72
Gold case. **CMV $6. MB, $9.**

GOLDEN BEAUTY 1957
Gold base box lined with gold acetate with gold plastic lid, holds Bright Night Beauty Dust, 4 oz. cologne, cream sachet and 1 dram perfume. **CMV $85.**

GOLDEN GLAMOUR SET 1958
Gold & white box holds Bright Night cologne mist, 1 dram perfume, cream sachet & beauty dust. **CMV $95. MB.**

BROCADE PERFUMED TALC 1969-72
(Left) 3 1/2 oz. brown & white cardboard. **CMV $1.50.**

SCENTED HAIR SPRAY 1969-72
(Right) 7 oz. brown & white can. **CMV $3.**

IF YOU LOVE TO LAUGH, GO TO THE BACK PAGE FOR INFO ON BUD HASTIN'S NEW JOKE BOOK AND HOW TO GET IT. LAUGH MORE AND LIVE LONGER.

BROCADE 4 OZ. COLOGNE 1967-72
(Left) Frosted ribbed glass with brown & white cap. **CMV $2. MB**

BROCADE COLOGNE MIST 1967-72
(Center) 3 oz. ribbed frosted glass with brown & white cap. Some lids have design only & some say Brocade on top. **CMV $2. MB.**

BROCADE COLOGNE MIST REFILL 1967-72
(Right) 3 oz. brown plastic coated bottle, white cap. **CMV $3. MB.**

MAGIC HOURS SET 1956
Gold & white box holds Bright Night 2 oz. toilet water & white cologne stick. **CMV $45.**

BROCADE PERFUME OIL 1967-69
(Left) 1/2 oz. frosted brown glass with gold cap. **CMV $5, MB.**
BROCADE 1/2 OZ. COLOGNE 1970-71
(Right) Ribbed clear glass with gold cap. **CMV $2. MB.**

BROCADE DELUXE GIFT SET 1967
Brown & white box with white lining holds Brocade beauty dust, perfume rollette & cream sachet. **CMV $35. MB.**

BROCADE COLOGNE SILK 1968-70
(Left) 3 oz. frosted bottle with gold cap. **CMV $2. MB, $4.50**
BROCADE FOAMING BATH OIL 1968--72
(Right) 6 oz. plastic bottle with gold cap. **CMV $2.**

BROCADE SOAP 1968
Brown & white wrapper. Came in Perfume Pair only. **CMV $4. mint.**

BROCADE BEAUTY DUST 1967-71
(Left) Brown ribbed plastic, patterned lid. **CMV $6, MB $9.**
BROCADE BEAUTY DUST 1971-75
(Right) Pattern printed cardboard, non-refillable. **CMV $4. MB.** Also came with upside down lettering. **CMV $6.**

BROCADE PERFUME ROLLETTE 1967-72
(Left) Brown frosted glass, gold cap with 4A design. Ribs horizontal. OSP $3. **CMV $3.**
(Inside Left) Same as above only no 4A design. **CMV $3.**
(Inside Right) Brown carnival glass, gold cap. Vertical ribs. **CMV $8.**
(Right) Brown frosted glass, brown & white paper band on cap. Ribs horizontal. **CMV $5.**

BROCADE PERFUMED SKIN SOFTENER 1969-72
(Left) 5 oz. ribbed sides, brown glass, designed top. **CMV $2. BO, $3.MB.**
BROCADE PERFUMED SKIN SOFTENER 1968-69
(Center) 5 oz. ribbed sides, brown glass, label printed on top. **CMV $3. MB**
BROCADE PERFUMED SKIN SOFTENER 1968 ONLY
(Right) Manufactured during glass strike, 5 oz. round smooth brown glass, label painted on top. **CMV $15. mint.**

MANAGER'S BROCADE DEMO KIT 1969
Brocade box holds round Brocade talc & cologne mist. **CMV $27.50 MB.**

BROCADE CREAM SACHET 1968-75
(Left) .66 oz. brown ribbed glass, designed cap. **CMV 50c.**
BROCADE CREAM SACHET 1967-68
(Center) .66 oz. brown ribbed glass, label on top. **CMV $2. MB.**
BROCADE TALC 1968
(Right) 2 3/4 oz. metal talc, brown, white and gold. Sold only in Perfume Pair set. **CMV $2.**

BROCADE PERFUME POWDER MIST 1967-74
(Left) 7 oz. brown & white painted can with gold cap. **CMV 50c.**
(Right) 7 oz. brown & white paper label with gold cap. **CMV $3.** Some came with 7 oz. weight in center label and some at bottom of can in front.

BUTTONS 'N BOWS

BUTTONS 'N BOWS NAIL POLISH 1961-63
(Left) Pink and white box holds nail polish with white cap. **CMV $8. in box, $6. bottle only.**
BUTTONS 'N BOWS LIPSTICK 1961-63
(Right) Pink and white box holds pink and white striped lipstick. **CMV $7. in box, $4. tube only.**

BUTTONS 'N BOWS CREAM LOTION 1962-63
(Left) 4 oz. pink plastic bottle with white cap, **CMV $6, MB. $10.**
BUTTONS 'N BOWS BUBBLE BATH 1962-63
(Right) 4 oz. pink plastic, white cap, pink lettering. **CMV $6, $10. MB.**
BUTTONS 'N BOWS
Cream lotion & bubble bath both came in solid pink plastic & clear frosted plastic bottle. Pink has pink letters. Frosted has white letters.

BUTTONS 'N BOWS SOAP 1961-63
Pink box & soap. Some buttons have thread through holes. **CMV $25. MB no threads, $27.50 with threads.** Two boxes are shown. Each box holds 2 bars. Boxes are same.

BUTTONS 'N BOWS COLOGNE 1960-63
(Left) 2 oz. clear glass, white cap, lettering pink, came with pink ribbon bow around neck.
CMV $12. MB, $9. BO.
BUTTONS 'N BOWS COLOGNE MIST 1960-63
(Center) 2 1/2 oz. pink plastic with white cap. Bottom is 2 shades of pink. **CMV $9., $12. MB.**
BUTTONS 'N BOWS ROLL-ON DEODORANT 1962-63
(Right) 1 3/4 oz. white and pink painted label on clear glass, pink cap. **CMV $8. BO, $12. MB.**

PRETTY CHOICE SET 1962-63
2 oz. frosted plastic bottle cream lotion, white cap. Cologne, clear glass, white cap, light pink ribbon on neck. Had choice of cream lotion or bubble bath. **CMV $30. MB.**

CUTE AS A BUTTON SET 1961-63
Pink & white box holds Buttons 'N Bows nail polish with white cap and pink & white lipstick. **CMV $17. MB.**

BUTTON BUTTON SET 1961-62
Pink & white box holds Buttons 'N bows 2 oz. cologne & beauty dust. **CMV $40. MB.**

BUTTONS 'N BOWS BEAUTY DUST 1960-63
(left) Pink & white cardboard box with clear plastic lid. **CMV $16.**
BUTTONS 'N BOWS CREAM SACHET 1960-63
(Right) Pink glass jar with white & pink lid. **CMV $9. BO, $12. MB.**

CAMEO

CAMEO SOAP ON A ROPE 1969
(Top Left) Blue box holds blue soap on white or blue & white rope. **CMV $7. - $12. MB.**
CAMEO SACHET 1961-63
(Top Right) Gold metal base holds pink painted over milk glass jar with white lid with lady's face. Came in Topaze, Cotillion, Somewhere. To A Wild Rose Persian Wood & Here's My Heart. **CMV $7. BO, $11. MB.**
CAMEO BROCH 1965
(Bottom) Gold brooch with pink & white lady's face. Came in Cameo Set only. **CMV $15. MB, $9. brooch only.**

CAMEO SET 1965
White, gold & green box holds Cameo compact, lipstick & Cameo brooch. **CMV $30.**
CAMEO LIPSTICK 1965-66
White lipstick with gold base & lady's face on top. **CMV $2. - $3. MB.**
CAMEO COMPACT 1965-66
White plastic with gold edge & pink lady's face on top. **CMV $6. CO, $8. MB.**

CAMEO SET 1973-74
Reddish brown plastic with white Cameo beauty dust 6 oz. Came in Sonnet, Moonwind, Hana Gasa, Charisma, Unforgettable, Rapture, Somewhere, Cotillion, Here's My Heart, Topaze, Occur!, To A Wild Rose. **CMV $4. BRUSH & COMB SET. CMV $3. MIRROR. CMV $2.**

CAMEO SOAP 1966
Blue & white box holds 4 white Cameo soaps. **CMV $20. MB.**

IF YOU LOVE TO LAUGH, GO TO THE BACK PAGE FOR INFO ON BUD HASTIN'S NEW JOKE BOOK AND HOW TO GET IT. LAUGH MORE AND LIVE LONGER.

CHARISMA

CHARISMA COLOGNE 1969-72
(Bottom Left) 4 oz. red glass, some are silver tip (rare) with red plastic cap trimmed in gold. **CMV $3.**
COLOGNE MIST 1968-76
(Bottom Right) 3 oz. red plastic coated, trimmed in gold. **CMV $1.**
PERFUME ROLLETTE 1968-76
(Bottom Center) .33 oz. red glass trimmed in gold. **CMV $1.**

CHARISMA CREAM SACHET 1968-76
(Left) .66 oz. red glass jar with red & gold lid. **CMV 50c.**
COLOGNE 1969-72
(Center) 1/2 oz. red glass, gold cap. **CMV $2.**
BEAUTY DUST 1968-76
(Right) 6 oz. red plastic powder box trimmed in gold. **CMV $6. MB, $3. CO.**

CHARISMA TRAY 1968-70
(Left) Dark red plastic with gold trim. 11" diameter. This one used as introduction. **CMV $8. MB.**
(Right) Lighter red plastic with gold rim. 10" diameter. **CMV $3. - $5. MB.**

CHARISMA COLOGNE SILK 1970-71
(Left) 3 oz. clear glass, red cap. **CMV $2. MB.**
COLOGNE SILK 1969
(Right) 3 oz. frosted glass, red cap. **CMV $3. MB.**

CHARISMA SCENTED HAIR SPRAY 1970-72
(Left) 7 oz. red can. **CMV $3.**
PERFUMED TALC 1970-76
(Inside Left) 3 1/2 oz. red cardboard. **CMV 50c.**
PERFUME POWDER MIST 1971-76
(Inside Right) 7 oz. red & gold can, gold top, painted label. No longer boxed. **CMV $1.**
PERFUMED POWDER MIST 1969-70
(Right) 7 oz. red & gold can, gold top, has paper label. Also came boxed. **CMV $3.**

CHARISMA SOAP 1975
(Top) 3 pink Charisma soap in special Christmas 1975 design box. **CMV $8. MB.**
CHARISMA SOAP 1970-76
(Bottom) Red box holds 3 bars. **CMV $6. MB.**

COTILLION

All white caps on 1961-74 Cotillion bottles will turn dark gray when exposed to sunlight. The gray or faded caps are not considered to be in mint condition.

COTILLION PERFUME 1945
3 dram bottle. Inset box with feather design.
CMV $90.00 MB.

COTILLION PERFUME 1951-52
3 dram glass stoppered swirl glass bottle. White, pink & blue flower design around neck with neck tag. Pink & white box. **CMV $125. MB, BO with tag & flower design $100.**

COTILLION SWIRL PERFUME 1948-50
3 dram glass stoppered is swirl glass design, gold neck tag. Purple & white flowered box. **CMV $75. mint, $100. MB.**

COTILLION PERFUME 1935 ONLY
1/4 oz. gold cap, green and yellow label & box. For 77th birthday of D. H. McConnell. **CMV $80. MB, $60. BO.**

COTILLION PERFUME 1945-47
(Left) 3 dram glass stopper bottle with gold neck tag. Came in blue, pink & white box as shown. **CMV $100. BO mint, $125. MB.**

COTILLION PERFUME 1939 ONLY
2 dram, ribbed cap with "A" on cap. Sold for one campaign only for 20c with purchase of other Avons. **CMV MB $75., $55. BO.**

COTILLION PERFUME 1936 ONLY
2 dram, gold ribbed cap. Sold for 20c July 7-27, 1936 only, with purchase of other Avons. In honor of mr. McConnell's 78th birthday. **CMV $80. MB, $60. BO.**

COTILLION TULIP PERFUME CHRISTMAS BOX 1935
Red & green Christmas box holds 1/4 oz. glass stoppered perfume with gold label. This bottle sold 1934-39. With this box 1935 Christmas only. **CMV $90. MB as shown.** See Misc. perfumes for other fragrances in same bottles.

COTILLION PERFUME 1934
1/4 oz. metal cap. First Cotillion bottle issued in honor of Mr. McConnell's birthday. **CMV $55. BO, $75. MB.**

COTILLION PERFUME 1937
2 dram, gold cap. **CMV $70. MB, $50. BO.**

COTILLION TOILET WATER 1938-39
Flowered box & label. 2 oz. bottle, white plastic cap. Sold for 20c with purchase of other Avons. May 2-22, 1939. CPC on box and back side of label. **CMV $52.50 MB, $37.50 BO mint.**

COTILLION PERFUME 1940 ONLY
2 dram, ribbed gold cap with "A" on top. Also came plain gold cap. Sold for 20c with purchase of other Avons. **CMV $75. MB, $55. BO.**

COTILLION PERFUME 1950
1/8 oz. pink cap. Very rare. **CMV $70.BO, $85.MB.**

COTILLION TOILET WATER 1946-49
2 oz. pink, gold or white cap. **CMV $35. MB, $25. BO mint.**

COTILLION BATH OIL 1962
(Left) 6 oz. pink & white plastic bottle. Came in Bath Bouquet set only. **CMV $6.**
COTILLION COLOGNE 1949-50
(Right) 2 oz. pink cap. **CMV $22.50 - $25. MB.** Toilet water in same design bottle & label. 2 oz. size, pink cap. **Same CMV.**

COTILLION CREAM SACHET 1951-53
(Left) White glass jar with pink & white lid. CMV $15.

COTILLION TOILET WATER 1950-53
(Right) 2 oz. pink cap, pink & white label & white box. Box came solid & with open window so label shows through. CMV $22. MB, $18. BO.

COTILLION BEAUTY DUST 1950-53
Pink & white container. CMV $20. mint, $25. MB.

COTILLION SOAP 1950-53
Pink & white box holds pink bars. CMV $37.50 MB.

COTILLION CREAM LOTION 1950-53
(Left) 6 oz. pink & white label, pink cap and pink & white box. CMV $22. MB, $18. BO.

COTILLION COLOGNE 1950-53
(Right) 4 oz. bottle with pink cap & label. CMV $22. MB, $18. BO.

COTILLION SOAP 1953-61
Pink & white box holds 3 pink or white bars. Box came as sleeve top with round edge white soaps. 1953-56 CMV $35. MB. 1956-61 came sleeve top box with 3 flat edge pink soaps. CMV $32.50 MB.

COTILLION BATH OIL 1950-53
6 oz. pink & white label & pink cap. Pink & white box. CMV $22. MB, $18. BO.

COTILLION SOAP 1961-67
Gold & white box holds 3 bars with gold centers. CMV $22.50 MB.

COTILLION TALC 1950-53
(Left) Pink & white can with pink cap. CMV $12., MB $15.

COTILLION BODY POWDER 1950-53
(Right) 5 oz. pink & white paper box, sifter top with metal lid & bottom. CMV $17., MB $20.

COTILLION TALCUM 1947 ONLY
(Left) Pink paper box, white shaker top. CMV $25., MB $30.

COTILLION TALCUM 1942-46
(Center) 2.75 oz. turquoise & white all paper box. War time. Paper top fits over top of box, shaker top. CMV without top $20. in mint. CMV $25. mint.

COTILLION TALCUM 1944-46
(Right) Turquoise & white paper box, plastic octagonal cap. CMV $25. mint.

COTILLION TALCUM BOX 1941 ONLY
Blue box with fan. 2.75 oz. can. Sold to Reps for 10c to use as a demonstrator. CMV $30. MB as shown.

53rd ANNIVERSARY COTILLION TALCUM 1939 ONLY
Special 53rd Anniversary box to first introduce Cotillion talcum. May 23 to June 12, 1939. 2.75 oz. turquoise & white can. This can sold 1939-43 then 1946-50. **CMV can only $10, in special 53rd box $25.**

COTILLION COLOGNE 1946-50
(Left) 6 oz. pink cap. **CMV $50. BO, $65. MB.**
COTILLION BODY POWDER 1946-50
(Center & Right) 4.5 oz. light pink cardboard. Blue metal sifter top. **CMV $15., Mb $20.** Came in sets 5 oz. size with pink & white plastic sifter top. **Same CMV.**

COTILLION TALCUM CHRISTMAS BOX 1943
Pale blue & pink outer box issued only at Christmas 1943 with cardboard large size talc. **CMV $35. MB as shown.**

COTILLION BEAUTY DUST 1962-63
Gold & white paper box with clear plastic lid with 4A design on lid. Came in 1962-63 Fragrance Magic sets only. **CMV $17. mint.**

COTILLION TALCUM 1938-50
2.75 oz. turquoise can. Box marked 2 3/4 oz. size. Can sold 1938-43 then 1946-50. **CMV $10. can only, $15. MB mint.**

COTILLION TALCUM 1940-43 THEN 1946-50
(Left) 14.5 oz. metal can, turquoise & white. **CMV $20., add $5. for CPC label.**
COTILLION TALCUM 1943-46
(Right) 14.5 oz. paper box used during war. Rare. **CMV $35.**

COTILLION BEAUTY DUST 1959-61
Pink plastic bottom, white plastic top with gold center. **CMV $6. CO, $12. MB.**

COTILLION PERFUMED TALC 1956-61
White can with pink cap & design. Also came just talc. **CMV $8. MB.**

COTILLION TALCUM CHRISTMAS BOX 1940-41
Special issue blue & white Christmas box holds regular issue metal can of Cotillion talcum in large size. RARE. **CMV $30. MB as shown.**

COTILLION BEAUTY DUST 1953-59
Pink paper sides with pink & white tin top. **CMV $12., MB $16.**

COTILLION

COTILLION FACE POWDER 1939-42
Gold & turquoise powder box. **CMV $8., MB $10. Add $3. for CPC label.**

COTILLION SACHET 1946-47
(Left) 1 1/4 oz. pink glass & cap with painted label. (Rare) Sold only in Cotillion Garland Set. Same set in 1947 was called Cotillion Duet. **CMV $20., MB $22.**
SACHET 1946-49
(Center) 1 1/4 oz. clear glass, pink cap, paper label. **CMV $16., MB $18.**
SACHET 1939-44
(Right) 1 1/4 oz. turquoise cap, clear glass, paper label. **CMV $12. BO, $16. MB.**

COTILLION CREAM SACHET 1961-75
(Left) .66 frosted glass with pink & white lid, gold or silver lettering. **CMV 25c.**
POWDER SACHET 1961-67
(Center) 9/10 oz. frosted glass with pink & white cap. **CMV $6. MB.**
SACHET 1944-45
(Right) 1 1/4 oz. paper box, pink plastic flowers on lid. **CMV $20. MB, $18. BO mint.**

COTILLION SACHET SPECIAL ISSUE BOX 1939
Special issue box is blue with lace design. Holds regular issue powder sachet. **CMV $18. MB as shown.**

COTILLION SACHET BOX 1941 ONLY
Special issue box to Avon ladies only, for 20c. Holds regular issue Cotillion sachet, 1939-44. **CMV $20. MB as shown.**

COTILLION SACHET 1937-38
1 1/4 oz. ribbed glass bottle with turquoise cap. **CMV $24. MB, $18. BO mint.**

COTILLION POWDER SACHET 1950-53
(Left) 1 1/4 oz. pink cap and pink & white label. **CMV $15., MB $20.**
POWDER SACHET 1957-61
(Center) 1 1/4 oz. or .9 oz. pink cap & pink bottom with painted label. Came light or dark pink bottom & also white or pink painted lettering. **CMV $9., MB $13.**
POWDER SACHET 1953-56
(Right) 9/10 oz. or 1 1/4 oz. clear glass, pink cap & pink painted label. Also white lettering (rare). **CMV $8., MB $12. White lettering $18.**

COTILLION SACHET VALENTINE BOX 1952
1 1/4 oz. pink cap. Came in gold, pink and white Valentine box. Rare in this box. **CMV $25. MB as shown.**

COTILLION VALENTINE SACHET 1952
1 1/4 oz. white cap. **CMV $25. MB.** See Misc. Powder Sachet section for nox. **CMV $18. BO mint.**

COTILLION SACHET 1937
(Left) Red & green box sold Christmas only for 25c, CPC on box & bottle. **CMV $25. MB, $18. BO mint.**
SACHET 1937
(Right) Blue & white box special issue. **CMV $25. MB.** Bottle only, ribbed glass, turquoise cap, sold 1937-38. **CMV $18. BO mint.**

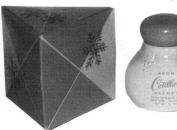

COTILLION SACHET CHRISTMAS BOX 1957
.9 oz. pink painted glass, pink cap. Bottle sold 1957-61. Pink, green and blue triangle box sold 1957 only. **CMV $15. MB as shown.**

COTILLION TALC 1953-54
4 oz. clear glass bottle with pink cap & pink or white (rare) painted label. 1955 was called Talcum in painted label, pink & white box. **CMV $15. each MB, $10. BO.**

COTILLION TALC 1950 ONLY
(Left) 2 oz. white cardbaord, pink top & bottom. Came in Always Sweet set only. **CMV $15.**
COTILLION PERFUMED BATH OIL 1959-61
(Right) 8 oz. pink plastic, pink cap. **CMV $5.**

COTILLION POWDER SACHET-NO LABEL 1957-61
Pink paint over clear glass, pink cap. Rare issue came with no painted label. Plain pink all over. **CMV add $5. to price of regular issue.**

COTILLION BATH OIL 1954-59
(Left) 4 1/2 oz. pink cap, pink painted label, pink & white box. **CMV $15. MB, $9. BO.**
CREAM LOTION 1954-61
(Right) 4 1/4 oz. pink cap & pink painted label, pink & white box. **CMV $12. MB, $8. BO.**

COTILLION COLOGNE MIST 1959-61
(Left) 3 oz. pink plastic coated bottle with white cap & paper label. **CMV $12. BO, $17. MB.**
COLOGNE MIST 1958-59
(Center) 3 oz. pink plastic coated bottle. **CMV $16. - $20. MB.**
COLOGNE MIST 1958 ONLY
(Right) Rare 3 oz. pink plastic bottle. **CMV $42.50 BO, $52.50 MB.**

COTILLION TOILET WATER 1953-61
(Left) 2 oz. gold cap, pink band around neck, pink painted label. **CMV $15. MB, $10. BO mint.** Some have white painted label.
4 OZ. COLOGNE 1953-61
(Right) Gold cap, pink band around neck, pink painted label. **CMV $15. MB, $10. BO mint.** Some have white painted label.

COTILLION TALC 1956-58
(Left) 3 oz. frosted glass with pink lid & paper label, pink & white box. **CMV $14. MB, $9. BO.**
BODY POWDER 1958-59
(Right) 3 oz. frosted glass with pink lid & paper label, pink & white box. **CMV $15. MB, $11. BO.**

COTILLION CREAM SACHET 1953-57
(Left) Pink lid, white glass bottom. **CMV $8., MB $10.**
CREAM SACHET 1957-61
Pink lid, pink glass bottom. OSP $1.50. **CMV $7., MB $9.**

91

COTILLION COLOGNE 1957 ONLY
(Left) 3 dram, white cap. Came in Fragrance Rainbow set only. CMV $8. BO, $10. with neck bow.

COLOGNE 1961 ONLY
(Right) 2 oz. gold cap, pink band around neck, painted label. CMV $20. - $22. MB.

COTILLION ENCHANTMENT SET 1951
Pink, white & green box holds Cotillion toilet water & cream sachet. CMV $60. MB.

COTILLION COLOGNE 1969-72
(Left) 1/2 oz. white cap, clear glass. CMV $1. BO, $2. MB.

PERFUMED OIL 1964-69
(Center) 1/2 oz. frosted glass with white cap. CMV $5. BO, $7. MB.

PERFUMED OIL FOR THE BATH 1963-64
(Right) 1/2 oz. frosted glass with white cap. CMV $7. BO, $9. MB.

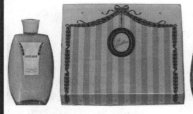

THE COTILLION SET 1950-52
Pink & white box with green lining holds Cotillion cream lotion & cologne. CMV $60.

COTILLION PERFUME TALC 1974-77
(Left) 3.5 oz. pink & gold cardboard. CMV $1.

CREAM SACHET 1975-78
(Inside Left) .66 oz. clear glass with gold & pink cap. CMV 50c.

PERFUME DEMI STICK 1975-78
(Center) .19 oz. white with pink & gold. CMV 50c.

COLOGNE MIST 1961-74
(Inside Right & Right) 3 oz. white plastic coated bottle with white cap. CMV $1. Same bottle with yellow plastic coated bottom. CMV $10. MB, $7. BO. 1975-76 issue has white cap, pink top & pink painted label. CMV $1.

JOLLY SURPRISE SET 1951-52
Pink & white box holds Cotillion powder sachet & 1 dram perfume in pink net lining. CMV $42. set.

COTILLION PERFUMED BATH OIL 1961-66
(Left) 6 oz. pink plastic bottle, white cap. CMV $1.

FAOMING BATH OIL 1966-74
(Right) 6 oz. pink plastic bottle, white cap. CMV $1. MB.

COTILLION BATH BOUQUET SET 1956 ONLY
Pink & white box holds 2 oz. Cotillion cologne, 2 oz. Cotillion bath oil & 1 bar of Cotillion soap. CMV $55.

COTILLION COLOGNE 1960 ONLY
4 oz. clear glass, gold cap, pink paper band around neck with pink painted label. Pink & gold box. CMV $22. in this box.

COTILLION BOUQUET SET 1958
Pink & white box holds Cotillion cologne mist & pink glass cream sachet. **CMV $65. MB.**

COTILLION BEAUTY DUST 1961-70
(Left) White frosted plastic bottom with clear plastic lid. **CMV $3. - $5. MB.** Some with yellow plastic bottom. **CMV $6. - $8. MB.**
PERFUMED TALC 1961-74
(Center) 2.75 oz. bright pink can with white cap. **CMV $1.**
PERFUMED SKIN SOFTENER 1964-73
(Right) 5 oz. pink glass jar with gold & white lid. Some came with silver lid. **CMV gold 50c, silver $1.** Regular issue came pink painted over clear glass. **CMV 50c.** Some came pink painted over white milk glass. **CMV $5.**
PERFUMED SKIN SOFTENER 1973-75
(Not Shown) 5 oz. pink plastic with white & gold cap. **CMV 50c.**

COTILLION COLOGNE 1961-71
(Left) 2 oz. frosted glass with white cap. **CMV $1. - $2. MB.**
COLOGNE 1961-63
(Right) 4 oz. frosted glass with white cap. **CMV $3.**

COTILLION CREAM LOTION 1961-68
(Left) 4 oz. pink plastic, white cap. **CMV $3..**
COTILLION BODY POWDER 1961-64
(Right) 4 oz. pink plastic, white cap. **CMV $6., MB $8.**

COTILLION DUET SET 1953-55
Pink & white flowered box with pink satin lining holds Cotillion 4 oz. cologne & Cotillion talc. **CMV $42. MB.**

COTILLION DELUXE SET 1953-55
Pink & white box flips open in center. Holds Cotillion 1 dram persume, 4 oz. cologne, powder sachet & talcum. Same set also came with lift off lid. **CMV $60. MB.**

THE COTILLION SET 1957
Pink & white box holds Cotillion beauty dust, cream sachet with white glass bottom & 4 oz. cologne. **CMV $45.**

COTILLION CAROL SET 1956
Pink & white box holds Cotillion cream sachet with white glass bottom & Cotillion talc. **CMV $35.**

COTILLION SCENTED HAIR SPRAY 1966-70
(Left) 7 oz. pink can. **CMV $3.**
PERFUMED POWDER MIST 1966-72
(Center) 7 oz. (1966-70) pink can has paper label & pink cap & came in white box lined in pink. **CMV $2.**
(Right) 7 oz. (1970-71) pink can, pink cap. Label was painted. Not boxed. **CMV $1.**

COTILLION

COTILLION BATH OIL 1955-56
(Left) 2 oz. clear glass bottle with pink cap, label pink & white. Came in That's For Me set only. **CMV $15.**

HAND LOTION 1949
(Right) 2 oz. clear glass bottle with pink & blue label, blue cap. Came in Your Charms & Hair-Ribbons set. **CMV $15.**

COTILLION TREASURES SET 1957
Gold, white & pink box holds 3 oz. bottles of Cotillion bath oil & cologne with gold caps, 1 pink bar of Cotillion soap. **CMV $75. MB.**

COTILLION PERFUME MIST 1964-68
(Left) 2 dram, pink & white metal with gold band. **CMV $6. - $7. MB.**

SPRAY PERFUME 1961-63
(Center) 2 dram, pink & white metal with gold band. **CMV $10. MB, $8. BO.**

SPRAY PERFUME 1960-61
(Right) Rose, white & gold box holds rose & gold metal spray container. **CMV $10. BO, $16. MB.**

COTILLION GARLAND SET 1954-55
Pink & white box holds 4 1/2 oz. Cotillion bath oil & cream lotion. **CMV $37.50 MB.**

COTILLION PRINCESS SET 1956
Pink, white & gold box holds Cotillion beauty dust & 4 oz. cologne. **CMV $40.**

ENCHANTMENT SET 1953-56
Pink & white box holds Cotillion powder sachet & 1 dram perfume. **CMV $37. MB.**

COTILLION TALC 1948
(Left) White, pink & blue paper container came in Hair Ribbon set only. **CMV $12.**

TALC 1951
(Right) 2 oz. blue, white & pink paper container. Came in 1951 Always Sweet set. **CMV $12.**

1 OZ. COTILLION COLOGNE 1957 ONLY
(Left) Pink cap. Came in Beautiful Journey set. **CMV $15.**

COLOGNE 1956 ONLY
(Center) 2 oz. white caps. Came in Bath Bouquet only. **CMV $20. mint.**

BATH OIL 1956 ONLY
(Right) 2 oz. white caps. Came in Bath Bouquet only. **CMV $20. mint.**

COTILLION DUO SET 1964
White, pink & gold box holds Cotillion powder sachet & 1 dram perfume. **CMV $22.50. MB.**

DEBUTANTE SET 1963
Pink, white & gold box holds Cotillion cologne mist & beauty dust. Comes in 2 different inner boxes. **CMV $20. MB.**

COTILLION DUET SET 1947-48
Pink box holds 2 oz. Cotillion toilet water with gold cap & powder sachet. **CMV $70. MB.**

ALWAYS SWEET SET 1951
White, blue & pink box with girls hat on lid, holds straw handbag containing Cotillion talc, 5/8 dram perfume & cream lotion with blue cap. **CMV $95. MB.**

HAIR RIBBONS SET 1948-49
Pink & white box has bottle of Avon hand lotion, Cotillion talc, 5/8 dram bottle of Cotillion perfume. Also came, this box, with hand lotion & Cotillion talc from 1949 Your Charm set. Set came with or without perfume. **CMV $65. with perfume, $50. without perfume.**

SOMEONE LIKE YOU SET 1961-62
Pink & white box holds Cotillion 2 oz. cologne & cream sachet. **CMV $22.**

COTILLION BATH ENSEMBLE SET 1950-52
Pink & white box holds 2 drawers with Cotillion talc, powder sachet & 2 bars of pink soap in top drawer. Bottom drawer holds Cotillion cream lotion, toilet water, bath oil & 1 dram perfume. **CMV $175. MB.**

COTILLION DEBUT SET 1961-62
White & gold box holds Cotillion beauty dust, cream sachet & cologne mist, in satin lined flip open compartment. **CMV $35.**

YOUR CHARMS SET 1949
White, blue & pink box with or without ribbon band around lid came with gold heart & arrow charm on lid. Box contains pink & blue paper box of Cotillion talc, 2 oz. Avon hand lotion, pink & blue label with blue cap, 5/8 dram Cotillion perfume with blue cap. Set came with & without perfume. **CMV $65. with perfume, $50. without perfume.**

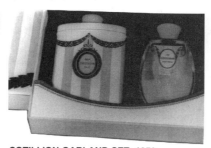

COTILLION GARLAND SET 1950
Pink, white & green box holds Cotillion talc & 2 oz. toilet water. **CMV $52.50.**

ALWAYS SWEET SET 1950
Pink & white box holds straw handbag with green & yellow ribbon & pink flower. Holds bottle of cream lotion with blue cap, Cotillion talc & 5/8 dram Cotillion perfume. **CMV $95. MB.**

COTILLION / COUNTRY GARDENS

COTILLION CLASSIC SET 1940-41
Satin lined box with people dancing on lid holds 2 oz. Cotillion toilet water & gold box of Cotillion talc. **CMV $67.50 MB.**

COTILLION ENCHANTMENT SET 1940-43
Silk lined gold & green box holds Cotillion powder sachet, 2 oz. toilet water & 1 dram perfume with gold cap. **CMV $95. MB.**

COUNTRY GARDENS

COTILLION FANTASY SET 1952
Pink & white Cotillion body powder with cream sachet on top under clear plastic lid. **CMV $40. MB.**

COTILLION GARLAND/COTILLION DUET SET 1946
Pink round box holds Cotillion toilet water & pink painted powder sachet. This set was introduced as Cotillion Duet then changed to Cotillion Garland for Christmas 1946. **CMV $80. MB.**

COUNTRY GARDEN FOAMING BATH OIL 1971-73
4" high, 6 oz. white glass bottle, white cap, green ribbon on neck. Came in Bird of Paradise, Elusive or Charisma. **CMV $5. MB.**

SOAP DISH & SOAP 1971-72
4" long white soap dish with bar of Country Garden soap. **CMV $6. MB.**

BEAUTY DUST 1971-72
4 1/2" high, 5 oz. white glass jar with white lid & greeen ribbon. Came in Bird of Paradise, Elusive or Charisma. **CMV $6. MB.**

POWDER SACHET 1971-73
3" high, 1 1/4 oz. white glass jar with white lid & green ribbon. Came in Bird of Paradise, Elusive or Charisma. **CMV $4. MB.**

COTILLION CLASSIC SET 1946-47
Pink flowered box holds Cotillion 6 oz. cologne & body powder. **CMV $95.**

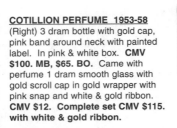

COTILLION PERFUME 1953-58
(Right) 3 dram bottle with gold cap, pink band around neck with painted label. In pink & white box. **CMV $100. MB, $65. BO.** Came with perfume 1 dram smooth glass with gold scroll cap in gold wrapper with pink snap and white & gold ribbon. **CMV $12. Complete set CMV $115. with white & gold ribbon.**

COTILLION ENCHANTMENT SET 1938-39
White box with satin lining holds Cotillion 2 dram glass stoppered perfume, 2 oz. Cotillion toilet water & powder sachet. **CMV $150. MB.**

COUNTRY KITCHEN

MOISTURIZED HAND LOTION
10oz. glass with pump dispenser. **CMV $3. MB.**

CERAMIC SALT & PEPPER SHAKERS
Made in Brazil. 4" high. set. **CMV $6. set MB.**

IF YOU LOVE TO LAUGH, GO TO THE BACK PAGE FOR INFO ON BUD HASTIN'S NEW JOKE BOOK AND HOW TO GET IT. LAUGH MORE AND LIVE LONGER.

COURTSHIP

COURTSHIP PERFUME 1938 ONLY
2 dram bottle, gold cap. **CMV $60. MB, $40. BO mint.**

COURTSHIP PERFUME 1940-44
Box holds 1/8 oz. bottle, gold cap and label. **CMV $25. mint, $35. MB as shown.**

COURTSHIP PERFUME 1937 ONLY
2 dram, gold cap. Sold for 20c with other purchase during Founders Campaign, July 6-26, 1937. **CMV $60. MB, $40. BO mint.** See Misc. Perfumes & Toilet Water for other Courtship bottles.

CRIMSON CARNATION

CRIMSON CARNATION TOILET WATER 1946-48
2 oz. gold or plastic caps. **CMV $40. BO, $55. MB.**

CRIMSON CARNATION PERFUME 1946-47
(Right) Blue & white box holds 3 dram bottle with white cap. **CMV $100. MB, BO $60.** See misc. perfumes for other Crimson Carnation perfumes.

CRYSTALIQUE

CRYSTALIQUE BEAUTY DUST 1972
(Left) Clear crystal plastic powder box & lid with gold base. **CMV $5. - $7. MB.**
CRYSTALIQUE BEAUTY DUST 1972
(Right) Clear glass came with choice of powder. Moonwind, Charisma, Regence, Elusive, Rapture, Occur!, Somewhere, Topaze, Cotillion, Unforgettable or Here's My Heart, with matching puffs. **CMV $11. - $13. MB.**

CRYSTALIQUE / DAISIES WON'T TELL

CRYSTAL BEAUTY DUST 1966
(Left) All glass powder dish. **CMV $20. - $22.50 MB.**

CRYSTAL COLOGNE 1966-70
(Right) 4 oz., 5 1/2" high glass bottle with matching plastic cap, gold trim. Came in Unforgettable, Rapture, Occur!, Somewhere, Topaze, Cotillion, Here's My Heart or To A Wild Rose. **CMV $5. MB.**

CRYSTALIQUE BEAUTY DUST 1979-80
Clear glass, holds all beauty dust refills. (Sold empty.) **CMV $5. MB.**

DAISIES WON'T TELL

DAISIES WON'T TELL BEAUTY DUST 1957
(Left) Blue, white & yellow paper powder box with girl on lid. **CMV $20. - $25. MB.**

DAISY FLUFF-ON 1959-60
(Right) Blue paper powder box with Daisy Puff & clear plastic lid. **CMV $12. - $16. MB.**

DAISIES WON'T TELL BEAUTY DUST 1956
Yellow, white & blue paper box. Short issue. **CMV $20. mint, $25. MB.** Also came with blue sided container.

DAISIES WON'T TELL CREAM SACHET 1963-64
(Left) Pink glass jar with white plastic lid. **CMV in box $11., jar only $9.**

CREAM SACHET 1959-61
(Right) Pink glass jar with floral metal lid. **CMV $11., MB $13.**

HEARTS 'N DAISIES 1958
(Left) Blue & white box holds 2 oz. Daisies Won't Tell cologne & pink pomade lipstick. **CMV $22. MB.**

LOVE ME - LOVE ME NOT 1959
(Right) Blue, white & green box holds Daisies Won't Tell spray cologne & cream sachet in pink glass. **CMV $30.**

DAISIES WON'T TELL BEAUTY DUST 1958
Blue & white box holds blue & white paper powder box with white daisy on top. **CMV $23. MB, beauty dust only $18. mint.**

DAISY SHAMPOO 1959-61
(Right) 4 oz. white plastic bottle & cap. **CMV $10. BO, $12. MB.**

DAISIES WON'T TELL CREAM LOTION 1956-57

(Left) Yellow & white box holds 2 oz. bottle with rib around center & white flower cap, painted label. **CMV $12. MB, $10. bottle only.**

HAND CREAM 1962-64

(Right) Pink tube with white flower cap. In pink & blue box. **CMV $7. in box, $5. tube only.**

DAISIES WON'T TELL COLOGNE WITH ATOMIZER 1956

Yellow, white & pink box holds 2 oz. bottle with rib around middle, white & gold spray atomizer. Short issue. **CMV $15., MB $20.**

DAISIES WON'T TELL COLOGNE 1958-62

(Left) 2 oz. white cap & painted label. **CMV $7. - $10. MB.** Same bottle came in Bubble Bath & Cream Lotion in sets only. **Same CMV.**

BUBBLE BATH 1956-57

(Center) 4 oz. bottle with rib around center. Painted label, white flower cap. **CMV $8., MB $10.**

COLOGNE 1957-58

(Right) 2 oz. cologne with rib around center in One I Love set and Daisies Won't Tell set. **CMV $12.**

DAISY DUST 1958-61

(Left) 2 oz. white plastic bottle & cap. **CMV $10. BO, $12. MB.**

DAISY CREAM LOTION 1958-61

(Center) 4 oz. white plastic bottle & cap. Two different labels. Newer has large letters & painted address at bottom. Older one is smaller letters & embossed address at bottom. **CMV $10. BO, $12. MB.**

DAISIES WON'T TELL SPRAY COLOGNE 1958-60

(Left) Pink plastic coated bottle with white cap. **CMV $10. BO, $12. MB.**

SPRAY COLOGNE 1957 ONLY

1 1/2 oz. blue plastic coated bottle with white c & painted label. **CMV $13., MB $15.**

COLOGNE 1962-64

(Right) 2 oz. glass bottle, white cap & painted label. **CMV $6. BO, $9. MB.**

DAISIES WON'T TELL COLOGNE MIST 1962-64

(Left) 2 oz. white plastic coated bottle with white cap and blue painted label. **CMV $7. BO, $9. MB.**

CREAM LOTION 1962-64

(Right) 4 oz. white plastic bottle and cap. Blue painted label. **CMV $6. BO, $8. MB.**

DAISY SOAP ON A ROPE 1963-64

(Left) Pink, white & yellow box holds white soap with yellow center on a white rope. **CMV $20. MB.**

DAISY SOAP ON A ROPE 1959-62

(Right) Blue, white & pink flowered box holds white Daisy soap with yellow center, on a blue rope. **CMV $20. MB.**

FAIRY TOUCH 1958

Blue and white box holds 2 blue & white tubes with yellow caps of Daisies Won't Tell hand cream. **CMV $16. MB.**

GAY DAISIES SET 1960
Blue, white & pink box holds daisy soap on a blue rope & choice of daisy bubble bath, daisy dust, cream lotion or daisy shampoo. **CMV $35. MB.**

FIRST RECITAL SET 1962-64
Pink & blue fold-over box holds Daisy soap on rope & choice of Daisy cream lotion, bubble bath or Daisy dust. **CMV $35. MB.**

DAISIES WON'T TELL BUBBLE BATH 1962-64
(Top Left) 4 oz. white plastic bottle & cap with blue painted label. CMV $8. MB.
DAISY DUST 1962-64
(Bottom Left) 2 oz. white plastic bottle & cap with blue painted label. **CMV $8. MB.**
HAND CREAM 1958-61
(Right) Blue & white box holds blue & white tube with both flat or tall yellow cap. **CMV $6. MB.**
2 oz. Bubble Bath is same type bottle. Came in One I Love set & Daisies Won't Tell set. **CMV $8.**

DAISY POMADE 1958-59
Blue & white flowered holder holds pink daisy pomade. Also came in lime green color. **CMV $12.50 in holder, $2. pomade only.**

PICK A DAISY SET 1963-64
Pink & blue box holds daisy soap on a rope & Daisies Won't Tell cream sachet. **CMV $32.50 MB.**

WEE TWO SET 1956
(Left) Blue, white & yellow box has two tubes with yellow caps of Daisies Won't Tell hand cream & cream shampoo. **CMV $18.**
DAINTY HANDS SET 1957
(Right) Pink, white & yellow box holds 2 tubes with pink hearts & yellow caps of Daisies Won't Tell hand cream. **CMV $18. MB.**

ONE I LOVE SET 1957 ONLY
Floral box contains 2 oz. cologne, cream lotion & bubble bath in Daisies Won't Tell. White flower caps with yellow centers. Any sets you find with pink caps are taken off Cotillion bottles and not considered a mint set. **CMV $50. MB.**

DAISY CHAIN GIFT SET 1963-64
Pink & white box holds 2 oz. Daisies Won't Tell cologne & pink tube of daisy hand cream. **CMV $22. MB.**

FIELD OF DAISIES SET 1958
Blue & white flowered box holds 2 oz. bottles of Daisies Won't Tell cologne, cream lotion with red ribbon & bubble bath. **CMV $50. MB.**

LITTLE CHARMER SET 1956
Black & white plastic basket with flowers on top holds Daisies Won't Tell 2 oz. cologne, gold pomade & tube of Daisy hand cream. **CMV $65. MB.**

BLOSSOMS SET 1956
Daisy box holds 2 oz. Daisies Won't Tell cologne with blue ribbon & gold pomade. **CMV $27.50 MB, gold pomade $5.**

DAISIES WON'T TELL SET 1957
Box holds 2 oz. each in bubble bath, cream lotion & cologne. White & yellow daisy caps. Came with outer sleeve. Also came Daisy Talc can in place of cream lotion. **CMV $60. MB.**

DAISY PETALS SET 1957
Yellow & white box with pink hearts holds 2 oz. Daisies Won't Tell cologne & lime yellow pomade lipstick in corner of box. **CMV $25. MB.**

DAISY BOUQUET SET 1959-60
Blue & white flowered box holds 4 oz. Daisy cream lotion, Daisy bubble bath & 2 oz. Daisy dust. **CMV $37.50 MB.**

DAISY TREASURES SET 1959
Pink box with yellow slide open cover with it. Light blue ribbon on daisy flower. Holds 3 bottles of nail polish with white caps & nail file. **CMV $60. MB.**

PRETTY BEGINNER SET 1961
Blue, white & yellow box holds Daisies Won't Tell 2 oz. cologne & choice of Daisy soap, Daisy dust, cream lotion, shampoo or bubble bath. **CMV $25, with soap $35. MB.**

DAISIES WON'T TELL SET 1956
Daisy box holds 2 oz. Daisies Won't Tell cologne & bubble bath with center rib on each & can of 3 1/4 oz. Daisy talc. **CMV talc can only $20., $60. MB with outer sleeve.**

MISS DAISY SET 1956
(Right) Daisy box holds Daisies Won't Tell 2 oz. cologne & beauty dust. Top of bottle sticks through top of box. **CMV $40.**

DAISY BOUQUET SET 1957
Blue, white & yellow box holds Daisies Won't Tell 2 oz. cologne, beauty dust & lime yellow pomade. **CMV $45. MB, yellow pomade $5.**

PLAYMATE SET 1956
Daisies carrying case holds Daisies Won't Tell 2 oz. cologne, cream lotion & gold or black pomade with plastic doll with movable arms with satin & net dress. Eyes open & shut, red hair. **CMV $90. MB.**

DAISY POMADE LIPSTICK 1962-64
Pink box holds pink with gold base lipstick. **CMV $4. MB.**

FIRST WALTZ SET 1960
Blue & white Daisies Wont't Tell box holds First Waltz nail polish & pink pomade. **CMV $20. MB.**

DAISY DARLING SET 1958
Blue box with daisies & red ribbon holds Daisies Won't Tell spray cologne & beauty dust. **CMV $42.50 MB.**

MY DOLLY SET 1957
White, yellow & green box holds Daisies Won't Tell 2 oz. cream lotion, cologne, pink or yellow pomade & plastic doll with movable arms, brown hair, blue hat, yellow dress trimmed in pink satin. **CMV $90. MB.**

DAISY PINK NAIL POLISH 1960
(Left) Blue & white box holds Daisies Won't Tell nail polish, white cap. **CMV $8. MB, $6. BO mint.**
FIRST WALTZ NAIL POLISH 1960
(Not Shown) Blue & white box holds Daisies Won't Tell nail polish, white cap. **CMV $8. MB, $6. BO mint.**
DAISY POMADE LIPSTICK 1960-61
(Right) Blue & white box holds pink & gold pomade in shades of 1st Waltz or Daisy Pomade. **CMV $6. MB.**

FIRST WALTZ LIPSTICK 1960
Blue flowered box holds pink lipstick. Came in Daisies Won't Tell. **CMV $6. MB.**

DAISY PINK SET 1960
Daisies box holds Daisy pink nail polish, white cap & pink metal pomade in box. **CMV $20. MB.**

DELFT BLUE

ELEGANTE

DELFT BLUE 1972-74
White milk glass with blue flowers.

SKIN-SO-SOFT SOFTENER
5 oz. **CMV $5. BO, $6. MB.**

FOAMING BATH OIL
5 oz. holds Patchwork, Moonwind or Sonnet. **CMV $7. MB, $6.BO.**

PITCHER & BOWL
5 oz. **CMV $10. MB, $7. BO & bowl.**

SOAP DISH & SKIN-SO-SOFT SOAP
3 oz. **CMV $6. MB.**

ELEGANTE BEAUTY DUST 1956-59
(Left) Red paper sides with tin top & bottom. Silver letters on lid. **CMV $15., MB $20.**
ELEGANTE COLOGNE 1956-59
(Inside Left) Red & silver box holds 4 oz. bottle with silver cap & neck tag & red ribbon. **CMV $40. MB, $20. BO with neck tag & ribbon.**
ELEGANTE TOILET WATER 1957-59
(Center) Red & silver box holds 2 oz. bottle with silver cap & neck tag & red ribbon. **CMV $40. MB, BO with tag & ribbon $20.**
ELEGANTE POWDER SACHET 1957-59
(Inside Right) 9/10 oz. bottle with silver cap. **CMV $12. BO, $17. MB.**
ELEGANTE CREAM SACHET 1956-59
(Right) .66 oz. jar with silver cap. **CMV $8. BO, $13. MB.**

ELEGANTE PERFUME 1956-59
Red & silver box holds 1/2 oz. bottle with silver cap & neck tag with red ribbon. **CMV $125. MB, $75. BO with neck tag & ribbon.**

Elegante fragrance line is the most beautiful packaging Avon ever did. It is very popular and very hard to find. To find these sets in mint condition is something to be proud to add to your collection.

SPARKLING BURGUNDY SET 1957
Round neck & silver box with red satin lining. Holds Elegante 4 oz. cologne, cream sachet, 1 dram perfume & beauty dust. **CMV $115. MB.**

SNOW DREAMS SET 1957
(Left) White box with red ribbon holds Elegante 2 oz. toilet water, cream sachet & 1 dram perfume in red wrapper. **CMV $75. MB.**

ELUSIVE

ELUSIVE BEAUTY DUST 1969-74
Pink plastic with gold or silver trim. **CMV $3. - $5. MB.**
ELUSIVE SAMPLES 1969-74
10 samples to a box. **CMV 50c.**
ROLLETTE 1969-75
.33 oz. frosted glass. **CMV 75c.**
PERFUMED DEMI STICK 1970-73
Paper center, white cap. **CMV $1.**
1/2 OZ. COLOGNE 1969-75
1/2 oz. pink frosted glass. **CMV $1.**
CREAM SACHET 1969-75
Pink frosted glass. OSP $3. **CMV 50c.**
PERFUMED SKIN SOFTENER 1970-72
Pink frosted glass. Lid came with gold or silver trim. **CMV $1.**
ELUSIVE TRAY 1970-71
Pink plastic, gold trim. **CMV $6. MB, $4. tray only.**

ELUSIVE SCENTED HAIR SPRAY 1970-72
(Back Left) 7 oz. pink can & cap with gold letters. **CMV $3.**
PERFUMED POWDER MIST 1971-74
(Back Inside Left) 7 oz. pink painted label. **CMV 50c.**
PERFUMED POWDER MIST 1970-71
(Back Center Left) 7 oz. pink paper label. **CMV $2.**
PERFUMED TALC 1971-74
(Back Center Right) 3 1/2 oz. pink paper container. **CMV 50c.**
COLOGNE MIST 1969-74
(Back Inside Right) 3 oz. pink plastic coated bottle. **CMV 50c.**
ELUSIVE FOAMING BATH OIL 1970-72
(Back Right) 6 oz. pink plastic with pink cap. **CMV .50c.**
PERFUMED SOAP 1970-74
(Front) 3 pink bars in pink box. **CMV $5. MB.**

ENGLISH PROVINCIAL

ENGLISH PROVINCIAL 1972-74
White milk glass with blue & pink flowers & aqua blue lid with flowers. Came in Charisma, or Bird of Paradise.
FOAMING BATH OIL
(Left) 8 oz. **CMV $2. MB, $1. BO.**
COLOGNE
(Inside Left) 5 oz. **CMV $2. MB, $1. BO.**
POWDER SACHET
(Inside Right) 1.25 oz. **CMV $2. MB, $1. BO.**
SOAP DISH & SOAP
(Right) 1.25 oz. **CMV $4. - $5. MB.**

ELUSIVE COLOGNE MIST 1969-74
(Left) Pink painted bottle with pink & gold cap. Paint doesn't go to bottom.
(Right) Later issue pink plastic coated bottle, pink & gold cap. **CMV painted $1., plastic coated 50c.**

FIELD FLOWERS

FIELD FLOWER PRODUCTS
COLOGNE MIST 1971-76
3 oz. green plastic coated over glass, yellow cap. **CMV $1.**
COLOGNE GELEE 1971-72
3 oz. green ribbed glass & orange cap. **CMV $1.50**
PERFUMED SKIN SOFTENER 1971-73
5 oz. green glass, bright or pale blue cap. **CMV $1.**
CREAM SACHET 1971-75
.66 oz. green ribbed glass with purple cap. **CMV 50c.**
PERFUMED POWDER MIST 1971-76
7 oz. green, white & pink can. **CMV 50c.** Also came with upside down label. **CMV $4.**
SOAP 1971-76
Flowered box holds yellow, pink 7 green flower bars. **CMV $6. MB.**
SCENTED HAIR SPRAY 1971-72
7 oz. pink & green can with green cap. **CMV $3.**
COLOGNE ICE 1976
1 oz. tube. **CMV $1.**

FIELD FLOWERS PERFUMED TALC 1970-73
(Left) 3 1/2 oz. green paper label. **CMV $1.** 1973-77 Perfumed Talc had pink label. **CMV 50c.**
DEMI STICK 1970-78
(Inside Left) Green paper band, white cap. **CMV 50c.**
FRAGRANCE SAMPLES 1970-77
(Inside Right) 10 samples in a box. **CMV 50c.**
COLOGNE SAMPLE 1970-78
(Right) Clear glass, white cap. **CMV 25c.**

FLOWER TALK

FLOWER TALK 1972-73
White with orange, blue, yellow, green & purple designs.
PERFUMED TALC
3.5 oz. **CMV $1.**
COLOGNE MIST
3 oz. **CMV $1.**
ROLLETTE
.33 oz. **CMV $1.**
DEMI STICK
.19 oz. **CMV 50c.**
SAMPLE FLOWER TALK
CMV 25c.
CREAM SACHET
.66 oz. **CMV $1.**

FIELD FLOWERS BATH BRUSH & SOAP 1971-72
Pink brush approx. 16" long & 5 oz. flower embossed pink soap. **CMV $8. MB.**

FLOWERTIME

VALENTINE GIFT SACHET 1952
In special red & white gift box. Came in Flowertime, Golden Promise, Quaintance or Cotillion. **CMV $15. MB as shown, $10. BO mint.**

FLOWERTIME POWDER SACHET 1950-53
(Left) 1 1/2 oz. with indented pink cap. **CMV $15. MB, $10. BO.**
FLOWERTIME TALC 1949-53
(Right) 5 oz. bottle with brass shaker top. **CMV $20. MB, $15. BO.**

FLOWERS IN THE WIND SET 1950-52
Blue & silver flip-open box with pink satin lining holds Flowertime cologne talc, powder sachet & 1 dram perfume. **CMV $95. MB.**

DOUBLY YOURS SET 1949
(Left) White & blue swing open box holds 2 oz. bottles of cologne with pink caps in Cotillion & Flowertime. **CMV $65. MB.**

FLOWERTIME / FOREVER SPRING

FOREVER SPRING

FLOWERTIME COLOGNE 1949-53
(Left) 4 oz. pink cap. **CMV $15. MB, $10. BO.**
Same bottle came in 2 oz. size in sets only.
CMV $10.
FLOWERTIME TOILET WATER 1949-53
(Center) 2 oz. pink cap. **CMV $15. MB, $10.
BO.**
FLOWERTIME POWDER SACHET 1949-50
(Right) 1 1/4 oz. bottle has flat or indented
pink cap. **CMV $15. MB, $10. BO.**

FOREVER SPRING BEAUTY DUST 1951-56
(Left) Green & white can. **CMV $20. - $25.
MB.**
FOREVER SPRING BEAUTY DUST 1956-59
(Right) Yellow & white paper box with tin top &
bottom. **CMV $16. - $20. MB.**

FOREVER SPRING PERFUME 1956-59
Yellow & white box with purple base holds
1/2oz. bottle with blue bird on yellow cap &
painted label. **CMV MB $100, BO with bird
$85.**

FLOWER CLUSTER SET 1949
Blue & gold box contains box of face powder,
gold lipstick & 1 dram Flowertime perfume.
CMV $50. MB.

FOREVER SPRING COLOGNE 1951-56
(Left) 4 oz. with yellow tulip cap & green
painted label. Came in green box. **CMV $20.
MB, $15. mint, BO.**
**FOREVER SPRING POWDER SACHET
1953-56**
(Right) 1 1/4 oz. bottle with yellow cap &
green painted label. Came in green box.
CMV $15. MB, $10. BO.

FOREVER SPRING PERFUME 1951-56
Yellow & green box with blue & green ribbon
holds 3 dram glass stoppered bottle blue
ribbon on neck & neck tag. $5. **CMV $110.
in box, $85. bottle only with tag & ribbon.**

FLOWERTIME SET 1949-52
Turquoise & gold box with satin lining holds 4
oz. Flowertime cologne & talc. **CMV $60. MB.**

**FOREVER SPRING 1 DRAM PERFUME
1951-52**
(Left) 1 dram, ribbed glass, gold cap.
Came in green felt folder. **CMV $15. in
sleeve, $10. BO.**
**FOREVER SPRING POWDER BOX
COLOGNE 1956**
(Right) 1/16 oz. size bottle came in
special beauty dust box set only. Came
tied to silk ribbon. **CMV $5. BO mint,
$10. mint with ribbon.**

FOREVER SPRING TOILET WATER 1951-56
2 oz. yellow tulip cap & green painted label.
Came in green box. **CMV $20. MB, $15. BO
mint.**

FOREVER SPRING CREAM SACHET 1956-59
(Left) Yellow glass bottom & cap with flowers
on all 3 lids shown. **CMV $8. - $11. MB.**
**FOREVER SPRING POWDER SACHET
1956-59**
(Center) 9/10 oz. yellow glass & cap. **CMV $9.
- $12. MB.**
**FOREVER SPRING BODY POWDER 1956-
59**
(Right) Frosted glass jar with flowered cap,
painted label. **CMV $12. BO, $17. MB.**

SPRING MOOD SET 1956
Yellow & white box holds Forever Spring body
powder & 4 oz. cream lotion in green glass.
CMV $40. MB.

SPRINGTIME SET 1956
Yellow & white box holds Forever Spring
beauty dust & 4 oz. cologne. **CMV $55.MB.**

FOREVER SPRING COLOGNE 1956-59
4 oz. bottle with blue bird on yellow cap,
painted label, yellow & white flowered box.
CMV $20. MB, BO with bird $15.

MERRY MERRY SPRING SET 1956
Yellow, white & blue box holds Forever Spring
2 oz. toilet water and cream sachet. **CMV
$37.50 MB.**

**FOREVER SPRING CREAM LOTION 1956-
59**
(Left) 4 oz. clear glass with yellow cap,
painted label. No bird on cap. Came in yellow
& white box. **CMV $14. MB, $12. mint BO.**
FOREVER SPRING TOILET WATER 1956-59
(Center) 2 oz. yellow cap with tiny blue bird,
painted label. Came in yellow & white
flowered box. **CMV MB $20., BO with bird
$15. mint.**
**FOREVER SPRING CREAM SACHET 1951-
56**
(Right) Green box holds white glass jatr with
green lid. **CMV $12. MB, $7. jar only mint.**

**FOREVER SPRING CREAM LOTION 1956-
59**
4 oz. green painted over clear glass bottle with
yellow cap. **CMV $18. BO mint, $25. MB.**

SPRING GODESS SET 1957
Yellow & white box holds Forever Spring beauty dust, cream sachet & 4 oz. cologne. **CMV $55. MB.**

FOREVER SPRING SET 1953
Green & white box with green net lining holds Forever Spring boby powder, cream sachet & 1 dram perfume in green felt sleeve. OSP $3.95. **CMV $55. MB.**

FOREVER SPRING SET 1952
Is same as above only did not have 1 dram perfume. **CMV $45. MB.**

SPRING MELODY SET 1952-53
Forever Spring body powder & cream sachet setting on top under clear plastic lid. **CMV $40. MB.**

FOREVER SPRING REPRESENTATIVE GIFT SET 1951
CMV $85. MB.

SPRING SONG SET 1953
Blue & green box holds Forever Spring 4 oz. cologne & 1 dram perfume. **CMV $45. MB.**

APRIL AIRS SET 1956-57
Yellow & white box with blue ribbon top holds Forever Spring body powder & cream sachet. **CMV $45. MB.**

SPRING CREATION SET 1953
Green box with net lining holds Forever Spring cream sachet & 1 dram perfume. **CMV$40.MB.**

SPRING CORSAGE SET 1951-52
Green box with clear plastic lid & bouquet of flowers holds Forever Spring 4 oz. cologne & 1 dram perfume. **CMV $55 MB.**

FOREVER SPRING BODY POWDER 1951-56
(Left) Green & white paper container. **CMV $15.**

FOREVER SPRING PERFUMED TALC 1957-59
(Right) 2.75 oz. yellow & white can, yellow capcap. **CMV $10., MB $12.**

GARDEN OF LOVE

GARDEN OF LOVE SWIRL PERFUME 1948 ONLY
3 dram glass stoppered bottle is swirl glass design with gold neck tag. Purple and white flowered box. **CMV $90. BO mint, $120. MB.**

GARDEN OF LOVE POWDER SACHET 1946-48
(Left) 1 1/4 oz. turquoise ribbed plastic cap and flowered label. **CMV $22.MB, $17. BO.**
GARDEN OF LOVE SACHET 1944-45
(Center) 1 1/4 oz. pink paper sachet. Came with pink plastic flower on lid. **CMV $18. mint, $23. MB.**
GARDEN OF LOVE POWDER SACHET 1940-46
(Right) 1 1/4 oz. bottle with black or turquoise metal cap. **CMV $20.MB, $15. BO.**

GARDEN OF LOVE PERFUME 1940-44
Orange lid, gold base box holds 3 dram glass stoppered bottle with gold neck tag. **CMV $100. mint BO, $130. MB.**

GARDENIA

GARDENIA PERFUME 1940-42
Gold speckled box holds 3/8 oz. bottle with gold octagonal cap. **CMV $50. BO mint., $80. MB.**

GARDENIA PERFUME "RIBBED" 1933-36
1/2 oz. ribbed glass with black octagonal cap. Came in gold box set. **CMV $45. mint.**
GARDENIA PERFUME "OCTAGONAL" 1933-36
6 sided bottle and black octagonal cap. Came in Little Folks set and Hankerchief set. **CMV $45. mint**

GARDENIA PERFUME 1948-52
3/8 oz. or 3 dram bottle with flowered cap, paper or painted label. Came in satin lined box with clear plastic lid. **CMV $80. MB, $40. BO mint.**

GOLDEN PROMISE

GOLDEN PROMISE BEAUTY DUST 1947-56
(Left) Standard issue gold and white can. **CMV $20. CO mint, $25. MB.**
GOLDEN PROMISE BEAUTY DUST 1947-51
(Right) Smaller than regular issue. Came in sets only. **CMV $20. mint.**

GOLDEN PROMISE PERFUME 1949 ONLY
(Left) 1/4 oz. glass bottle fits in gold metal case. Came in Golden Duet & Evening Charm Sets. **CMV $25.**
GOLDEN PROMISE CREAM SACHET 1953-56
(Center) White glass, square base with yellow flowered top. **CMV $9. BO, $13. MB.**
GOLDEN PROMISE BODY POWDER 1947-56
(Right) Gold and white shaker top can. **CMV $16. CO mint, $20. MB.**

GOLDEN PROMISE POWDER SACHET 1952-56
(Left) 1 1/4 oz. yellow plastic cap. **CMV $12. MB, $9. BO.**
GOLDEN PROMISE POWDER SACHET 1951-52
(Center) 1 1/4 oz. gold cap. **CMV $12. MB, $9. BO.**

GOLDEN PROMISE

GOLDEN PROMISE PERFUME 1947-50
Gold and white flip open box holds 1/2 oz. bottle with gold cap and painted label. **CMV $175.00 MB. $100.00 BO. mint.**

GOLDEN PROMISE PERFUME 1954-56
Gold and white box holds 1/2 oz. bottle with flat glass stopper and gold & white label. **CMV $125. MB. $90. BO. mint.**

GOLDEN PROMISE BODY POWDER CHRISTMAS DEMO 1947
Regular issue talc in gold box given to Avon ladies in special Merry Christmas demo box. **CMV $30. MB with outer box shown.**

GOLDEN PROMISE PERFUME 1950-54
Gold & white box holds 3 dram glass stoppered bottle with gold base label and neck cord. **CMV $125.MB. bottle with label and cord $100. Mint.**

GOLDEN PROMISE 3 PIECE SET 1947-49
Gold and white box holds Golden Promise 1 dram perfume, 4 oz. cologne, and beauty dust. **CMV $85. MB.**

GOLDEN PROMISE SET 1950-51
Gold box with clear plastic cover and gold tie down ribbon holds Golden Promise 4 oz. cologne and beauty dust. **CMV $65. MB.**

GOLDEN PROMISE SACHET 1948
Special gold box, 62nd Anniversary issue. 1 1/4 oz. ribbed gold plastic cap or threaded brass cap. **CMV $22. MB as shown.**

GOLDEN PROMISE COLOGNE 1947-56
4 oz. painted label, gold cap. **CMV $20.BO. $25. MB.**
GOLDEN PROMISE TOILET WATER 1953-56
2 oz. gold cap & painted label. **CMV $20.BO. $24.MB.**

GOLDEN PROMISE PERFUME GIFT 1947
Clear bottle, gold cap. Label is gold with red lettering, says "Golden Promise Perfume with Best Wishes of Avon Products Inc., Pasadena, Cal." Came in gold box with same statement. **CMV $75. MB, $50. BO.**
GOLDEN JEWEL SET 1953-54
White and gold box with gold jewel on front. Holds Golden Promise 2 oz. Toilet Water and 1 dram Perfume. Toilet Water cap fits through top of box. **CMV $40. MB.**

HANA GASA

HAPPY HOURS

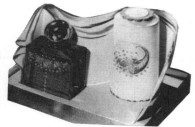

GOLDEN PROMISE 2 PIECE SET 1947-49
Gold and white box holds Golden Promise 4
oz. cologne and body powder. **CMV $65. MB.**

HANA GASA FRAGRANCE SAMPLES 1970-74
10 in a box. **CMV 50c box.**
HANA GASA COLOGNE SAMPLE 1970-74
Sample bottle, white cap. **CMV 25c.**
COLOGNE 1970-75
1/2 oz. clear glass, yellow cap. **CMV $1,
$1.50 MB.**
PERFUME ROLLETTE 1970-74
Yellow painted glass, yellow cap. **CMV $1.**
CREAM SACHET 1970-75
.66 oz. yellow painted over milk glass with
yellow lid. **CMV 50c.**
HANA GASA BEAUTY DUST 1970-76
6 oz. yellow plastic. **CMV $5. MB.**

HAPPY HOURS TALC 1948-49
2 3/4 oz. metal shaker cap. Sold in sets only.
CMV $20. mint.
HAPPY HOURS COLOGNE 1948-49
1 oz. plastic cap. Came in sets only. **CMV
$20. mint.**
HAPPY HOURS PERFUME 1948-49
3 drams, pink cap. Rare. Came in sets only.
CMV $50. mint.

GOLDEN PROMISE DELUXE SET 1952-54
Gold box with clear plastic lid and gold satin
lining holds Golden Promise 4 oz. cologne,
powder sachet, 1 dram perfume and body
powder. Gold ribbon around box. **CMV $100.
MB.**

HANA GASA HAIR SPRAY 1971
7 oz. yellow can, **CMV $3.**
**HANA GASA PERFUME POWDER MIST
1971-74**
7 oz. yellow can. **CMV $1.**
PERFUME TALC 1971-74
3 1/2 oz. yellow cardboard. **CMV $1.**
COLOGNE MIST 1970-76
3 oz. yellow plastic coated glass, yellow cap.
CMV $1.
HANA GASA SOAP 1971-75
3 yellow bars in pink and yellow box. **CMV $5.
MB.**

MEMENTO SET 1948-49
Blue and pink box holds Happy Hours Cologne
and Perfume. **CMV $95. MB.**

GOLDEN DUET SET 1949
Small gold purse holds Lipstick and gold metal
case with 1/2 dram bottle of Golden Promise
perfume inside. **CMV $35. mint, $40. MB.**

HAPPY HOURS SET 1948-49
(Left) Pink and blue box holds Happy
Hours Talc, Cologne and Perfume. **CMV
$112.00 MB.**

STAR BOUQUET SET 1948-49
Green and pink box holds Happy Hours Talc
and Cologne. **CMV $75. MB.**

HAWAIIAN WHITE GINGER

HAWAIIAN WHITE GINGER TALC 1968 ONLY
(Left) 2.75 oz. green and white talc sold in perfume pair only. **CMV $2.**
TALC 1968-73
(Center) 3.5 oz. multi-colored cardboard, gold letter label. **CMV $1.** 1974-77 Talc came with pink letter label. **CMV 50c.**
BEAUTY DUST 1972
(Right) Multi-colored cardboard. **CMV $4. mint, $5. MB.**

COLOGNE MIST 1971-72
2 oz. Light green glass bottle with white cap. **CMV $1. MB.**
AFTER BATH FRESHENER 1965-67
5 oz. bottle with white painted label and cap. Also came with and without gold 4A design. **CMV $6. MB..**

HELLO SUNSHINE

HELLO SUNSHINE PRODUCTS 1979-80

LIP BALM
Pink, white and yellow. **CMV 50c.**
HAND CREAM
White, yellow and pink. 1.5 oz. tube. Green cap. **CMV 50c.**
FUN SHINE NAIL TINT
.5 oz. clear glass, pink cap. **CMV 75c MB.**
COLOGNE
2.5 oz. clear glass, yellow cap. Yellow and pink decal on glass. **CMV $1.**

HAWAIIAN WHITE GINGER CREAM SACHET 1968-72
Both .66 oz. green frosted jars and flowered caps. Short jar 1967, same as Lily of the Valley jar. **CMV $2.** Tall green jar in 1969. **CMV $1.**

HAWAIIAN WHITE GINGER COLOGNE MIST 1972-76
2 oz. clear glass bottle with clear plastic cap with inner cap of green, red and white. **CMV 75c.**
ROLLETTE 1972-74
.33 oz. clear bottle, white cap with colored band. **CMV 50c.**
DEMI STICK 1970-78
.19 oz. green, red & white, white cap. **CMV 50c.**
CREAM SACHET 1973-78
.66 oz. glass jar, white, green and red cap. This has 3 different lid labels. Early one - no zip code. .66 oz. Next - zip but no numbers. Doesn't have weight on lid. Later ones have zip and numbers but no weight on lid. **CMV 50c.**
FLORAL DUET HAWAIIAN WHITE GINGER SET 1972-73
Came with Rollette and bar of soap. **CMV $5. MB.**
HAWAIIAN WHITE GINGER SOAP 1970-78
3 oz. single bar soap (same as shown in set). **CMV $1.**
FRAGRANCE KWICKETTES 1969-75
(Not shown) Box holds 14 packettes. **CMV $1. box.**

HER PRETTINESS

HER PRETTINESS LIP KISSES 1970-71
Lip Pomade, tubes blue and white, pink and white, orange and white in cherry, chocolate or peppermint. Mirror on back side of cap. **CMV $2. each, MB.**

BATH FRESHENER 1967-72
(Left) 6 oz. glass bottle with white cap. **CMV $2.**

HER PRETTINESS ENCHANTED COLOGNE MIST 1969-72
Brown tree base holds 3 oz. cologne mist in green bubble top and green bird spray button. **CMV $7. MB.**

MAGIC MUSHROOM CREAM SACHET 1969-72
Green, pink and blue plastic. **CMV $4.**

LADY BUG FRAGRANCE GLACE 1969-72
Red, black and green plastic bug. **CMV $4. MB.**

LOVE LOCKET FRAGRANCE GLACE 1969-71
Gold locket and chain, in yellow, gold and pink box. **CMV $10. MB.**

SECRET TOWER ROLLETTE 1969-72
Red cap on bottle. **CMV $3. MB.**

ROYAL FOUNTAIN CREME SACHET 1970
Blue base with silver and gold fountain top. Contains Her Prettiness Creme Sachet. **CMV $5. MB.**

HER PRETTINESS TALC 1970-71
3 1/2 oz. flowered box. **CMV $2.**

HER'S MY HEART PERFUME 1946-48
1/2 oz. glass stoppered bottle with painted label and pink neck ribbons. Bottle is tied to pink satin heart shaped base and box. **CMV $140. MB. BO with ribbon, $100. mint.**

HER PRETTINESS ART REPRODUCTION PRINT 1969-70
14" x 18" pink, green and white, was free purchase of any Her Prettiness products. Came in cardboard tube with Her Prettiness sticker and a poem "Her Prettiness Serves Ten in The Garden". **CMV $8., three pieces. $4. print alone.**

HERE'S MY HEART PERFUME 1948-49
1/2 oz. glass stoppered heart shaped bottle. Painted label, pink satin ribbon and heart shaped box and base. Very rare. **CMV $125. BO mint, $175. MB.**

PRETTY ME DOLL 1969-71
5 oz. plastic bottle with gold hair, cap and pink neck ribbon. Holds Powdered Bubble Bath. 6 1/2" high. **CMV $8.MB.**

FLOWER BELLE COLOGNE MIST 1969-72
Blue top with yellow base has 2 oz. Her Prettiness Cologne Mist. **CMV $4.**

BRUSH AND COMB SET 1969-72
Pink box with yellow comb and brush. **CMV $5.**

BUNNY PUFF 1969-72
3 1/2 oz. white plastic rabbit with pink fluff tail. Holds Her Prettiness Talc. **CMV $5.**

BUNNY FLUFF PUFF 1976
Reissued - Same except holds Pink & Pretty. **CMV $4.** Also has R on bottom for reissue. 1979 reissue in yellow rabbit. It is shown in children's toy section.

HER PRETTINESS COLOGNE SAMPLE 1969-72
1/8 oz. clear glass white cap. Painted label. Came in envelope. **CMV $1. mint in envelope.**

HERE'S MY HEART PERFUME OIL FOR THE BATH 1963
1/2 oz. painted label and white beaded cap. Came in blue and white box.Hard to find. **CMV $12. MB. $8. BO.**

1/2 OZ. COLOGNE 1970-71
1/2 oz. painted label, white beaded cap, blue and white box. **CMV $1. BO, $2. MB.**

HERE'S MY HEART

HERE'S MY HEART COLOGNE SPECIAL ISSUE 1961
Blue and white box (short issue) holds 4 oz. cologne. **CMV $16. MB as shown.**

HERE'S MY HEART PERFUME OIL 1964-68
1/2 oz. painted label and white beaded cap. Came in blue and white box. **CMV $8. MB..**

LOTION SACHET 1958-61
1 oz. blue plastic coated bottle with white beaded cap and painted label. Blue and white box. **CMV $ 5. MB, .**

2 OZ. COLOGNE 1961-68
2 oz. white beaded cap and painted label, blue and white box. First introduced in red and white rose box. **CMV in rose box $8. In blue box $3..**

COLOGNE MIST 1958-76
3 oz. blue plastic coated bottle with white beaded cap and painted label. Blue and white box. **CMV $1.**

HERE'S MY HEART PERFUMED BATH OIL 1960-66
6 oz. blue plastic, white beaded cap. **CMV $2. MB.**

FOAMING BATH OIL 1966-68
6 oz. blue plastic, white beaded cap. **CMV $2 MB.**

HERE'S MY HEART COLOGNE MIST 1957-58
3 oz. blue plastic coated bottle with indented heart, 2 hearts on gold cap. Also plain lid. **CMV $18. BO mint, $23. MB.**

HERE'S MY HEART TOILET WATER 1959-62
2 oz. painted label and white beaded cap. Came in blue and white box. **CMV $5. MB, $2. BO.**

4 OZ. COLOGNE 1960-63
4 oz. bottle with white beaded cap and painted label. Came in blue and white box. **CMV $5. MB, $2. BO.**

POWDER SACHET CHRISTMAS BOX 1959
Blue box with gold butterflies sold Christmas only 1959 with choice of powder sachet in Here's My Heart, Persian Wood, Nearness, Cotillion (pink painted), Bright Night and To A Wild Rose. **CMV $15. each MB as shown.**

HERE'S MY HEART PERFUME ROLLETTE 1967-68
.33 oz. ribbed glass, smooth gold cap. **CMV $3.MB.**

PERFUMED CREAM ROLLETTE 1963-65
.33 oz. 4A embossed bottle with gold cap. **CMV $3.MB..**

HERE'S MY HEART POWDER SACHET 1960-66
9/10 oz. blue glass, white beaded plastic cap. **CMV $8 MB.**

POWDER SACHET 1958-60
Blue and white plastic squeeze bottle with white beaded cap. **CMV $10. MB.**

DEMI STICK 1975-78
.19 oz. blue and white, white cap. **CMV $1.MB.**

CREAM SACHET 1976-77
.66 oz. clear glass, gold, blue and white lid. **CMV $1. MB. .**

LOTION SACHET 1958
1/2 oz. clear glass fan shaped bottle with blue cap. Came in Here's My Heart and Persian Wood. Came in Wishing set only. **CMV $8. each MB, $4. BO.**

HERE'S MY HEART BODY POWDER 1961-63
4 oz. blue plastic bottle with white beaded cap, painted label. **CMV $8. MB, $5. BO.**

HERE'S MY HEART SOAP 1962-65
(Left) Blue and white box holds 2 white heart shaped soaps. **CMV $25. MB.**

114

HERE'S MY HEART CREAM LOTION 1958-68
4 oz. bottle with painted label and white beaded cap. **CMV $2. MB.**

SPRAY PERFUME 1958-63
Blue, white and gold box holds blue tin container with gold cap with hearts on top. **CMV $12. MB.**

HERE'S MY HEART PERFUME SAMPLE 1950
With gold lid. **CMV $30.**

HERE'S MY HEART LOTION SACHET 1957-58
1 oz. blue plastic coated bottle with hearts on gold cap, painted label. **CMV $10. MB, $5. BO.**

SENTIMENTAL HEART SET 1961
Blue box with blue satin lining holds Here's My Heart cologne mist and beauty dust. **CMV $32.50. MB.**

HERE'S MY HEART PERFUMED SOAP 1965-66
3 oz. white soap in blue and white wrapper. **CMV $3.**

PERFUME MIST 1964-68
2 dram blue and white metal with gold band. **CMV $5. MB.**

ROMANTIC MOOD SET 1960
Blue and white box with blue satin lining with Here's My Heart cologne mist, cream sachet and beauty dust.. **CMV $40. MB.**

HEART FELT SET 1964
Blue and white box holds Here's My Heart 2 oz. cologne and cream sachet. **CMV $25. MB.**

HERE'S MY HEART SOAP 1966-67
Blue and white box holds 3 heart shaped bars. **CMV $25. MB.**

HERE'S MY HEART PERFUMED TALC 1958-62
2.75 oz. blue and white can, white beaded cap. **CMV $1. CO, $3. MB.**

SCENTED HAIR SPRAY 1966-70
7 oz. blue and white can, 4A on cap. **CMV $3.**

PERFUMED TALC 1962-72
2.75 oz. blue and white can with white cap. **CMV $1.**

HERE'S MY HEART CREAM SACHET 1959-75
.66 oz. white beaded cap. Came blue painted over clear glass. **or blue paint over white milk glass. CMV $1.**

PERFUMED SKIN SOFTENER 1964-73
5 oz. painted over milk glass or clear glass jar with gold and white lid. **CMV $1.**

HERE'S MY HEART BEAUTY DUST 1958-70
White plastic powder box with beaded edge. Some with yellow lid and white handle. **CMV $10.** white issue. **CMV $ 5. MB.**

HEARTS IN BLOOM SET 1964
Blue and white box holds Here's My Heart cologne mist, cream sachet and cream lotion. **CMV $40. MB.**

HERE'S MY HEART SOAP 1959-64
Blue and white box, holds 2 white heart shaped bars. **CMV $25. MB.**

SWEETHEARTS SET 1958
Blue and white heart shaped box with white satin lining and white rose on lid. Holds Here's My Heart cologne mist, and plastic powder sachet or lotion sachet. **CMV $50. MB.**

HEART O'MINE SET 1959
Blue and white box with blue heart on lid with white rose and blue satin lining. Holds Here's My Heart cologne mist, cream sachet, beauty dust and spray perfume. **CMV $50. MB.**

NEW REMEMBRANCE SET 1963
Blue and white box holds Here's My Heart cologne mist and beauty dust. **CMV $35. MB.**

TWO HEARTS GIFT SET 1961
Blue and white box holds 2 oz. Here's My Heart cologne and cream sachet. **CMV $30.. MB.**

HONEYSUCKLE

HONEYSUCKLE FLORAL DUET SET 1972-73
Box came with Rollette and bar of soap. **CMV $5. MB.**

IMPERIAL GARDEN

IMPERIAL GARDEN COLOGNE MIST 1973-77
3 oz. white with orange flowers and gold stems. 2 different designs as pictured. **CMV $2. MB. each.**

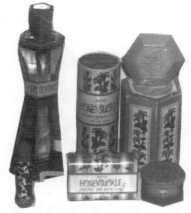

HONEYSUCKLE AFTER BATH FRESHENER 1967-72
8 oz. bottle with orange cap and center band label. **CMV $1.MB.**
PERFUMED TALC 1967-77
3 1/2 oz. yellow and white paper container. **CMV $1.50**
SOAP 1968-69
6 sided box holds 3 yellow bars. **CMV $9. MB.**
PERFUMED DEMI STICK 1970-74
.19 oz. yellow, green and white. Yellow cap. **CMV $1. MB.**
COLOGNE MIST 1971-72
2 oz. yellow glass bottle, yellow cap. **CMV $1 .MB.**
PERFUMED SOAP 1967-78
3 oz. bar in yellow and orange wrapper. **CMV $3.**
CREAM SACHET 1967-75
.66 oz. yellow frosted glass with orange lid. **CMV $1. MB.**

IMPERIAL GARDEN CERAMIC VASE TEST 1973
Test vase from factory never sold by Avon. Has gold band around top of cap and bottom is glazed over Avon. Blue and green flowers on front different from regular issue. **CMV $25.**

IMPERIAL GARDEN PERFUME TALC 1974-76
3.5 oz. white, gold and orange, cardboard.
CMV 50c.
IMPERIAL GARDEN BEAUTY DUST 1974-ONLY
6 oz. white plastic with orange and gold. **CMV $7. MB.**

IMPERIAL GARDEN CERAMIC VASE 1973-75
Some came with short neck and tall cap and some with long neck and short caps. White with orange flowers and gold stems. 18 oz. ceramic vase. Bath crystals. 7" high. **CMV $20. MB.**
COLOGNE MIST 1973-77
3 oz. **CMV $1.MB.**
CREAM SACHET 1973-77
.66 oz. **CMV $1. MB**
ROLLETTE 1973-77
.33 oz. **CMV $1.MB.**
SAMPLE BOTTLE COLOGNE 1973-77
CMV $1. MB.

IMPERIAL GARDEN PERFUMED SOAP 1974-76
Three 3 oz. cakes white soap. Came in white and orange box. **CMV $9. MB.**
PERFUMED POWDER MIST 1974-77
7 oz. orange painted can, white lid. **CMV 50c.**
PERFUMED SKIN SOFTENER 1974-76
5 oz. orange plastic, white and gold cap. CMV.50c.
IMPERIAL GARDEN COASTERS 1973
4 white plastic, orange design. **CMV $25. MB set.**

JARDIN D'AMOUR
See Misc. Perfume & Powder Section for additional Jardin D'Amour bottles.

JARDIN D'AMOUR PERFUME 1930s
1 oz. clear glass bottle with frosted glass stopper. Silver & blue CPC label. Very rare. **CMV $150. mint.**
JARDIN D'AMOUR SACHET 1926-30
Brass cap, silver & blue label. Rare. **CMV $85. mint.**

JARDIN D'AMOUR PERFUME 1929-33
2 oz. glass stoppered bottle. Orange box. Label on top of bottle. **CMV $85. BO mint, $135. MB.**

JARDIN D'AMOUR PERFUME 1926-33
Orange box with gold base for 1 oz. glass stoppered bottle. Black label at neck. **CMV $85. BO, $135. MB.**

JARDIN D'AMOUR PERFUME SET 1954 ONLY
Blue & gold bucket with gold tie down cord. Holds 1 1/2 oz. bottle with gold label, clear plastic cap with blue stone in gold set. Bottom of bucket holds 1 dram perfume. Came in blue, white & gold lay down box. **CMV MB. complete $200, 1- 1/2 oz. bottle in bucket mint $175, 1 dram perfume $15, 1 1/2 oz. bottle only $50. mint.**

JARDIN D'AMOUR VANITY COMPACT 1926-32
Silver compact. **CMV $40. MB. compact only $35. mint.**

JASMINE SOAP 1936-45
Turquoise & gold box holds 3 embossed bars. **CMV $47.50 MB.**

JASMINE & ROYAL JASMINE

JARDIN D'AMOUR SACHET 1932-36
1 1/4 oz. ribbed glass jar, black cap. **CMV $25. mint BO, $30. MB.**

JASMINE SOAP 1934-36
Beige & gold box holds 3 bars. **CMV $50. MB.**

ROYAL JASMINE SOAP 1954-59
Box holds 3 bars, with round or flat edges. Box lid lifts off. **CMV $28. MB.**
ROYAL JASMINE SOAP 1959-66
Same box only lid flips back and not off. The soap has flat edges. **CMV $27. MB.**

JASMINE SOAP 1946-53
Black flowered box holds 3 bars. **CMV $45. MB.**

JARDIN D'AMOUR TALC 1926-36
Frosted glass with brass shaker top. Front paper label. **CMV $60. BO mint, $75. MB.**

JASMINE GIFT SOAP 1966-67
Floral box contains 3 yellow Jasmine soaps. **CMV $25. MB.**

JASMINE SOAP 1948-49
(RIGHT) Christmas only. Black flowered box holds 3 white bars. **CMV $45. MB.**

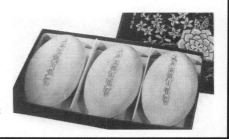

JASMINE AFTER BATH FRESHENER 1964-68
8 oz. glass bottle with yellow cap & painted label. Yellow flowered box. **CMV $2. BO, $3. MB.**

PERFUMED SOAP 1964-67
3 oz. bar in yellow flowered wrapping. **CMV $2.**

CREAM SACHET 1967-72
.66 oz. yellow frosted glass with gold & white lid. **CMV 50c.**

PERFUMED TALC 1964-68
3 1/2 oz. yellow flowered paper container with plastic shaker top. **CMV $2.**

JASMINE SOAP 1939 ONLY
Gold striped box holds 3 bars. Avon on back of soap. **CMV $60. MB.**

JASMINE BATH SALTS 1936-44
9 oz. glass jar, turquoise lid. **CMV $20. BO mint, $25. MB.**

ROYAL JASMINE BATH SALTS 1954-57
Yellow & white flowered box holds 8 oz. bottle with yellow cap. **CMV $25. MB, $20. BO.**

FANTASY IN JASMINE SET 1942-44
Green box holds 2 bars Jasmine soap & 9 oz. Jasmine bath salts with turquoise lid. **CMV $75. MB.**

JASMINE POWDER SACHET 1946-50
(Left) 1 1/4 oz. bottle with black cap & label. Came in black box. **CMV $20. MB, $15. BO.**

JASMINE DUSTING POWDER 1947-50
(Right) 13 oz. black & gold tin can with pink flowers on lid. **CMV $25., MB $30.**

ROYAL JASMINE BATH OIL 1957-59
Yellow, white & green box holds 8 oz. bottle with yellow cap and flowered label. **CMV $25. MB, $20. BO.**

JASMINE TOILET WATER 1946-48
2 oz. gold cap, also came in black flowered box. Turquoise box shown. **CMV MB $40., $30. BO.**

FANTASY IN JASMINE 1946-47
Black box with pink flowers holds 2 bars of Jasmine soap & 9 oz. bottle of Jasmine bath salts. **CMV $75 MB.** Set also came with 2 bottles in boxes of 1 1/4 oz. Jasmine sachet in place of soaps. **CMV with boxed sachets $100. MB.**

JASMINE BATH SALTS 1945-52
(LEFT) 9 oz. clear glass with black cap & label. Label came with either a large or small pink flower on front. Came in black box. **CMV $40 MB, $30. BO.**

FANTASY IN JASMINE SET 1945 ONLY
Black box with pink flowers holds Jasmine bath salts & 2 Jasmine soaps. **CMV $77.50 MB.**

BATH ENSEMBLE SET 1940-43
Blue flowered flip open box holds Jasmine bath salts, Jasmine 2 oz. toilet water, 2 bars of Jasmine soap & can of dusting powder. **CMV $150. MB set.**

LAVENDER

LAVENDER SACHET 1944-45
Beige box holds 2 lavender wrapped cakes of sachet. One set is wrapped in clear cellophane with a flowered band. The other set is wrapped in lavender flowered paper, no band. Some boxes have label printed on box & some boxes plain. **CMV $25. MB.**

FANTASY IN JASMINE SET 1956-57
White box with yellow flowers holds 2 bars Royal Jasmine soap & 2 oz. Royal Jasmine bath oil with white cap & black label. **CMV $45. MB, 2 oz. bath oil $25. BO.**

ROYAL JASMINE SET 1954-57
Yellow & white flowered box holds 8 oz. Royal Jasmine bath salts & bar of Royal Jasmine soap. **CMV $40. MB.**

FANTASY IN JASMINE SET 1940
Blue box with flowers holds 9 oz. Jasmine bath salts & 2 bars soap or 2 Powder Sachets boxed. **CMV $100. MB.**

LAVENDER BLOSSOMS 1935-38
Lavender & pink box holds package of Lavender Blossoms. **CMV $40. MB.**

FANTASY IN JASMINE SET 1948
Black box with pink flowers holds 2 bars Jasmine soap & 2 oz. Jasmine toilet water. **CMV $75. MB.**

JASMINE POWDER SACHET 1949
(Left) 1 1/2 oz. clear glass bottle, black cap & label. **CMV $20. - $25. MB.**
JASMINE TOILET WATER 1949
2 oz. black cap & label. **CMV $35., MB $40.**

LAVENDER SACHET CAKES 1946-48
(Top) Box holds 2 flower design wrapped cakes of sachet. **CMV $30. MB.**
LAVENDER SACHETS 1945-46
(Bottom) Beige box holds 2 foil wrapped cakes of sachet. Plain band. **CMV $30. MB.**

LAVENDER SOAP 1935 ONLY
Box holds 3 lavender bars of soap. **CMV $75. MB.**

LAVENDER TOILET WATER 1938-43
(Left) 4 oz. lavender cap. **CMV $35. BO, $40. MB. CPC on box, 1938-39 add $5.**
LAVENDER TOILET WATER 1945-46
(Right) 4 oz. lavender cap. **CMV $40. BO, $45. MB.**

LAVENDER SOAP SET 1945
Pink box holds 3 Lavender embossed bars. OSP 85c. **CMV $60. MB.**

LAVENDER SOAP SET 1946 ONLY
Box holds 3 lavender bars of soap. **CMV $60. MB.**

LAVENDER TOILET WATER 1946-48
(Left) 4 oz. pink cap. **CMV $35. BO, $40. MB.**
LAVENDER TOILET WATER 1934-37
(Right) 4 oz. ribbed bottle with blue or gold cap. Lavender label, box shown used 1934-36. **CMV $45. mint BO, $55. MB.**

LAVENDER TOILET WATER 1934-37
4 oz. ribbed glass, gold cap, pink & lavender box. Box shown used 1936-37. **CMV $45. BO, $55. MB.**

LAVENDER POWDER SACHET 1961-68
.9 oz. pink & white label & neck band, glass & plastic stopper. **CMV one with 4A design in place of size $4. BO, $7. MB. CMV on 9 oz. $20. MB, $15. BO.** Box on right is 1965, box in center is regular issue.

LAVENDER ENSEMBLE SET 1941 ONLY
Box holds 2 Lavender sachet cakes, bottle of Lavender toilet water & 2 Lavender bars of soap. **CMV $100. MB set.**

LAVENDER ENSEMBLE SET 1934-38
Lavender box holds 4 oz. Lavender toilet water, 2 bars Lavender soap & package of Lavender Blossoms. **CMV $125. MB set, Lavender Blossoms only $50. MB.**

LAVENDER BOUQUET SACHET PILLOWS 1977-78
Pink box holds 6 satin lavender filled sachet pillows. Came with pink ribbon around them. **CMV $4.**

LAVENDER ENSEMBLE SET 1938 ONLY
Lavender flip open box holds 4 oz. Lavender toilet water with same label as 1934 Lavender toilet water, 2 bars of Lavender soap, 2 Lavender sachet cakes. **CMV $100. MB, $45. BO.**

LILAC

LAVENDER ENSEMBLE 1938-40
Lavender flip open box with cardboard liner holds 4 oz. Lavender toilet water, 2 bars of Lavender soap wrapped in lavender paper & 2 sachet cakes with lavender band around them. **CMV $100. MB.**

LAVENDER ENSEMBLE SET 1945-46
Blue, pink & white with silver bottom holds 4 oz. Lavender toilet water, 2 bars Lavender soap & 2 sachet cakes. **CMV $100. MB.**

LILAC TOILET WATER 1940
2 oz. gold ribbed cap with "A" on top, gold label. Blue box. Has Avon Products Inc. label. **CMV $35. BO mint, $40. MB.** Same bottle sold 1934 to 1939 only bottom of label says Toilet Water & does not say Avon Products. CPC pn backside of label. **Same CMV as above.**

LAVENDER ENSEMBLE SET 1940-43
Lavender flowered box with satin lining holds 4 oz. Lavender toilet water, 2 bars of Lavender soap & 2 Lavender sachet cakes. **CMV $100. MB.**

LAVENDER ENSEMBLE SET 1946-48
Blue & pink flowered flip open box holds 4 oz. bottle, pink cap of Lavender toilet water, 2 pink bars of Lavender soap & 2 paper wrapped cakes of sachet. **CMV $100. MB.**

LAVENDER SET 1939
Yellow box with lavender, green & pink flowers holds 4 oz. Lavender toilet water, 2 cakes Lavender soap & 2 sachet cakes with plain lavender color paper ribbons. **CMV $125. MB.**

LAVENDER ENSEMBLE 1946
(LEFT) Blue, pink & green flowered box with satin lining holds 2 bars of Lavender soap, 4 oz. bottle of Lavender toilet water & 2 flower wrapped cakes of sachet. **CMV $100. MB.**

LILAC AFTER BATH FRESHENER 1964-68
8 oz. glass bottle with pink cap & pink or white painted label. Pink box. **CMV $2.**
PERFUMED TALC 1964-76
3 1/2 oz. pink paper container with plastic shaker top. **CMV $1.**
PERFUMED DEMI STICK 1970-76
.19 oz. lavender label with white cap & bottom. **CMV 50c.**
PERFUMED DEMI STICK 1968-70
.19 oz. lavender label & cap & bottom. **CMV $1.**
PERFUMED SOAP 1964-67
1 bar in pink flowered wrapping. **CMV $3. MB.**
CREAM SACHET 1967-75
.66 oz. purple frosted glass with gold & white lid. **CMV 50c.**
CREAM SACHET 1975-76
.66 oz. clear glass, white cap with lilacs on top. **CMV 50c.**

LILAC SOAP 1966
Lavender box holds 3 piece lavender soap in cellophane wrapper. **CMV $17. MB.**

LILAC SOAP 1968-77
Box holds lavender bars. **CMV $10. MB.**

LILY OF THE VALLEY

LILY OF THE VALLEY TOILET WATER 1946-49
Green box holds 2 oz. bottle with gold cap & label. **CMV $40. MB, $30. BO.**

LILY OF THE VALLEY SOAP 1966-68
Green box holds 2 green cakes. **CMV $25. MB.**

LILY OF THE VALLEY AFTER BATH FRESHENER 1964-68
8 oz. glass bottle with green cap, painted label in green or white letters, green box. **CMV $2. MB.**

PERFUMED TALC 1964-70
3 1/2 oz. green paper container with plastic shaker top. **CMV $1.50.**

PERFUMED SOAP 1964-67
3 oz. bar with green & white flowered wrapping. **CMV $3. MB.**

LILY OF THE VALLEY TOILET WATER 1949-52
2 oz. white cap. **CMV $45. MB, $35. BO.**

LILY OF THE VALLEY PERFUME 1948-52
3 dram bottle with flower cap. Came in satin lined box with clear plastic lid. **CMV $80. MB, $40. BO.**

LILY OF THE VALLEY PERFUME 1952-54
3 dram, white cap, white satin lined box. **CMV $85. MB, $40. BO.** Also came in Gardenia.

IF YOU LOVE TO LAUGH, GO TO THE BACK PAGE FOR INFO ON BUD HASTIN'S NEW JOKE BOOK AND HOW TO GET IT. LAUGH MORE AND LIVE LONGER.

LILY OF THE VALLEY TOILET WATER 1934-40
2 oz. gold ribbed cap, "A" on top. Gold front label. **CMV $35. BO, $40. MB.**

LILY OF THE VALLEY / LITTLE BLOSSOM

LILY OF THE VALLEY CREAM SACHET 1974 ONLY
(Left) .66 oz. clear embossed glass with white cap with flowers. First issued with this jar. **CMV $1.**
CREAM SACHET 1975-76
(Center) .66 oz. clear ribbed glass with white cap with flowers. **CMV $1.**
PERFUME DEMI STICK 1974-76
(Right) .19 oz. white with flowers. **CMV $1.**

LILY OF THE VALLEY PRODUCTS 1979-80
COLOGNE ICE STICK
(Left) Yellow & green plastic. **CMV 50c.**
PERFUMED TALC
(Center) 3.5 oz. cardboard sides, plastic bottom & top. **CMV 25c.**
CHATEAU OF FLOWERS BOOK
(Right) Green hardback book on story of Lily of the Valley. Book does not say Avon on it. Must be in Avon box cover as shown. **CMV $2. MB.**

LITTLE BLOSSOM

LITTLE BLOSSOM LIP & NAIL TINT 1982-83
Lip tint on left, pink cap, no box. Nail tint in .5 oz. plastic bottle, white cap, boxed. **CMV $1. each.**

LITTLE BLOSSOM FINGER PUPPET WITH DEMI STICK SET 1982-83
(Left) box holds small finger puppet & blue, white & pink Demi Stick. **CMV $4. MB.**
LITTLE BLOSSOM LIGHT SWITCH COVER
(Right) Box holds blue & green light switch plate with pink flowers. **CMV $4. MB.**

LITTLE BLOSSOM WHISPER SOFT COLOGNE 1981-82
1.5 oz. clear glass painted decor. Pink cap. **CMV $2. MB.**
CHEEKY ROSE BLUSH 1981-82
Pink & white plastic jar. **CMV $1. MB.**
CHEERFUL LIP TINT 1981-82
White flowered tube, pink cap. **CMV $1. mint, no box.**
LITTLE BLOSSOM SCENTED PICTURE FRAME 1981-82
Pink plastic frame 4 1/2" x 4 1/2" has scented fabric picture of little blossom. **CMV $6. MB.**

LITTLE BLOSSOM BUBBLE BATH PACKETS 1983
Flowered box holds 10 packets. **CMV $1. MB.**

LITTLE BLOSSOM & FRIENDS 1983-84
(RIGHT) Shaker talc with puff sets. 2 oz. talc & small hand puff. Choice of
LITTLE BLOSSOM
Pink
DAISY DREAMER
Yellow
SCAMPER LILY
Orange
CMV $4. each set.
MINI DOLLS
2 1.4" high soft plastic, choice of Little Blossom, Daisy Dreamer, Scamper Lily. each. **CMV $2. each.**
DAB O COLOGNE
.45 oz. rollette, choice of Little Blossom in Whisper Soft, Daisy Dreamer in Secret Wishes & Scamper Lily in Sparkle Bright. **CMV $2. each.**

LUCY HAYS

LUCY HAYS PERFUME 1936 ONLY
2 dram, gold cap. Sold for 20c with other purchase to celebrate Mr. & Mrs. McConnell 51st wedding anniversary. Lucy Hays was Mrs. McConnell's maiden name. Sold March 3 to 23, 1936 only. **CMV $85. MB, $65. mint BO.**

LULLABYE SET 1955-56
Blue & pink box holds baby oil & baby powder. **CMV $45. MB.**

LULLABYE

LULLABYE BABY TALC 1946-50
5 oz. pink paper container with pink & white plastic top & bottom. **CMV $35. MB, $30. talc only mint.**

LULLABYE BABY OIL 1946-50
6 oz. clear glass bottle, back side flat. Pink cap & painted label. **CMV $50. MB, $40. BO.**

LULLABYE BABY CREAM 1946-50
White milk glass jar with pink lid & label. **CMV $30. MB, $25. jar only.**

LULLABYE BABY SOAP 1946-50
Plastic wrapper with pink painted bow & flowers on wrapper. **CMV $25. mint.**

LULLABYE BABY SET 1951-55
Blue, pink & white box holds baby lotion, baby talc, lanolin baby soap. **CMV $75. MB.**

LULLABYE BABY SET 1946-50
Pink box holds Lullabye baby oil, Lullabye baby soap, Lullabye baby cream & Lullabye baby talc. **CMV $150. MB.**

LULLABE BABY SET 1964-66
Pink & blue box holds 2 bars baby soap & choice of Tot 'N Tyke baby oil, baby lotion or baby shampoo. **CMV $27.50 MB.**

LUSCIOUS

LUSCIOUS PERFUME AWARD 1950
(Left) Gold & purple box holds 3 dram, ribbed glass stopper. Stopper different from regular issue. Given when Luscious was first issued. **CMV $150. MB, $100. BO.**

LUSCIOUS PERFUME 1950
(Right) 1 dram clear bottle with gold cap & label. Came in brown felt wrapper. **CMV $12. BO, $18. in wrapper.**

LUSCIOUS PERFUME 1950-55
(Left) 1 dram, painted label with smooth gold cap. Came in felt wrapper. **CMV in wrapper $15., $10. mint BO.**

LUSCIOUE PERFUME 1955-56
(Right) 1 dram, painted label, embossed gold cap. Came in felt wrapper. **CMV in wrapper $15., $8. BO.**

LUSCIOUS PERFUME 1950
3 dram glass stoppered bottle, came with painted label or with gold neck tag label. **CMV $125. MB, $100. BO.**

MARIONETTE

MARIONETTE PERFUME 1940-44
(Left) 1 dram bottle, plastic cap. CMV $25. BO, $30. MB.

MARIONETTE PERFUME 1938
(Right) 1/4 oz. size. Gold ribbed cap with "A". CPC on label. Sold in honor of Mr. McConnell's birthday. CMV $50. MB, $40. BO.

MARIONETTE TOILET WATER 1939-40
2 oz. plastic cap, long front label. CMV $45. MB, $35. BO.

MERRIMENT

JOLLY SURPRISE 1955
Pink & blue flip open box holds choice of 4 oz. bottle of Merriment cologne, or bubble bath with pink caps. CMV $55. each MB, $40. BO.

MISS LOLLYPOP

MARIONETTE SACHET SPECIAL ISSUE BOX 1940 ONLY
(Left) Short issue blue & pink box holds regular issue marionette powder sachet on left in 1 1/4 oz. size. Sold for 20c with regular order. CMV $30. MB in this box only.

MARIONETTE SACHET 1938 ONLY
(Right) 1 1/4 oz. ribbed glass bottle with turquoise plain metal cap or ribbed plastic turquoise cap. CMV $25. BO, $30. MB.

MARIONETTE TOILET WATER 1940-46
2 oz. gold ribbed cap & gold label. Also came with plastic caps. CMV $30. BO mint, $35. MB.

MARIONETTE SACHET 1938-46
1 1/4 oz. with turquoise plain metal cap or ribbed turquoise plastic cap. Shown with regular issue box. CMV $20. MB, $15. BO.

MISS LOLLYPOP COLOGNE BOOT 1967-69
2 oz. glass boot with gold cap & red tassel. Red & white box. CMV $8. MB.

MISS LOLLYPOP CREAM SACHET 1967-70
(Left) .66 oz. dark or light yellow glass jar with white kitten on red, white & pink cap. Kittens eyes are blue or black, head also turns on some. CMV $5. MB. Also came with white base. CMV $7. MB.

COLOGNE MIST 1967-70
(Right) 3 oz. pink plastic coated bottom with red band, white hat with red & yellow ribbon. CMV $6. MB.

MISS LOLLYPOP POWDER MITT 196870
Yellow, orange & white plastic mitt filled with powder. Pink & white box. CMV $5. MB.

SOAP & SPONGE 1967-70
Pink soap & 9" long sponge. Pink & white box. CMV $12. MB.

MISS LOLLYPOP LIP POPS 1967-69
(3 on Left) Girls face on handle. Pink lemonade, cherry, raspberry, peppermint & cola. CMV $4. MB.

ROLLETTE 1968-69
(Center) Pink, yellow & white cap. 1/3 oz. size. CMV $3. MB..

PERFUMED TALC 1968-70
(Right) 3 1/2 oz. paper container with plastic shaker top. CMV $5. MB.

MOONWIND

MISS LOLLYPOP HAND CREAM 1968
(Left) 2 oz. white plastic tube, white boots & purse, yellow cap. **CMV $3.**
HAND CREAM 1968
(Right) 2 oz. white plastic tube, black boots & purse, yellow cap. **CMV $3.**

MOONWIND PERFUMED SOAP 1975-78
3 cakes blue soap. Blue & silver lid slides over gold box. **CMV $10. MB.**

MISS LOLLYPOP POWDERETTE 1967-68
(Left) 3 1/2 oz. container of perfumed talc, red plume on top is long handled puff. **CMV $10. MB.**
PRETTY TOUCH 1969
Yellow, pink, green & orange plastic light switch plate. OSP 29c with purchase of Miss Lollypop items. Hard to find. Sold only 1 campaign. **CMV $9. MB.**

MOONWIND COLOGNE & BATH OIL 1973
4 oz. clear glass bottles, gold caps. Came in Treasure Chest set only. **CMV $4.**

MOONWIND FRAGRANCE 1971-78
All are blue trimmed in silver.
COLOGNE MIST 1971-75
3 oz. blue with silver painted top. **CMV $1.**
COLOGNE MIST 1975-80
Blue with flat top, 2.7 oz. size. **CMV 50c.**
PERFUME ROLLETTE 1971-76
1/3 oz. **CMV 50c.**
BEAUTY DUST 1971-76
6 oz. **CMV $3. - $6. MB.**
PERFUMED POWDER MIST 1972-77
7 oz. silver or blue caps. **CMV 50c.** Some upside down painted label. **CMV $8.**
PERFUMED SKIN SOFTENER 1972-73
5 oz. blue glass. **CMV 50c.**
CREAM SACHET 1971-75
.66 oz. **CMV 50c.**
PERFUMED SOAPS 1972-73
3 bars, blue, in blue box. **CMV $7. MB.**
FOAMING BATH OIL 1972
(Not Shown) 6 oz. **CMV $1.**

NEARNESS

MISS LOLLYPOP LIP POP 1967
(Left) 1st issue pink & white dots, mirror top with face on back. **CMV $5 MB.**
LIP POP 1968
(Right) Same box came with 2 pink & white dot lip pops, no mirror top. **CMV $5. MB.**

MISS LOLLYPOP ICE CREAM PUFF 1968-70
(Left) 3 1/2 oz. yellow plastic bottom with pink fluff. Holds talc. **CMV $4. BO, $6. MB.**
DOUBLE DIP BUBBLE BATH 1968-70
(Right) 5 oz. orange & white plastic bottle, red cap. **CMV $4. BO, $5. MB.**

PRETTY ME 1968
(RIGHT) Box with white plastic tray holds Miss Lollypop perfume rollette & lip pop in choice of peppermint, pink lemonade, cherry, raspberry or cola. **CMV $12. MB.**

NEARNESS BODY POWDER 1956-58
Frosted glass bottle with blue cap & label. Blue & gold box. **CMV $13. MB, $10. BO.**
NEARNESS PERFUMED TALC 1957-61
Blue can & cap. **CMV can only $5., $7. MB.**
NEARNESS POWDER SACHET 1956-61
1 1/4 oz. blue glass bottle with blue cap & label. **CMV $10. MB, $7. BO.** Also came .9 oz. size. **Same CMV.**

NEARNESS

NEARNESS TOILET WATER 1956-61
2 oz. bottle with blue cap & see through label on back side. Came in blue & gold box. **CMV $15. MB, $10. BO.**

NEARNESS COLOGNE 1955-61
4 oz. bottle with blue cap & see through label on back side. Came in blue & gold box. **CMV $15. MB, $10. BO.**

NEARNESS PERFUME 1955-59
Blue satin draw bag holds clam shell with pearl & 1/2 oz. bottle with blue cap & see through label on back side. **CMV in bag $100, $50. BO.**

NEARNESS COLOGNE 1957 ONLY
(Left & Center) 1/2 oz. clear glass. Sold in Gems & Crystals set only. Came with 2 different caps. Available in 4 fragrances. **CMV $7.**

NEARNESS CREAM SACHET 1955-61
(Right) Blue glass bottom, blue metal cap. **CMV $5. BO, $8. MB.**

NEARNESS BEAUTY DUST 1959-61
Plastic pearl color lid with lavender rim & turquoise bottom. General issue. **CMV $15. MB, $10. CO.** Rare issue came all lavender matching rim & bottom. **CMV $18. MB, $13. CO.**

NEARNESS 1 DRAM PERFUME 1955-59
(Left) 1 dram, clear smooth glass, gold scroll cap. Came in blue felt wrapper. **CMV $8. Mint**

TWO PEARLS SET 1956-57
(Right) Blue & gold box with 2 pearls on lid holds Nearness body powder & cream sachet. **CMV $40. MB.**

NEARNESS CHARM 1957
Blue box holds Nearness toilet water & can of talc. **CMV $40. MB.**

NEARNESS COLOGNE MIST 1957-59
(Left) 3 oz. blue plastic coated bottle with blue cap, blue & gold box. **CMV $20. MB, $15. BO mint.**

NEARNESS COLOGNE MIST 1959-61
(Right) 3 oz. blue plastic coated bottle with pearl on pearl colored cap. Cap will turn gray in sunlight & not considered mint. Blue & gold box. **CMV $15. BO mint, $20. MB.**

NEARNESS SEA SHELL NECKLACE 1956 ONLY
Gold finished pendant with pearl on fine chain. Came only in Always Near set. **CMV $25.**

NEARNESS BEAUTY DUST 1956-59
Blue cardboard container with tin bottom. **CMV $20. MB, $15. CO, mint. CMV $22. for special 1956 Christmas issue box as shown, MB.**

ALWAYS NEAR SET 1956
Blue sea shell box with pink satin lining holds Nearness 2 oz. toilet water, 1 dram perfume & gold sea shell necklace with pearl. **CMV $75. MB.**

SEA MIST SET 1958
Blue & gold box with net lining holds Nearness cologne mist & cream sachet. **CMV $60. MB.**

NEARNESS GIFT PERFUME COMBO SET 1956
1/2 oz. Nearness perfume on the clam shell in blue satin bag. Came with 1 dram Nearness perfume in blue felt wrapper in white box & outer sleeve. **CMV $130. MB.**

CIRCLE OF PEARLS 1957
Blue plastic box with blue plastic cover holds Nearness 2 oz. toilet water, cream sachet & pearl necklace. **CMV $75. MB.**

OCCUR!

OCCUR! POWDER SACHET 1963-67
(Left) 9/10 oz. black glass & cap, painted label. **CMV $7. MB, $5. BO.**
OCCUR! CREAM SACHET 1963-75
(Center) .66 oz. black glass & cap. 2 caps: 1 says Occur!, 1 says Occur! Cream Sachet. **CMV 50c.**
OCCUR! CREAM SACHET 1976-78
(Right) .66 oz. clear glass with black & gold lid. **CMV .50c.**

OCCUR! CREAM LOTION 1964-68
(Left) 4 oz. gold cap & painted label. Came in black & gold box. **CMV $4. MB, $2. BO.**
OCCUR! 1/2 OZ. COLOGNE 1970-71
(Center Left) 1/2 oz. size with gold cap & painted letters. Came in black & gold box. **CMV $1. BO, $2. MB.**
OCCUR! PERFUME OIL 1964-69
(Center Right) 1/2 oz. gold cap & painted label. Came in black & gold box. **CMV $6. MB, $4. BO.**
OCCUR! 2 OZ. COLOGNE 1964-71
(Right) 2 oz. bottle with gold cap & painted label. Came in black & gold box. **CMV $1. BO, $2. MB.**

OCCUR! PERFUMED TALC 1964-74
(Left) 2.75 oz. black can & cap, gold painted label. **CMV $1.**
OCCUR! FOAMING BATH OIL 1966-74
(Center) 6 oz. black plastic bottle with gold cap & painted label. Came in black & gold box. **CMV $2. MB.**
OCCUR! COLOGNE MIST 1963-76
(Right) 3 oz. black plastic coated bottle with gold cap & painted label. Came in black & gold box. Older issue was gold bottom under plastic coating. Came with & without 3 oz. on front of bottle. **CMV $2.**

OCCUR! SOAP 1965-67
Black & gold box holds 3 yellow bars. **CMV $15. MB.**

OCCUR! BEAUTY DUST 1971-75
6 oz. black cardboard, non-refillable. **CMV $5. MB.**
OCCUR! BEAUTY DUST 1963-70
Black plastic box with gold handle on black lid. **CMV $3. - $5. MB.**
OCCUR! PERFUMED SKIN SOFTENER 1964-72
5 oz. black painted over white milk glass or clear glass jar with black & gold lid. **CMV $1.** ALso came white milk glass painted black or solid black glass. **CMV $3. each.**
OCCUR! PERFUMED SOAP 1965-68
Black wrapped soap. **CMV $2.**

OCCUR! PERFUMED BATH OIL 1964-65
6 oz. black plastic bottle with gold cap & painted label. Black & gold box. **CMV $2. BO, $4. MB.**

OCCUR! PERFUME OIL FOR THE BATH 1963
(Left) Black & gold box holds 1/2 oz. bottle with gold cap & painted label. **CMV $8. MB.**
OCCUR! COLOGNE MIST 1963-66
(Center & Left) 2 oz. frosted glass with black cap & gold painted label. Came in black & gold box. **CMV $4. BO, $6. MB.** Also came with 4A embossed bottle with black neck label & gold plastic cap. **CMV $5. MB, $3. BO.**

OCCUR! / ORCHARD BLOSSOMS / PATTERNS

OCCUR! SCENTED HAIR SPRAY 1966-70
(Left) 7 oz. black can with black cap. **CMV $3. .MB.**
PERFUME ROLLETTE 1965-69
(Center Left) .33 oz. gray ribbed carnival glass, gold cap. **CMV $3. MB.**
PERFUMED CREAM ROLLETTE 1963-65
(Center Right) .33 oz. 4A embossed bottle with gold cap. **CMV $2. MB..**
OCCUR! PERFUME MIST 1963-68
(Right) Gold box holds 2 dram black & gold metal case with white cap. **CMV $3. MB.**

ORCHARD BLOSSOMS

ORCHARD BLOSSOMS COLOGNE 1941-45
(Left) 6 oz. bubble sided bottle, short front label has tree with flowers on it. pink cap. **CMV $30. BO, $40. MB.**
ORCHARD BLOSSOMS COLOGNE 1945-46
(Right) Same as above with long blue & white front label, pink cap. **CMV $45. MB, $35. BO.**

PETAL OF BEAUTY 1945-46
Blue & white box holds 6 oz. Orchard Blossoms cologne and blue & white box beauty dust. **CMV $100. MB.**

PETAL OF BEAUTY 1943-44
Blue box with pink satin lining holds 6 oz. Orchard Blossoms cologne & blue feather design beauty dust or Apple Blossom beauty dust. **CMV $100. MB.**

OCCUR! FRAGRANCE FORTUNE SET 1964-65
Black & gold box holds Occur! 2 oz. cologne & 1/2 oz. perfume oil. Both have gold **CMV $30. MB.**

OCCUR! DELUXE SET 1965
Black & gold box holds Occur! beauty dust, perfumed skin softener & cologne mist. **CMV $35.**

PATTERNS

PATTERNS 1969
TRAY 1969-70
10" black plastic tray with gold edge when held to light shows purple, red, gray (these are transparent). There is an opaque black one-rare. **CMV red, gray & purple $5. MB,** Reissued in 1975. Black (no light comes through) **$8.**
POWDER SHADOW COMPACT 1969-70
Black & white plastic.
LIPSTICK 1969-70
CREAM SACHET 1969-74
COLOGNE MIST 1969-72
PERFUME ROLLETTE 1969-74
PATTERNS PERFUME GLACE RING 1969-70
gold ring with black set. **CMV $6. MB**
All others CMV $1. each.

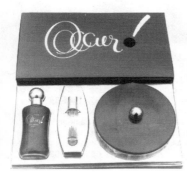

OCCUR! ELEGENCE SET 1964
Black & gold box holds Occur! 4 oz. cream lotion, perfumed talc & 2 oz. cologne. **CMV $35. MB.**

OCCUR! SOPHISTICATE SET 1963-64
(Left) 3 oz. Occur! cologne mist, perfume cream rollette & beauty dust. Black & gold box. **CMV $35. MB.**

PENNSYLVANIA DUTCH

PENNSYLVANIA DUTCH DECANTERS 1973-76
Yellow painted over clear glass with orange fruit and yellow caps. **All items CMV $4. MB.**
HAND & BODY LOTION 1973-76
10 oz. came in Patchwork or Sonnet only.
COLOGNE DECANTER 1973-74
(Salt or pepper shaker) Holds Moonwind, Patchwork or Sonnet. 4 oz.
FOAMING BATH OIL 1973-76
6 oz.
POWDER SACHET SHAKER 1973-75
1.25 oz.
PERFUMED SKIN SOFTENER 1973-76
5 oz.

PERSIAN WOOD

PERSIAN WOOD MIST 1959-64
(Left) 3 oz. red plastic coated glass, gold crown cap. Came in red & gold box. **CMV $6. MB.**
COLOGNE MIST 1964-76
(Center) 3 oz. red plastic coated glass, gold crown cap. Came in red & gold box. **CMV $1. - $2. MB.**
PERFUME OIL FOR THE BATH 1963
(Right) 1/2 oz. bottle with gold cap, painted label. Came in red & goldbox. **CMV $10. MB.**

PERSIAN WOOD CREAM LOTION 1961-66
(Left) 4 oz. clear glass, gold lettering, gold cap. Came in red & gold box. **CMV $5. MB, $3. BO.**
PERFUMED BATH OIL 960-66
(Center) 6 oz. red plastic bottle with gold cap. Came in red & gold box. **CMV $4. MB.**
BODY POWDER 1961-63
(Right) 4 oz. red plastic bottle with gold cap, in red & gold box. **CMV $10. MB.**

PERSIAN WOOD COLOGNE 1962-63
2 1/2 oz. clear glass, gold cap. Red label on front of flat sided bottle. Came in Refreshing Hours set only. **CMV $10.**
CREAM SACHET 1975-76
.66 oz. clear glass, red & gold cap. **CMV .50c**

PERSIAN WOOD PERFUME OIL 1964-66
Red & gold box holds 1/2 oz. bottle, white lettering & gold cap. **CMV $8. MB, $5. BO.**
PERSIAN WOOD COLOGNE 1961-66
2 oz. clear glass, gold lettering, gold cap. In red & gold box. **CMV $6. MB, $4. BO.**
PERSIAN WOOD COLOGNE 1960-63
Red & gold box holds 4 oz. bottle with gold lettering & gold cap. **CMV $10. MB, $6. BO.**

PERSIAN WOOD TOILET WATER 1959-61
(Left) 2 oz. gold cap, painted label. Came in red & gold box. **CMV $6. MB, $4. BO.**
PERSIAN WOOD MIST 1957-59
(Center) 3 oz. red plastic coated glass, smooth gold cap. Came in red & gold box. **CMV $6. BO, $8. MB.**
PERSIAN WOOD MIST 1956-59
(Right) 3 oz. red plastic coated glass, raised gold cap with 4A on top. Came in red & gold box. **CMV $8. MB, $6. BO.**

PERSIAN WOOD POWDER SACHET 1957-66
(Left) 1 1/4 oz. red plstic squeeze bottle, gold cap, red & gold box. **CMV $7. MB, $4. BO.**
LOTION SACHET 1957-61
(Right) Red plastic coated, gold cap. Came in red & gold box. **CMV $4. BO, $7. MB.**

PERSIAN WOOD PERFUMED SKIN SOFTENER 1960-64
(Left & Center) 5 oz. off-white glass bottom with straight sides. Red & gold cap with either curved or straight sides. **CMV $5. MB, $3. BO.**
PERFUMED SKIN SOFTENER 1964-66
(Right) 5 oz. white glass, round bottom, red & gold cap. **CMV $3. BO, $4. MB.**

PERSIAN WOOD PERFUMED TALC 1958-62
(Right) Red & gold box holds red can with brass cap & trim. **CMV $4. MB.**

PERFUMED TALC 1962-68
(Left) Same as above only with a white or red plastic cap. **CMV $3. MB.**

PERSIAN WOOD BEAUTY DUST 1957-60
(Left) Red glass bottom with red & gold tin lid. Lid also came in cardboard just like tin lid shown. Same CMV. **CMV $12. mint, $17. MB.**

PERSIAN WOOD BEAUTY DUST 1960-66
(Right) White plastic with red design around gold handle. **CMV $8. mint, $12. MB.**

PERSIAN WOOD 4 OZ. COLOGNE 1960-62
Red & gold flip open box holds 4 oz. Persian Wood cologne. **CMV $20. MB.**

PERSIAN WOOD CREAM SACHET 1959-76
(Left to Right) .66 oz. red bottom with smooth gold lid. **CMV $6. MB.** Gold embossed cap with curved sides. **CMV $4. MB.** Same cap with straight sides. **CMV 50c.** Came red paint over clear or milk glass.

PERSIAN WOOD BEAUTY DUST REFILL 1960s
Box holds plain paper refill pack with red powder puff. **CMV $6. MB.**

PERSIAN WOOD SET 1964
Red & gold box with white lining holds Persian Wood cream sachet & 1 dram perfume. **CMV $22. MB.**

PERSIAN WOOD PERFUME MIST 1963-67
(Left) 2 drams, red base, white cap, in gold box. **CMV $4. MB.**

SPRAY PERFUME 1957-63
(Right) 2 dram, red metal with gold cap, red & gold box. **CMV $7. MB.**

PERSIAN WOOD BEAUTY DUST 1962-63
(Right) Red paper sides with gold writing around sides & clear plastic top. Came in Fragrance Magic sets only. **CMV $15. mint.**

PERSIAN WOOD FANCY SET 1957-58
Red & gold box with red lining holds Persian Wood mist & lotion sachet or powder sachet. **CMV $40. MB.**

PINE & ROYAL PINE

PERSIAN WOOD INTRIGUE SET 1963-64
Red & gold box holds Persian Wood mist, cream lotion & perfumed cream rollette. **CMV $37.50 MB.**

PERSIAN MAGIC SET 1961-62
Red & gold box holds Persian Wood 2 oz. cologne & cream sachet. **CMV $25. MB.**

PERSIAN TREASURE SET 1959-60
Fancy gold box with white satin lining holds Persian Wood mist, 2 oz. toilet water, perfume spray & cream sachet. **CMV $60. MB.**

PERSIAN LEGEND SET 1961-62
Red & gold box with red satin lining holds Persian Wood mist & beauty dust. **CMV $40. MB.**

ROYAL PINE BATH SALTS 1954-57
8 oz. clear glass with green lid. Green & brown label. **CMV $20. - $25. MB.**

ROYAL PINE BATH OIL 1957-59
8 oz. bottle with green cap & pine cones on label in yellow, white & green box. **CMV $10. MB**

PINE BATH SALTS 1953
8 oz. clear glass jar, green lids, painted pine branch. Came in 2 different ways. Both came in 1953 Royal Pine set only. **CMV $30. each mint.**

ROYAL PINE BATH OIL 1963-68
8 oz. green plastic bottle & cap. **CMV $3. MB,**

PINE SOAP 1959
Plain green box with gold printing on lid. 3 green flat edge bars. **CMV $32.50 MB.**

PINE SOAP 1940 ONLY
Special box holds 3 green bars of Pine soap. **CMV $45. MB.**

PINE BATH OIL 1942-51
6 oz. flat sided bottle with turquoise cap. **CMV $22.BO. Mint $30. MB.**

PINE BATH OIL 1944-45
(Left) 6 oz. flat sided bottle with green cap & brown label. **CMV $25. MB, $20. BO.**

ROYAL PINE BATH OIL 1955-57
(Center) 6 oz. flat sided bottle, green cap. OSP $1.25. **CMV $20. BO, $25. MB.**

PINE BATH OIL 1955-56
(Right) 2 oz. pink cap. Pink & white curtain label. Came in "That's for Me Set" only. **CMV $15.**

ROYAL PINE SET 1954-57
Pine covered box holds 8 oz. jar with green lid of Royal Pine bath salts & green bar of Pine soap. **CMV $35. set, $20. BO.**

PINE SOAP SUBSTITUTE 1940
3 green bars of pine soap came in brown and green box that was the Royal Pine set box. A letter from Avon stating the regular soap boxes were not available & Royal Pine set box was substituted. Rare, with letter. **CMV $45. MB with letter as shown.**

PINEHURST SET 1955-57
Pine box holds 2 green bars of Pine soap & 4 oz. bottle of Pine bath oil with green cap. **CMV $55. MB.**

PINE BATH OIL 1955-57
4 oz. bottle with green cap. Came in Pinehurst Set only. **CMV $20.**

ROYAL PINE SET 1953
Pine box holds 1 bar of Pine soap & 8 oz. jar with green lid & pine cone & branch painted on bottle. OSP $1.25. **CMV $45.**

ROYAL PINE SET 1940-43
Pine comes on lid of box, holds 2 green bars of Pine soap & 6 oz. bottle of Pine bath oil with brown label. **CMV $60. MB.**

PINE SOAP 1940-59
(Top) Green box with pine cone on lid holds 3 green round bars of Pine soap. **CMV $30.MB.**

ROYAL PINE SOAP 1959-65
(Bottom) Same design box & same design on soap, only edge of soap is flat instead of round. **CMV $25. MB.**

BREATH OF PINE SET 1940
Box holds 9 oz. bottle of Pine bath salts & 2 green bars of Pine soap. **CMV $60. MB.**

BREATH OF PINE SET 1940-42
Green & white box holds 2 green bars of Pine soap & 9 oz. bottle of Pine bath salts. **CMV $60. MB.**

TOWERING PINE SET 1941-42
Pine comes on lid of box, holds Apple Blossoms body powder, green bar of Pine bath soap & 6 oz. bottle of Pine bath oil with tulip A on label. **CMV $85. MB.**

ROYAL PINE SET 1943
Beige box with pine cones & crest on lid, holds 6 oz. Royal Pine bath oil with brown label & 2 bars Pine soap. Came in 2 different size boxes as shown. **CMV $70. MB each set.**

PRETTY PEACH

PRETTY PEACH "SODA" COLOGNE MIST 1964-67
2 oz. pink plastic coated bottle with pink top with white flowers & blue straws. Came in 2 different silver stands. OSP $2.50. **CMV $8. each MB, $5. BO mint.**

PRETTY PEACH EAU DE COLOGNE FOREIGN 1960s
Peach cap & painted label. **CMV $10.**
FOREIGN PRETTY PEACH HAND CREAM
CMV $6.

PRETTY PEACH CREAM SACHET 1964-67
Yellow glass jar with peaches on lid. **CMV $8. MB, $5. jar only.**
PEACH POMADE 1964-67
Foam peach with green leaf holds pomade lipstick. **CMV $18. MB.**

PRETTY PEACH CREAM LOTION & BUBBLE BATH 1964-67
4 oz. pink plastic bottle with peach on cap, painted label, pink box. **CMV $6. - $8. MB each.**

PRETTY PEACH SOAP 1964-66
Pink box holds 2 peach halves & brown seed center soap. **CMV $25. MB.**

PRETTY PEACH COLOGNE 1964-67
2 oz. bottle with peach cap with green leaf & painted label. Pink box. **CMV $8. MB..**

PRETTY PEACH NECKLACE 1965
Small peach on gold chain. Came in Peach Delight Set only. **CMV $20. - $25. on card.**
SACHET SAMPLES 1964-67
Box holds 10 peach shaped samples of cream sachet packets. **CMV $5. box of 10.**

PRETTY PEACH TALC PUFF 1965-66
Pink box holds pink & white puff filled with powder. **CMV $6. MB, puff only $2. mint.**

PRETTY PEACH SOAP ON A ROPE 1964-67
(Left) 5 oz. peach shaped soap on white rope. **CMV $20. MB**
PERFUMED TALC 1964-67
(Center) 2 1/2 oz. pink & white paper container. **CMV $8. MB.**
BEAUTY DUST 1964-67
(Right) Pink & white cardboard box. **CMV $10., MB $14.**

QUAINTANCE

JUST PEACHY SET 1964-65
Pink & white box holds Peach soap on a rope
& Peach pomade. **CMV $45. MB.**

PEACH SURPRISE SET 1964
Pink & white box holds Pretty Peach 2 oz.
cologne with choice of 4 oz. bubble bath or
cream lotion. **CMV $22. MB.**

BUTTONS 'N BOWS SONG SHEET 1949
Green song sheet with words to help sell
Quaintance products. 4 1/4" wide x 6 1/2"
high. **CMV $5.**

PEACH DELIGHT SET 1965
Box holds Pretty Peach necklace, beauty dust
& cologne. **CMV $55. MB set.**

PRETTY PEACH PRINCESS 1965-66
Box holds Pretty Peach talc & cream sachet.
CMV $20. MB.

QUAINTANCE PERFUME 1950
White box with white lace trim holds 3 dram
perfume with plain red cap & green leaf. **CMV
$125. MB.**

PEACH SMOOTH SET 1965
Peach box holds 2 tubes of Pretty Peach hand
cream. **CMV $15. MB, $5. tube only mint.**

MISS AVON SET 1964-65
Blue & black plastic case holds Pretty Peach
cologne, bubble bath, perfumed talc & 10 Lip
Dew samples in a bag. Also talc samples.
CMV $50. set in blue case, $60. set MB.

QUAINTANCE DIARY PERFUME 1949-56
3 dram glass bottle, painted label, rose
flowered cap & green leaf. Box green felt.
Diary has white cover with red rose &
turquoise design. **CMV $100. MB.**

PEACHY KLEEN SET 1966-67
Pink box holds pink & white sponge & soap.
CMV $15. Set MB. soap & sponge only $9.

QUAINTANCE POWDER SACHET 1948-56
.9 oz. clear glass, white cap & painted label.
Cap same as Bright Night without stars, but
came this way. Very rare. **CMV $15. BO, $20.
MB.**

QUAINTANCE DIARY PERFUME AWARD 1949

Given to Representatives in 63rd anniversary campaign for selling 63 pieces of Avon. Green felt cover trimmed in gold, holds 3 dram bottle with rose flowered cap & painted label, green leaf around neck. Not shown in picture. Must have leaf to be mint. 63rd anniversary inscribed inside cover. **CMV $100. MB.**

62nd ANNIVERSARY QUAINTANCE COLOGNE 1948 ONLY

1st issued in white lace design box. 4 oz. size. Given to Reps for selling 62 Avon items on 62nd anniversary celebration. **CMV $65.MB.**

QUAINTANCE BEAUTY DUST 1948-57

Red rose on tin lid, white paper sides & tin bottom, white box. CMV $20. MB, $12. **beauty dust only mint.**

QUAINTANCE BODY POWDER 1948-56

(Left) 5 oz. red & white paper box, shaker top. **CMV $16. MB, $12. CO.**

QUAINTANCE PERFUME 1948-50

(Right) 1 dram size with red rose cap, painted label in large or small lettering. Blue & white box. **CMV $50. MB.**

QUAINTANCE COLOGNE 1948-56

4 oz. clear glass, green painted label, ribbed corners, rose cap with green leaf. **CMV $15. MB, $10. BO.**

QUAINTANCE 2 OZ. COLOGNE 1948-50

2 oz. bottle with rose cap, painted label & ribbed corners. Came in Quaintance Set & Quaintance Bow Knot Set only. **CMV $20. MB.**

QUAINTANCE TOILET WATER 1953-56

2 oz. clear glass, green painted label, ribbed corners, rose cap with green leaf. **CMV $20. MB, $15. BO.**

DAINTINESS SET 1956

White box with pink & blue ribbon holds 2 oz. bottles of Quaintance cream lotion & cologne with blue caps & blue bar of Quaintance soap. **CMV $60. MB.**

QUAINTANCE POWDER SACHET 1948-56

(Left) 9/10 oz. or 1 1/4 oz. clear glass with red cap, painted label. **CMV $12. MB.**

QUAINTANCE POWDER SACHET 1948 ONLY

(Right) 9/10 oz. clear glass with red cap & larger painted label. CMV $20. MB. Also came in 1 1/4 oz. size with large size label. **CMV $20. MB.**

QUAINTANCE BATH OIL 1949-56

(Left) 4 oz. clear glass, white painted label. Rose on cap. **CMV $20. MB.**

QUAINTANCE CREAM LOTION 1949-56

(Right) 4 oz. clear glass, white painted label. Rose cap. **CMV $15. MB.**

QUAINTANCE COLOGNE 1955-56

2 oz. bottle with blue cap, came in Daintiness Set and Bath Bouquet Set. CMV $15. Quaintance cream lotion in same sets. **CMV $12.**

QUAINTANCE CREAM SACHET 1953-56

White square glass jar with red rose on white cap. **CMV $12. MB.**

QUAINTANCE SACHET 63RD BIRTHDAY BOX 1949

Regular issue powder sachet came in special issue Avon's 63rd Birthday box. **CMV $15. MB as shown.**

QUAINTANCE SACHET VALENTINE BOX 1952
Short issue box at Valentine time. Holds regular issue powder sachet. **CMV in this box $22. mint.**

QUAINTANCE BATH OIL 1955-56
2 oz. pink cap, pink & white label. Came in That's For Me set only. **CMV $15. mint.**

DAINTINESS SET 1955
White box with pink & blue ribbons, holds 2 oz. bottles of perfumed deodorant & Quaintance cologne with blue caps & blue bar of Quaintance soap. **CMV $55. MB.**

QUAINTANCE SOAP 1955-56
3 blue bars with embossed bows. **CMV $40. MB.**

BATH BOUQUET SET 1955
White & blue box with red rose on lid holds 2 oz. bottles of Quaintance cream lotion & cologne with blue caps. Blue bar of Quaintance soap. **CMV $52. MB.**

ROSE GAY SET 1954-56
Blue & white box holds Quaintance 4 oz. cream lotion & body powder. **CMV $55. MB.**

GAY BONNET SET 1948
White hat shaped box with black ribbon & red rose around hat lid contains gold lipstick & 1 dram bottle of Quaintance perfume with rose cap. **CMV $125. MB.**

QUAINTANCE ROSE GAY SET 1950-51
Blue & white box with red rose holds Quaintance body powder & 4 oz. cream lotion. **CMV $55. MB.**

LEISURE HOURS SET 1954-55
Blue & yellow fold up box holds 4 oz. Quaintance bath oil & cream lotion. **CMV $55.**

MISS QUAINTANCE SET 1952-53
Blue & white octagonal box holds Quaintance body powder & 4 oz. cream lotion. **CMV $50. MB.**

QUAINTANCE HARMONY SET 1952-53
Box with blue ribbon on clear plastic lid holds 4 oz. Quaintance cream lotion & cologne. **CMV $50. set MB, 4 oz. cologne with rose cap $20.**

QUAINTANCE HARMONY SET 1950-51
White box with blue ribbon over clear plastic lid holds Quaintance 4 oz. cologne & body powder. **CMV $50. MB.**

BEAUTY MUFF SET 1949
(Left) Red, white & blue box with blue ribbon on lid contains white lambswool muff with 1 dram Quaintance perfume with rose cap & gold lipstick. **CMV $135. MB.**

BEAUTY MUFF SET 1950
(Right) Same set & box only came with 1 dram gold scroll top perfume. **CMV $65. MB.**

QUAINTANCE SET 1948
Blue & white box contains 2 oz. Quaintance cologne & powder sachet. Both have red caps. **CMV $55. MB.**

QUAINTANCE BOW KNOT SET 1950
Box holds Quaintance 2 oz. cologne & powder sachet. **CMV $55. MB.**

QUAINTANCE HARMONY 1954-55
Blue & white flip open box holds Quaintance cologne & cream lotion. **CMV $50. MB.**

RAPTURE

RAPTURE FOAMING BATH OIL 1966-72
6 oz. blue plastic bottle & cap. **CMV $1.**
PERFUMED BATH OIL 1965-66
6 oz. blue plastic bottle & cap. **CMV $1. MB.**
CREAM LOTION 1965-68
4 oz. blue plastic bottle & cap. **CMV $1. MB.**

RAPTURE COLOGNE MIST 1966 ONLY
2 oz. medium blue glass, gold trim.
COLOGNE MIST 1966 ONLY
2 oz. dark blue glass, no gold trim.
COLOGNE MIST 1965-66
2 oz. very light, appears almost frosted glass.
CMV each $2. MB.

RAPTURE PERFUME OIL 1964-69
(Top Left) 1/2 oz. green glass & cap. **CMV $6. MB.**
RAPTURE COLOGNE 1964-71
(Top Center) 2 oz. blue glass & cap. **CMV $2. MB.**
RAPTURE COLOGNE MIST 1964-74
(Top Right & Bottom Two) 3 oz. turquoise plastic coated cap, all have gold letters. **CMV $1.50 MB.** Pictured above with regular issue box on right & special issue 1970 box on left. **Add $2. for 1970 box.**

RAPTURE SCENTED HAIR SPRAY 1966-70
(Left) 7 oz. blue can. **CMV $3. MB.**
RAPTURE PERFUMED TALC 1965-72
(Left Center) 2.75 oz. blue can. **CMV $1. MB.**
(Right Center) Foreign Rapture perfume talc is 2.75 oz. blue can, but shorter than U.S. can. **CMV $2. MB.**
RAPTURE BEAUTY DUST 1971-74
(Right) 6 oz. blue & gold cardboard. **CMV $4. MB.**

RAPTURE DELUXE SET 1965
Turquoise box contains beauty dust, perfumed skin softener & cologne mist in Rapture. **CMV $32.50.**

RAPTURE RHAPSODY SET 1964-65
Rapture powder sachet, 1 dram perfume & 2 oz. cologne sit on blue velvet, trimmed in gold. Rapture mirror in center with 2 doves on mirror. **CMV $30. tray, set mint, $40. set MB.**

RAPTURE POWDER SACHET 1964-66
(Left) 9/10 oz. blue frosted glass with blue lid with 2 white doves. **CMV $6. MB.**
CREAM SACHET 1964-75
.66 oz. dark purple glass jar with 2 white doves on purple plastic lid. **CMV 50c.**
RAPTURE PERFUMED SOAP 1966-67
3 oz. soap in turquoise wrapper. **CMV $4.**

RAPTURE / REGENCE

RAPTURE PERFUMED SKIN SOFTENER 1964-73
5 oz. with blue & gold lid. Came blue painted over clear glass. **CMV $1.** ALso came blue painted over white milk glass. **CMV $2.**

RAPTURE BEAUTY DUST 1964-70
Light blue plastic, white doves on lid. **CMV $3. CO. $5. MB.**

RAPTURE SOAP 1965-68
Blue box holds 3 blue bars with 2 doves embossed. **CMV $20. MB.**

RAPTURE 1/2 OZ. COLOGNE 1969-72
1/2 oz. green cap. **CMV $2. MB.**

RAPTURE PERFUMED CREAM ROLLETTE 1964-65
Gold cap, embossed 4A design on 1/3 oz. bottle. **CMV $2. MB.**

RAPTURE PERFUMED ROLLETTE 1965-69
1/3 oz. blue ribbed glass, goldcap. **CMV $4. MB.**

REGENCE

REGENCE PERFUME 1966-69
1 oz. frosted glass bottle & stopper, trimmed in gold, green & white box. Gold neck tag. **CMV $20. BO, $30. MB.**

REGENCE PERFUME 1966-69
1/2 oz. frosted glass with gold plastic cap. Bottle trimmed in gold, green & white box. Gold neck tag. **CMV $15. BO, $25. MB.**

REGENCE CREAM SACHET 1968
.66 oz. clear glass painted gree. Green & gold tone cap & base. Sides are smooth, no design. **CMV $4. MB.**

REGENCE HAND MIRROR 1966
(Left) Green & gold metal 4 1/2" long. Came in Regence gift set. **CMV $10. MB, $7. mirror only.**

REGENCE FRAGRANCE SAMPLE 1967-71
Foil packet. **CMV $1. box of 10.**

REGENCE 1/2 OZ. COLOGNE 1970-71
(Left) 1/2 oz. clear glass bottle with gold cap. **CMV $2. MB.**

PERFUME OIL 1968-69
(Inside Left) 1/2 oz. gold cap. Came with either clear bottom label or gold neck tag label. **CMV $6. MB.**

COLOGNE 1967-69
(Center) 2 oz. gold cap. **CMV $2. MB.**

COLOGNE SILK 1968-70
(Inside Right) 3 oz. gold cap, frosted glass bottle. **CMV $2. MB.**

SKIN-SO-SOFT 1968-70
(Right) 6 oz. gold cap. **CMV $2. MB...**

REGENCE 4 OZ. COLOGNE 1969-71
4 oz. gold cap. **CMV $2.**

FOAMING BATH OIL 1969-72
6 oz. light plastic bottle with gold cap. **CMV $1. MB.**

COLOGNE MIST REFILL 1966-71
3 oz. green plastic coated. **CMV $2. MB.**

REGENCE CREAM SACHET 1966-67
(Left) Green painted glass with green paper band. Green & gold cap, gold base. **CMV $2. MB.**

CREAM SACHET 1968-75
(Right) Solid green glass, green plastic cap. **CMV $1.** Both also came green painted over clear or milk glass. **Same CMV.**

REGENCE COLOGNE MIST 1966-71
(Left) 3 oz. green & gold plastic. Base is gold on older ones and green on newer ones. **CMV gold base $3, green base $2. MB..**
HAIR SPRAY 1968-71
(Center) 7 oz. green & gold with green cap. **CMV $3. MB.**
REGENCE BEAUTY DUST 1966-73
(Right) Green & gold plastic bottom, clear plastic lid with gold crown. Paper side older, **CMV $8. MB.** Plastic side newer, **CMV $5. MB, $2. less each for no box.**

REGENCE GIFT SET 1966
Green box holds cream sachet, cologne mist, green & gold hand mirror. **CMV $37.50. MB.**

ROSE GERANIUM BATH OIL 1943-50
6 oz. flat sided bottle has Tulip A label, pink cap. **CMV $20. BO, $25. MB.**

ROSE GERANIUM SOAP 1966-67
Flowered box holds 4 flower shaped soaps. **CMV $20. MB.**

REGENCE PERFUME ROLLETTE 1967-68
.33 oz. ribbed glass, smooth gold cap. **CMV $2. MB.**
PERFUME ROLLETTE 1969-73
.33 oz. ribbed glass & green cap. **CMV $1. BO.**
PERFUMED GLACE 1967-70
(Right) Green & gold box holds green & gold glace compact. **CMV $8. MB, $5. compact only.**

REGENCE PERFUME SKIN SOFTENER 1968-71
(Left) 5 oz. ribbed glass, small silver edged cap. Gold center & multi color cap. **CMV $2.**
REGENCE PERFUMED SKIN SOFTENER 1971-74
(Center) 5 oz. ribbed glass, large silver edged, gold center & multi-color green cap. **CMV $3.**
REGENCE PERFUMED SKIN SOFTENER 1967-68
(Right) 5 oz. green ribbed glass, small silver edge cap with gold center & plain green cap. **CMV $3. MB.**

ROSE GERANIUM LIQUID SOAP FRA-GRANCE 1942 ONLY
(Left) 6 oz. flat sided bottle came in Rainbow Wings and Bath Bouquet Set only. **CMV $45. MB.**
ROSE GERANIUM BATH OIL 1943-48
(Right) 6 oz. flat sided bottle, pink cap. **CMV $20. BO, $25. MB.**

ROSE GERANIUM

REGENCE TALC 1968-72
(Left) 3 1/2 oz. green paper box. **CMV $1.**
REGENCE PERFUMED POWDER MIST 1967-72
(Right) 7 oz. greencan with gold cap, painted label. **CMV $1, with paper label $3.**

ROSE GERANIUM BATH OIL 1957-58
8 oz. bottle with red cap. **CMV $15. MB, $10. BO.**

ROSE GERANIUM AFTER BATH FRESH-ENER 1964-68
8 oz. glass bottle with rose colored cap, red flowered box. **CMV $2. MB.**
PERFUMED TALC 1964-66
3 1/2 oz. rose covered paper container with plastic shaker top. **CMV $3. MB.** ALso came with upside down label. **CMV $8.**
PERFUMED SOAP 1964-66
3 oz. bar with rose design wrapping. **CMV $3.**

ROSES ROSES

ROSES PERFUME TALC 1974-77
3.5 oz. pink and gray cardboard. **CMV 25c.**
TOUCH OF ROSES SOAP 1976-78
3 oz. pink soap, pink and gray wrapper. **CMV $2.**
ROSES ROSES SOAP 1974-75
3 oz. pink soap, pink wrapper with floral band. **CMV $2.**
PERFUMED SKIN SOFTENER 1973-76
5 oz. pink plastic with pink and gold metal lid. **CMV 25c.**
SACHET OF ROSES CREAM SACHET 1975-78
.33 oz. clear glass with pink metal lid. **CMV .50c.**

PERFUMED SOAP 1982
(Left) 3 oz. bar. **CMV $2**
ROSES ROSES PERFUMED SOAP BAR 1976
(Right) 3 oz. bar wrapped in red paper. Short issue. **CMV $2.**

GLOW OF ROSES PERFUMED CANDLE 1972-73
4 1/2" high, pink frosted glass. **CMV $8. MB.**
SCENT OF ROSES DECANTER 1972-73
6 oz. red glass jar with gold lid, filled with Cologne Gelee. **CMV $5. MB.**
DEW OF ROSES PERFUMED SKIN SOFTENER 1972-73
5 oz. frosted pink glass jar with gold lid. **CMV $2.MB.**
SCENT OF ROSES COLOGNE GELEE 1972-76
3 oz. clear or tinted glass jar, gold lid. **CMV $2. MB.**

MIST OF ROSES COLOGNE MIST 1972-77
3 oz. pink plastic coated bottle, gold cap.**CMV $1. MB.**
TOUCH OF ROSES PERFUMED SOAP 1972-77
Pink box holds 3 pink flowered soaps. **CMV $9. MB.**
ROSES CREAM SACHET 1972-75
.66 oz. pink glass jar with pink rose on gold lid. Also came in clear glass. **CMV $1.**
All other Roses products CMV 25c.

SILK & HONEY

SILK & HONEY MILK BATH 1970-71
6 oz. gold plastic milk can bottle with flowers around neck. **CMV $4.**

SILK & HONEY PERFUME SOAP 1970-76
3 oz. gold and yellow wrapper. **CMV $3.**
SILK & HONEY BANK 1969
Yellow plastic Beehive Bank. **CMV $15.MB.**

BATH GELEE 1969-70
4 oz. gold frosted glass jar with gold beehive lid and gold spoon. **CMV $7. MB. with spoon.**

SMALL WORLD

SMALL WORLD PRODUCTS 1970-73
(Back row left to right)
COLOGNE (SPLASHU) 1970-72
2 oz., 4 1/2" high. **CMV $7. MB.**
BUBBLE BATH (BUBBLY-O-BATH) 1970-71
5" high, 5 oz. green plastic bottle. **CMV $10. MB.**
PERFUMED TALC 1971-73
3 1/2 oz. blue paper container. **CMV $4.**
(Front row left to right)
LOVE CAKES SOAP 1970-73
3 pink heart shaped bars in blue box. **CMV $9. MB.**
ROLLETTE 1971-72
3" high, .33 oz. Indian design. **CMV $3.**
DEMI STICK 1970-73
3" high with pink cap. **CMV $2. MB.**
PIN PAL PERFUME GLACE 1970-71
Black hair, white and red body. **CMV $5., $7. MB.**
NON-TEAR SHAMPOO (POOLU) 1970-71
5 1/2" high, red bottle, black hair. **CMV $7. MB**
COLOGNE MIST (HEIDI) 1970-71
3 oz. 5" high, purple bottle, yellow hair. **CMV $6. MB.**

SMALL WORLD PRODUCTS 1970-73
(Back row left to right)
CREAM LOTION (WENDY) 1971-72
5 oz, 5" high cowgirl plastic bottle. **CMV $8. MB.**
BUBBLE BATH (BRITISH MISS) 1971-72
4 1/2" high, 3 oz. pink plastic bottle. **CMV $8. MB.**
COLOGNE MIST (GIGI) 1971-72
5" high, 5 oz. blue plastic coated bottle with white collar and blue & red hat. **CMV $8. MB.**
NON-TEAR SHAMPOO (SENORITA) 1971-72
5" high, 5 oz. orange plastic bottle with pink flower in hair on cap. **CMV $12. MB.**
(Front row left to right)
CREAM SACHET 1971-72
.66 oz. white jar with pink and white lid. **CMV $3. MB.**
LIPKINS 1970-73
3" high with pink, yellow and orange caps in Dutch Chocolate, Tropical Fruit or French Mint. **CMV $3. each MB.**
LOVE DOVE CREAM SACHET 1970-73
White jar and dove lid. **CMV $4., $5. MB.**

SMALL WORLD SUCKER 1970
Sent to representatives at introduction of Small World. Red and yellow wrapper says "Avon Watch for the Small World". **CMV $25. mint.**
SMALL WORLD PERFUME GLACE 1971-72
Blue and white polka-dots. **CMV $6. MB.**
SMALL WORLD GLACE WATCH 1971
Orange with striped band. **CMV $15. MB.**

SOMEWHERE

ALL CONTAINERS PRICED EMPTY
See front of book for Grading Examples on Mint Condition

SOMEWHERE PERFUME 1961-63
1 oz. pink jewel cap, jewels in glass around bottom of bottle. Has 4 butterflies on lid. **CMV $80. MB, $50. BO.**

SOMEWHERE PERFUMED SKIN SOF-TENER 1964-66
5 oz. pink glass jar with pink and gold lid. **CMV $2. MB.**
SOMEWHERE PERFUMED SOAP 1965
3 oz. pink soap with pink & white wrapper. **CMV $4. mint.**

SOMEWHERE PERFUMED OIL FOR THE BATH 1963
1/2 oz. clear glass, white lettering, pink cap. **CMV $7. BO, $10. MB.**
SOMEWHERE PERFUMED OIL 1964-66
1/2 oz. clear glass, white lettering, pink cap. **CMV $5. BO, $7. MB.**

SOMEWHERE BATH OIL 1962-66
6 oz. pink plastic bottle and cap. **CMV $2.MB.**
SOMEWHERE COLOGNE MIST 1961-66
3 oz. pink plastic coated glass, pink jeweled
lid. **CMV $3. BO, $5. MB.**

SOMEWHERE CREAM LOTION 1963-66
4 oz. pink lid without jewels. **CMV $3., $5.
MB.**
SOMEWHERE COLOGNE 1961-66
2 oz. pink jeweled lid. **CMV $3, $5. MB.**

SOMEWHERE TALC 1962-66
2 3/4 oz. pink can and lid. **CMV $3., $5. MB.**
**SOMEWHERE 2 DRAM PERFUME MIST
1964-66**
White lid, pink bottom, gold band. **CMV $4.
MB.**

SOMEWHERE BEAUTY DUST 1967-70
White plastic with green around bottom. Gold
handle. **CMV $10. MB, $6. CO.**
PERFUME TALC 1968
3 1/2 oz. green cardboard with gold trim.
Came with Fluff Puff set. **CMV $2.**

SOMEWHERE DUSTING POWDER 1961-66
Pink plastic bottom, clear plastic top with pink
jeweledcrown .**CMV $10.MB.**

PERFUME MIST AWARD 1961
Given to each representative sending in an
order during the 75th Anniversary Campaign.
This was also the introduction to a new
fragrance - Somewhere. **CMV $15. MB.**

UNFORGETTABLE SET 1962-63
Pink, yellow and blue box holds Somewhere
Cologne Mist, Cream Sachet and Beauty Dust.
CMV $45. MB.

SOMEWHERE POWDER SACHET 1962-66
1 1/4 oz. pink glass bottom, pink jeweled lid.
Also came in .9 oz. **CMV $6. MB, $4. BO.**
SOMEWHERE CREAM SACHET 1962-66
Pink glass and pink jeweled lid. **CMV $1. $3.
MB.** Some came pink paint on milk glass.
Same CMV.

**SOMEWHERE POWDER SACHET 1967
ONLY**
(Left) 9/10 oz. white glass bottom, white and
gold cap with green ribbon. Issued during
bottle strike in 1967. Bottom is same as
Wishing Powder Sachet. **CMV $15. - $20.
MB.**
SOMEWHERE POWDER SACHET 1966-68
9/10 oz. white glass, green label, white lid with
gold band. Hard to find. **CMV $12. MB, $10.
BO.**

SOMEWHERE PRODUCTS 1966-67
(Left to Right)
CREAM SACHET 1966-75
White glass trimmed in green and gold. .66 oz.
CMV 50c.
SKIN SOFTENER 1966-72
Green and gold lid, 5 oz. glass jar. Came in
green paint over clear glass. **CMV $1,** or
green paint over white milk glass. **CMV $1.**
PERFUME OIL 1966-69
1/2 oz. green label, gold cap. **CMV $4., $6.
MB.**
COLOGNE 1966-71
2 oz. gold cap. **CMV $1.**
COLOGNE MIST 1966-76
3 oz. green plastic coated, gold cap, green
label. **CMV $1.**

SOMEWHERE
(Green and White design)
CREAM SACHET 1976
Gold and green lid. **CMV 50c.**
DEMI STICK 1975-76
CMV 50C.
COLOGNE 1970-71
1/2 oz. gold cap. **CMV $2. MB, $1. BO.**
CREAM LOTION 1967-68
4 oz. gold cap. **CMV $2. MB.**
SOMEWHERE TALC 1973-76
3.5 oz. green cardboard, round container.
CMV $1.

SOMEWHERE SOAP 1966-68
Green and white box holds 3 bars. **CMV $18. MB.**

SOMEWHERE SOAP 1962-66
Pink box holds 3 bars with embossed name.
CMV $24. MB.

SOMEWHERE SOAP 1968-69
3 white bars in green box. **CMV $15. MB.**

SOMEWHERE PERFUME MIST 1966-68
2 dram, white cap, green bottom. **CMV $2. MB.**

DREAMS OF SOMEWHERE SET 1964
Box holds 2 dram bottle of Somewhere Perfume Mist, 6 oz. Beauty Dust and 4 oz. bottle of Cream Lotion. **CMV $40. MB.**

SOMEWHERE SCENTED HAIR SPRAY 1966-71
7 oz. green can. **CMV $3.**
SOMEWHERE SOAP 1966-67
Single bar in green wrapper. **CMV $4.**
SOMEWHERE TALC 1966-72
2 3/4 oz. green and white can, green cap.
CMV $1.

DREAM CASTLE SET 1964
Pink and white box holds 2 oz. bottle of Somewhere Cologne and Cream Sachet.
CMV $30. MB.

SONNET

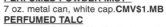

SONNET PRODUCTS 1973-78
(White and gold design)
PERFUMED POWDER MIST
7 oz. metal can, white cap.**CMV$1.MB**
PERFUMED TALC
3.5 oz. cardboard with plastic top and bottom. Rare upside down label. **CMV $5.**
CREAM SACHET
.66 oz. jar.**CMV .50c**
BEAUTY DUST
6 oz. plastic puff. **CMV $2., $5. MB.**
PERFUMED SKIN SOFTENER
5 oz. plastic jar.**CMV.50c**
PERFUMED ROLLETTE
.33 oz. bottle.**CMV .$1.MB.**
COLOGNE MIST
3 oz. spray bottle. 1st issue 1973. Issued with no gold ring around neck. **CMV $2.**
1973-78 issued with gold ring around neck.
CMV 50c.

SONNET POWDER SACHET 1975-78
1.25 oz. white and gold cardboard. **CMV $1.**
SONNET PERFUMED SOAP 1976-78
3 oz. white bar with gold and white wrapper.
CMV $2.
SONNET PERFUMED SOAP 1974-75
3 oz. white with multi-colored center. **CMV $3.**
SONNET PERFUMED DEMI STICK 1974-78
White and gold. **CMV $1..**

SONNET BODY POWDER 1941-43
Flat sifter top, scroll box. **CMV $22. MB, CO $18. mint.**
SONNET PERFUME POWDER MIST (double stamped label) 1973-77
Regular issue can came out with double stamp label on entire can. Rare. **CMV $5.**

FRAGRANCE MIST SONNET 1940-42
Blue and gold box holds 2 oz. Sonnet Toilet Water, gold cap and label and Spray atomizer. Also came in other fragrances. See Fragrance Mist Sets of 1940s. **CMV $50. MB, $35. BO mint.**

SONNET COLOGNE & SONNET SKIN SO SOFT BATH OIL 1973
4 oz. clear glass bottles, cap is gold. Came in Treasure Chest set only. **CMV $4. each.**

BLUE BIRD SET 1943-44
Blue and white box, blue satin lining holds feather design face powder, cardboard or plastic lipstick and Sonnet or Apple Blossom Body Powder. **CMV $75 00 MB..**

SONNET SET 1941-42
Satin lined lavender box holds 2 oz. Sonnet Toilet Water with gold top atomizer & Sonnet Body Powder. **CMV $75. MB.**

SONNET TOILET WATER 1941 ONLY
2 oz. purple cap and label. 2 different labels. One has yellow dress on box and label and the other has green dress on box and label. **CMV $30. BO, $40. MB each.**

STRAWBERRY

SONNET PERFUMED SOAP 1974-77
3 oz., three pink oblong shaped bar soap, in gold and white box. **CMV $5. MB.**
SONNET PERFUMED SOAP 1972-74
3 oz. three pink round shaped bars of soap, in gold and white box. **CMV $6. MB.**

SONNET TOILET WATER 1941-46
2 oz. gold ribbed cap and gold front label. **CMV $30. BO mint, $35. MB.**
SONNET BODY POWDER 1941-43
Special issue box, angel on box, blue and white paper container with plastic shaker top. **CMV $25. MB as shown, $18. CO.**

STRAWBERRY PORCELAIN NAPKIN RINGS & SOAP SET 1978-79
Box holds 2 porcelain napkin rings and 1 red strawberry shaped soap. Porcelain made in Brazil. **CMV $10. MB set.**

SWAN LAKE

STRAWBERRY BATH GELEE 1971-72
4 oz. red strawberry base and gold cap and spoon. **CMV $4., $6. MB.**
STRAWBERRY GUEST SOAP 1971-72
Red box holds 3 strawberry soaps. **CMV $7. MB.**
STRAWBERRY BATH FOAM 1971-72
4 oz. red glass and top, 6" high. **CMV $5. MB.**

BIG BERRY STRAWBERRY 1973-74
10 oz. red plastic with green cap top. Holds Bath Foam. **CMV $2., $3. MB.**
BERRY NICE STRAWBERRY COMPACT 1979-80
Small red and green plastic holds lip gloss. **CMV $3. MB.**
STRAWBERRY FAIR SHOWER SOAP 1979-80
Red strawberry soap on a green rope. **CMV $8. MB.**

STRAWBERRY PORCELAIN DEMI CUP CANDLETTE 1979-80
Box holds 4" saucer and 2 1/4" high cup. Strawberry design. Made in Brazil for Avon 1978 on bottom of each. **CMV $7. MB.**

STRAWBERRY PORCELAIN SUGAR SHAKER & TALC 1979
Box holds white porcelain shaker and 3.5 oz. box of strawberry perfumed talc. Made in Brazil. Avon 1978 on bottom of shaker. **CMV $12. MB set.** Early orders and demos had 1978 on bottom of sugar shaker and regular issue had only "Avon" and no date on bottom. Talc only **CMV $2., shaker only CMV $8. no date, CMV $10. 1978 date.** Talc also came with upside down label from factory by mistake. **CMV $5. upside down label on talc.**

STAWBERRIES & CREAM BATH FOAM 1970
4 oz. white milk, red cap and design, or orange cap and design. **CMV for red cap $7, orange cap $5.**
STRAWBERRY FAIR SOAP 1969-70
Red soap in yellow plastic basket with green grass, wrapped in cellophane and bow. **CMV $10. MB.**

SWAN LAKE BATH OIL 1947-49
6 oz. flat sided bottle, pink cap, painted label. **CMV $55., $65. MB.**
SWAN LAKE COLOGNE 1947-50
4 oz. pink cap, painted label. **CMV $45. BO, $55. MB.**

SWAN LAKE 3 PIECE SET 1947-50
Blue and white box holds 9 oz. blue boxes of Swan Lake Bath Salts, Body Powder and 4 oz. cologne with white cap. **CMV $125. MB.**

SWAN LAKE 2 PIECE SET 1947-49
Blue and white box holds 6 oz. Swan Lake Bath Oil and 9 oz. blue box of Swan Lake Body Powder. **CMV $100. MB.**

SWAN LAKE BODY POWDER 1947-49

9 oz. blue, pink and white paper box. Came with swan or ballerina on side. **CMV $30.,** **$35. MB.** Also came 4 1/2 oz. size in sets. **CMV $30. mint.**

SWAN LAKE BATH SALTS 1947-49

9 oz. blue, pink and white paper box. **CMV $30., $35. MB.**

TO A WILD ROSE

TO A WILD ROSE PERFUME 1955-59

Pink & white box holds 1/2 oz. white glass bottle with pink cap & painted label. **CMV $35. BO, $70. MB.**

TO A WILD ROSE TOILET WATER 1956-62

(Left) 2 oz. white glass, pink cap, has paper flower band around base. **CMV $10. BO, $12. MB.**

PERFUME OIL FOR THE BATH 1963

(Right) 1/2 oz. white glass, pink cap, pink & white box. **CMV $10. MB, $8. BO.**

TOILET WATER 1956

(Not Shown) 1/2 oz. size. Same size & design as perfumed oil shown above. White glass with pink cap & lettering. Came in Special Date Set, rare. **CMV $27. mint.**

TO A WILD ROSE PERFUME 1950-56

(Left) Pink flowers on pink & blue box. 3 dram bottle with blue cap & flower around neck. **CMV $110. MB, BO with tag $75.**

SPRAY PERFUME 1960-63

(Right) Red, white & gold box holds pink & white metal spray perfume with pink flowers. **CMV $11. MB, spray only $7.**

TO A WILD ROSE COLOGNE 1957

(Left) 2 oz. white glass with paper label, pink cap. Came in Trilogy Set only. **CMV $16. mint.**

LOTION 1957

(Right) 2 oz. white glass with paper label & pink cap. Came in Trilogy Set only. **CMV $16. mint.**

TO A WILD ROSE 2 OZ. COLOGNE 1961-68

(Left & Center) 2 oz. white glass, pink letters & cap. Came with & without painted flowers around base. **CMV $3.MB.**

SPRAY PERFUME REFILL 1960-63

(Right) Box holds small metal refill. **CMV $4. MB, $2. refill only.**

TO A WILD ROSE CREAM LOTION 1965-68

(Left) 4 oz. painted label, white glass, pink cap. **CMV $5. MB.**

CREAM LOTION 1956-65

(Right) 4 oz. white glass, pink cap, paper label. **CMV $5. BO, $7. MB.**

TO A WILD ROSE COLOGNE 1970-71

(Left) 1/2 oz. white glass with pink cap & letters. **CMV $3. MB, $1. BO.**

PERFUMED TALC 1962-72

(Center) 2 3/4 oz. white & pink can with pink cap. **CMV $1.**

TALC 1954-55

(Right) Blue can & cap with pink flowers. **CMV $8. MB.**

TO A WILD ROSE COLOGNE 1955-63

4 oz. white glass bottle, pink cap, has flowered paper border around base. **CMV $10. BO, $12. MB.**

BODY POWDER 1950-55

5 oz. blue paper container, 2 different bottoms. One is refillable from the bottom. **CMV $15. - $20. MB.** Some issued as shown with To A Wild Rose Body Powder on side & some only say Avon Body Powder.

TO A WILD ROSE BODY POWDER 1955-59
(Left) 4 oz. white glass & cap with rose on lid, paper label around bottom, pink letters. **CMV $10. BO, $13. MB.**

BODY POWDER 1961-63
(Center) 4 oz. white hard plastic bottle, white lid with roses. Also came 3 oz. size & with short issue pink cap. **CMV $12. pink cap. CMV $8. BO, $10. MB.**

BODY POWDER 1955-59
(Right) 4 oz. white glass & cap with rose on lid, paper label. **CMV $10. BO, $13. MB.**

TO A WILD ROSE 4 OZ. COLOGNE 1960-61
Pink, green & white Christmas box holds 4 oz. white glass bottle with pink cap & neck ribbon. No flower band around base, but also came with a paper flower band around base as shown. **CMV $25. in box pictured.**

TO A WILD ROSE 4 OZ. COLOGNE 1960-61
Pink & white box holds 4 oz. white glass bottle, pink cap, painted label, pink silk ribbon on neck. **CMV $15. BO with ribbon mint, $17. MB.** Came with and without painted flowers around base.

TO A WILD ROSE CREAM SACHET 1950-55
(Left) Blue cap with pink flowers, white glass, 3 cornered shape. **CMV $10. MB, $8. BO.**
(Center) Same shaped jar as one on right only has blue lid as on the left jar. Lid will not interchange with jar on right. Also came with white lid, label on bottom with no zip code, is older. Rare. **CMV $9. BO, $11. MB.**

CREAM SACHET 1955-72
(Right) White glass, white lid with painted rose. **CMV $1. MB.**

TO A WILD ROSE COLOGNE MIST 1958-59
3 oz. white plastic coated over clear glass, pink cap. Came with or without embossed rose on lid. **CMV $15 MB.**

TO A WILD ROSE SOAP 1966-67
3 oz. white embossed soap in pink & green wrapper. **CMV $4.**

TO A WILD ROSE BATH OIL 1956-59
4 oz. white glass bottle with pink cap. **CMV $12. MB, $10. BO.** 2 oz. white glass bottle with pink cap, same label came in Trilogy set only. **CMV $15.**

TO A WILD ROSE TALC 1956-62
(Left) White can with pink flowers & cap. **CMV $5. - $7. MB.** Add $4. for 1959 Christmas box shown.

FOAMING BATH OIL 1966-68
(Right) 6 oz. white plastic bottle with pink cap. **CMV $1. BO, $2. MB.**

TO A WILD ROSE BEAUTY DUST 1964-70
White plastic trimmed in pink. **CMV $4. $6.MB.**

PERFUMED SKIN SOFTENER 1959-70
5 oz. white glass, pink & white lid. **CMV $2.**

TO A WILD ROSE BEAUTY DUST 1950--55
Blue can with flowers on lid. **CMV $15. CO, $20. MB.**

TO A WILD ROSE PERFUMED BATH OIL 1959-61
8 oz. white plastic bottle with pink cap. **CMV $3. MB.**

PERFUMED BATH OIL 1961-66
(Not Shown) Same only 6 oz. size. **CMV $3. MB.**

TO A WILD ROSE COLOGNE MIST 1959-75
(Left) 3 oz. white plastic coated with pink flower on cap. **CMV $2. MB.**
COLOGNE MIST 1976
(Not Shown) 3 oz. white bottle, pink letters, pink cap, no flower. **CMV 50c.**
PERFUMED MIST 1964-68
(Right) 2 dram, pink & white, gold band. **CMV $4. MB, $2. mist only.**

TO A WILD ROSE TALC 1969
2.75 oz. pink & white can, pink cap. Came in 1969 Perfumed Pair set only. **CMV $2.**
BATH OIL 1955-56
2 oz. pink cap & label. Came in "That's Me Set" only. **CMV $15. mint.**

TO A WILD ROSE SCENTED HAIR SPRAY 1966-69
7 oz. pink & white can, pink cap. **CMV $3.**
PERFUMED POWDER MIST 1968-73
7oz. pink & white can, 2 different labels. **CMV paper label $4, painted label $2.** each.

TO A WILD ROSE POWDER SACHET 1955-67
White glass, white lid with painted rose. Paper band around bottom with roses. Came in 9 oz. & 1.25 oz. **CMV $7. BM, $6. BO.**
PERFUME OIL 1964-68
1/2 oz. white glass, pink letters & cap. **CMV $6. BO, $8. MB.**

TO A WILD ROSE BEAUTY DUST 1962-63
(Left) Pink & green flowers, clear platic top, cardboard. Came in Fragrance Magic Sets only. **CMV $16. mint.**
BEAUTY DUST 1955-59
(Right) Pink ball on top, trimmed in pink, tin lid & bottom. Sides cardboard. **CMV $12. - $16. MB.**

TO A WILD ROSE TOILET WATER 1950-55
(Left) 2 oz. blue cap, with or without embossed roses. Three cornered bottle. **CMV $20. MB, $15. BO.**
CREAM LOTION 1953-55
(Right) 4 oz. blue cap & label, with or without embossed roses. **CMV $15. BO, $17. MB.**

TO A WILD ROSE SACHET 1953-55
1 1/4 oz. blue cap with embossed flower on top. Blue box. **CMV $15. MB, $12. BO mint.**

BATH BOUQUET SET 1955
White & pink box holds To A Wild Rose 2 oz. cologne & cream lotion with white caps & 1 bar of soap. **CMV $55. MB.**

TO A WILD ROSE BATH OIL 1953-55
4 oz. bottle with blue cap, with or without embossed roses. Blue label. **CMV $20. MB, $17. BO.**

TO A WILD ROSE COLOGNE OR CREAM LOTION 1954
2 oz. clear glass with blue caps. Came in Bath Bouquet Set. **CMV $17.50 each mint.**

MISS COED SET 1954
Blue box holds three 2 oz. bottles of To A Wild Rose cologne, cream lotion & bath oil. All have white caps. **CMV $75. set, $17.50 each bottle.**

TO A WILD ROSE COLOGNE 1950-55
4 oz. clear glass, blue cap, blue label. **CMV $20. MB, $16. BO.**
POWDER SACHET 1953-55
1 1/4 oz. blue smooth top cap, blue label, clear glass. **CMV $12. - $15. MB.**
CREAM SACHET 1975-76
.66 oz. clear glass jar, red & gold lid. **CMV 50c.**

TO A WILD ROSE COLOGNE, BATH OIL, CREAM LOTION 1954
2 oz. clear glass with white cap, blue label. Came in Miss Coed Set only. **CMV $17.50 each.**

TO A WILD ROSE COLOGNE OR CREAM LOTION 1955
2 oz. clear glass with white caps. Came in bath bouquet Set. **CMV $15. each mint.**

TO A WILD ROSE BATH OIL & COLOGNE 1956
Both 2 oz. bottles with white caps. Came in 1956 Bath Bouquet Set only. **CMV $15. each mint.**

TO A WILD ROSE SOAP 1969-73
Floral box holds 3 white bars. **CMV $7. MB.**

TO A WILD ROSE SOAP 1952-56
White box holds 3 white bars. **CMV $26.50**
TO A WILD ROSE SOAP 1954
Blue box of 3 bars. **CMV $30. MB.**

TO A WILD ROSE SOAP 1957-68
Pink & white box holds 3 bars in 2 different size boxes. **CMV large box $25. MB, small box $20. MB.**

BATH BOUQUET SET 1956
White & pink box holds To A Wild Rose cologne & bath oil with white caps & 1 bar of soap. **CMV $55. MB.** Also came with 2 bath oils as substitutes.

BATH BOUQUET SET 1954
Pink & blue box. To A Wild Rose 2 oz. cologne & cream lotion with blue caps & white soap. **CMV $55. MB.** One box has sleeve top and one with a lift off lid. Came with and without flowers on bottom of box.

SWEETHEART SET 1956
White & pink box holds To A Wild Rose beauty dust & 4 oz. cologne. **CMV $47.50 MB.**

ROSES ADRIFT SET 1957
Pink & white box holds To A Wild Rose beauty dust, cream sachet & cologne. **CMV $52.50 MB.**

SPRAY OF ROSES SET 1961
White & pink box with pink satin lining holds To A Wild Rose beauty dust & cologne mist. **CMV $30. MB.**

TO A WILD ROSE SPECIAL DATE SET 1956
Pink & gold box holds black lipstick, powder pak & 1/2 oz. of To A Wild Rose Toilet Water. **CMV $45. MB.**

ADORABLE SET 1955-56
Pink & white box with pink flowers on top holds To A Wild Rose body powder & cream sachet. **CMV $35. MB.**

HOLIDAY ROSES SET 1963-64
Box holds To A Wild Rose beauty dust, splash cologne, cream lotion, with paper label. Same set in 1964 with painted label. **CMV $37. each set MB.**

ADORABLE SET 1956
Pink & white box with pink ribbon on lid holds To A Wild Rose body powder & cream sachet. **CMV $35. MB.**

A SPRAY OF ROSES SET 1958
Pink & white box holds To A Wild Rose cologne mist & cream sachet. **CMV $37. MB.**

LOVELY AS A ROSE SET 1961
Pink & white box holds 2 oz. To A Wild Rose cologne & cream sachet. **CMV $20. MB.**

WILD ROSES SET 1953
To A Wild Rose body powder with cream sachet on top. Pink ribbon around set. **CMV $40. MB.**

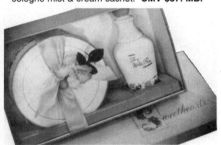

SWEETHEARTS SET 1955
Pink & white box holds To A Wild Rose beauty dust with pink ribbon & 4 oz. cologne. **CMV $55. MB.**

WILD ROSES SET 1964
Multi-pink flowered box holds 2 oz. bottle of To A Wild Rose cologne & cream sachet. **CMV $25. MB.**

TRILOGY SET 1957
(Left) Box holds 3 To A Wild Rose 2 oz. bottles of bath oil, cream lotion & cologne. **CMV $60. MB.**

PETAL OF BEAUTY SET 1953
Pink box holds blue & pink satin bag, all blue bag, or all pink bag with To A Wild Rose 4 oz. cologne & beauty dust with 5/8 dram perfume, "Small Square Bottle" with ribbon tied around it. Inside beauty dust. **CMV $75. MB. Bag & contents only $55.** 1950-52 set sold without 5/8 dram perfume. **CMV $65. MB, $50. in bag with no box mint.**

TO A WILD ROSE SET 1950-52
Blue & pink box holds To A Wild Rose body powder & 4 oz.cologne. **CMV $60. MB.**

PETAL OF BEAUTY 1954-55
Blue & pink box with blue ribbon around outside holds 4 oz. cologne & beauty dust. **CMV $62.50 MB.**

ANNIVERSARY SPECIAL SET 1956
Pink & white box holds 2 cans of To A Wild Rose talc. **CMV $20. MB.**

PINK BELLS SET 1955
Pink box holds 2 blue cans of To A Wild Rose talc. **CMV $25. MB.**

ROSE PETALS SET 1953-54
Two clear glass bottles, blue caps, holds bath oil & cream lotion. **CMV $57.50 MB.**

TOPAZE
See Stockholders Gift section for 1960 Topaze Treasure Set.

TOPAZE PERFUME OIL 1963-69
(Left) 1/2 oz. gold cap & painted label. **CMV $4., MB $6.**
PERFUME OIL FOR THE BATH 1963
(Center) 1/2 oz. gold cap, painted label. **CMV $40. BO, $45. MB.**
1/2 OZ. COLOGNE 1970-71
(Right) Gold cap & painted label. **CMV $2. MB.**

TOPAZE PERFUME 1959-63
1 oz. amber glass & amber jeweled glass stopper. Bottle cut like a gem. In yellow & white box. **CMV $135. MB, $85. BO.**

TOPAZE PERFUME 1935 ONLY
1/4 oz. gold cap, gold & white label & box. Introducing Topaze for the 50th wedding anniversary of Mr. and Mrs. D. H. McConnell. **CMV BO $50., $70. MB.**

TOPAZE 4 OZ. COLOGNE 1959-63
(Left) Gold cap. **CMV $8. in plain yellow box, $4. BO.**
2 OZ. COLOGNE 1960-71
(Right) Gold cap, painted label. **CMV $1. MB**

TOPAZE PERFUME MIST 1964-68
(Left) 2 dram yellow bottle, white top with gold band, box gold. **CMV $2. - $4. MB.**
SPRAY PERFUME 1959-63
(Right) Yellow box holds 2 dram metal spray perfume, gold top & yellow bottom. **CMV $7. - $12. MB.**

TOPAZE 4 OZ. GIFT COLOGNE 1959-61
Gold cap, clear glass in yellow & gold satin lined box. **CMV $20. MB as shown.**

TOPAZE BEAUTY DUST 1960-70
(Left) Yellow plastic bottom, white lid with yellow jewel. **CMV $5. MB.**
PERFUMED SKIN SOFTENER 1964-72
(Right) 5 oz. yellow painted over white milk glass or clear glass, gold & white lid. **CMV $1. MB.**

TOPAZE TREASURE SET 1960
Box holds 2 oz. cologne and beauty dust. **CMV $40.**

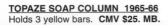

TOPAZE SOAP COLUMN 1965-66
Holds 3 yellow bars. **CMV $25. MB.**

TOPAZE PERFUME ROLLETTE 1965-69
.33 oz. ribbed carnival glass, gold cap. **CMV $2. MB.**
SCENTED HAIR SPRAY 1966-70
7 oz. yellow can. **CMV $3.**

TOPAZE BATH OIL 1961-66
(Left) 6 oz. yellow plastic bottle & cap. **CMV $1.**
FOAMING BATH OIL 1966-73
(Center) 6 oz. yellow plastic bottle and cap. **CMV $1.**
BODY POWDER 1961-63
(Right) 4 oz. yellow plastic bottle & cap. **CMV $4. - $6. MB.**

GOLDEN TOPAZE 1960-61
Gold box with plastic cover holds Topaze Cream Sachet, Cologne Mist and Beauty Dust. **CMV $40. MB.**

CREAM LOTION 1959-67
(Left) 4 oz. clear glass, yellow cap. **CMV $2.** ALso came with yellow cap with jewel, rare. **CMV $8.**
TOPAZE COLOGNE MIST 1959-68
(Right) 3 oz. yellow plastic coated, yellow jewel on lid, in round yellow box. **CMV $3. in round box.** 1969-76 issue came in square box. Same bottle. **CMV $1.**

TOPAZE POWDER SACHET 1959-67
Both 9/10 oz. yellow glass, yellow caps. common issue with large cap. **CMV $6. MB, CMV small cap $7. MB.**

TOPAZE PERFUMED TALC 1961-62
(Left) 2 1/4 or 2 3/4 oz. yellow round can & cap. **CMV $5., $7. MB.**
TOPAZE PERFUMED TALC 1962-74
(Right) 2 3/4 oz. yellow & white can, yellow cap. **CMV $1.**

UNFORGETTABLE

TOPAZE SOAP 1961-64
Yellow box holds 2 bars of Topaze soap. **CMV $22. MB.**

TOPAZE SETTING SET 1964
Yellow box holds 2 oz. bottle of Topaze Cologne and Powder Sachet. **CMV $25. MB.**

TOPAZE TEMPLE OF LOVE 1960-61
Yellow and gold. Holds yellow and white plastic holder. Came with .75 oz. Topaze Cream Sachet. **CMV MB $20., $10. holder only. $6. for .75 oz. Cream Sachet only.**
CREAM SACHET 1960-75
.66 oz. yellow paint on clear or milk glass, yellow cap. **CMV .50c**

TOPAZE JEWEL SET 1961
Gold box holds Topaze Cologne Mist and Cream Lotion. **CMV $30. MB.**

TOPAZE ELEGANCE 1963
Gold and white box holds Topaze Beauty Dust, 4 oz. Creme Lotion, and 2 oz. Cologne. **CMV $35. MB.**

GOLDEN GEM SET 1961
Gold box holds 2 oz. Topaze Cologne and Cream Sachet in .75 oz. size. **CMV $25. MB.**

TOPAZE PRINCESS SET 1964
Gold box holds Topaze 3 oz. Cologne Mist and 4 oz. Cream Lotion. **CMV $25. MB.**

UNFORGETTABLE SOAP 1965-68
(Right) Orange box holds 3 orange soaps with gold centers. **CMV $20. MB.**

UNFORGETTABLE PERFUME OIL 1965-69
(Left) Clear glass, gold cap, no neck trim.
(Center Left) Clear glass, gold cap, cut out gold neck trim.
(Center Right) Clear glass, gold cap, solid gold neck trim, scalloped edge.
(Right) Solid gold neck trim with smooth edge.
CMV $7. MB. ea.

UNFORGETTABLE BEAUTY DUST 1965-70
Pink plastic trimmed in gold. **CMV $6. MB.**
SKIN SOFTENER 1965-73
5 oz. pink painted over clear or milk glass, pink & gold lid. **CMV $1.**

UNFORGETTABLE COLOGNE 1970-71
1/2 oz. with gold cap. **CMV $2. MB.**
PERFUMED TALC 1966-74
2 3/4 oz. pink can & cap. **CMV $1.**

UNFORGETTABLE POWDER SACHET 1966-68
All are .9 oz.
(Left) Pink glass, gold pattern printing & gold cap. No neck trim.
POWDER SACHET 1965 ONLY
(Center Left) Pink glass, gold lettering, cap & trim. Neck trim has cut out pattern.
(Center Right) no trim
POWDER SACHET 1965 ONLY
(Right) 9 oz. pink glass, gold lettering, cap & trim. No holes in trim. **CMV $6. MB. each.**

UNFORGETTABLE SCENTED HAIR SPRAY 1966-71
(Left) 7 oz. orange & gold cn. **CMV $3.**
BEAUTY DUST 1971-73
(Center Left) Orange & gold 6 oz. cardboard box. **CMV $3. mint, $5. MB.**
PERFUMED POWDER MIST 1968-72
(Center Right & Right) 7 oz. orange & gold can, 2 different labels painted on paper. **CMV $1. - $3. paper.**

UNFORGETTABLE DELUXE SET 1965
Gold & white box holds beauty dust, cream sachet & cologne mist. **CMV $32.50 MB.**

UNFORGETTABLE COLOGNE MIST 1965-76
(Left & Center) 3 oz. pink plastic coated, gold cap. Two different gold trims around neck. **CMV $1. with holes in gold trim, $4. on solid gold neck trim.**
CREAM SACHET 1965-75
Pink painted over clear or milk glass bottom with gold plastic cap & gold trim. **CMV $1.MB.**

UNFORGETTABLE PERFUMED SOAP 1965
(Left) 3 oz. pink & gold wrapper. **CMV $4.**

UNFORGETTABLE HEIRLOOM 1965-66
Gold & white tray holds 1 2/ oz pink & gold cardboard perfumed talc. **CMV $15.** 9/10 oz. powder sachet, gold cap & 1/2 oz. perfume oil with gold cap. For set **CMV $30. - $40. MB.**

VIOLET BOUQUET

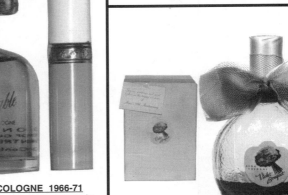

UNFORGETTABLE CREAM LOTION 1966-68
(Left) 4 oz. orange plastic bottle with gold cap. **CMV $2. MB.**
FOAMING BATH OIL 1966-72
(Right) 6 oz. orange plastic bottle with gold cap. **CMV $2. MB.**

UNFORGETTABLE COLOGNE 1966-71
(Left) 2 oz. gold cap, painted label. **CMV $2.**
PERFUME MIST 1964-68
(Right) 2 dram, rose colored bottom, white cap, gold trim, all metal. **CMV $3. MB.**

VIOLET BOUQUET REPRESENTATIVE GIFT 1945
Avon's 59th Anniversary gift to each representative. Violet colored net ribbon around white cap. 16 oz. crackle glass bottle. **CMV $150. mint, $175. MB.**

VIOLET BOUQUET COLOGNE 1946-49
6 oz. bottle. Came in different color caps.
CMV $80. MB, $50. BO. mint

WHITE MOIRE SOAP 1946-49
Blue & white box, white bow tie soap. **CMV $50. MB.**

WHITE MOIRE

WHITE MOIRE SACHET 1946
White cap & small plain paper label. **CMV $20. BO, $25. MB.**

WHITE MOIRE BODY POWDER 1945-49
(Left) 5 oz. or 4 1/2 oz. size, blue & white paper container with plastic sifter top, came in blue & white box. CMV $30. MB, $25. CO mint.

WHITE MOIRE COLOGNE 1945-49
6 oz. bubble sided bottle with white or blue cap. Blue & white label. CMV$50. BO. $75. MB.

WHITE MOIRE POWDER SACHET 1948-49
(Left) 1 1/4 oz. clear glass, blue and white label, blue cap. CMV $20. MB, $15. BO.
POWDER SACHET 1946-47
(Right) 1 1/4 oz. clear glass, white or blue plastic cap. CMV $15. BO, $20. MB. Both bottles pictured have same label.

WHITE MOIRE SACHET 60th ANNIVERSARY BOX 1946
1 1/4 oz. regular issue bottle, white cap. Came in special issue blue & white box with white ribbon and blue & silver tag saying "Avon Diamond Anniversary 60th Year". **CMV $30. MB as shown.**

WHITE MOIRE SET 1945-49
(Right) Blue & white box with white silk bow on lid contains 6 oz. White Moire cologne with white cap. Blue & white label. Also 5 oz. White Moire body powder, blue & white cardboard. **CMV $115. MB.**

WISHING

WISHING COLOGNE 1947
4 oz. bottle with gold cap, painted label. Same bottle as Golden Promise cologne. Came in fancy open front & top box. Given to Avon Representatives for calling on 61 customers during 61st Anniversary Campaign in campaign 9 - 1947. **CMV $85. BO, $110. MB.**

WISHING BATH OIL 1964-66
6 oz. white plastic bottle, gold lettering, white box. **CMV $10. MB, $7. BO.**

WISHING BEAUTY DUST 1963-67
4 oz. white plastic trimmed in gold. **CMV $10. MB.**
PERFUMED SKIN SOFTENER 1964-69
5 oz. white glass jar with gold & white lid. **CMV $3. MB.**

WISHING TOILET WATER 1952

(Left) 2 oz. white cap. Same as Flowertime bottle. **CMV $25. BO, $30. MB.**

TOILET WATER 1947-49

(Right) 2 oz. white cap. **CMV $35. MB, $30. BO.** Also came in gold 61st Anniversary box. **CMV $40. MB.**

WISHING PERFUME OIL 1964-67

(Left) 1/2 oz. clear glass, white cap, gold lettering with small gold wishbone on gold string. White box. **CMV $8. BO, $10. MB.**

WISHING COLOGNE 1963-67

(Right) 2 oz. clear glass, white cap, gold lettering with gold wishbone on neck, white box. **CMV $7. MB, $4. BO.**

SECRET WISH SET 1963 65

White box holds Wishing perfumed talc & 4 oz. cream lotion. **CMV $20. MB.**

WISHING COLOGNE MIST 1963-70

(Left) 2 1/2 oz. white plastic coated, gold trim. Gold wishbone on neck, white box. **CMV $3. BO, $5. MB.**

BUBBLE BATH 1963-66

(Center) 4 oz. white plastic bottle & cap, white box. **CMV $5 MB, $3. BO.**

WISHING CREAM LOTION 1963-67

(Right) 4 oz. white plastic bottle & cap. White box. **CMV $6. MB, $4. BO.**

WISHING SCENTED HAIR SPRAY 1966-67

7 oz. white can with gold lettering, white cap. **CMV $10.**

PERFUMED SOAP 1965-66

3 oz. white soap with white & gold wrapper. **CMV $5. mint.**

WISHING NECKLACE 1964-65

22K gold wishbone necklace came in Charm of Wishing set only. **CMV $25. in small pink & white box, $17. necklace only.**

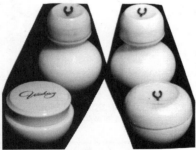

WISHING POWDER SACHET 1964-68

(Back Two) 9/10 oz. white glass bottom. Bottle on right has white plastic cap, bottle on left has yellow plastic cap, not faded. Both have wishbone in center of cap. White box. **CMV yellow cap $10., white cap $6., add $2. MB each.**

WISHING CREAM SACHET 1963-70

(Front Two) White glass bottom with white plastic cap, gold wishbone in center of cap. Also came with Wishing written on lid. **CMV $2. with wishbone, $25. with Wishing lettering.**

WISHING PERFUME MIST 1965-67

2 dram, white metal, gold trim, white box. **CMV $4. MB.**

PERFUMED TALC 1963-66

2.75 oz. white can, gold lettering. **CMV $4.**

WISHING DUETTE 1964-65

White, gold & pink box holds Wishing cream rollette & cream sachet. **CMV $22. MB.**

WISHING SET 1963 ONLY

White & gold box holds Wishing 2 oz. cologne & cream sachet. **CMV $25. MB.**

CHARM OF WISHING SET 1964-65
Gold & white box holds Wishing beauty dust, cologne mist & 22K gold plated Wishbone necklace on 9" chain. **CMV $62.50 MB.**

WISH COME TRUE SET 1963-64
White & gold box holds Wishing bubble bath & 2 oz. cologne with wishbone on neck. **CMV $26. MB.**

WISHING DATE SET 1965
White & gold box holds Wishing perfume skin softener, perfume rollette & white vinyl covered Wishing date book. **CMV $32.50 MB.**

WISHING SOAP 1963-66
White box holds 3 white Wishbone embossed soaps. **CMV $25. MB.**

WISHING PERFUMED PAIR 1964
White box holds Wishing perfumed talc & bar of soap in white wrapper. **CMV $19. MB.**

YOUNG HEARTS

YOUNG HEARTS TALC 1952-53
1 2/3 oz. cardboard talc. Came in sets only. **CMV $20.**
YOUNG HEARTS COLOGNE 1952-54
2 oz. cologne with pink cap and painted label. **CMV $30. BO mint.**
YOUNG HEARTS BUBBLE BATH 1952-54
2 oz. pink cap and painted label. **CMV $30. BO mint.**

YOUNG HEARTS 1952-54
1 dram perfume, pink cap and painted label. Came in sets only. **CMV $60.** !/2 oz. Toilet Water with pink cap and painted label. Came in sets only. **CMV $30.** 1 oz. Cologne with pink cap. Came in sets only. **CMV $30.**

KIDDIE COLOGNE 1954-55
2 oz. bottle of Young Hearts Cologne has pink cap with white foam dog head on cap, in yellow, white and blue box. **CMV $50. MB, $25. BO. Add $15. for foam head on BO mint.**
YOUNG HEARTS BUBBLE BATH 1954-55
White foam dog head on pink cap, in yellow, white & blue box. **CMV $25. BO. Add $15. for foam head on BO mint. $50. MB.**

YOUNG HEARTS KIDDIE BUBBLE BATH 1952-54
2 oz. bottle with pink cap and white foam cat head on cap. Blue and white box, painted label. **CMV $50. MB with foam head. $30. BO. Add $10. for foam head.**
YOUNG HEARTS KIDDIE COLOGNE 1952-53
2 oz. bottle with white foam cat head over pink cap, painted label. Blue and white box. **CMV $50. MB with cat head. $30. BO. Add $10. for foam head.**

YOUNG HEARTS TALC 1954-55
Pink and white metal can.
COLOGNE
Pink cap.
BUBBLE BATH
Pink cap. All 3 came in sets only **CMV $25.ea.Mint**

FOR YOUNG HEARTS SET BOTTLES 1945-46
Each are 2 oz. frosted glass with pink caps. In Cotillion Toilet Water, Cream Lotion and Bubble Bath. **CMV $20. each.**

YOUNG HEARTS SACHET 1945-46
Box holds two pink lace net sachets with pink ribbons on each end and flower in the middle. Refills for the Young Hearts set. **CMV $40. MB.**

RAIN DROPS 1952
Red umbrella bag holds 1 oz. Young Hearts Cologne, Perfume and Cream Lotion. All have pink caps. **CMV $125. MB.**

YOUNG HEARTS CREAM LOTION 1954
Bottle has pink cap, in pink and white heart shaped box. **CMV $25. MB, $20. BO.**

YOUNG HEARTS BEAUTY DUST 1954-55
Blue, white and yellow paper box. **CMV $20., $25. MB.**

RAIN DROPS 1953
Red umbrella hand bag holds Young Hearts Cologne, Pomade and Cream Lotion. Pink caps. **CMV $95. set MB.**

YOUNG HEARTS CREAM LOTION 1952-53
2 oz. pink cap. Came in sets only. **CMV $20. mint.**

YOUNG HEARTS POLISH REMOVER 1952-53
2 oz. pink cap. Came in "N Everything Nice set only. **CMV $20. mint.**

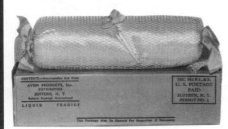

YOUNG HEARTS SACHET 1945-46
One pink lace net with pink ribbons on each end. Came in For Young Hearts set only. **CMV $25. MB.**

RAIN DROPS SET 1954-55
Red umbrella hand bag holds Young Hearts Cologne, Pomade and Cream Lotion. **CMV $90. set MB.**

HONEY BUN SET 1953
Blue and pink round box holds 2 1/2 oz. Young Hearts Toilet Water with pink cap and gold Pomade Lipstick. **CMV $50. MB.**

HONEY BUN SET 1954-55
Young Hearts Cologne and gold lipstick in
white, blue and yellow box. **CMV $50. MB.**

YOUNG HEARTS SET 1953
Blue and white box holds Young Hearts
Cologne, Bubble Bath and Talc. **CMV $100.
MB.**

LITTLE DOLL SET 1954-55
Plastic doll with blond hair. Blue dress is a
zipper handbag containing Young Hearts
Cream Lotion, Cologne and Gold Pomade.
CMV $115. set MB.

HONEY BUN SET 1954
Blue, white and yellow box holds Young Hearts
Toilet Water, and gold Pomade Lipstick. **CMV
$50. MB.**

FOR YOUNG HEARTS SET 1945-46
Pink box holds three 2 oz. frosted glass bottles
of Cotillion Toilet Water, Cream Lotion and
Bubble Bath. All have pink caps. Pink net
sachet in top box. **CMV $110. set MB, or
$22.50 each bottle, $20. for net sachet.**

YOUNG HEARTS SET 1954-55
Cologne, Talc, and Bubble Bath with pink caps
and pink hearts on label, in pink and white
box. **CMV $85. MB.**

MISS FLUFFY PUFF SET 1954-55
Young Hearts Beauty Dust and Cologne in
blue and pink. Pink cap in pink and white box.
CMV $60. MB.

HONEY BUN SET 1952
Pink and white 8 sided box holds Young
Hearts Toilet Water and gold Pomade Lipstick.
CMV $50. MB.

NEAT & SWEET SET 1954-55
Young Hearts Cologne and Cream Lotion with
pink heart shaped soap. Pink caps in yellow,
white and blue box. 1955 set came with green
and gold spray atomizer. **CMV $85. MB, $95.
for atomizer set.**

'N EVERYTHING NICE SET 1952
Box holds Young Hearts Cream Lotion, pink
cap. Polish Remover, pink cap. Nail Polish,
white cap. Emery board and orange stick.
CMV $60. MB.

MEN'S AFTER SHAVES & COLOGNES

YOUNG HEARTS SET 1952
Blue, white and pink box holds Young Hearts Cologne, Talc and Bubble Bath. **CMV $85. MB.**

DELUXE AFTER SHAVE "WOOD TOP" 1961-63
6 oz. Some have gold letters on bottle, some have gold paper labels. Came in Deluxe Electric Pre-Shave Lotion, Deluxe After Shave Lotion, After Shave Lotion Spicy, Electric Pre-Shave Lotion Spicy. **CMV each $25. MB, $20. BO mint.** 4 different fragrances.

AFTER SHOWER FOR MEN 1959-60
8 oz. gold cap with gold foil on neck & gold neck cord with Stage Coach on bottom. **CMV with foil top & tag, $30. mint, $40. MB.**

AFTER SHAVING LOTION 1932-36
4 oz. black caps. Two different yellow paper labels. **CMV $30. BO mint each, $40. MB.**

'N EVERYTHING NICE SET 1953
Box holds Young Hearts Cream Lotion, Polish Remover with pink caps and Nail Polish, white cap, Emery Board and Orange Stick. **CMV $65. MB.** Top different from back of lid.

VIGORATE AFTER SHAVE 1959-60
8 oz. clear glass with white cap. Bottle indented on bottom with carriage. Box is black with red ribbon, gold bottom, plastic white insert on top with gold carriage. **CMV $20. BO mint, $35. MB.**

COLOGNE FOR MEN 1946-49
6 oz. maroon cap. Shield on paper label. **CMV $35. BO. Mint In 2 different maroon boxes, $50. MB.**

4A AFTER SHAVE 1964-66
6 oz. 4A painted on clear glass, black cap with gold mirror on top. **CMV $15. BO, $20. MB.**

FRAGRANCE TRADITIONS COLOGNE FOR MEN. 1995
3.4 oz. glass stoppered bottles in choice of Rugger, LoverBoy, Clint, Windjammer, & Trazarra. Each bottle & box has the date on front when the fragrance was introduced. **CMV $1. ea. MB empty.**

HOLIDAY VINTAGE MINI COLOGNE 1995
.5 oz ribbed glass bottles, gold caps. Special black box with red strips sold only during Xmas season 1995. Choice of Aures 1985, Everest 1975, Legacy 1988, Signet 1987, & Taiwinds 1971. Must be in this red & black short issue box. **CMV $2.ea. MB.**

DEODORANT FOR MEN 1948-49
2 oz. maroon cap & label. **CMV $10.**
COLOGNE FOR MEN 1948 ONLY
2 oz. size, maroon cap. Came in 1948 Pleasure Cast set only. **CMV $15.**

AFTER SHAVING LOTION SAMPLE 1936-40
(Left) Maroon cap. CPC on back label. **CMV $35. mint.**
AFTER SHAVE LOTION SAMPLE 1940-49
(Center) 1/2 oz. maroon cap. **CMV $35.**
HAIR TONIC SAMPLE 1939
(Right) 1/4 oz. maroon cap. **CMV $40. - $45. MB.**
HAIR LOTION SAMPLE 1940s
(Not Pictured) Same as 1/4 oz. Hair Tonic. **Same CMV.**

AFTER SHAVES MISC. 1965-66
2 oz. with 4A on black caps. Came in Island Lime, Blue Blazer, Leather, Tribute, Spicy, Bay Rum, Original, 4A After Shaves, Leather All Purpose Cologne & After Shower Cologne. Came in Bureau Organizer, Fragrance Wardrobe & After Shave Selection sets only. **CMV each $8. MB, 10 different $5. BO. Add $3. for Blue Blazer.**

GENTLEMEN'S CHOICE 1969-70
Red & silver box holds 2 oz. embossed bottles with silver, gold & black caps. Came in Excalibur, Wild Country, Tribute, Leather & Windjammer cologne. **CMV $4. BO. $6. MB.**

AFTER SHAVE 1975-79
(Left) 5 oz. clear glass, brown cap. Came in Deep Woods, Everest, Oland, Tai Winds, Wild Country & Clint. Different labels, same bottles. **CMV $1.MB. each.** Issued in 1981-82 in 4 oz. size. Same shape in Wild Country, Weekend, Trazarra & Clint. **CMV $1.**
GIFT COLOGNE FOR MEN 1974-75
(Center) 2 oz. clear glass with gold cap. Came in Wild Country, Deep Woods, Oland or Tai Winds. **CMV $1. MB.**
GIFT COLOGNE FOR MEN 1975-76
(Right) 2 oz. clear glass, gold cap. Choice of Wild Country, Tai Winds, Deep Woods or Oland. **CMV $1.MB.**

GENTLEMEN'S SELECTION 1970
2 oz. each with gold caps. Came in COlogne in Oland, Tribute, Excalibur, Leather, Wild Country & Windjammer. **CMV $2. BO, $3. MB.**

COLOGNE ACCENT FOR MEN 1979-80
(Left) .5 oz. clear glass. Blue cap, blue & silver box. **CMV $2. MB.**
GIFT COLOGNE FOR MEN 1978-79
(Center) 2 oz. clear glass, black cap. Holds Everest, CLint, Wild Country or Deep Woods cologne. **CMV $2. MB.COLOGNE MINIATURE FOR MEN 1978-79**
(Right) 5 oz. clear glass, brown cap. Holds Wild Country, Clint, Everest or Trazarra. **CMV $2. MB.**

AFTER SHAVING LOTION 1936-49
4 oz. maroon cap, maroon & cream colored box. **CMV $30. MB, $22. BO.**

EAGLE ORGANIZER BOTTLE 1972
(Left) 3 oz. clear glass, eagle embossed, gold cap. Came in set only in Deep Woods & Tai Winds. **CMV $5. each.**

GIFT COLOGNE FOR MEN 1976
(Right) 2 oz. came in Deep Woods, Tai Winds, Wild Country, Everest or Oland. **CMV $1. MB.**

CJ GIFT EDITION COLOGNE 1982-83
.5 oz. mini cologne. Clear glass, gray cap, Christmas box. **CMV $3. MB.**

CREAM HAIR LOTION 1948-49
4 oz. maroon cap. **CMV $20., $25. MB.**

SERVICE KIT AFTER SHAVE BOTTLE 1951-52
4 oz. clear plastic with red cap. **CMV $12.**

COLOGNE SPRAY FOR MEN 1970-72
4 oz. silver can with red cap in Leather, brown cap in Wild Country, and tan cap in Oland. This can leaked & most boxes were ruined. **CMV $3. each MB.**

STYPTIC CREAM 1936-49
Maroon & ivory tube. **CMV $8., $15. MB.**

SHAVING STICK 1936-49
Avon on maroon base on Soap Stick. Maroon box. **CMV $20. MB.**

GIFT COLOGNE FOR MEN 1980
(Left) .5 oz. black cap, clear glass. Choice of Trazarra, Wild Country, Clint, Weekend, Light Musk, Cool Sage, Brisk Spice or Crisp Lime. **CMV $2. MB.**

COLOGNE MINIATURE FOR MEN 1977-78
(Right) 5 oz. smoked glass, black cap. Came in Clint, Everest or Wild Country. **CMV $2. MB.**

COUNTRY CHRISTMAS COLOGNE 1982
(Left) 2 oz. ribbed, clear glass, green cap & box. Came in Country Christmas set only in men's cologne. **CMV $2. MB.**

COLOGNES FOR MEN 1979-82
(Right) 3 oz. clear glass bottle. Gold caps. Choice of Brisk Spice, Cool Sage, Light Musk or Crisp Lime. Came in box. **CMV $2. each MB.**

HAIR TONIC EAU DE QUININE 1936-38
For normal, dry or oily hair. 6 oz. turquoise cap. **CMV $15.** Also came in 16 oz. size, **$25. BO, $30. MB.**

TALC FOR MEN 1943-46
Maroon & ivory colored cardboard. One on left also came with black octagonal cap as shown and also with maroon or black round cap. One on right was smooth top. You punched holes in it. **CMV $35. each mint.**

TALC FOR MEN 1929 ONLY
(Left) Green can. **CMV $55. mint.**
TALC FOR MEN 1930-36
(Right) Greenish yellow can, black cap. Came with plain black cap & sifter cap. **CMV $45. mint.**

HAIR TONIC 1938-39
(Left) 6 oz. clear glass, maroon cap and label. **CMV $30. BO mint, $40. MB.**
HAIR LOTION 1940-49
(Right) 6 oz. maroon cap & box. **CMV $40. MB, $30. BO mint.** Some labels say "formerly Hair Tonic".

STICK DEODORANT FOR MEN 1959-61
2 3/4 oz. black & red plastic container. Came with two different caps, 1 flat, 1 indented. **CMV $12. each, $15. MB.**

SHAVING BOWL 1953-56
Wood Shaving Bowl, green label. No center handle. **CMV $30., $40. MB.**
SHAVING BOWL 1949-53
Wood Shaving Bowl, green label with red center handle. **CMV $35., $45. MB.**

ORIGINAL AFTER SHAVE SPRAY 1965-66
5 1/2 oz. green can with red cap. **CMV $4. CO, $10. MB.**
TALC FOR MEN 1949-58
2 5/8 oz. green can, red cap. **CMV $6., $8. MB.** Also came in 2.6 oz. size.

SHAVING STICK 1934-36
(Left) Nickel metal container. **CMV $50. MB, $40. mint only.**
SHAVING STICK 1929-33
(Right) Green metal can. CPC on lid. **CMV $50. CO mint, $60. MB.**

LATHER & BRUSHLESS SHAVING CREAM 1949-59
Green tubes, flat red caps, used in 1949-56. Tall red caps used 1957-59. **CMV $10. each MB, $8. tube only mint.**

KWICK FOAMING SHAVE CREAM 1955-57
10 oz. green & white can, pointed red cap. **CMV $4., $7. MB.**
SAME CAN 1957-58
With flat red top, red cap. **CMV same.**

SHAVING STICK 1949-57
Green & red box holds Shaving Soap Stick with red plastic base. **CMV $15. MB.**
STYPTIC CREAM 1949-57
1/3 oz. green tube with red cap. **CMV $10., MB $15.**

SHAVING CREAM SAMPLE 1949-58
1/4 oz. green tubes of lather & brushless shaving cream, red caps. **CMV $6. each mint.** Also came in 1/2 oz. size sample tubes. **CMV $8. each mint.**

COLOGNE FOR MEN 1949-58
All three sizes have red caps & silver labels, 6 oz. size. 1949-57 **CMV $15. MB.** 4 oz. size 1952-57 came in sets only. Also with green label. **CMV $9.** 2 oz. size 1949-58 **CMV $6.**

COLOGNE FOR MEN SAMPLE 1949-58
1/2 oz. red cap, silver label. **CMV $25. MB.**
AFTER SHAVING LOTION SAMPLE 1949-58
1/2 oz. red cap, green label. **CMV $5.**

ORIGINAL SOAP ON A ROPE 1966-68
White bar with embossed carriage. **CMV $25. MB.**
ORIGINAL AFTER SHAVE 1965-69
4 oz. green label, red cap & red & green box. **CMV $4. BO, $6. MB.**

CREAM HAIR DRESS 1949-57
2 1/4 oz. green tube & box. Came with flat or tail red cap. **CMV $15. MB.**

DEODORANT FOR MEN SAMPLE 1949-58
1/2 oz. bottle with red cap, green label. **CMV $25. mint.**

COLOGNE FOR MEN 1952-57
4 oz. clear glass bottle with red cap. Label is green & red. **CMV $9.**

BRUSHLESS SHAVING CREAM 1959-62
(Left) 5 oz. black & white tube, red cap. **CMV $7. MB.**
LATHER SHAVING CREAM 1959-62
(Center) 5 oz. black & white tube, red cap. **CMV $8. MB.**
KWICK FOAMING SHAVE CREAM 1958-62
(Right) 6 oz. black & white can, red cap. **CMV $6. MB.**

DEODORANT FOR MEN 1954-57
4 oz. red cap & green label. Came in sets only. **CMV $7. MB.**
DEODORANT FOR MEN 1949-58
2 oz. red cap & green label. **CMV $6. MB.**

AFTER SHAVE LOTION 1949-58
4 oz. bottle with silver label & red cap. **CMV $7. MB.**
AFTER SHAVE 2 OZ. 1957
Silver label. Came in Good Cheer set only. **CMV $8.**

FIRST CLASS MALE 1953-56
6 oz. cologne for men, box red & white. **CMV $25. MB as shown.**

TRIUMPH 1957
Special issue box holds 6 oz. cologne for men. Silver label, red cap. **CMV $25. MB.**

KING FOR A DAY 1957
Box holds 4 oz. bottle of Electric Pre-Shave Lotion or choice of cologne for men, or 4 oz. deodorant for men. All had red caps. **CMV $25. MB.**
ELECTRIC PRE-SHAVE LOTION 1957-58
4 oz. red cap, silver label. **CMV $10. MB.**

ROYAL ORDER 1957 ONLY
Red & green box holds 6 oz. cologne for men. Silver label. **CMV $25. MB.**

HAIR LOTION 1949-58
4 oz. silver label & red cap. **CMV $7. BO, $12. MB.**
CREAM HAIR LOTION 1949-58
4 oz. bottle, silver label, red cap. **CMV $7. BO, $12. MB.**
AFTER SHAVE LOTION 1953-54
4 oz. silver label, red cap,same bottle as above. **CMV $15.**

HAIR LOTION 1 OZ. 1953-54
1 oz. bottle with red cap & green label. **CMV $20. BO, $25. MB.**
CREAM HAIR LOTION 1 OZ. 1953-54
1 oz. bottle with red cap, green label. **CMV $10. BO, $25. MB in trial size box.**
LIQUID SHAMPOO 1953-54
1 oz. bottle with red cap & green label. **CMV $22. BO, $27. MB.**

AFTER SHAVE LOTION SAMPLE 1958-62
(Left) 1/2 oz. red cap, black & white label. **CMV $8. MB.**
AFTER SHAVE LOTION 1958
(Center) 2 oz. red cap. Came in sets only. **CMV $6. MB.**
AFTER SHAVE LOTION 1958-62
(Right) 4 oz. red cap, black & white label. **CMV $4.MB.**

COLOGNE FOR MEN 1953-54
4 oz. green label, red cap. Came in Before & After set only. **CMV $15.**

ELECTRIC PRE-SHAVE LOTION 1959-62
4 oz. red cap, black & white label. **CMV $12. MB, $8. BO.**
AFTER SHAVING LOTION PLASTIC 1960-62
3 1/2 oz. white plastic bottle with red cap. Came in Overnighter Set only. **CMV $4.** 2 oz. After Shave, red plastic & cap as above came in 1959 Lamplighter Set. **CMV $4.**
SPRAY DEODORANT FOR MEN 1959-62
2 3/4 oz. white plastic bottle with red cap. **CMV $5. MB, $3. BO.** 1 1/2 oz. size in white plastic, red cap, came only in 1959 Lamplighters Set. **CMV $5.**

COLOGNE FOR MEN 1958-59
4 oz. black glass, red cap. **CMV $15. MB, $10. BO.**
AFTER SHOWER SAMPLE 1959-62
1/2 oz. black glass, red cap. **CMV $6.**
AFTER SHOWER FOR MEN 1959-62
4 oz. black glass, red or gold cap. **CMV $12. MB.**

COLOGNE FOR MEN 1958
2 oz. red cap, black & white label. Came in Happy Hours Set only. **CMV $7. BO.**
DEODORANT FOR MEN 1958-62
2 oz. red cap. **CMV $8. MB, $6. BO.**

VIGORATE AFTER SHAVE 1960-62
4 oz. frosted glass bottle, gold or red caps. 2 different painted labels. **CMV $10., $15. MB.**

DELUXE STICK DEODORANT NORMAL 1962-63
2 1/2 oz. brown & gold plastic bottle. **CMV $8. MB.**
STICK DEODORANT FOR MEN A SPICY FRAGRANCE 1961-62
2 3/4 oz. brown & gold plastic holder. **CMV $9., $11. MB.**

AFTER SHOWER FOR MEN 1959-60
2 oz. black plastic bottle with red cap. **CMV $4. MB.**
AFTER SHAVE 1959-60
2 oz. red plastic bottle & cap. Came in 1959 Lamplighter Set. **CMV $4. MB.**

AFTER SHAVE FOR DRY & SENSITIVE SKIN 1960-61
2 oz. white plastic bottle with red cap. **CMV $7. BO, $10. MB.** Also came in 2 3/4 oz.
CREAM HAIR LOTION 1960-61
2 oz. or 2 3/4 oz white plastic bottle with red cap. Came in 1st Prize Set only. **CMV $7. MB.**

CREAM HAIR LOTION 1962-65
4 oz. white plastic bottle, red cap. **CMV $10. MB, $7. BO.**
LIQUID HAIR LOTION 1962-65
4 oz. clear glass bottle, red cap. **CMV $12. MB, $8. BO.**
HAIR TRAINER 1962-65
4 oz. white plstic bottle, red cap. **CMV $10. MB, $7. BO.**

STAGE COACH EMBOSSED BOTTLES 1960-61
2 oz. size. Red or white caps. Came in First Prize Set only in After Shower for Men. Vigorate, Deodorant for Men, After Shave Lotion, Electric Pre-Shave Lotion, Liquid Hair Lotion. **CMV each $18. MB, $10. BO.**
1961 ONLY
4 oz. size with white cap came in Spice After Shave Lotion. **CMV $10. BO, $14. MB.**
1960-61
8 oz. size with gold metal cap, came in Spice After Shave Lotion. After Shave Lotion, Vigorate & After Shower for Men. **CMV each $17., with indented gold cap $25. MB.**

DELUXE TALC FOR MEN 1962-63
4 oz. brown can. **CMV $8., $10. MB.**
DELUXE FOAM SHAVE CREAM 1962-63
6 oz. brown can & cap. Regular or mentholated. **CMV $8.. MB.**

AFTER SHAVE LOTION SPICY 1962-65
ELECTRIC PRE-SHAVE LOTION SPICY
AFTER SHOWER COLOGNE FOR MEN
ORIGINAL AFTER SHAVE LOTION
VIGORATE AFTER SHAVE LOTION
Each bottle is 4 oz. size with red caps. **CMV each $7. MB.**

DELUXE AFTER SHAVE AFTER SHOWER SPRAY 1962-63
(Left) 5 1/2 oz. brown can, gold cap. **CMV $8.. MB.**

AFTER SHOWER POWDER SPICY 1961 ONLY
(Center) 4 oz. brown can. **CMV $12.. MB.**

AFTER SHAVE AFTER SHOWER SPRAY LOTION - A SPICY FRAGRANCE 1961-62
(Right) 5 1/2 oz. brown can, gold cap. **CMV $12. MB.**

VIGORATE AFTER SHAVE AFTER SHOWER SPRAY 1963-65
ORIGINAL AFTER SHAVE AFTER SHOWER SPRAY SPICY 1963-65
AFTER SHAVE AFTER SHOWER SPRAY SPICY 1963-65
AFTER SHOWER COLOGNE SPRAY 1963-65
5 1/2 oz. each. White can with red caps. **CMV $4. MB. ea.**

MEN'S SQUEEZE BOTTLE 1963-64
2 oz. white plastic bottles with red caps & letters. Came in Vigorate, Spicy & Original After Shave Lotions, Electric Pre-Shave Lotion, Spicy Liquid Hair Lotion, Hair Trainer, Cream Hair Lotion, After Shower Cologne for Men, Liquid Deodorant for Men, gentle or Plain. Came only in 1964 Christmas Trio Set & 1965 Jolly Holly Day Set. **CMV $3. each.**

TALC FOR MEN SPICY 1962-65
3 oz. white can, red cap. **CMV $7. MB.** Also came in 3.1 oz. size.

ROLL ON DEODORANT FOR MEN 1960-63
1 3/4 oz. white plastic with red cap. **CMV $5. MB.**

STAND UP HAIR STICK 1962-65
1 1/2 oz. white plastic, red cap. **CMV $3. MB.**
ROLL ON DEODORANT FOR MEN 1963-66
1 3/4 oz. glass bottle, red cap. **CMV $3. MB.**
SPRAY DEODORANT FOR MEN 1962-66
2 3/4 oz. white plastic bottle, red cap. Came in gentle, normal or plain. **CMV $3. MB.**
LIQUID DEODORANT FOR MEN - GENTLE OR PLAIN 1962-65
4 oz. & 2 oz. clear glass bottle, red cap. **CMV 2 oz. $6. MB. 4 oz. $7. MB.**

AFTER SHAVE FOR DRY OR SENSITIVE SKIN SPICY 2 OZ. 1962-65
LATHER SHAVE CREAM SPICY 4 OZ. 1962-65
All three white tubes with red caps. **CMV $3., $6. each MB.**
LATHER SHAVE CREAM 1962-63
4 oz. tube, red cap. **CMV $4. mint, $6. MB.**

BODY POWDER FOR MEN 1967-68
6 oz. maroon cardboard box. **CMV $8.mint $15. MB.**

LIQUID HAIR LOTION 1966-70
(Bottles) 4 oz. clear glass bottle with white cap. **CMV $2. MB.** 1970-71 bottle is white, red cap, 6 oz. plastic. **CMV $1. MB.**
HAIR DRESS 1966-71
(Tubes) 4 oz. tube in Cream Clear & Clear for Extra Control. **CMV $1. MB.** Also came in 3 oz. tube. **CMV $1. MB. each.**

CREAM HAIR LOTION 1958-62
4 oz. white plastic bottle, red cap. **CMV $4. MB.**
HAIR LOTION 1958-62
4 oz. clear glass, red cap, black & white label. **CMV $4 MB.** Glass bottle on right also came in Deer Head box on left. **CMV $8. MB.**

AFTER SHOWER COLOGNE SPRAY 1962
5.5 oz. white can & cap. **CMV $7 MB..**
FOAM SHAVE CREAM SPICY 1962-65
6 oz. white can, red cap. Came in regular or
mentholated. **CMV $6. MB, $4. BO.** Came
with tall or flat red caps as shown.

ELECTRIC PRE-SHAVE LOTION 1966-72
(Left) 4 oz. white cap. **CMV $1. MB.**

HAIR GUARD & HAND GUARD 1958 ONLY
Both 2 oz. bottles with red caps. Came in
Avon Guard set only. **CMV hand guard $16.,
hair guard $20.**

CREAM HAIR LOTION 1966-69
4 oz. white plastic bottle with red cap and red
label. Regular issue **CMV $1.MB.** Very short
issue sold 1966 only with red cap and red
label with black border. **CMV $2. MB.**

FOAMY BATH FOR CLEANER HIDES 1957
(Left) 2 oz. red cap, cow hide on label. Came
in Trading Post set only. **CMV $20.**
**HAIR TRAINER FOR TRAINING WILD HAIR
1957**
(Right) 2 oz. red cap, cow hide on label.
Came in Trading Post set only. **CMV $20.**

SKIN CONDITONER FOR MEN 1969-73
(Center) 5 oz. black glass, red lid and red &
black label. **CMV $2.50 MB.**
**ALL PURPOSE SKIN CONDITIONER FOR
MEN 1966-68**
(Right) 5 oz. black glass, tan lid, gold label.
CMV $5. MB.

TALC FOR MEN 1959 ONLY
(Left) Black & white can, red cap. **CMV $12.
MB..**
**AFTER SHOWER POWDER FOR MEN
1959-62**
(Right) 3 oz. black & white can, red cap.
CMV $7. MB.

BATH OIL 1969-72
(Left) 4 oz. black glass bottle, red cap. **CMV
$2. MB.**
AFTER SHAVE SOOTHER 1969-72
(Center) 4 oz. frosted glass bottle with red
cap. **CMV $2. MB.**
**PROTECTIVE HAND CREAM FOR MEN
1969-72**
(Right) 3 oz. black plastic tube with red cap.
CMV $2. MB.

AFTER SHOWER FOAM FOR MEN 1965-67
(Left) 4 oz. silver can, black & red cap. Came
in silver box. **CMV $4. BO, $6. MB.**
BATH OIL FOR MEN 1965-67
(Right) 4 oz. silver paint over clear glass, red
cap & red Avon plastic tag on gold neck cord.
Came in silver box. **CMV $7. MB.**

HAIR TRAINER BOXES 1958-61
(Left to Right) 4 oz. red plastic bottle with
1958 box on left, 1962 box center, 1960-61 on
right. 1959 box came with boxer on front of
box. **CMV add $5. for each box mint, $1.
BO.**

HAIR TRAINER 1957-58
(Left) 6 oz. clear glass bottle with white or
blue cap. Came in 1957 Hair Trainer Set.
CMV $20.
HAND GUARD & HAIR GUARD 1951-52
(Right) 2 oz. clear glass with blue cap; hair
guard has red cap. Label is red, white &
black. Came in Changing of the Guard set
only. **CMV $20. each.**

HAND GUARD & HAIR GUARD 1954-57
2 oz. red cap on Hair Guard. 2 oz. green cap
on Hand Guard. Both came in Back Field set
& Touchdown set. Hair Guard also came in
Pigskin Parade set. **CMV $18. each.**
CREAM HAIR LOTION 1955
2 oz. clear glass, red cap. Came in Space
Scout set only. Rare. **CMV $25.**

BAY RUM

**All Men's Product lines 1975 or newer are
no longer collectable because of little or no
interest and mass production. Only soaps
& sets in this catagory are collectable after
1975.**

**ANTI-PERSPIRANT DEODORANT FOR MEN
1971-74**
(Left) 4 oz. red, white & black can. **CMV
$1.MB..** With upside down label, **CMV
$6.MB..**
LIQUID DEODORANT FOR MEN 1966-70
(Inside Left) 2 oz. red cap. **CMV $2. MB.**
STICK DEODORANT FOR MEN 1968-70
(Inside Right) 2.25. oz. red, white & black
plastic. **CMV $2.**

TODAY'S MAN SHAVE CREAM 1975-76
(Left) 5 oz. white with red & black design,
black cap. **CMV 1. MB..**
**TODAY'S MAN HAND CONDITIONER 1975-
76**
(Center) 5 oz. white plastic tube with black &
red design, black cap. **CMV $1. MB.**
**TODAY'S MAN AFTER SHAVE FACE
CONDITIONER 1975-76**
(Right) 5 oz. white with red & black, black
cap. **CMV $1. MB.**

BAY RUM GIFT SET 1964
Green box holds 4 oz. Bay Rum after shave
with black cap & green 4 oz. paper Bay Rum
talc for men. **CMV $35. MB.**

HAIR TRAINER LIQUID 1958-74
(Left) 4 oz. red plastic bottle, white cap. **CMV
$1.**
ATTENTION CREAM HAIR DRESS 1959-62
(Center) 4 oz. red & white tube, red cap.
CMV $8. MB.
STAND UP HAIR STICK 1958-65
(Right) Red & white container with white cap.
CMV $3. - $7. MB.

BAY RUM SOAP 1964-65
Green box holds 2 Bay Rum shaped soaps.
CMV $27.50, MB.

BAY RUM 1936-49
4 oz. maroon cap. 2 different labels. Both bottles have indented shoulders. Also came in 8 & 16 oz. size. **CMV $22. BO, $30. MB each.**

BAY RUM AFTER SHAVE 1964-65
(Left) 4 oz. clear glass, black cap. **CMV $10. MB.**

BAY RUM JUG 1962-65
(Center) 8 oz. white painted bottom, green top over clear glass, black cap. Bay Rum after shave. **CMV $6. BO mint, $12. MB.**

BAY RUM TALC 1964-65
(Right) 4 oz. green paper container. **CMV $10.**

BLACK SUEDE

BLACK SUEDE PRODUCTS 1980-84
Basic Color is tan & black.
GIFT SOAP & CASE 1980 ONLY
Black plastic soap case & soap. **CMV $5. MB.**
SOAP BAR ONLY
CMV $1. mint.
SOAP ON A ROPE
CMV $4. MB.
All other products 25c each.

BLEND 7

BLEND 7 PRODUCTS 1973-74
SOAP ON A ROPE 1973-76
5 oz. yellow with black cord. CMV $6. MB.
All other products .50c each.

BLUE BLAZER AFTER SHAVE 1964-68
6 oz. blue glass with red square cap over small red cap. Horses on labels, came in gold or silver & with or without lines across horses. Some labels have 6 oz. at bottom of horse label. **CMV $15. MB., $12. BO.**
BLUE BLAZER SOAP ON A ROPE 1964-68
Blue soap on white rope. **CMV $20. MB, $10. soap only mint.**

BLUE BLAZER

BLUE BLAZER FOAM SHAVE CREAM 1964-65
(Not Shown) 6 oz. blue can, red cap. **CMV $10. MB, $7. CO.**
AFTER SHAVE SPRAY 1964-65
(Left) Blue 6 oz. can, red cap. **CMV $10. MB, $7. CO.**
TALC 1964-65
(Center) 3 1/2 oz. blue paper box. **CMV $12. MB, $9. CO.**
HAIR DRESS 1964-67
(Right) 4 oz. blue tube, red cap. **CMV $8. MB, $6. TO.**

BLUE BLAZER 1 SET 1964-65
Blue & red box holds 6 oz. Blue Blazer after shave lotion & Blue Blazer soap on a rope. **CMV $50. MB.**

BLUE BLAZER DELUXE SET 1965
Blue & red box holds 6 oz. Blue Blazer after shave, Blue Blazer spray deodorant & silver Blue Blazer emblem tie tac. **CMV $67.50 MB.**

BLUE BLAZER TIE TAC 1964
Silver Blue Blazer emblem tie tac. Came in Blue Blazer Deluxe Set only. In blue & red box. **CMV $22. MB, $10. pin only.**

BRAVO AFTER SHAVE 1969
(Left) 4 oz. bottle with black cap, pink label. **CMV $3. MB.**
BRAVO AFTER SHAVE 1970-72
(Right) 4 oz. black cap, pink label with black border around label. **CMV $2. MB.**

SANTA'S HELPER 1970
Green box holds 4 oz. Bravo After Shave. Box came with foam stick on decorations. **CMV $8. MB only.**

BLUE BLAZER SOAP & SPONGE SET 1966-67
Red & blue box holds bar of blue soap and red & blue sponge. **CMV $22.50 MB.**

BRAVO

BRAVO AFTER SHAVE TOWELETTES 1969-72
Pink & black box holds 100 sample packets. **CMV $7. MB or 10c per sample.**

BLUE BLAZER II SET 1964-65
Blue & red box holds Blue Blazer talc & spray deodorant. **CMV $25.**

CLINT

CLINT AFTER SHAVE 1977-79
(Left) 5 oz. glass bottle, brown cap. **CMV $1.50.**
CLINT SHOWER SOAP 1977-78
(Center) Soap on green or white rope. **CMV $5. MB.**
CLINT COLOGNE 1976-79
(Right) 5 oz. bottle with Clint painted on front. **CMV $1. MB..** Also came in 4 oz. size, same design and CMV.

BLUE BLAZER SPRAY DEODORANT 1964-67
2.75 oz. blue plastic bottles, red caps. One bottle has lines on horse design & 1 plain. The plain one is hardest to find. **CMV $8.** Different label on right. **CMV $7. with 2.75 oz. on front side.**

BRAVO AFTER SHAVE SAMPLE 1969-72
Box of 10 samples. **CMV $1.50 MB.**
BRAVO TALC 1969-72
3.5 oz. pink & black paper container. **CMV $1.50.**

CLINT TRAVEL KIT 1977
Comes empty, gray, maroon & green bag.
CMV $6. MB.
CLINT SOAP 1977-78
3 oz. soap. **CMV $1.50.**
All other Clint products CMV 25c.

EVEREST

EVEREST SOAP ON A ROPE 1975-79
(Left) Blue soap, white rope **CMV $3. MB.**
EVEREST SOAP BAR 1977-79
(Top) Blue wrapped 3 oz. bar. **CMV $1. mint.**
All other Everest products CMV 50c.

ISLAND LIME SOAP 1966-68
Green soap on a rope. **CMV $22. MB.** Two
different weave designs on soap.

EXCALIBUR

CLINT GIFT SET 1977-78
(Left) Gray & green box with outer sleeve.
Came with Clint soap on a rope & 5 oz. Clint
cologne. **CMV $12. MB.**
CLINT TRAVEL SET 1977
(Right) Cardboard 1.5 oz. talc & 3 oz. Clint in
plastic bottle with maroon cap. **CMV $6. MB.**

ISLAND LIME

**ISLAND LIME AREOSOL DEODORANT
1966-67**
(Left) 4 oz. green & yellow checked can &
green cap. **CMV $3. MB.**
ISLAND LIME AFTER SHAVE 1969-73
(Center & Left) 6 oz. green frosted glass &
green cap with yellow letters. **CMV $1.50.
MB.** 1973-74 issue has gold cap, green
letters. **CMV $2. MB.**

EXCALIBUR COLOGNE 1969-73
6 oz. gold cap. Bottom of bottle appears to
have rocks in glass. **CMV $6 MB.** Rare issue
came with sword pointing to right side low end
of rocks. **CMV $15. mint.**

DEEP WOODS

DEEP WOODS PRODUCTS 1972-79
AFTER SHAVE 1976-79
(Left) 5 oz. brown cap. **CMV 50c.MB.**
SHOWER SOAP ON A ROPE 1972-75
(Center) **CMV $6. MB.**
SHOWER SOAP ON A ROPE 1976-79
(Right) **CMV $6. MB.**
DEEP WOODS SOAP BAR 1977-78
(Top) Brown wrapped soap, 3 oz. bar. **CMV
$1. mint.**
All other products CMV 50c.

ISLAND LIME SPRAY TALC 1974-76
(Left) 7 oz. green & yellow with dark green
cap. **CMV $1. MB.**
ISLAND LIME AFTER SHAVE 1966-69
(Right) First issue 6 oz. dark yellow basket
weave. **CMV $12. MB,** 1967 issue has light
yellow weave on clear. 1968 issue has light
green weave. **CMV $10. MB. ea.** All 66 to 68
are clear glass bottles. 1969 issue is green
glass bottle & low issue. **CMV $20. MB.** All
have green & yellow caps. . Came with small
or large flowers on caps.

EXCALIBUR SOAP ON A ROPE 1969-71
(Left) Blue soap on a rope. **CMV $10. MB.**
EXCALIBUR SPRAY TALC 1970-72
(Right) 7 oz. black can & cap. **CMV $1.**

LEATHER

LEATHER SOAP 1966
One bar in brown & red box. **CMV $18. MB.**

ALL PURPOSE COLOGNE LEATHER 1966
(Left) 4 oz. black cap, red label. Came in Fox Hunt set only. **CMV $10.**
AFTER SHAVE LOTION LEATHER 1968
(Right) 3 oz. red cap, clear glass. Came in Boots & Saddle set only. **CMV $5.**

LEATHER AEROSOL DEODORANT 1966-67
(Left) 4 oz. tan & red can with black cap. **CMV $5. MB - $3.** can only.
LEATHER SPRAY TALC 1969-72
(Right) 7 oz. tan & red can, black cap. **CMV $2.**

OLAND

OLAND GIFT SET 1970
Brown and silver box holds bar of Oland soap, 31/2 oz. Oland talc & 6 oz. Oland cologne. **CMV $15. MB.**

OLAND COLOGNE 1970-77
6 oz. embossed bottle with brown cap. **CMV $2.. MB.**
OLAND SOAP ON A ROAP 1970-77
Tan bar of soap on green rope with plastic "O". OSP $4. **CMV $7 MB** with plain rope (no "O"). **CMV $5. MB.**
OLAND SPRAY TALC 1970-77
7 oz. brown spray can with brown cap. OSP $3. **CMV $1.**

OLAND SPRAY TALC 1970-72
(Left) 7oz. can with O on brown cap. Painted label on can is upside down. Can was filled & sold by Avon by mistake. **CMV $5.**

OLAND AFTER SHAVE & COLOGNE 1970
3 1/2 oz. clear glass with gold cap. Came in Master Organizer only. **CMV $5. each.**

SPICY

SPICY AFTER SHAVE 1967-74
4 oz. clear glass, black cap, **CMV $1. MB.** 4 oz. amber glass with black cap. **CMV $2. MB**

SPICY SOAP SET 1965-66
Five brown bars. OSP $2. **CMV $22.50 MB**

COLOGNE PLUS SPICY 1965-67
2 oz.. gold ribbed cap. **CMV $20. MB.**
AFTER SHAVE LOTION 1965-67
4 oz. tan cap. **CMV $7. MB.**

TALC FOR MEN - SPICY 1967-74
3 1/2 oz. brown & white container. **CMV $1. MB.** Upside down label **CMV $5 MB..**
AFTER SHAVE SPRAY - SPICY 1965-67
5 1/2 oz. Bamboo style can, gold cap. **CMV $6. MB.**

AFTER SHAVE FOR DRY OR SENSITIVE SKIN - SPICY 1967-75
2 oz. black, brown & white tube, brown or white cap. One has all white letters. **CMV $2.** One has black over print on white letters. Hard to find. **CMV $4.**

SPICY AFTER SHAVE SAMPLES 1961
Plastic sample tubes of Spicy After Shave Lotion. Full box of 30. Same samples also came in Cream Hair Dress. Rich Moisture Cream & Dew Kiss. **CMV 25c each sample or $7. for full box of 30 mint.** Comes in 2 different boxes.

TALC FOR MEN - SPICY 1965-67
3 1/2 oz. Bamboo style box. **CMV $5. MB**
AFTER SHAVE SPRAY - SPICY 1965-67
5/12 oz. Bamboo style can, tan cap. **CMV $5. MB.**

AFTER SHAVE FOR DRY OR SENSITIVE SKIN - SPICY 1965-67
2 oz. tan & white tube, tan cap. **CMV $4. MB.** Upside down label on right is rare. **CMV $8.MB.**

SPICE AFTER SHAVE LOTION SAMPLES 1961
Small white envelope holds 2 plastic samples. **CMV $3.**

OATMEAL SOAP - SPICY 1967-76
(Left) Large bath size & 3 oz. size in brown & white wrapper. **OSP 60c. CMV $2.**
OATMEAL SOAP - SPICY 1965-67
(Right) Brown & white wrapping. **OSP 49c. CMV $7**

FORE N AFTER SPICY 1966
Spicy box holds 4 oz. Electric Pre-Shave Lotion Spicy & 4 oz. After Shave Lotion Spicy. White caps on both & wood grained paper label. **OSP $1.96. CMV $22. MB.**
ELECTRIC PRE-SHAVE & AFTER SHAVE LOTIONS - SPICY 1966
4 oz. white caps & wood grained paper labels. Came in Fore N After Set only. **CMV $7. ea.**

SPICY THREE SET 1965
Brown box holds 2 bars of Spicy Oatmeal Soap & Spicy Talc for Men. **CMV $22.50 MB.**

OVERNIGHTER 1965-66
Brown vinyl zippered bag holds Spicy Talc, 4 oz. Spicy After Shave Lotion & bar of Spicy Oatmeal soap for men. **CMV $25. MB.**

TWICE SPICE 1967
Brown striped box holds 4 oz. Spicy After Shave Lotion & Spicy Talc for Men. **CMV $17. MB.**

FIRST EDITION SPICY 1965
Book type box holds 4 oz. Spicy After Shave Lotion & Spicy Talc for Men. **CMV $25. MB.**

SPORTS RALLY

CHRISTMAS WREATH 1965
Gold box holds two 4 oz. bottles of Spicy After Shave Lotion with tan caps. **CMV $20. MB.**

SPICY TREASURES 1968
Brown chest type box holds 4 oz. Spicy After Shave Lotion & 3 1/2 oz. Talc for Men. **CMV $17. MB.**

SPORTS RALLY BRACING LOTION 1966-68
4 oz. glass bottle with blue cap. **CMV $2 MB,**
BRACING TOWELETTE 1966-68
Blue & white box holds 12 packets. **CMV $1 MB.**
SPORTS RALLY SOAP ON A ROPE 1966-68
4 oz. soap on white rope. **CMV $15. MB.**
AEROSOL DEODORANT 1966-68
4 oz. red, white & blue can, white cap. **CMV $2. MB.**

SPORTS RALLY HAIR DRESS 1966-68
4 oz. red & white tube, red cap. **CMV $3. MB.**
SPORTS RALLY ALL PURPOSE TALC 1966-68
3 1/2 oz. blue & white cardboard container. **CMV $2. MB.**
SPORTS RALLY CLEAR SKIN SOAP 1966-68
2 bars with blue band around them. **CMV $4. ea. bar, $10. set.**
SPORTS RALLY CLEAR SKIN LOTION 1966-68
4 oz. white plastic bottle, red cap. **CMV $1. MB**

HOLIDAY SPICE 1965
Brown & white box holds Spicy Talc for Men & 4 oz. Spicy After Shave Lotion. **CMV $22.50 MB.**

SPICE 'O' LIFE SET 1966 ONLY
Box holds Spicy Talc for Men & 4 oz. After Shave Lotion. Came out at Fathers Day. **CMV $22.50 MB.**

TAI WINDS

TRIBUTE

TRIBUTE AFTER SHAVE SAMPLES 1963-68
Box holds 30 foil samples. **CMV $5. MB.**

TRIBUTE SOAP 1966-67
Blue & silver box holds 2 white bars with blue & silver centers. **CMV $20. MB.**
TRIBUTE SOAP 1963-66
Single bar in blue box. **CMV $25. MB.**

TRIBUTE COLOGNE FOR MEN 1964-66
4 oz. blue & silver top, cap & neck tag. **CMV $12. MB.**
TRIBUTE ALL PURPOSE COLOGNE 1967-68
4 oz. blue & silver top, cap & neck tag. **CMV $12. MB.** Later issues had no tags. **CMV $6. MB.**

TRIBUTE SHAVE SET 1964-65
Blue box holds 6 oz. After Shave Lotion & can of Foam Shave Cream. **CMV $35. MB.**

TAI WINDS COLOGNE 1971-79
5 oz. green glass, blue-green cap & yellow ribbon. **CMV $1. MB.**
SPRAY TALC 1971-76
7 oz. blue-green & yellow can. **CMV $1.**
AFTER SHAVE 1971-75
5 oz. clear glass, blue-green cap, yellow ribbon. **CMV $1.50. MB.**
SOAP ON A ROPE 1972-79
Yellow soap on rope. **CMV $5. MB.**

TRIBUTE AEROSOL DEODORANT 1963-67
3 oz. blue & silver can & cap. **CMV $6. MB,** 4 oz. size same can, 1967 only. **CMV $6. MB.**
TRIBUTE CREAM HAIR DRESS 1963-66
4 oz. blue & silver tube & cap. **CMV $8. MB.**
TRIBUTE FOAM SHAVE CREAM 1963-66
6 oz. blue & silver can & cap. Came in regular & mentholated. **CMV $6. MB.**

TAI WINDS GIFT SET 1971-72
5 oz. green glass bottle with green cap. Yellow bands, 5 oz. embossed soap. **CMV $15. MB.**

TRIBUTE AFTER SHAVE LOTION 1963-68
(Left) 6 oz. silver & blue cap. **CMV $6. mint.**
TRIBUTE AFTER SHAVE 1968-72
(Right) 4 oz. blue label, blue & silver cap. Same bottle also reads After Shave Lotion on label. **CMV $2.50 mint.**

TRIBUTE TALC 1963-66
4 oz. blue & silver can, blue cap. **CMV $6.**
mint.
**TRIBUTE AFTER SHAVE AFTER SHOWER
SPRAY 1963-66**
5 1/2 oz. blue & silver can & cap. **CMV $6.**
mint.

TRIBUTE GIFT SET NO. 2 1963-64
Blue & silver box holds 6 oz. Tribute After
Shave Lotion, Talc & Aerosol Deodorant.
CMV $35. MB.

**WILD COUNTRY SOAP ON A ROPE 1967-
76**
Ivory colored bar with bulls head in center.
Round. **CMV $5. MB.**
FOAM SHAVE CREAM 1970-73
11 oz. brown can. **CMV $1.**
SPRAY TALC 1969-77
7 oz. brown can. **CMV $2. With special
upside down label, CMV $5.**
AFTER SHAVE 1971-76
4 oz. silver label & black cap. **CMV $1.**
TALC 1971-74-78
3 1/2 oz. brown shaker top container.**CMV
50c.** Reissued in 1978.
COLOGNE
6 oz. bottle with silver cap & label. **CMV $2.
MB.**
ALL PURPOSE COLOGNE 1968-80
6 oz. silver cap & label. **CMV $1. MB.**
SOAP ON A ROPE 1976-78
Not shown, squared side, not round. **CMV
$4. MB.**

WILD COUNTRY

TRIBUTE SPRAY TALC 1969-72
7 oz. blue can. **CMV $1.** Upside down label,
rare. **CMV $10.**
TRIBUTE SHAMPOO 1964-66
Blue & silver tube. **CMV $5. MB.**
**TRIBUTE ELECTRIC PRE-SHAVE LOTION
1963-66**
4 oz. blue & silver cap. **CMV $8. MB, $5. BO.**

WILD COUNTRY PRODUCTS 1976-80
**All products for this design period 25c.
Soap $1. Belt Buckle $3.**

TRIBUTE GIFT SET NO. 1 1963-64
Blue & silver box holds Tribute Talc, Foam
Shave Cream & After Shave After Shower
Spray. **CMV $35. MB.**

WILD COUNTRY TRAVEL SET 1977
Box holds 1.5 oz. talc and 3 oz. after shave in
plastic bottle with brown cap. **CMV $5. MB.**
WILD COUNTRY GIFT SOAP 1977-78
Metal container holds 5 oz. bar of white Wild
Country soap. **CMV $5. MB.** Also came with
label printed upside down on bottom of can.
CMV $8.

WILD COUNTRY SADDLE KIT 1970-71
Brown & white cowhide kit holds Wild Country
6 oz. cologne, Foam Shave Cream & Spray
Talc. **CMV $12. MB.**

WILD COUNTRY HAND CREAM 1973-74
3 oz. brown & white plastic tube with brown
cap. **CMV $1.75.**
WILD COUNTRY DEODORANT 1975-77
4 oz. brown & white can, white cap. **CMV
75c. With upside down label, $8.**

WINDJAMMER

CANADIAN WINDJAMMER SOAP ON A ROPE 1973
CMV $12. MB.
WINDJAMMER SPRAY TALC 1968
7 oz. blue can. CMV $3. Also came in 4 oz. size. CMV $4. MB.

WINDJAMMER COLOGNE 1968-69
(Left) 5 oz. blue glass bottle & cap with ring. Painted label. CMV $8. MB.
WINDJAMMER COLOGNE 1969-72
(Right) 5 oz. blue glass & cap with blue paper label. CMV $3.50 MB.

COLOGNES - MISC.

All Colognes 1975 or newer have little value to collectors. If they are not pictured in this book, we suggest you do not collect them. No new colognes will be added to this book 1984 or newer.

REFRESHING COLOGNE 1940-41
4 oz. bottle with turquoise cap and label. Turquoise box. CMV $35. MB, $30. BO.

INHALANT COLOGNE 1936-40
4 oz. bottle with turquoise cap and label. Turquoise and white box. CMV $35. MB, $30. BO.

HEADACHE COLOGNE 1931-36
(LEFT) 4 oz. ribbed glass bottle with dark blue cap & silver label. CMV $50. BO, $60. MB.

WILD COUNTRY BODY POWDER 1967-68
6 oz. brown & white cardboard box. CMV $8. mint, $12. MB.
WILD COUNTRY COLOGNE SPRAY 1969-70
2-1/2 oz. white coated plastic bottle with silver cap. CMV $4. MB.

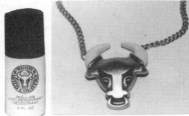

WILD COUNTRY ROLL ON DEODORANT 1978
2 oz. white & brown plastic bottle. CMV 50c.
WILD COUNTRY PENDANT 1978
Silver & ivory bull head. Neck chain for men. Avon on back. CMV $4. MB.

BE MY VALENTINE MINI COLOGNE 1984
His & Her's cologne in 2 separate 1/2 heart boxes, .5 oz. clear glass, red cap on hers, black on his, choice of Odyssey, Foxfire, Timeless, Candid, Ariane, Tasha, Pavi Elle & Soft Musk for her & Rugger Musk for Men, Black Suede, Wild Country for him. **CMV $2. each MB.**

GOLD CAP ROCKER COLOGNE 1967-68
1/2 oz. gold round cap. Came in Brocade, Regence, Unforgettable, Rapture, Occur!, Somewhere, Topaze, Cotillion, Here's My Heart, To A Wild Rose, Persian Wood and Wishing. **CMV $4. MB.**

FLAT TOP ROCKER COLOGNE 1959-62
1/2 oz. flat plastic cap. Came in Persian Wood, Here's My Heart, Cotillion, To A Wild Rose, Topaze, Somewhere, Regence, Bright Night and Nearness. **CMV $6. MB. Add $1. for Nearness and Bright Night.**

COLOGNE MINIATURE FOR MEN 1977-78
(Left) 1/2 oz. Came in Clint, Everest or Wild Country. Smoked glass, gray cap. **CMV $1. MB.**

CHRISTMAS CANDLE COLOGNE DECANTER 1977
(Center) 1 oz. green glass. Came in Charisma, Sweet Honesty, Topaze or Moonwind. **CMV $2. MB.**

FRAGRANCE FACETTES 1977
(Right) 1/2 oz. colognes. Came in Moonwind, Charisma, Topaze, Occur, Unforgettable, Here My Heart, Cotillion, Sweet Honesty, Sonnet or Bird of Paradise, with gold cap. **CMV $1. MB.**

BO MEANS BOTTLE ONLY MINT.
CMV MEANS CURRENT MARKET VALUE MINT.

BATH CLASSIC 1962-63
1 1/2 oz. clear glass with gold design & gold cap. Came in Bath Classic Set only. Came in Somewhere, Cotillion, Topaze, Here's My Heart, Persian Wood, & To A Wild Rose. **CMV $10. BO mint.**

POWDER BOX COLOGNE 1956
1/16 oz. Came in Beauty Dust only with ribbons attached. In Cotillion, Forever Spring, Golden Promise, To A Wild Rose & Quaintance. **CMV $11. BO, $13. mint with ribbon.**

DEMI COLOGNE 1973-75
1/2 oz. clear glass, gold cap. Came in Imperial Garden, Patchwork, Sonnet, Moonwind, RosesRoses, Field Flowers, Bird of paradise, Charisma, Unforgettable, Topaze, Occur!, Here's My Heart. **CMV $1. MB.**

FAN ROCKER 1962-63
1/2 oz. cologne, gold cap with neck cord. Came in To A Wild Rose, Here's My Heart, Persian Wood, Cotillion, Somewhere, Topaze. **CMV $6. MB. WITH CORD.**

COLOGNE 1975-77
2 oz. clear glass with gold cap. Name of cologne on side in gold. Came in Moonwind, Charisma, Topaze, Sonnet. **CMV 50c.**

DEMI-COLOGNE 1975-76
Pepper Mill Shape. 1/2 oz. clear glass with gold cap. Holds Sonnet, Moonwind, Charisma, Patchwork, Somewhere, Topaze, Occur!, Cotillion. **CMV $1. MB.**

FRAGRANCE COLOGNES 1956
(Left) 3 dram bottle with white painted label and cap. Came in Fragrance Rainbow set only in Nearness, Cotillion, Bright Night & To Wild Rose. **CMV $15. mint.**

BEAUTY DUST COLOGNE 1953-55
(Right) 5/8 dram bottle with no label & flat white or round white cap. Came in Beauty Dust at Christmas only. Each had a silk neck ribbon with gold edge. Quaintance, blue ribbon; To A Wild Rose, pink ribbon; Forever Spring, purple ribbon; Cotillion, pink ribbon; Nearness, pink ribbon; Elegante, red ribbon. **CMV with ribbon $12., $8. BO.**

DAZZLING PERFUME 1969-75
(Left) 1/8 oz. gold cap. Came in Unforget-table, Rapture, Occur!, Somewhere, Topaze, Cotillion, Here's My Heart, To A WIld Rose, Charisma, Brocade, Regence, Bird of Paradise, Elusive & Moonwind. **CMV $2. MB.**

MINUETTE COLOGNE 1969-70
(Center) 1/2 oz. gold cap. Elusive, Charisma, Brocade, Regence, Unforgettable, Rapture, Somewhere, Topaze, Occur!, Cotillion. **CMV $2. MB.**

FRAGRANCES FLING COLOGNE 1968-69
(Inside Right) 1/2 oz. gold cap. Came in Charisma, Brocade, Regence, Occur!, Unforgettable, Rapture, Somewhere, Topaze, Cotillion, Here's My Heart, To A WIld Rose, Wishing, Persian Wood. **CMV $4. MB.**

COLOGNE RIVIERA 1968
(Left) 4 oz. silver cap & silver on bottle. Unscrew bottom of bottle & reverse metal to make stand for bottle. Came in Brocade & Regence. **CMV $7. MB.**

COLOGNE CLASSIC 1967-68
(Center) 4 oz. spiral bottle with gold cap, came in Here's My Heart, To A Wild Rose, Somewhere, Topaze, Cotillion, Unforgettable, Rapture, Occur!. **CMV $5. MB.**

GIFT COLOGNE 1969
(Right) 4 oz. gold cap. Came in Topaze, To A Wild Rose, Somewhere, Here's My HEart, Cotillion & Rapture. **CMV $5. MB.**

COLOGNE PETITE 1976-79
(Left) 1/2 oz. Came in Charisma, Moonwind, Topaze, Here's My Heart, Unforgettable, Sweet Honesty, Cotillion, Occur!, Persian Wood, Regence, Rapture and Brocade. Gold cap. **CMV 50c. MB.**

ULTRA COLOGNE 1977-78
(Center and right) .33 oz. Came in Unspoken, Emprise, Ariane, Timeless, Candid. Came with silver or gold caps. **CMV 50c MB.**

1/2 OZ. COLOGNE 1953-55
(Left) 1/2 oz. size with white cap & painted label. Came in Cupids Bow, Fragrance Tie Ins, Fragrance Rainbow & Special Date Set only. Came in Forever Spring, Cotillion, Quaintance & To A WIld Rose, Bright Night. **CMV $10. each mint.**

REFRESHING HOURS COLOGNE 1962-63
(Right) 2 1/2 oz. gold cap, front side of bottle is flat, trimmed in gold. Came in Somewhere, Topaze, Cotillion, Here's My Heart, Persian Wood, To A Wild Rose Cologne. Came in Refreshing Hours Set only. **CMV $8. mint.**

COIN FAN BOTTLES 1958
1/2 oz. clear glass with turquoise caps. Box pink & gold. Came either cologne or lotion sachet, choice of To A WIld Rose, Cotillion, Nearness, Forever Spring, Bright Night, Elegante, Here's My Heart & Persian Wood. Came in Wishing Coin Set only. **CMV each, $8. MB.**

1/2 OZ. GEMS IN CRYSTAL COLOGNES 1957 ONLY
1/2 oz. bottle in 2 different shapes. Both came with pointed & flat top plastic caps. Each came in To A Wild Rose, Cotillion, Bright Night, Nearness. Each has matching tops and labels. All came in Gems in Crystal Set only. **CMV $15. flat top, $18. pointed cap.**

COLOGNE 1/2 OZ. 1977-78
.5 oz. Came in Field Flowers, Honeysuckle, Hawaiian White Ginger, Apple Blossom, Raining Violets, Roses Roses, Lily of the Valley. Different fragrances came with different colored caps. **CMV$1.50 MB.**

COLOGNE SILK 1966-70
3 oz. frosted glass bottle, gold cap, colored neck labels. Came in Here's My Heart, To A Wild Rose, Somewhere, Topaze, Cotillion, Unforgettable, Rapture, Occur!. **CMV $3. MB.**

BUD VASE COLOGNE 1968-69
4 oz. gold neck trim, colored paper label in Here's My Heart, To A Wild Rose, Somewhere, Topaze, Cotillion, Unforgettable, Rapture, Occur!. **CMV $3. MB.**

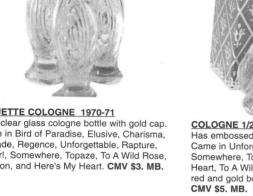

MINUETTE COLOGNE 1970-71
5 oz. clear glass cologne bottle with gold cap. Came in Bird of Paradise, Elusive, Charisma, Brocade, Regence, Unforgettable, Rapture, Occur!, Somewhere, Topaze, To A Wild Rose, Cotillion, and Here's My Heart. **CMV $3. MB.**

COLOGNE 1/2 OZ. 1966
Has embossed leaves in glass, gold cap. Came in Unforgettable, Rapture, Occur!, Somewhere, Topaze, Cotillion, Here's My Heart, To A Wild Rose or Wishing. Came in red and gold box in Renaissance Trio only. **CMV $5. MB.**

ANNIVERSARY COLOGNE PETITE 1979
(Left) .5 oz. clear glass, gold cap, special box. Comes in Regence, Persian Wood, Rapture or Brocade. **CMV $1. MB.**
COLOGNE CLASSIQUE 1979-80
(Center) .5 oz. clear glass, gold cap. Comes 11 fragrances. **CMV $1. MB.**
PURSE CONCENTRE 1979-80
(Right) .33 oz. octagonal shaped bottle. Different color stripe on cap for 9 different fragrances. **CMV $1. MB.**

CLASSIC FRAGRANCE NOTE 1983
.5 oz. clear glass, black cap. Cologne in choice of Moonwind, Charisma, Topaze, Occur!, Sweet Honesty, Wild Jasmine, Willow, Tea Garden or Amber Mist. **CMV $1. MB.**

SILKEN SCENTS COLOGNE 1980-82
1.7 oz. clear glass. Sold with Silken Scents Scarf Set. **CMV $1. MB.**

ULTRA FRAGRANCE JEWELS 1982
(Left) .33 oz. clear glass jewel shaped bottle, gold cap. **CMV $1. MB.**
VINTAGE FRAGRANCE COLLECTION COLOGNE 1982
(Center) Pineapple shaped bottle, gold cap. Red & green box. Choice of .5 oz. cologne in Cotillion, Here's My Heart, Regence, Persian Wood, Brocade or Rapture. **CMV $1. MB.**
COUNTRY CHRISTMAS COLOGNE 1982
(Right) .33 oz. clear glass. Choice of Foxfire, Odyssey, Timeless, Tasha, Candid, Ariane. In Christmas box, came in set only. **CMV $1.MB.**

ULTRA COLOGNE .33 OZ. 1978-79
.33 oz. clear glass. Came in gold & silver caps in Timeless, Ariane, Tempo, Candid, Emprise, Unspoken. Each comes with different color bands on caps & different boxes. **CMV $1. MB.**

1/2 OZ. HEART SHAPED COLOGNE 1964-66
Left is gold band on plastic cap. Came in Unforgettable, Rapture, Occur!, Cotillion, Somewhere, Topaze, Here's My Heart, Persian Wood, To A WIld Rose, and Wishing.**CMV $5. MB.**
HEART SHAPED EAU DE COLOGNE (Foreign)
(Right) No gold band around plastic cap. **CMV $8. MB.**

CRYSTAL DROP COLOGNE 1980
(Left) Red Xmas box, .5 oz. clear glass, gold top. Choice of Moonwind, Charisma, Topaze, Occur!, Sweet Honesty, Zany, Sportif or Country Breeze. **CMV $1. MB.**
ULTRA COLOGNE .33 OZ. 1980-81
(Right) .33 oz. clear glass, gold or silver caps. Choice of Tempo, Candid, Timeless, Ariane, Emprise, Unspoken, Tasha & Foxfire. **CMV $1. MB.**

SNOW FLAKE COLOGNE 1957-58
1/8 oz. round white caps. Came in Beauty Dust only in Cotillion, Forever Spring, To A Wild Rose, Nearness, Elegante, & Bright Night. No labels on bottles. **CMV $9. each.** Flat top bottle came in all Beauty Dust at Christmas 1963. **CMV $8. each.**

FRAGRANCE FACETS 1973
.5 oz. gold cap. Came in Brocade & all fragrances. **CMV $2. MB.**

COLOGNE GEMS 1966-69
1 oz. clear glass with flat plastic top. Came in Cotillion, Rapture, Unforgettable, Somewhere, Occur!, Topaze, Here's My Heart & To A Wild Rose. **CMV $4. MB.**

COLOGNE STICK 1952-56
Turquoise plastic cologne stick came in Golden Promise, Cotillion, Quaintance, Forever Spring & To A Wild Rose. 1956 only Nearness & Bright Night came in white plastic of same design. **CMV each $10.**

COLOGNE & COLOGNE MIST SPECIAL ISSUE BOXES
Each was sold with choice of fragrance on a short selling period.
COLOGNE 1968
(Left) **CMV $2. box.**
COLOGNE 1969
(Inside Left) **CMV $2. box.**
COLOGNE MIST 1974
(Inside Right) **CMV $1. box.**
COLOGNE MIST 1971
(Right) **CMV $1. box.**

Continued on next page

ULTRA SHIMMER COLOGNE DECANTER 1981
(Left) .75 oz. octagonal shape clear glass, gold cap. Choice of Timeless, Foxfire, Tasha, Odyssey. In gold box dated 1981. **CMV $1. MB.**
CLASSIC MINIATURE COLOGNE 1981-82
(Inside Left) Small .33 oz. clear glass, gold cap. Choice of Tasha, Foxfire, Odyssey, Candid, Timeless, Unspoken, Ariane, Emprise. In gold box dates 1981. **CMV $1. MB.**
FLUTED PETITE COLOGNE 1981-82
(Inside Right) .5 oz. clear glass, gold cap, 4" tall. Choice of Moonwind, Topaze, Charisma, Occur!, Sweet Honesty, Zany or Country Breeze. **CMV $1. MB.**
CHRISTMAS CHARMER COLOGNE 1981
(Right) .33 oz. clear glass, red cap. Came with Country Charmer Candlestick. Zany or Charisma. **CMV $1. BO.**

COLOGNE STICK 1956-58
White plastic with colored caps. Came in Nearness, Bright Night, Cotillion, Quaintance, To A Wild Rose, Forever Spring, Came in blue, white & gold pape ornament at Christmas only. **CMV in ornament $20., stick only $6.**

COLOGNE STICK 1956-58
White plastic with colored cap. Gold, white & red paper ornament package. Christmas only in 1957-58. Came in Nearness, Elegante, Bright Night, To A Wild Rose, Forever Spring, Cotillion. **CMV stick only $6., MB $20.**

COLOGNE STICKS CHRISTMAS PACKAGING 1953-54
(Left) Green & red on white cardboard, pink ribbon on top. **CMV $20. MB.**
COLOGNE STICK CHRISTMAS PACKAGING 1952 ONLY
(Right) Red & white candy striped cardboard, red ribbon top. **CMV $20. MB.**

CRYSTAL GLORY 1962-64
(Left) Does not say Spray Essence on cap. Plastic gold top & base. 1 oz. refillable bottle. Came in Topaze, Somewhere, Cotillion, Here's My Heart, Persian Wood, To A Wild Rose. **CMV $6. MB.**

CRYSTAL GLORY SPRAY ESSENCE 1962-64
Gold top & base. Same fragrances as above. **CMV$6. MB.**

SILVER TOP CRYSTAL GLORY SPRAY ESSENCE 1962
Metal on top & base is silver instead of gold. Rare. Same fragrances as above. **CMV $20.MB.**

CRYSTAL GLORY REFILL 1962-64
(Right) 1 oz. spray bottle fits inside Crystal Glory bottle. Came in all fragrances above. **CMV $3. MB.**

SPRAY ESSENCE 1959-66
(Left) 1 oz. black plastic coated, gold & blue lid. Came in Cotillion, To A Wild Rose, Bright Night, Nearness, Persian Wood, Here's My Heart, Somewhere 1962-66. Rapture, Occur! 1965-66. **CMV $5. MB.**

ESSENCE DE FLEURS 1957-59
(Right) 1 oz. black plastic coated, gold & blue lid. Came in Nearness, Elegante, To A Wild Rose, Cotillion, Bright Night & Forever Spring. **CMV $7. MB.**

CHRISTMAS BOX 1965
Special issue box used by Avon at Xmas 1965 for several different products. **Add $4. to value of product for this short issue box.**

COLOGNE MIST 1969-70
(Left) 2 oz. gold cap, frosted glass. Came in Charisma, Brocade, Elusive & Regence. **CMV $1. MB.**

SPRAY ESSENCE 1969-71
(Right) 1 1/4 oz. gold cap, ribbed glass. Came in Charisma, Brocade, Regence.**CMV $1. MB.**

COLOGNE MIST 1968-72
(Left) 2 oz. gold cap, gold & white band. Came in Here's My Heart, Topaze, To A Wild Rose, Somewhere, Cotillion, Occur!, Roses Roses & Unforgettable. **CMV $1. MB.**

COLOGNE MIST 1963-66
(Right) Embossed bottles with gold plastic caps, came with black & gold paper label and green & gold cloth type label and green & white paper label. Held 2 oz. of Occur!, Somewhere, Topaze, Cotillion, Persian Wood, Here's My Heart & To A WIld Rose.**CMV $3. each MB.**

COLOGNE MIST 1966-68
(Left) 2 oz. gold cap with 4A design on cap. Came in Here's My Heart, To A Wild Rose, Somewhere, Topaze, Cotillion, Unforgettable, Rapture, Occur!. **CMV $1. BO, $2. MB each.**

SPRAY ESSENCE 1966-67
(Right) 1 1/4 oz. palstic coated glass with gold cap. Came in Here's My Heart, To A Wild Rose, Wishing, Somewhere, Topaze, Cotillion, Rapture, Unforgettable, Occur! **CMV$2. MB.**

COLOGNE MIST SPECIAL ISSUE BOXES
(Left) Each came in choice of fragrance & was sold for a short period.

COLOGNE MIST 1975
(Left)

COLOGNE MIST 1975
(Inside Left)

COLOGNE MIST 1976
(Inside Right)

ULTRA COLOGNE SPRAY 1978
(Right)
Add $2. to CMV of each bottle for each box shown.

SPRAY ESSENCE 1967-70
1 1/4 oz. All had gold caps. Eight different fragrances with 8 different colored bands around neck. Unforgettable, Rapture, Occur!. Somewhere, Topaze, Cotillion. Here's My Heart, To A WIld Rose. **CMV $4. MB.**

CREAM SACHETS - MISC.

Cream sachets 1975 or newer have been dropped from this book & no new ones will be added due to little collector interest.

PURSE SPRAY ESSENCE 1970-76
(Left) 1/4 oz. glass bottle with gold cap in Elusive, Charisma, Brocade, Regence, Unforgettable, Rapture, Occur!, Somewhere, Topaze, Cotillion, Bird of Paradise & Hana Gasa. **CMV $1. MB.**

COLOGNE MIST 1971-75
(Right) 2 oz. silver top. Came in Bird of Paradise, Hana Gasa, Elusive, Charisma, Brocade & Regence. **CMV $1. MB.**

CREAM SACHET BOXES
Special short issue boxes came with cream sachets in several fragrances. Left to Right: 1956,1964,1958,1954. **CMV see bottle in each fragrance line & add $5. each for these boxes.**

CREAM SACHET CHRISTMAS BOX 1957
Special issue at Christmas. Pink & white, came in choice of Cotillion, Forever Spring, Bright Night, To A Wild Rose, Elegante cream sachet. See bottle in each fragrance line and **add $6. for this box.**

DECORATOR COLOGNE MIST 1972
4 oz. plastic coated bottle in color to match fragrance. Long gold cap with top matching fragrance color. Came in Moonwind (deep blue), Charisma (crimson red), Bird of Paradise (pale blue) & Field Flowers (spring green). **CMV $3. MB.**

CREAM SACHET JARS 1973-75
Clear ribbed glass jar with colored border on lid & colored flower to match fragrance. .66 oz. came in Gardenia, Violet, & Carnation. **CMV $1 each.**

CREAM SACHET DECOR 1960
Ribbed clear plastic with removable bottom sold for 50c at Xmas with purchase of cream sachet in Bright Night, Nearness, Cotillion, To A Wild Rose, Persian, Wood & Here's My Heart. **CMV $8. holder only, $12. MB.**

CREAM SACHET 1957
(Left) White jar with green, yellow or pink lid. Came in Cotillion, To A Wild Rose, Bright Night & Nearness. Came in Rainbow Set. **CMV $8.**

CREAM SACHET PETITES 1956
(Right) Plastic cream sachet came in Cotillion, Bright Night, Nearness, To A Wild Rose. Came in Cream Sachet Petites Sets only. 4 different colors. **CMV $10. each MB.**

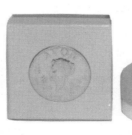

MAGNOLIA CREAM SACHET 1974-76
(Left) .66oz. clear embossed glass with white lid and pink & yellow on flower. **CMV $1. MB.**

MAGNOLIA DEMI STICK 1974-77
(Inside Left) .19 oz. white with floral colored center. **CMV $1. MB.**

HYACINTH DEMI STICK 1974-77
(Right) .19 oz. white with pink flowers.**CMV $1. MB.**

CREAM SACHET CHRISTMAS BOX 1958
Special issue box came with choice of cream sachet in To A Wild Rose, Cotillion, Forever Spring, Nearness, Bright Night, Elegante. **CMV See jar in each fragrance line and add $5. for this box.**

CREAM SACHET 1958
.3 oz. white glass jar. Turquoise flower lid. Came in 1958 Wishing Trio set., Pink & gold box. **CMV $10. MB**

SENTIMENTS CREAM SACHET 1969
1/2 oz. clear glass jar, gold lid, 4A design on lid. Came in Scentiments Set only in Unforgettable, Rapture, Occur!, Somewhere, Topaze or Cotillion. **CMV $4. BO.**

POWDER SACHETS, - MISC

POWDER SACHET 1939-48
1 1/4 oz. glass bottle with turquoise cap & label. Came in Jardin D'Amour 1939-40, Ariel 1939-42, Cotillion 1939-46, Garden of Love, turquoise or black cap 1940-46, Attention 1942-48, Marionette 1939-46 **CMV $10 each BO. $15. MB**

TURN-OF-CENTURY POWDER SACHET SHAKER 1973-75
(left) 1.25oz. clear glass with solid gold cap. Came in Roses Roses, Charisma, Unforgettable. **CMV $5. MB.**
POWDER SACHET SHAKER 1972-73
(right) 3 1/2" high, 1.25 oz. white glass jar with gold cap. Came in Moonwild, Bird of Paradise, Unforgettable, Field Flowers. **CMV $5. MB.**

POWDER SACHET 1969-70
(Left) 1 1/2 oz. Painted red over clear glass, red neck bow with silver lid. Comes in Cotillion, Charisma, Unforgettable & To A Wild Rose. **CMV $7. MB**
POWDER SACHET 1970-71
(Right) Crystal-like glass bottle holds 1 1/4 oz. of powder sachet in Elusive, Charisma, Unforgettable, & Topaze. **CMV $6. MB.**

POWDER SACHET 1936-38
1 1/4 or 2 oz. ribbed glass with turquoise cap & label. Came in Ariel 1936-38, Cotillion 1937-38, Marionette 1938 only, Jardin D'Amour 1936-38 or Jardin Sachet. All prices are mint only. **CMV $20. each BO. $25. MB**

POWDER SACHET 1944-45
1 1/4 oz. pink paper sachet boxes. Came in Attention, Garden of Love, Cotillion, Marionette. Pink plastic flower on lid. **CMV $15. each - $22. MB**

POWDER SACHET 1930-32
(left) Clear glass bottle with brass cap & silver & blue label. Came in Ariel and Jardin D'Amour. **CMV $60. mint.**

POWDER SACHET 1934-36
(right) 1 1/4 oz. ribbed glass bottle with dark blue cap & silver & blue label. Came in Jardin D'Amour & Ariel. **CMV $28. each mint - $33. MB**

CROWN TOP POWDER SACHET 1965-66
.9 oz. frosted bottle with gold cap. Came in Perfume Pillowette Set in Rapture, Wishing, Occur, Lavender, Somewhere, Topaze, Cotillion, Here's My Heart, To A Wild Rose. **CMV $8. MB**

POWDER SACHET CHRISTMAS BOX 1952 only
Special issue red & green box for all powder sachets at Christmas. Came in Cotillion, Golden Promise, Quaintance & Flowertime. **CMV See bottle in each fragrance line & add $7. for this box.**

POWDER SACHET CHRISTMAS BOX 1963
(Left) Short issue box came in 6 fragrances at Christmas. **Add $5. to CMV of bottle for this box.**

POWDER SACHET CHRISTMAS BOX 1965
(Right(High top boot design box was short issue. Came in 8 fragrances. **Add $5. to CMV of bottle for this box.**

POWDER SACHET CHRISTMAS BOX 1958
Special issue pink & white box came with powder sachet in choice of To A Wild Rose, Cotillion, Forever Spring, Nearness, Bright Night, Elegante. **See jars in each fragrance line for CMV & add $5. for this box.**

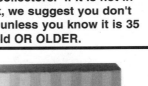

POWDER SACHET CHRISTMAS BOX 1956
Special issue Christmas box came with choice of 6 fragrances. **Add $5. to CMV of bottle for this box.**

PERFUMED TALC CHRISTMAS BOX 1958
Special issue Christmas box for perfumed talc in choice of To A Wild Rose, Cotillion, Nearness & Forever Spring. **Check fragrance line for MB CMV on talc & add $7. for this box.**

PERFUMED TALC SPECIAL ISSUE CHRISTMAS BOXES
(Left to Right) 1966 Christmas, 1967 Christmas, 1969 Christmas, 1970 Christmas. Each came in choice of talc. **Add $2. each box to CMV of the talc it holds, MB.**

VALENTINE GIFT SACHET 1952
Short issue box in red & white. Came in Flowertime, Golden Promise, Cotillion & Quaintance. Cotillion came in same design, different shaped box. **Add $8. CMV to price of each bottle for this box.**

PERFUMED TALCS - MISC.

All Talcs 1960 or newer have little value to collectors. If it is not in this book, we suggest you don't collect it unless you know it is 35 YEARS old OR OLDER.

PERFUMED TALC CHRISTMAS BOX 1959
Short issue box in choice of 6 fragrances of talcs. **Add $7. CMV for this box to price of talc, MB.**

FLORAL PERFUMED TALC 1959-60
Lavender & white can. Matching box. **CMV $7. MB.**

POWDER SACHET CHRISTMAS BOX 1957
Pyramid shaped box in pink, green, blue & white. Came in To A Wild Rose, Forever Spring, Cotillion, Nearness, Bright Night & Elegante powder sachet. **Short issue - RARE.** See bottle in each fragrance line & **add $8. for this box mint.**

TOILET WATERS - MISC.

TOILET WATER 1940 ONLY
(Left) 2 oz. plastic caps, blue & gold label with tulip. Came in Cotillion, Vernafleur, Lily of the Valley, White Rose, Lilac, Trailing Arbutus, Marionette, Lilac Vegetal. **CMV $35. BO mint, $45. MB.**

TOILET WATER 1940-46
(Center) 2 oz. gold ribbed cap & gold label. Also came with plastic caps. Came in Cotillion, Jasmine, Marionette, Lilac, Lily of the Valley, Trailing Arbutus, Apple Blossom, Sonnet & Attention. **CMV $30. BO mint, $40. MB.**

TOILET WATER 1935-40
(Right) 2 oz. gold cap with A on top of cap. Blue & gold tulip label. CPC on back of label. Came in same as 1st toilet water on left. **CMV $35. BO mint, $45. MB.**

TOILET WATER 1933-34
2 oz. ribbed bottle came in Trailing Arbutus, Vernafleur, Lily of the Valley, White Rose, Lilac Vegetal. Black or blue cap. **CMV $50. BO mint, $60. MB.**

PERFUMES - MISC.

1/4 OZ. TULIP PERFUME 1934-39
Glass stopper, gold label with tulip. Came in Lucy Hays, Topaze, Jardin D'Amour, Bolero, Cotillion, Ariel, Narcissus, Rose, Lily of the Valley, Trailing Arbutus, Gardenia, Sweet Pea, Marionette, Courtship. **CMV $75. BO, $90. MB.**

GIFT ATOMIZER PERFUME 1931-34
1 oz. red glass bottle with screw on metal top & white squeeze bulb. Came in Atomizer Set No. 6 only. Does not say Avon or CPC. Also comes in green glass. **CMV $85.**

7 DRAM TULIP PERFUME 1934-39
Glass stoppered bottle, gold label with tulip. Came in Jardin D'Amour, Bolero, Cotillion, Ariel, Narcissus, Rose, Lily of the Valley, Trailing Arbutus, Gardenia, Sweet Pea, Marionette, Topaze, Courtship, Lucy Hays. **CMV $125. MB, $100. BO.**

7 DRAM TULIP PERFUME 1934-39
Glass stopper, gold label with tulip. Came in Lucy Hays, Topaze, Jardin D'Amour, Bolero, Cotillion, Ariel, Narcissus, Rose, Lily of the Valley, Trailing Arbutus, Gardenia, Sweet Pea, Marionette, Courtship. **CMV $125. MB, $100. mint.**

1/8 OZ. PERFUME OR 1 DRAM 1946-50
Gold box, gold label. Some have metal gold caps. Came in Crimson Carnation, Lily of the Valley, Gardenia, Cotillion, Golden Promise, Garden of Love, Ballad, Quaintance, Flowertime. **CMV $20., Crimson Carnation $30. Add $7. each MB.** Also came in Gold Box set of 1947-49.

1/8 OZ. PERFUME 1940-42
(Left) 1 dram or 1/8 oz. gold cap & label. Came in Cotillion, ballad, Gardenia, Garden of Love, Apple Blossom, Marionette, Trailing Arbutus, Lily of the Valley, Sweet Pea. **CMV $25. BO mint, $35. MB.**

1/8 OZ. PERFUME 1940-44
(Right) Gold metal or plastic caps & gold label. Came in Garden of Love, Gardenia, Marionette, Sweet Pea, Lily of the Valley, Trailing Arbutus, Ballad, Courtship, Apple Blossom, Cotillion. **CMV $25. BO mint, $30. MB**

RIBBED PERFUME 1933-36
(Left) 1/2 oz. ribbed glass bottle with black octagonal cap & gold label. Came in Gold Box set in Bolero, 391, Gardenia, Ariel, Vernafleur. **CMV $45. mint.**

PERFUMES 1933-36
(Right) Small six sided bottles with silver label & black caps. Came in Ariel, Bolero, Gardenia, Trailing Arbutus, 391, Vernafleur. Came in Little Folks set & Handkerchief set. **CMV $45. mint.**

FLORAL PERFUMES 1944-45
3 dram gold cap & labels. Came in yellow feather design box in Ttrailing Arbutus, Cotillion, Gardenia, Sweet Pea, Lily of the Valley, Marionette. 2 different boxes. **CMV $60. BO mint with tag, $90. MB.**

2 DRAM TULIP PERFUME 1934-39
1/4 oz. or 2 drams, gold cap & label with tulip. CPC on back of label & Avon on bottom of bottle. Came with 2 different labels as shown. Came in Jardin D'Amour, Bolero, Cotillion, Ariel, Narcissus, Rose, Lily of the Valley, Trailing Arbutus, Gardenia, Sweet Pea, Marionette, Courtship, Lucy Hays, Topaze. **CMV $65. MB, $55. BO mint.**

VALENTINE'S DAY PERFUME 1941
1/8 oz. clear glass bottle with gold cap with Ballad perfume. Box red & white. Came in several fragrances. **CMV $75. MB.**

BOUQUET PERFUMES 1940-44
3 dram, glass stopper, box is gold base & orange lid. Came in Garden of Love, Apple Blossom, Marionette, Courtship, Cotillion. Gold neck tag. **CMV $100. BO mint, $135. MB.**

PERFUME 1946-50
(Left) 1/8 oz. clear glass, gold cap, painted label. Available in Crimson Carnation, Lily of the Valley, Gardenia, Cotillion, Golden Promise, Garden of Love, Ballad, Quaintance, Flowertime. **CMV $20. BO, $25. MB.**
5/8 DRAM PERFUME 1954 ONLY
(Right) Came in 1954 House of Charms set only. Blue caps, pink, blue & white label. Came in Cotillion, Quaintance, To A Wild Rose, Golden Promise, Lily of the Valley. Rare. **CMV $22. each.**

PERFUME 1937-46
1/8 oz. bottle on right has flower on label with 3 branches on each side. Came in sets only in Gardenia, Cotillion, Narcissus, Trailing Arbutus, Sweet Pea. **CMV $15. each.** White, blue, red, green or yellow plastic caps. 2 dram size or 1/4 oz. on left came in 1939-40 Gold Box sets & Little Folks sets in same fragrances and caps. **CMV $25. each.**

FLORAL PERFUIMES 1946-47
Blue & white box holds 3 dram bottle with plastic cap. Came in Crimson Carnation, Gardenia, Lily of the Valley. **CMV $75. MB, $50. BO. Crimson Carnation, CMV $100. MB, $60. BO.**

BO MEANS BOTTLE ONLY MINT IN NEW CONDITION. **CMV** MEANS CURRENT MARKET VALUE IN NEW CONDITION. **AS AVON BOXES GET (30 TO 40 YEARS) OLDER OR MORE, THEY BECOME MORE VALUABLE. MINT-BOXES ARE VERY IMPORTANT.**

ONE DRAM GIFT PERFUME 1958
1 oz. smooth clear glass bottle, cap either smooth or embossed. Box is blue, white & gold. Choice of Elegante, Nearness, Bright night, Forever Spring, To A Wild Rose or Cotillion. **CMV $20. MB as shown, $5. BO.**

1/8 OZ. PERFUME 1946-53
(Left) Flower on label, plastic cap. Came in Trailing Arbutus, Cotillion, Crimson Carnation, Quaintance, Lily of the Valley, Sweet Pea. Came in Fair Lady, Your Charms & Hair Ribbons sets. **CMV each $15. Crimson Carnation & Sweet Pea, CMV $25. mint.** Same label came out on 5/8 dram size "smaller bottle" but has no size on label. **Same CMV.**

1/8 OZ. PERFUMES 1941-45
(Right) 1/8 oz. 2 different flat gold caps & also plastic caps. White paper label. Came in Courtship, Sweet Pea, Lily of the Valley, Trailing Arbutus, Marionette, American Ideal, Apple Blossom, Cotillion, Ballad, Gardenia, Garden of Love. **CMV $30. mint BO, $40. MB.**

FLORAL PEFUME 1940-42
3/8 oz. gold cap & label in gold speckled box. Came in Sweet pea, Gardenia, Trailing Arbutus, Lily of the Valley. **CMV $50. BO mint, $80. MB.**

PERFUMES 1950
5/8 dram each. Quaintance, Cotillion, Golden Promise, Luscious. Green, blue, pink & yellow caps. Came in Avon Blossoms set. **CMV $12. each mint.**

PERFUMES FOR SIZE COMPARISON ONLY
(Left to Right) 2 dram or 1/4 oz., 1/8 oz. or 1 dram, 5/8 dram, 5/8 dram.

PERFUMES 5/8 DRAM 1951-53
Bottle with pink, yellow, green or blue caps came in Cotillion, Quaintance, Forever Spring, Golden Promise, Luscious, Lily of the Valley. Came in 1952-53 House of Charm, 1951 Always Sweet Set & Sweet As Honey Beehive Set. **CMV $12. each, mint.**

1/8 OZ. PERFUME 1946 ONLY
(Left) 1/8 oz. plastic cap. Came in Gardenia, Cotillion, Garden of Love, Lily of the Valley, Trailing Arbutus, Sweet Pea. **CMV $25. BO, $30. MB each mint.**

1/8 OZ. PERFUME 1941-46
(Right) 1/8 oz. size, white paper label, gold metal caps & plastic caps. Came in Gardenia, Sweet Pea, Courtship, Apple Blossom, Cotillion, Trailing Arbutus, Lily of the Valley, Garden of Love, Marionette. **CMV $25. BO, $30. MB.**

391 PERFUME 1931-33
(Left) Silver & blue box holds 1 oz. glass stopper. Blue ribbon on neck. **CMV $125. BO, $150. MB.**

391 PERFUME FLACONETTE 1931-33
(Center) Small embossed bottle with glass stopper with long dabber. Brass cap with 391 on it. **CMV $85. BO, $95. MB.**

391 PERFUME 1933-36
(Right) 1/2 oz. ribbed glass bottle with black octagonal cap. Came in Gold Box set. **CMV $45. mint.**

BOUQUET PERFUMES 1945-47
Blue, pink & white box holds 3 dram glass stoppered bottle with gold neck tag. Came in Cotillion, Courtship, Garden of Love. **CMV $125. MB, $100. BO.**

1 OZ. HEART PERFUME 1963-71
Gold box, 4A insignia on glass stopper. Gold neck tag. Came in Unforgettable & Occur!, Somewhere, Topaze, Cotillion, Here's My Heart, Persian Wood, Rapture, To A Wild Rose. **CMV $25. BO, $45. MB.**

PERFUMES "1 DRAM" 1955-59
Clear smooth glass, gold scroll cap with felt like wrapper. Nearness, gray; Bright Night, black; Elegante, maroon; To A Wild Rose, pink; Forever Spring, green; Cotillion, gold. Simulated grain leather, Luscious, 1st issue 1950 tan; Here's My Heart, blue. **CMV $10. each in wrapper mint, $5. BO, $12. MB.**

BOUQUET PERFUMES 1944 ONLY
Blue & pink box holds 3 dram perfume, glass stopper. Came in Marionette, Cotillion, Garden of Love. Gold neck tags. **CMV $140. MB, $100. BO with tag.**

ROCKER PERFUME 1959-63
White box holds 1 oz. bottle with flat glass stopper with 4A on top. Gold cord criscrossed bottle with white tag label. Came in Here's My Heart, Persian Wood, To A Wild Rose, Bright Night, Nearness, Cotillion. **CMV BO with tag $25.MINT, $35. MB.**

PERFUME 1953-54
Green and pink fold out box holds 1 dram ribbed glass bottle with gold scroll cap. Came in To A Wild Rose, Cotillion, Forever Spring, Quaintance, Golden Promise, Luscious, Ballad. **CMV $25. MB as shown.**

CHRISTMAS PERFUME 1955
1 dram, gold cap in red, white, blue and gold Christmas box. Came in To A Wild Rose, Cotillion, Forever Spring, Golden Promise, Luscious and Quaintance. **CMV $25. MB.**

VALENTINE PERFUMES 1953
1 dram perfume came in To A Wild Rose, Forever Spring. Cotillion, Golden Promise, Quaintance. **CMV $25. MB as shown.**

PERFUMES "1 DRAM" 1950-55
Ribbed bottles with gold caps came in Cotillion, Quaintance, Ballad, Golden Promise, Gardenia, Lily of the Valley, Forever Spring and To A Wild Rose. **CMV $12. MB, $8. BO.**

WITH LOVE PERFUMES 1951-52
(Left) Pink heart box opens to 1 dram ribbed bottle and cap in Lily of the Valley, To A Wild Rose, Luscious, Quaintance, Golden Promise, Cotillion, Ballad, Flowertime, Gardenia. **CMV $25. MB as shown.**
CHRISTMAS BELL PERFUME 1951
(Right) Gold bell box holds 1 dram, ribbed bottle and cap in Forever Spring, To A Wild Rose, Luscious, Cotillion, Flowertime, Quaintance, Golden Promise, Ballad, Gardenia and Lily of the Valley. **CMV $25. MB as shown.**

PERFUME CREME ROLLETTE 1963-65
4A embossed bottles with gold caps. Came in Here's My Heart, Persian Wood, To A Wild Rose, Cotillion, Somewhere, Topaze and Wishing, Occur! and Rapture. **CMV $3. MB.**

PERFUME HALF OUNCE 1971
1/2 oz. bottle with clear plastic top in a pink and gold box. Came in Somewhere, Topaze, Cotillion, Unforgettable, Rapture, Occur!, Regence, Brocade, Charisma, Elusive. **CMV $16. MB.**

PERFUME FLACON 1966-67
(Left) 1 dram, gold ribbed cap, ribbed glass. Came in Here's My Heart, Wishing, To A Wild Rose, Somewhere, Topaze, Cotillion, Unforgettable, Regence, Rapture, Occur!. **CMV $4. MB.**

TOP STYLE PERFUME 1959-62
(Right) Shown with general issue box. 1 dram size, gold cap. Came in Topaze, Persian Wood, Here's My Heart, To A Wild Rose, Cotillion, Bright Night and Nearness. **CMV $5. MB.**

ONE DRAM PERFUME GOLD BOX 1964-65
(Center) 4A embossed gold box. Ribbed bottle, gold cap. Came in Somewhere, Topaze, Cotillion, Here's My Heart, Persian Wood, Occur!, To A Wild Rose, Wishing, Rapture and Unforgettable. On left, same bottle sold in regular issue box. 1962-66. **CMV $6. MB in gold box.** 1965 Christmas special issue box on right. **CMV $8. MB, CMV regular issue box $3. MB.**

GOLDEN GIFT PERFUME 1961
Blue, gold and green box holds 1 dram top style perfume. Came in Cotillion, To A Wild Rose, Nearness, Bright Night, Somewhere, Here's My Heart, Persian Wood, Topaze. **CMV $13. MB.**

1/2 OZ. PERFUME 1969-72
(Left) Pink box holds jewel like clear glass bottle 4" high. Comes in Elusive, Charisma, Brocade, Regence, Unforgettable, Rapture, Occur!, Somewhere, Topaze, Cotillion. **CMV $13. MB.**

PERFUME 1966-69
(Right) 1/2 oz. gold cap, metal leaves around base. White and gold box. Came in Unforgettable, Rapture, Occur!, Somewhere, Topaze, Cotillion, Here's My Heart, To A Wild Rose, Wishing. **CMV $18. MB.**

TOP STYLE CHRISTMAS PERFUME 1959-60
Sold only at Christmas time in box shown. Came in all regular fragrances of Top Style perfume. **CMV $17. MB in this box only.**

PERFUME ROLLETTES 1965-69
.33 oz. glass bottles available in Somewhere, Topaze, Cotillion, Here's My Heart, To A Wild Rose, Wishing, Regence, Occur!, Rapture, Unforgettable, Brocade and Persian Wood. Issued in carnival glass or clear ribbed glass. **CMV clear, $2. MB. CMV carnival $6. MB. Box pictured is 1966 Christmas box. Add $2. extra for this box.**

PERFUME "1 DRAM" 1951-53
Vertical ribbed bottle and ribbed gold cap with scroll on cap. Came in Cotillion, Golden Promise, Qauintance, To A Wild Rose, Forever Spring. **CMV $8. MB.**

PERFUME OILS

PERFUME OIL PETITES (PIN CUSHION) 1966
5/8 dram, clear bottle, gold cap and label. Came in Pin Cushion Set only. Came in Somewhere, Wishing, Occur!, Rapture, Topaze, To A Wild Rose, Here's My Heart, Unforgettable, Cotillion. **CMV $5. each mint.**

PERFUME PENDANT 1972-75
Gold with 2 simulated half pearls, 32" chain. Came in Sonnet or Moonwind perfume. **CMV $10. MB, Pendant only $5.**

PERFUME OIL 1969-73
(Left) 1/2 oz. gold caps. Came in Elusive, Rapture, Hana Gasa, Charisma, Brocade, Moonwind, Regence, and Bird of Paradise, Unforgettable and Occur!. **CMV $3. MB.**
BULLET PERFUME OIL 1965
(Right) 5/8 dram, gold top. Came in Wishing, Somewhere, Occur!, Rapture, To A Wild Rose, Topaze, Unforgettable, Here's My Heart, Cotillion. Came in Fragrance Ornaments Set only. **CMV $8. with holder, $4. BO.**

JEWEL PERFUME OIL 1964-65
(Left) 5/8 dram, gold cap. Perfume Oil came in Jewel Collection only. Came in Cotillion, Topaze, Persian Wood, Here's My Heart, To A Wild Rose. **CMV $6. each mint.**

GOLDEN MOMENTS PENDANT PERFUME 1971-72
Antiqued brass pendant on 32" gold chain. Holds 1/8 oz. perfume in Moonwind, Bird of Paradise, Elusive, Charisma. **CMV pendant on chain only $10. mint, $16. MB.**
PERFUME PENDANT 1970
Gold pendant with ruby teardrop, holds 1 dram liquid perfume. Comes in Charisma, Elusive, Brocade and Regence. **CMV $15. MB, $10. pendant only mint.**

SCENTIMENT PERFUME ROLLETTE 1973-74
(Left) .33 oz. white base with blue bird and pink flowers, gold trim and cap. Holds Moonwind, Patchwork, Sonnet. **CMV $4. MB.**
SCENTIMENT PURSE SPRAY ESSENCE 1974
(Right) .25 oz. blue plastic coated bottom, white and pink bird design on paper label with gold cap. Came in Field Flowers, Bird of Paradise or Charisma. **CMV $6. MB.**

AVON BOTTLES MISC.

HEART STRINGS PERFUME FLACON 1986
(LEFT) .18 oz. gold cap. **CMV $2. MB.**
ULTRA PERFUME 1984
(RIGHT) Gold box holds .6 oz. perfume, glass stopper. **CMV $2. MB.**

LIQUID POWDER 1930-36
4 oz. ribbed glass bottle with dark blue cap, silver and blue label. **CMV $40. MB, $35. BO.**
LOTUS CREAM 1930
4 oz. ribbed glass. Rare with flowered label. **CMV $50. BO, $60. MB.**

Misc. Avon Bottles are very high production items and most collectors are no longer interested in them unless they are very old, "1950s or older". We have removed all plastic bottles and most bottles back to the 50s or newer from this book. They have little or no value to most collectors. All plastic SSS bottles have been dropped from this book because of no value to collectors. BOXES are very important to most collectors, and become more valuable with age 35 years old & older.

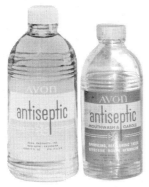

ANTISEPTIC MOUTHWASH 1955-59
(Left) 7 oz. white cap. Label says antiseptic only. **CMV $7. BO, $10. MB.**
ANTISEPTIC MOUTHWASH 1959-68
(Right) 7 oz. white cap. **CMV $6. MB.**

HAIR TONIC EAU DE QUININE FOR OILY HAIR 1931-36
1 pint size. Silver metal cap. (For dry hair, same price and date). **CMV $45. MB, $40. BO.**
HAIR TONIC EAU DE QUININE 1931-36
6 oz. ribbed glass bottle with dark blue cap with silver and blue label. Came in Tonic for Dry Hair and for Oily Hair. **CMV $40. MB, $35. BO.**

ANTISEPTIC 1932-36
(Left) Metal cap, green label. 6 oz. size. **CMV $35. MB, $30. BO.** Also came in 12 oz. size with same label. **CMV $40. MB, $35. BO.**
ANTISEPTIC 1936-40
(Right) 6 oz. metal cap. Turquoise box and label. **CMV $35. MB, $30. mint BO.**

ANTISEPTIC 1940-50
(left) 6 oz. clear glass bottle with turquoise cap. Early issue had metal cap. Also came in 12 oz. size. **CMV 6 oz. size $12..MB. CMV 12 oz. size $16. BO, $20. MB.** Add $5. for CPC label.
ANTISEPTIC ONLY 1946
(right)6 oz. round bottle, black cap. 2 different labels. Rare. **CMV $45. MB, $40. BO.**

ASTRINGENT 1936-54
2 oz. and 4 oz. size with turquoise caps. **CMV $15. MB. $10. BO. each mint.** Add $5. for CPC label.

LIQUID POWDER RACHEL OR PEACH 1936-41
(Right) 4 oz. green cap, clear glass. **CMV $20. MB, $15. BO.** Add $5. for CPC label on box.

ASTRINGENT 1930-36
Came in 2 and 4 oz. size as pictured on right for size comparison. Both are ribbed glass bottles with dark blue caps and silver and blue labels. **CMV $40. MB, $35. BO. mint each size.**

AVON BOTTLES - MISC., ETC.

COCONUT OIL SHAMPOO 1951-55
6 oz. bottle with turquoise cap and label.CMV
$17. MB, $12. BO.
PRE-SHAMPOO OIL 1936-38
2 oz. bottle with turquoise cap and label. CMV
$22. MB, $18. BO. Add $5. for CPC label on
bottle in box.

SKIN FRESHENER 1954-58
2 oz. bottle with turquoise cap and label.
Came in Beautiful You Set, A Thing of Beauty
Set, For Your Beauty Set and Happy Traveler
Set with white cap. **CMV $2. MB.**

COCONUT OIL SHAMPOO 1951-55
1 pint bottle with black pouring or flat black
cap. **CMV $22. BO, $27.50 MB.**
LIQUID COCONUT OIL SHAMPOO 1956-57
1 pint with green label and double pouring cap.
CMV $17. BO, $22. MB.

SKIN FESHENER 1954-65
4 oz. bottle with green cap and label. CMV $1.
each. 1965 bottle has For Dry Skin and For Normal
Skin added to label. **CMV$2. MB.**
ASTRINGENT 1954-65
4 oz. bottle with green cap & label. **CMV $2. MB,**
ASTRINGENT FRESHENER FOR OILY SKIN 1965
Same 4 oz. bottle as 1954-65 Astringent only name
is changed. **CMV $2. MB.**

BRILLIANTINE 1931-36
2 oz. ribbed glass bottle with dark blue
cap and silver and blue label. CMV $45.
MB, $40. BO.

SKIN FRESHENER 1930-36
2 or 4 oz. ribbed glass, blue or black cap.2 oz.
size came in sets only. **CMV $40. BO, $45.**
MB each.

NAIL CLIPPER 1960s
Avon on nail clippers. We have no information on this. **Rare. CMV $5.**

LOTUS CREAM 1936-44
4 oz. clear glass, green cap. **CMV $17. MB, $12. BO.** ·
Add $5. for CPC label on bottle in box. Came with 2
different labels and 2 different boxes.

SKIN FESHENER 1955
Rare 2 oz. glass bottle with embossed flowers
around neck. Turquoise cap. Came in 1955
Happy Traveler Set only. **CMV $12. mint.**
LOTUS CREAM 1930-36
(Left) 4 oz. ribbed glass bottle, blue cap.
CMV $40. MB, $35. BO.

BATH SALTS 1954-57
8 oz. bottle with turquoise cap and label.
Came in Jasmine and Pine. **CMV $15. MB,
$10. BO.**

BATH SALTS 1929-30
10 oz. bottle with metal lid, silver & blue label,
Ribbed glass sides. **CMV $60. BO. $75. MB.**

CREME HAIR RINSE 1953-55
6 oz. clear glass bottle with green cap and
label. **CMV $4. MB.**
CREME LOTION SHAMPOO 1954-56
6 oz. bottle with turquoise cap, painted label.
1956 label has 4A design. **CMV $4. MB.**

BATH SALTS SAMPLE 1933-37
Ribbed glass bottle with blue cap. Came in
Ariel, Vernafleur. **CMV $60.** Pine and
Jasmine **CMV $55. each.**

BATH SALTS 1931-33
(Right) 10 oz. ribbed glass bottle with blue lid,
silver label. 2 different labels. **CMV $60. MB,
$40. BO.**
BATH SALTS 1933-37
(Left) 8 1/2 oz. ribbed glass jar with dark blue
cap. Came in Ariel & Vernafleur from 1933-37,
Pine & Jasmine from 1935-37. **CMV $60. MB,
$40. BO.**

CREME LOTION SHAMPOO 1956 only
6 oz. clear glass, green cap. **CMV $3. MB,**
LIQUID COCONUT OIL SHAMPOO 1956-57
6 oz. clear bottle with green cap, painted label.
CMV $3. MB.
CREME HAIR RINSE 1956
6 oz. bottle with white cap and painted label
with 4A design. **CMV $3 MB.**

BATH SALTS 1936
8 1/2 9 oz. glass jars with turquoise lids from
1936-44, small paper label. 9 oz. jars from
1943-53 came in Ariel, 1936-44, Pine 1936-44
then 46-53, Vernafleur 1936-44, Attention
1936-44, and Jasmine 1936-44 then 46-48.
See Attention Fragrance for regular issue
box. **CMV $20. BO. $30. MB.**

BATH SALTS 1943-45
5 oz. and white paper containers Came in
Attention, Jasmine, Pine, and Vernafleur. each.
CMV $25. each mint, $30. MB.

SKIN FRESHENER 1936-54
(Left to Right) 2 and 4 oz. bottles. Both 4 oz.
bottles in center have 2 different labels.
Turquoise caps. **CMV $10. MB, $5. BO.**

LIQUID SHAMPOO 1937-50

6 oz. turquoise cap. Indented top of bottle.
MCV $20. MB, $15. BO. Add $5. for CPC label on bottle in box.

BRILLIANTINE 1936-54

2 oz. green cap and label, 3 different labels.
CMV $20. MB, $15. BO. Add $5. for CPC label.

LIQUID SHAMPOO 1943-45

6 oz. round shoulder bottle, black cap. This bottle is rare with round shoulders. **CMV $30. BO, $35. MB.**

SOAPLESS SHAMPOO 1946-49

6 oz. turquoise cap. **CMV $20. BO, $25. MB.** Also came in 16 oz. round size with same label. 1946-49. **CMV $20. BO, $25. MB.**

PRE-SHAMPOO OIL 1931-36

2 oz. ribbed glass bottle with dark blue cap, silver and blue label. **CMV $40. MB, $35. BO.**

LIQUID SHAMPOO 1930-36

(Left) 1 pint size, metal cap. **CMV $35. BO, $40. MB.**

LIQUID SHAMPOO 1931-36

(Right) 6 oz. ribbed glass bottle with dark blue cap and silver and blue label. **CMV $40. MB, $35. BO.**

LIQUID SHAMPOO 1937-50

1 pint size with raised pouring or flat metal or black cap.**CMV $20. BO, $25. MB. 1937-39 has CPC label $30.**

SKIN SO SOFT 1966-67

(Left) 1 oz. gold cap with painted leaf. Came in set of three only. Unforgettable, Rapture, Occur!, Somewhere, Topaze, Cotillion, Here's My Heart, To A Wild Rose, Wishing. **CMV $3. MB.**

SKIN SO SOFT 1969

(Center) 1 oz. gold cap & paper label. Came in Unforgetttable, Rapture, Occur!, Some-where, Topaze, Cotillion, To A Wild Rose & Here's My Heart. **CMV $4. MB.**

SKIN SO SOFT SCENTED BATH OIL 1969-70

(Right) 2 oz. clear glass bottom, clear plastic top. This top is the same as the clear Just II. Came in Charisma, Brocade, Rapture, Unforgettable, Occur!, Here's My Heart, Cotillion, To A Wild Rose & Regence**CMV $4. MB.**

ROSE WATER, GLYCERINE & BENZOIN 1926

(Left) 4 oz. ribbed bottle with cork stopper, front and neck label. **CMV $60. BO, $75. MB.** See CPC bottles for different label.

ROSE WATER, GLYCERINE & BENZOIN 1930-36

(Right) 4 oz. ribbed glass bottle, blue cap. **CMV $40. BO, $45. MB.** Regular issue box in center. **Add $5. for 1935 special issue Christmas box shown on right.**

INSECT REPEL-LENT "ALLIED PRODUCTS" 1941

2 oz. clear bottle - A war-time division of Avon Products. **CMV $30.**

FOUNDATION LOTION 1950-51
2 oz. bottle with turquoise cap. Formerly called Finishing Lotion. **CMV $20. MB, $15. BO.**

LEG MAKE-UP 1943-49
4 oz. clear glass with turquoise cap on left. 2 different bottles as shown. **CMV $20. MB, $15. Bo each.**

WAVE SET 1936-44
4 oz. bottle with turquoise cap and label. **CMV $20. MB, $15. BO. Add $5. for CPC label on bottle in box.**

DEODORANT 1931-36
2 oz. ribbed glass bottle with silver label and dark blue cap. **CMV $40. MB, $35. BO.**

BATH OILS - MISC. 1965
Came in Bath Bouquet Set only. 2 oz., gold cap and label. Came in Rapture, Occur!, Somewhere, Topaze, Cotillion, Here's My Heart, To A Wild Rose and Wishing. **CMV $3 each.**

ROSE WATER, GLYCERINE & BENZOIN 1936-44
4 oz. bottle with turquoise cap. **CMV $17. MB, $12. BO. Add $5 for CPC label on bottle in box.**

WITCH HAZEL 1936-48
4 oz. green cap and label. Also came with black cap. **CMV $15. BO, $20. MB. Add $5 for CPC label on bottle in box.** (Also came in 8 and 16 oz. size).

FINISHING LOTION 1938-50
2 oz. clear glass bottle **CMV $17. MB, $12. BO. Add $5. for CPC label on bottle**

WAVE SET 1930-36
4 oz. ribbed glass bottle with dark blue cap, and silver and blue label. **CMV $40. MB, $35. MB.**

WITCH HAZEL 1930-36
4 oz ribbed glass bottle with dark blue plastic cap, green label. **CMV $45. MB, $40. BO.** Also came in 8 and 16 oz. size.

DEODORANT 1936-48
(Left) 2 oz. turquoise cap and label. **CMV $20. MB, $14. BO. Add $5. for CPC label on bottle in box. 1946-48** came with black applicator with sponge end. **CMV $25. MB, $20. BO.**

LIQUID DEODORANT 1944-45
(right) 2 oz. turquoise cap with applicator. **CMV $20. BO, $25.MB.**

AVON BOTTLES - MISC., ETC.

STICK DEODORANT 1961-62
1 3/4 oz. white cap, green glass jar with painted label. CMV $5., $9. MB.

STICK DEODORANT 1956-61
Green cap and label on clear glass jar, 2 different caps. Older has 4A design on top and newer one has "New" spelled on lid. CMV $6., $9. MB. each.

TOILET WATER, CREAM, LOTION & BUBBLE BATH 1945
All are 2 oz size, frosted glass and pink caps. Came in 1945 Young Hearts Set. CMV $20. each. Toilet Water is in Cotillion fragrance.

NAIL POLISH 1936-37
Clear glass with turquoise cap. CPC label. CMV $15. BO - $20. MB.

DOUBLE DARE NAIL POLISH 1946-47
1 oz. black cap, red paper label. CMV $8. BO, $12. MB.

CUTICLE SOFTENER 1936-39
1.2 oz. bottle with turquoise cap. CPC on label. CMV $15. BO, $20. MB.

OILY POLISH REMOVER 1955-62
2 oz. white cap and label. CMV $4. MB.

NAIL POLISH 1931-36
Ribbed glass bottle with black octaginal cap. Gray and blue box. CMV $30. MB.

POLISH REMOVER & CUTICLE SOFTENER 1931-36
Both 1/2 oz. ribbed glass, black 8 sided caps. Silver labels. CMV $25. each BO, $30. MB.

OILY POLISH REMOVER 1946-50
2 oz. bottle with turquoise cap. CMV $15. MB, $10. BO.

OILY POLISH REMOVER 1950-53
2 oz. white cap. CMV $6. BO, $10. MB.

NAIL POLISH 1950-54
1/2 oz. bottle with white cap and gold line through label. Came in nail polish, cuticle softener, cling-tite, oily polish remover, clear nail polish and double coat. CMV $3. EA. MB.

NAIL POLISH 1954-58
With 4A design on label, came in long last nail polish, cuticle softener, silvery base, top coat, oily polish remover. CMV $2. ea. MB.

NAIL POLISH 1938-50
1/2 oz. and 1/4 oz bottle came in polish remover, cream polish, cuticle softener, cuticle oil, oily polish remover, nail polish base and top coat. 1946-50 same bottles and labels with black caps. Also came in double coat, nail polish and cling-tite. CMV $2. BO, $5 MB.

HAND LOTION 1943-50
4 oz. clear glass, turquoise cap. CMV $7. MB, $3. BO.

CREAM LOTION 1951
2 oz. bottle with blue cap. Came in 1951 Always Sweet Set. **CMV $18.**

CREAM LOTION 1950-51
2 oz. clear glass with turquoise cap, label has red, yellow and blue streamers. Came in 1951 Always Sweet Set and 1950 Jolly Surprise. **CMV $12.**

BUBBLE BATH 1948-51
4 oz. bottle with blue cap. Round blue and pink box with top of bottle sticking through lid. **CMV $25. MB, $15. BO.**

BUBBLE BATH 1951-58
Same bottle as above in a square box of same design. **CMV $20. MB, $15. BO.**

FASHION FILM 1954-58
(Left) 1 oz. white cap. **CMV $3. BO. $5. MB.**

FASHION FILM 1951-54
(Center) 1 oz. white cap. **CMV $5. BO. $8. MB.**

FASHION FILM 1958-61
(Right) 1 oz. pink cap. **CMV $4. BO. $7. MB.**

INSECT REPELLENT 1959-65
2 oz. bottle with red and white caps. **CMV $5. MB, $3. BO.**

CREAM LOTION 1942-49
6 oz. pink cap, back side of bottle is flat. Flowered box shown sold in 1942 only. **CMV $30. MB, $20. BO.**

BUBBLE BATH 1944-48
Blue and white box with pink ribbon holds 8 oz. bottle with blue cap and label. **CMV $45. MB, $35. BO mint.**

BEAUTIFUL JOURNEY BOTTLES 1957
1 oz. clear glass bottles came in Beautiful Journey Set only. Pink caps. Came in hand lotion, skin freshener, deep clean, deodorant and Cotillion cologne. **CMV $5. each.**

CREAM LOTION BOX 1942-43
Box shown sold 1942-43 only. 6 oz. flat sided bottle with pink cap sold 1942-49. as pictured. **CMV $30. MB as shown, $20. BO mint.**

LIQUID TWIN-TONE 1944-45
2 oz. bottles. **CMV $15. BO, $20. MB.**

EYE AND THROAT OIL 1967
1 oz. gold cap. Issued during glass strike in 1967 only. Short issue. **CMV $2. BO, $4. MB.**

LIQUID ROUGE 1954-59
(Right) 1/8 oz. gold embossed cap. **CMV $7. MB, $5. BO.**

LIQUID ROUGE 1959-66
(Left) 1/4 oz. smooth brass cap, 2 different labels. **CMV $5. MB, $3. BO.**

SUN CREAM 1943-48
4 oz. clear glass, turquoise cap. **CMV $10. MB, $5. BO.**

POLISH REMOVER 1936-40
(Left) Has Good Housekeeping seal on turquoise and gold label. Black cap. **CMV $15. BO, $20. MB.**
POLISH REMOVER 1936-39
(Right) 1/2 oz. bottle, turquoise cap. CPC on label. **CMV $15. BO, $20. MB.**

SUN LOTIN 1954
2 oz. bottle, white cap. Came in camping kit set only. **Rare CMV $22.**
SUN FOAM 1955-57
Peach colored can and cap. **CMV $6. MB, $3. CO.**
HAND LOTION 1954-58
4 oz. green cap and label. **CMV $1. BO, $2. MB.**

HAND LOTION & PUMP 1963-64
8 oz. gold stripes on bottle, gold and white pump. Also came without gold neck band. **CMV $3. MB, $1. BO.**
LOTION LOVELY 1964-65
8 oz. gold painted label. Came in Wishing, Here's My Heart, Persian Wood, To A Wild Rose. Somewhere, Topaze, Cotillion. Occur!, Rapture. **CMV $4. MB, $1. BO.**

SUN LOTION 1949-58
4 oz. bottle with white cap. Montreal label to 1954. **CMV $11.** Pasadena label 1954-58. **CMV $10. BO, $12. MB.**

HAND LOTION 1950 ONLY
4 oz. clear glass, turquoise cap and label. **CMV $7. BO, $12. MB.**
HAND LOTION 1950
4 oz. pink cap. Same bottle as Cotillion of that period. This was a substitute bottle. Rare. **CMV $12. MB, $7. BO.**

HAND LOTION 1948
(Left) 2 oz. glass bottle with blue cap. Came in 1948 Hair Ribbons Set. **CMV $5.**
HAND LOTION ROSE WATER, GLYCERINE & BENZOIN LOTION 1942 ONLY
(Right) 6 oz. flat sided bottle. Came in sets only. **CMV $20. mint.**

HAND LOTION 1951-54
4 oz. pink or white plastic cap, blue and pink label. **CMV $10. MB, $5. BO.**

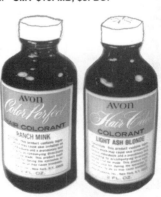

COLOR PERFECT HAIR COLOR 1971-72
2 oz. brown glass with white cap. **CMV $1.50.**
HAIR COLOR COLORANT 1969
2 oz. brown glass with white cap. has 4A on cap. **CMV $3.**

PROPER BALANCE VITAMINS 1979-81
3 different bottles, 60 and 100 size. Proper balance for the whole family. Womens Vitality, Dieters Support. **CMV $5. each MB.**

ULTRA SHEER LIQUID FOUNDATION 1966-67
1 oz. gold top, embossed bottle. **CMV $1. MB.**
ULTRA SHEER NATURAL VEIL 1968-74
1 oz. embossed bottle, same as Liquid Foundation only named changed. **CMV $1. MB.**
EYE & THROAT OIL 1965-72
1 oz. gold cap, painted label. **CMV $1. MB.**

VITA MIGHTS FOR KIDS 1980-81
Vitamins for kids, bottle of 100 tablets. **CMV $7. MB.**

IF YOU LOVE TO LAUGH, GO TO THE BACK PAGE FOR INFO ON BUD HASTIN'S NEW JOKE BOOK AND HOW TO GET IT. LAUGH MORE AND LIVE LONGER.

SKIN SO SOFT 1970
(Left) Clear glass container holds 2 oz. Skin-So-Soft, gold cap. Comes in Bird of Paradise, Elusive, Charisma, Brocade, Unforgettable, Field Flowers, Occur!, Rapture & To A Wild Rose. **CMV $2. MB.**
SKIN SO SOFT "2 OZ." 1971-72
(Right) 2 oz. 7 layer glass bottle with gold cap. 4 1/2" high. Came in Bird of Paradise, Elusive, Charisma, Brocade, To A Wild Rose. **CMV $3. MB.**

DEW KISS DECANTER 1973
(Left) 4 oz. clear glass with gold cap. **CMV $1. MB.**
DEW KISS DECANTER 1974
(Center) 4 oz. clear glass with gold cap. **CMV $1.MB.**
DEW KISS 1960-66
(Right) 1 1/2 oz. pink lid, gold string with pink and gold tag, with 4A design. **CMV $3. MB, $1. BO.**

BEAUTY DUST, POWDERS, TALC - MISC.

All Powders newer then 1975 are not pictured and have little or no value to collectors.

DUSTING POWDER 1945-48
6 oz. blue and white cardboard with ladies face on lid. Also contained Apple Blossom Beauty Dust. **CMV $25. $30. MB.**
DUSTING POWDER 1936-49
13 oz. turquoise and beige can with "A" on top. 1st (1936-39) issue has CPC on bottom. **CMV $30.** 1940-49 Avon Products label only. **CMV $20., $25. MB.** There are at least 3 different varieties of the 1936-49 metal dusting powder. One has a deeply indented bottom, shining silver, with CPC on it, another has a slightly indented dull silver bottom, no CPC on it.

DUSTING POWDER 1930-34
(Left) 8 oz. blue and silver square can. **CMV $40. MB, $30. CO mint.** Gold can, blue letters came in sets only. **CMV $50. mint.**
DUSTING POWDER 1926-29
(Right) Gold metal can with black stripes. Came in Daphne, Vernafleur, Trailing Arbutus, California Rose, Baby Powder and Super Rite Talcum. **CMV $50. MB, $40. CO.**

BEAUTY DUST CHRISTMAS BOX 1944
Special issue Christmas box. Holds feather design paper container of beauty dust. **CMV $27. MB as shown, beauty dust only mint, $22.**

DUSTING POWDER 1935-36
13 oz. metal gold colored can. Came in Bath Ensemble Set only. **CMV $35. mint.**
DUSTING POWDER 1935-36
Same as gold can only general issue was silver and blue can. **CMV $30. CO mint, $40. MB.**

DUSTING POWDER CHRISTMAS BOX 1943
Outer box special issue for Christmas. Holds square cardboard beauty dust. **CMV $50. MB as shown.**

DUSTING POWDER REFILL 1930-36
Gray box holds plain paper wrapped box of powder. **CMV $25. MB.**

DUSTING POWDER 1943-46
13 oz. paper box, turquoise and ivory. **CMV $35. MB, $30. BO mint.**

DUSTING POWDER CHRISTMAS BOX 1940-41
Special issue blue and white Christmas box holds regular issue metal can of dusting powder. **CMV $35. MB as shown.**

DUSTING POWDER 1943-44
Turquoise and white paper box. **CMV $35., $40. MB.**

DUSTING POWDER MOTHERS DAY BOX 1941
Special issue lavender box with white lace holds regular issue dusting powder. Sold during Mothers Day. **CMV $35. MB as shown.**

BEAUTY DUST REFILL 1965
White outer box holds colorful inner box with plain beauty dust refill. Came in choice of Persian Wood, Cotillion, To A Wild Rose, Somewhere, Topaze, Occur!, Here's My Heart, and Rapture. **CMV $7. as shown MB.**

FACE POWDER 1930-36
Silver and blue paper box came in Ariel and Vernafleur. **CMV $17. MB, $12. CO mint.**

(Left to Right)
BEAUTY DUST 1942-48
6 oz. blue feather design cardboard. Came in Avon Beauty Dust and Apple Blossom **CMV $20., $25. MB.**
FACE POWDER 1942-48
1 3/4 oz. blue feather design cardboard. **CMV $8. mint, $12. MB.**
HEAVENLIGHT FACE POWDER 1946--48
2 1/2 oz. same feather design paper box. **CMV $8., $12. MB.**
ROUGE 1942-49
Blue feather design, paper container on right. **CMV $5., $8. MB.**
FEATHER DESIGN LIPSTICK 1942-46
Blue plastic top and bottom with cardboard sides. Also came with red plastic top and bottom. **CMV $5., $9. MB.**

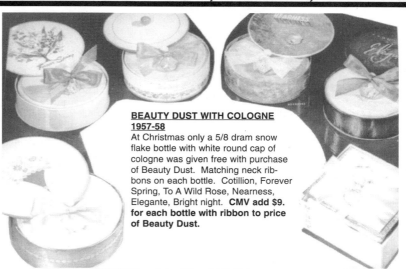

DUSTING POWDER REFILL 1936-49
Round cardboard container. Came in Jasmine or Avon dusting powder. **CMV $15. MB. Add $5. for CPC label.**

BEAUTY DUST WITH COLOGNE 1957-58
At Christmas only a 5/8 dram snow flake bottle with white round cap of cologne was given free with purchase of Beauty Dust. Matching neck ribbons on each bottle. Cotillion, Forever Spring, To A Wild Rose, Nearness, Elegante, Bright night. **CMV add $9. for each bottle with ribbon to price of Beauty Dust.**

BEAUTY DUST DEMO 1966-68
White box, came in choice of beauty dust refill and different fragrance empty container. Both came boxed. Used by Reps C10, 1966. **CMV $11. MB.**

BEAUTY DUST WITH COLOGNE 1956
At Christmas only a 5/8 dram bottle with white falt cap and neck ribbon came in Beauty Dust. Elegante with red ribbon, nearness, lavender ribbon, Cotillion, and To A WIld Rose, pink ribbons, Forever Spring, purple ribbon, Quaintance, blue ribbon. Each ribbon has gold edge. **Add $12. to each Beauty Dust if bottle has ribbon.**

FACE POWDER 1936-39
3" diameter, turquoise and cream container, cardboard. Came in Cotillion, Ariel or Vernafleur fragrance. Choice of natural, rose, peach, Rachel No. 1, Rachel No. 2, orchre, orchre-rose and suntan shades. **CMV $10. MB, $6. CO.**

BEAUTY DUST WITH COLOGNE 1953-55
At Christmas only a 5/8 dram bottle of cologne with silk ribbon came in Beauty Dust in Quaintance, To A WIld Rose, both pink and white. Also blue container Golden Promise, Forever Spring and Cotillion. **CMV add $12. to price of Beauty Dust if bottle has ribbon and $10. without ribbon.**

SHEER MIST FACE POWDER 1955-57
Turquoise cardboard with white and pink flowers and gold 4A design on lid. **CMV $5. MB.**

SHEER MIST FACE POWDER 1958-59
2 1/2 oz. white cardboard box with pink rose on lid and pink rim around edge. **CMV $3.MB.**
FACE POWDER 1960-63
Same design as Sheer Mist only has plastic lid, no pink rim. **CMV$2. MB.**
FASHION FINISH FACE POWDER 1963-67
1 1/2 oz. white plastic box. **CMV 1. MB.**

ELITE FOOT POWDER 1943-46
Maroon and cream colored paper box. 2.75 oz. Black screw off octagonal cap. **CMV $25. mint.**
ELITE FOOT POWDER 1943-46
2.75 oz maroon and white victory paper box. Flat punch out top with paper lift off lid.**CMV $25. mint.**

ELITE POWDER 1943-46
Turquoise and white paper boxes in family size.(large) **CMV $30.** Regular size **CMV $20.** Three different caps, plastic cap, punch out top and punch out top with paper top and bottom cover. **Same CMV.**

ELITE POWDER 1931-36
Silver and blue can with blue cap is general issue in regular size on right. **CMV $25.** Family size 1 ln. can on left. **CMV $30. Add $5. MB.**
ELITE POWDER 1934-35
Same design and shape cans. Came in sets only in gold and blue cans. **CMV small size $35. Large family size $35. Add $5. each MB.**

TOOTH POWDER 1936-49
Box holds 2 1/4 oz. turquoise and white can. Silver slide open cap. **CMV $10., $15. MB.**

ELITE POWDER 1936-48
Large family size on left, turquoise and white can. **CMV $25., $30. MB.**
ELITE POWDER 1936-54
2.9 oz. or 3 oz. size on right, turquoise and white can, 2 different boxes. **CMV $10. CO, $14. MB. Add $3. for CPC label.**

SMOKERS TOOTH POWDER 1932-36
Green cap **CMV $35. MB, $25. CO.**

HEAVENLIGHT FACE POWDER 1944
(Left) General issue feather design paper box. Shown in 1944 pink design box. 2 1/2 oz. contents. Powder only sold in 1944-48. **CMV $12. MB as shown. Powder box only $8.**

TALCUM POWDER 1930-32
Silver and blue can came in regular and family size. **CMV $35., $40. MB.** 1 lb. family size **CMV $35., $45. MB.**

SMOKERS TOOTH POWDER SAMPLES
(Left) 1936-40 small 1/4 oz. turquoise and white can. CPC label, turquoise sifter cap. **CMV $35. mint.**
(Right) 1940-49 Same can only has chrome lift off cap. **CMV $30. mint.**
(Center) Same can, has small chrome cap. **CMV $30.**

TOOTH POWDER 1930-36
(Left) Green metal can. **CMV $32. MB, $25. CO mint.**
TOOTH POWDER 1936-50
(Right) Turquoise and white metal can, silver cap. **CMV $15. MB, $10. CO.**

SMOKER'S TOOTH POWDER 1944-46
Turquoise and white paper container. Plastic cap. **CMV $20. mint. $25. MB.**

(Left to Right)
SMOKERS TOOTH POWDER 1936-49
Metal cap, 3 1/2 oz. turquoise and white can. **CMV $16., $20. MB.**
SMOKERS TOOTH POWDER 1950-54
3 1/2 oz. turquoise and white can, turquoise tilt cap. **CMV $14., $19. MB.**
SMOKERS TOOTH POWDER 1946-50
3 1/2 oz. turquoise and white can, turquoise plastic cap. **CMV $14., $19. MB.**

AMMONIATED TOOTH POWDER 1949 ONLY
3 oz. turquoise can and tilt cap. This can with this style cap was a very short issue. **CMV $18. MB, $13. can mint.**

TOOTH POWDER 1943-46
Flat metal top, paper side container. 3 oz. size. Turquoise and white. **CMV $25. MB, $20. CO mint.**

ELITE POWDER 1943-46
2.75 oz. or 3 oz. paper box. **CMV $18. mint. $23. MB.**
TOOTH POWDER 1943-46
3 oz. paper box. **CMV $20. mint. $25. MB.**
SMOKERS TOOTH POWDER 1943-46
3 1/2 oz. paper box with metal top and bottom. **CMV $20. mint. $25. MB.** All are turquoise and white.

AMMONIATED TOOTH POWDER 1949-55
3 oz. turquoise and white can with turquoise lid. **CMV $10. $15. MB.**

AQUA DENT 1958-66
7 oz. green color can with white cap. **CMV $1.,
$3. MB.**

TALC FOR MEN 1936-49
Maroon and cream colored can with maroon
cap. **CMV $15. MB, $10. CO.**
SMOKERS TOOTH POWDER 1938-49
Maroon and cream colored can. Came in
Men's Sets only. **CMV $16. mint.**

BEAUTY DUST 1960-61
3 oz. white plastic bottle, has paper label or
painted label, turquoise cap. This came in
Modern Simplicity Set only. Came in Cotillion,
To A Wild Rose and Here's My Heart. **CMV
$5.**

**SMOKERS TOOTH POWDER "PAPER"
1943-46**
(Left) Maroon and cream paper sides, tin top
and bottom. **CMV $20. mint, $25. MB.**
TALC FOR MEN "PAPER" 1943-46
(Right) Maroon and cream paper container.
metal screw on cap in black or maroon. **CMV
$20. mint.**

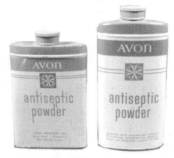

ANTISEPTIC POWDER 1956-62
(Left) 3 oz. gray and white can, red cap. **CMV
$2. MB.**
ANTISEPTIC POWDER 1962-64
(Right) 3 oz. gray and white can, red cap.
CMV $2. MB.
ANTISEPTIC POWDER 1965-68
Same as 1962-64 can only 2 3/4 oz. size.
CMV $2. MB.

BATH BOUQUET TALC 1965
1 1/2 oz. green paper box. Came in Bath
Bouquet Set only in all fragrances of that set.
CMV $4. mint.

**POWDER PUFF COMPACT REFILLS 1960-
70s**
2 different puffs and package for compacts.
CMV $3. each mint.

POWDER PAK PUFFS REFILL 1940s
Envelope holds 2 compact puff refills. **CMV
$5. mint.**
POWDER PUFF REFILLS 1960s
Envelope holds 2 puff refills. **CMV $3.**

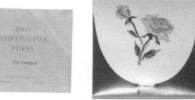

SACHET PILLOWS 1963
Green and white holder contains powder
sachet pillow. Came 6 to a pack. **CMV for
set of 6, $5. mint.**

**HEAVY DUTY POWDERED HAND CLEANS-
ER 1973-76**
10 oz. blue, white, pink and black cardboard
with plastic top and bottom. **CMV $1. mint.**

COMPACTS & LIPSTICKS - MISC.

Compacts & Lipsticks 1975 or newer have been dropped from this book due to mass production & little collector interest. Only the very decorative items & items in the kids lines will be included in the future.

DUSTING POWDER PUFF 1940s-50s
Envelope holds Avon puff. **Rare. CMV $10.**

TRIM TONE COSMETIC STOCKING 1940s
Beige with gold band, box turquoise.**CMV $25. MB.**

MASCARA COMPACT 1933-36
Blue and silver metal compact. **CMV $30. BO, $35. MB.**

COMPACT 1930-32
Silver metal compact in single size. & double size. **CMV $30. each, $40. MB.**

DRESSING TABLE ROUGE 1930-36
Silver and blue paper box. **CMV $12. BO, $17. MB.**
LIIPSTICK 1932-36
Blue and silver metal tube. **CMV $20., $25. MB.**

NAIL WHITE & NAIL CUTICLE CREAM 1937-39
Both turquoise and white small metal cans. Came in Manicure Set only. **CMV $7.**
COMPACT 1932-33
Octaganal shaped blue and gold. Avon lid shown closed and open. Came in 1932-33 Vanity Set only. **CMV $30. mint.**

FAN COMPACT 1931-33
Silver and blue compact. **CMV $30. BO, $40. MB.**

TRIPLE COMPACT 1931-33
Blue and silver compact. Avon on lid. **CMV $35. $40. MB.**

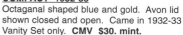

NAIL WHITE & NAIL CREME 1931-36
Both small silver and blue or gold and blue cans. Came in Manicure Sets only. **CMV $8. mint.**

SINGLE ROUGE COMPACT 1930-36
Blue and silver metal compact. OSP 52c.
CMV $20., $25. MB.
EYE LASH CREAM 1930-33
Blue compact with mirror, same as above rouge compacts. **CMV $20. - $25. MB.**

DOUBLE COMPACT 1934-36
Blue and silver compact and puffs.**CMV $30. BO, $35. MB.**

COMPACT REFILLS 1931-36
Avon on small and large size, blue and silver puff and refill cake. Came in gray box. **CMV $4. each. MB.**

CREME ROUGE COMPACT 1930-36
Blue metal compact as above. **CMV $20. $25. MB.**

FACE POWDER SAMPLE 1936-42
Cream colored metal can. Came in Vernafleur, Ariel in 5 shades. **CMV $5. CPC label $2. MB.**

DRESSING TABLE ROUGE 1936-42
Turquoise and gold cardboard with turquoise and white box. Came in 5 shades. **CMV $5. $8. MB. Add $2. for CPC. label.**

POWDER ROUGE REFILL 1936-42
Turquoise and white box. Refill fits double compacts. **CMV $6. MB.**

CREME ROUGE COMPACT 1936-42
Turquoise and gold metal case. **CMV $9. MB.**

SINGLE ROUGE COMPACT 1936-42
Turquoise and gold metal case. **CMV $7., $9. MB.**

Most lip sticks, chap sticks lip balms & compacts no longer pictured in this book are worth 25c to $1.00, depending on age. Most collectors only want 1950s & older. No new items of this type will be added in the future. As with any thing collectible, after 40 or more years, things start to have value just because of age and hard to find. Keep this in mind as you collect.

MASCARA 1949-52
Gold metal case. **CMV $8. MB. $5. case only.**

LIPSTICK PLASTIC 1942-46
Blue feather design plastic lipstick. **CMV $8. MB. lipstick only $4.**

CHAP STICK 1943-45
Olive green metal case. Lipstick Anti Chap and Sunburn Protective Hot Climate. Avon Products, Inc., New York on label. Given to G.I.'s in World War II in first aid kit. **CMV $25. BO.**

CHAP CHECK 1956-59
(Left) Small white plastic tube, red cap. **CMV $3.**

CHAP CHECK 1960-73
(Center) Is same color as above only longer tube. **CMV $1.**

CHAP CHECK 1951-55
(Right) Small turquoise and white plastic tube. 1/10 oz. size. **CMV $4.**

MASCARA COMPACT 1936-41
Turquoise and gold. **CMV $12., $15. MB.**

LIPSTICK 1936-41
Turquoise and gold. **CMV $8. BO $10 MB.**

CAPTIVATORS COMPACT & LIPSTICK 1969
Leapord, Zebra, and Tiger design plastic compacts. **CMV $5. MB each.** Matching lipsticks, **CMV $3. MB.**

FLOWER PRINT COMPACT & LIPSTICK 1967
4 compacts with matching lipsticks. Designs are Sunflower, Daisy, Poppy, and Carnation. Compacts **CMV $3., $5. MB.** Lipsticks **CMV $2., $3. MB.** Also came in flower print nail polish. See Misc. Bottles.

JEWELED LIPSTICK 1968-69
Gold lipstick with simulated diamond.**CMV $6. MB.**
JEWELED COMPACT 1968-69
Gold powder compact with simulated diamonds. **CMV $12. MB.**

ROUGE PUFFS REFILLS 1940's
(Left) Avon package holds 3 small turquoise rouge double compact puffs. **CMV $3.**
POWDER COMPACT PUFFS REFILLS 1940's
(Right) Avon package holds 2 turquoise puff refills. **CMV $3. mint.**

JEWELED LIPSTICK 1954
Gold Christmas box holds gold lipstick with jewel on top. **CMV $15. MB.**
JEWELED LIPSTICK 1954-56
Gold lipstick with white jewel on top. **CMV lipstick only $8. MB.**

COMPACT & LIPSTICK DELUXE 1967-69
Gold compacts. **CMV $8. MB.** Gold lipstick **CMV $5. MB.**

MASCARA COMPACT 1941-48
Gold metal, bamboo design. Sold 1942-43 then 1946-48. **CMV $12., $15. BO.**
BAMBOO LIPSTICK 1941-48
Gold metal bamboo design. **CMV $6., $8. MB.**
BAMBOO SINGLE ROUGE COMPACT 1941-48
Gold metal bamboo design. **CMV $7., $9. MB.**
BAMBOO CREME ROUGE COMPACT 1941-48
Gold metal bamboo design. **CMV $7., $9. MB.**

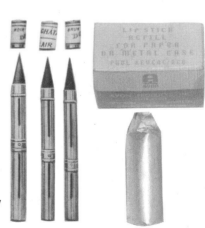

EMPRESS LIPSTICK 1970-71
Green, blue and gold lipstick. **CMV $3. MB.**

EMPRESS COMPACT 1970-71
Green, blue and gold compact. **CMV $5. MB.**

FACE POWDER COMPACT 1943-44
Feather design cardboard compact with mirror inside. 3 1/2 " across. **CMV $20., $25. MB.**

CPC EYEBROW PENCILS 1916-20
Metal tubes. **CMV $15. each, $25. MB.**
LIPSTICK REFILL 1944
(Right) Foil wrapped lipstick in plastic case, for metal or paper case. Came in green and white box. 2 different boxes. Some are white top, green bottom as shown or reversed. **CMV $10. MB.**

BAMBOO COMPACT 1941-49
Gold metal, bamboo design. Double size.
Single size in same design. Sold 1942-43
then 1946-49. **CMV $15. $20. MB.**

MASCARA 1943-49
Blue and white feather design paper box.
CMV $14. BO $17. MB.
FACE POWDER SAMPLE 1942-49
Blue and white feather design, metal case or
paper box in 1943-46. **CMV $4. BO.**
HEAVENLIGHT COMPACT 1943-45
Blue plastic or metal with white feather, came
in rouge or face powder. Rouge is smaller.
CMV $8., $10. MB.
EYE SHADOW 1945-49
Blue plastic compact with white feather. Same
as 1943 Rouge feather compact above. **CMV
$7., $9. MB.**

NAIL WHITE PENCIL 1941-48
White plastic pencil in turquoise box.Avon on
pencil. **CMV $2. pencil only $5. MB.**

COMPACTS 1936-42
Single compact. Double compact. Both
turquoise and gold metal. **CMV $15., $20.
MB.**

VIOLET NUTRI CREAM 1930-34
(Left) White jar, metal lid, silver & blue label. 2 & 4 oz. size.
CMV $40. MB. $30. jar only.

CLEANSING CREAM 1930-34
(Right) 4 oz. white glass ribbed jar with aluminum lid. Silver & blue label. **CMV $30. jar only mint.- $40. MB.**

ROSE COLD CREAM 1930-34
(Left) 2 & 4 oz. white glass ribbed jars with aluminum lids. Silver & blue labels.**CMV $40. MB - $30 jar only.**

BLEACH CREAM 1932-33
(Right) 3 oz. frosted glass jas, metal lid, silver & blue label.
CMV $50. - $60. MB.

CREAM JARS - MISC. 1933-36
Ribbed white glass jar with blue metal caps. Following came in 2 & 4 oz. size. Rose Cold Cream, Violet Nutri Cream; 4 oz. size only in Cleansing Cream; 2 oz. size only in Bleach Cream, Vanishing Cream, Tissue Cream.**CMV $30. $35. MB.**

CREAM JARS - MISC. 1936-55
This style bottle was sold from 1935-55. Came in Tissue Cream, Rose Cold Cream, Special Formula Cream, Foundation Cream, Violet Protective Cream, All Purpose Cream, Bleach Cream, Cleansing Cream, Night Cream, Violet Nutri Cream, Complexion Cream, Super Rich Cream, 1947 Special Dry Skin Cream, 1948 Facial Mask Cream. White glass jars came in small, medium, and large size with turquoise metal caps. Paper caps were used 1943-46. **CMV $4. each.** Add $3. each for turquoise paper caps. **CMV with CPC labels on jar or box 1936-39 $8. jar only. $12. CPC label on box.**

ANTISEPTIC CREAM 1954-55
3 1/2 oz. large size jar only. **CMV $4., $7 MB.**

CREAM DEODORANT 1954-59
White glass jar, turquoise lid. **CMV $4. BO. $2.50 jar only.**

   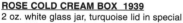

ROSE COLD CREAM BOX 1939
2 oz. white glass jar, turquoise lid in special short issue design box. CPC on box. **CMV $25. MB as shown.**

ROSE COLD CREAM SPECIAL ISSUE BOX 1942
Special issue blue & pink rosebud box holds regular issue large size jar of Rose Cold Cream. **CMV $25. MB.**

CREAM DEODORANT 1939 Only
(Left) White glass jar, turquoise lid. This is Rare. **CMV $16. MB $12. jar only, mint.**

TISSUE CREAM 1930-34
(Left) Ribbed white glass, metal lid, silver & blue label. 2 oz. size. **CMV $35., $40. MB.**

VANISHING CREAM 1931
(Right) 2 oz size white glass jar with aluminum lid. Silver & blue label. **CMV $40 BO. $35. jar only.**

213

CREAM CAKE 1955-57
(Left) Avon in center of pink lid, white glass bottom. **CMV $3 - $4. MB.**

CREAM CAKE 1948-55
(Right) Dove on top of pink lid. white glass bottom. **CMV $4 - $5. MB.**

ROSE COLD CREAM SPECIAL ISSUE BOX 1941
Special issue rose color box with girls face on side. Came with regular issue middle size jar of Rose Cold Cream for 10c. with regular orderCMV **$20. MB as shown.**

COLOR PICK-UP LIQUID 1946-50
(Left) 1 oz. clear glass bottle with turquoise cap. **CMV $8. - $11. MB.**

COLOR PICK-UP CREAM 1946-54
(Right) 17/8 oz. white glass jar with turquoise lid. **CMV $6. - $10. MB.** Also came in 1 oz. jar. Same lid & jar.

CREAM SHAMPOO 1953
4 oz. jar very short issue. RARE. CMV $17. MB - $10. jar only.

ROSE COLD CREAM BOX 1940
1 3/4 oz. jar if Rose Cold Cream came in special issue box for Reps to use as demonstrator only. Cost Reps 10c. **CMV $20. MB as shown.**

TWIN TONE MAKE-UP 1943-46
(Left) 1 7/8 oz. white jar, turquoise paper lid & metal lid. **CMV metal lid $9. - paper lid $12.**

TWIN TONE MAKE-UP 1943-46
(Right) 7/8 oz. white glass jar, turquoise paper lid. **CMV $10 - $14. MB.**

RICH MOISTURE CREAM 1954
(Left) 1 1/2 & 3 1/2 oz. turquoise glass jars with turquoise plastic lids. **CMV $3 - $4. MB.**

CREAM FOUNDATION 1963-66
(Right) 1 oz. white glass jar with white plastic lid with gold center.CMV **$1. MB.**

COLOR PICK-UP CREAM 1946
7/8 oz. white glass jar, turquoise lid.CMV **$15. BO. $18. MB.**

HAND CREAM 1945 Only
3 1/2 oz. clear glasss jar, turquoise lid. Rare **CMV $25. - $32. MB.**

COLOR PICK-UP CREAM 1946-47
Painted over twin tone lid. 1 7/8 oz. white glass jar with green lid. **CMV $12. $16. MB.**

CAKE MAKE-UP 1947-54
(Bottom) 1 3/4 oz. pink base, white cap. **CMV $3. - $5. MB.**

RICH MOISTURE CREAM 1954-57
Turquoise jar & cap in 2 oz & 3 1/2 oz. size. Came with 2 different size neck & caps **CMV $3 each size MB. $2. jar only.**

STRAWBERRY COOLER 1956
Frosted glass jar with strawberry on white lid.
CMV $2. - $3. MB.

NAIL BEAUTY 1954-57
1 oz white jar with white lid. CMV $3 - $4.
MB.

CREAM DEODORANT 1936-54
1 oz. white glass jar, turquoise lid. CMV $7.
jar only. $12. MB. Add $4. for CPC label.

AVON CREAMS 1954-61
(Left to Center) White glass jar with green lid
& label. Came in : Hormone Cream, Super
Rich Cream, Cleansing Cream & Antiseptic
Cream in large & small jars. CMV $2. each.
$3. MB.

COLOR PICK UP CREAM 1955-57
(Left) White glass jar with pink lid. CMV $6.
each MB, $4. jar only.
WHITE VELVET CREAM 1961-65
(Inside Left) 3 1/2 oz. white glass jar with 4A
on turquoise lid. CMV $1. - $2. MB.
POLISH REMOVER PADS 1963-66
(Inside Right) White glass jar with red lid,
holds 20 pads. CMV $2. - $3. MB.
ANTISEPTIC CREAM 1954-58
(Right) 3 1/2 oz. white glass jar with gray lid.
CMV $2. - $3. MB.

NAIL & CUTICLE CREAM 1940-50
(Left) 1 oz. white glass jar, turquoise lid. CMV
$5. - $8 MB.
NAIL BEAUTY 1951-54
(Right) 1 oz. white glass jar, white lid. CMV
$4 - $5. MB.

SKIN-SO-SOFT VANITY JAR 1973-74
(Left) 5 oz. clear glass with antiqued gold lid.
CREAM SACHET VANITY JAR 1973-75
(Center) 1 oz. clear glass with antiqued silver
lid. Holds Field Flowers, Charisma or Topaze.
**RICH MOISTURE CREAM VANITY JAR
1973**
(Right) 5 oz. clear glass with antiqued silver
lid. CMV $2. each. MB.

IF YOU LOVE TO LAUGH, GO TO THE BACK PAGE FOR INFO ON BUD HASTIN'S NEW JOKE BOOK AND HOW TO GET IT. LAUGH MORE AND LIVE LONGER.

AVON NET HAIR SPRAY 1954-57
Green & white, white caps. Came in 5 oz. size.
. **CMV $4. MB, $2. each CO.**

SPRAY CANS - MISC.

All Spray Cans 1960 & newer are mass produced & have little value to most collectors. We have dropped most spray cans 1960 or newer for this reason. All Avon spray cans not pictured in this book 1960 or newer would not have a value over 25c each. We suggest you do not collect them unless they are very old. New spray cans will not be added to this book in the future. We suggest you collect 1950s and older in cans & jars.

AVON NET HAIR SPRAY 1957-58
White & pink spray can came in 5 & 11 oz. sizes. **CMV $5. each.**
AVON NET FOR FINE HAIR 1958-60
5 oz. blue & white can & cap. **CMV $2.**
AVON NET REGULAR 1959-64
5 oz. pink & white can & cap. **CMV $2.**
LATHER FOAM SHAMPOO 1956
Green cap & can, short issue. **CMV $3. mint.**

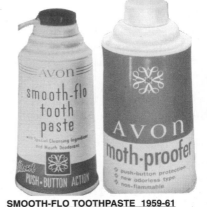

SMOOTH-FLO TOOTHPASTE 1959-61
(Left) 5 1/2 oz. white, red & gray metal can, red cap. **CMV $2.**
MOTH PROOFER 1956-60
(Right) 12 oz. red & white spray can, white cap. **CMV $2.**
MOTH PROOFER 1968-72
11 oz. red & white spray can with white cap.
CMV $1.

KLEAN AIR 1956-58
(Left) 12 oz. blue & white spray can with white cap. Mint scented. **CMV $5. mint.** Also came 3 oz. pink & white. Same shape can. **CMV $3.**

TUBES - MISC.

Tubes 1965 or newer have been dropped from this book due to mass production & little or no interest to most Avon collectors. Only fancy decorated or cute kids type tubes are considered collectable after 1965. All other tubes not pictured in this book unless they are very old should not be collected for future value.

TO means Tube Only CMV-- CurrenMarket Value. OSP - Original Selling Price.

MENTHOL WITCH HAZEL 1914
OSP 25c. **CMV $45. MB, $40. TO mint.**
WITCH HAZEL CREAM 1914
Small & large tube. OSP 25c & 50c. **CMV $45. MB, $40. TO mint.**

WITCH HAZEL CREAM 1904
OSP 2 oz. tube 25c, 6 oz. tube 50c. **CMV $50. MB, $45. TO mint.**
ALMOND CREAM BALM 1904
OSP 2 oz. tube 25c, 6 oz. tube 50c. **CMV $50. MB, $45. TO mint.**

WITCH HAZEL CREAM 1908
2 & 6 oz. size tubes. OSP 25c & 50c. **CMV $50. each MB, $40. TO mint.**
ALMOND CREAM BALM 1908
2 & 6 oz. size tubes OSP 25c & 50c. **CMV $50. each MB, $40. TO.**

WITCHHAZEL CREAM 1923
Large & small green tube. OSP 30c & 59c. **CMV $40. MB, $35. TO mint.**

MENTHOL WITCH HAZEL CREAM 1909
2 oz. tube, 1sr issue. OSP 25c. **CMV $45., $50. MB.**

BAYBERRY SHAVING CREAM SAMPLE 1925
Small sample tube in sample box. Comes with instruction sheet. **CMV $70. MB.**
MENTHOL WITCH HAZEL CREAM 1923
Green tube. OSP 33c. **CMV $35. MB, TO mint, $30.**

AMBER CREAM SHAMPOO OR AMBER GEL 1948-50
Turquoise & white tube with blue cap **CMV $8. MB, $4. TO.**
CREME SHAMPOO 1955-60
Green and white tube, **CMV $10. MB, $6. TO.**

CREME SHAMPOO WITH LANOLIN 1960-62
Green & white box holds yellow tube with turquoise cap. **CMV $6. MB.**
WITCH HAZEL CREAM SAMPLE 1925
Green tube, says on back "Not for sale Sample". **CMV $45. MB, $40. TO mint.**

MENTHOL WITCH HAZEL CREAM 1930-36
Green & black tube. OSP 50c. **CMV $20.**
MB, $15. TO mint.
WITCH HAZEL CREAM 1930-36
Green & black tube OSP 75c. **CMV $20. MB,**
$15. TO mint.

ALMOND CREAM BALM 1910
Tube came in 2 sizes. OSP 25c & 50c. **CMV**
$45. MB, $40. TO mint.
COLD CREAM TUBE 1923
Large & small tube. OSP 23c & 45c. **CMV**
$30. TO mint, $40. MB.

SEN-DEN-TAL 1936-42
(Left) Turquoise & white tube. OSP 36c.
CMV $20. MB, TO mint $15.
SEN-DEN-TAL 1933-36
(Right) Green tube of tooth paste. OSP 35c.
CMV $25. MB, $20. TO mint.

WITCH HAZEL CREAM 1936-44
Turquoise & white tube OSP 52c. **CMV $15.**
MB, TO mint $12.
MENTHOL WITCH HAZEL CREAM 1936-44
Maroon & ivory colored tube. OSP 37c. **CMV**
$20. MB, TO mint $15.

TAKE ALONG HAND CREAM 1980
1 oz. tube in Vita Moist red design, or Rich
Moisture blue design. **CMV 50c each.MB.**
CREME SHAMPOO 1959
2.4 oz. yellow tube & turquoise cap. Yellow &
blue box. OSP 69c. **CMV $5. MB, $3. TO.**

BAYBERRY SHAVING CREAM 1923
Green tube, came in Gentlemens Shaving Set.
CMV $35. mint, $40. MB.
STYPTIC PENCIL 1923
White pencil. OSP 10c. **CMV $10. ,$15. MB.**
BRUSHLESS SHAVING CREAM 1936-49
Maroon & ivory tube. OSP 41c. **CMV $20.**
MB, $15. TO mint.

CREME SHAMPOO 1949-58
(Top) Green tube with blue or white cap. OSP
59c. **CMV mint TO $5., $8. MB.**
CREME SHAMPOO 1954-5
(Bottom) Green tube with white cap. OSP 59c.
CMV $8., MB, mint TO $6.

BAYBERRY SHAVING CREAM 1930-36
Green tube. OSP 35c. **CMV $25. MB, $20.**
TO mint.
BRUSHLESS SHAVING CREAM 1935-36
Green & black tube, OSP 51c. **CMV $25.**
MB, $20. TO mint.

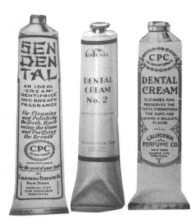

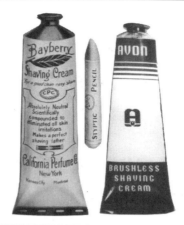

SEN-DEN-TAL 1921-33
Yellow tube. OSP 47c. **CMV $35. MB, $30 TO mint.** Also came in small sample tube. **CMV $35. mint.**

DENTAL CREAM NO. 2 1932-36
Green tube. OSP 35c. **CMV $25. MB.**

DENTAL CREAM 1915-33
OSP 23c. 1915-23 tube was pink, 1923-33 tube was light blue. **CMV pink tube mint $40., blue tube mint $35. Add $5. for box.**

BAYBERRY SHAVE CREAM 1923
Green tube. OSP 33c. **CMV $40. MB, $35. TO mint.**

SHAMPOO CREAM 1923
Yellow tube. OSP 48c. **CMV $40 MB, $35. TO mint.**

SHAVING CREAM 1936-49
Maroon & ivory tube. OSP 36c. **CMV $20. MB, TO mint $15.**

HAIR DRESS 1931-36
(Left) Silver tube. OSP 37c. **CMV $25. MB, $20. TO mint.**

HAIR DRESS 1936-49
(Center) Maroon & ivory colored tube. OSP 37c. **CMV $20. MB, TO mint $15.**

CREAM HAIR DRESS 1962-65
(Right) 4 oz. white tube. Red cap. Stage coach on tube. OSP 89c. **CMV $4., $6. MB.**

HAND CREAM NEW YEAR BOX 1943
Regular issue tube of hand cream. Came in special short issue Flower designed box. RARE. OSP 15c. **CMV $17. MB as shown.**

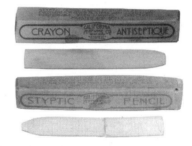

STYPTIC PENCIL 1925
White stick in CPC box. Came in Humidor Set box in French and English. **CMV $25. MB.**

HAND CREAM CHRISTMAS BOX 1934
(Left) Green & red box, short issue, holds silver tube of hand cream. OSP 10c with regular order. **CMV $18. MB as shown.**

HAND CREAM 1934
(Right) Regular issue, gray box holds silver tube of hand cream. OSP 52c. **CMV $12., TO mint $15. MB.**

DENTAL CREAM 1912
Metal tube, paper label. OSP 25c. **CMV $50. mint, $75. MB.**

ALMOND CREAM BALM 1908
Metal tube. OSP 50c. **CMV $45. mint, $55. MB.**

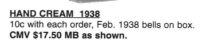

HAND CREAM 1938
10c with each order, Feb. 1938 bells on box. **CMV $17.50 MB as shown.**

TUBES - MISC.

HAND CREAM INTRODUCTORY 1934-36
Blue & silver tube. OSP 52c. **CMV $25. MB as shown, $20. TO mint.**

HAND CREAM SPECIAL ISSUE BOX 1941
Special issue flowered box holds regular issue tube of hand cream. Sold for 10c with regular order. **CMV $15. MB as shown.**

67th ANNIVERSARY HAND CREAM DUO 1953
Box holds two 2 1/2 oz. tubes of hand cream. OSP $1.10. **CMV $20. MB.**

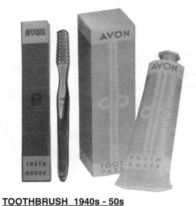

HAND CREAM DUO 1953
Box holds 2 tubes 2 1/2 oz. size of hand cream. Turquoise & white. OSP $1.18. **CMV $18.50 MB.**

HAND CREAM CHRISTMAS BOX 1935
Silver tube of hand cream came in special issue Christmas box for 10c with regular order. **CMV $17.50 MB as shown.** Same box came with Tulip 'A' tube of Hand Cream on right in 1936. **CMV $15. MB.**

TOOTHBRUSH 1940s - 50s
Turquoise and white box with Tulip A holds 1 Avon tooth brush. OSP 50c. **CMV $3.50 MB.**
TOOTHPASTE 1935-36
Red, white and green tube. OSP 23c. **CMV $17.50 MB as shown, tube only mint $12.**

HAIR BEAUTY 1956
Blue box holds two 2 oz. tubes of creme shampoo. OSP $1.29. **CMV $17.50 MB.**

HAND CREAM SPECIAL ISSUE BOX 1940
Special issue box is rose and white color. Has hand and flower on box with tulip A in flower. Sold for 10c. Holds regular issue hand cream tube. **CMV $16. MB as shown.**

HAND CREAM SPECIAL ISSUE BOX 1939
Short issue box came with regular issue, tube of hand cream for 10c with regular order. **CMV $17.50 MB as shown.**

CARE DEEPLY HAND CEAM 1974
2 tubes 4 oz. in pink, blue, orange & purple box. **CMV $4. MB.**

HAND CREAM CHRISTMAS PACKAGING 1964
Special Christmas boxes in pink, blue and white, came with choice of green tube of 3 oz. hand cream, 4 oz. white plastic bottle of hand loiton, pink and white 3 3/4 oz. tube of moisturized hand cream and 2 1/4 oz. turquoise and white tube of Silicone Glove. CMV $4. each MB.

MERRY CHRISTMAS HAND CREAM DUO 1953 ONLY
2 turquoise & white metal tubes of hand cream in Merry Christmas box. OSP $1.10. **CMV $20. MB.**

HAND CREAM SPECIAL ISSUE BOX 1942
Special issue box with flower design holds regular issue tube of hand cream. OSP 10c. **CMV $16. MB as shown.**

DOUBLY YOURS 1954
Rose box holds 2 tubes of Avon Hand Cream. OSP $1.18. **CMV $17. MB.**

CLEANSING CREAM SAMPLE 1936
(Left) 1/4 oz. tube, black or turquoise cap. **CMV $6.,** CPC label add $4.
CLEANSING CREAM 1957
(Right) 2 1/2 oz. white tube with gray band, turquoise lettering. OSP 59c. **CMV $3., $4. MB.**

FOR BEAUTIFUL HANDS 1956 ONLY
Blue flowered box holds 2 tubes of 2 3/4 oz. hand cream. OSP $1.10. **CMV $16. MB.**

CHRISTMAS TREASURE BOX 1960 ONLY
Red and green box holds turquoise tube of hand cream. OSP 69c. **CMV $7. MB as shown.** Tube only $2. mint.

MERRY CHRISTMAS TWIN FAVORITES 1956 ONLY
Green & red box holds 2 tubes of hand cream. OSP $1.18. **CMV $18. MB.**

FOR BEAUTIFUL HANDS 1954
2 1/2 oz. turquoise and white tubes with hand cream, turquoise caps. One tube with "Lanolin added" other regular issue. Box bouquet red roses. OSP $1.10. **CMV $17. MB.** In 1955 same box came with 2 tubes of hand cream like in the 1954 Merry Christmas Hand Cream, Duo. **CMV $17. MB.**

ROSEMINT FACIAL MASK 1962-71
(Left) 3 oz. pink and white tube. **CMV $2. MB.**

TUBES - MISC.

MERRY CHRISTMAS HAND CREAM DUO 1954
Red & white box holds two green tubes of Avon Hand Cream. OSP $1.10. **CMV $17. MB.**

HAND CREAM 1955-62
(Left) Turquoise tube and cap. Flat cap sold 1955-57 2 1/2 oz. tube. Tall cap sold 1957-62 2.65 oz. **CMV $3. flat cap MB, TO $2. flat cap mint $1. less on tall cap tubes.**
HAND CREAM 1937-54
(Right) 2 1/2 oz. turquoise and white tube. OSP 52c. **CMV $8. MB, TO mint $4.**

MOISTURIZED HAND CREAM CHRISTMAS BOX 1963 ONLY
3 3/4 oz. pink and white tube pictured with special issue Christmas box. **CMV $3. MB TO sold 1957-67, CMV TO $1.**
SILICONE GLOVE CHRISTMAS BOX 1963 ONLY
(Right) 2 1/4 oz. turquoise and white tube in special issue CHristmas box. **CMV $3. MB, TO sold 1960-69, CMV TO $1.**

HAND CREAM FOR MEN DOUBLE PAK 1966-68
Box holds 2 black & orange tubes. OSP $2.50. **CMV tubes $2. each. $8. set MB.**

HAND CREAM WITH LANOLIN 1954
2 1/2 oz. tube. OSP 59c. **CMV $12. MB, $10. TO mint.**
SPECIAL FORMULAS CREAM 1940-43
Turquoise & white tube. OSP 78c. **CMV $12. MB TO mint $9.**

MERRY CHRISTMAS GIFT BOXES 1958-59
Special issue gift box came with choice of Moisturized Hand Cream, pink and white tube. OSP 79c. Avon Hand Cream, turquoise tube. OSP 59c. Silicone Formula Hand Cream, white tube. OSP 98c. **CMV $10. MB as shown each.**

HAND CREAM 1963-69
3 oz. turquoise tube, white caps (top) tube older, (bottom) newer. Two different labels. (1963-69) $1. and (1970-73) **CMV 50c.**

FALL BAZAAR GIFT BOX 1955
Special issue Christmas box holds 2 turquoise tubes of hand cream. OSP 89c. **CMV $17. MB.**

PORE CREAM 1936-39
(Left) Turquoise & white tube. OSP 78c.
CMV $20. MB, $15. TO mint.
PORE CREAM 1930-36
(Right) Silver & blue tube. OSP 78c. **CMV
$25. MB, $20. TO mint.**

TOOTH PASTE SPECIAL ISSUE BOX 1938
Short issue box holds regular issue tooth
paste. Cost 10c with regular order. **CMV
$17.50 MB as shown.**

DEPILATORY 1931-34
Silver tube. OSP 75c. **CMV $17.50 MB, $12.
TO mint.**
DENTAL CREAM 1948-53
Red cap, red, white & blue tube. OSP 43c.
CMV $6. MB TO mint $4.

FLUFFY CLEANSING CREAM 1947
LIQUEFYING CLEANSING CREAM 1947
Both tubes are pink 2 1/4 oz. Came in 1947
Cleansing Cream Demo Kit only. Was never
sold to public. Very rare. **CMV $20. each.**

TOOTH PASTE SPECIAL ISSUE BOX 1937
Regular issue tooth paste came in special
issue box for 10c with regular order. **CMV
$17.50 MB as shown.**

TOOTHPASTE 1940
Special Box, OSP 10c with good order from
Rep. in Sept. 1940. **CMV $18. MB as shown.**

NIGHT CREAM 1948
SPECIAL DRY SKIN CREAM 1948
Both tubes are blue 2 1/4 oz. size. Came in
1948 Skin Care Demo Kit. Was never sold to
public. Very rare. **CMV each $20. mint full.**

AMMONIATED TOOTHPASTE 1949-55
Green & white tube. OSP 49c. **CMV $8. MB,
$5. TO mint.**
DENTAL CREAM 1936-44
Turquoise & white tube. OSP 26c. **CMV $10.
MB, $7. TO mint.**

TOOTHPASTE SPECIAL BOX 1939
OSP 10c with order October 1939. **CMV $18.
MB as shown.**

DENTAL CREAM 1933-36
(Left) Green tube. OSP 25c. **CMV $20. MB, $15. TO mint.**
TOOTHPASTE NO. 2 1936-48
(Center) Turquoise and white tube. OSP 23c. **CMV TO $10. mint, $15. MB.**
TOOTHPASTE 1936-48
(Right) Turquoise and white tube. OSP 23c. **CMV $12. MB, TO mint $7.**

CHLOROPHYL TOOTHPASTE 1953-56
Green & white tube, green cap. OSP 49c. **CMV $8. MB, TO mint $5.**
TOOTHPASTE 1953-56
Blue & white tube, white cap. OSP 49c. **CMV $8. MB, TO mint $5.** Also came in 3/4 oz. sample tube. **CMV $5. mint.**

SMOKERS TOOTHPASTE 1941-50
Maroon & cream colored tube. OSP 39c. **CMV $18. MB, $15. TO mint.**

SMOKERS TOOTHPASTE 1957-67
Red & white & grey tube. White cap. OSP 50c. **CMV $2.50 MB, $1. TO mint.**
DENTAL CREAM WITH AVONOL 1957-63
Red, white & gray tube, white cap. OSP 50c. **CMV $3. MB, TO $1.**

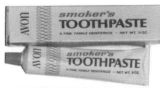

SMOKERS TOOTHPASTE 1964-67
5 oz. white tube, blue cap. OSP 79c. **CMV $1.50. MB.**
PREMIUM TOOTHPASTE 1964-66
5 oz. white tube, red cap. OSP 89c. **CMV $1.50 MB.**
CREAM DEODORANT 1964-67
OSP 69c. **CMV $1.50, $2. MB.**

SILICONE FORMULA CREAM 1957-61
White tube, small turquoise cap. OSP 98c. **CMV $2. MB, TO $1.**
MOISTURIZED HAND CREAM 1957-67
Pink & white tube, small white cap. OSP 79c. **CMV $2. MB, TO $1.**

ANTISEPTIC CREAM 1957-60
1 3/4 oz. tube white & gray & red with red cap. OSP 69c. **CMV $1. - $2. MB.**

CLEARLY GENTLE BABY "BEAR" PRODUCTS 1983
Each item has bear in blanket design.
BABY BATH
1 oz. tube.
BABY CREAM
1 oz. tube.
BABY OIL
1 oz. plastic bottle. **CMV $1. each. MB.**

RABBIT LIP BALM AND HAND CREAM 1983
Both have pink caps and rabbit on side. Hand cream is 1.5 oz. tube. No box. **CMV $1. each.**

STARS & STRIPES TO GO AFTER TAN MOISTURIZER 1982 ONLY
1 oz. bottle, red cap. No box. **CMV $1.**
SUNTAN LOTION
1 oz. tube, red cap, no box. **CMV $1.**

SAMPLES & DEMON-STRATOR KITS

CLOWNING AROUND BODY SOAP 1982
1.5 oz. tubes in red, yellow or blue. **CMV $1. MB. each.**

SEASONAL SMOOTHERS HAND CREAM 1982
1.5 oz. tubes in blue, red or green. **CMV $1. MB. each.**

SANTA'S HELPER HAND CREAM & LIP BALM 1980
Lip balm is green, red & white. Care Deeply hand cream is red, white & green. 1.5 oz. tube. Sold together with no box. **CMV $2. mint set.**

HOT STUFF 1981-82
Tanarifics Tanning lotions. 3.75 oz. Yellow tube. **CMV 50c.**

COOL IT 1981-82
Tanarifics Tanning Lotion 3.75 oz. blue tube. **CMV 50c.**

DELIVERY BAGS
(Left) 1929 black leatherette. **CMV $30.**
(Middle) 1948 black leatherette front opening lays flat. **CMV $20.** (Right) 1942 black leatherette. **CMV $20.**

CPC SALES MANAGERS DEMO BAG 1913
Leather bound straw bag used by early day Avon ladies to show their products. Measures 14" wide, 4" deep. 10" high. Does not say CPC on case. **CMV $75. mint.** Also came with CPC Products label on inside lid. Same design case only size is 17" x 11 1/4" x 4" deep. **CMV $100.**

FRUIT FOR ALL HAND CREAM & LIP BALM 1981
Lip balm & 1.5 oz. mathcing tube of hand cream in strawberry, grape or orange. **CMV $2. each set.**

DEMO BAG 1937
Simulated ostrich leather holds Avon sales catalog & room for 4 demo packages. Used by Avon Reps. **CMV $35. bag only mint.**

DELIVERY BAG 1941-43
Black imitation leather waterproof bag used by Reps to deliver Avon products. Base of bag measures 15 1/2" long, 7" wide. 10" high and has a 21 inch zipper. Cost a Rep $1.49. **CMV $15. mint.**

DELIVERY BAG PRIZE 1944
Black waterproof bag, zipper top, metal buttons on bottom to set on. Given to Reps for placing order of $150. or more. Used to deliver Avon products. **CMV $15. mint.**

DELIVERY BAG 1950s
Black leatherette. **CMV $17. mint.**

SAMPLES & DEMONSTRATOR KITS

SALES BAG 1953
Black bag used by Avon reps in early 50s.
CMV $22. mint.

DELIVERY BAG 1970s
White, blue & green design used by Avon
ladies. **CMV $6.**

DELIVERY BAG 1976
(Left) Blue brocade bag used by Avon Reps to
make delivery of Avon products. **CMV $3.**
BEAUTY SHOWCASE DEMO BAG 1976
(Right) Used by Avon Reps to carry Avon
demonstration products. Matching blue brocade. **CMV $3.**

BEAUTY SHOWCASE BAG 1960s (early)
(Right) Two tones blue with black trim. Used
by Reps. **CMV $6.**
BEAUTY SHOWCASE BAG 1960s (late)
(Left) Two toned blue & blue trim. Used by
Reps. **CMV $5.**

DELIVERY BAG 1960s
Used by Avon Reps. **CMV $25.**

HAND CARE DEMONSTRATOR KIT 1953
Box holds 2 bottles of nail polish, 1 tube of
hand cream, jar of nail beauty. **CMV $40. MB.**

DELIVERY BAG 1960s
Two toned blue, silver 4A emblem under handle. **CMV $6.**

BEAUTY SHOWCASE BAG 1970s
Blue & green vinyl came with blue plastic holder for samples. **CMV $10. for both or $5.
each.**

REPRESENTATIVES DEMO BAG 1970
White background with bright colored flowers.
Silver 4A emblem under handle. **CMV $6.
mint.**

IF YOU LOVE TO
LAUGH, GO TO THE
BACK PAGE FOR
INFO ON BUD
HASTIN'S NEW
JOKE BOOK AND
HOW TO GET IT.
LAUGH MORE AND
LIVE LONGER.

**REPRESENTATIVE DEMONSTRATOR KIT
1948**
Black leather kit. **CMV $90. mint.**

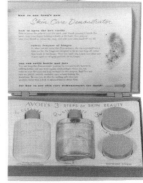

DEMONSTRATOR KIT 1942 ONLY
Box holds jar of cream deodorant & a bar of Lemonol soap. **CMV $45. MB.**

REPRESENTATIVE DEMO KIT 1940
Box holds jard of cleansing cream, night cream, foundation cream & bottle of skin freshener. **CMV $50. MB.**

SKIN CARE DEMONSTRATOR 1956
Plastic case holds plastic bottle of Deep Clean Cleansing Cream, 1 oz. glass bottle of Skin Freshener, 2 white jars of Rich Moisture & Hormone Cream & plastic spoon.. **CMV $37.50 MB.**

MAKE-UP TRIO DEMO KIT 1936
Brown box holds 1 3/4 oz. box of Ariel Suntan Face Powder, turquoise & gold rouge compact in Crusader red & matching lipstick in Crusader red. Came with fold out display card. **CMV $60. MB.**

PACK UP YOUR SKIN TROUBLES DEMONSTRATOR KIT 1953
Cardboard carrying case holds jars of cleansing cream & tissue cream & 4 oz. bottle of astringent. **CMV $50. MB.**

DEMONSTRATOR KIT 1946
Box holds tube of toothpaste & hand cream & bottle of antiseptic. **CMV $45.**

SHAMPOO DEMO KIT 1947
Box holds 2 bottles of soapless & liquid shampoo. For Reps only. **CMV $50. mint.**

BEAUTY COUNSELOR DEMO KIT SAMPLES 1956-60
(Front row left to right) White plastic jars with turquoise caps. Came in Vita Moist Cream, Strawberry Cooler, Rich Moisture Cream. **CMV $6. each.** (Back row left to right) Skin Freshener, clear glass, white cap, **$10.** Deep Clean Cleansing Cream, white plastic, gold lettering, white cap, **CMV $6.** Rouge, clear glass, white cap. **CMV $6. each.**

HAND LOTION & HAND CREAM DEMO KIT 1948
Demo box holds tubes of hand cream & 4 oz. bottle of hand lotion. Not sold. Used by Reps to sell products. **CMV $30. MB.**

SAMPLES & DEMONSTRATOR KITS

SKIN CARE DEMO KIT 1952
Flip open display box holds 1 jar each of Cleansing Cream and Night Cream and a bottle of skin freshener. Used by Reps to show products. CMV $35. MB.

FACIAL DEMO KIT 1940s
Green lid box with pink base holds white glass jars of cleansing cream, night cream, foundation cream & 4 oz. bottle of skin freshener. All have turquoise caps. Used by Reps to demonstrate facial products. CMV $45. MB.

CLEANSING CREAM DEMONSTRATOR KIT 1942
Box holds jar & 3 sample tubes of cleansing cream. CMV $35. MB.

DEMONSTRATOR KIT 1949
Demo box holds tubes of hand cream and creme shampoo and jar of perfumed deodorant. Used by Reps to show products. CMV $35. MB.

CLEANSING CREAM DEMONSTRATOR KIT 1951
Demo box holds 2 white glass jars with turquoise lids of Cleansing Creams & 1 jar of Night Cream. Used by Reps to show products. CMV $25. MB. Comes in 2 different boxes.

FACIAL DEMONSTRATOR KIT 1942
Box holds 3 tubes of night cream, jar of night cream, foundation cream & 4 oz. bottle of skin freshener. CMV $50. MB.

CLEANSING CREAM DEMO KIT 1947
Box with lady's face on lid holds tube of liquifying & fluffy cleansing cream. Pink tubes, 2 1/4 oz. each. Tubes were never sold to public. For Reps only. CMV Rare $45. MB.

CLEANSING CREAM SAMPLE SET 1940s
Box holds 10 turquoise 1/4 oz. sample tubes of cleansing cream. Also came with 2 stacks of Your Skin Can Be Beautiful pamphlets. CMV $35. MB.

SKIN CARE DEMO KIT 1948
Demo box holds blue 2 1/4 oz. tube of Fluffy Cleansing Cream, 4 oz. bottle of Skin Freshener & tube of Special Dry Skin Cream. Not sold to public. Used by Reps as demonstrator. CMV $55. MB.

DENTAL DEMO KIT 1949
Box holds tube of Ammoniated toothpaste and can of Ammoniated tooth powder. Not sold to public. Used by Reps to show products. CMV $40. MB.

HAND CREAM SAMPLES 1938
Box of 24 1/4 oz. turquoise & white tubes. CMV $3. each tube, mint complete $100.
CLEANSING CREAM SAMPLES 1938
Same box as hand cream samples. Box of 24 1/4 oz. tubes. CMV $3. each tube mint, complete set $100.

PERFUME DEMO KIT 1940-41
Green & gold box holds three 1 dram bottles with colored caps. Perfume samples set used by Representatives. Came in Marionette, Garden of Love, Coitllion & Gardenia. **CMV $67.50 MB.**

BIRTHDAY CAKE 1951
Blue & white box holds foam cake with five 1 dram ribbed perfumes. To A Wild Rose, Golden Promise, Cotillion, Quaintance & Flowertime. This was a demonstrator kit, for Reps. **CMV $90.** cake & bottles only mint, **$125. MB.**

PERFUME SAMPLES 1947-50
Small sample tubes with glass vials of perfume inside. Gardenia, Lily of the Valley, Crimson Carnation, Luscious, Garden of Love, Ballad, Quaintance & Golden Promise. **CMV $20. each with vials.** Here's My Heart, FLowertime, Quaintance & Cotillion came in pink or blue tubes. **CMV $15. each mint.**

76th ANNIVERSARY CELEBRATION DEMO KIT 1962
(right) Pink cardboard box holds 2 oz. Cotillion cologne, Cotillion cream sachet, 2 oz. perfumed deodorant, 6 oz. Rosiest Spray Sachet, Silver Notes Eye Shadow & Hi Light Shampoo. **CMV $30.**

PERFUME SAMPLE 1964
Small 1/8 oz. bottle came in Occur!, Somewhere, Cotillion, Topaze, Here's My Heart, Persian Wood, To A WIld Rose. **CMV $8. each.**

PERFUME SAMPLE 1932
Very small glass vial with cork stopper in envelope. Came in Gardenia, Jardin D'Amour, Bolero, Cotillion, Ariel, Narcissus, Rose, Lily of the Valley, Sweet Pea, Trailing Arbutus. CPC on package. **CMV $18. each in envelope mint.**

GARDEN OF LOVE PERFUME SAMPLE 1940
Small bottle with metal cap in sample envelope. Also came in Ballad, Trailing Arbutus, Cotillion, Gardenia, Merriment, Sweet Pea, Courtship, Lily of the Valley, Jardin D'Amour. **CMV $18. each in envelope only. Add $2. for CPC on envelope.**

PERFECT BALANCE MANAGER'S DEMO KIT 1974
Contained Tissue-Off cleansing cream, Toning Freshener, night cream, Wash-Off cleansing lotion, Toning astringent, night time moisturizer. **CMV $20. MB.**

MANAGERS DEMO KIT 1965
White box holds eye & face make-up. **CMV $55. MB.**

PRIMA NATURA PRODUCTS INTRODUCTION DEMO KIT FOR MANAGERS ONLY 1970
White Avon embossed box holds Creme of Soap, Night Veil Concentrate, Toning Freshener, Moisturizing Freshener. **CMV $25.**

SAMPLES & DEMONSTRATOR KITS

MAKE-UP DEMO CASE 1979
Large tan vinyl case. **CMV $5. MB.**

77th ANNIVERSARY DEMO SET 1963
Demo kit for Avon Reps on 77th Anniversary. Top of box has rose in left corner & says "Celebrating Avon's 77th Anniversary." Box holds 2 oz. cologne mist with 4A's embossed on side, jar of cream foundation, 4 oz. skin-so-soft & petti pat compact. **CMV $35. MB.**

FASHION MAKEUP GROUP COLLECTION 1977
Demo kit used by Reps to sell Fashion Makeup products. Box is black & gold with white base. Outside sleeve. Cost Rep $5.47. **CMV $8. MB complete.**

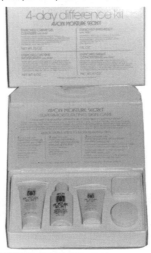

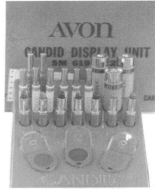

ENVIRA MAKE-UP DEMO KIT & PRODUCTS 1979-80
Pink lid box with outer sleeve & white plastic inner base holds 1 each of Envira Products which are also sold separate: Conditioning Make-up, Pure Color Blush, Gentle Eye Color, Pure Color Lipstick, Soft Eye Definer, Conditioning Mascara. **CMV complete set in demo box, mint, $7.50.**
SAMPLES CONDITIONING MAKE-UP
Box of 10.
SAMPLES OF PURE COLOR BLUSH
Box of 10. **CMV 25c. All products listed each.**

MOISTURE SECRET KIT 1980
Outer sleeve holds white and pink plastic case. 4 small pink plastic containers of creams. **CMV $7. MB.**

CANDID MANAGERS DISPLAY 1976
Orange plastic display for Avon managers to display new Candid products. Base holds 7 Candid lipsticks, 6 eye colors, 2 mascaras, 3 cheek colors & three 1 1/2 oz. bottles of make-up. **CMV complete full set MB $45., empty items 25c each, base only $15.**

FRESH LOOK MAKE-UP DEMO KIT 1979
Used by Reps only. Peach color box. **CMV $8. MB.**

REP'S DEMO & ORDER CASE 1970
Blue plastic snap shut case. Has order pad & fragrance samples & color brochures. **CMV $10. mint.**

COLORWORKS DEMO KIT 1977
Silver & white box with outer sleeve holds Oil Free Liquid Makeup, Oil Free Cheekblush, Supershine Lip Gloss, Lasting Eye Shadow & Lashes, Lashes Mascara. Used by Reps to sell new Colorworks products. Rep cost $4.50. **CMV $8. MB complete.**

TIME CONTROL DEMO KIT 1980
Black & pink box & sleeve has small white hour glass & .75 oz. plastic bottles of Time Control. Plus 6 more bottles in box. Used by Reps as demo kit. **CMV $8. MB.**

MOISTURE SECRET SKIN CARE KIT 1978
White & pink plastic kit holds pink plastic tubes of Moisture Secret Enriched Creme gel Cleanser, Enriched Freshener & Enriched Daytime Moisturizer. All with PMB and pink plastic jar of Enriched Night Concentre. All are trial size. Came with outer sleeve over kit. **CMV $6. MB.**

CANDID MAKEUP DEMO KIT 1977
For Reps only. Box lid Candid is in different position than regular set sold. Came with outer sleeve and says (Not for Resale) on back side. Box holds 5 items. Makeup, lip color, eye color, cheek color, mascara with lash builders. **CMV $10. MB with outer sleeve only.** Sold to public for $10.95. **Same CMV.**

ACCOLADE DEMO KIT 1982
Carmel color plastic case holds Accolade products for Avon managers. **CMV $20. mint.**

FACE POWDER DEMO PALETTE 1940s
Green palette holds 5 Tulip "A" metal samples in Ariel & Vernafleur. **CMV $32. mint.**

BEAUTY FLUID SAMPLE KIT 1980
Given to President's Club member Reps. Box has outer sleeve. Silver & brown box & sleeve. Holds 3 oz. bottle of beauty fluid & pack of tissues. **CMV $12. MB.**

MAKING EYES DISPLAY 1976
Plastic base used by managers to display new turquoise color eye makeup products. Base holds 12 powder eye shadows, 5 dream eye shadows, 2 eye shadow wands, 3 mascaras, 3 brow & liner pencils. **CMV $25. MB as shown full. Products 25c each empty. CMV base only $5.**

REPRESENTATIVE DEMO CASE 1936
Black case with metal mirror in lid. Handle is on opposite side of lid opening. Inner shelf is dark blue & lifts out of case. Storage area under shelf. Case came complete with 1936 sales catalog, 1/4 oz. glass stopper perfume in Cotillion, metal cap 1/4 oz. perfume in Gardenia, blue & silver lipstick & rouge compact, silver box of face powder, ribbed glass bottle of skin freshener (2 oz.), astringent 92 oz.), Lotus Cream (4 oz.), Rosewater Glycerin & Benzoin (4 oz.). All with black caps. 2 oz. jars of vanishing cream & tissue cream & 4 oz. jars of cleansing cream. **CMV $700. MB complete set.**

GIFT DISPLAY ENSEMBLE DEMO 1943
A special hand carrying box used by Reps at Christmas time to show Christmas sales items & sets. **To determine price of this kit, look up each set & get their price, then add $25. for this demo box.**

GIFT DISPLAY ENSEMBLE DEMO 1942
A special hand carrying box used by Reps at Christmas time. Came with several sets to show customers. **To determine price of this kit, look up each set & get price. Then add $25. for the demo box.**

DEMO KIT - CHRISTMAS 1941
For Representatives only. **CMV complete $350.00 mint.**

REPRESENTATIVE DEMO CASE 1930s
Black case held sets & demo products & catalog. No price established. **Case only $75. mint.**

BEAUTY COUNSELOR DEMO KIT 1959-60
Black shoulder bag with outside pocket holds removable turquoise & white plastic inner case with Avon & 4A design on lid containing 3 white plastic jars with turquoise lids holding .46 oz. of Rich Moisture Cream, Vita Moist Cream & Strawberry Cooler, 1 oz. glass bottle sample of Skin Freshener, 1 1/4 oz. white plastic sample bottle Deep Clean Cleansing Cream, 17 sample bottles of Liquid Powder, 5 liquid rouge samples in small bottles, 45 gold metal lipstick samples & 16 plastic shaker powder samples. **CMV $200. complete & mint.**

FACE POWDER DEMONSTRATOR PALETTE 1957
Turquoise board holds 10 samples with clear plastic tops. **CMV $10. mint.**

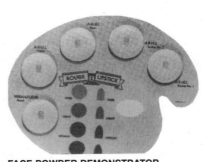

FACE POWDER DEMONSTRATOR PALETTE 1938
Board holds 5 samples in Ariel & Vernafleur. **CMV $20. mint.**

FACE POWDER DEMONSTRATOR PALETTES
HEAVENLIGHT 1946-49
(Left) Blue board holds 9 feather design samples. **CMV $15. mint**
FACE POWDER PALETTE 1949-54
(Right) Turquoise board holds 8 to 10 samples. **CMV $10. mint.**
FACE POWDER PALETTE 1954-55
(Bottom) Turquoise board holds 10 samples. **CMV $10. mint.**

FACE POWDER DEMONSTRATOR PALETTE 1942
Board holds 8 paper box samples. **CMV $15. mint.**

HEAVENLIGHT FACE POWDER SAMPLE PALETTE 1946
Each pink sample has Heavenlight written across each top. **CMV $15.mint**

FACE POWDER DEMONSTRATOR PALETTE 1940
Board holds 8 metal samples. **CMV $20. mint.**

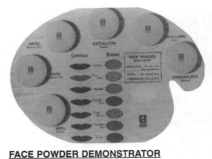

FACE POWDER DEMONSTRATOR PALETTE 1940
Board holds 6 metal samples in Ariel, Cotillion & Vernafleur. **CMV $20. mint.**

FACE POWDER PALETTE DEMONSTRATOR 1950s
Board holds 10 sample powders. Came in pink envelope. Used by Reps. Same palette came in different envelopes. **CMV $10. with envelopes mint.**

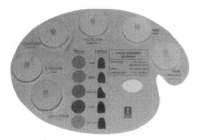

FACE POWDER DEMONSTRATOR PALETTE 1939
Board holds 6 different face powder samples with tulip A on lid in Cotillion, Ariel or Vernafleur. **CMV $20. mint.**

HEAVENLIGHT FACE POWDER SAMPLE 1940s
Blue metal case, white feather on lid. **CMV $2. mint.**

FACE POWDER SAMPLES 1949-55
(Left) Green metal samples. **CMV $1. each mint.**
FACE POWDER SAMPLE 1930-36
(Right) Small silver can, came in Ariel or Vernafleur. **CMV $2. mint.**

FACE POWDER SAMPLE SET 1942
Box holds 30 metal face powder samples. **CMV $45. set MB, $1. each sample.** Also came with CPC Avon label. **CMV $65. set MB.**

HEAVENLIGHT FACE POWDER SAMPLES 1946-49
Box holds 30 feather design samples. **CMV $35. MB.** Samples came both in cardboard & tin.

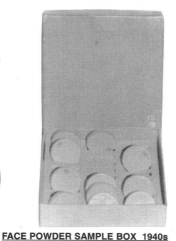

FACE POWDER SAMPLE BOX 1940s
Light green box holds 30 plain blue face powder samples. Avon on back. **CMV $25. box complete mint.**

LIPSTICK SAMPLES
(Left) 1947 red box holds 30 brass samples. Also came 2 boxes in a plain carton from Avon. **CMV $30. CMV $60. box of 2 sets.**
(Right) 1951 white plastic tray holds 30 brass lipstick samples. **CMV $25. mint.**

LIPSTICK DEMONSTRATOR 1952
Box holds 4 full size gold embossed lipsticks & 1 refill. Used early to mid-50s. **CMV $30. MB.**

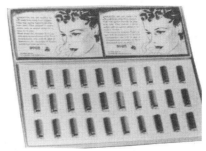

LIPSTICK DEMONSTRATOR 1940
Box holds 30 metal lipstick samples, with cards. **CMV $35. MB with all 30 cards.**

NEW CUSTOMER KIT 1936-40
Turquoise box holds 30 turquoise metal lipstick samples with 30 sample cards. **CMV $45. set MB with all cards.**

SAMPLES & DEMONSTRATORS KITS

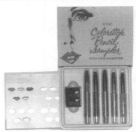

FACE POWDER SAMPLES 1942
Box holds 30 blue feather design samples.
CMV $42. MB.

CREAM CAKE SAMPLES 1949-55
Holds 6 shades of cream cake. **CMV $8. mint.**

LIPSTICK DEMONSTRATOR CASE 1942
Box holds 30 turquoise plastic or metal samples or 30 brass bamboo samples. **CMV $40. MB.** Lady's face on top of box.

COLORSTICK PENCIL SAMPLER 1977
Plastic base with sleeve lid holds color chart & 5 Colorstick pencils & brown plastic 2 hole pencil sharpener, marked Avon. Used by Reps to sell Colorstick products. **CMV $2. MB complete.**

COLOGNE DEMONSTRATOR SET 1956
1 dram bottles of To A Wild Rose, Forever Spring, Bright Night, Nearness, Elegante & Cotillion. All different color caps, in pink & gold box. **CMV $15. MB.** Also came out in Canada in all white caps. **CMV $15. MB.**

FACE POWDER SAMPLES 1940-50s
Avon envelope holds 10 sample packets of face powder. **CMV $3. mint.**

FRAGRANCE SAMPLES - WOMEN'S 1960
(Top) Pink & gold box holds ten 1 dram bottles, white caps. **CMV $12. MB.**
LIPSTICK JEWEL ETCHED SAMPLES 1949-EARLY 1950s
(Bottom) Box holds 30 metal lipstick samples. **CMV $30. MB.**

BATH FRESHENER SAMPLES 1968
Colored caps, 7 samples. **CMV $6. MB.** 14 samples, white caps. **CMV $7. MB.**

FACE POWDER DEMO SAMPLES 1949-50
Pink & white feather box holds 50 demo packets of face powder. Used by Reps. Packets are different. Was not sold to public. **CMV $15. MB.**

DEMONSTRATOR KIT 1940
(Right) Box with gold Avon seal on lid holds lipstick sample box, face powder palette, box of face powder & 30 cotton puffs. **CMV complete set $75. MB.**

FRAGRANCE COLOGNE SAMPLES 1965
Pink & gold box holds 10 cologne samples with white caps. **CMV $7. MB.**

LIPSTICK PACKS 1950s
Two different packs of 10 brass lipsticks. **CMV $6. complete pack or 50 sample pack, brass. CMV $15. complete.**

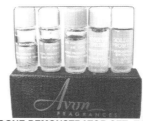

COLOGNE DEMONSTRATOR SET EARLY 1950s
1 dram bottles of Cotillion, Quaintance, Forever Spring, Golden Promise & To A Wild Rose. In green & gold box. Came in 5 & 6 bottle sets. **CMV $17. MB.**

NOSE GAY LIPSTICK DEMO KIT 1960
White foam, pink ribbon & flowers. Holds 4 white lipsticks. Came only in plum, orange, peach & cherry blossom. Made up like flower bouquet. **CMV $65. mint.**

LIPSTICK SAMPLE 1940
Gold metal case on display card. Came in 2 different size & style cards as shown. **CMV $1. on card, lipstick only 25c.**
LIPSTICK SAMPLE 1938
Same card as 1940 card only came with turquoise metal lipstick sample. **CMV $1. on card, mint.**

CUSTOM CONDITIONER 1971-72
(Left) 3/4 oz. bottle with white cap. Used in Avon beauty shops for professional use only. **CMV $10.**
NEW DIMENSION EXTRA & REGULAR 1971-72
(Right) 3/4 oz. glass bottle. Used in Avon beauty shops for professional use only. Top of bottle must be broken to use contents. **CMV $10.**

EYE SHADOW DEMONSTRATOR CARD 1960
Six gold metal eye shadow tubes. **CMV $2. mint.**

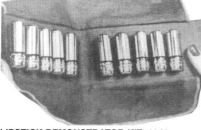

LIPSTICK DEMONSTRATOR KIT 1949
Black flannel roll-up kit holds 10 gold full size lipsticks. **CMV $30. mint.**

LIPSTICK DEMONSTRATOR 1953
Green leatherette zippered case holds 5 gold lipsticks. **CMV $27.50 mint.**

LIPSTICK DEMONSTRATOR 1961
A demonstrator piece sold to representatives for $1.35. Black plastic base with clear lucite dome. Came with silver deluxe lipstick with 4A on top (wrong lipstick shown in case). **CMV $22. MB.**

MEN'S AFTER SHAVE SAMPLES
Two on left are 1960s. Box red & silver, bottles have red caps. **CMV $10. MB.** Two on right are late 60s & early 70s. Box is red woven design & black, bottles have red caps. Came with 2 different outer sleeves as shown on top. **CMV $6. each MB.**

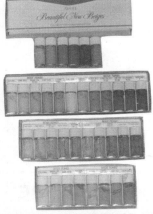

FOUNDATION DEMONSTRATOR 1960s
Clear glass bottles with white plastic lids. (Top to bottom) 6 bottle set, 12 bottle set; 10 bottles set. Front row 8 bottle set. **CMV all sets $5. MB.**

HARMONY ROUGE SAMPLES 1956
(Left) 5 sample bottles. **CMV $15.**
COLOGNE SAMPLES 1950
(Right) Green box holds 6 samples, colored lids. **CMV $12. MB.**
COLOGNE SAMPLES 1968
(Bottom) Green box with woven design holds 7 samples, all have yellow caps. **CMV $5. MB.**

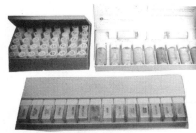

LIPSTICK SAMPLES 1960s-70s
(Top Left) Turquoise plastic box holds 40 white plastic lipstick samples. **CMV 10c each sample or $5. MB complete.**
LIQUID POWDER SAMPLES 1967
(Top Right) Box of 12 samples, clear plastic top. **CMV $5. MB.**
POWDER SAMPLES 1958
(Bottom) 14 samples, square container. **CMV $7. MB.**

FRAGRANCE DEMO KIT 1978-83
Plastic demo kit holds 6 sample bottles of Avon fragrance. **CMV $2. mint.**

FOUNDATION MAKEUP DUO 1977
(Left) Box holds 7 Even-Tone foundation tubes with white caps. Marked not for resale on back. **CMV $2. MB.**
COLORCREME MOISTURE LIPSTICKS DEMO SET 1978
(Right) Fruit basket design box holds 15 small white plastic sample lipsticks & 1 full size lipstick in silver & blue tube. Box came with outer sleeve. **CMV $2. MB.**

TRIBUTE AFTER SHAVE SAMPLES 1963
(Left) Box of 10. **CMV $5.**
OCCUR! CREAM SACHET SAMPLES 1965
(Center) Box of 30. **CMV each $5.**
CREAM HAIR DRESS SAMPLES 1961
(Right) Box of 30 tubes. **CMV $5. MB, each tube 25c.**

TISSUE DEMONSTRATOR 1949
Small packet of Avon tissues for demonstrations. **CMV $12. mint.**

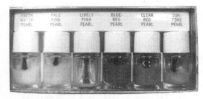

NAIL POLISH DEMONSTRATOR 1957
Six 1/2 dram bottles with white caps. **CMV $20. MB.**

FOUNDATION MAKEUP DEMO 1973
Box holds 7 bottles with white caps. Used by Reps only. **CMV $3. MB.**

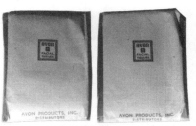

FACIAL TISSUE SAMPLES 1937-44
Beige & green paper wrapper. **CMV $10. mint.**

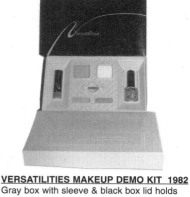

EYE SHADOW TRY-ONS 1964
Demo paper container with 50 match samples, double sided. **CMV $6. mint.** Eye shadow Try-Ons also came with 15 match samples. **CMV $5. mint.**

FLAVOR BUDS TOOTHPASTE SAMPLE 1950s
Red & white box with foil tear off samples. **CMV $7. MB.**

VERSATILITIES MAKEUP DEMO KIT 1982
Gray box with sleeve & black box lid holds black & gray lipstick & Versatilities nail polish & eye makeup. Used by reps for demo. **CMV $5. MB.**

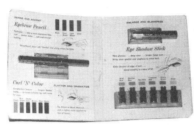

POWDER SACHET PACKETS 1950s
Came in all fragrances, 10 in an envelope. **CMV $1. each or $7. for packet of 10 mint.**

NEW BEAUTY FOR EYES DEMO 1960
Cardboard card opens up with 6 brass lipstick samples, brass eye shadow stick, eyebrow penil & curl 'n' color. Used by Reps. **CMV $4. mint.**

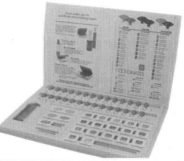

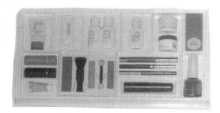

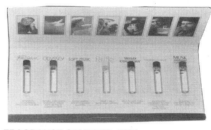

BEAUTY MAKE-UP DEMOS KIT
Came in gray box. **CMV $5. MB.**

FRAGRANCE SAMPLER 1984
Gold box holds 7 one inch vials of fragrance, 4 womens & 3 mens. **CMV $4. MB.**

COORDINATES MAKEUP DEMONSTRATOR 1983
Plastic display case used by Avon reps to show makeup products. Size 11" x 16". Red & white lip stick sample tubes, nail enamel fan demo, eye shadow, blush colors. **CMV $10. MB.**

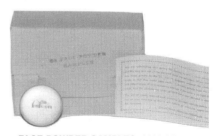

FACIAL TISSUES DEMO 1940s
Plain box of Avon Tissue used as demo for reps. **CMV $20. mint.**

FACE POWDER SAMPLE 1941
(Left) 1 metal face powder sample of Tulip "A" design on round card. Silverback says "Avon Products 1 dollar." **CMV $6. mint.**
FACE POWDER SAMPLE MASTERPIECE 1941
(Right) Blue card holds Tulip "A" metal samples of Rose & Ochre Rose. **CMV $7. mint.**

FACE POWDER SAMPLES 1930-36
Plain box of 30 silver & blue metal samples. With CPC card inside. **CMV $30. MB.**

PAPER ITEMS - SALES CATALOGS

CPC CALLING CARD 1896
(Left) Has list of products on back side and CPC Co., 126 Chambers St., New York on front. **CMV $25.**

CPC SALES CATALOG 1896
(Right) Small 30 page booklet on products. Contains no pictures. Rare. **CMV $75.**

INSTRUCTIONAL MANUAL 1912
(Left) Used by CPC Slaes Managers. **CMV $50.**

CATALOG CPC 1912
(Center) 64 page sales catalog used by Reps. **CMV $150.**

WOMEN BEAUTIFUL BOOKLET 1909
(Right) Small booklet on massage cream. **CMV $35.**

CPC SALES CATALOG 1916-29
On bottom is black hard bound CPC Sales Catalog with 32 to 40 color pages. Book is 10 1/2" x 16" in size. The hard bound book was first issued in 1916 in the big size and last used in 1921. Gold lettering on front. 1922-1929 the black catalog is soft cover and 34 pages in color. 10" x 14 1/2" in size. These catalogs are usually not dated and very hard to find. **CMV range from $25. in very bad condition to $150 for a mint, new condition catalog.** Each year a new book was issued.

BABY BOOK 1920
(Left) **CMV $50.**

CATALOG CPC 1898
(Center) 62 page sales catalog. Only has illustrations, not pictures of products. Book is dated 1898. **CMV $200.**

CATALOG CPC 1897
(Right) 62 page sales catalog. Book is dated 1897. **CMV $200.**

CPC MAIL ORDER CATALOG 1916-18
(Left) 4 1/2" x 6" gray cover 40 page booklet sent to customers in areas where CPC Reps did not call. Rare. **CMV $150.**

CPC CATALOG 1898
(Right) 5" x &' size blue cover and 64 pages in blue paper. Used by CPC Reps to sell products. Eureka Trade Mark on back cover. Very rare. **CMV $200.**

CATALOGS CPC
1900 CPC Catalog shown on top left, top right **1898**, bottom right 1908 and bottom left is **1915**. Each one shows the item sold during that period by CPC and gives prices. **1915** was the last small catalog printed. **1916** they went to the large black hard bound color books. For comparison of size, the **1896** is 4 1/2" wide and 6 5/8" high. **CMV $150.**

CATALOGS - AVON 1930-57
1930-36 10" x 7" dark blue, silver Avon on cover. **CMV $20. to $30 depending on condition.**
1936-48 7 1/4" x 10 1/2" size, green cover, gold tulip A. **CMV $20 . to $30.**
1948-54 7 1/4" x 10 1/2" green cover, Avon in gold letters. **CMV $10. to $15.**
    Bottom row left to right.
1954 A special gold cover catalog for Honor Presidents Award Reps. **CMV $20 each.**
1954-57 General issue was green cover 7 1/2" x 10 1/2", gold Avon and 4A design. **CMV $10.**
1956 Honor Award - Red cover catalog gold Avon and 4A design. **CMV $15.** Each of these catalogs was made to install or remove pages. The dates given reflect the years that each cover was issued. Each catalog was changed each year on the inner pages.

OUTLOOKS 1905-74
Outlooks were first printed in 1905 and given only to sales Reps. of CPC and Avon. They were to show new items coming out and also show awards they could win. The Outlook was discontinued in 1974 and the name was changed to "Avon Calling". Outlooks were given for each sales campaign during the year. **CMV 1905 to 1930, $5. to $15.; 1930 to 1939, $2 to $5.; 1940 to 1949 $1. to $5.; 1950 to 1959, $1 to $4.; 1960 to 1965, $1. to $3.; 1960 to 1969, 50c. to $1.; 1970 to 1976 10c. to 25c. each.**

POCKET CATALOG 1937
A small fold out leaflet brochure left with the customer to buy Avon products. **CMV $25. mint.**

CPC LADY INTRODUCTION CARD 1930's
3 1/2" x 5 1/4" card used by Reps. to introduce themselves to customers. **$4. mint.**

CHRISTMAS AVON CATALOGS
Starting in the early 1930's thru 1956, Avon printed a special Christmas Sales Catalog showing many gifts never sold at any other time. These catalogs are rare and hard to find. **CMV 1930's, $40. each. 1940's $35. each. 1950's $15. each.**

CHRISTMAS CATALOG 1967
In upper right part of picture is special hard bound edition. **CMV $8. mint.**

SALES BROCHURES 1920's 30's
Fold out sales brochures given to customers by CPC and Avon Representatives. Each one shows all items sold in regular sales catalog. These are rare and in color. Left to right 1926, **CMV $40.; 1929, CMV $35.; 1931-36, CMV $30.** A 1933 brochure is laid out on bottom to see all the products offered.

CPC CALENDAR 1910
9" wide, 12 5/16" high. Printed in 6 colors. Given to all customers with order of 75c. or more. **CMV $250. in New Condition**

CPC CALENDAR 1909
Given only to best CPC customers. **CMV $300. in New Condition**

CALENDAR 1967
Avon Calling calendar. **CMV $8. mint.**

CALENDAR - AVON 1979-80
Large Avon calendar given to customers by Avon Reps. Came in big envelope each year. **CMV $1. each mint in envelope.**

ORDER BOOK 1981
(Bottom) Green & white **CMV 50c.**
ORDER BOOK 1982
(Top) Pink & white **CMV 50c.**

CPC INTRO BOOKLET 1928
(Left) 30 page booklet used by Reps to start selling Avon. **CMV $30. mint.**
CPC ORDER BOOKLET 1922
(Right) Used by Reps. to keep records of their orders. **CMV $25 mint.**

ORDER BOOK CPC AVON 1930
(Left) **CMV $15. mint.**
CUSTOMER LIST BOOKLET 1930
(Center) 8 pages. **CMV $5. mint.**
CPC CUSTOMER LIST BOOKLET 1928
(Right) 12 pages. **CMV $8. mint.**

ORDER BOOK CPC 1926
Order book used by Reps. shown with CPC envelope and announcement of new head-quarters address in New York. **CMV $25 as shown.**

ORDER BOOKS (Left to right)
1933, 37, 42 Far right 1939 green order book cover. **CMV $15. each mint.**

ORDER BOOK COVER 1940
Dark green cover for order book imprinted with tulip "A" and name of representative. Given for sales during 1940 Founders Campaign. **CMV in envelope $20. - book only $15 mint.**

ORDER BOOK 1960's 70's
Misc. Avon Order Books used by Reps. **CMV 50c. each.**

ORDER BOOKS
(Left to right) 1920's CPC on cover (white cover). **CMV $20.**
1930's Tulip A design (white cover) **CMV $15.**
1940's Script A design (blue cover). **CMV $10.**
1950's 4A design (green cover). **CMV $5.**
1960's 4A design (white cover). **CMV $2.**
All must be in new condition for CMV given.

BUSINESS INTRO BOOK 1935
(Left) 20 page booklet on how to be a Avon Lady. Used by Reps. **CMV $5.**
BUSINESS INTRO BOOK 1931
(Right) 17 page booklet on how to be an Avon lady. Used by Reps. **CMV $5.**

AVON FACIAL TISSUE 1937-44
Turquoise & white paper box. Rare **CMV $20 mint.**

ORDER BOOK 1960
(Left) **CMV $2.**
CALL TAG PADS 1958
(Right) Pad of tear off sheets left by Avon lady. **CMV $3. pad.**

FACIAL TISSUES 1932-36
Box of 160 tissues. **CMV $30. mint.**

ADDRESS BOOK 1930's - 40's
(Left) Green leather, gold A design. **CMV $10.**
HONOR AWARD BOOK COVER 1956
(Center) Red plastic, gold design. **CMV $7.50.**

CLEANSING TISSUE 1930-32
Wrapped in cellophane. Package of 135 sheets. **CMV $15. mint.**

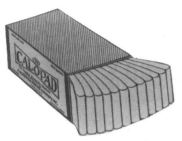

CALOPAD SANITARY NAPKINS 1926
Cardboard box holds 12 napkins. **CMV $75. MB. Extremely Rare.**

CPC FIVE HUNDRED CLUB CERTIFICATE 1930's
Sent to a representative when she completes $500. worth of net business. **CMV $25. mint.**

BEAUTY SERVICE BOOK 1935
30 page booklet showing how to apply Avon cosmetics. Used by Reps. Came in Avon CPC envelope. **CMV $10 mint with envelope.**

CPC BOOKLET
(Left) Cover says "Introducing You To The CPC". **CMV $30.**
GREAT OAK BOOKLET 1945
(Right) 20 page, blue cover. Given to Reps. in 1945. Written by D.H. McConnell, founder of CPC in 1903. Came with letter from Russel Rooks who became President of Avon. Rare. **CMV $50. with letter.**

EARLY 1930's CPC AVON FIVE HUNDRED CLUB
Certificate given to representatives for selling $500 worth of Avon products. **CMV $20. each, mint.**

50TH ANNIVERSARY GOLD QUILL PEN & LETTER 1936
Sent to representatives to announce the 50th year celebration. The circle stands for the "Avon Family Circle", the feather and quill indicated the opportunities to "Feather Your Nests". Comes complete with attached 50th anniversary letter. It folds in center. Did not come separate. **CMV complete as pictured $50. mint.**

PAVING THE WAY 1937
Booklet used by the Reps. in 1930's to help train them for better sales. Tulip A on cover. **CMV $8.**

McCONNELL LETTER BOOK 1930
174 pages of letters from Managers to D. H. McConnell, Avon Founder. Rare. No price established.

CPC SALES REP CONTRACT 1930's
Used to sign up CPC Reps. for sales in early 1930's. Came in CPC Avon business envelope. Shown also with Customer List booklet & booklet "Now You are in Business for Yourself." **CMV $25 complete as shown.**

PROMISE TO MYSELF BOOKLET 1953
23 page booklet published by Irene Nenemaker & Avon Products, Inc. **CMV $10.**

BEAUTY SERVICE BOOKLET 1934
24 page beauty tip book. **CMV $10.**

MANAGERS INFORMATION BOOKLET 1945
8 1/4" x 9" - 18 page booklet for managers to show new Avon Reps. for general information on Avon products. The cover of this booklet is the same artwork Avon Products used to make the 1977 National Association of Avon Clubs plate advertised in C26-77 Avon Calling. **CMV $15.**

CHILDREN'S COLOR BOOKS 1960's - 70's
Small World, Mickey Mouse, Peanuts, I Wish I Could. **CMV $2. each.**

MANAGERS SALES MEETING NOTEBOOK 1962
Campaign 15,16,17,18 sales meeting plans. Red and white Christmas tree. **CMV $25.**

ROSE STAMPS 1961
Page of 75 rose stamps for Avon Rep use in C-2-1961. Stamps say " Avons 75th Year". **CMV $20.**

AD DISPLAYS 1950's
Magazine advertising on hardbacks. **CMV $15 each.**

IF YOU PAID MORE FOR ANY AVON COLLECTIBLE IN THIS BOOK IN THE LAST 2 YEARS & FEEL YOU PAID A FAIR PRICE. SEND THIS INFORMATION TO BUD HASTIN, PO BOX 9868, KANSAS CITY, MO. 64134 SO HE CAN CHANGE THE PRICE IN HIS NEXT BOOK. REMEMBER THAT AVON TIMES EACH MONTH REFLECTS THE AVERAGE GOING PRICE ON MOST AVONS. IF YOU DON'T GET AVON TIMES. YOU MAY PAY TO MUCH .

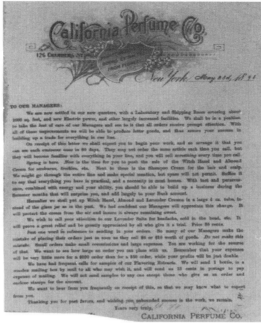

CPC INK BLOTTER 1912
Used by Reps in early 1900s. **CMV $35.**

CATALOG - HONG KONG 1978
Avon sales catalog from Hong Kong. **CMV $6.**

LETTER FROM CPC 1896
On CPC letterhead. Letter to CPC managers.
CMV $45.

CPC INSTRUCTIONAL MANUAL 1920
14 page booklet used to train early day
Avon Reps. Tells them how and what to
do to be a sales lady for CPC. No pictures. **CMV $25.**

CPC D. H. McCONNELL LETTER 1900s
On CPC letterhead. Hand written by D. H.
McConnell, founder of Avon to his factory
workers. **CMV for any hand written D. H.
McConnell letter dated 1890s to 1930s
would be $25. to $50. depending on buyer.**
Note that most later years McConnell's signa-
ture is rubber stamped and not hand written.

SALES MANAGERS CONTRACT 1913
Paper agreement for Avon ladies in early
1900s. Signed by D. H. McConnell, founder of
Avon. **CMV $25.**

**CPC CHRISTMAS GREETING CARD EARLY
1900s**
1c post card sent out at Christmas time. 126
Chambers Street, New York is the return
address. **CMV $25.**

War Time Hat-Avon 1942
Paper hat marked Avon on inside. **CMV $50.**

PLACE MATS 1971
Four Seasons - Robert Woods signed plastic place mats for Avon. Had choice of one of the four when you bought certain products. **CMV $3. each.**

DEPOT MANAGERS CONTRACT CPC 1909
Paper agreeement between CPC and sales lady. **CMV $40. mint.**

GEORGE WASHINGTON REPRESENTATIVE GIFT LETTER 1976
Folder (on left) and a copy of a letter George Washington wrote from Mt. Vernon. Given at sales meeting in February. **CMV $5. mint.**

LETTER FROM AVON 1936
Misc. letters from Avon may vary in price depending on the year. Any letters personally signed by D. H. McConnell, founder of Avon in his own handwriting should be worth at least $25. Letter shown is a copy. **CMV $15. mint.**

SHAVING PADS 1908
(Left) Girl holding flowers on cover. **CMV $60. mint.**
SHAVING PADS 1915
(Right) Lady with big flower on hat on cover. **CMV $60.**

HERITAGE ALMANAC 1975
1975 calendar given to District Managers only. Duplicate of 1929 calendar, each page shows different outlook. Limited edition, 2,678 given. **CMV $25.**

SHAVING PADS 1900's
2 different-(Left) with lady and (Right) with Joe Jefferson. **CMV $60. each.**

DESIGNERS COLLECTION CHRISTMAS CARDS 1971
Box of 25 Avon Christmas cards, all the same design. Came in 36 different designs. No. 1 shown. Back of each card marked Avon Products, Inc. & gives the card number. **CMV each card 50c. to $1.**

DESIGNER COLLECTION CHRISTMAS CARD SAMPLE SET 1971
Box of 36 different Avon Christmas cards used by Avon Reps. for sales. Short issue. **CMV $35. complete set.**

DESIGNERS COLLECTIONS CHRISTMAS CARD CATALOGUE DEMONSTRATOR 1971
Large spiral bound picture album holds 1 each of 36 different Christmas cards sold by Avon in 1971. **CMV $75. complete, mint with all 36 cards, album only, no cards, $45.** Never sold to public.

PERFECTION - ALL PRODUCTS

Grading condition is paramount. CMV can vary 60-90% on condition.

SILVER PLATE POLISH 1906
4 oz. glass bottle with metal cap. **CMV $100., $125. MB.**

SILVER CREAM POLISH 1923
8 oz. metal can. **CMV $40. mint.** 16 oz. can. **CMV $45. mint. Add $5. MB.**

CPC SILVER CREAM POLISH 1918
6 oz. jar, metal lid. **CMV $85. mint.**

PERFECTION SILVER CREAM POLISH 1931-41
1/2 lb. brown, orange and white can. **CMV $30. MB, $25. can only mint.**

PERFECTION SPOTS OUT 1943-46
9 1/2 oz. glass jar, white metal lid. **CMV $22., $27. MB.**

PERFECTION KWICK METAL POLISH 1943-46
11 oz. glass jar with white metal cap.**CMV $40-$50 MB. Rare.**

PERFECTION SILVER CREAM POLISH 1943-46
10 1/2 glass jar with white metal lid. **CMV $22., $27. MB.**

PERFECTION SILVER CREAM POLISH 1941-52
Green, brown and white. 8 oz can. Sold 1941-43 then 1946-52. **CMV $15 mint, $20. MB.**

MOTHICIDE 1925
1 lb. metal can on right. Paper label around can is in English and French. **CMV $60. mint. CMV as shown with spots $20.** 1/2 lb. metal can on left, **CMV $50. mint.**

SILVER CREAM POLISH 1943
Stick on white and green label over name of other products on can. Used during shortage of products during war. **CMV $25. mint with label shown.**

MOTHICIDE 1925
1/2 lb. metal can with blue label. **CMV $65. MB. $50. can mint only.**

MOTHICIDE 1943-46
Glass jar with white lid, green and white label-Rare. **CMV $30, $40 MB.** Green white and bronze label. **CMV $20., $30. MB.**

LIQUID SPOTS OUT 1934-41
4 oz. bottle. Orange, brown and white label. Black cap. **CMV $30. MB. $25. BO.**

PERFECTION MOTHICIDE 1931-41
1/2 lb. orange, brown and white can. **CMV $25. MB, $20. can only mint.** Add $5. for CPC label.

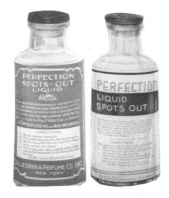

PERFECTION SPOTS OUT LIQUID 1929
(Left) 4 oz. bottle with CPC on black cork stopper and blue label. **CMV $45. MB. $40. BO.**
PERFECTION LIQUID SPOTS OUT 1931-34
(Right) 4 oz. size. CPC on cork stopper. **CMV $40. MB. $32.50. BO**

LIQUID SPOTS OUT 1946-58
4 oz. green smooth or threaded cap. 2 different labels. One box brown and one box bronze. **CMV $20. MB., $15. BO.**

MOTHICIDE 1923
1/2 lb. metal can 3 1/4" across. Paper label in English and French. **CMV $40. mint.**

SPOTS OUT 1920
Metal can. **CMV $70., can only mint $85. MB.**

PERFECTION MOTHICIDE 1954-57
8 1/2 bronze metal can, green top, three different edges on lid. Sold 1954-57. **CMV $10.** Red metal can sold 1957 only. **CMV $12.. $16. MB.**

LIQUID SPOTS OUT 1925-29
4 oz. clear glass bottle, black cork cap. blue label. **CMV $50. MB, $45. BO mint.**

SPOTS OUT 1923
8 oz metal can. **CMV $40. mint.** 16 oz. can not shown, **CMV $45. mint.** Add $10 each MB.

SPOTS OUT 1931-41
1/2 LB. ORANGE, BROWN AND WHITE CAN.
CMV $25. MB. $20. can only mint.

SHOE WHITE 1915
Box holds 5 oz. sack of Shoe White Powder.
CMV $90. MB.

SHOE WHITE 1920
Green box holds 5 oz. sack of powder. CMV
$100.00 MB.

SPOTS OUT 1941-43
8 oz. green, brown and white can. Sold 1941-
43 then 1946-48. CMV $20., $25. MB.

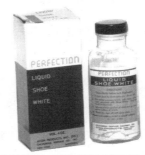

PERFECTION LIQUID SHOE WHITE 1931-35
(Right) Box holds 4 oz. bottle with cork stopper. Brown, orange and white label. CMV
$25., $30. MB.
LIQUID SHOE WHITE 1928-30
(Left) 4 oz. glass bottle with cork stopper.
CMV $50. MB, $45. BO mint.

PERFECTION LIQUID SHOE WHITE 1935-41
Box holds 4 oz bottle with brown cap. Brown,
orange and white label. CMV $25., $30. MB.

LIQUID SHOE WHITE SAMPLE 1935-41
(Center) 1/2 oz. black cap. CPC on label.
CMV $40. Also with Avon Products label only
white cap. CMV $25.
LIQUID SHOE WHITE SAMPLE 1935-41
(Left) Same as above, different label. CMV
$40.
LIQUID SHOE WHITE SAMPLE 1941-57
(Right) 3/4 oz. white cap, green and brown
label. CMV $35.

KWICK CLEANING POLISH SAMPLE 1922
Small sample can issued for one month on
introduction of this product. Rare. CMV $75.

PERFECTION LIQUID SHOE WHITE 1941-57
4 oz. green smooth or threaded cap. Two different labels. CMV $10. BO, $15. MB.

KWICK CLEANING POLISH 1922
8 oz. metal can, brown label. CMV $70. MB.
$55. can only. Also came in 16 oz. can. CMV
$75. MB. $60. can only mint.

KWICK METAL POLISH 1925
1/2 lb. metal can with brown label. CMV $60.,
$45. only mint.

PERFECTION KWICK METAL POLISH 1931-41
1/2 lb. orange, brown and white can. **CMV $35. MB. $30. can.**
KWICK METAL POLISH 1954-57
Green & brown 13 oz. can on right. Two different lids. **CMV $30. mint.**

PERFECTION LAUNDRY CRYSTALS PERFUMED 1941-48
Green, brown and white can with green lid holds 13 crystals. Metal top and bottom and paper sides. Sold 1941-46. All metal sold 1946-48. **CMV $20 each mint.**
PERFECTION LAUNDRY CRYSTALS PERFUMED 1943-46
All cardboard war time packaging. **CMV $30. mint.** Also came with white top and bottom. 4 different labels.

PERFECTION LAUNDRY CRYSTALS 1931-36
Brown, orange and white paper box. **CMV $30. MB.**
LAUNDRY CRYSTALS PERFUMED 1934-36
(Right) Brown, white and orange box holds 13 white crystals. **CMV $30. mint.**

LAUNDRY CRYSTALS PERFUMED 1938-41
Brown, orange and white paper sides, tin top and bottom. Top cut out to be used as bank. Held 13 crystals. Came with Avon and CPC labels. **CMV $30. Avon label, $40. CPC label.**

POWDERED CLEANER 1928-31
12 oz blue box. **CMV $75. mint $90 MB.**

POWDERED CLEANER 1931-34
Red, white and blue. 16 oz. can. **CMV $75. mint. $90. MB.**

FURNITURE POLISH 1912
8 oz. 1/2 pint bottle, cork stopper, clear glass. **CMV $100., $125. MB.**

PERFECTION PREPARED STARCH 1941-48
8 oz. brown, green and white can. Two different labels. Shiny top or painted top. **CMV $20 mint. $25. MB.** 1943-46 had paper sides. **CMV $20 mint.**

PERFECTION POWDERED CLEANER 1934-41
16 oz. orange, brown and white can. Two different labels. Cardboard sides, metal bottom. **CMV $25. MB. $20 can only mint.**

CARPET RENOVATOR 1906
Box holds 1 bar of soap. **CMV $85. MB.**

PERFECTION - ALL PRODUCTS

PERFECTION FURNITURE POLISH 1936-41
12 and 32 oz. brown, orange and white can.
Three different labels. **CMV $15., $20. MB.**
CMV 32 oz. size $20., $25. MB.

FURNITURE POLISH 1915
(Left) 8 oz. clear glass bottle, cork stopper.
CMV $85. BO mint. $100. MB. Same label
is on rare amber bottle.

PERFECTION FURNITURE POLISH 1943-46
(Right) 12 oz. bottle, metal cap. Two different
labels. Green and white label, and white and
bronze. **CMV green and white add $5.**
CMV $22., $30. MB.

PERFECTION FURNITURE POLISH 1931-36
12 oz. brown, orange and white can. **CMV**
$20., $30. MB.

FURNITURE POLISH 1944 Only
12 oz. bottle, black cap. **CMV $40. BO. $50.**
MB.

FURNITURE POLISH 1916
12 oz metal can with green label. **CMV $80.**
MB. $65 can only mint. Also came in qt.
size. & 1/2 gal. size.**CMV $75. mint.**

FURNITURE POLISH 1915
8 oz. amber glass, cork stopper. Very rare.
CMV $150. bottle only mint. $175. MB.

FURNITURE POLISH 1904
8 oz glass botle. This bottle may be dark
amber glass or clear. Eureka trade mark on
neck label. Cork stopper. **CMV $100. BO**
mint. $140. MB.

CPC FURNITURE POLISH 1906
(Right Center) 8 oz. bottle with cork stopper.
Came as round or square bottle, same label.
CMV $100., $125. MB.

FURNITURE POLISH 1912
(Left) 8 oz. bottle, cork stopper, label also
read for automobile bodies. **CMV $125. MB,**
$100. BO mint.

FURNITURE POLISH 1925
12 oz. metal can with blue label on right. OSP
48c. Same as above only in 32 oz. on left,
blue metal can. Back side labels in French on
both cans. **CMV $70. can only mint, $85.**
MB each.
12 oz. can on right has a different cap. **Same**
CMV

BAKING POWDER SAMPLE 1936-41
Orange, brown and white 1 oz can, 2 1/4"
high. Two different size samples. Rare. **CMV**
$40 each mint.

PERFECTION MACHINE OIL 1941-48
3 oz. brown, green and white can. Sold 1941-
43 then 1946-48. **CMV $15. MB. $10. can**
only.

PERFECTION AUTO POLISH 1933-36
1 pt. brown, orange and white can. Two different labels. **CMV $50. MB. $40 can only. Rare.**

POWDERED CLEANER 1943-46
16 oz. paper can, green, bronze and white. **CMV $20. mint. $25. MB.**
POWDERED CLEANER 1941-43 then 1946-57
16 oz. paper sides with metal top and bottom. Green, bronze, and white. **CMV $15., $20. MB** Five different labels & a Canada label.

CARPET RENOVATOR SOAP 1915-20
Paper box with one bar carpet soap, 2 different boxes shown. First issued about 1893. **CMV $90. each mint.**

AVON POWDERED CLEANER SAMPLE 1928-31
Small blue, orange and white paper box. 3 oz. size sample. CPC on label Rare. **CMV $100 mint.**

PERFECTION PREPARED STARCH 1931-41
6 oz. brown, orange and white can. Sold 1931-36. **CMV $25., $30. MB.** Same can in 8 oz. size sold 1936-41, two different labels as shown. **CMV $20., $25. MB.**

AUTO LUSTRE 1930-33
(Left) Blue 1 pt. can. **CMV can only $75 mint. $90. MB.**
AUTO LUSTRE SAMPLE 1930-33
(Right) 1 oz. blue metal can. Rare. **CMV $90.**

OLIVE OIL 1895
8 oz. glass bottle with cork stopper. **CMV $105 .00 MB. $85. BO. mint.** Also came in 1 pt., 1 qt., 1/2 gal, and 1 gal size. **CMV $125. rare.**
OLIVE OIL 1905
16 oz. bottle. **CMV $100. mint, rare.**

FURNITURE POLISH 1941
All green, bronze and white metal can. 12 oz. can 1941-43 then 1946-48. **CMV $12., $15. MB.** 16 oz can 1948-51. **CMV $12.** 32 oz can 1941-43 **CMV $25.** Add $5 MB.

PERFECTION MACHINE OIL 1943-46
3 oz. smooth side glass, metal cap. **CMV $20. BO, $25. MB.**
MACHINE OIL "RIBBED SIDE"
Short issue 3 oz. ribbed sided bottle, metal cap. Came in two different boxes as shown. **CMV $25. BO, $30. MB.**

OLIVE OIL 1915
8 oz. glass bottle with cork stopper. **CMV $110. MB, $90. BO. Mint.** Also came in 16 oz., 1 qt, 1/2 gal., 1 gal. size. **CMV $100, $125 MB, rare.**
BAKING POWDER 1915
16 oz. container. **CMV $80. MB, $65. container only mint..** Also came in 1 lb. and 5 lb. size. **CMV $100.00 mint.**

CPC EASYDAY OR SIMPLEX AUTOMATIC CLOTHES WASHER 1918
Made of pure zinc. Washer is 11" high and 9" in diameter. Has Easyday name on top and Pat. July 4, 1916. **CMV $100.**
CPC MARVEL ELECTRIC SILVER CLEANER 1918
Metal plate has Marvel name and Pat. Jan. 11, 1910. **CMV $50.00**

SUPREME HUILE D'OLIVE OIL 1923
Green & yellow can in 1 pt. size. **CMV $75. MB, $60. can only mint.** Also came in qt,. size can. **CMV $85. MB, $70. can only mint.**

PERFECTION MACHINE OIL 1931-41
3 oz. brown, orange and white can. Two different labels. **CMV $18 MB., $12.50 can only mint.**

EXTRACT OF LEMON 1908
16 oz. glass stopper. **CMV $150. BO mint. $175. MB.**

PERFECTION OLIVE OIL 1931-41
1 pt. orange, brown and white can. Two different labels. **CMV $45. MB, $35. can only.**

FRUIT FLAVORING 1908
2 oz. embossed Fruit California Perfume Co. Flavors. Had paper label on reverse side. **CMV $35. BO, $100.** mint with paper label, **$125. MB.** Some came with reversed "A" in California. **Add $5 for reversed "A".**

BAKING POWDER 1943-46
16 oz. paper contianer used during the war. **CMV $40 mint.**

VANILLA TONKA AND VANILLAN FLAVOR EXTRACT 1910
2 or 4 oz. glass bottle, cork stopper. Comes in 17 flavors. **CMV $100 mint. $125. MB.**

FLAVORING EXTRACTS 1908
Came in 1,2,4 and 8 oz. sizes with cork stoppers. Also came in 1 pt. and 1 qt. with glass stoppers. Flavors are almond, banana, celery, cinnamon, jamaica, ginger, lemon, maple, nutmeg, orange, onion, peppermint, pineapple, pistachio, rasberry, rose, strawberry, vanilla, tonka and vanillin, vanilla pure and wintergreen. The 2 oz. bottles are

embossed "California Perfume Co. Fruit Flavors" on back side, paper label on front. OSP 1 oz 25c. 2 oz. 45c. 4 oz. 90c. 8 oz. $1.75. 16 oz. $3.25. **CMV each $100 mint with label. CMV $125. embossed bottle with no label. $25. CMV 1 pt. and 1 qt size $125. BO, $150. MB with label and glass stopper.**

FLAVORING EXTRACT 1905-08
(Left) 8 oz and 16 oz. bottle, glass stopper. Came in all flavors listed under smaller bottles of 1893 Flavoring Extracts. **CMV $150. BO. $175. MB.**

FLAVORING EXTRACTS 1900-12
(Right) 2 oz. bottle shown is same as 4 oz. botle. Paper label. Came in almond, banana, blood orange, celery, cinnamon, cloves, lemon, nutmeg, onion, orange, peach, pear, peppermint, pineapple, pistachio, quince, jamaica ginger, rasberry rose, strawberry, vanilla and wintergreen. **CMV $100. MB, $85 BO mint.** Also came in 16 oz., 1 qt, 1/2 gal, and 1 gal. **CMV $125. BO, $150. MB.**

PERFECTION SAMPLES 1941
Sample size each. Perfection flavor sample came 20 in a box for 50c. Baking powder came in 16 for 50c. **CMV flavoring bottle. $20. each. Baking powder $45. each.**

BAKING POWDER 1906
1/2 and 1 lb can. **CMV $100. mint.**
BAKING POWDER 1906-15
5 lb container, paper label, metal can. **CMV $70. mint.** Pictured next to 1923-30 1 lb. can, for size comparison.

IF YOU LOVE TO LAUGH, GO TO THE BACK PAGE FOR INFO ON BUD HASTIN'S NEW JOKE BOOK AND HOW TO GET IT. LAUGH MORE AND LIVE LONGER.

PERFECTION MENDING CEMENT 1933-41
Brown, orange, and white tube. **CMV $12.
MB. Tube only $10. mint.**
PERFECTION MENDING CEMENT 1941-48
White, green, and brown tube. **CMV $12. MB.
$10 tube only mint.**

**PERFECTION BAKING POWDER 1941-43-
46-48**
16 oz. red and white can, cardboard sides,
metal top or all metal can and top. **CMV $20.
mint, $25. MB.** Also came 1946-48 all metal
can. Screw on lid. **CMV $50. Rare**

KWICK METAL POLISH 1941-48
8 oz. green, brown and white can. Sold 1941-
43 then 1946-48. **CMV $35., $45. MB.**

PERFECTION BAKING POWDER 1923-30
(Left) 1 lb can. Also came in 1/2 lb. and 5 lb.
sizes. **CMV $60. mint. $65. MB.**
PERFECTION BAKING POWDER 1931-41
(Right) 1 lb. orange, brown and white can.
CMV $25., $30. MB. Add $5 for CPC label.

EXTRACTS - FRUIT FLAVORING 1898
2 oz. clear glass. Fruit Flavors California
Perfume Co. embossed on backside.
Pineapple and wintergreen or rose. Cork stop-
per. **CMV $110. BO mint., $130. MB.**
ROOT BEER EXTRACT 1915
2 oz. cork stopper, clear glass. Very rare.
CMV $100. mint, $125. MB.

FLAVORING EXTRACT 1934-41
8 oz. bottle plus cap. Came in vanilla, tonka,
lemon, almond, orange, peppermint, wintergreen, pure vanilla, black walnut and maple.
CMV $35. MB. $25. BO.

HARMLESS RED COLORING 1915
2 oz. clear glass, cork stopper. **CMV $75.
mint with label. $90. MB.**
RASBERRY FLAVOR 1908
1 oz. size CPC New York Label. **CMV $50.
$75. MB.**

SAVORY COLORING 1915
3 oz. clear glass bottle, cork stopper. 3 oz.
size is rare. **CMV $80. with mint label.
$100.00 MB.**

PERFECTION CAKE CHEST 1941-42

Brown and red designed cake chest has coloring set in can, 2 oz. bottles of lemon and almond extract, 2 oz. bottles of maple and black walnut flavoring, and 4 oz. bottle of vanilla. All bottles have red plastic caps. Can of baking powder, recipe book, cake chest is same as 1938 to 1941. Avon Perfection in bottom of cake pan. **CMV set complete $110. MB. Chest only $35. mint.**

NO ALCOHOL FLAVORING SET 1920-21

Set came with five small tubes and one large tube. Choice of vanilla, lemon, pineapple, banana, maple, almond, orange, strawberry, jamaica, ginger, peppermint, nutmeg, wintergreen, cinnamon, rose, celery onion, pistachio, and rasberry. **CMV $200. MB.**

NO ALCOHOL FLAVOR IN TUBES 1921

Metal tubes came in small and large size, available in flavors as set. **CMV small tube $40. large tube $45. mint.**

NO ALCOHOL FLAVORS 1923

Lemon and vanilla only in small and large size tubes. **CMV $40. MB. tube only $30 mint.**

PERFECTION CAKE CHEST 1938-41

Gold, red, brown, black cake chest. Contains can of baking powder, coloring set of 4 oz. vanilla extract. 2 oz each of lemon and almond extract, 2 oz each of black walnut and maple flavors. All have metal caps, recipe book. Avon Perfection in bottom of cake pan. **CMV set complete $135. MB. chest only $35. mint.**

PERFECTION CAKE CHEST 1933-38

Blue and gold cake pan 10 1/2" in diameter contains Perfection coloring set, metal caps. Can of Perfection baking powder. Bottles contain lemon, maple, black walnut, almond and vanilla flavoring and recipe book. Avon Perfection in bottom of cake pan. **CMV set complete $135. MB. chest only $50 mint. $70. MB.**

VEGETABLE COLORING 1908

2 oz. or 4 oz. clear glass. Front white paper label. Embossed Fruit Flavors on back side. **CMV $100 mint, $125. MB.**

SAVORY COLORING 1915

8 oz. clear glass. Cork stopper. Rare in 8 oz. size. **CMV $125 mint - $150. MB.**

FOOD FLAVORING SET 1914

Box holds 2 oz. bottle of vanilla tonka, a 2 oz bottle of lemon, and four 1 oz bottles of any other flavor. **CMV $450. for set. MB.**

FLAVORING EXTRACT SET 1920

Box holds two 2 oz. bottles and four 1 oz. bottles of any flavor desired. 1,2 and 4 oz. bottles shown. **CMV $450. set MB.**

IMITATION VANILLAN COUMARIN VANILLA AND TONKA FLAVOR 1939-41

4 oz. red cap. **CMV $15.BO. $20. MB.**

PERFECTION BLUE COLORING 1919
1 oz. size. Black & white label. Cork stopper.
New York-Montreal label. **CMV $75. mint.**
NUTMEG FLAVORING 1906
2 oz. cork stopper. Eureka Trade Mark label.
CMV $100. mint.
JAMAICA GINGER FLAVORING 1919
1 oz., cork stopper. **CMV $75. mint.**

**PERFECTION CONCENTRATED COLORING
1920-30**
(Right) 2 oz. No coloring listed on label. Cork
stopper. **CMV $45. BO mint. $55. MB.**
VEGTABLE COLOR SAMPLE 1900
(Left) Small clear glass vial with cork stopper.
CMV $50. mint.

SAVORY COLORING 1923-30
(Left) 2 and 3 oz. bottle with yellow labels and
brown letters, cork stoppers. Came in red, yellow, blue, brown, and green. Also came with
brown label and yellow letters. **CMV each
with mint label $45., $55. MB.** 1/2 oz. bottle came in Coloring Set only. **CMV same as
above.**
PERFECTION SAVORY COLORING 1931-34
(Right) 4 oz. cork stopper. CPC label. **CMV
$35. MB. $30. BO.**

PERFECTION EXTRACT 1934-41
Metal caps on 1/2 oz. 2, 4 and 8 oz. bottles.
Flavors are vanilla, tonka, lemon, almond,
orange, peppermint, wintergreen, pure vanilla,
black walnut, maple. **CMV each 2 oz. and 4
oz. $12.50 each; 8 oz. size $20.; CMV
each 1/2 oz. size $12.**

**CONCENTRATED FLAVORING EXTRACT
1923-30**
8 oz. size with handle. Same label as 1923-30
extracts. This bottle is very rare with handle.
Label in poor condition. **CMV $75. mint.**
**PERFECTION FLAVORING EXTRACT 1923-
30**
2 oz. clear glass bottle, cork stopper. Lemon,
orange, grape, cherry, rasberry, loganberry.
CMV $50., $60. MB.

**VANILLA TONKA & VANILLAN FLAVOR
SAMPLE 1910**
(Left) Small sample bottle, clear glass, cork
stopper. **CMV $100. mint. $125. MB.**
**"EXTRACT CONCENTRATED" VANILLA
EXTRACT 1906**
(Right) 2 and 4 oz. glass bottle with cork stop-
per. **CMV $100., $125. MB.**

PERFECTION COLORING 1934-41
1/2 oz size in green, yellow, blue and brown.
Came in Coloring Set. **CMV $15 each.** 2 oz.
size in same colors plus red. **CMV $17.** 4
oz. size in savory coloring. All have metal
caps. **CMV $17. Add $3. each MB.**

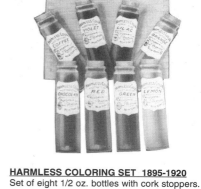

VANILLA TONKA VANILLAN SPECIAL ISSUE BOX 1937
Regular issue 2 oz. bottle in special issue box for 15c. with regular order. **CMV $25. MB as shown.**

FOOD COLORING 1941-48
Red plastic caps. Savory coloring came in 4 oz. bottle. Red, Yellow, Blue, Brown and Green came in 2 oz. bottles. All but Red and Savory coloring came in 1/2 oz bottles in coloring set. **CMV $12. each size, $15. each MB.**

HARMLESS COLORING SET 1895-1920
Set of eight 1/2 oz. bottles with cork stoppers. Came in wood box. Lemon, chocolate, lilac, coffee, orange, red, violet and green. **CMV $400. set MB. or $45. each bottle.**

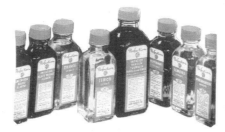

SAVOURY COLORING 1941-48
4 oz. bottle with the word Savoury spelled different. Regular spelling is Savory. **CMV $15 BO. $18. MB.**
PERFECTION IMITATION VANILLAN COUMARIN VANILLA AND TONKA SAMPLE 1939-41
1/4 oz. size bottle. Metal cap. **CMV $25. mint.**

PERFECTION FLAVORING EXTRACTS 1941-48
Vanilla and lemon came in 2 and 4 oz. sizes. 2 oz size only in maple, black walnut, orange, peppermint, almond, wintergreen. All have red plastic caps. **CMV $9 each 1/2 oz. size came in Extract Set only. CMV $12., $15. MB. ea.**

FOOD FLAVORING DEMONSTRATOR SET 1909
Black leather covered wood case holds 24 1 oz bottles of food flavoring. Original Selling Price to Reps was $2. **CMV mint with all labels $1800.00 complete and MINT.**

VANILLA TONKA 1/4 OZ. SAMPLE 1934-39
(Right) 1/4 oz. size, 2 3/8" high, metal cap. On right shown next to 1/2 oz. size, on left that came in food flavor sets. **CMV $25. 1/4 oz. size sample mint. CMV 1/2 oz. size $15. mint.**

HARMLESS COLORS SET 1915
Wood box with slide open lid, paper label on top. Holds eight 1/2 oz. bottles with cork stoppers. Paper labels on top of cork and front of bottles also. Came in chocolate, lemon, green, red, coffee, violet, lilac, and orange. **CMV $350.00 MB.**

HARMLESS COLORS SET 1920
Cardboard box holds eight 1/2 oz. bottles with cork stoppers. Red, chocolate, green, coffee, lemon, velvet, orange, lilac. **CMV $300.00 MB.**

FLAVORING EXTRACT SET 1912
Black leather grain case with double handles and snaps. Holds 20 one ounce bottles of food flavor extract. Used by Reps. to show products. **CMV $1500. complete set mint.**

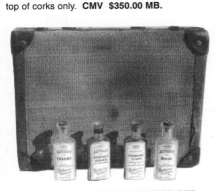

HARMLESS COLORS SET 1910-15
Wood box, slide open lid, holds 8 1/2 oz. bottles with cork stoppers. Red, chocolate, green, coffee, lemon, velvet, orange, lilac. Labels on top of corks only. **CMV $350.00 MB.**

FOOD FLAVORING DEMONSTRATOR SET 1900
Straw covered wood case holds 20 bottles of food flavoring extracts. **CMV complete set mint $1500.00**

PERFECTION COLORING SET 1920-30
Bottles of green, yellow, blue and brown in 1/2 oz. size. Red in 2 oz. size. All have cork stoppers. Came with CPC Cook Booklet. **CMV $250.00 MB.**

FRUIT FLAVORS BROCHURE 1923
Introducing new line of CPC Perfection fruit flavors. 1 page. **CMV $20.**

CAKE CHEST PRODUCT BOX 1930's
CPC box with list of all contents that came in Perfection Cake Chest. **CMV $15 box only.**

FOOD COLORING DIRECTIONS 1930's
Came in Perfection Food Coloring sets. CPC on back **CMV $15. mint.**

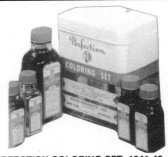

PERFECTION COLORING SET 1941-48
Orange, brown and white can holds 2 oz. red coloring and 1/2 oz. each of yellow, brown, blue and green coloring, red plastic cap. **CMV $65 MB.** Set came with Avon Recipe Booklet. Add $10. for Recipe Booklet. Can only $15. mint. This set also came in 1934-41 can. Only can is marked Avon and not CPC. Came with red caps and 1941-48 labels.. **CMV $70. MB.** Same set came 1942 only with matching caps to color content. Rare. **CMV $85. set MB.**

PERFECTION COLORING SET 1934-41
Orange, brown and white metal cans hold four 1/2 oz. bottles in blue, yellow, brown and green coloring and 2 oz. bottle of red. All have plain metal caps, or all color caps. Rare. Came with Perfection Cook Booklet **CMV $75. MB. Can only $15. mint.**

PERFECTION FLAVORING EXTRACT SET 1930-34
In orange, brown and white can, has 2 oz. vanilla and 1.2 oz. each of almond, lemon, peppermint, and wintergreen extract. All have cork stoppers. **CMV $125.00 Set mint. Can only $15. mint.**

PERFECTION RECIPE BOOKS 1930's 1940's

Came in food coloring or flavoring sets. At lest four different booklets. **CMV $15. each mint.** 1920 far right **CMV $25.**

PERFECTION FLAVORING SET 1941-48

Red, white and bronze can holds 2 oz. bottle of vanilla, 1/2 oz. bottle of maple, black walnut, almond and lemon. All have red plastic caps. **CMV $60. complete set mint.** Set came with Avon Recipe Booklet in can. Add $10 for Recipe Booklet. **Can only $12 mint.**

PERFECTION FLAVORING EXTRACT SET 1934-41

Orange, brown, and white metal can holds four 1/2 oz. bottles in wintergren, peppermint, almond and lemon, and a 2 oz. bottle of maple. All have metal caps. Came with Perfection Cook Booklet. **CMV booklet only $12. CMV $75. MB can only $15. mint.**

PERFECTION COLORING SET 1930-34

Brown and orange paper box. Red coloring in 2 oz. size brown, blue, yellow, green coloring in 1/2 oz. size. All have cork stoppers. **CMV $160. MB. Box only $20. mint.**

AVON FACIAL SETS

WARNING!! Condition is very important on sets. CMV can vary up to 90% from poor to mint condition.

FACIAL SET 1936-37

Turquoise flip up box holds Ariel face powder, 2 oz. jar cleansing cream, tissue cream & 2 oz. bottle of astringent. All products are marked CPC. Also came with packet of tissues. **CMV $50. MB.**

FACIAL SET 1941-48

Green box contains jar of cleansing cream, foundation cream, night cream with green lids. Skin freshener, 2 oz. green cap & box of face powder, blue and white feather design, 2 packs of Avon facial tissues. Jars had green or white metal lids. **CMV $50. MB. Add $10 set for white lids.**

FACIAL SET 1937-38

Green box contains choice of 2 oz. bottle of skin freshener or astringent, green caps, 2 oz. jar of cleansing cream, 1 oz. jar of tissue cream and Ariel of Vernafleur face powder. **CMV $65. MB.**

FACIAL SET 1933-36

(left) Silver & blue box contains 2 oz. jar of cleansing cream & 1 oz. jar of tissue cream, 1 bottle of astringent, silver box of Ariel face powder, package of tissues. **CMV $110.00 MB.**

FACIAL SET 1938-40
Green box holds 4 oz. bottles of astringent & Lotus cream, jars of tissue cream & cleansing cream and box of face powder in Ariel or Cotillion. **CMV $65. MB.**

GOLD BOX SET 1933-36
Gold box contained three 1/2 oz. bottles of Vernafleur, Ariel, 391, Bolero or Gardenia. Black caps. **CMV $125. MB.**

GOLD BOX SET 1941-44
Pink & gold box contains 1/8 oz. perfumes in Gardenia, Cotillion & Trailing Arbutus. White caps, pink & gold box. **CMV $90. MB.**

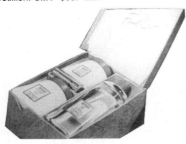

FACIAL SET FOR DRY SKIN 1949-54
Green box contains Fluffy cleansing cream, skin freshener, special dry skin cream & lipstick
SAME SET FOR OILY SKIN
Contained liquifying cleansing cream, astringent, night cream, & lipstick. **CMV $50 MB each set.**

GOLD BOX SET 1937-38
Gold box holds three 1/8 oz. bottles of Cotillion, Narcissus, & Gardenia perfumes. **CMV $85. MB.**

GOLD BOX 1945-46
Pink & white box holds three 1/8 oz. bottles in Crimson Carnation, Gardenia & Cotillion perfume. **CMV $85. MB>**

GOLD BOX SETS

GOLD BOX 1939-40
Gold open front box holds 3 bottles of perfume in Gardenia, Cotillion, Narcissus or Trailing Arbutus. White plastic caps on all. **CMV $90. MB.**

GOLD BOX 1944
Ribbons & flower design box holds three 1/8 oz. perfumes in Trailing Arbutus, Cotillion, And Gardenia. **CMV $90. MB.**

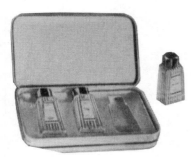

GOLD BOX SET 1932
Metal gold with black strips. Can holds 3 1/2 oz. ribbed glass bottles of 391, Ariel and Vernafleur perfume. All have black octagonal caps. This is the same metal can as the 1925-30 manicure set. **CMV $140.00 MB.**

GOLD BOX SET 1947-48
Three 1/8 oz. perfume bottles, gold caps, pink labels. Ballad, Garden of Love, Cotillion. **CMV $85. MB.**

GOLD BOX SET 1949
Turquoise plastic bottom with gold insert, clear plastic lid contains three 1 dram bottles of Cotillion, Flowertime, & Golden Promise perfumes. All have gold caps and labels. **CMV $80. MB.**

MAKEUP ENSEMBLE SETS

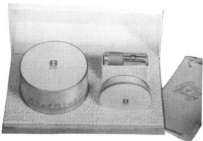

MAKE-UP ENSEMBLE 1939-40
Box holds can of face powder in choice of Cotillion, Ariel or Vernafleur, and table rouge in green & gold boxes. Lipstick in green & gold. **CMV $40. MB.**

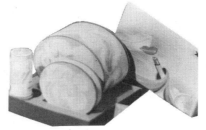

MAKE-UP ENSEMBLE 1945
Lipstick designed box holds feather design face powder, lipstick & rouge. Also came with metal bamboo lipstick. **CMV $37. MB.**

MAKE-UP ENSEMBLE 1947 Only
White, pink box with Eiffel Tower on box holds pink & blue feather design powder with bamboo lipstick & rouge. **CMV $45. MB.**
MAKE-UP ENSEMBLE 1948
Same except lipstick gold with swirl design around bottom. **CMV $45. MB.**

MAKE-UP ENSEMBLE 1943-44
Blue and pink box holds feathered box of face powder, rouge & plastic or cardboard lipstick. **CMV $40 MB.**

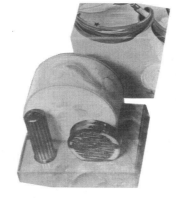

MAKE-UP ENSEMBLE 1946 Only
Pink & blue feather design box holds gold bamboo lipstick, rouge, & box of face powder. **CMV $45. MB.**

MAKE-UP ENSEMBLE 1949-51
Blue, pink and white box contains face powder, gold lipstick, & rouge. Eiffel Tower on box. **CMV $35. MB.**

MANICURE SETS

WARNING!! Grading condition is paramount on sets. CMV can vary 50% to 90% on grade.

MAKE-UP ENSEMBLE 1941-42
Box contains face powder, rouge in feather design, turqoise & gold lipstick. **CMV $40. MB.**

MAKE-UP ENSEMBLE 1952-53
Turquoise & gold box holds compact, lipstick & face powder or powder pak. **CMV $35. MB.**

MANICURE SET NO. 1 1930
Silver box holds 2 small bottles of nail polish remover. Black caps. Booklet "What Story Do Your Hands Tell?" came with set. **CMV $65. MB.**

MANICURE SETS

MANICURE SET NO. 1 1936-37
Green & white box has bottles of nail polish & polish remover with 2 rolls of cotton & booklet " What Story Do Your Hands Tell?" **CMV $45. MB.**

MANICURE SET NO. 2 1937
Turquoise & white lid, gold inside box holds cans of nail white & nail cream, bottles of nail polish remover, cuticle softener & nail polish, orange stick, nail file, 3 cotton rolls in glass tube & booklet "What Story Do Your Hands Tell?" **CMV $80. MB.**

ROYAL WINDSOR SET 1941-44
Blue box holds choice 1/2 oz. nail polish base & 1/2 oz. cream polish or 1/2 oz. top coat. **CMV $17. MB as shown**

MANICURE SET NO. 2 1931-36
Silver box holds 3 small ribbed glass bottles of polish remover, nail polish, cuticle softener. All have black caps. Two small silver cans of nail white & nail cream, 1 fingernail file & booklet "What Story Do Your Hands Tell?" **CMV $110. MB.** Same set also came with no stripe on box as shown & 2 different listings inside box as shown.

MANICURE SET NO. 1 1938-49
Turquoise box holds 1/2 oz. nail polish and cream polish, 2 cotton rolls and booklet "What Story Do Your Hands Tell?" CPC on box, 2 different boxes. Some say Manicure Set No. 1 at top of box and some at bottom of box. **Add $5 for CPC box. CMV $30. MB.**

MANICURE SET NO. 2 1940
Brown case holds fingernail file, orange stick, white Avon nail white pencil, 1/2 oz bottles of clear or cream nail polish, polish remover, cuticle softener & cuticle oil. Turquoise or black caps. **CMV $60. MB.**

MANICURE SET DELUXE 1941-43
Same set as above only name changed. **CMV $60 MB.**

MANICURE SET NO.2 1938-39
Brown case holds orange stick, nail file, can of nail white, nail cream, bottles of cuticle softener, cream polish & polish remover. **CMV $60. MB>**

TWOSOME SET 1938-49
Turquoise & white box holds 1/2 oz. of nail polish & 1/2 oz. of cuticle softener, 2 cotton rolls & booklet "What Story Do Your Hands Tell?" CPC on box in 1938-39. **Add $5 for CPC box. CMV $30.**

NAIL POLISH THREESOME 1938-49
Turquioise & white box holds 1/2 oz. double coat, 1/2 oz. nail polish, 1/2 oz oily polish remover, 2 rolls cotton & booklet. **CMV $42.50**

THREESOME SET 1942-43
Pink & white box has 3 small bottles with turquoise caps of cream polish, nail polish base & oily polish remover. Comes with story booklet on hands. **CMV $40 MB.**

DELUXE MANICURE SET 1950-51
Black & red box holds three 1/2 oz. bottles of nail polish, 1/2 oz. bottle of clear nail polish, 1/2 oz. bottle cuticle softener, 1 orange stick, 1 white nail white pencil & booklet. **CMV $25. MB.**

MANICURE SET DELUXE 1944-49
Black & red bag holds 5 bottles of nail polish, top coat, nail polish base, cuticle softener, oily polish remover. All have black or turquoise caps. White nail white pencil, orange stick & 2 nail files. **CMV $45. MB.**

MANICURE SET DELUXE 1949
Same black & red bag only holds 4 bottles with turquoise caps in Cling Tite nail polish, nail polish remover & cuticle softener. **CMV $40 MB.**

NAIL POLISH TWOSOME 1945-50
Turquoise box holds 1/2 oz. bottles of cream polish & cuticle softener and small 30 page booklet. **CMV $30. MB.**

AVON THREESOME SET 1948-49
Red, white & green tray with green box holds three 1/2 oz. bottles with white caps for oily polish remover, Cling Tite & nail polish. **CMV $30. MB.**

AVON THREESOME SET 1950-52
Red & white box holds 3 nail polish bottles with white caps. **CMV $30. MB.**

DELUXE MANICURE SET 1950-52
Black & red box holds bottles of cuticle softener, nail polish, oily polish remover & Cling Tite. **CMV $25. MB.**

MANICURE SET DELUXE 1953-54
Gray case holds 1/2 oz. bottles of cuticle softener, nail polish, double coat, 2 oz. oily polish remover, white caps on all. **CMV $25. MB.**

DELUXE MANICURE SET 1955
White plastic with gold dots, red lining holds oily nail polish remover, cuticle softener, Silvery Base, choice of nail enamel, all white caps & emery board. **CMV $25. MB.**

LITTLE FAVORITE SET 1955
Plastic turquoise case holds bottles of nail polish, oily polish remover & cuticle softener, all have white caps. **CMV $20. MB.**

POLKA DOT SET 1956-57
Red & white plastic case holds 1/2 oz. bottles of nail polish, top coat & 2 oz. oily polish remover. **CMV $20. MB.**

MANICURE SET DELUXE 1956-57
Pink plastic container holds 1/2 oz. bottles of polish remover, cuticle softener, silvery base, top coat & polish. All have white caps. **CMV $25. MB.**

COLOR CHANGE SET 1957
Pink, turquoise & gold design on white plastic case, holds 2 oz. bottle, white cap, oily polish remover & top coat & nail polish. **CMV $20. MB.**

NAIL CARE KIT 1979-80
Blue plastic kit holds 5 bottles of nail care products & 3 emery boards & 1 cuticle stick. **CMV $5. complete. MB.**

NAIL CARE KIT 1978-79
Same as above only beige color alligator grain case. **CMV $5. MB.**

COLOR BAR SET 1958
White plastic tray holds 4 bottles of nail polish or silvery base coat, top coat & cuticle softener. Mix or match. **CMV $15 complete - $20. MB**

MANICURE KIT 1966
Gold & white plastic case holds 1 bottle of nail enamel, long last base coat, enamel set, cuticle remover cream, nail beauty, 10 nail enamel remover pads, emery board & orange stick. **CMV $15 complete set MB.**

PERFUME PAIR SETS

MANICURE DELUXE SET 1959
Box holds cuticle softener, silvery coat, oily polish remover, top coat & cream polish. **CMV $25. MB.**

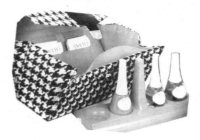

MANICURE BEAUTI-KIT 1968-69
Black & white vinyl case holds 1/2 oz. bottles of nail enamels, 1 oz. plastic tube cuticle conditioner, 1 oz. plastic tube cuticle remover, 10 enamel remover pads, 1/2 oz. bottle of enamel set, long-last top coat, & emery boards. Red plastic tray. **CMV $8. MB.**

PERFUMED PAIR 1962
Box holds 2 1/4 oz. can of perfumed talc & perfumed soap in Somewhere, Topaze, Cotillion, Persian Wood, Here's My Heart, & to A Wild Rose. **CMV $15. MB.**

MANICURE PITITE SET 1960-61
Black vinyl case holds top coat, oily polish remover & cream or pearl nail polish, White caps. **CMV $15 MB.**

NAIL BUFFER SET 1974
Box holds .25 oz. tube of nail buffing cream & nail buffer. **CMV $1.50 MB.**

DELUXE MANICURE SET 1960-61
Black vinyl case holds silvery base, oily polish remover, cuticle softener, top coat & cream nail polish. All have white caps. **$20. MB.**

PERFUMED PAIR 1964
Box holds perfumed talc & soap in Here's My Heart, Persian Wood, To A Wild Rose, Somewhere, Topaze, Cotillion. **CMV $14. MB.**

PERFUMED PAIR 1966
Brown, gold & white box holds 2 3/4 oz. perfumed talc & wrapped soap in Unforgettable, Rapture, Occur!, Cotillion, Somewhere, Topaze, Here's My Heart, To A Wild Rose & Wishing. **CMV $11. MB.**

PERFUMED PAIR 1968
Box holds 2 3/4 oz. can of talc and matching soap in Brocade, Regence, Unforgettable, Hawaiian White Ginger, Honeysuckle & To A Wild Rose. **CMV $8. MB.**

PERFUMED PAIR 1974-75
1.5 oz. perfumed talc & .5 oz. cologne. Choice of Roses Roses, Unforgettable, Cotillion, Sonnet or Moonwind. Came in 2 different boxes. **CMV $6. MB.**

PURSE SETS WOMEN

PERFUMED PAIR 1967
Box contains perfumed talc and matching soap. Comes in Unforgettable, Here's My Heart, To A Wild Rose, Somewhere, Topaze, Cotillion, Rapture & Occur!. **CMV $10. MB.**

PERFUMED PAIR 1970
Each box contains perfumed talc & matching soap in Hawaiian White Ginger, Honeysuckle, Elusive, Blue Lotus, Bird of Paradise, & Charisma. **CMV $7. MB.**

EVENING CHARM SET 1949
Black purse holds gold compact, lipstick & 1 dram bottle in gold metal case with Golden Promise perfume. Also came with beige purse. **CMV $30. MB.**

EVENING CHARM SET 1952
Gold purse holds 1 dram perfume, lipstick & gold deluxe compact. **CMV $30. MB.**

PERFUMED PAIR 1963
Gold & white with perfumed talc & bar of soap in To A Wild Rose, Here's My Heart, Persian Wood, Topaze, Somewhere, & Cotillion. **CMV $14 each set MB.**

PERFUMED PAIR 1969
Box holds perfumed talc & bar of soap in Charisma, Brocade, Blue Lotus, White Ginger, Honeysuckle, & To A Wild Rose. **CMV $8. MB.**

LADY FAIR SET 1956
Gold box holds 1 dram prefume, gold lipstick & red leather billfold. **CMV $35. MB.**

EVENING CHARM SET 1953
Choice of black velvet bag or brocade bag. Came with 1 dram embossed top perfume, gold deluxe & gold jeweled lipstick **CMV $35. MB.**

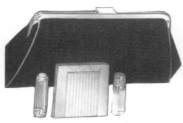

DRESS UP SET 1955
Black & gold purse with gold satin lining holds 1 dram perfume, jeweled lipstick & deluxe gold compact. **CMV $30. MB.**

IN STYLE SET 1957
Black satin purse holds Persian Wood spray perfume, white compact, gold lipstick & black coin purse. **CMV $30. MB.**

EVENING CHARM SET 1951
Brocade hand bag, or black satin bag with gold trim. Came with same contents as 1953 Evening Charm Set listed. **CMV purse only $6. complete set MB $30.**

EVENING CHARM SET 1955
Gold brocade purse. Has Avon tag inside. Also came in matching black satin bag. Holds 2 dram embossed top perfume, gold deluxe compact, and gold jeweled lipstick. **CMV $30. MB.**

MAKE-UP TUCK IN SET 1957
Black striped purse contains pink powder-pak, liquid rouge, & lipstick. **CMV $30. MB.**

EVENING CHARM PURSE 1953
Avon box holds black velvet purse. Avon on tag inside. **CMV $15 MB. purse only $6.**

DRESS UP SET 1955-56
Black & gold reversible purse holds 1 dram perfume, gold compact & jeweled lipstick. **CMV $30. MB.**

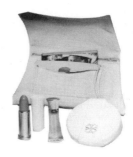

PAK PURSE SET 1959
White leather purse holds lipstick, 1 dram perfume & compact. **OSP $8.95 CMV $20. MB.**

EVENING CHARM SET 1954
Choice of black velvet or white brocade purse with 1 dram perfume, gold deluxe compact & jeweled lipstick. Both have zipper tops. **CMV $30. MB.**

AROUND TOWN SET 1956
Black leather bag holds gold lipstick, powder compact, 1 dram perfume & cologne stick. **CMV $30. MB.**

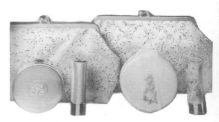

MODERN MOOD SET 1963
Gold & white or pink & gold purse holds deluxe compact & lipstick. On left: **CMV $17.50 MB.** Or pearl pink compact & floral fashion lipstick (on right). **CMV $20. MB.**

HIGH STYLE SET 1960
Blue satin lined bag holds gold deluxe compact & lipstick. **CMV $20 MB.**

DELUXE TWIN SET 1962
Blue clutch bag holds deluxe compact & lipstick. **CMV $20. MB.**

IF YOU LOVE TO LAUGH, GO TO THE BACK PAGE FOR INFO ON BUD HASTIN'S NEW JOKE BOOK AND HOW TO GET IT. LAUGH MORE AND LIVE LONGER.

MENS SETS OF 1930'S

WARNING!! Grading condition is paramount on sets. CMV can vary up to 90% on grade.

ON THE AVENUE SET 1958
Black purse holds Top Style lipstick & Top Style compact with Here's My Heart or Persian Wood sparay perfume. **CMV $30. MB.**

PURSE COMPANIONS SET 1964
Brocade beige purse with pockets to hold floral fashion lipstick & cameo compact. Same set in 1965 only with cameo lipstick. **CMV $20. each set MB.**

HEADLINER FOR BOYS 1938-39
Maroon & gray striped box holds tubes of Hair Dress & Tooth Paste with Tooth Brush. **CMV $65 mint.**

GOING STEADY SET 1960
Gray bag holds white compact & lipstick. Purse does not say Avon on it. **CMV $10. MB.**

BEAUTY BOUND SET 1964
Black leather handbag deluxe compact & lipstick & choice of creme rollette. **CMV $30. MB.**
BEAUTY BOUND SET 1965
Same set as 1964 only with perfume rollete instead of creme rollette. **CMV $30. MB.**

MODERN MOOD SET 1961
Gold & white sequin bag holds deluxe lipstick & compact. **CMV $20. MB.**

EVENING LIGHTS PURSE SET 1965
White box with gold purse came with deluxe compact, lipstick, & perfume rollette. **CMV $20. MB.**

MEN'S PACKAGES 1936-37
Maroon box holds can of Talc for Men, 4 oz. After Shave Lotion, turquioise can of Smokers Tooth Powder and tube of Shaving Cream. **CMV $100. MB.**

SMOKERS TRIO 1938-39
Green box holds 6 oz. Antiseptic, Tooth Brush
and green can of Smokers Tooth Powder.
CMV $80. MB.

ASSORTMENT NO. 7 FOR MEN 1931-34
Avon box holds can of Talc for Men, 4 oz. bottle of Bay Rum and tube of Bayberry Shaving
Cream, 2 yellow Cannon wash cloths and 1
yellow Cannon towel. **CMV $110.00 set mint.**

ASSORTMENT FOR MEN 1931-36
Green box holds tube of Shaving Cream and
green can Talc for Men with choice of 4 oz.
Bay Rum or 2 oz. Lilac Vegetal. **CMV $110.00
MB.**

MENS TRAVEL KIT 1936-38
Leather case 7 1/4" x 6 1/2" x 2". Holds 4 oz.
After Shave Lotion, Talc for Men, Shaving
Cream and tube of Styptic. **CMV $90 mint.**

ASSORTMENT FOR MEN 1936-37
Wood grained paper box holds tube of
Shaving Cream and can of Talc for Men with
choice of 4 oz. Bay Rum or After Shave Lotion.
CMV $85. MB.
**ESQUIRE SET OR COUNTRY CLUB SET
1938-39**
Same set as above and same price, only
name changed. **CMV $85. each set.**

MEN'S TRAVEL KIT 1933-36
Black leather case 7 1/4" x 6 1/2" x 2". Holds
green tube of Bayberry Shaving Cream, 4 oz.
After Shave Lotion, Styptic Pencil and green
can of Talc for Men. **CMV $110.00 MB.**

MEN'S TRAVEL KIT 1938-40
Brown leather zipper case holds maroon can
of Talc for Men, tube of Shaving Cream,
Styptic, and 4 oz. After Shave Lotion. **CMV
$85. MB.**

VALET SET 1938-39
Speckled box holds 4 oz. After Shave, maroon
can of Talc for Men, Smokers Tooth Powder &
tube of Shaving Cream. **CMV $100.00 set
mint.**

HAIR TREATMENT SET FOR MEN 1931-35
6 oz. Liquid Shampoo, 2 oz. Pre-Shampoo, 6
oz. Hair Tonic, All have blue caps. Silver tube
Hair Dress. White box. **CMV $135.00 MB.**

BRUSHLESS SHAVING SET 1937-39
Speckled box holds 4 oz. After Shave Lotion,
maroon can of Talc for Men, and tube of
Brushless Shaving Cream. **CMV $85. MB.**

CHRISTMAS BOXES 1930
Special issue boxes came with seven different
Avon sets at Christmas, 1931. **CMV $25.
added to price of set for this box.**

MEN'S SHAVING SET 1934-35
Wood grained box holds 4 oz. After Shave Lotion, can of Talc for Men, Smokers Tooth Powder and tube of Bayberry Shaving Cream. **CMV $175.00 set.**

TRAVEL KIT FOR MEN 1938
Tan leather like case with zipper. Holds tube of Styptic Cream, 4 oz. after shave lotion, tube of shaving cream, can of Talc for Men. **CMV $80. MB.**

CHRISTMAS SET NO. 49 1934
Red and green holly design box holds 2 white and green linen hand towels. 4 oz. bottle of Vanilla Tonka and Vanilla Extract in box with tube of Mending Cement in box. Rare set. Comes with outer sleeves with Set No. 49 on sleeve. **CMV $115.00 MB with sleeve.**

ASSORTMENT FOR MEN NO. 1 & NO. 2 1936
Avon box holds can of Talc for Men, tube of Bayberry Shaving Cream and choice of ribbed glass bottle after shave or Bay Rum. **CMV $110.00 MB.**

WOMEN'S SETS OF 1930'S

WARNING!! Grading condition is paramount on sets. CMV can vary up to 90% on grade.

BATH ENSEMBLE SET 1935
Box contains Jasmine Bath Salts, 2 bars Jasmine Bath Soap, Avon Dusting Powder in silver can and bottle of Trailing Arbutus Toilet Water. **CMV $185.00 MB.**

CHRISTMAS PERFUME SET 1933
Small blue box with winter snow scene holds 4 octagonal shaped perfumes with black caps. Came in choice perfumes. **CMV $275.00 Very Rare.**

ASSORTMENT SET FOR WOMEN 1931-32
Contains 2 bars Verna Fleur Toilet soap, blue and silver can Avon Dusting Powder, bottle of Verna Fleur Bath Salts, 1 bath towel and 2 wash cloths. All in orange and blue box. **CMV $160.00 MB.**

SHAVING CABINET 1930-34
White enamel cabinet with mirror on door. Cabinet is 8" high, 6 1/2" wide and 2 3/8" deep. Label on door reads "Gem Micromatic Shaving Cabinet, Avon Products" **CMV $90.00 empty mint.**

BATH ENSEMBLE SET 1936-39
Plaid box holds 9 oz. Jasmine Bath Salts, 2 oz. Trailing Arbutus Toilet Water, 2 bars of Jasmine Soap and can of Beauty Dust. **CMV $160.00 MB.**

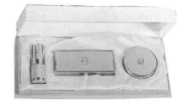

CHARMER SET 1938-41
Satin lined box contains lipstick, mascara and rouge. All green and gold. **CMV $60.00 MB.**

HAIR TREATMENT SET FOR WOMEN 1931-35
Contains Liquid Shampoo, Pre-Shampoo Oil, Wave Set, and Hair Tonic. All have blue plastic caps, blue and white box. **CMV $180.00 MB.**

HARMONY SET 1937
Blue and white box contains Lily of the Valley Toilet Water, gold cap and label. White milk glass jar with turquoise cap of Rose Cold Cream and turquoise and white tube Hand Cream. **CMV $75. MB.**

MAYFAIR SET 1939
Blue lid box holds 2 dram glass stoppered bottle of Bolero Perfume box of Face Powder and turquoise double compact. **CMV $110.00 MB.**

WINGS TO BEAUTY SET 1938-40
Hinged lid box holds 4 oz. bottle of Lotus Cream and choice of Ariel or Cotillion Face Powder and choice of astringent or skin freshener. **CMV $75. MB.**

VANITY SET 1932-33
Gray velvet lined box contains blue and gold double Compact and Lipstick. **CMV $70. MB.**

VANITY BOOK SET 1936-37
Satin lined box holds green and gold Compact and Lipstick. **CMV $50. MB.**

SPORTS WISE SET 1938-40
Same set as 1936-37. Vanity Book only name changed. **CMV $50. MB.**

COLONIAL SET 1939
Blue and gold box holds 2 dram Gardenia Perfume and Face Powder in choice of Ariel or Cotillion. **CMV $75. MB.**

VANITY BOOK SET 1931-32
Silver and blue box contains blue and silver Compact and Lipstick. **CMV $80. MB.** Also came in Christmas box. **CMV $90. MB.**

VANITY BOOK SET 1934-35
Blue and silver box holds blue and silver compact and lipstick. **CMV $70. MB.**

HANDKERCHIEF SET 1936 Only
Avon box holds 2 perfume bottles of Bolero and Ariel. **CMV $90. MB.**

LYRIC SET 1937
White and gold box holds Trailing Arbutus Toilet Water, turquoise and white can, Daphne Talcum, turquoise and white can, turquoise cap, white jar, turquoise lid cold cream. **CMV $75. MB.**

VANITY BOOK SET 1933
Silver and blue box contains blue and silver double Compact and Lipstick. **CMV $75. MB.**

PERFUME HANDKERCHIEF SET 1937-38
Two 1/8 oz. bottles of Gardenia and Cotillion Perfume on four colored handkerchiefs. **CMV $70. MB.**

PERFUME HANDKERCHIEF SET 1933-36
Two small bottles of Ariel and 391 perfume or Bolero, with black caps, 4 handkerchiefs under green and red flower cutout. **CMV $85. MB.**

HANDKERCHIEF SET 1939 Only
Gardenia and Cotillion Perfumes with 4 handkerchiefs. **CMV $75. MB.**

FAIR LADY SET 1939-42
Green, yellow and white flowered box with gold base holds 4 perfumes in Narcissus, Gardenia, Cotillion, Trailing Arbutus, or Sweet Pes. Each came in different caps. **CMV $100.00 MB.**

ATOMIZER SET NO. 6 1931-33
Blue and silver box contains red 1 oz. glass bottle with atomizer with Vernafleur perfume in 1 oz. bottle with cork stopper. Set comes in 2 different boxes. **CMV $160.00 MB.**

THREESOME SET 1934-35
Silver and blue box contains Compact Face Powder and 2 dram bottle Bolero Perfume. **CMV $110. MB.**

THREESOME SET 1936-37
Box has green and gold compact, box of face powder and glass stoppered 3 dram bottle of Bolero Perfume. **CMV $115.00 MB.**

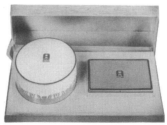

POWDER COMPACT SET 1936-37
Box holds box of face powder and green and gold compact. **CMV $50. MB.**
ARISTOCRAT SET 1938
Same set as Powder Compact Set only name changed in 1938. **CMV $50. MB.**

BATH DUET 1937-39
Box holds turquoise and white can of Daphne Talc with choice of bath salts in Jasmine, Pine, Ariel, or Vernafleur. **CMV $55. MB.**

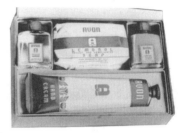

BEAUTY KIT FOR FINGERS 1938-39
Green box holds bar of Lemonal soap, turquoise tube of hand cream, bottle of polish remover and cream or nail polish. **CMV $75. MB.** Same set also came in gold design box as substitute.

SPECTATOR SET 1939
Turquoise and white box holds 2 dram bottle with gold cap ot Trailing Arbitus Perfume, lipstick and rouge compact. **CMV $80. MB.**

TRIO GIFT SET 1936
Box holds 2 oz. Trailing Arbutus toilet water with tulip label and gold ribbed cap. Silver can of Daphne Talcum and ribbed glass. Ariel powder sachet. **CMV $110.00 MB.**

WOMEN'S SETS OF 1930's

TRIO SET 1934-35
Red and blue box contains Trailing Arbutus Toilet Water, Daphne Talcum and Ariel Sachet. **CMV $115.00 MB.**

GIFT SET "A" 1935
Satin lined box contains face powder in Ariel or Vernafleur and 2 dram bottle of Gardenia perfume with gold ribbed cap. **CMV $85. MB.**

GIFT SET "A" 1936-37
Box has box of face powder, 3 dram size of Ariel, Vernafleur or Gardenia perfume with gold caps. **CMV $75. MB.**

GIFT SET "B" 1936-37
Green and silver box holds green and gold lipstick and rouge with 3 dram Trailing Arbutus perfume with gold cap. **CMV $90. MB.**

GIFT SET "B" 1935
Box contains blue and silver lipstick and rouge compact and 2 dram bottle of Trailing Arbutus perfume. **CMV $95. MB.**

GIFT SET "D" 1935
Blue and yellow box contains choice of Ariel or Vernafleur face powder in silver and blue box and 2 dram Ariel perfume with gold cap and Ariel sachet with silver label. **CMV $105.00 MB.**

GIFT SET "D" 1936
Blue and yellow box contains Ariel or Vernafleur face powder in green and gold and 2 dram Ariel perfume with gold cap and Ariel powder sachet with black cap. **CMV $90. MB.**

GIFT SET "F" 1936-37
Box holds green and gold compact, lipstick and box of face powder in Ariel or Vernafleur. **CMV $60. MB.**
MASTERCRAFT SET 1938
Same set as Gift Set "F" only name changed in 1938. **CMV $60. MB.**

GIFT SET "F" 1935
Red and gold box contains blue compact, face powder in Ariel or Vernafleur and lipstick. **CMV $85. MB.**

GIFT SET "K" 1936-37
Blue and gold box has green and gold lipstick and compact and 2 dram perfume with gold cap. **CMV $90. MB.**
EMPRESS SET 1938
Same set as Gift Set "K" only name is changed. **CMV $90. MB.**

GIFT SET NO. 19 1934
Red and green box contains Deluxe Hair Brush, toothpaste, 1 bar of Savona soap, bottle of antiseptic and tube of Dental Cream No. 2. **CMV $110.00 MB.**

GIFT SET "K" 1935
Box contains blue compact, 2 dram perfume in Gardenia and blue and silver lipstick. **CMV $115.00 MB.**

GIFT SET "W" 1936-37
Satin lined box holds two ribbed bottles of nail polish and polish remover, green and gold lipstick and rouge. **CMV $80. MB.**

GIFT SET "W" 1935
Box contains nail polish, lipstick, rouge compact and polish remover. **CMV $105.00 MB.**

GIFT SET NO. 21 1936-37
Striped box holds turquoise and white box face powder, turquoise and white cake rouge, turquoise and gold lipstick. **CMV $60. MB.**

GIFT SET NO. 21. 1933-35
Contains box of face powder and table rouge. Silver and blue. Blue lipstick in green, white and red box. **CMV $65. MB.**

GIFT SET NO. 24 1934
Holly decorated box contained box of face powder, rouge and jar of vanishing cream. **CMV $85. MB.**

GIFT SET NO. 36 1934
Red and green box contains bottle of Rosewater Glycerine, can of Daphne Talcum and Vernafleur Bath Salts. **CMV $175.00 MB.**

MEN'S SETS OF 1940'S

WARNING!! Grading condition is paramount on sets. CMV can vary up to 90% on grade. Refer to front of book for grading.

MODERN NIGHT 1946-49
Maroon and white box holds 2 oz. Deodorant for Men, can of Talc for Men and 4 oz. After Shaving Lotion. **CMV $95. MB.**

PLEASURE CAST SET 1948
Blue box holds 2 oz. bottles with maroon caps in Deodorant for Men and tube of Brushless or Regular Shaving Cream. **CMV $75. MB.**

VALET SET 1945-46
Maroon & ivory box holds 4 oz. After Shave Lotion, tube of Shaving Cream, Talc for Men and Smokers Tooth Powder. Both came in maroon paper containers with flat top lids and also pouring lids with caps. **CMV $125.00 MB.**

ARMY & NAVY KIT 1943-46
Blue and red box holds tube of Brushless Shaving Cream, maroon paper box of Elite Foot Powder and paper carton of Tooth Powder. **CMV $100.00 MB.**

ESQUIRE SET 1940-41
Maroon box holds 4 oz bottle of Bay Rum, tube of shaving cream, can of talc for men. **CMV $90. MB.**

MEN'S SETS OF 1940'S

ARMY & NAVY KIT 1941-42
Blue & red box with Eagle on lid, holds 4 oz. After Shave Lotion, maroon tube of Brushless Shaving Cream and maroon can of Elite Powder. Each in maroon & ivory boxes. **CMV $90 MB.**

VALET SET 1940-42
Maroon and white box holds 4 oz. After Shaving Lotion, maroon cans of Talc for Men, Smokers Tooth Powder and tube of Shaving Cream. **CMV $100.00 MB.**

MENS TRAVEL KIT 1946-49
Brown flip open leather case holds can of Talc for Men, 4 oz After Shaving Lotion, Styptic Cream and choice of tube of Shaving Cream or Brushless Shaving Cream. **CMV $85. MB.**

TRAVELER KIT 1946-49
Maroon & white box holds 4 oz. After Shaving Lotion, maroon tubes of Smokers Tooth Paste and Shaving Cream. **CMV $75. MB.**

VALET SET 1946-49
Maroon box holds maroon can of Smokers Tooth Powder, Talc for Men, 4 oz. After Shaving Lotion and tube of Shaving Cream. **CMV $90. MB.**

COUNTRY CLUB SET 1943-46
Maroon and white box holds 4 oz. After Shave Lotion, 2 5/8 oz. paper box of Talc for Men and 3 oz. tube of Shaving Cream. Talc came with flat paper top lid or cap lid as shown. **CMV $90. MB.**

VALET SET 1943-45
Maroon & ivory box holds 4 oz. After Shave Lotion, 3 oz. tube in box of Shaving Cream, 2 5/8 oz. paper talc, 3.5 oz. paper side, tin flat top and bottom Smokers Tooth Powder. **CMV $115.00 MB.**

TRAVELER SET 1941-45
Maroon and ivory box holds 4 oz. After Shaving Lotion, maroon tubes of Smokers Tooth Paste and Shaving Cream. **CMV $75. MB.**

COUNTRY CLUB SET 1940-42
Maroon and ivory box holds 4 oz. After Shaving Lotion, maroon can of Talc for Men and tube of Shaving Cream. **CMV $90. MB.**

COUNTRY CLUB SET 1943-46
Maroon and white box holds 4 oz. After Shave Lotion, maroon flat top paper box of Talc for Men and tube Shaving Cream. **CMV $90. MB.**

ARMY NAVY KIT 1943
Blue box with eagle holds turquoise can of Elite powder, 4 oz. of After Shave and maroon tube of Brushless Shaving Cream. **CMV $85. MB.**

COUNTRY CLUB SET 1946-49
Maroon and white box holds tube of Shaving Cream, 4 oz. After Shaving Lotion and can of Talc for Men. **CMV $85. MB.**

BRUSHLESS SHAVE SET 1940-42
Maroon and ivory box with man fishing, maroon can of Talc for men and tube of Brushless Shave Cream. **CMV $85. MB.**

COMMODORE SET 1943-46
Maroon and white box holds 4 oz. After Shave Lotion, 2 white handkerchiefs and maroon paper box of Talc for Men. **CMV $90. MB.**

BRUSHLESS SHAVE SET 1943-46
Maroon and white box holds tube of Brushless Shave Cream, 4 oz. After Shave Lotion and maroon paper box of Talc for Men. **CMV $90. MB.**

BRUSHLESS SHAVE SET 1946-49
Maroon and white box holds can of Talc for Men, tube of Brushless Shaving Cream, and 4 oz. After Shaving Lotion. **CMV $85. MB.**

OLYMPIC SET 1946-49
Maroon and white box holds tube of Shaving Cream, 6 oz. bottle of Hair Lotion and 4 oz. After Shaving Lotion. **CMV $95. MB.**

WOMEN'S SETS OF 1940'S

WARNING!! Grading condition is paramount on sets. CMV can vary up to 90% on grade.

COUNTRY CLUB SET 1939-41
Box holds 4 oz. bottle of After Shave, tube of Shaving Cream, can of Talc for Men. **CMV $80. MB.**

OLYMPIC SET 1940-46
Maroon and ivory box holds 6 oz. bottle of Hair lotion, tube of Shaving Cream and 4 oz. After Shave Lotion. **CMV $95.00 MB.**

COMODORE SET 1940-42
Maroon and ivory box holds 4 oz. After Shaving Lotion, maroon can of Talc for Men and 2 white handkerchiefs. **CMV $90. MB.**

MENS TRAVELERS SET 1941-42
(left) Brown leather snap case with maroon & black strip inside case & lid. Holds 4 oz. After Shaving Lotion, 3.5 oz. tube of brushless shaving cream. Maroon 2 5/8 oz. can of talc for men & tube of styptic cream. All products came in original maroon & ivory color boxes. **CMV $100.00 set MB.**

BEAUTY BASKET SET 1947
Straw basket with pink ribbon holds two 6 oz. bottles of Avon Cream Lotion and Rose Gardenia Bath Oil. Both bottles are flat on the back side and have pink caps. **CMV $55. basket mint with bottles, $75. MB.**

LITTLE JEWELS SET 1944-45
Pink box holds 3 paper powder sachets in 11/4 oz. Cotillion, Attention, Garden of Love. **CMV $65. MB.**

RAINBOW WINGS SET 1943-44
Box holds 6 oz. bottles of Cream Lotion and Rose Geranium Bath Oil with pink caps. Both bottles are flat on one side. Butterflies on box. **CMV $65. MB.**

COLOR CLUSTER SET 1948
Red and gold box contains gold lipstick, gold rouge and 1/2 oz. nail polish with green cap. **CMV $45. MB.**

MINUET SET 1942
Box with music notes on lid, satin lined holds lipstick, powder compact, rouge, and face powder. All are blue and white feather design. **CMV $75. MB.**

RAINBOW WINGS SET 1945-46
Pink box holds two 6 oz. flat sided bottles of Cream Lotion and Rose Geranium Bath Oil. Pink net ribbon on top of box. **CMV $75. MB with net.**

MAYFAIR SET 1940
Blue box contains 1 dram perfume with gold cap. Green & gold compacts & box of face powder in Ariel or Cotillion. **CMV $75. MB.**

MINUET SET 1943-44
Pink and blue box with yellow satin lining holds blue plastic rouge compact, cardboard feather design lipstick, Cotillion perfume with gold cap and neck tag, and blue satin sachet pillowette. **CMV $110. MB.**

SPECTATOR SET 1940
Box contains green and gold rouge, 1 dram Garden of Love perfume, gold cap, green and gold lipstick. **CMV $65. MB.**

DOUBLE DARE SET 1946
Red and gold box holds bottle of Double Dare nail polish and gold Bamboo lipstick. **CMV $50. MB.**

LEADING LADY SET 1946 ONLY
Red, blue and gold box holds Bamboo lipstick and nail polish. **CMV $45. MB.**

COLOR CLUSTER SET 1946-47
Red and gold box holds gold Bamboo lipstick and rouge with 1/2 oz. nail polish with black cap. **CMV $50. MB.**

COLOR MAGIC THREE PIECE SET 1949-50
Multi-colored box holds gold lipstick, gold rouge and 1/2 oz. nail polish with green cap. **CMV $50. MB.**

BEAUTY MARK 1948
Red and gold box contains gold lipstick and 1/2 oz. nail polish with green cap. **CMV $40. MB.**

MILADY SET 1940-41
Satin lined box contains two small bottles of perfume in Gardenia, Cotillion, Apple Blossom or Ballad & white lace edged hanky. **CMV $85. MB.**

MR. & MRS. SET 1940-43
Blue & pink box contains smokers tooth-powder, after shaving lotion for men, Cotillion toilet water & Cotillion talcum for women. **CMV $140.00 MB.**

COLOR MAGIC TWO PIECE SET 1949-50
Multi-colored box contains gold lipstick and 1/2 oz. nail polish with green cap. **CMV $40. MB.**

COLONIAL DAYS SET 1943
6 oz. clear glass bottle, pink cap, cream lotion & cardboard body powder, shaker cap. **CMV $65. MB.**

BATH BOUQUET SET 1943-44
Blue box holds 6 oz. of Rose Geranium bath oil & Apple Blossom beauty dust. **CMV $75. MB.**

BATH DUET SET 1940-43
Blue, pink & white box box holds can of Daphne or Cotillion talc & choice of Jasmine, Pine, Ariel or Vernafleur bath salts. **CMV $60. MB.**

PEEK-A-BOO SET 1944 ONLY
Blue, white & pink box with yellow satin lining holds cardboard compact covered with pink satin & white net. Cake rouge in blue plastic compact & cardboard feather design lipstick. **CMV $60. MB.**

RECEPTION SET 1941-42
Satin lined box holds gold compact, blue box of face powder & 1/8 oz. perfume. **CMV $75. MB.**

WOMEN'S SETS OF 1940s

COLONIAL SET 1940
Blue box holds 1 dram Garden of Love perfume, gold cap & label & box of face powder. **CMV $55. MB.**

TANDEM SET 1941
(Left) Box holds gold bamboo compact & turquoise & gold lipstick. **CMV $50. MB.**
TANDEM SET 1942
(RIght) Same set only with matching bamboo lipstick. **CMV $50. MB.**

FAIR LADY SET 1945-47
Blue & white box holds 4 small bottles with colored caps of perfume in Cotillion, Lily of the Valley, Gardenia, Garden of Love, Trailing Arbutus & Sweet Pea. **CMV $75. MB.** Also came with all blue caps.

COLONIAL SET 1940-41
Feather face powder & Garden of Love perfume in blue box. **CMV $60. MB.**

ELYSIAN SET 1941-42
Satin lined box contains lipstick, rouge & 1 dram perfume with gold cap. **CMV $85. MB.**

PEEK-A-BOO SET 1943
Pink & blue box with yellow satin lining holds blue & white feather design cardboard compact, cardboard lipstick & rouge. **CMV $65. MB.**

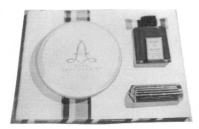

THAT'S FOR ME SET 1947-49
Multi-colored box contains choice of cream cake or cake makeup, gold lipstick & 1/2 oz. nail polish. **CMV $40. MB.**

WINGS TO BEAUTY SET 1941
Red designed box contains choice of two 2 oz. skin conditioner, atringent, finishing lotion or Lotus cream, and box of face powder. **CMV $55. MB.**

FRAGRANT MIST 1950
Turquoise & gold box holds 2 oz. toilet water with green & gold atomizer in the choice of Flowertime, Cotillion, Lily of the Valley & Wishing. **CMV $50. MB.**

ORCHID SET 1940
Red & white box, green & gold lipstick & rouge. Cream polish with green cap.**CMV $55.**

PERFUMED DEODORANT SET 1947-54
Turquoise box holds two 2 oz. bottles of perfumed deodorant. **CMV set $15. MB.**

MEN'S SETS OF 1950s

WARNING!! Grading condition is paramount on sets. CMV can vary up to 90% on grade.

FAIR LADY SET 1948--49
Pink & blue box contains four 1/8 oz. perfumes in Lily of the Valley, Garden of Love, Quaintance, Gardenia & Cotillion. All have blue caps. **CMV $85. MB.**

MERRIMENT SET 1940-42
Rouge, lipstick & eyebrow pencil. All green & gold. **CMV $45. MB.**

HANDKERCHIEF SET 1940-42
Box holds white, pink, blue & yellow handkerchiefs, 1/8 oz. Cotillion perfume with red cap. Gardenia perfume with blue cap. **CMV $60. MB.**

FRAGRANT MIST SET 1940-42
Blue & gold box holds 2 oz. toilet water with gold or plastic cap & label and spray atomizer. Came in Cotillion, Marionette, Sonnet, Jasmine or Apple Blossom. **CMV $50. MB.**

COMMODORE SET 1949-53
Stage coach on green flip open box holds 2 oz. cologne & 2 oz. deodorant for men & green tube of brushless or lather shaving cream. **CMV $55. MB.**

GROOMING GUARDS SET 1959
Black flip open box with red inner box holds can of After Shower Powder for Men, 2 oz. Spray Deodorant for Men in white plastic & tube of Attention Cream Hair Dress & choice of 4 oz. After Shower for Men or After Shaving Lotion. **CMV $60. MB.**

COAT OF ARMS SET 1958
Red, white, blue & gold box holds 6 oz. Kwick Foaming Shave Cream, 2 oz. Deodorant for Men & 2 oz. After Shave Lotion. **CMV $40. MB.**

PARADE DRESS SET 1953-54
Red, white & blue soldier box holds 1 oz. bottle of liquid shampoo, 1 oz. cream or liquid hair lotion & 1 bar of Dr. Zabriskie's Soap. **CMV $75. MB.** Set also came with 2 shampoos & 1 hair lotion with no soap. **Same CMV.**

CHANGING THE GUARD SET 1952
Red, white & blue guard house box holds 2 oz. hair guard with red cap. Came with outer box. **CMV $70. MV.**

GOOD MORNING SET 1955-56
Red box with geese holds choice of two 4 oz. bottles of cream or liquid hair lotion. **CMV $26. MB.**

ATTENTION SET 1957
Red & green box holds two 4 oz. bottles in after shave lotion & choice of liquid or cream hair lotion. **CMV $35. MB.**

PIGSKIN PARADE SET 1955
(Left) Red & green box holds tube of creme shampoo, youths toothbrush, chap check, 2 oz. bottle of hair guard & a plastic football. **CMV $65. MB.**
TOUCHDOWN SET 1956-57
(Right) Green, red & gold box holds 2 oz. bottles of hair guard with red cap, hand guard with green cap & small football soap. **CMV $65. MB.**

SPACE SHIP SET 1953
Blue box holds plastic spaceship with tubes of chlorophyll toothpaste, creme shampoo & toothbrush. **CMV $60. MB.**

HAIR TRAINER & COMB SET 1957
6 oz. bottle, white or blue cap, red & white label. Came in box with comb. **CMV $25. BO, $40. MB.**

MAN'S WORLD SET 1957
Box has choice of 2 cream or liquid hair lotions in 4 oz. size. **CMV $30. MB.**

SMOOTH SHAVING SET 1954
Green tubes with red caps has choice of brushless or lather shaving cream. **CMV $25. MB.**

BEFORE & AFTER SET 1953-54
Silver, white & green box opens up to 4 oz. cologne for men & choice of cream or liquid hair lotion. **CMV $45. MB.**

PLEASURE SHAVE SET 1949-51
Green box holds green can of talc for men, wood shaving bowl & 4 oz. after shave lotion with silver label. **CMV $75. MB.**

BACKFIELD SET 1954
Red & green box holds 2 oz. bottle of hair guard with red cap, 2 oz. hand guard with green cap, tube of chap check & small brown football soap. **CMV $70. MB.**

PERSONAL NOTE SET 1954-56
Green & red box holds 4 oz. cologne & deodorant for men with green label & gold ball point pen. **CMV $60. MB.**

PLEASURE SHAVE SET 1952-54
Green box with red & white barber pole holds 2 tubes of shaving cream in choice of brushless or lather. **CMV $25. MB.**

DELUXE TRIO SET 1949-51
Stage coach on green flip open box with green & red inner box. Holds choice of 4 oz. cream or liquid hair lotion, 2 oz. deodorant for men & 2 oz. cologne for men. **CMV $60. MB.**

DELUXE TRIO SET 1952
Same as 1949 set only has green removable lid. **CMV $60. MB.**

QUARTET SET 1953-54
Green & red box holds 2 tubes of shave cream brushless or lather, 2 oz. deodorant for men, green label & 4 oz. after shave lotion with silver label. **CMV $60. MB.**

OUT IN FRONT SET 1959
Box with soldier on horse holds 4 oz. cream or liquid hair lotion & 2 3/4 oz. spray deodorant for men in white plastic bottles. **CMV $30. MB.**

KING PIN SET 1953
Red & green box holds two 4 oz. bottles of after shave lotion wrapped in green King Pin wrappings. **CMV $45. MB.**

HI PODNER SET 1950-51
White box holds 2 red leatherette cowboy cuffs with tubes of cream hair dress & ammoniated toothpaste or dental cream and toothbrush. **CMV $70. MB.** 1952 Hi Podner set is same except tube of cream hair dress was replaced with green tube of creme shampoo. **CMV $70. MB.**

GOOD CHEER SET 1957
Man playing bass fiddle on green & red box. 2 oz. bottles of cologne, deodorant & after shave lotions. All have red caps. **CMV $45. MB.**

COUNTRY CLUB SET 1949-51

Green flip open box with red inner box, holds green can of talc for men, 4 oz. after shaving lotion & choice of lather or brushless shaving cream. **CMV $55. MB.**

COUNTRY CLUB SET 1952-53

Stage coach on green box lid with inner box in red. Holds green talc for men, 4 oz. after shave lotion & tube of brushless or lather shave cream. **CMV $55. MB.**

TOP OF THE MORNING SET 1956

Red, white, green & silver box holds can of Kwick Foaming shave cream & 2 oz. after shave lotion. **CMV $45. MB.**

COUNTRY CLUB SET 1954-55

Red box holds green can of talc for men, 4 oz. after shaving lotion & tube of brushless or lather shaving cream. **CMV $60. MB.**

Country Club Set 1956

Came in green box with golf ball & red flag on lid & red lined box. Same contents as 1954 set. **CMV $60. MB.**

SPORT WISE SET 1954

Red, white & green box holds two 4 oz. bottles of after shave lotions. **CMV $30. MB.**

ROUGN 'N' READY SET 1953

White, red & green box holds 4 oz. cream hair lotion, chap check & Dr. Zabriskie's soap. **CMV $47.50 MB.**

YOUNG MAN SET 1950

(Left) Red, white & green box holds tubes of cream hair dress & creme shampoo, comb & nail file in brown leather case. **CMV $60. MB.**

LAMPLIGHTER SET 1959-60

(Left) Lamp post on covered box. 2 oz. bottle of after shave lotion, 1 1/2 oz. white plastic bottle of spray deodorant for men & 2 oz. black plastic bottle of after shower for men. All have red caps. **CMV $45. MB.**

AVON GUARD SET 1958

(Right) Red & blue box holds 2 bottles of hair guard & hand guard with red caps, white Avon rocket soap sits on top of bottles. **CMV $65. MB.**

CAPTAIN OF THE GUARD SET 1959

White tube, red cap of cream hair dress and white plastic bottle, red cap of spray deodorant for men. **CMV $40.**

SAILING, SAILING SET 1957

4 oz. clear glass, red cap, silver label. Choice of any 2 bottles of after shaving lotion, electric pre-shave lotion or deodorant for men. **CMV $30. MB.**

REFRESHING HOURS SET 1957
Red & green hourglass box holds 4 oz. after shaving lotion & 4 oz. deodorant for men. **CMV $30. MB.**

HAPPY HOURS SET 1958
Coo-coo clock on black & brown box. 2 oz. cologne, deodorant & after shave lotion. All have red caps. **CMV $40. MB.**

MORE LOVE THAN MONEY SET 1956
Red, black & gold box holds 4 oz. cologne for men, 4 oz. after shave lotion & 2 oz. deodorant for men. Brown leather wallet with a new 1956 penny in it. **CMV $55. MB.**

PENNY ARCADE SET 1954-55
Red & white with center foil mirror, holds tubes of cream hair dress, creme shampoo & chlorophyll toothpaste, toothbrush & chap check. **CMV $70. MB.**

TRIUMPH SET 1959
Triumph box holds choice of 5 combinations of two 4 oz. after shave lotions or electric pre-shave lotion & after shave lotion or after shave lotion & after shower powder for men. **CMV each set $30. MB.** Electric pre-shave lotion & after shower for men in black glass, or after shower powder for men & after shower for men in black glass. **CMV $30. MB. ea. set.**

SHAVE BOWL SET 1955-56
Bronze box holds wood shave bowl & bronze 4 oz. deodorant for men. **CMV $55. MB.**

SEND OFF SET 1957
Red, white & black box holds two 4 oz. after shave lotions. **CMV $30. MB.**

TWO SUITER SET 1953-54
Two different olive tan box with airlines painted on sides. Holds choice of two 2 oz. deodorants for men or one 2 oz. deodorant and 4 oz. after shave or 2 oz. deodorant and 2 oz. cologne for men. Sold at Father's Day. **CMV $60. MB, light color box, $70. MB dark color box.**

FATHER'S SAIL DAY SPECIAL SET NO. 1 1957
Box with sailboat holds two 4 oz. bottles of after shave with silver labels. Also came with choice of 4 oz. after shave and green can of talc for men or 4 oz. deodorant & 4 oz. after shave lotion. **CMV $35. MB.**

PLEASURE CAST SET 1955
Green & white box holds two 4 oz. bottles of after shaving lotion. **CMV $30. MB.**

MEN'S SETS OF 1950s

MODERN DECOY SET 1958
Blue & brown box with ducks on lid holds silver Paper Mate Capri pen, 4 oz. cream hair lotion & choice of 4 oz. after shave lotion, cologne, deodorant or electric pre-shave lotion. **CMV $40. MB.**

TRADING POST SET 1957
Red & brown box holds 2 oz. bottle of foamy bath & hair trainer. Both have red caps. **CMV $40. MB.**

FLYING HIGH NO. 1 & NO. 2 SET 1955
Red & green box has 4 oz. after shave lotion & 4 oz. deodorant for men. No. 2 box has 4 oz. deodorant for men & green can talc for men. **CMV $35. each set MB.**

CAROLLERS SET 1959-60
Xmas box with red & gold base holds red & black stick deodorant for men & black and white can of after shower powder for men & choice of 4 oz. after shower for men in black glass of electric pre-shave lotion or after shave lotion. **CMV $55. MB.**

SPACE SCOUT SET 1955
Blue box holds wall charts of planets, toothbrush, white toothpaste, bottle of hair guard, tube of antiseptic cream & chap check. **CMV $60. MB.**

ROUND THE CORNER SET 1955
Red & white striped box holds 2 oz. deodorant for men & can of Kwick Foaming shave cream. **CMV $35. MB.**

STAGE COACH SET 1958
Yellow stage coach box holds 2 oz. bottles of hair trainer & foamy bath. Both have red caps. **CMV $40. MB.**

SATURDAY NIGHT SET 1955
Plaid box holds 4 oz. deodorant for men, plaid bow tie & choice of 4 oz. cream or liquid hair lotion. **CMV $50. MB.**
VARSITY SET 1956
Same set as Saturday Night only name changed. **CMV $50. MB.**

MONEY ISN'T EVERYTHING SET 1957
Red box with money written all over lid, holds 4 oz. cologne for men, 4 oz. after shave lotion & 2 oz. deodorant for men, plus brown leather billfold. **CMV $60. MB.**

MERRILY SET 1957
Red, white & green box holds can of Kwick Foaming shaving cream, 2 oz. deodorant for men & 2 oz. after shave lotion. **CMV $30. MB.**

PLEASURE CAST NO. 2 SET 1954
(Left) Green & white box holds 4 oz. after shave lotion & green can of talc. **CMV$35.MB.**
PLEASURE CAST NO. 1 SET 1954
(Right) Red & white box holds 2 oz. deodorant for men & 4 oz. after shave lotion. **CMV $35. MB.**

HOLIDAY HOLLY SET 1957
Green & white box holds 4 oz. after shave lotion & green can of talc for men. **CMV $30. MB.**

CLASSIC SET 1954
Red & white box with horse head on box holds green can of talc for men, 2 oz. deodorant green label, 4 oz. cologne, silver label, all have red caps. **Rare. CMV $80.**

BEFORE & AFTER SET 1956
Red & silver box holds 4 oz. electric pre-shave lotion & 4 oz. after shave lotion. **CMV $30. MB.**

NEW DAY SET 1957
Red top box holds 4 oz. electric pre-shave lotion & 4 oz. after shaving lotion. **CMV $30. MB.**

AVON CLASSIC SET 1952-53
Silver & green box holds 2 oz. deodorant for men, green talc for men & 4 oz. cologne for men. **CMV $55. MB.**

CUFFLINKS SET 1957
Black velour covered box holds 2 gold cufflinks and 4 oz. cologne & deodorant for men. **CMV $55. MB.**

BLACK SHEEP 1954-56
Red, white, green & black box holds black sheep soap with gold bell on neck & 4 oz. cologne for men & 4 oz. deodorant for men. **CMV $100.00 MB.**

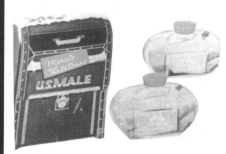

U.S. MALE SET 1952-53
Green & white mailbox choice of two 4 oz. after shave lotions or 4 oz. after shave lotion & 2 oz. deodorant for men. **CMV $40. MB.**

CLASSIC SET 1951
Green box holds 4 oz. cream hair lotion, tan bar of soap & 2 oz. deodorant. set. **CMV $65. MB.**

OVERNIGHTER SET 1956-57
Brown alligator type bag holds 2 oz. after shaving lotion & 2 oz. deodorant for men, & choice of 4 oz. cream or liquid hair lotion. **CMV $45. MB.**

MEN'S SETS OF 1950s

VALET SET 1951
Green flip open box holds 2 oz. deodorant for men & tube of brushless or lather shaving cream & 4 oz. cream or liquid hair lotion. **CMV $50. MB.**

AVON SERVICE KIT 1953-54
Green & red box holds tan plastic apron with 4 oz. plastic bottle of after shaving lotion with red cap, tube of brushless shaving cream, chlorophyll toothpaste, Dr. Zabriskie's soap, comb & toothbrush. . **CMV $55. MB.**

HAPPY HOURS SUBSTITUTE SET 1958
Outer sleeve marked Happy Hours Sub holds tan vinyl case with 2 oz. cologne, after shave lotion & deodorant. This is a rare set. Factory ran out of regular issue box & used overnighter case for short period. **CMV $45. set MB.** Must have outer sleeve.

VALET SET 1949-50
Green box with choice of green can talc for men or shaving soap & 4 oz. cologne for men. **CMV $50. MB.**

AVON SERVICE KIT 1951-52
Red & green box holds canvas apron with 4 oz. plastic bottle of after shaving lotion with red cap, Dr. Zabriskie's soap, tube of brushless shaving cream, toothpaste, toothbrush & comb. **CMV $55. MB.**

OVERNIGHTER SET 1958
Tan case holds 2 oz. deodorant for men & 2 oz. after shaving lotion & choice of 4 oz. liquid or cream hair lotion. **CMV $35. MB.**

MAN'S SAMPLE CASE SET 1953
Very rare brown leather case has three partitions inside to hold a Gilette brass razor, 1/2 oz. green sample tube brushless shaving cream 3/4 oz. blue, white & green sample toothpaste tubes, 1 oz. bottle liquid shampoo, green label, 1 oz. bottle cream hair lotion, green label, 1/2 oz. bottle shaving lotion, green label, 1/2 oz. bottle deodorant for men, green label, 1/2 oz. bottle cologne for men, silver label. All bottles have red caps. **CMV $125. complete set mint.**

ON THE GO SET 1957
Brown leatherette bag holds green can of talc for men, 2 oz. deodorant for men, 4 oz. after shave lotion & can of shaving cream in choice of Kwick Foaming lather, brushless or electric pre-shave lotion. **CMV $50. MB.**

THE TRAVELER SET 1956
Brown leatherette bag holds choice of shaving cream in Kwick, lather or brushless, 4 oz. after shaving lotion, green can talc for men, 2 oz. deodorant for men & styptic cream. **CMV $50. MB.**

WOMEN'S SETS OF 1950s

WARNING!! Grading condition is paramount on sets. CMV can vary up to 90% on grade.

NEAT TRAVELER SET 1958
Tan soft leather case holds 2 oz. deodorant for men, 4 oz. after shaving lotion choice of Kwick Foaming, lather or brushless shaving cream or electric pre-shave lotion & choice of cream or liquid hair lotion. **CMV $45. MB.**

CMV means Current Market Value Mint.

MEN'S TRAVELING KIT 1953-55
Choice of brown leatherette or plaid case. Holds 4 oz. after shave lotion, 2 oz. deodorant for men, styptic cream, green can of talc for men and tube of Lather Shaving Cream. **CMV $55. MB.**

DELUXE TRIO SET 1953-56
Tan leatherette bag holds 2 oz. cologne for men & 2 oz. deodorant for men & choice of 4 oz. cream or liquid hair lotion. Avon on bag. Fold open top, no zipper. **CMV $45.**

LADY BELLE SET 1954-55
White bell shaped box trimmed in blue & gold has two 1 dram perfumes. Ribbed glass with gold cap. Choice of Cotillion, To A Wild Rose, Golden Promise, Quaintance, Bright Night or Forever Spring. **CMV $60. MB.**

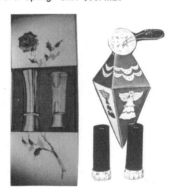

TOPS STYLE BEAUTY SET 1959
(Left) Red & white box holds lipstick & 1 dram perfume Top Style perfume. **CMV $25. MB.**
TWO LOVES SET 1956
(Right) Box holds 2 black lipsticks. **CMV $25. MB.**

CONCERTINA SET 1954
Two gold fashion lipsticks in red, white & green box. **CMV $35. MB.**

TWO LOVES SET 1955
Red, white, blue & gold Christmas tree ornament box holds 2 gold fashion lipsticks. **CMV $35. MB.**

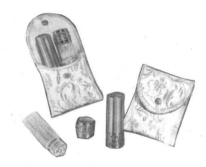

AVONETTE SET 1950-51
Blue & white brocade bag holds 1 dram perfume & deluxe gold lipstick. **CMV $18. - $25. MB**

2 LIPS SET 1959
Two white enamel lipsticks, white box with pink & gold design. **CMV $15. MB.**

287

TWO LOVES SET 1957
Red Christmas tree hang on box came with black fashion lipstick & liquid rouge. **CMV $35. MB.**

JEWELED LIPSTICK 1955
(Left) Blue & gold box with gold lipstick with pearl & rhinestones on top. **CMV $20. MB.**
CHARMER SET 1955
(Right) White, gold & red brocade case holds jeweled lipstick & 1 dram perfume. **CMV $25. mint.**

FASHION FIRSTS SET 1958
White & gold box holds 2 light tan fashion lipsticks. **CMV $15. MB.**

PRECIOUS PEAR SET 1953
Gold bell box holds 1 dram perfume in Golden Promise, Quaintance, Cotillion, To A Wild Rose & Forever Spring. **CMV $75. MB.**

FRAGRANCE RAINBOW SET 1954
Flowers on top of box. Choice of Cotillion, To A Wild Rose, Forever Spring, Quaintance. Cologne in 1/2 oz. bottles, white caps & painted labels. **CMV $70. MB.**

FRAGRANCE RAINBOW SET 1956
Box holds four 3 dram bottles with white painted caps. Came in To A Wild Rose, Nearness, Bright Night, Cotillion, Quaintance & Forever Spring. **CMV $75. MB.**

FRAGRANCE TIE INS SET 1953
White box with bows holds four 1/2 oz. bottles with white caps. Came in Cotillion, Forever Spring, Quaintance & To A Wild Rose cologne. **CMV $70. MB.**

SWEET AS HONEY SET 1951
Foam beehive holds four 5/8 dram bottles of perfume in Cotillion, Quaintance, Golden Promise, Luscious, Forever Spring & To A Wild Rose. All have different colored caps. **CMV MB $115.00 Beehive and bottles only $90. mint.**

AVON BLOSSOMS SET 1950
Four 1/8 oz. or 5/8 dram perfume bottles set in white foam with wire fence behind it. Flowers around bottles. Plastic cap. Quaintance, Cotillion, Luscious and Golden Promise. **CMV $85. set only, $100.00 MB.**

CREAM SACHET PETITES SET 1956
Gold box holds 4 plastic cream sachets in blue boxes. Came in Cotillion, Bright Night, Nearness and To A Wild Rose. **CMV $55. set, $10. each jar MB.**

CUPID'S BOW SET 1955
White and pink box holds four 1/2 oz. bottles of cologne with white caps. Bright Night, To A Wild Rose, Quaintance and Cotillion. **CMV $70. MB.**

AVONETTE SET 1953-54
Black case holds 1 dram perfume & gold
deluxe lipstick. **CMV $20 - $25. MB.**

HOLIDAY FASHION SET 1953
White box holds 2 gold fashion lipsticks in
green holly leaves. **CMV $25. MB.**

TIME FOR BEAUTY SET 1952
Blue, white & pink box with pink ribbon holds
gold lipstick & nail polish. **CMV $30. MB.**

HOUSE OF CHARMS SET 1952-53
With windows open. You find four 1/8 oz. or
5/8 dram bottles or perfume: Lily of the Valley,
Cotillion, Golden Promise or Quaintance. In
pink box, all blue caps. **CMV $100.00 MB.**

HOUSE OF CHARMS PERFUMES
Shown only to identify size & labels, Left
square bottle is 1954 set only. Center bottle
has same label as short one on left issued in
1953-54. Right one issued 1952-53 sets only.

HOUSE OF CHARM SET 1954
Pink box holds four 5/8 dram bottles of per-
fume with turquoise caps or white caps.
Choice of To A Wild Rose, Cotillion, Golden
Promise or Quaintance. **CMV $110.00 MB.**

BEAUTY PAIR SET 1957
White, blue & yellow box with 2 black & pink
fashion lipsticks. **CMV $30. MB.**

LITTLE LAMBS SET 1954-56
Box holds 2 lamb soaps and can of baby powder. Two different boxes. One has 2 lambs &
the other has 2 lambs holding an umbrella.
CMV $80. each set MB.

THAT'S FOR ME SET 1955-56
Pink box holds four 2 oz. bottles with pink caps
of bath oil. Quaintance, To A Wild Rose,
Cotillion & Pine. **CMV $85. MB.**

GEMS IN CRYSTAL SET 1957
1/2 oz. bottles of Nearness, Bright Night, Cotillion &
To A Wild Rose. Pointed plastic caps. **CMV with flat
top caps (left) $65., with pointed caps (right) $75.
MB.**

OVER THE RAINBOW SET 1957
Blue box holds 4 cream sachet jars in Cotillion, To A Wild Rose, Bright Night and Nearness. Jars are white glass with green and yellow and have two pink lids. **CMV $50. set MB, $55. MB with outer box as shown, $8. each jar.**

WISHING COIN TRIO SET 1958
Blue and gold box. Holds choice of cream sachet, lotion sachet and 1/2 oz. cologne in To A Wild Rose, Cotillion, Nearness, Forever Spring, Bright Night, Elegante, Here's My Heart and Persian Wood fragrances. Blue caps on all three. **CMV $40. MB.**

SINGING BELLS SET 1956
White bell box holds 2 cans of talc in Cotillion or To A Wild Rose. **CMV $20. MB.**

JOLLY SURPRISE SET 1950
Pink, white and green Santa box holds 2 oz. cream lotion, nail polish and 1 dram perfume in ribbed glass. **CMV $55. MB.**

SILVER WINGS SET 1954
Box holds cream sachet and body powder in choice of To A Wild Rose, Quaintance, Golden Promise or Forever Spring. **CMV $40. each set MB.**

CHRISTMAS ANGELS SET 1953-55
Blue and white box holds gold lipstick and cream sachet in To A Wild Rose, Quaintance, Cotillion, Forever Spring and Golden Promise. To A Wild Rose pictured sold 1955 only and 1953-54 came with older 3 corner white jar with blue cap. Both are same CMV. **CMV $30.**

SHOWERS OF STARS SET 1955
Silver box with fluff on top holds cream sachet and body powder in choice of Golden Promise, Quaintance and Forever Spring. **CMV $40. MB.**

BATH DELIGHTS SET 1955
Box holds bottle of Avon Bubble Bath and shoice of body powder in Golden Promise, Quaintance or Forever Spring. **CMV $50. MB.**

SUNNY HOURS SET 1952-53
White umbrella holds 1 dram perfume and deluxe gold lipstick. **CMV MB $50. Umbrella and contents only $30. mint.**

SPECIAL DATE SET 1955
Blue and white box holds gold lipstick, 2 different powder paks and 1/2 oz. Cotillion Toilet water.   **CMV $40. MB.**

MODERN MOOD SET 1957
Pink and gold box holds 2 cans of talc in choice of Cotillion or To A Wild Rose. Same box in blue and gold holds 2 cans of talc in choice of Nearness or Forever Spring. **CMV $25. each set MB.**

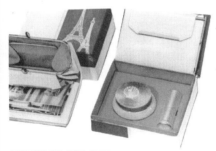

TRI COLOR SET 1957
Blue and white box holds Nearness or choice of cream sachet, gold satin sheen lipstick and white leather purse trimmed in gold.**CMV $45. MB.**

CLASSIC STYLE SET 1958
Black and gold box holds Top Style lipstick and gold Top Style compact. **CMV $20. MB.**

AVON JEWELS SET 1957
Box contains liquid rouge, nail and longlife gold lipstick.   **CMV $25. MB.**

LADY FAIR SET 1950-51
Red, white and silver box holds gold Deluxe Lipstick and bottle of nail polish. **CMV $30. MB.**

TOP STYLE SET 1955-56
Box holds gold lipstick, 1/2 oz. nail polish and liquid rouge. **CMV $25. MB.**

BEAUTY PAIR SET 1954
Red and gold box holds golds Deluxe Lipstick and nail polish. **CMV $25. MB.**

MAKEUP MATES SET 1958
Green box holds lipstick and face powder. **CMV $20. MB.**

TOUCH OF PARIS SET 1958
Box holds white lipstick and compact. **CMV $15. MB.**

GADABOUTS SET 1954-55
Gold and white box holds turquoise and white compact and gold lipstick. **CMV $20. MB.**

GADABOUTS SET 1952-53
Gold and white box holds compact and cologne stick. Both are turquoise in color. **CMV $25. MB.**

COLOR CORSAGE SET 1954-55
Turquoise box of face powder with gold lipstick on top. **CMV $25. MB.**

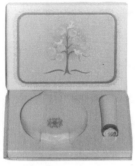

PEARL FAVORITES SET 1959
Blue, green and white box holds white compact and white enamel lipstick. **CMV $20. MB.**

BEAUTY BOUND SET 1955-56
Turquoise and white plastic compact, jeweled lipstick. Box pink and turquoise. **CMV $20. MB.**

ADORABLE SET 1950-51
White box holds blue satin with white lace pillow with powder pak and lipstick inside. **CMV $35. MB.**

ADORABLE SET 1950
Foam holder has powder pak and gold lipstick. Trimmed in blue feathers and pink ribbon and flowers. Came in green box. **CMV $35. mint as shown.**

FRAGRANCE MIST SET 1951-52
Turquoise box with pink and gold inside holds 2 oz. toilet water and 1 dram perfume in choice of Cotillion, Flowertime and Lily of the Valley. **CMV $50. MB.**

BEAUTIFUL JOURNEY SET 1957
Pink zippered bag holds 1 oz. bottles of Cotillion cologne, Deep Clean Cleansing Cream, Deodorant, Hand Lotion, Skin Freshener and 1/2 oz. jar of Rich Moisture Cream with peach colored cap. **$10. each bottle, $15. Cotillion cologne, $7. Rich Moisture Cream. CMV set $70. MB.**

HAND BEAUTY SET 1955
Pink box holds two 4 oz. bottles of hand lotion with turquoise caps. **CMV $20. MB.**

FOR YOUR LOVELINESS SET 1954-55
Green and silver box holds 3 1/2 oz. jar of Moisture Cream and choice of 4 oz. bottle of Hand Lotion or Skin Freshener. **CMV $20. MB.**

SPECIAL SET 1951
Blue and pink Christmas box holds 2 bottles of hand lotion. **CMV $30. MB.**

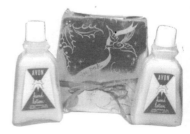

TWIN PAK SET 1952-53
Silver box holds 2 bottles of hand lotion. White caps, red ribbon on box. **CMV $30. MB.**

SAFE JOURNEY SET 1958
Gold and white zippered travel kit holds 6 plastic containers of Perfumed Talc, Hand Lotion, Lotion Sachet, Cleansing Cream, Rich Moisture Cream and Deodorant. **CMV $35. mint.**

DRAMATIC MOMENTS SET 1958
Essence de Fleurs Cologne Mist and paper box of powder in blue box. Came in To A Wild Rose, Cotillion, Forever Spring. Nearness, Elegante and Bright Night. **CMV $40. MB.**

BEAUTIFUL YOU SET 1958
Pink and white box with ladies face holds 3 1/2 oz. Rich Moisture Cream, 2 oz. of Skin Freshener and Rich Moisture Suds or Deep Clean. **CMV $20. MB.**

FOR YOUR BEAUTY SET 1956
Blue and gold box holds Cleansing Cream in plastic bottle, 2 oz. bottle of Skin Freshener and Rich Moisture Cream in jar. **CMV $20. MB.**

CLEAR-IT-SKIN CARE KIT 1959
White box holds shampoo and lotion in white plastic bottles and bar of Clear Skin soap. **CMV $20. MB.**

DOUBLY YOURS SET 1956
Blue and gold box holds two bottles of hand lotion. **CMV $20. MB.**

HAND BEAUTY SET 1954
Red box holds two bottles of hand lotion. **CMV $20. MB.**

FOAM 'N' SPRAY SET 1955
Green box holds can of Avon Hair Spray and 6 oz. bottle of Cream Lotion Shampoo. **CMV $20. MB.**

BOUQUET OF FRESHNESS SET 1957
Pink and lavender box holds two 2 oz. bottles of Perfumed Deodorant. **CMV $15. MB.**

SHOWER OF FRESHNESS SET 1956
Turquoise and white box holds 2 bottles of Perfumed Deodorant. **CMV $15. MB.**

FASHION JEWELS SET 1954-55
Black velvet case holds 1 dram perfume, jeweled lipstick and gold compact. **CMV $40. MB.**

WOMEN'S SETS OF 1950s

HIGH FASHION SET 1950-54
Black case with white satin lining holds 1 dram perfume, gold lipstick, gold compact and gold rouge compact. **CMV $45. MB.**

SPECIAL NAIL CARE SET 1955-57
Red and white box contained Silvery Base and Top Coat. **CMV $10. MB.**

HOME PERMANENT REFILL KIT 1951
Kit contains 4 oz. permanent wave lotion. **CMV $25.** Neutralizer, end tissues. **CMV $45. MB set.**

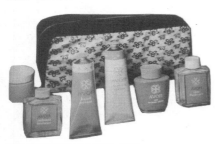

HAPPY TRAVELER SET 1955-56
Black bag with pink and blue stripes holds Cleansing Cream, Skin Freshener, Rich Moisture Cream, Hand Cream, Flowing Cream Deodorant, 1 empty plastic jar, packette of tissues. **CMV $35. MB.**

A THING OF BEAUTY SET 1957
White, pink and black box holds 6 oz. Avon Cleansing Cream, 2 oz. Skin Freshener and 3 !/2 oz. Rich Moisture Cream. **CMV $25. MB.**

HAPPY VACATION SET 1953
Plastic bag and tie string says Avon Happy Vacation. Bag holds Cotillion Talc, toothpaste, cream deodorant and tube of Ammoniated Toothpaste. **CMV $60. MB.**

HAPPY TRAVELER SET 1954
Black and white bag holds Perfumed Deodorant, Hand Cream, Rich Moisture Cream, Skin Freshener, Cleansing Cream and a plastic jar. **CMV $35. MB.**

HAPPY TRAVELER SET 1955
Black zipper bag with pink and blue stripes. Came with pack of Kleenex tissues, 2 turquoise and white plastic jars, tube of hand cream and cleansing cream and rare 2 oz. bottle of skin freshener with turquoise cap. **CMV $35. mint, $40. MB.**

CAMPING KIT 1954
Navy blue cotton twill draw string bag. Came with 2 oz. Sun Lotion, Chap Check, Antiseptic Cream and choice of either Creme Shampoo or Cream Hair Dress. **Value complete set $50. MB.**

HAPPY VACATION SPECIAL GIFT BAG SET 1951
Folder has plastic bag and Avon tie tag to hold cream deodorant, toothpaste, toothbrush and Cotillion Talcum, all boxed. **CMV $7. as pictured.**

MEN'S SETS OF 1960's

WARNING!! Grading condition is paramount on sets. CMV can vary up to 90% on grade.

CHRISTMAS CALL SET 1965
Red box holds two 4 oz. bottles of Original After Shave Lotion. Red caps. **CMV $20. MB.**

FRAGRANCE CHEST 1966-67
Brown chest type box holds four 1 oz. bottles with silver caps, of after shave lotion in Tribute, blue glass; Leather in amber glass; Spicy in clear glass; Island Lime in green glass. **CMV $40. MB. With outer sleeve $37. as pictured.**

MEN'S FRAGRANCE WARDROBE SET 1965
Red box holds three 2 oz. bottles of after shave lotion in choice of Set A: Leather, Blue Blazer, After Shower Cologne; Set B: Leather, Tribute, Spicy; Set C: "4-A", Tribute, Original; or Set D: Spicy, Bay Rum, Original. **CMV $33. each set boxed with sleeve.**

ORIGINAL SET 1965
Horse box holds two 4 oz. bottles of Original after shave with red caps. **CMV $20. MB.**

MEN'S AFTER SHAVE CHOICE SET 1967-68
Black box holds 2 oz. after shave lotion in Wild Country with silver cap; Leather with gold cap; & Tribute with blue cap. Late issue set came with all silver or gold caps. **CMV $18. MB.**

AFTER SHAVE SELECTION SET 1966
Father's Day box holds three 2 oz. bottles in choice of Leather all purpose lotion for men, Blue Blazer, Island Lime, Tribute, after shave lotion Spicy, Bay Rum, Original & 4A after shave lotions. **CMV $33. boxed with outer sleeve.**

FIRST PRIZE SET 1960
Black, gold & red box holds three 2 oz. embossed Stage Coach bottles in choice of after shower for men, "Vigorate" after shaving lotion, cream hair lotion, deodorant for men, liquid hair lotion, electric pre-shave lotion, after shave for dry or sensitive skin. **CMV $55. set of 3 MB with outer sleeve.**

BUREAU ORGANIZER 1966-67
Wood grained plastic tray is 12 1/4" x 5 1/4". Came with 2 oz. botlles with black 4A embossed caps in Tribute after shave lotion, Blue Blazer after shave, Spicy after shave & Leather all purpose cologne. **CMV $50. MB, tray $15.**

GENTLEMAN'S COLLECTION SET 1968
Brown plastic box holds three 2 oz. bottles with gold, silver & bronze caps. Came in Leather, Windjammer & Wild Country cologne. **CMV $20. MB.**

FOX HUNT SET 1966

Fox hunt box holds two 4 oz. bottles with black caps in Leather all purpose cologne. **CMV $30. MB.**

AFTER SHAVE CADDY 1968

6 oz. rectangular bottle with silver cap & top fits in brown plastic box. Came in Leather & Island Lime after shave. **CMV $14. MB.**

GOLD MEDALLION GIFT SET 1961

Gold box holds three individual men's grooming products in 2 oz. glass or plastic bottles. Glass bottles are: Spicy after shave lotion, Vigorate after shaving lotion, after shaving lotion, after shower lotion, electric pre-shave lotion, liquid hair lotion & deodorant for men. Plastic bottles are: after shave for dry sensitive skin & cream hair lotion. Set of 3 bottles. **CMV $55. MB with outer sleeve.**

DELUXE SET FOR MEN 1962-63

Brown & gold box holds can of deluxe foam shave cream, deluxe after shave, after shower spray & deluxe stick deodorant normal. Box has outer sleeve. **CMV $45. MB.**

CHRISTMAS TRIO FOR MEN SET 1964

Winter scene box holds three 2 oz. red & white plastic bottles of any three of: Spicy after shave lotion, Original after shave lotion, "Vigorate" after shave lotion, after shower cologne, Spicy electric pre-shave lotion, liquid deodorant for men, liquid hair lotion, cream hair lotion or hair trainer. **CMV $15. MB.**

COLOGNE TRILOGY SET 1969-70

Brown & gold plastic box holds three 1 1/2 oz. bottles with gold caps & labels in Wild Country, Windjammer & Excalibur cologne. Box is 6" high. **CMV $18. MB.**

STRUCTURED FOR MEN SET 1969

Silver box holds black plastic stair step base with 3 oz. bottles of Glass, Wood & Steel cologne. **CMV $15. MB, bottles & base only $10.**

JOLLY HOLLY DAY SET 1963

Green & white box holds three 2 oz. white plastic bottles with red caps in choice of Vigorate, Spicy & Original after shave lotions, electric pre-shave lotion, liquid or cream hair lotion, hair trainer, after shower cologne for men, & liquid deodorant for men - gentle. **CMV $15. MB.**

KING FOR A DAY 1965

Box holds 3 white plastic bottles with red caps in choice of any 3 after shave lotion. Spicy, Original & Vigorate after shave, after shower cologne for men, cream or liquid hair lotion, liquid deodorant for men, electric pre-shave lotion. **CMV $15. MB.**

SMART MOVE SET 1967
Orange & black box holds three 2 oz. plastic bottles of after shave. Original or Spicy in red, Tribute or Spicy in black. White bottle came in both Original or Spicy. **CMV $20. MB.**

TAG-ALONGS SET 1967
Box holds 3 1/2 oz. red plastic bottle of after shave lotion Spicy & tan 3 oz. plastic bottle of Squeeze Spray deodorant. Both have black caps. **CMV $12. MB. Bottles only $3. each.**

FOR GENTLEMEN SET 1961
Black, gold & red box holds 4 oz. plastic cream hair lotion, roll-on deodorant for men, choice of Vigorate or after shower for men in 8 oz. embossed Stage Coach bottle and choice of 6 oz. Kwick foaming shave cream or 4 oz. electric pre-shave lotion. **CMV $62.50 each set MB, 2 different sets are shown.**

THE TRAVELER SET 1969
Box holds 2 plastic bottles in Bravo or Spicy after shave & spray deodorant. **CMV $10. MB.**

OVERNIGHTER SET 1968
Black box holds 3 oz. white plastic bottle of Squeeze Spray deodorant & 3 1/2 oz. black plastic bottle of Spicy after shave lotion. **CMV $10. MB.**

BOOTS & SADDLE SET 1968
Cowhide type box holds 3 oz. bottles of Leather after shave lotion with red cap & Wild Country after shave with black cap. **CMV $15. MB.**

MEN'S TRAVEL KIT 1963-64
Black leather bag holds can of after shave, after shower spray, Spicy, tube of cream hair dress, toothbrush, smokers toothpaste, spray deodorant for men & choice of foam shave cream, Spicy or electric pre-shave lotion. **CMV $32.50 MB.**

DASHING SLEIGHS SET 1960-61
Black, gold & red box holds 4 oz. plastic bottle of cream hair lotion, can of after shower powder for men, roll-on deodorant for men & choice of Vigorate or after shower for men in 8 oz. embossed stage coach bottle. **CMV $62.50 MB.**

TRAVEL DELUXE SET 1962
Tan plastic bag with front & top zipper. Holds only 2 items, after shave lotion & roll-on deodorant as pictured. Outer sleeve lists only 2 contents. **CMV $35. MB.**

UNDER THE MISTLETOE SET 1962-63
Green box holds 4 oz. electric pre-shave lotion Spicy & After Shave lotion Spicy. Red caps. **CMV $20. MB.**

OVERNIGHTER SET 1960-62
Tan plastic travel case holds after shaving lotion, roll on deodorant for men & cream hair lotion, cream hair lotion or hair trainer. **CMV $25. MB.**

GOOD CHEER SET 1962-63
Red & gold box holds Spicy talc for men & choice of Spicy or Original after shave lotion. **CMV $20. MB.**

TRAVEL DELUXE SET 1959-60
Brown leather case holds after shave lotion, choice of spray deodorant for men, 4 oz. hair lotion in cream or liquid or Attention & choice of shave cream in Kwick foaming, lather or brushless or electric pre-shave lotion. **CMV $35. MB.**

CHRISTMAS CLASSIC SET 1962-63
Blue box holds choice of two 4 oz. bottles of "Vigorate' after shave lotion, after shower cologne for men, original after shave lotion. **CMV $20. MB.**

HOLIDAY GREETINGS SET 1964
Gold box holds 4 oz. bottle of electric pre-shave lotion Spicy & after shave lotion Spicy. **CMV $20. MB.**

HOLLY TIME SET 1962-63
Red white and green box holds choice of 2 plastic bottles in cream hair lotion or liquid hair lotion in glass bottle. **CMV $20. MB.**

HOLLY STAR SET 1964
Red, white and green box holds 4 oz. each of after shave lotion, Spicy & 3 oz. talc for men, Spicy. **CMV $20. MB.**

MEN'S TRAVEL KIT 1966
Brown travel bag holds smoker's toothpaste, clear hair dress, Spicy after shave lotion, Spicy talc for men, aerosol deodorant & choice of electric pre-shave lotion or foam shave cream in regular or mentholated. **CMV $30. MB.**

SANTA'S TEAM SET 1964 Only
Blue box holds 4 oz. each of after shave lotion Spicy & liquid deodorant for men. **CMV $20. MB.**

CHRISTMAS DAY SET 1962-63
Partridge box holds 4 oz. liquid deodorant for men - gentle choice of Spicy or Original after shave lotion. **CMV $15. MB.**

CHRISTMAS MORNING SET 1964
Red & gold box holds two 4 oz. bottles of after shave lotion Spicy. **CMV $15. MB.**

WOMEN'S SETS OF 1960'S

WARNING!! Grading condition is paramount on sets. CMV can vary up to 90% on grade.

FRAGRANCE FLING TRIO 1968
1/2 oz. cologne gold cap. Set of three. Came in Occur!, Charisma, Brocade, Regence, Unforgettable, Rapture, Somewhere, Topaze, Cotillion, Here's My Heart, Wishing, To A Wild Rose, Persian Wood. **CMV $15. MB.**

FRAGRANCE GOLD SET 1964
Box holds 3 heart shaped 1/2 oz. colognes in Occur!, Somewhere, Wishing, Topaze, Cotillion, Here's My Heart, Persian Wood, To A Wild Rose. **CMV $20. MB.**

COLOGNE GEMS SET 1966-67
Gold & white box contains two 1 oz. Gem colognes, clear glass with plastic caps. Came in Unforgettable, Rapture, Occur!, Somewhere, Topaze, Cotillion, Here's My Heart, To A Wild Rose. **CMV $12. MB.**

FRAGRANCE ORNAMENTS SET 1965
Three bottles 5/8 dram perfume oil. Same as the Bullet bottle. White paper trimmed in gold. Gold & white box. Set A: Wishing, Somewhere, Occur!; Set B: Rapture, Topaze, To A Wild Rose; Set C: Unforgettable, Here's My Heart, Cotillion. **CMV $35. MB.**

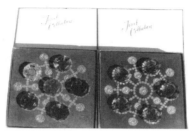

JEWEL COLLECTION SET 1964
(Left) With 6 gem shaped bottles of perfume oil & gold caps. Blue and gold box. Somewhere, Topaze, Cotillion, Persian Wood, Here's My Heart, To A Wild Rose. **CMV $35. MB.**

JEWEL COLLECTION- CANADASET 1964
(Right) Box is same as American set only center bottle hole is not punched out. Came in Somewhere, Topaze, Cotillion, Here's My Heart, To A Wild Rose in perfume oils, 5/8 dram each. Very rare set. **CMV $100.00 MB.**

FRAGRANCE FAVORITES SET 1965
Box holds 3 heart shaped 1/2 oz. colognes in Unforgettable, Rapture, Occur!, Cotillion, Somewhere, Topaze, Here's My Heart, Persian Wood, To A Wild Rose, Wishing. **CMV $20. MB.**

PERFUME OIL PETITES SET PIN CUSHION 1966
Gold box with red velvet pin cushion top & inner box holds three 5/8 dram heart shaped bottles with gold caps & labels. Came in choice of Wishing, Somewhere, Occur, Rapture, Topaze, To A Wild Rose, Here's My Heart, Unforgettable, Cotillion. **CMV $35. MB.**

RENAISSANCE TRIO 1966-67
Box holds 3 boxes with 1/2 oz. colognes in Unforgettable, Rapture, Occur!, Somewhere, Topaze, Cotillion, Here's My Heart, To A Wild Rose & Wishing. **CMV $20. MB.**

FRAGRANCE GOLD DUET 1965
Two heart shaped 1/2 oz. colognes in gold & white box. Came in Rapture, Occur!, Cotillion, Somewhere, Topaze, Here's My Heart, Persian Wood, To A Wild Rose, Wishing & Unforgettable. **CMV $20. MB.**

GIFT MAGIC SET 1960
Flat rocker bottles in same set that sold in 1967-68 with round cap rocker bottles. **CMV $20. MB.**

GOLDEN HEIRLOOM CHEST SET 1968
6" long gold metal, glass lid. Red velvet in bottom of chest. Avon on bottom. Came in perfume rollette in Brocade or Regence & deluxe refillable gold lipstick. Came in pink box. **CMV complete set in box $35. chest only $25.**

STAR ATTRACTIONS SET 1965
Box contains 1/2 oz. cologne & metal lipstick in Rapture, Occur!, Somewhere, Topaze, Cotillion, Here's My Heart, Persian Wood, To A Wild Rose, and Wishing. **CMV $20. MB.**

GOLDEN RINGS SET 1960
Red & gold box holds 2 pink & white lipsticks. **CMV $15. MB.**

GIFT MAGIC SET 1967-68
3 1/2 oz. clear glass rocker bottle with gold label & lid. Box red & purple with gold & white sleeve. Came in choice of Brocade, Regence, Unforgettable, Rapture, Occur!, Somewhere, Topaze, Cotillion, Here's My Heart, To A Wild Rose, Wishing, & Persian Wood. **CMV $15. MB.**

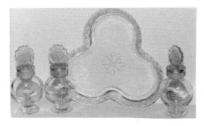

FRAGRANCE VANITY TRAY SET 1966
Three hearts on tray. 1/2 oz cologne. Heart shaped bottles on glass tray with Avon insignia on tray. **CMV $3. tray $4. MB. Colognes CMV $2. each- $4. MB. CMV set $20. MB.**

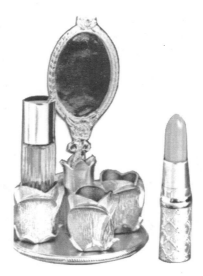

GOLDEN VANITY SET 1965-66
Gold metal stand with removable mirror in center. Came with perfume rollettte & gold refillable lipstick. **CMV complete set $30. MB. Stand with mirror only $15.**

VANITY SHOWCASE SET 1964-65
Silver & gold plastic holder. Avon on bottom. Came with 1 dram ribbed perfume & deluxe silver lipstick with 4A on top. **CMV complete set $20. in box-holder only $9.**

MANICURE TRAY SET 1967
Dark brown plastic tray with 4A design. Came with tubes Nail Beauty & Cuticle Remover, 1/2 oz. bottle of Double Coat & Nail Enamel with white caps & box of 10 enamel Remover Pads, 1 orange stick & emery board. **CMV complete set $16. MB. tray only $5. Also came in amber color tray. CMV $10 tray.**

MANICURE TRAY 1962-64
Clear plastic, Avon on bottom, 4A design. Came with 3 oz. bottle of Oily Polish Remover, 1/2 oz. bottle of Nail Polish & Base Coat or Double Coat & 2 tubes of Cuticle Remover & Nail Beauty. **CMV complete set $15. MB. tray only $3.**

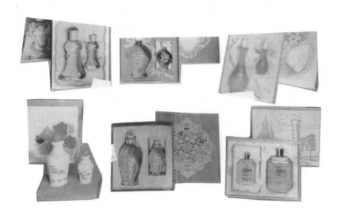

FRAGRANCE FORTUNE SET 1964
Matching boxes hold 2 oz. cologne & 1/2 oz. perfume oil in Somewhere, Here's My Heart, Cotillion, To A Wild Rose, Persian Wood & Topaze. **CMV $30. MB.**

FRAGRANCE MAGIC SET 1962-63
Matching boxes holds cologne mist & beauty dust with claer plastic top. Came in To A Wild Rose, Persian Wood, Here's My Heart, Somewhere, Cotillion, & Topaze. **CMV $35. MB each.**

MODERN SIMPLICITY SET 1960-61
Lavendar blue & white box contains soap, 4 oz. bath oil, 3 oz. beauty dust in choice of Cotillion, To A Wild Rose & Here's My Heart. **CMV $45. MB.**

LADIES CHOICE SET 1960
Matching boxes hold 4 oz. cologne & beauty dust in Cotillion, Persian Wood, To A Wild Rose, Here's My Heart, **CMV $40. each set MB.**

FLOWER FANTASY SET 1965
Floral box holds cream sachet & Perfume rollette in Wild Rose, Wishing, Somewhere, Cotillion, Topaze, & Occur!. **CMV $15. each MB. $18. with carnival glass rollette.**

TWO LOVES SETS 1956-60
Matching boxes hold cologne mist & cream sachet in To A Wild Rose, Here's My Heart. **CMV $23. 1959 only for Persian Wood CMV $27. Bright Night CMV $30.**

VANITY TRAY SET 1968
Brown plastic tray. Came with brown plastic fashion lipstick shown on right & perfume rollette in choice of Unforgettable, Rapture, Occur!, Here's My Heart or To A Wild Rose. **CMV complete set $11. MB. tray only $6. MB.**

SPLASH & SPRAY SET 1968
Purse size cologne spray & 2 1/2 oz. splash cologne botle with refill funnel. Both trimmed in gold. Gold box. Came in Brocade, & Regence, Unforgettable, Somewhere and Topaze. **CMV $20. MB.**

SCENTIMENTS SET 1968-69
Gold, white & silver box holds cream sachet & perfumed rolette in Brocade, Regence, Unforgettable, Rapture, Occur, Somewhere, Topaze, or Cotillion. **CMV $12. MB.**

PERFUMED PILLOWETTES SET 1965
Box contains two sachet pillows & gold top powder sachet in Occur!, Somewhere, Cotillion, Topaze, Here's My Heart, To A Wild Rose, and Wishing. **CMV $22. MB.**

FLOWER FANTASIES SET 1963-64
Cream sachet & cream rollette in Here's My Heart, Persian Wood, To A Wild Rose, Cotillion, Somewhere, Topaze, Occur!. **CMV $17. MB.**

SCENTIMENTS SET 1969
Box holds 1/2 oz. clear glass with gold cap with cream sachet in Unforgettable, Rapture, Occur!, Somewhere, Topaze or Cotillion with 4A embossed soap. **CMV $10 MB. Each fragrance came with different color soap.**

TWO LOVES SET 1970
Cream sachet & perfume rollette in Elusive in pink & gold box. Bird of Paradise in turquoise & gold box and Charisma in red & gold box with white , gold or red liner. **CMV $12 each MB.**

JUST TWO SET 1965
3 oz. each, Tribute after shave, black glass; clear Rapture cologne with gold tags. **CMV $50 MB. bottles only with tags. $15. each.**

TWO LOVES SET 1969
Red & gold box with red felt inside holds perfume rollette & cream sachet in Charisma, Brocade or Regence. **CMV $12. Brocade is gray inside box.**

MERRY FINGERTIPS SET 1967
Pink velvet box holds 2 bottles of nail polish. **CMV $10 MB.**

MERRY LIPTINTS SET 1967
Red flocked sleeve holds 2 white & gold Encore lipsticks with boxes to match sleeve but not flocked. **CMV $9. MB.**

TWO LOVES SET 1967
Gold & green box has cream sachet & perfume rollette in Unforgettable, Rapture, Occur!, Somewhere, To A Wild Rose, Topaze, Cotillion, Here's My Heart. **CMV $13. MB.**

FASHION STAR SET 1963
Blue, pink and white box holds two Fashion lipsticks. **CMV $10. MB.**

FASHION TWINS SET 1965
Multi-colored box holds 2 Cameo lipsticks. **CMV $10. MB.**

COLOR TRICK SET 1962
Blue & gold foil box has 2 black Fashion lipstick tubes, gold bottom. **CMV $15. MB.**

CANDY CANE TWINS SET 1966
Candy cane box holds 2 cameo lipsticks. **CMV $20. MB.**

CLEVER MATCH SET 1962
Pink & red box holds black lipstick & nail polish with white cap. 1961 set same only has white plastic lipstick with pink flowered top. **CMV $10. MB.**

GOLDEN ARCH SET 1964
Gold arch box holds 2 floral Fashion lipsticks. **CMV $17.50 MB.**

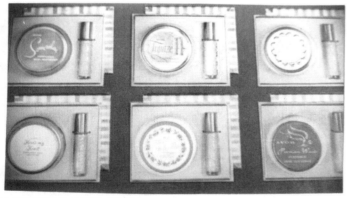

BEAUTY SCENTS SET 1963-64
Box holds 5 oz. perfumed skin softener & matching perfume creme rollette in Somewhere, Topaze, Cotillion, To A Wild Rose, Here's My Heart, & Persian Wood. **CMV $16. MB.** 1965 Beauty Scents issued same box but with perfume rollette and dropped Persian Wood and added Rapture and Occur! **CMV $15. each MB. $17 with carnival glass rollette.**

COLOR NOTE SET 1963
Gold & white box holds bottle of nail polish & pink Fashion lipstick. **CMV $10. MB.**

TOUCH-UP TWINS SET 1963-64
Multi-colored box holds perfume cream rollette in Here's My Heart, Persian Wood, To A Wild Rose, Somewhere, Topaze, Cotillion, Occur! **CMV $17. MB.**

HAWAIIAN DELIGHTS SET 1962-63
Box holds 4 bottles of nail polish. White caps. **CMV $15. MB.**

COLOR GARDEN SET 1964
Red & white floral box holds 4 nail polish bottles with white caps. Came with pearl or cream polish only. **CMV $20. MB.**

TOUCH-UP TWINS SET 1965
Angel box holds deluxe lipstick & perfume rollette in Here's My Heart, Wishing, To A Wild Rose, Somewhere, Topaze, Cotillion, Rapture, Occur! **CMV $10 Add $2 for carnival glass rollette.**

BATH BOUQUET SET 1963
8 oz. plastic bottle of bath oil & soap in Royal Jasmine, Royal Pine, Rose Geranium. **CMV $10. MB.**

BATH BOUQUET SET 1964
Pink & white plastic 6 oz. bottle of perfumed bath oil & perfumed soap in Topaze, Somewhere, To A Wild Rose, Persian Wood, Here's My Heart & Cotillion fragrances. **CMV $10. each MB.**

PAIR TREE SET 1964
Gold, white, & blue holds nail polish & floral lipstick. **CMV $15. MB.**

BATH BOUQUET SET 1965
Green box contains 1 1/2 oz. green cardboard talc, 2 oz. bath oil & 1/2 oz. cologne in Here's My Heart, To A Wild Rose, Wishing, Somewhere, Topaze, Cotillion, Rapture & Occur!. **CMV $35. MB.**

SLEIGH MATES SET 1966
Red and gold box holds Fashion Cameo lipstick & bottle of nail enamel. **CMV $20. MB.**

CLASSIC HARMONY SET 1960
Red, white & gold box holds Top Style lipstick compact & perfume. Came in choice of shades & fragrances. **CMV $25 each.**

REFRESHING HOURS SET 1962-63
Red & white box holds 2 3/4 oz can of perfumed talc & 2 1/2 oz. bottle of cologne in Somewhere, Topaze, Cotillion, Here's My Heart, Persian Wood, & To A Wild Rose. **CMV $25. each set.**

PARIS MOOD SET 1959-60
Gift set came with spray essence, beauty dust & cream sachet in Persian Wood, Here's My Heart, Cotillion, To A Wild Rose, Bright Night & Nearness fragrances. **CMV $47. MB.** See stockholders gifts for additional information.

FRAGRANCE DUETTE SET 1966
Blue and gold box holds 2 oz. splash on cologne & perfumed rollette in Occur!, Rapture & Unforgettable. **CMV $15. MB.**

BATH SPARKLERS SET 1965
Silver box holds 3 colored tubes of bubble bath powder in Lilac, Jasmine & Lily of the Valley. **CMV $25. MB.**

BEGUILING SET 1960
Multi-colored box holds spray essence & cream sachet in Bright Night, Nearness, To A Wild Rose, Cotillion. Here's My Heart & Persian Wood. **CMV $15. MB.**

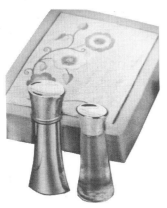

PARTY FUN SET 1960
Blue & gold box holds gold lipstick & 1 dram perfume in Topaze, Here's My Heart, Persian Wood, Cotillion, To A Wild Rose, Bright Night, Nearness. **CMV $20. MB.**

FRAGRANCE GEMS SET 1962-63
Box holds creme sachet & cream lotion in Topaze, Cotillion, Somewhere, Persian Wood, Here's My Heart & To A Wild Rose. **CMV $12. MB.**

BATH CLASSIC SET 1962-63
1 1/2 oz. with gold design, gold cap in gold box with large red powder puff. Box has clear plastic top. Cologne came in Somewhere, Cotillion, Topaze, Here's My Heart, Persian Wood & To A Wild Rose. **CMV $35. MB.**

BATH BOUQUET SET 1963
Gift box holds 8 oz. plastic bottle of bath oil & soap in Lily of the Valley, Lilac. **CMV $10. each MB.**

FASHION TWIN SET 1962
Blue & white silk cosmetic case holds gold & black compact & lipstick. **CMV $15. MB.**

DECORATION GIFT SET 1964
Purple, gold & white box holds cream sachet & spray essence in Here's My Heart, Persian Wood, To A Wild Rose, Somewhere, Cotillion & Topaze. **CMV $15. MB.**

WOMEN'S SETS OF 1960s

BATH BOUQUET SET 1962
White & gold box holds 6 oz. pink & white plastic bottle of bath oil & wrapped soap in Somewhere, Cotillion, Here's My Heart, Topaze, Persian Wood, Royal Jasmine, Rose Geranium, Royal Pine, Floral & To A Wild Rose. **CMV $12. MB.**

KEEPSAKES SET 1967-68
Gold, floral & white box holds 3 oz. cologne mist, perfume rollette in Occur!, Rapture & Unforgettable. **CMV $10. MB.**

MANICURE TRAY 1965-66
White plastic tray & tissue holder. Came with pink box of Kleenex Tissue with 4A design on box. 8 1/2 x 6 x 3 inches. **CMV tray only $5., MB $7. Avon Kleenex box mint $7. Complete set MB $15.**

FRAGRANCE CHIMES SET 1966
Red & gold box holds perfumed talc & cream sachet in Rapture, Occur!, Unforgettable, Somewhere, Topaze, Cotillion, Here's My Heart & To A Wild Rose & Wishing. **CMV $10. MB.**

FLORAL MEDLEY SET 1967
Floral box contains perfumed talc & cream sachet in Honeysuckle, Jasmine, Lily of the Valley, Lilac. **CMV $10. each set MB.**

FLORAL ENCHANTMENT SET 1963-64
Floral box holds cologne mist & cream sachet in Occur!, Persian Wood, Here's My Heart, To A Wild Rose, Topaze, Somewhere & Cotillion. Came with 2 different bottles. **CMV $15. MB.**

FLOWER BATH SET 1964
Talc & 2 bars of soap in choice of Lily of the Valley, Lilac, Jasmine & Rose Geranium. **CMV $10. MB.**

FLORAL TALC TRIO 1965
Floral box holds three 3 1/2 oz. talcs in Lily of the Valley, Lilac & Jasmine. **CMV $12.50 MB.**

MAKING EYES SET 1961-62
Blue & green box with checkerboard top holds Eye Shadow Stick, Curl 'N' Color & Eyebrow Pencil. Box came with outside sleeve. **CMV $15. MB.**

PRETTY NOTIONS SET 1965
Pink vinyl case contains pink compact & Cameo lipstick. **CMV $4 set only, $6. MB.**

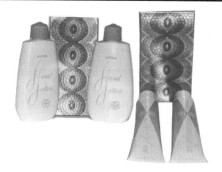

DOUBLE PAK SET 1965
Box in green, pink & red foil design. Came with choice of 2 tubes of moisturized hand cream or Avon hand cream or silicone glove or bottle of hand lotion as shown. **CMV $10. MB.**

FLUFF PUFF SET 1967
Issued during bottle strike. Green box holds 2 boxes 3.5 oz. of powder. White plastic bottle, gold base & pink puff. Does not say Avon. Came in Unforgettable, To A Wild Rose, Cotillion, Regence. **CMV $18. MB.** Regence came in dark pink & light pink & green. Green is rare. **CMV green only $25. MB.**

FLUFF PUFF SET 1969
Cardboard talc, blue & gold design on white, puff white with marbleized handle, white knob with 4A. Came 3 different colors: Rapture, turquoise; Occur!, yellow; & Unforgettable, coral. **CMV $10. MB.**

FLUFF PUFF SET 1967
Floral box contains one puff & beauty dust. White plastic. Comes in Unforgettable, To A Wild Rose, Cotillion & Regence. **CMV $12. MB.** Also came in white puff Regence. **CMV $20.**

FLUFF PUFFS SET 1968
3 1/2 oz. talc & matching puff comes in Somewhere with green puff, Honeysuckle with yellow puff, Here's My Heart with blue puff & To A Wild Rose with pink puff. **CMV $10. MB.**

ON THE WING SET 1959-60
Blue plastic bag holds choice of perfumed talc in Here's My Heart, Persian Wood, To A Wild Rose, Nearness, Cotillion & Floral. Skin freshener, deep clean & 2 oz. plastic bottle of choice of 1 1/2 oz. jar of Vita Moist or Rich Moisture cream. **CMV $30. MB.**

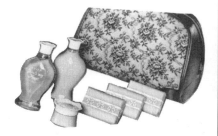

ROLL-A-FLUFF SET 1967-70
Fluff holds 3 1/2 oz. beauty dust. Red puff is Charisma. Green puff is Regence. White puff is Brocade. Gold top & handle. **CMV $15. MB.**

WOMAN'S TRAVEL KIT 1963-64
White floral bag holds moisturized hand cream, perfumed talc, 4 oz. Skin-So-Soft, 2 oz. perfumed deodorant & choice of night cream. **CMV $25. MB.**

TOTE ALONG SET 1962
Tapestry bag holds 4 oz. cologne & cream lotion, cream sachet, 3 cakes of wrapped soap in Somewhere, Topaze, Cotillion, Here's My Heart, Persian Wood & To A Wild Rose. **CMV $32. MB.**

WOMEN'S TRAVEL KIT 1965-66
Yellow floral "hat box" contains cream deodorant, Skin-So-Soft, hand cream, white Velex Cleansing cream, Hormone cream, Rich Moisture, Vita Moisture & Cream Supreme. **CMV complete set $15. MB, hat box only $6.**

BATH LUXURY SET 1966-67
Box holds 4 oz. bottle of Skin-So-Soft & pink bath sponge. Came with 2 different sponges. Coarse as shown & fine grain. **CMV $11. MB.**

FRAGRANCE TRIO SET 1966
Box holds 3 bottles of Skin-So-Soft, 1 oz. each, gold cap. In choice of Unforgettable, Rapture, Occur!, Somewhere, Topaze, Cotillion, Here's My Heart, To A Wild Rose & Wishing. **CMV $12. MB.**

FRAGRANCE GIFT SET FOR MEN 1979
Box holds choice of After Shave in plastic bottles in Cool Sage, Brisk Spice, or Light Musk or the same fragrance in cologne in glass bottles & matching talc. **CMV cologne set glass. $4. MB. CMV Plastic $3. MB.**

SKIN-SO-SOFT COMPLIMENTS SET 1967
Box holds 3 oz. box of Satin Talc & 2 bars of SSS soap. **CMV $9. MB.**

SKIN-SO-SOFT SMOOTHIES SET 1968
Box holds 4 oz. bottle of Skin-So-Soft & 3 oz. Satin Talc. **CMV $8. MB.**

COLLECTORS ORGANIZER SET 1971 ONLY
Plastic brown duck holds two 3 oz. bottles of Cologne & After Shave. Tai Winds & Wild Country. Painted duck design on bottles & gold caps. 1 yellow bar of duck soap. **CMV $30. MB.**

WILD MALLARD SET 1978
Brown and green ceramic organizer and white Clint Soap On A Rope. Bottom says "Made in Brazil for Avon, May 1978". **CMV $16. - $20. MB.** Also came no date.

BATH MATES SET 1964-65
Box holds 4 oz. bottle Skin-So-Soft bath oil & cakes of soap. **CMV $11. MB.**

SHOWER MATES SET 1965
Green & white box holds 4 oz. can of after shower foam & 2 bars of SSS soap. **CMV $11. MB.**

WOMEN'S SETS OF 1970s

WARNING!! Grading condition is paramount on sets. CMV can vary up to 90% on grade.

WHALE ORGANIZER SET 1973
Brown plastic whale holds 2-3 oz. ivory milk glass bottles and 5 oz. bar of soap. Came in Blend 7 or Deep Woods After Shave and Cologne. **CMV $35. MB.**

MASTER ORGANIZER SET 1970
Wood grained plastic flip open box, holds choice of 3 1/2 oz. Cologne or After Shave in Oland with tan bar of soap or Excalibur with blue bar of soap. **CMV $45. MB. Only 14000 sets made.**

AMERICAN EAGLE BUREAU ORGANIZER SET 1972
Plastic case, wood carved like finish. Case holds 2 clear glass bottles with embossed eagles & a 5 oz. bar of soap. The bottles hold 3 oz. One has cologne and one after shave. Came in Deep Woods or Tai Winds. **CMV $30. MB.**

TREASURE CHEST SET 1973
White plastic chest with deep purple velour inside & on top. Bottles are clear glass with white on front & gold rose & gold cap. One bottle holds 4 oz. Skin-So-Soft, other holds 4 oz. cologne in Moonwind or Sonnet. Soap 5 oz. in Moonwind (blue) or Sonnet (pink). **CMV $27.50 MB.**

ULTRA FLUFF SET 1970
Box holds 3 1/2 oz. beauty dust, 1/8 oz. perfume, Lamb's Wool Puff & white pedestal dish in Brocade, Charisma & Regence. **CMV $12. MB.**

TRAVEL SET FOR MEN 1974-75
Brown box holds 3 oz. white plastic bottle with white cap. Choice of Deep Woods, Wild Country, Oland or Spicy After Shave and 1.5 oz. brown plastic bottle, white cap of Talc in choice of same fragrances. Short issue. OSP $4. **CMV $5. MB.**

LIGHTS & SHADOWS COLOGNE SET 1969-72
(Left) Lights is clear glass & gold cap. Shadows is smoked glass & cap. 2 oz. each. **CMV $6. MB.**

MINUETTE DUET SET 1973
5 oz. cologne in clear bottle with gold cap. 1.5 oz. talc in paper cylinder with Christmas scene. Came in set of Unforgettable, To A Wild Rose, Occur!, Somewhere, Topaze or Cotillion. **CMV $5. MB.**

IF YOU LOVE TO LAUGH, GO TO THE BACK PAGE FOR INFO ON BUD HASTIN'S NEW JOKE BOOK AND HOW TO GET IT. LAUGH MORE AND LIVE LONGER.

FRAGRANCE FANCY SET 1972-75
Pink, blue & white. Has .33 oz. rollette & 1.5 oz. perfumed talc. Choice of Unforgettable, Somewhere, Cotillion, Occur!, Topaze, Here's My Heart or Rapture. **CMV $4. MB.**

FLUFF PUFF SET 1977-78
Perfumed talc dispenser. Pink plastic holder approx. 11 1/2" long. Came with 2 oz. cardboard talc in Roses Roses or Sonnet. **CMV $5. MB.**

HAIR COLOR SET 1969
2 oz. brown glass bottle of hair color & 2 oz. white plastic bottle of cream developer in blue box. Short issue. **CMV $16. MB.**

PRECIOUS PAIR SET 1971-73
Multi-colored box holds matching 1 1/2 oz. perfumed talc & 1/2 oz. cologne in Occur!, Rapture, Unforgettable, Somewhere, Topaze & Cotillion. **CMV $5. MB.**

SOPHISTICURL SET 1971
A salon permanent wave used only in Avon Beauty Salons. Box holds 4 oz. bottle of waving lotion and 3.75 oz. white tube of neutralizer. **CMV $10. set MB.**

BUILT-IN BODY SALON PERMANENT WAVE SET 1971
White box holds 4 oz. bottle of waving lotion & 4 oz. bottle of neutralizer. Used only in Avon Beauty Salons and not sold. **CMV $12. MB.**

FRAGRANCE TREASURES SET 1973-75
.66 oz. clear glass cream sachet with pink & gold lid. Pink & gold soap wrapper & box. Choice of Sonnet, Charisma or Moonwind. **CMV $4. MB.**

HAIR PERFECT SET 1971-74
Blue & white box holds 2 oz. brown glass bottle of Color Perfect & 2 oz. white plastic bottle of cream developer. **CMV $4. MB.**

EMPRISE PERFUME 1977-80
Box holds 1/4 oz. bottle with glass stopper with plastic base seal. **CMV $10. BO, $14. MB.**

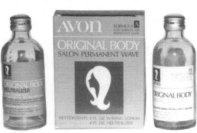

FRAGRANT NOTIONS SET 1978-79
Floral design box with gold & blue felt inner box holds .33 oz. bottle, gold cap & porcelain thimble with Avon stamped in bottom. Box came with outside sleeve. Choice of Ariane or Timeless cologne. **CMV $5. MB.**

ORIGINAL BODY SALON PERMANENT WAVE SET 1971
Pink box holds 4 oz. bottle of neutralizer and waving lotion. Used only in Avon Beauty Salons. Not sold. **CMV $12. MB.**

EMPRISE ULTRA GIFT SET 1977-78
Box came with 1.8 oz. Ultra cologne spray and .33 oz. Ultra purse concentre. **CMV $11.50 MB.**

MEN'S SETS OF 1980s

CURL SUPREME SALON PERMANENT WAVE SET 1971
Purple box holds 3.75 oz. white tube of neutralizer & 4 oz. bottle of waving lotion. Used only in Avon Beauty Salons. Not sold. **CMV $12. MB.**

SWEET HONESTY GIFT SET 1977-78
Came with 2 oz. cologne and 2 perfumed soaps. **CMV $7. MB.**

TIMELESS GIFT SET 1976
Amber bottles with gold caps. Box yellow & gold. Contains Ultra cream sachet & cologne mist. **CMV $10. MB.**

TIMELESS ULTRA GIFT SET 1977-78
Box came with 1.8 oz. Ultra cologne spray and .33 oz. Ultra perfume rollette. **CMV $10. MB.**

COUNTRY CHRISTMAS COLLECTION FOR HIM SET 1982
Green plastic box with green outer sleeve, holds matching bar of soap, talc 1.5 oz. & 2 oz. ribbed clear glass bottle, green cap cologne in choice of Clint, Weekend, Black Suede or Wild Country. **CMV $12. MB. with sleeve.**

TRAVELER GIFT SET 1981
Green and red box with deer, holds 1.5 oz. deer decor Talc and 2 oz. plastic After Shave in own box, in choice of Weekend, Wild Country, Black Suede. **CMV $5. MB set.**

UNSPOKEN ULTRA GIFT SET 1976-77
Box came with 1.8 oz. Ultra cologne spray and .33 oz. Ultra perfume rollette. **CMV $10. MB.**

BUCKAROO GIFT SET FOR BOYS 1981
Brown leather look box holds 2 oz. Buckaroo Talc and matching tan 2 oz. plastic bottle of Buckaroo Cologne for Boys. **CMV $8. MB set.**

NATURALS AFTER SHAVE & SOAP SET 1981
Wood look box holds 3 oz. plastic bottle and bar of soap to match box. Choice of Crisp Lime, Brisk Spice, Light Musk. **CMV $5. MB.**

HOWDY PARDNERS SET 1982-83
Box holds 2 oz. Talc & 2 oz. plastic bottle of Buckaroo Cologne with 2 piece blue cowboy hat cap. **CMV $7. MB.**

MEN'S SETS OF 1980s

GIFT COLLECTION FOR MEN SET 1984
Triangle box holds 1 oz. talc, deodorant & after shave conditioner. Choice of Wild Country, Cordovan, Musk for Men or Black Suede. **CMV $2. MB.**

GENTLEMEN'S GIFT COLLECTION 1986
Box holds 3.5 oz. Talc & 3 oz.cologne in choice of Wild Country "shown" Musk for Men, or Black Suede. **CMV $6. set MB.**

FERAUD POUR HOMME GIFT SET 1987
Black box holds grey,black & white neck tie & 2.5 oz. cologne. **CMV $16. MB.**

MEN'S TRAVELER GIFT SET SET 1985
Box holds 2 oz. after shave deodorant & small bar soap. Choice of Black Suede, Wild Country, Cordovan, Musk for Men. **CMV $4. MB.**

AURES GIFT SET 1986
Box hold 4 oz. Aures after shave & soap on a rope.. **CMV $7. MB.**
AMERICAN CLASSIC GIFT SET
Box hold 4 oz. American Classic after shave & soap on a rope.. **CMV $7. MB.**

HOLIDAY TRADITIONS DELUXE GIFT SET 1987
Box hold 3 oz. bottles of Mens Cologne & After Shave & Soap Dish. Same set as in 1989 Avon Classic Gift Set only different box. **CMV $10.**

SIGNET GIFT SET 1988
Box Hold 3.5 oz. cologne & ballpoint pen Personal initials for bottle. **CMV $15. MB**

FERAUD POUR HOMME GIFT SET 1985
(Top). Box holds cologne, soap & talc. **CMV $10. MB.**
GENTLEMEN'S GIFT SET 1985
(Bottom). Box holds 3 oz. cologne in flannel pouch & can of talc.Choice of Cordovan, Black Suede, Musk for Men, or Wild Country. **CMV $6. set MB.**

FERAUD POUR HOMME GIFT SET 1986
Black box holds 2.5 oz. after shave & razor with clear black plastic handle. **CMV $10. MB.**

MEN'S FRAGRANCE DUO SET 1980
Brown box holds choice of 5 oz. After Shave and1 1/2 oz. Talc in Wild Country, Trazarra, Weekend or Clint. **CMV $4. MB each set.**
NATURALS AFTER SHAVE SAMPLER SET 1980-81
Box holds 3 plastic bottles of Brisk Spice, Crisp Lime and Light Musk After Shave. **CMV $2 MB.**

BRISK SPICE GIFT SET 1988
Box hold Soap on a Rope & 4.5 oz. Cologne.. **CMV $8. MB.**

WOMEN'S SETS OF 1980s

WARNING!! Grading condition is paramount on sets. CMV can vary up to 90% on grade.

BLACK SUEDE KEY RING GIFT SET 1989
Box holds cologne, key ring & talc. **CMV $12. MB**

GENTLEMAN'S GIFT COLLECTION 1989
Giftbox holds 3.3 oz. talc. . **CMV $5. MB**

WILD COUNTRY GIFT SET 1989
Box holds tin box with choice of Wild Country or Wild Country Musk in Cologne, Deodorant & After Shave Conditioner.**CMV $10. MB**

AVON CLASSIC GIFT SET 1989
Box holds soap, cologne & after shave. **CMV $10. MB**

FLORAL ACCENT GIFT SET 1982
Box holds 1 oz. cologne & matching trim handkerchief. Choice of Wild Jasmine & Honeysuckle in yellow trim; Hawaiian White Ginger or Field Flowers in green trim; Roses Roses or Sweet Honesty in pink trim. **CMV $5. MB each set.**

ENVIRA SKIN CARE KIT 1982
Handle carton holds .5 oz. tube of conditioning cleansing cream, .5 oz. plastic bottles of clarifying toner & protective moisturizing lotion. **Short issue. CMV $2. mint set.**

HOLIDAY TAPESTRY GIFT SET 1981
Red & green handle carry box holds green & red tapestry design 1.5 oz. talc & 1.8 oz. cologne spray in choice of Occur!, Topaze, Moonwind, Charisma, Sweet Honesty or Zany. Colognes come in own box. **CMV $5. MB set.**

HOLIDAY GIFT SET ULTRA 1981
Red & green carry box holds gold 1.5 oz. talc & 1 oz. Ultra cologne spray in gold box. Choice of Timeless, Candid, Ariane, Tempo or Tasha. **CMV $5. MB.**

LEGACY GIFT SETS 1988
Box holds sun glasses & choice of After Shave or Cologne. **CMV $12. MB each.**

HOLIDAY GIFT SOAP SET 1981
Red & green handle box holds 3 bars soap in gold wrappers. Choice of mix & match in Tasha, Foxfire, Odyssey, Candid, Timeless, Unspoken, Ariane or Emprise. **CMV $7. MB set.**

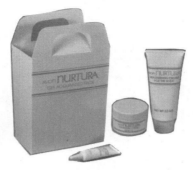

NUTURA GET ACQUAINTED PACK SET 1982
Carry carton holds tube of 2.5 oz. Replenishing body cream, .25 oz. eye cream & 1 oz. jar of Replenishing cream. Short issue. **CMV $4. mint set.**

APPLE BLOSSOM TIME SET 1983
Fancy box from early Avon days holds .5 oz. bottle of Apple Blossom cologne. Box has outer sleeve. **CMV $7. MB.**

COLORCREME & ULTRA WEAR GIFT SET 1980
Blue & red box holds blue & silver Colorcreme moisture lipstick & Ultra Wear nail enamel. Each item in own box inside set box. **CMV $4. MB.**

TOCCARA DELUXE GIFT SET 1982
Blue box holds white bar of soap & jar of renewable creme cologne. Short issue. **CMV $9. MB.**

GAY NINETIES SET 1983
Fancy box from early Avon days holds .5 oz. of White Lilac cologne. Box has outer sleeve. **CMV $7. MB.**

FANTASQUE GIFT COLLECTION SET 1983
Black box, gray plastic liner holds Eau de Cologne Flacon spray, 5 oz. Perfumed Body Veil & .5 oz. Perfumed Bath Essence. **CMV $6.50 MB.**

COUNTRY CHRISTMAS COLLECTION FOR HER SET 1982
Red & tan plastic box & outer sleeve holds matching soap, talc & .33 oz. cologne. Choice of Odyssey, Timeless, Tasha, Foxfire, Ariane or Candid. **CMV $9. MB.**

GOLD STAMPS SET 1982
Blue & gold box sleeve holds small bottle of golden fixative & small container of Beauty Dust & plastic stamps. **CMV $6. MB.**

HALLOWEEN MAKE A FACE KIT 1982
Carton box holds jar of Make a Face Base, blue lid, 3 pomettes of face color, orange, black & blue. **CMV $6. MB.**

COORDINATES SET 1982
White & red box holds small red checked bag marked Avon. Comes with choice of 2 of 4 different coordinates make up products, lipstick & nail enamel shown. Each boxed separately. **CMV $4.50 set MB.**

NAIL ACCENTS SET 1982
Yellow container box holds .5 oz. top shield & packet of 3 sheets of decals. **CMV $3. MB.**

GIFT COLLECTION FOR WOMEN 1984
Triangle box holds 1 oz. bath foam, Talc & 1 oz. cologne. Choice of Pavi Elle, Odyssey or Soft Musk. **CMV $3. MB.**

GILDED PERFUME SET 1985
Gold & black box holds .33 oz. cologne & .6 oz. perfume in Pavi Elle, Soft Musk or Odyssey. **CMV $6. MB.**

FANTASQUE ELEGANT EVENING SET 1985
Black box holds .33 oz. cologne & black earrings. **CMV $10. MB.**

PEARLS & LACE CLASSIC COLLECTION SET 1985
Pink box holds 1.5 oz. cologne spray & pair of pearlized earrings. **CMV $8. MB.**

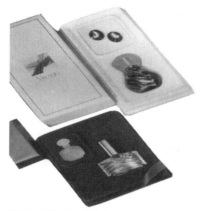

VIVAGE RADIANCE GIFT SET 1985
Box holds blue earrings & .33 oz. cologne. **CMV $9. MB.**

SOFT MUSK GILDED PERFUME SET 1985
Box holds .06 oz. perfume & .33 oz. cologne. **CMV $7. MB.**

CELEBRATION OF BEAUTY SET 1985
Black plastic box holds makeup. **CMV $6. MB.**

IMARI GIFT SET 1986
Maroon box holds .33 oz. cologne purse spray & pair of red & gold enamel like earrings. **CMV $11. MB.**

ROARING TWENTIES SET 1983
.5 oz. bottle of Trailing Arbutus cologne. Fancy blue & gold box. **CMV $7. MB with outer sleeve.**

CELEBRATION SAMPLER SET 1983
Trial size products given to customers 1 campaign only for $7.50 purchase. Box holds trial size tubes of Care Deeply Hand Cream, Aqua Clean Shower Gel, Nutura Creamy Wash Off Cleanser & small bottle of Naturally Gentle Shampoo. **CMV $6. set MB.**

GOING TO GRANDMA'S HOUSE SET 1982
Carton box holds 1.25. oz. white plastic bottles with turquoise caps of bubble bath for children & Little Blossom Whisper Soft Cologne, 1 small green Child's toothbrush. **CMV $5. MB.**

WOMEN'S SETS OF 1980s

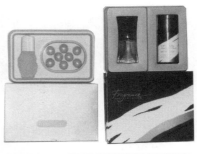

PEARLS & LACE FRAGRANT TREASURE GIFT SET 1986
Pink box holds 8 bath pearls & .33 oz. cologne. **CMV $5. MB.**

FRAGRANCE DUET COLLECTION SET 1986
Box holds .33 oz. cologne spray & 1.5 oz. Perfumed Talc in choice of Soft Musk "shown", Pavi Elle, Odyssey & Pearls & Lace. **CMV $4. MB.**

SOMERSAULTS PASTEL TALC & PUFF SETS 1986
2 oz. talc with Tallulah in pink, Zippy in yellow, and Miss Pear in green puff. **CMV $3. MB.ea.**

NUTRAFRESH GIFT SET 1987
Box holds tubes of Cleansing Buffing Gel, After Bath Moisturizer & 1 oz. Bar of Soap. **CMV $5. MB.**

LAVENDER FLORAL GIFT SET 1987
Box holds 4 oz. Lavender Floral toilet water & bar of soap. **CMV $5. MB.**

FANTASQUE GIFT SET 1986
Black box holds 1 oz. cologne spray & 2 bars of soap. **CMV $12.. MB.**

ENGLISH COUNTRY GIFT SET 1988
Box holds 1 oz. Cologne Spray & Beauty Dust. **CMV $7. MB.**

(Left to Right)
FRAGRANCES INDULGENCE SET 1987
Box holds 1 oz. Cologne Spray & Jar of Perfumed Skin Softener. **CMV $8. MB.**

FRAGRANCE TREASURES SET 1987
Box holds 1 oz. Cologne Spray & 5 oz. Perfumed Beauty Chest. **CMV $8. MB.**

FRAGRANCE LUXURIES SET 1987
Box holds 1 oz. Cologne Spray & 5.75 oz. Shimmering Body Lotion. **CMV $8. MB.**

SILK TAFFETA GIFT SET 1986
Box holds 2 square goldtone earrings & .33 oz. cologne spray in choice of Soft Musk, Pavi Elle, Odyssey or Pearls & Lace. **CMV $7. MB.**

SWITCH GIFT SET 1982
Blue sleeve over red box. Holds 7 oz. New Vitality Shampoo, 10 oz. Care Deeply lotion, Lots O' Lash, Ultra Wear Eye Shadow & 3 oz. Beauty Fluid. This set was given to first people around U.S. to call in on radio advertisement to switch to Avon Products. Rare. **CMV $30. MB.**

MEN'S SETS OF 1990s

CREME DE LA FLEUR GIFT SET 1988
Box holds 4 oz. creme bath 7 2 bars of soap.
CMV $9. MB

IMARI HOLIDAY TRIO GIFT SET 1988
Maroon Box holds soap, talc & cologne spray.
CMV $15. MB.
FACETS GIFT SET 1988
Blue box holds cologne spray & .25 oz.
perfume. **CMV $15. MB.**

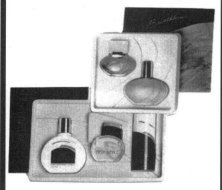

BREATHLESS SENSUAL TREASURES GIFT SET 1988
Box holds cologne spray & body veil. **CMV $17. MB.**
FIFTH AVENUE FRAGRANCE ESSENTIALS GIFT SET 1988
Box holds body lotion, cologne spray, talc.
CMV $16. MB

BLACK SUEDE PEN & PENCIL GIFT SET 1994
Box holds Black Pen & Pencil Set, 3.25 oz. cologne, 4 oz. After Shave Conditioner and Talc.
CMV $16. MB.

TRAVELER GIFT SETS 1994
Zippered Travel bag 9 3/4" long, 6 1/4" wide, 6" high holds 3.4 oz. cologne, 2 oz. After Shave Conditioner, 2 oz. Roll On deodorant in choice of Trail Blazer or Triumph. **CMV $15. ea set.MB.**

VALENTINE GIFT SET FOR MEN 1995
6 different color boxes holds men's cologne and After Shave Conditioner in choice of Black Suede, Sea Zone, Musk for Men, Trail Blaz er, Wild Country, Triumph. **CMV $10. MB for ea. set.**

SEA ZONE MARINE FRESH GIFT SET 1994
Blue box holds 3.4 oz. Sea Zone cologne, After Shave Soother, Body Talc, and 5 oz. Marine Fresh Soap.
CMV $20. MB.

SHAVING ESSENTIALS GIFT SET 1993
Black and gray box holds 3.25 oz. cologne, 4 oz. Shaving Cream and Plastic and Metal razor. Choice of Triumph and Black Suede. **CMV $15. MB.**

IF YOU LOVE TO LAUGH, GO TO THE BACK PAGE FOR INFO ON BUD HASTIN'S NEW JOKE BOOK AND HOW TO GET IT. LAUGH MORE AND LIVE LONGER.

MENS SETS OF 1990s

MEN'S COLOGNE SAMPLER GIFT SET 1990
Box holds .5 oz. cologne in Wild Country, Musk & Black Suede. **CMV $8. MB.**

GROOMING TRAVELER GIFT SET 1991
Box holds fragrance. Choice of deodorant talc 1.75 oz., after shave conditioner 2 oz., after shave lotion 2 oz. & roll on deodorant 2 oz. Short issue. **CMV $6. MB.**

TRIUMPH TOILETRY KIT GIFT SET 1992
Black & red nylon bag 9.5" long holds full size Triumph Cologne, Talc & After Shave Conditioner. **CMV $16. MB.**

BLACK SUEDE ARMY KNIFE GIFT SET 1992
Box holds black swiss style knife 2.25" long, Black Suede Cologne, After Shave Conditioner & Roll on Deodorant. **CMV $15. MB.**

AVON SPORTS CAR GIFT SET 1991
10.5" x 5" black plastic car caddy holds choice of 3.3 oz. cologne & 2 oz. after shave conditioner. Black box. Short issue. **CMV $14. MB.**

HIP PACK GIFT SET 1992
Black nylon hip bag holds 4 oz. after shave conditioner, 2 oz. roll on deodorant & cologne in choice of Black Suede, Everafter for Men, Musk for Men or Wild Country. **CMV $15. Set.**

BLACK SUEDE ADDRESS BOOK GIFT SET 1991
Box holds black & silver address book, 3.25 oz. cologne, 4 oz. after shave conditioner. Short issue. **CMV $12. MB**

CLEAN UP HITTER GIFT SET 1990
Box holds 2 oz. baseball soap & bat toothbrush. **CMV $5. MB**

HOT LINE SPRING FLING SET FOR BOYS 1992
Round Box holds tube of shampoo, bar of soap & .5 oz. cologne. **CMV $7. MB.**

UNDENIABLE FOR MEN TOILETRY GIFT SET 1992
Nylon zipper bag holds cologne, after shave conditioner & deodorant talc. **CMV $16. Set. MB.**

MY FIRST SHAVE KIT SET 1991
Box holds 2 oz. after shave & gray plastic toy shaver. **CMV $7. MB.**

MEN'S FRAGRANCE GIFT TIN SET 1993
Tin can holds 2 oz. cologne, 5 oz. soap on a rope & 2 oz. tube of after shave conditioner in choice of Undeniable or Black Suede. **CMV $10. MB.**

CANISTER GIFT SET 1994
Black cardboard round weights and measure canister box holds 2 ozs. Men's Cologne and 2 oz. tube of After Shave Conditioner. Choice of 8 fragrances. Sold 2 times only. **CMV $8. set MB.**

MEN'S FRAGRANCE GIFT TIN SET 1993
Box holds 4 3/4" high round Tin can with world map on side. Holds 2 oz. Cologne and After Shave Conditioner 2 oz. tube. Choice of Bl ack Suede or Undeniable for Men. **CMV $10. set MB.**

CLASSICAL CANISTER GIFT SET 1994
Black round marbleized box holds 2 oz. Mini cologne and 2 oz. After Shave conditioner and 5 oz. Soap on a Rope. Choice of Triumph or Black Suede. Short issue. **CMV $12. MB**

WILD COUNTRY BELT BUCKLE GIFT SET 1993
Box holds 4 oz. cologne, 4 oz. After Shave Conditioner and Metal Wild Country belt buckle. No belt. Very short issue. **CMV $13. MB.**

GROOMING TRIO GIFT SET 1993
Wire basket holds Men's Soap on a Rope, Roll On deodorant and 3.4 oz cologne in Trail Blazer or Undeniable for Men. **CMV $17. MB.**

TOTALLY MUSK FOR MEN/WOMEN'S SET 1993
Box holds 4 1/4 oz. sample size bottles of Soft Musk Cologne, Night Magic Evening Musk, Musk for Men and Wild Country Musk. **CMV $9. MB.**

BEGUILING HOLIDAY GIFT SET 1990
IMARI HOLIDAY GIFT SET 1990
Both sets come in blue & gold tin box. Each holds cologne spray, body talc & body creme. Also came in Night Magic Evening Musk or Soft Musk. **CMV $14.50 ea. MB.**

IMARI FANTASY CREATION GIFT SET 1991
Box holds 21" wide fan with stand & 1.2 oz. cologne. Short issue. **CMV $14. MB.**

MOTHERS DAY COZY COTTAGE SET 1991
House shaped box holds choice of 4 fragrances in perfumed skin softener cologne spray & talc. Short issue. **CMV$10. MB.**

FLORAL PRINT TIN GIFT SET 1991
8" x 6.75" x 3.75" flowered tin box has choice of Imari, Night Magic Evening Musk or Soft Musk with cologne spray, perfumed talc & perfumed skin softener. **CMV $10. Set ea. MB.**

HOLIDAY CELEBRATIONS GIFT SET 1991
Bamboo chest box holds cologne spray, talc & prefumed skin softener in choice of fragrances. Short issue. **CMV $12. MB.**

LOVE STRUCK GIFT SET 1992
7.5" red wicker heart box holds choice of Imari, Everafter or Beguiling, in Eau de Cologne spray, body creme & body talc. Short issue. **CMV $13. Set MB.**

FLORAL FANTASIES NAIL CARE SET 1991
Red & White flowered round box holds nail brush, emery board, nail advantage, nail strengthener & cuticle repair cream. **CMV $9. MB.**

LOVING SENTIMENTS BOUQUET GIFT SET 1991
Black & pink rose box holds .5 oz. cologne splash in choice of 6 fragrances. **CMV $5. MB.**

DECORATIVE HOLIDAY GIFT SET 1992
(Right) Winter ice skating scene on metal box 8.5" x 6.25" x 3.1/2". Choice of 7 ladies fragrances with cologne spray, silky moisture lotion & satin cologne rollette. **CMV $14.50 Set MB.**

IMARI ELEGANCE GIFT SET 1992
Box holds Imari eau de cologne spray, purse spray & hand cream. **CMV $20. MB.**

JEWEL OF LOVE GIFT CARD 1992
Flower fold out display box holds .5 oz. mini cologne. Short issue. **CMV $5. MB.**

BEAUTY TIME MANICURE SET 1990
Pink box holds 2 nail polish & 1 tube of hand cream. **CMV $5. MB.**

FRAGRANCE KEEPSAKE GIFT SET 1992
Flowered box 8" x 5" x 2.25" holds choice of 4 fragrances with 3 bars of soap, 1 oz. cologne spray & 2 oz. tube of body creme. **CMV $15. Set MB.**

MINNIE'N ME GIFT SET 1990
Box holds Minnie'N Me 2 oz. talc & bubble bath. **CMV $5. MB**

ENCHANTED CASTLE GIFT SET 1991
Castle box holds Shimmering cologne rollette, hand cream & bubble bath. **CMV $5. MB.**

ENCHANTED EVENING GIFT SET 1992
Colorful hexagon box 6.5" across holds Limited Edition Perfume, eau de cologne spray & fragranced body creme in Undeniable fragrance. **CMV $12. Set. MB.**

BEAUTY TIME MAKE UP KIT 1990
Pink heart box holds 3 Crayola make up sticks. **CMV $4. MB.**

PRACTICE MAKES PERRFECT GIFT SET 1992
Pink & blue ballet plastic purse holds 1.5 oz. tubes of non tear shampoo & bubble bath. Box of Kitty Ballerina soap. **CMV $6. MB.**

VICTORIAN PROMISE GIFT SET 1992
Tin can holds 3.5 oz. cologne spray, 3.5 oz. perfumed talc & 5 oz. skin softener in choice of ladies fragrance. **CMV $15. MB.**

MINNIE'N ME GIFT SET 1990
Box holds 2 oz. talc & 2 oz. tube of bubble bath. **CMV $5. MB.**

BATHOSAURUS GIFT SET 1992
Box holds 2.5" dinosaur brush & tubes of non tear shampoo & gritty hand cleanser. **CMV $6. MB.**

WOMEN'S SETS OF 1990s

KALEIDOSCOPE SPRING FLING SET FOR GIRLS 1992
Pink & yellow box holds tube of shampoo, soap & .5 oz. cologne. **CMV $7. MB.**

LUXURY GIFT SET 1991
4" x 8" Round flowered box. Fragrance, choice of Imari, Everafter, Splendor and Beguiling in Cologne Spray, Body Creme & Perfumed Talc. Short issue. **CMV $18. ea set. MB.**

IMARI FRAGRANT TREASURES GIFT SET 1994
Red and gold box holds 1.2 oz cologne spray and 5 oz perfumed dusting powder. **CMV $16. MB.**

BLOSSOM GARDEN MANICURE SET 1992
Display box comes with 3 bottles of nail tint. **CMV $5. MB.**

MESMERIZE ENCHANTING GIFT SET 1993
Blue box holds solid brass bowl, potpouri and 1.7 oz. cologne spray. **CMV $19. MB.**

INSPIRE FRAGRANCE GIFT SET 1993
Box holds crystal heart pendant on 20" chain and 1.7 oz Inspire Cologne. Sold 1 time only. **CMV $19. MB.**

PINK BUBBLE GUM GIFT SET 1993
Box holds 1.5 oz. tubes of bubble bath, body lotion, non tear shampoo & lip balm. **CMV $5. MB.**

IMARI LUXURY GIFT SET 1993
Red and gold box holds 1.2 oz cologne spray and .5 oz cream sachet in red plastic tray 7 1/4 X 10". **CMV $20. MB.**

PERLE NOIRE COLLECTION DU SOIR SET 1994
Black and gold box holds 1.6 oz. Eau de Toilette and perfumed body talc. Lid has gold tassel. **CMV $20. MB.**
CASBAH LUXURIOUS HOLIDAY COLLECTION SET 1994
Box holds 2" long blue and gold earrings and 1.7 oz. Casbah Eau de Toilette spray. **CMV $25. MB.**

CABBAGE PATCH KIDS TEA SET 1994
Box holds plastic tea set for kids. **CMV $13. set MB.**

CONTRAST FASHION FRAGRANCE GIFT SET 1993
Black and white polka dot box with red ribbon holds 1.7 oz cologne spray and 5 oz skin softener. **CMV $15.MB.**

FRAGRANCE ELEGANCE GIFT SET 1993
Blue and pink box 7 1/2 X 3 1/4" holds cologne spray and body talc in choice of Mesmerize, Imari, Inspire, Undeniable. **CMV $19. MB.**

SENTIMENTAL TREASURES FRAGRANCE COLLECTION 1994
Box hold four .5 oz colognes, Cotillion, Sonnet, Somewhere, Unspoken. set. **CMV $15. MB.**

FESTIVE HAT BOX GIFT SET 1993
Red octagonal box holds choice of 1.5 oz cologne spray and perfumed skin softener. **CMV $14. MB.**

NIGHT MAGIC EVENING DELIGHTS GIFT SET 1994
Blue box holds 1.5 oz cologne spray, 5 oz perfumed skin softener, .33 purse spray. **CMV $14. MB.**

CLASSIC PERFUME COLLECTION SET 1995
Red box holds miniature 1/8 oz bottles of perfume in Soft Musk, Lahana, Imari, Night Magic Evening Musk and Mesmerize. **CMV $15. MB.**

PARFUM GIFT SET 1993
Pink box holds .25 oz. perfume in frosted glass bottle and glass stopper. Choice of Lahama, Mesmerize, or Contrast. **CMV $15. MB.**

MESMERIZE BEAUTIFUL ENCHANTMENT GIFT SET 1994
Blue box holds 1.7 oz cologne spray in a blue zippered cosmetic purse, gold trim. **CMV $16. MB.**

PARFUMS CREATIFS DEMO SET 1993
Purple box holds 3 spray toilet waters in Casbah, C'est Moi, and Perle Noire. Sold only to Reps. to demonstrate to customers. **CMV $25. set MB.**

UNDENIABLE HOLIDAY ELEGANCE PURSE SPRAY GIFT SET 1994
Box holds 1.7 oz cologne spray, 5 oz Body Creme and .33 oz purse spray. **CMV $15. MB.**

SMALL LUXURIES FRAGRANCE COLLECTION 1994
Gold and black box holds small size colognes in Provocative, Mesmerize, Imari and Undeniable. **CMV $15. MB.**

WOMEN'S SETS OF 1990s

HOLIDAY LIPSTICK COLLECTION SET 1994
Box holds 4 different lipsticks from choice of 16 shades. **CMV $2.. MB.**

SOOTHING SEAS AROMATHERAPY GIFT SET 1994
Box holds jar of bath salts and tube of bath gel. **CMV $7. MB.**

TRANQUIL MOMENTS AROMATHERAPY IRIDESCENT GIFT SET 1994
Box holds 6 oz. Body Lotion and 8 oz. Foam bath. Both sets sold 2 times only. **CMV $7. MB.**

AVON ESSENTIALS GIFT SET 1994
Pick and white rose carton holds any 2 products in choice of Rose Shower Gel or Rose Hand and Body Lotion. Short issue. set. **CMV $5. MB.**

HOLIDAY ELEGANCE LIPSTICK SET 1993
Red box holds 3 red lipsticks. **CMV $3. MB.**

BUBBLE BATH GIFT SET 1993
Box holds 6-1 oz. plastic bubble baths. **CMV $2. MB.**

BEAUTY AND THE BEAST VANITY SET 1993
Box holds hand mirror, nail tint and lip gloss. **CMV $5. MB.**

HALLOWEEN MAKEUP KIT 1994
Box holds 4 face and body make up sticks and **CMV $4. MB.**

BUBBLE BATH TRIAL SIZE GIFT SET 1994
Box holds 6 different 1 oz. plastic bubble bath samples. **CMV $2. MB.**

PEPPERMINT ROSE GIFT SET 1993
Pink box holds 1 oz. talc, 1.5 oz. Body Lotion and 1 oz. Rose Soap. **CMV $8. MB.**

BILLOWING BUBBLES GIFT SET 1993
Pink box holds 8 oz. plastic bubble bath and 5 oz. pink soap on a rope. **CMV $5. MB.**

SOOTHING SEA'S TRIAL SIZE SET 1994
Blue and white box hold .5 oz sizes in Foaming bath salts, Nourishing Body Cream, Polishing Bath and Shower Gel, Smoothing Talc. **CMV $5. MB.**

TRANQUIL MOMENTS TRIAL SIZE SET 1994
Purple and white box holds 1 oz. Foam Bath, 1 oz. Body Lotion, .5 oz. Bath and Shower Gel and Talc .5 oz. **CMV $5. MB.**

BABY SITTERS CLUB GIFT SET 1994
Set holds cologne rollette, white soap and 4 oz. body cream. **CMV $7.MB.**

1957-1973 STOCKHOLDER'S CHRISTMAS GIFTS

Stockholders gifts were special packaged Avon items sent to each share holder of Avon Stock at Christmas each year. A special stockholders greeting card was sent with each gift & a stockholders gift is not mint or complete without this card.

They were first sent in 1957 & discontinued at Christmas 1973. They are considered quite hard to find.

There are only 2 years of stockholders gifts not shown. If you have any of the following 2 complete sets with card, please contact Bud Hastin. 1957 set had Persian Wood Perfume Mist & Beauty Dust. 1959 set had

Topaze Spray Perfume & Cologne Mist. Also listed as After Shower for Men. This could be 1 complete set or 2 different. 1 for men & 1 for women. Also listed for 1960 is 8 oz. Spice After Shave Lotion. This again sounds like 2 different items for 1960. All the other years are pictured & priced.

STOCKHOLDERS GIFT 1958
Satin lined box with large ribbon across lid and stockholders card. Holds Here's My Heart beauty dust, sachet lotion & Top Style lipstick. **CMV $65. MB.**

REGENCE COLOGNE MIST STOCKHOLD-ERS GIFT 1966
White, green and gold box. Given to stockholders on introduction of Regence, says "Your introduction to a fragrance masterpiece by Avon". **CMV $40. MB.**

STOCKHOLDERS GIFT 1961
Box with stockholders Christmas card, holds Cotillion beauty dust, cream sachet & cologne mist. This set is same as 1961-62 Cotillion Debut, only with special card. **CMV $60. MB.**

STOCKHOLDERS GIFT 1964
White flip open box with 4A design on both sides of lid, holds 4A after shave and Rapture 2 oz. cologne. With stockholders card. **CMV $60. MB.**

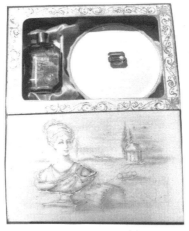

TOPAZE TREASURE STOCKHOLDERS GIFT 1960
Yellow & gold satin lined box holds Topaze Beauty Dust & 2 oz. cologne. Came with stockholders card. This was a general issue gift that was also sold. **CMV $40. MB., $55. MB with stockholders card.**

STOCKHOLDERS GIFT 1962
Flip open box with Avon printed all over lid. Holds Bay Rum jug after shave & Skin So Soft bud vase. With stockholders card. **CMV $65. MB.**

STOCKHOLDERS GIFT 1967
Brown brocade design box holds 1st Edition Book after shave & Brocade 4 oz. cologne. **CMV $40. MB.**

STOCKHOLDERS GIFT 1970
Bird of Paradise Cologne Mist in foam box. Gold band around box. Came with card from Avon as Christmas gift to stockholders. **CMV $22.50 MB with card only.**

STOCKHOLDERS GIFT 1963
Box opens in center with double lid to show 3 oz. Occur! cologne mist & Tribute after shave. Stockholders card. **CMV $50. MB.**

STOCKHOLDERS GIFT 1968
A special gift given to Avon stockholders. Short pony in Windjammer & Charisma Cologne Mist, set in white foam. **CMV set $32.50 MB.**

STOCKHOLDERS MEETING GIFTS 1970's
A special wrapped Avon product is given to each stockholder attending the Annual Avon Stockholders Meeting. Each gift comes with a special card which states "With the compliments of the Board of Directors, Officers and Employees of Avon Products, Inc.". **CMV $15. to $20. each mint with card only.**

STOCKHOLDERS GIFT 1971
White foam box with blue felt band. Contains Moonwind Cologne Mist. **CMV $25. MB with card.**

DEEP WOODS STOCKHOLDERS GIFT 1972
Brown foam box shaped like a log, card on top, with brown ribbon and gold sticker, contains Deep Woods Cologne. **CMV $25. MB.**

STOCKHOLDERS GIFT 1965
Box with stockholders card & Just Two set. **CMV $80. MB.**

IMPERIAL GARDENS STOCKHOLDERS GIFT 1973
Cream sachet in white styrofoam with orange & gold ribbon. Also has card. **CMV $18. MB.**

STOCKHOLDERS GIFT 1969
Pink foam box holds Elusive Cologne Mist & Perfume Rollette. Ribbon around box. **CMV $27.50 MB.**

MEN'S DECANTERS TRANSPORTATION

EXTRA SPECIAL MALE 1977-79
(Left) 3 oz. blue glass, dark blue cap and white plastic roof. Separate American eagle and red striped stick on decals. Came in Deep Woods or Everest After Shave. CMV $8. MB

MUSTANG '64 1976-78
(Right) 2 oz. size blue glass and blue tail cap. Came in Spicy or Tai Winds. CMV $7. MB.

WINNEBAGO MOTOR HOME 1978-79
(Top) 5 oz. white painted over clear glass. Stick on trim decals. Holds Wild Country or Deep Woods After Shave. CMV $10. MB.

STANLEY STEAMER 1978
(Bottom) Silver, 5 oz. silver paint over clear glass. Came in Tai Winds or Deep Woods After Shave. CMV $12 MB.

BIG MACK 1973-75
6 oz. green glass with beige bed. Holds Oland or Windjammer After Shave. CMV $8 MB.

FERRARI '53' 1974-75
(Left) 2 oz. dark amber glass with plastic closure. Came in Wild Country After Shave or Avon Protein Hair Lotion for Men. CMV $8 MB.

THUNDERBIRD '55 1974-75
(Right) 2 oz. blue glass with blue plastic closure. Came in Wild Country or Deep Woods After Shave. CMV $8. MB.

FOUR WHEEL DRIVE DECANTER 1987
3 oz. black glass. Stick on decals. Holds After Shave. CMV $8 MB.

PIERCE ARROW '33 1975-77
(Left) 5 oz. dark blue sprayed glass with beige plastic cap. Came in Wild Country or Deep Woods After Shave. CMV $10. MB.

STOCK CAR RACER 1974-75
(Right) 5 oz. blue glass with blue plastic cap. Holds Wild Country After Shave or Electric Pre-Shave Lotion. CMV $8. MB.

HOT WHEELS 1997
lst in series. Father & Son collector pack. Avon marked mattel package of 2 diecast metal cars. Choice of Mercedes, Mustang & Corvette. Each set of cars must be in the package and unopened to be a Avon Collectible. CMV for this set and all future Hot Wheels Sets marked Avon. CMV $6.00 ea. set mint unopened.

CHRYSLER TOWN & COUNTRY '48 1976
4.25 oz. off red painted over clear glass. Beige plastic top. Came in Everest or Wild Country. CMV $10. MB.

GREYHOUND BUS '31 1976-77
5 oz. blue painted over clear glass. Blue plastic front cap. White plastic roof will pop off. Came in Avon Spicy or Everest. CMV $8 MB.

RED SENTINEL "FIRE TRUCK" 1978-79
4 piece decanter. Engine is 3 1/2 oz. clear glass painted red. Holds Wild Country or Deep Woods After Shave. Plastic hook and ladder center section and 6 oz. rear red plastic section holds talc. Comes with stick on decals. CMV $13. MB.

FORD EDSEL 1958 DECANTER 1995
3 oz. blue green glass, holds "original" after shave. 5 1/4" long. CMV $10. MB

THE CAMPER 1972-74
5 oz. green glass truck with After Shave. 4 oz. Talc in beige plastic camper. Came in Deep Woods or Oland. CMV $12. MB.

1973 FORD RANGER PICK-UP 1978-79
5 oz. blue paint over clear glass, blue plastic bed cap. Stick on decals. Came in Wild Country or Deep woods. CMV $9. MB.

ROLLS ROYCE 1972-75
6 oz. beige painted over glass with dark brown and silver plastic parts. Came in Deep Woods or Tai Winds After Shave. CMV $13. MB.

TRIUMPH TR-3 '56 1975-76
(Left) 2 oz. blue-green glass with plastic cap. Came with Spicy or Wild Country After Shave. CMV $8. MB.
PORSCHE DECANTER '68 1976
(Right) 2 oz. amber glass with amber plastic cap. Holds Wild Country or Spicy After Shave. CMV $8 MB.

GOLD CADILLAC 1969-73
(Left) 6 oz. gold paint over clear glass. Came in Oland & wild Country After Shave. CMV $14. MB.
SILVER DUESENBERG 1970-72
(Right) 6 oz. silver paint over clear glass. Came in Oland & Wild Country After Shave. CMV $13 MB.

BUGATTI '27 1974-75
6.5 oz. black glass with chrome colored plastic trim. Came in Wild Country or Deep Woods Cologne or After Shave. CMV $12. MB.

STUDEBAKER '51 1975-76
(Left) 2 oz. blue glass with blue plastic parts. Holds Avon Spicy or Wild Country. CMV $8 MB.
CORVETTE STINGRAY '65 1975
(Right) 2 oz. green glass with green plastic cap. Holds Wild Country, Deep Woods or Avon Spicy After Shave. CMV $8 MB.

SURE WINNER RACING CAR 1972-75
(Left) 5.5 oz. blue glass with blue cap. Came in Sure Winner Bracing Lotion and Wild Country. CMV $8. MB.
JAGUAR CAR DECANTER 1973-76
5 oz. jade green glass with green plastic trunk over cap. Holds Deep Woods or Wild Country After Shave. CMV $10. MB,

'37 CORD 1974-76
7 oz. yellow painted with yellow plastic cap and black plastic top. Came in Tai Winds or Wild Country After Shave. CMV $12. MB.

JEEP RENEGADE 1981-82
3 oz. black glass, stick on decals. Tan plastic top. Black cap. Sure Winner Bracing Lotion or Trazerra Cologne. CMV $9. MB.

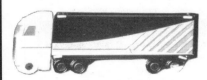

'36 FORD 1976-77
5 oz. orange paint over clear glass. Plastic stick on hub caps and grill. Came in Tai Winds or Oland. CMV $10. MB.

10-FOUR TRUCK DECANTER 1989
2.1/2 oz. truck holds after shave. CMV $8. MB.
SPEEDBOAT DECANTER 1989
7" long blue glass boat with stick on decals. Holds after shave. CMV $8. MB.

THUNDERBIRD 1955 FORD 1995
3 oz. blue glass. Holds sea zone after shave. 5 1/4" long. CMV $10.00 MB

VOLKSWAGON RABBIT 1980-82
3 oz. blue glass and blue plastic cap. Comes with silver stick on windows and hub caps. Choice of Light Musk Cologne or Sure Winner Bracing Lotion. CMV $8. MB.

BUICK SKYLARK '53 1979-80
(Left) 4 oz. emerald green glass and cap. Stick on decals. Came in Clint or Everest After Shave. CMV $11. MB.
VANTASTIC 1979-80
(Right) 5 oz. burgundy color glass. Stick on decals. Comes in Wild Country or Everest After Shave. CMV $8. MB.

BLUE VOLKSWAGON 1973-74
(left) 4 oz. light blue painted with plastic cap. Holds Oland or Windjammer After Shave. CMV $8. MB.
BLACK VOLKSWAGON 1970-72
(Right) 4 oz. black glass with black plastic cap. Holds Wild Country, Spicy or Electric Pre-Shave Lotion. CMV $8. MB.
RED VOLKSWAGON 1972
(Center) 4 oz. painted red with red cap. Came in Oland or Wild Country After Shave or Sports Rally Bracing Lotion. CMV $8. MB.

MINI-BIKE 1972-73
(Left) 4 oz. light amber glass coated over clear glass with light amber plastic wheel and silver handlebars with yellow grips. Came in Wild Country After Shave, Sure Winner Bracing Lotion, or Protein Hair Lotion for Men. CMV $8. MB.
ROAD RUNNER DECANTER 1973-74
(Right) 5.5 oz. blue glass with blue plastic front wheel, silver handle bars with black grips. Holds Sure Winner Bracing Lotion or Wild Country After Shave. CMV $9. MB.

SUPER CYCLE 1971-72
(Left) 4 oz. gray glass. Came in Wild Country, Island Lime or Sports Rally Bracing Lotion. CMV $9. MB.
SUPER CYCLE II 1974-75
(Right) Issued in blue glass. Came in Wild Country and Spicy After Shave. CMV $9. MB.

AVON OPEN GOLF CART 1972-75
(Left) 5 1/2" long, green glass bottle with green plastic front end, red plastic golf bags. Holds 5 oz. Wild Country or Windjammer After Shave. Came in light or darker green glass. CMV $10. MB.
SNOWMOBILE 1974-75
(Right) 4 oz. blue glass with yellow plastic front and back runners. Came in Oland or Windjammer After Shave. CMV $9. MB.

HARVESTER TRACTOR 1973-75
5.5 oz. amber glass with amber plastic front. Holds Wild Country After Shave or Protein Hair Lotion for men. CMV $14. MB.
'55 CHEVY 1975-76
5 oz. sprayed green glass with white plastic parts. Holds Wild Country or Electric Pre-Shave Lotion. CMV $11. MB.

TOURING T SILVER 1978
6 oz. silver plated over clear glass. May, 1978 on bottom. Came in Deep Woods or Everest. CMV $12. MB.

STERLING SIX SILVER 1978
7 oz. plated over clear glass. Came in Tai Winds or Deep Woods After Shave. May 1978 on Bottom. CMV $11. MB.

1914 STUTZ BEARCAT 1974-77
(Left) 6 oz. red painted with black plastic seats and cap. Came in Oland or Blend 7 After Shave. CMV $9. MB.
1936 MG DECANTER 1974-75
(Right) 5 oz. red painted with red plastic cap and white plastic top. Came in Avon Blend 7, Tai Winds or Wild Country After Shave. CMV $10. MB.

MAXWELL '23 DECANTER 1972-74
(Left) 6 oz. green glass with beige plastic top and trunk over cap. Came in Deep Woods or Tribute Cologne or After Shave. CMV $9. MB.

COVERED WAGON 1970-71
6 oz.. 4 1/2" long. Dark amber glass bottom, white painted top and gold cap. Came in Spicy and Wild Country After Shave. **CMV $10. MB.**

SIDE WHEELER 1971-72
5 oz. dark amber glass, black plastic stacks, silver cap, brown label. Came in Wild Country and Spicy After Shave. **CMV $11. MB. Reissued 1976 in Tai Winds gold cap, white label, same CMV.**

COUNTRY VENDOR 1973
5 oz. brown glass with brown plastic top, has picture of fruits and vegetables on side. Holds Wild Country or Avon Spicy After Shave. **CMV $10. MB.**

STRAIGHT 8 1969-71
(Left) 5 oz. dark green glass with black trunk cap. No. 8 on hood. Came in Wild Country, Windjammer, and Island Lime After Shave. Label says "Avon for Men" **CMV $10 MB.**

STRAIGHT 8 1973-75
(Left) 5 oz. green glass. Came in Wild Country and Island Lime After Shave. Label says Avon-Keep out of reach of children. **CMV $10 MB.**

DUNE BUGGY 1971-73
(Right) 5 oz. blue glass, silver motor cap. Came in Spicy After Shave, Liquid Hair Lotion and Sports Rally Bracing Lotion. **CMV $10. MB.**

1926 CHECKER CAB 1977-78
5 oz. yellow painted over clear glass. Black plastic trunk cap and top. Stick on decal hub caps, bumper and checker design. Came in Everest or Wild Country. **CMV $10. MB.**

TOURING T 1969-70
(Left) 6 1/2" long, 6 oz. black glass with black plastic top and tire cap. Came in Excalibur or Tribute After Shave. **CMV $12. MB.**

MODEL A 1972-74
(Right) 4 oz. yellow painted over clear glass, yellow cap. Holds Wild Country or Leather After Shave. **CMV $10. MB.**

ARMY JEEP 1974-75
4 oz. olive drab green with plastic closure. Came with Wild Country or Avon Spicy After Shave. **CMV $10. MB.**

GOLDEN ROCKET 0-2-2 1974-76
(Right) 6 oz. smoky gold over clear glass with gold plastic cap. Came in Tai Winds or Wild Country After Shave. **CMV $10. MB.** Factory reject from factory is indented sides and gold coated. **CMV $20.**

STERLING SIX 1968-70
7 oz. came in 4 different shades of amber glass, black tire cap, rough top roof. Came in Spicy, Tribute, Leather After Shave. **CMV $10. MB.** Smooth top in very light amber glass. **CMV $45. MB.**

STERLING SIX II 1973-74
7 oz. green glass with white tire cap. Came in Wild Country or Tai Winds After Shave. **CMV $8. MB.**

ELECTRIC CHARGER 1970-72
(Left) 5 oz. black glass with red cap and red side decals. Came in Spicy, Leather or Wild Country After Shave. **CMV $10. MB.**

STAGE COACH 1970-77
(Right) 5 oz. dark amber glass with gold cap. Came in Wild Country, Tai Winds or Oland After Shave. 1977 issue has "R" on bottom for reissue, hard to find silver cap. **CMV $7 MB.for reissue. CMV $10. MB.**

FIRST VOLUNTEER 1971-72
6 oz. gold coated over clear glass. Oland or Tai Winds Cologne. **CMV $14. MB.**

1910 FIRE FIGHTER 1975
(Right) 6 oz. painted over glass with red plastic back. Came in Wild Country or Tai Winds After Shave. **CMV $9. MB.**

VOLKSWAGON BUS 1975-76
(Left) 5 oz. red painted glass with silver gray motorcycle plastic closure. Set of 4 "decorate-it-yourself" labels come with each decanter. Came with Tai Winds After Shave or Sure Winner Bracing Lotion. **CMV $10. MB.**

THE THOMAS FLYER 1908 1974-75
(Right) 6 oz. white painted glass with red and blue plastic parts with white tire cap on back. Came in Wild Country or Oland After Shave. **CMV $12. MB.**

REO DEPOT WAGON 1972-73
5" long, 5 oz. amber glass with black plastic top and cap. Holds Tai Winds and Oland After Shave Lotion. **CMV $12. MB.**

CEMENT MIXER 1979-80
3 piece bottle. Front section is dark amber glass. Comes in Wild Country or Everest After Shave. Center plastic section connects to 6 oz. pale yellow plastic rear section bottle. Holds talc. Has stick on decals. **CMV $14. MB.**

STATION WAGON 1971-73
6 oz. green glass car with tan plastic top. Came in Wild Country or Tai Winds After Shave. **CMV $12. MB.**

PACKARD ROADSTER 1970-72
6 oz. light amber glass and matching plastic rumble seat cap. Came in Oland and Leather Cologne. 6 1/2" long. **CMV $12. MB**

TRAIN 1876 CENTENNIAL EXPRESS DECANTER 1978-86
5.5 oz. dark green glass with stick on trim decals. Holds Wild Country or Everest After Shave. **CMV $12. MB.** Reissues 1986.

STANLEY STEAMER 1971-72
5 oz. blue glass bottle with black plastic seats and tire cap. Came in Wild Country or Windjammer After Shave. **CMV $10. MB.**

HIGHWAY KING 1977-79
4 oz. green glass bottle with white plastic center connection piece and rear section is 6.5 oz. white plastic talc bottle. Came in Wild Country or Everest. **CMV $14. MB.**

CABLE CAR DECANTER 1974-75
4 oz. green painted over clear glass has plastic green and white top. Came in Wild Country or Avon Leather. **CMV $12. MB.**

HAYNES APPERSON 1902 1973-74
(Right) 4.5 oz. green glass with green plastic front over cap. Has silver tiller steering rod. Holds Avon Blend 7 or Tai Winds After Shave. **CMV $10. MB.**

ATLANTIC 4-4-2 DECANTER 1973-75
5 oz. silver over clear glass with silver plastic parts. Holds Deep Woods or Leather After Shave or Cologne. **CMV $14. MB.**

BIG RIG 1975-76
3.5 oz. blue glass cab with 6 oz. white & blue plastic trailer. Cab holds After Shave, trailer holds Talc in Wild Country or Deep Woods. **CMV $16. MB.**

700E HUDSON LOCOMOTIVE 1993
Black porcelain train is 9" long, 1.5" wide & 2.25" high. Wood base 10.5 x 4". **CMV $45. MB.**

CAPTAINS PRIDE 1970
6 oz. bottle with ship decal, tan cap & blue neck label. Sits on black plastic stand. Came in Oland & Windjammer After Shave. **CMV $10. MB.**

CANNONBALL EXPRESS 4-6-0 1976-77
3.25 oz. black glass, black cap. Came in Deep Woods or Wild Country or After Shave. **CMV $11. MB.**

AMERICAN SCHOONER 1972-73
4.5 oz. blue glass with blue plastic end over cap. Some are blue painted over clear glass. Came in Oland or Spicy After Shave. **CMV $12. MB.**

VIKING DISCOVERER 1977-79
4 oz. blue-green glass & matching plastic cap. Red & white metal sail. Black plastic sail post. Came in Wild Country or Everest. **CMV $12. MB.**

GENERAL 4-4-0 1971-72
5 1/2 oz. dark blue glass and cap. Came in Tai Winds or Wild Country After Shave. **CMV $14. MB**

BLUE COMET LIONEL CLASSIC TRAIN 1991
(Top) Blue porcelain train figurine on wood base with name plate. Base size 9.75" x 3.75" **CMV $40. MB.**
NO. 381E LOCOMOTIVE 1992
(Bottom) Green porcelain train on 9.75" x 3.75" wood base with metal plaque **CMV $45. MB.**

"LIONEL" SANTA FE F3 DIESEL ENGINE 1992
3rd in series of Lionel Trains. Train engine is 9" long x 2.25" high. Red & silver painted porcelain figurine on a wood base with brass plaque. **CMV $45. MB.**

GONE FISHING DECANTER 1973-74
5 oz. lt. blue boat with white plastic man, yellow fishing rod. Came in Tai Winds or Spicy. **CMV $12. MB.**

CLASSIC SPORTS CAR DECANTER 1990
2 oz. blue glass car with stick on decals. Holds
Wild Country After Shave. **CMV $8. MB.**
CORVETTE DECANTER 1988
3 oz. black glass 1988 Corvette holds after
shave. **CMV $8. MB.**

SPIRIT OF ST. LOUIS 1970-72
6 oz. silver paint over clear glass. Came in
Windjammer & Excalibur After Shave. 7 1/2"
long. **CMV $12. MB.**

GOODYEAR BLIMP 1978
2 oz. silver gray paint over clear glass, blue
letters. Came in Everest or Wild Country After
Shave. **CMV $9. MB.**

AUBURN BOATTAIL SPEEDSTER 1983-84
1st in series. Black & red ceramic car figurine.
8 1/2" long. Dated 1983. **CMV $30. MB.**

HISTORIC FLIGHT "1903 FLYER" 1986
3/3/4" high pewter plane. Wood base.
CMV $20. MB.
SPIRIT OF ST. LOUIS 1986
4 1/2" wide pewter plane with wood base.
CMV $20. MB.
PEWTER CAR COLLECTION 1984
Wood base with '63 Corvette, '63 Riviera,
'55 Thunderbird, '57 Chrysler 300, and '64
Mustang. **CMV $15. each MB.**

1964 1/2 MUSTANG DECANTER 1994
3 oz. green glass bottle and cap holds Wild Country cologne. 5 1/2" long. **CMV $10. MB..**

JEEP DECANTER GIFT SET 1993
Box holds 3 oz. blue glass jeep decanter with
tan plastic top, and multi-function pocket knife.
Jeep holds Trailblazer cologne. **CMV $20. set
MB. Jeep only, $10.00 Mint.**

LIONEL GG-1 ELECTRIC ENGINE TRAIN 1994
Made of Hardford porcelain. 9" long, 2 3/4" high
train on wood base with brass name tag. Base is 10
1/2" X 4". **CMV $45. MB.**

CORD CAR '1937' 1984
9" long car, yellow. **CMV $30. MB.**

**CLASSIC CAR COLLECTION 1930's
ROADSTER 1995**
7" long wood base holds removable yellow &
black die cast metal car. Tires & doors move.
CMV $15. MB

**CLASSIC CAR COLLECTION 1930's
TOURING SEDAN 1996**
3rd in series. Die cast blue metal car, 4 1/2"
long by 1 1/2" high. Doors open, tires move.
Wood base. **CMV $15.00 MB.**

1950's SPORTS CONVERTIBLE 1996
2nd in series. Red metal convertible with
plastic parts. 6 1/4" long wood base is dated.
CMV $15. MB

COLLECTOR'S STEIN 1976-79
Hand made ceramic blue stein. Made in Brazil and numbered on bottom. Came with 8 oz. plastic bottle of Everest or Wild Country. **CMV $40. MB.**

SPORTING MINIATURE STEIN 1983-84
5" tall ceramic stein. Hunting scene on side. **CMV $15. MB.**

BLACKSMITH STEIN 1985
Ceramic stein, pewter top, Made in Brazil & numbered. **CMV $40. MB.**
SHIP BUILDER STEIN 1986
Both ceramic steins 8 1/2" high, numbered on bottom. Pewter lids. **CMV $50. each MB.**

BIG SHOT MUG - TEST AREA 1983
Chrome plated brass jigger about 2 1/2" inches high. Comes with or without stick on initials. Sold only in Test area in Mid-West. **CMV $40. in white test box.**

AGE OF THE IRON HORSE STEIN 1982-84
8 1/2" ceramic stein made in Brazil. Numbered and dated. Metal top. Has train design on side. Sold Empty. **CMV $40. MB.**

GREAT AMERICAN FOOTBALL STEIN 1982-83
9" high ceramic stein made in Brazil. Metal flip top. **CMV $40. MB.**

WRIGHT BROTHERS MUG 1985
3" high. Hand painted porcelain mug. **CMV $16. MB.**
LEWIS & CLARK MUG 1985
Hand painted porcelain mug. 3" high. **CMV $16. MB.**

MINIATURE STEINS 1982-83
4 1/2" to 5 1/2" high ceramic steins. Choice of Tall Ships, Vintage Cars or Flying Classics. Each numbered and dated 1982. **CMV $15. each MB.**

WESTERN ROUND UP MINI STEIN 1983-84
5" mini ceramic tan & white stein, made in Brazil and numbered on bottom. Cowboys on side. **CMV $15. MB.**
ENDANGERED SPECIES MINI STEIN 1983-84
Blue and white 5" mini stein, moose and goat on side. **CMV $15. MB.**

IRON HORSE MINI STEIN 1985
5 1/4" high ceramic stein. **CMV $15. MB.**
GREAT AMERICAN BASEBALL STEIN 1984
Ceramic stein 8 3/4" high , Metal top, Made in Brazil. **CMV $40. MB.**

DUCKS OF AMERICAN WILDERNESS STEIN 1988
8 3/4" high ceramic stein. Duck on top of lid.
CMV $45. MB.

FLYING CLASSIC CERAMIC STEIN 1981
6th in series, 9 1/2" high blue ceramic stein made in Brazil and numbered on the bottom. Sold empty. Metal Top. **CMV $38 MB.**

SPORTING STEIN DECANTER 1978
9" tall, ceramic stein marked on bottom "Made in Brazil for Avon Products 1978". Came with choice of 8 oz. Trazarra or Wild Country cologne with gold cap in red plastic bottle. Each stein is numbered on the bottom. **CMV $35 MB.**

CAR CLASSIC STEIN 1979-80
9" high ceramic stein made in Brazil & numbered on the bottom. Comes with 8 oz. plastic of Trazarra Cologne.**CMV $40.00 MB**

WESTERN ROUND-UP CERAMIC STEIN 1980
(Left) 8 1/2" high. Made in Brazil and numbered on the bottom. Metal top. Comes with 8 oz. plastic bottle of Wild Country or Trazarra cologne.**CMV $40. MB.**
CASEY AT THE BAT TANKARD 1980
(Right) 6" high beige opaque glass. Comes with a 4 oz. Casey plastic bottle of Wild Country or Weekend After Shave. **CMV $16. MB.**

HUNTER'S STEIN 1972
8 oz. nickle plated over clear glass, has gray and black plastic bottle inside. Holds Deep Woods or Wild Country After Shave. **CMV $15. MB.**

STEIN – SILVER 1968
(Left) 6 oz. silver paint over clear glass, silver cap. Came in spicy, Windjammer & Tribute After Shave. **CMV $12. MB.**
STEIN – SILVER 1965
(Right) 8 oz. silver paint over clear glass, silver cap. Came in Tribute, Spicy, Blue Blazer, & 4A After Shave. **CMV $12. MB.**

TALL SHIPS STEIN 1977
Ceramic stein, pewter handle and lid. Came with 8 oz. red plastic bottle of Clint or brown plastic of Wild country cologne for men. Silver cap. Each stein was hand made in Brazil and numbered on the bottom. **CMV $40. MB.**

TALL SHIPS SHORT STEIN 1978
Smaller stein on right was sold in Trend Setter test area and was later changed to larger regular issue size on left. Both marked Avon on bottom and numbered. **CMV $60 small stein MB.**

AMERICAN ARMED FORCES STEIN 1990
9 1/4" high ceramic stein with pewter bald eagle lid. **CMV $45. MB.**

GOLD RUSH STEIN 1987
8 1/2" high ceramic stein - gold trim. **CMV $40.**

RACING CAR STEIN 1989
9 1/4" high ceramic stein. Has pewter race car on lid. **CMV $50. MB.**

ENDANGERED SPECIES MINI STEINS 1990
American Bald Eagle or Asian Elephant 5 1/4" ceramic mini steins with pewter lids. **CMV $20. MB.**

INDIANS OF THE AMERICAN FRONTIER STEIN 1988
9" high ceramic stein. Indian design. **CMV $40. MB.**

ALL AMERICAN SPORTS FAN MUG & POPCORN 1983
5 1/2" high clear glass mug with red white and blue design. Comes with red white and blue cannister of popcorn. **CMV $8. set MB., or $4 mug only.**

FISHING STEIN 1990
8 1/2" high ceramic Fish stein. **CMV $45. MB.**

FIRE FIGHTER'S STEIN 1989
9" high ceramic stein. Gold Bell lid & trim. **CMV $55. MB.**

GIANT PANDA MINI STEIN 1991
JAGUAR MINI STEIN 1991
Both ceramic steins are 5.5" high with pewter lids. **CMV $20. ea. MB.**

GREAT DOGS OUTDOOR STEIN 1991
9" ceramic stein with pewter lid. Hunting dogs on side. Tan, brown & green stein. **CMV $45. MB.**

CHRISTOPHER COLUMBUS STEIN 1992
12" high ceramic stein with pewter lid. Dated & numbered on bottom. **CMV $45. MB.**

FANCY FOOTWORK WESTERN MUG 1991
Tan ceramic mug 4.75" tall. Came with package of almond nuts.**CMV $12. MB**

PERFECT COMBO MUG & POPCORN 1982
Box holds 12. oz. clear glass mug with geese on side & 10 oz. gold foil wrapped can of popcorn. **CMV $10. MB set, mug only $5.**

MOUNTAIN ZEBRA STEIN 1992
Zebra on side.
SPERM WHALE STEIN 1992
Whale on side.
Both ceramic steins are 5.5" high. Pewter lids. **CMV $20. ea. MB.**

IRON HORSE SHAVING MUG 1974-76
White milk glass mug holds 7 oz. plastic bottle with gold cap. Came in Avon Blend, Deep Woods or Avon Leather After Shave. **CMV $7. MB. $3. mug only.**

CONQUEST OF SPACE STEIN 1991
9.75" blue ceramic stein with astronaut pewter lid, numbered and dated on bottom. **CMV $45. MB.**

WINNERS CIRCLE STEIN 1992
10" high ceramic horse racing stein with pewter lid.**CMV $45. MB.**

WILD WEST STEIN 1993
8.5" high ceramic rust color stein with pewter lid. Indian chief on top of lid. **CMV $50. MB.**

COUNTRY AND WESTERN MUSIC STEIN 1994
8 1/4" high brown ceramic stein with pewter lid. Numbered and dated. **CMV $40. MB.**

BASKETBALL STEIN 1993
Century of Basketball tan ceramic stein 9 1/2"
high. Pewter lid. **CMV $50.**

WILDLIFE STEIN 1995
9 1/2" high ceramic stein with Eagle pewter
lid. Dated on bottom. **CMV $45. MB.**

TRIBUTE TO RESCUE WORKERS STEIN 1997
9 1/2" high blue & gray stoneware stein. Pewter lid.
CMV $45. MB.

FATHER CHRISTMAS STEIN 1994
9 1/2" high ceramic stein and pewter lid.
Numbered and dated. **CMV $40. MB.**

**SALUTE TO THE POSTAL SERVICE STEIN
1996**
9 1/2" high ceramic stein with pewter lid.
Dated & numbered on bottom. **CMV $45.
MB.**

**TRIBUTE TO THE NORTH AMERICAN WOLF
STEIN 1997**
9 1/2" high ceramic stein with pewter lid. **CMV $45.
MB.**

CHRISTMAS CAROL STEIN 1996
9 1/2" high tan ceramic stein with pewter lid.
Dated on bottom. **CMV $45. MB.**

AMERICA THE BEAUTIFUL STEIN 1998
9 1/2" high stoneware stein. Pewter lid.
Dated 1998. **CMV $45. MB.**

KNIGHTS OF THE REALM STEIN 1995
King Arthur on side of 9 1/2" ceramic blue stein.
CMV $50. MB.

AMERICAN EAGLE TANKARD 1997
7 1/4" high clear glass mug with Eagle on side. Pewter lid. **CMV $20. MB.**

MAJESTIC FOREST TANKARD 1995
6 1/2" high clear glass with "deers" head on top of pewter lid. **CMV $20. MB.**

ENDANGERED WETLANDS TANKARD 1996
6" tall etched glass tankard with duck pewter lid. **CMV $25. MB.**

GREAT KINGS OF AFRICA STEIN's 1997
3 different ceramic steins. Each are 5 3/4" high. Choice of '**SHAKA"**, **"AKHENATON", &
"HANNIBAL'.** **CMV $30. each MB.**

**MICHAEL JORDAN COMMEMORATIVE
TANKARD 1997**
18 oz. ceramic mug with Michael Jordan of the Chicago Bulls on the side. **CMV $20. MB.**

**WINSTON CUP 25TH ANNIVERSARY
TANKARD 1996**
20 oz. porcelain mug. Has 10 past car raceing champs on side. **CMV $20. MB.**

**COTTAGE COLLECTION MUGS
1997**
(Left) Hand painted 10 oz. ceramic mugs. Choice of pink **TOWNHOUSE,** yellow **BAKERY,** tan **COTTAGE,** or blue **FLORIST** mug. **CMV $8. ea. MB.**

MEN'S DECANTERS

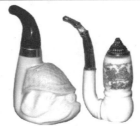

AMERICAN EAGLE PIPE 1974-75
5 oz. dark amber glass with gold plastic top & black handle. Holds Wild Country or Tai Winds Cologne. **CMV $10. MB.**

CALABASH PIPE 1974-75
3 oz. yellow gold sprayed glass with yellow gold plastic cap & black plastic stand. Holds Wild Country or Deep Woods After Shave. **CMV $10. MB.**

UNCLE SAM PIPE 1975-76
3 oz. white opal glass with blue band & blue plastic stem. Holds Wild Country or Deep Woods After Shave. **CMV $8. MB.**

PONY EXPRESS RIDER PIPE 1975-76
3 oz. white milk glass with black plastic stem. Holds Wild Country or Tai Winds Cologne. **CMV $9. MB.**

CORNCOB PIPE 1974-75
3 oz. amber glass with black plastic stem. Holds Wild Country or Avon Spicy. **CMV $6. MB.**

COLLECTOR'S PIPE 1973-74
3 oz. brown glass with black stem. Holds Deep Woods or Windjammer After Shave or Cologne. **CMV $8. MB.**

WILD MUSTANG PIPE 1976-77
3 oz. white paint over clear glass. Holds Wild Country or Deep Woods cologne. **CMV $10. MB.**

BULL DOG PIPE 1972-73
6 oz. cream colored milk glass with black stem. Came in Wild Country or Oland After Shave or Cologne. **CMV $10. MB.**

DUTCH PIPE 1973-74
2 oz. white milk glass, blue design, silver handle & cap. Came in Tribute or Tai Winds Cologne. **CMV $10. MB.**

PIPE FULL DECANTER 1971-72
2 oz. brown glass with black stem. Holds Spicy, Oland, Tai Winds or Excalibur After Shave. **CMV $8. MB.**

PIPE FULL DECANTER 1972-74
2 oz. lt. green glass with brown plastic stem. Holds Tai Winds or Spicy After Shave. **CMV $7. MB.**

PHILADELPHIA DERRINGER 1980-82
2 oz. dark amber glass with gray stick on parts & gold trim. Came in Light Musk or Brisk Spice After Shave. **CMV $10. MB.**

PIPE DREAM 1967
6 oz. dark amber glass, black cap, tan plastic base. Came in Spicy, Tribute & Leather After Shave. **CMV $15 BO, $22. MB.**

PIPE DREAM CLEAR TEST 1967
6 oz. clear glass factory test bottle. Very rare. **CMV $250.**

PONY POST MINIATURE 1973-74
1.5 oz. clear glass with gold cap & ring. Holds Oland or Spicy After Shave. **CMV $6. MB.**

PONY POST 1972-73
5 oz. bronze paint over clear glass with bronze cap & nose ring. Holds Tai Winds or Leather After Shave. **CMV $9. MB.**

PONY POST "TALL" 1966-67
8 oz. green glass with gold cap & nose ring. Holds Island Lime, Tribute or Leather After Shave. **CMV $17. MB, $10. BO.**

PEPPERBOX PISTOL '1850"---1979
(Top) 3 oz. silver plated over clear glass barrel bottle with gold and brown plastic handle cap. Came in Everest or Tai Winds. **CMV $9. MB, $6. BO.**

PEPPERBOX PISTOL 1982-83
Reissued in gold tone instead of silver came in Clint and Wild Country. **CMV $11. MB.**

DERRINGER 1977
(Bottom) 2 oz. gold plated over amber glass. Came in Deep Woods or Wild Country. **CMV $9. MB.**

MINIATURE VOLCANIC REPEATER PISTOL DECANTER 1986
1.4 oz. amber glass. **CMV $12. MB.**

SHORT PONY DECANTER 1968-69
(Right) 4 oz. green glass, gold cap. Came in Wild Country, Windjammer, Spicy, Leather or Electric Pre-Shave. **CMV $10. MB.**

BLUNDERBUSS PISTOL 1780 1976
(Top) 12 1/2" long, 5.5 oz. dark amber glass, gold cap & plastic trigger. Came in Everest & Wild Country. **CMV $13. MB**

THOMAS JEFFERSON HAND GUN 1978-79
(Bottom) 10" long, 2.5 oz. dark amber glass with gold & silver plastic cap. Holds Deep Woods or Everest cologne. **CMV $10. MB.**

DUELING PISTOL 1760 1973-74
(Top) 4 oz. brown glass with silver clamp on parts, silver cap. Holds Deep Woods or Tai Winds After Shave. **CMV $12. MB.**

DUELING PISTOL II 1975
Same as above but black glass & gold plastic parts. Came in Wild Country or Tai Winds. **CMV $12. MB.**

COLT REVOLVER 1851 1975-76
(Bottom) 3 oz. amber glass with silver plastic barrel. Holds Wild Country or Deep Woods After Shave. **CMV $12. MB.**

TWENTY PACES 1967-69
3 oz. each, 10" long. Gold paint over clear glass, gold cap. Red paper labels on end of barrel. Came in All Purpose Cologne, Wild Country & Leather After Shave. **CMV brown box lined with red $50.**, **black lined box $120**, **blue lined box $160**. Very rare gun with raised sight did not break off in glass mold. **CMV $100. Raised sight gun only. Regular issue guns $15. each mint.**

LONGHORN STEER 1975-76
5 oz. dark amber glass with amber plastic head, ivory colored horns. Holds Wild Country or Tai Winds After Shave. **CMV $10. MB.**

OLD FAITHFUL 1972-73
5 oz. brown glass with brown plastic head & gold keg. Holds Wild Country or Spicy After Shav **CMV $10. MB.**

HOLIDAY MINI COLOGNE 1991
.5 oz. ribbed bottle, green cap. Short issue Christmas box. Choice of 7 mens fragrances. **CMV $3. MB as shown**

GAS PUMP - REMEMBER WHEN DECANTER 1979-80
4 oz. clear glass painted yellow, white top, yellow cap. Came in Light Musk or Cool Sage. **CMV $15. MB.**

VOLCANIC REPEATING PISTOL DECANTER 1979-80
2 oz. silver coated over clear glass. Silver & pearl plastic handle. Holds Wild Country or Brisk Spice Cologne. **CMV $10. MB.**

MAJESTIC ELEPHANT 1977
5.5 oz. gray painted over clear glass. Gray head cap. Came in Wild Country or Deep Woods. **CMV $11. MB.**

AT POINT DECANTER 1973-74
5 oz. reddish brown glass with reddish brown plastic head. Came in Deep Woods or Tribute. **CMV $9. MB.**

SNOOPY SURPRISE 1969-71
5 oz., 5 1/2" high. White glass with blue or yellow hat & black ears. Came in Wild Country, Excalibur After Shave & Sports Rally Bracing Lotion. **CMV $12. MB.**

PHEASANT 1972-74
5 oz. brown glass with green plastic head. Holds Oland or Leather After Shave. **CMV $10. MB.**

CANADA GOOSE 1973-74
5 oz. brown glass with black plastic head. Holds Deep Woods, Wild Country or Everest After Shave or Cologne. **CMV $10. MB.** Reissued in 1976 in smaller box in After Shave only. **Same CMV.**

NOBLE PRINCE 1975-77
4 oz. brown glass with plastic head. Holds Wild Country After Shave or Electric Pre-Shave Lotion. **CMV $8 MB.**

CLASSIC LION 1973-75
8 oz. green glass with green plastic head. Holds Wild Country, Tribute After Shave or Deep Woods Emollient After Shave. **CMV $9 MB.**

FAITHFUL LADDIE 1977-79
4 oz. light amber glass & amber head cap. Came in Wild Country or Deep Woods. **CMV $8. MB.**

KODIAK BEAR 1977
6 oz. dark amber glass & head. Came in Wild Country or Deep Woods. **CMV $8. MB.**

PONY EXPRESS 1971-72
5 oz. brown glass with copper colored man on cap. Came in Avon Leather or Wild Country After Shave. **CMV $10. MB.**

BUCKING BRONCO 1971-72
6 oz. dark amber glass horse with bronze plastic cowboy cap. Came in Oland or Excalibur. **CMV $10. MB.**

SPORT OF KINGS DECANTER 1975
5 oz. amber glass with plastic head. Holds Wild Country, Avon Spicy or Avon Leather After Shave. **CMV $10. MB.**

AMERICAN BUFFALO 1975-76
5 oz. amber glass with amber plastic head & ivory colored horns. Holds Wild Country or Deep Woods After Shave. **CMV $10. MB.**

PHEASANT DECANTER 1977
Same bottle as 1972-74 issue only came in Deep Woods or Wild Country and box is smaller than early issue. **CMV $9. MB.**

WILDERNESS CLASSIC 1976-77
6 oz. silver plated over clear glass. Silver plastic head. Came in Sweet Honesty or Deep Woods. **CMV $11. MB.**

WESTERN BOOT 1973-75
5 oz. dark amber glass bottle, silver cap & clamp on spurs. Came in Wild Country or Leather. **CMV $8. MB.**

ALASKAN MOOSE 1974-75
8 oz. amber glass with cream colored plastic antlers. Holds Deep Woods or Wild Country After Shave. **CMV $11. MB.**

TEN-POINT BUCK 1973-74
6 oz. reddish brown glass with reddish brown plastic head & gold antlers. Holds Wild Country or Leather After Shave. **CMV $11. MB.**

DUCK AFTER SHAVE 1971
3 oz. glass bottles with gold caps & ducks painted on sides. Came in Collector's Organizer Set only in Tai Winds & Wild Country After Shave. **CMV $4. each.**

BIG GAME RHINO 1972-73
4 oz. green glass with green plastic head over cap. Came in Spicy or Tai Winds After Shave. **CMV $8. MB.**

BLACKSMITH'S ANVIL 1972-73
4 oz. black glass with silver cap. Came in Deep Woods or Avon Leather After Shave. **CMV $8. MB.**

MALLARD DUCK 1967-68
6 oz. green glass, silver head. Came in Spicy, Tribute, Blue Blazer, Windjammer After Shave. **CMV $13. MB.**

MALLARD-IN-FLIGHT 1974-76
5 oz. amber glass with green plastic head. Holds Wild Country or Tai Winds Cologne or After Shave. **CMV $10. MB.**

AMERICAN EAGLE 1971-72
6" high, dark amber glass with silver eagle head. Holds 5 oz. Oland or Windjammer After Shave. **CMV $10. MB.**

AMERICAN EAGLE 1973-75
Eagle is black glass with dark gold head. **CMV $9. MB.**

CAPTAIN'S CHOICE 1964-65
(Right) 8 oz. green glass with green paper label, gold cap. Came in Spicy & Original After Shave Lotion, Electric Pre-Shave Lotion, Spicy After Shower Cologne for Men & Vigorate After Shave Lotion. **CMV $9.. $15. MB.**

CAPITOL DECANTER 1976-77
4.5 oz. white milk glass with white cap & gold tip. Came in Spicy or Wild Country After Shave. **CMV $8. MB.**

CAPITOL DECANTER 1970-72
5 oz. amber glass or clear glass coated amber, gold cap. Came in Leather & Tribute After Shave. **CMV $10. MB.**

WILD TURKEY 1974-76
6 oz. amber glass with silver & red plastic head. Holds Wild Country or Deep Woods After Shave. **CMV $9. MB.**

QUAIL DECANTER 1973-75
5.5 oz. brown glass, gold cap. Came in Avon Blend 7, Deep Woods or Wild Country After Shave. **CMV $9. MB.**

REVOLUTIONARY CANNON 1975-76
2 oz. bronze spray over glass with plastic cap. Holds Avon Spicy or Avon Blend 7 After Shave. **CMV $8. MB.**

HOMESTEAD DECANTER 1973-74
4 oz. brown glass with gray plastic chimney over cap. Holds Wild Country After Shave or Electric Pre-Shave. **CMV $8. MB.**

WISE CHOICE OWL 1969-70
4 oz. silver top, light amber bottom. Came in Excalibur or Leather After Shave. **CMV $9. MB.**

RADIO 1972-73
5" high dark amber glass with gold cap & paper dial on front. Holds 5 oz. liquid Hair Lotion, Wild Country or Spicy After Shave. **CMV $9. MB.**

MEN'S DECANTERS

KING PIN 1969-70
(Left) 4 oz. 6 1/2" high. White glass & cap, red label. Came in Wild Country & Bravo After Shave. CMV **$8. MB.**

STRIKE DECANTER 1978-79
(Right) 4 oz. white milk glass, white cap. Red painted on AMF designs. Came in Sweet Honesty of Wild Country. CMV **$5. MB.**

BOOT "SILVER TOP" 1965-66
8 oz. amber glass, silver cap with hook on cap. Came in Leather All Purpose Lotion for Men. CMV **$8. MB.**

BOOT "GOLD TOP" 1966-71
8 oz. amber glass with hook on cap. Came in Leather All purpose Cologne for Men. CMV **$7. MB.** Gold top boot with no hook on cap is 1971-72 with Leather Cologne. CMV **$7. MB.**

BOOT SPRAY COLOGNE 1967-70
3 oz. tan plastic coated with black cap. Came in Leather All Purpose Cologne in early issues. CMV **$6. MB. & Leather Cologne Spray in later issues. CMV $5. MB.**

SURE WINNER BASEBALL 1973-74
White ball with dark blue lettering, blue base contains Liquid Hair Trainer. CMV **$6 MB.**

FIRST DOWN 1970
5 oz. brown glass, white plastic base. Came in Wild Country or Sports Rally Bracing Lotion. CMV **$8. MB.**

FIRST DOWN 1973-74
5 oz. brown glass, white base. Came in Deep Woods & Sure Winner Bracing Lotion. CMV **$8. MB**

RAM'S HEAD 1975-76
5 oz. white opal glass on brown plastic base. Holds Wild Country or Avon Blend 7 After Shave. CMV **$7 MB.**

MINUTEMAN 1975-76
4 oz. white opal glass with plastic top. Holds Wild Country or Tai Winds After Shave. CMV **$10. MB.**

OPENING PLAY 1968-69
6 oz. each, 4" high. Gold caps, white plastic face guards. Came in Sports Rally Bracing Lotion, Spicy & Wild Country After Shave. Shiny gold over blue glass was issued one campaign only, on last campaign Open Play was sold. CMV **Shiny gold $25., BO $30. MB. Dull gold over blue glass with blue stripe CMV $12. MB. Dull gold over blue glass, no stripe, CMV $16. MB.**

THEODORE ROOSEVELT 1975-76
(Left) 6 oz. white paint over clear glass. Came in Wild Country or Tai Winds After Shave. CMV **$10. MB.**

THOMAS JEFFERSON 1977-78
(Right) 5 oz. white paint over clear glass. White head cap. Came in Wild Country or Everest After Shave. CMV **$9. MB.**

LONG DRIVE 1973-75
4 oz. brown glass with black cap. Holds Deep Woods After Shave or Electric Pre-Shave Lotion. CMV **$7. MB.**

TEE-OFF DECANTER 1973-75
3 oz. white golf ball on a plastic yellow tee & fits into a green plastic green. Holds Protein Hair Lotion for Men. CMV **$7. MB.**

MARINE BINOCULARS 1973-74
Black over clear glass with gold caps. One side holds 4 oz. Tai Winds or Tribute Cologne, other side holds 4 oz. Tai Winds or Tribute After Shave. CMV **$12. MB**

PASS PLAY 1973-75
5 oz. blue glass with white soft plastic top over cap. Came in Sure Winner Bracing Lotion or Wild Country After shave. CMV **$11. MB.**

PERFECT DRIVE 1975-76
4 oz. green glass with white plastic top over cap. Holds Avon Spicy After Shave or Avon Protein Hair/Scalp Conditioner. CMV **$11. MB.**

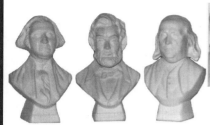

PRESIDENT WASHINGTON 1974-76
6 oz. white spray over clear glass, white plastic head. Holds Wild Country or Tai Winds After Shave. 1976 came in Deep Woods or Tai Winds After Shave. **CMV $8. MB.**

PRESIDENT LINCOLN 1973
6 oz. white spray over clear glass, white plastic head. Holds Wild Country or Tai Winds After Shave. **CMV $12. MB.**

BENJAMIN FRANKLIN 1974-76
6 oz. white spray over clear glass, white plastic head. Holds Wild Country or Tai Winds After Shave. **CMV $8. MB.**

PRESIDENT LINCOLN BRONZE 1979
6 oz. bronze tone over clear glass. Dated 1979 on bottom. Also came no date on bottom. Holds Deep Woods or Everest After Shave. **CMV $11 MB.**

PRESIDENT WASHINGTON BRONZE 1979
6 oz. bronze tone over clear glass. Dated 1979 on bottom. Holds Wild Country or Tai Winds After Shave. **CMV $11 MB.**

CHESS PIECE "BROWN" (THE ORIGINAL SET)
3 oz. dark amber glass with silver toned tops.
SMART MOVE 1971-72
Came in Tribune & Oland Cologne. **CMV $8. MB.**
Smart move came in Wild Country After Shave or Protein Hair/Scalp Conditioner. **CMV $5. MB.**
THE KING 1972-73
Came in Tai Winds or Oland After Shave. **CMV $8. MB.**
THE KING 1973-78
The King came in Wild Country or Oland. **CMV $5. MB.**
THE QUEEN 1973-74
Came in Tai Winds or Oland After Shave. **CMV $7. MB.**
THE QUEEN 1974-78
The Queen came in Wild Country or Deep Woods After Shave. **CMV $5. MB.**
THE ROOK 1973-74
Came in Oland & Spicy After Shave. **CMV $7. MB.**
THE ROOK 1974-78
The rook came in Wild Country, Avon Blend 7 or Avon Protein Hair Lotion for Men. **CMV $5. MB.**
THE BISHOP 1974-78
Came in Wild Country, Avon Blend 7 or Avon Protein Hair Lotion for Men. **CMV $5. MB.**
THE PAWN 1974-78
Came in Wild Country, Oland or Electric Pre-Shave Lotion. **CMV $8. MB.**
(Pieces needed for one side are 2 Smart Moves, 1 King, 1 Queen, 2 Rooks, 2 Bishops, 8 Pawns.) Early issues Chess Pieces do not have to have name on label.

CHESS PIECE DECANTER (THE OPPOSING SET)
3 oz. silver over clear or amber glass with amber plastic tips. **CMV $5. MB, Pawns CMV $8. MB. Silver over clear are hard to find.**
SMART MOVE II 1975-78
Came in Wild Country After Shave, Avon Protein Hair Lotion or Avon Protein Hair/Scalp Conditioner for Men.
THE KING II 1975-78
Came in Avon Spicy After Shave or Avon Protein Hair Lotion.
THE QUEEN II 1975-78
Came in Avon Spicy After Shave or Avon Protein Hair/Scalp Conditioner.
THE ROOK II 1975-78
Came in Wild Country After Shave or Protein Hair Lotion for Men.
THE BISHOP II 1975-78
Came in Avon Spicy After Shave or Avon Protein Hair Lotion for Men. **CMV $5. MB.**
THE PAWN II 1975-78
Came in Avon Spicy After Shave or Avon Protein Hair/Scalp Conditioner for Men.
(Pieces needed for one side are 2 Smart Moves, 1 King, 1 Queen, 2 Rooks, 2 Bishops, 8 Pawns.)

WASHINGTON BOTTLE 1970-72
5 1/2" high, 4 oz. bottle with gold eagle cap. Holds Spicy or Tribute After Shave. **CMV $6. MB..**

LINCOLN BOTTLE 1971-72
5 1/2" high, 4 oz. bottle with gold eagle cap. Holds Wild Country or Leather After Shave. **CMV $6. MB.**

RAINBOW TROUT 1973-74
(Left) Plastic head over cap. Holds Deep Woods or Tai Winds. **CMV $10. MB.**
SEA TROPHY 1972
(Right) 5.5 oz. lt. blue with plastic blue head over cap. Came in Wild Country or Windjammer After Shave. **CMV $12. MB.**

AVON CALLING '1905 DECANTER 1973
7 oz. brown glass with brown plastic top, has gold bell & black plastic receiver. Holds 7 oz. After Shave and .75 oz. Talc. Came in Wild Country or Avon Spicy. **CMV $14. MB.**

AVON CALLING FOR MEN 1969-70
8 1/2" high, 6 oz. gold paint over clear glass, gold cap, black mouth piece, black plastic ear piece. Holds 1 1/4 oz. Talc. Came in Wild Country and Leather Cologne. **CMV $14. MB.**

WESTERN SADDLE 1971-72
5 oz. brown glass with brown cap, sets on beige fence. Came in Wild Country or Avon Leather After Shave. **CMV $12. MB.**

GOOD SHOT 1976-80
(Left) 2 oz. plastic bottle, gold cap. Red bottle in Wild Country or Brisk Spice After Shave and yellow bottle in Deep Woods or Cool Sage After Shave. **CMV $4. MB. Add $5. for cap on wrong end.**

WILD WEST" BULLET" 1977-78
(Right) 1.5 oz. bronze plated over clear glass. Silver top. Wild Country or Everest. **CMV $5. MB.**

GET THE MESSAGE DECANTER 1978-79
(Left) 3 oz. black glass with silver & black plastic top. Came in Clint or Sweet Honesty. **CMV $8. MB.**

NO CAUSE FOR ALARM DECANTER 1979-80
(Right) 4 oz. silver plated over clear glass. Silver plastic top. Came in Deep Woods, or Tai Winds. **CMV $8 MB.**

MIXED DOUBLES TENNIS BALL 1977-78
(Left) 3 oz. light green flock over clear glass. Green cap base. Came in Sweet Honesty Body Splash or Avon Spicy. **CMV $6. MB.**

SURE CATCH 1977
(Right) 1 oz. white milk glass, with red cap, yellow tassel, black eyes. Came in Spicy or Wild Country. **CMV $6. MB.**

FIRM GRIP 1977-78
(Left) 1.5 oz. silver plated clear glass. Came in Wild Country or Everest. **CMV $7. MB.**

WEATHER VANE 1977-78
(Right) 4 oz. red painted over clear glass. Silver top with black horse weather vane. Came in Wild Country or Deep Woods. **CMV $7. MB.**

ARCTIC KING 1976-79
(Left) 5 oz. blue glass bottle, silver bear cap. Came in Everest only. **CMV $7. MB.**

BOLD EAGLE 1976-78
(Right) 3 oz. gold plated over clear glass, gold top. Came in Tai Winds or Wild Country. **CMV $8. MB.**

WHALE ORGANIZER BOTTLES 1973
3 oz. ivory milk glass with dark blue design. Holds After Shave & Cologne in Deep Woods or Avon Blend7. Sold only in Whale Organizer. **CMV $7. each.**

BLOOD HOUND PIPE 1976
5 oz. lt. tan paint over clear glass, brown & silver cap. Came in Wild Country or Deep Woods After Shave. **CMV $10. MB.**

CHIEF PONTIAC CAR ORNAMENT CLASSIC 1976
4 oz. black ribbed glass with silver Indian. Came in Tai Winds or Deep Woods After Shave. **CMV $11. MB.**

NBA DECANTER 1977-80
(Left) Came with your choice of individual NBA team labels. Came in Wild Country or Sure Winner Bracing Lotion. 6 oz. dark amber glass. Silver top. **CMV $8. MB.**

NFL DECANTER 1976-77
(Right) Came with your choice of NFL team emblem out of 28 member clubs of the National Football League. Came in Wild Country or Sure Winner Bracing Lotion. 6 oz. black glass with silver top. **CMV $8. MB.**

INDIAN CHIEFTAIN 1972-75
(Left) 4 oz. brown glass with gold cap. Came in Avon Spicy After Shave or Avon Protein Hair Lotion for Men. **CMV $7. MB.**

INDIAN TEPEE DECANTER 1974-75
(Right) 4 oz. amber glass with brown plastic cap. Holds Wild Country or Avon Spicy. **CMV $6. MB.**

MOTOCROSS HELMET 1976-78
6 oz. white plastic bottle with stick on decals, blue plastic face guard cap. Came in Wild Country or Avon Protein Hair Lotion for Men. **CMV $8. MB.**

REMEMBER WHEN GAS PUMP 1976-77
(Left) 4 oz. red painted over clear glass. Red & white plastic cap. Came in Deep Woods or Wild Country. **CMV $15.. MB.**

ONE GOOD TURN "SCREWDRIVER" 1976
(Right) 4 oz. clear glass, silver cap. Came in Tai Winds or Avon Spicy. **CMV $7. MB.**

SUPER SLEUTH MAGNIFIER 1979
10" long. Bottom is dark amber glass and top is real magnifying glass. Came in Wild Country or Everest After Shave. **CMV $9. MB.**

COUNTRY LANTERN 1979
4 oz. clear glass painted red. Red wire handle. Holds Wild country or Deep Woods After Shave. **CMV $8. MB.**

GENTLEMEN'S TALC 1979
3.75 oz. green can. Holds Clint, Trazarra or Wild Country Talc. **CMV $2. mint, no box.**

STATUE OF LIBERTY DECANTER 1986
7 1/2" high. Dark amber glass base. Gold top. Holds men's or women's fragrance. **CMV $10. MB.**

SCIMITAR 1968-69
10' long, 6 oz. gold paint with red windows over clear glass, gold cap. Came in Tribune & Windjammer After Shave Lotion. **CMV $25. MB.**

BIG BOLT 1976-77
(Left) 2 oz. silver plated over clear glass. Silver cap. Came in Deep Woods or Wild Country. **CMV $4. MB.**

DURACELL SUPER CHARGE 1976-78
(Center) 1 1/2 oz. black glass with bronze & silver cap. Came in Spicy or Everest. **CMV $4. MB.**

RIGHT CONNECTION "FUSE" 1977
(Right) 1.5 oz. clear glass, with gold & brown cap. Came in Oland or Wild Country. **CMV $4. MB.**

LOVER BOY AFTER SHAVE 1980
(Right) 3 oz. clear glass. Red letters and cap. Red box, **CMV $3. MB.**

FESTIVE MINI COLOGNE 1994
.5 oz. bottle of men's Cologne in 7 different fragrances. Special short issue Xmas box. **CMV $1. .MB.**

LITTLE BROWN JUG DECANTER 1978-79
Brown glass, tan plastic cap. Beige painted sides. Holds 2 oz. Deep Woods or Tai Winds After Shave. **CMV $3. MB.**

QUAKER STATE POWERED HAND CLEANER 1978-79
12 oz. cardboard sides and gold plastic top and bottom. Holds heavy duty powdered hand cleaner. **CMV $3. MB.**

DAD'S PRIDE & JOY PICTURE FRAME 1982-83
6 1/2" long clear glass. Holds pictures. **CMV $8. MB.**

TRIBUTE SILVER WARRIOR 1967
6" high, 6 oz. silver & blue paint over clear glass, silver cap. Came in Tribute After Shave. **CMV $23. MB, All blue glass $30 mint.**
TRIBUTE RIBBED WARRIOR 1971-73
6" high, 6 oz. clear ribbed glass, silver cap. Came in Tribute Cologne. **CMV $11. MB.**
TRIBUTE RIBBED WARRIOR 1968-71
6" high, 6 oz. frosted glass, silver cap. Came in Tribute Cologne. **CMV $11. MB.**

HEART TO HEART COLOGNE SPLASH 1992
.5 oz. heart embossed bottles of ladies and mens colognes. Ladies, red cap & box. Mens, black cap and red box. Half heart on each box. Short issue. **CMV $2. MB ea.**

ROOKIE COLOGNE FOR BOYS 1980-81
2.5 oz. clear glass. Red cap & label. **CMV $2. MB.**
AVON'S FINEST DECANTER 1980-81
2 oz. dark amber glass. Gold tone cap. Comes in Clint or Trazarra cologne. **CMV $3. MB.**
BOOTS 'N SADDLE DECANTER 1980-81
7 1/2" high, 7 oz. dark amber glass. Silver label, brown leather look wrap around label. Choice of Wild Country or Weekend After Shave. **CMV $4. MB.**

WEATHER-OR-NOT 1969-71
5 oz. dark amber glass, regular issue on left, gold cap. Came in Leather & Oland, Tribute, Wild Country & Spicy After Shave. **There are 5 different Thermometers starting with 20 below, 10 below, 0, 10 above, & 20 above. All same price. CMV $13. MB.**
SUPER SHIFT 1978
4 oz. black glass bottle with silver & black shifter cap. Came in Sure Winner Bracing Lotion or Everest Cologne. 7" high. **CMV $7. MB.**

VIKING HORN 1966
7 oz. dark amber glass with gold cap & decoration. Came in Spicy, Blue Blazer & Original After Shave. **CMV $20. MB.**

DESK CADDY 1977-80
Brown cork desk caddy holder, silver top made in Spain. Holds 4 oz. clear glass bottle of Clint cologne, red letters, silver cap or Wild Country. **CMV $7. MB.**

DEFENDER CANNON 1966
6 oz. 9 1/2" long, amber glass, brown plastic stand, gold cap, & gold center band, small paper label. Came in Leather, Island Lime & Tribute After Shave. **CMV $15 bottle & stand mint, $22. MB.**

GAVEL 1967-68
5 oz. dark amber glass with brown plastic handle. 8" long. Came in Island Lime, Original, & Spicy. **CMV $14. BO, $20. MB.**

FATHERS DAY SPORTS COLOGNE 1991

.(Right) 5 oz. cologne in special short issue boxes. Choice of Tennis, Golf, Soccer, Bowling, Baseball or Basketball boxes. **CMV $2. ea. MB.**

POT BELLY STOVE 1970-71

(Above rightr) 5" high, 5 oz. black glass bottle with black cap. Came in Bravo or Excalibur After shave. **CMV $10. MB.**

FIRST CLASS MALE 1970-71

(Left) 4 1/2" high, 4 oz. blue glass with red cap. Came in Bravo or Wild Country after Shave or Liquid Hair Lotion. **CMV $8. MB.**

DAYLIGHT SHAVING TIME 1968-70

6 oz. gold paint over clear glass. Came in Spicy, Wild Country, Windjammer, Bravo & Leather After Shave. **CMV $14. MB.**

WESTERN CHOICE (STEER HORNS) 1967

Brown plastic base with red center, Holds 2-3 bottles with silver caps. Came in Wild Country & Leather After Shave. **CMV $15. BO. mint. $25. MB.**

PAID STAMP 1970-71

5" high, dark amber glass with black cap & red rubber paid stamp on bottom. Holds 4 oz. of Spicy or Windjammer After Shave. **CMV $10. MB.**

SWINGER GOLF BAG 1969-71

5 oz. black glass, red & silver clubs. Came in Wild Country & Bravo After Shave. **CMV $11. MB.**

BAY RUM KEG 1965-67

(Right) 6 oz. brown & silver paint over clear glass bottle. **CMV $15. BO, $22. MB.**

DECISIONS 1965

8 oz. red painted labels, black caps with red centers that say Panic Buttons. Came in Spicy After shave Lotion. **CMV $22. MB, $15. BO.**

CASEY'S LANTERN 1966-67

10 oz. gold paint on clear glass bottle gold caps. Came in Leather After Shave in red window & Island Lime in green window. **CMV amber & green $55. MB, Red $45 MB, BO $10 less each mint.**

INKWELL 1969-70

(Right) 6 oz. amber with purple tint, black cap with gold or silver pen. Came in Windjammer & Spicy After Shave. **CMV $12. MB.** (Left) Factory test. No value established.

TOWN PUMP 1968-69

8" high black glass bottle with gold cap & plastic shoe horn. Holds 6 oz. of Leather, Windjammer, Wild Country. **CMV $13. MB.**

CLOSE HARMONY (BARBER BOTTLE) 1963

8 oz. white glass bottle, gold painted letter & neck band. <u>White cap with or without tip.</u> Came in Spicy & Original After Shave, Vigorate & After Shower Cologne. **CMV $25 MB.**

DOLLARS 'N SCENTS 1966-67
8 oz. white glass bottle with green dollar painted on silver cap. Came in Spicy After Shave. Red rubber band around bottle. **CMV $20. MB, $12.. BO. mint.**

TOP DOLLAR SOAP ON A ROPE 1966-67
White 1886 dollar soap. **CMV $30 MB.**

ALPINE FLASK 1966-67
8 oz. 8 3/4" high, brown glass, gold cap & neck chain. Came in Spicy, Original, Blue Blazer & Leather After Shave. **CMV $30. MB, $25. BO. mint.**

JUST A TWIST 1977-78
2 oz. silver plated over clear glass. Came in Sweet Honesty or Deep Woods. **CMV $6. MB.**

HARD HAT 1977-78
4 oz. yellow paint over clear glass. Yellow plastic base. Came with seven decals. Came in Everest or Deep Woods. **CMV $6. MB.**

AVON CLASSICS 1969
6 oz. each Leather in clear & dark amber glass. Wild Country in light & dark amber glass & clear glass. Tribute After Shave in clear glass, light & dark amber glass. All bottle caps & labels must match color, gold or silver. **CMV $8. MB.**

FIRST EDITION 1967-68
6 oz. gold cap. Came in Bay Rum, Wild Country & Leather After Shave. **CMV $9. MB.**

GENTLEMAN'S REGIMENT COLLECTION 1982-83
Talc in beige tin can, No box, **CMV $2.**

SHAVING MUG AND SOAP
Beige in color glass mug and matching bar of soap. **CMV $15. MB.**

SHAVING BRUSH
Beige plastic brush. **CMV $3. MB.**

AFTER SHAVE DECANTER
4.5 oz. clear glass painted beige. Gold cap. Fragrance choice was Wild Country or Black Suede. **CMV $6. MB.**

NO PARKING FIRE PLUG 1975-76
(Left) 6 oz. red painted glass with red cap. Came in Wild Country After Shave or Electric Pre-Shave. **CMV $8. MB.**

FIRE ALARM BOX 1975-76
(Right) 4 oz. red painted glass with black cap. Came in Avon Spicy After Shave, Avon Protein Hair Lotion or Electric Pre-Shave. **CMV $7. MB.**

ROYAL ORB 1965-66
8 oz. round bottle, gold cap, red felt around neck. Came in Spicy & Original After Shave. Red letters painted on bottle common issue. **CMV $20. BO. mint, $27. MB. White letter Orb $75.**

KING OF HEARTS DECANTER 1990
Plain .9 oz. bottle of after shave in King of Hearts card box. **CMV $3. MB.**

ANGLER 1970
5 oz., 4 1/2" high blue glass with silver reel cap & trim. Came in Windjammer & Wild Country After Shave. **CMV $12. MB.**

EIGHT BALL DECANTER 1973
3 oz. black glass with black cap & white 8. Came in Spicy After Shave, Avon Protein Lotion for Men, or Electric Pre-Shave Lotion. **CMV $7. MB.**

BARBER POLE 1974-75
3 oz. white milk glass with red & blue paper striped label & white plastic cap. Holds Avon Protein Hair/Scalp Conditioner or Wild Country After shave. **CMV $7. MB.**
BARBER SHOP BRUSH 1976
1.5 oz. brown glass with black & white plastic brush cap. Came in Tai Winds or Wild Country Cologne. **CMV $7. MB.**

BUFFALO NICKEL 1971-72
5 oz. plated over clear glass with matching cap. Came in Spicy, Wild Country After Shave or Liquid Hair Lotion. **CMV $10. MB.**
INDIAN HEAD PENNY 1970-72
4 oz. 4" high. Bronze paint & cap over clear glass. Came in Bravo, Tribute, Excalibur After shave. **CMV $10. MB.**

AFTER SHAVE ON TAP 1974-75
(Left) 5 oz. dark amber glass with gold plastic spigot cap. Holds Wild Country or Oland After Shave. **CMV $7. MB.**
AFTER SHAVE ON TAP 1976
5 oz. amber glass, red spigot cap. Holds Spicy or Wild Country. **CMV $7. MB.**
TRIPLE CROWN 1974-76
(Right) 4 oz. brown glass with red plastic cap. Holds Spicy After Shave or Avon Protein Hair/Scalp Conditioner. **CMV $6. MB.**

LIBERTY DOLLAR 1970-72
(Left) 6 oz. silver paint over clear glass, silver cap with eagle. 6" high. Came in Oland, and Tribute After Shave. **CMV $10. MB Same bottle only gold, Rare $40. MB.**
TWENTY DOLLAR GOLD PIECE 1971-72
(Right) 6 oz. gold paint over clear glass. Gold cap. Came in Windjammer After Shave & Electric Pre-Shave Lotion. **CMV $10. MB.**

IT'S A BLAST 1970-71
(Left) 5 oz. 8 1/2" high, gold paint over clear glass, black rubber horn on cap. Came in Oland or Windjammer After Shave. **CMV $13. MB.**
MAN'S WORLD 1969-70
(Right) Brown plastic stand holds 6 oz. globe. Gold paint over clear glass, gold cap. Came in Bravo, Windjammer & Tribute After Shave. 4" high. **CMV $14. MB.**

ELECTRIC GUITAR DECANTER 1974-75
6 oz. brown glass with silver plastic handle. Came in Avon Sure Winner Bracing Lotion or Wild Country After Shave. **CMV $12. MB.**
TOTEM POLE DECANTER 1975
6 oz. dark amber glass with plastic cap. Holds Wild Country, Deep Woods or Avon Spicy After Shave. **CMV $10. MB.**

LIBERTY BELL 1971-72
(Left) 5 oz. light amber glass coated over clear glass, brown cap. Came in Tribute or Oland After Shave or Cologne. **CMV $10. MB.**
LIBERTY BELL 1976
(Right) 5 oz. sprayed bronze with bronze cap. Came in Oland or Deep Woods After Shave. **CMV $9. MB.**

SMOOTH GOING OIL CAN 1978
1.5 silver plated over clear glass. Came in Deep Woods or Everest After Shave. **CMV $6. MB.**

BREAKER 19 1977-79
(Left) 2 oz. black glass with black & silver plastic cap. Wild Country or Sweet Honesty. **CMV $6. MB.**
COLEMAN LANTERN 1977-79
(Right) 5 oz. green painted over clear glass. Green cap, silver bail handle. Came in Wild Country or Deep Woods. **CMV $10. MB.**

CAPTAINS LANTERN 1864 1976-77
(Left) 7 oz. black glass with black plastic cap & gold ring. Came in Wild Country or Oland After Shave. **CMV $8. MB.**
WHALE OIL LANTERN 1974-75
(Right) 5 oz. green glass with silver toned plastic top & base. Holds Wild Country, Oland or Tai Winds. **CMV $8. MB.**

AUTO LANTERN DECANTER 1973
Shiny gold with amber windows. Left bottle holds 5 oz. Oland or Deep Woods After Shave. Right base holds 1.25 oz. Oland or Deep Woods Talc. **CMV $15. MB.**

SUPER SHAVER 1973
4 oz. blue glass with gray plastic top. Holds Sure Winner Bracing Lotion or Avon spicy After Shave. **CMV $7 MB.**
BOTTLED BY AVON 1973
(Right) 5 oz. clear glass with silver lift off cap, holds Oland or Windjammer After Shave. **CMV $7 MB.**

JUKE BOX 1977-78
4.5 oz. amber glass, silver top. Came in Sweet Honesty or Wild Country. Came with decals. **CMV $7. MB.**
AVON ON THE AIR 1975-76
3 oz. black glass with silver plastic stand. Holds Wild Country, Deep Woods or Spicy After Shave. **CMV $7. MB.**

STOP! DECANTER 1975
5 oz. red plastic with white plastic base. Holds Wild Country After Shave or Sweet Honesty After Bath Freshener. **CMV $4. no box.**
STOP 'N GO 1974
4 oz. green glass with green cap. Holds Wild Country or Avon Spicy After Shave. **CMV $7 MB.**

"HAMMER" ON THE MARK DECANTER 1978
8 1/2" long dark amber glass with silver top holds 2.5 oz. of everest or Wild Country After Shave. **CMV $7. MB.**
ON THE LEVEL DECANTER 1978
3 oz. silver coated over clear glass holds Everest or Deep Woods After Shave. **CMV $6. MB.**

PIANO 1972
(Left) 4" high, 4 oz. dark amber glass piano with white music stack cap. Holds Tai Winds or Tribute After Shave Lotion. **CMV $10. MB.**
FIELDER'S CHOICE 1971-72
(Right) 5 oz. dark amber glass, black cap. Came in Sports Rally Bracing Lotion, Liquid Hair Trainer, or Wild Country After Shave. **CMV $10. MB.**

STAR SIGNS DECANTER 1975
4 oz. black glass with gold cap. Came in Sweet Honesty Cologne or Wild Country After Shave. Came blank with choice of one of 12 Zodiac signs sticker to apply. **CMV $5 MB each.**
SPARK PLUG DECANTER 1975
1.5 oz. white milk glass with gray cap. Holds Wild Country, Tai Winds or Avon Spicy After Shave. **CMV $5 MB.**

#1 DAD DECANTER GIFT BOX 1989
.9 oz. bottle holds after shave in special box. **CMV $3. MB.**

FUTURA 1969
5 oz., 7 1/2" high, silver paint over clear glass, silver cap. Came in Excalibur & Wild country Cologne. **CMV $12.50 MB**

WORLD'S GREATEST DAD DECANTER 1971
4 oz. clear glass, red cap. Came in spicy or tribute After Shave or Electric Pre-Shave Lotion. **CMV $4 MB.**

DUTCH BOY HEAVY DUTY POWDER HAND CLEANER 1979-80
12 oz. blue and white paper sides. Yellow plastic top, gray bottom. No box. **CMV $3. mint.**

BATH BREW DECANTER 1979-80
4 oz. dark amber glass, gold cap. Brown box. Holds Wild Country Bubble Bath. **CMV $4. MB.**

WEEKEND DECISION MAKER DECANTER 1978-79
3 oz. green and white painted over clear glass. Green top. Holds Wild Country or Tai Winds After Shave. **CMV $6. MB**

THERMOS PLAID BRAND DECANTER 1978-79
3 oz. white milk glass. Red cap and plaid design. Holds Wild Country After Shave or Sweet Honesty Body Splash. **CMV $4. MB**

DOMINO DECANTER 1978-79
1.5 oz. black glass with white spots. Holds Everest or Tai Winds After Shave. **CMV $4. MB**

HANKERCHIEF SAVINGS BANK 1988
Ben Franklin 4 1/2" high metal bank with white hankerchief inside. **CMV $4. MB.**

ON TAP MUG DECANTER 1979
4 oz. clear glass with white plastic top. Holds Wild Country or Deep Woods After Shave. **CMV $7. MB.**

PAUL REVERE BELL DECANTER 1979
4 oz. clear glass painted gold. Brown and silver handle. 1979 stamped in bottom. Holds Clint After Shave or sweet Honesty Body Splash. **CMV $8. MB.**

U.S. OLYMPIC TEAM DECANTER 1996
5 oz. frosted glass, gold cap. Holds triumph cologne. **CMV $20. MB**

TIME FOR DAD MINI COLOGNE 1990
.33 oz. bottle with Avon clock on face. Short issue. **CMV $3. MB.**

BIG WHISTLE DECANTER 1972
4 oz. blue glass with silver cap. Came in Tai Winds or Spicy After Shave or Electric Pre-Shave Lotion. **CMV $8. MB.**

OPENING PLAY DECANTER 1995
(Right) Dated 1995, 6 oz. clear glass, blue cap & face guard. Holds Triumph cologne. **CMV.$12. MB.**

JOAN WALSH ANGLUND FIGURINES 1987
Choice of Christmas Wishes, Boy or The Night Before, Girl. Hand painted porcelain. 4" high. **CMV $15 ea. MB.**

FOREST FRIENDS FIGURINES 1988
2" high land painted. Choice of Easter Fun, Sunday Best and Springtime Stroll. **CMV $5 ea. MB.**

BEARY CUTE BEAR BANK 1990
6" high ceramic bank. **CMV $15 MB.**

HUMMINGBIRD PORCELAIN FIGURINE 1989
7 1/2" high hand painted porcelain. **CMV $60. MB.**

POINSETTIA SEASONS IN BLOOM 1986
(Right) Red porcelain flower. **CMV $28. MB.**
MAGNOLIA SEASONS IN BLOOM 1986
(Left) Yellow, white and green porcelain flower. Both have Avon label. **CMV $28. MB.**

MOTHER'S LOVE BUNNY FIGURINE 1990
Hand painted porcelain. Baby 1 1/4" high, Mother 2 1/2" high. **CMV $10. set MB.**

FOREST FRIENDS MINI FIGURINES 1987
Choice of Story Time, Sleigh Ride, or All Tucked In. 2" high by 2 1/4" wide ea. **CMV $5 ea.**

BEAR COOKIE JAR 1985
Brown ceramic cookie jar. **CMV $25.**
BABY BEAR BANK 1986
Ceramic blue & tan bank with small green & white bear blanket. Comes with iron on letters. **CMV $7. MB.**

PANDA SWEETHEART FIGURINE 1990
Boy and girl hand painted porcelain. 2 1/2" high. **CMV $10. set MB.**

IRIS FLOWER FIGURINE 1987
8" long porcelain Iris. Marked Avon. **CMV $35. MB.**

PEACE ROSE FIGURINE 1987
7" long porcelain yellow rose. Marked Avon. **CMV $35 MB.**

HOLIDAY HUGS BEAR FIGURINE SET 1990
Papa Bear and Mama Bear with baby. Both 2 5/8" high and dated on bottom. **CMV $10. MB.**

FIGURINES, GLASS, PORCELAIN & CERAMIC - MEN'S / WOMEN'S

GOD BLESS MY DOLLY FIGURINE 1990
3" high porcelain in choice of Black or White girl. **CMV $15. ea. MB.**

CHRISTMAS TREE POMANDER 1986
9" high green ceramic tree. Comes with wax chips. **CMV $17. MB.**

IMAGES OF HOLLYWOOD 1983-84 - SCARLETT O'HARA
1st in a series of porcelain figurine, 4 1/2" high. Vivian Leigh as Scarlett O'Hara. **CMV $35. MB.**
RHETT BUTLER FIGURINE 1984-85
Clark Gable figurine, 5 3/4" high. **CMV $40 MB.**

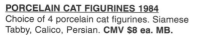

PORCELAIN CAT FIGURINES 1984
Choice of 4 porcelain cat figurines. Siamese Tabby, Calico, Persian. **CMV $8 ea. MB.**

MOTHERS DAY FIGURINE "A MOTHERS LOVE" 1995
Porcelain figurine 5 1/2" high, 5 1/4" long. dated on bottom. **CMV $20. MB.**

BUNNY MATES SALT & PEPPER SHAKERS 1983
Bunny box holds two small ceramic white rabbit shakers. **CMV $12. MB.**
CLAUS & COMPANY SANTA'S HELPERS SALT & PEPPER SHAKERS 1983
Red box holds two small green and red ceramic boy and girl salt & pepper shakers. 2 1/2" high. **CMV $10 MB.**

FRED ASTAIRE FIGURINE 1984
6 3/4" high porcelain. 3rd in series. **CMV $35. MB.**
GINGER ROGERS FIGURINE 1984
4th in series. 6" high porcelain. **CMV $35. MB**

SUMMER FUN FIGURINE 1986
(Right) 3 1/2" wide porcelain figurine by Jessie Wilcox Smith. **CMV $27. MB.**
GIVING THANKS FIGURINE 1986
(Left) 3 1/4" wide porcelain figurine by Jessie Wilcox Smith. **CMV $27. MB.**

JUDY GARLAND FIGURINE 1985
5 1/2" high porcelain. **CMV $35. MB.**
CHRISTMAS FIGURINE 1984
6 3/8"" high porcelain. Dated Christmas 1984. **CMV $40. MB.**

JOAN WALSH ANGLUND FIGURINE COLLECTION 1986-87
(Top) 3 1/2" high porcelain figurines is "School Days" & "My ABCs". 1986 "Magic Slippers" & "Home Run" is 3 3/4" high. **CMV $12. ea. MB.**
JESSIE WILCOX SMITH FIGURINES 1986
(Bottom) 3 1/2" wide porcelain figurines choice of "Be My Valentine", "Springtime", & "Helping Mom".**CMV $28. ea. MB.**

355

MOTHERS DAY FIGURINE "LITTLE THINGS" 1983-84

(Left) 3 3/4" high hand painted porcelain boy figurine. **CMV $18. MB.**

MOTHERS DAY FIGURINE "CHERISHED MOMENTS" 1983-84

(Right) 4" high hand painted porcelain girl figurine. **CMV $18. MB.**

JOY TO THE WORLD MUSICAL FIGURINE 1985

(Left to Right) Small porcelain figurine, music base. **CMV $20. MB.**

EASTER CHARM FIGURINE 1985

4" high porcelain. Dated Easter 1985. **CMV $15. MB.**

MOTHERS TOUCH FIGURINE 1984

Shiny glaze porcelain. Mother's Day figurine. **CMV $35. MB.**

KEEPING THE CHRISTMAS TRADITION 1982

Hand painted porcelain figurine dated 1982. 2nd in Christmas Memories Series. **CMV $49. MB.**

SHARING THE CHRISTMAS SPIRIT FIGURINE 1981

First in a series of Christmas figurines from Avon. Dated 1981. 6" high. **CMV $45. MB.**

WE WISH YOU A MERRY CHRISTMAS FIGURINE 1986

(Left) 3 1/2" wide porcelain figurine with music box base. **CMV $18. MB.**

A WINTER SNOW FIGURINE

(Right) Porcelain figurine by Jessie Wilcox Smith. **CMV $27. MB.**

McCONNELLS CORNER TOWN SHOPPERS 1982

(Right) 3" high ceramic figurine. Bottom says Christmas, 1982. **CMV $10. MB.**

SUMMER BRIDE FIGURINE 1986

6" high white porcelain. **CMV $25. MB.**

CARDINAL FIGURINE 1985

Red porcelain bird.

BLUEBIRD FIGURINE 1986

Blue, orange & white porcelain bird . On both birds **CMV $32. ea. MB.**

MY PET FIGURINE 1973

(Left) Green & brown, white kitten, ceramic figurine. 1973 embossed in ceramic & printed on box. **CMV $40. MB.**

JENNIFER FIGURINE 1973

(Right) Pastel turquoise dress & hat figurine. 1973 embossed in ceramic & printed on box. Some came with flowers in center of hat & some with flowers on the right side of hat. **CMV $45. Both issued from Springdale, Ohio branch only.**

MRS. CLAUS SUGAR BOWL & CREAMER 1983-84

Red, white and green ceramic sugar bowl & creamer. **CMV $13. ea. MB.**

BEST FRIENDS PORCELAIN FIGURINE 1981

(Left) 6" high boy figurine. Dated 1981. **CMV $19. MB.** 1 made in Taiwan and 1 in Japan.

MOTHER'S LOVE PORCELAIN FIGURINE 1981

(Center) 5 1/2" high girl figurine holding a baby. Bottom tan painted label is dated 1981. Made in Taiwan sticker is tan color. **CMV $19. MB.**

MOTHER'S LOVE FIGURINE ADVANCED 1981

(Right) Factory sample. About 75 were given by Avon Products Inc. to Avon collectors at the 10th Annual National Association of Avon Collectors Convention in Long Beach, California. These factory samples do not have Avon label on bottom & is 1/4" higher. Made in Taiwan, label is green. Rare. Came in plain box. **CMV $100. Mint.**

WISHFUL THOUGHTS 1982-83
5 1/2" high porcelain figurine. Blue & white.
CMV $15. MB.

MOTHER'S LOVE PORCELAIN FIGURINE TEST PRODUCTS 1981
24 were given to Avon collectors at the 10th Annual National Association of Avon Collectors Convention on the Queen Mary Ship June 1981. It is not in the regular issue box & figurine is not marked on bottom. Came with letter from Avon as very rare. **CMV $150 with letter & plain box.**

CHRISTMAS PORCELAIN FIGURINE 1983
5 1/2" high hand painted porcelain figurine. Called **"Enjoying the Night Before Christmas."** Dated Christmas 1983. **CMV $45 MB.**

FRIENDS FOR KEEPS FIGURINE 1991
3 1/4" high porcelain. **Tender Memories series.** Black or white child & pup. **CMV $15. ea. MB.**

PURR-FECT LOVE FIGURINES 1991
Tender Memories Collection Black or White child porcelain figurines with kittens. 3 1/4" high. **CMV $15. ea. MB.**

CIRCUS BEAR COLLECTION FIGURINES 1993
4 different bisque porcelain figurines. **PIERRE THE RING MASTER** 4 1/2" high. **BETTINA THE BALLERINA** 51/4" high. **MARCELLO THE MAGICIAN** 4 1/4" high. **ULYSSES THE UNICYCLIST** 41/4" high. **CMV $20. ea. MB.**

LITTLE MOMENTS FIGURINE 1998
Precious Moments by Enesco made only for avon. 4" high bisque porcelain girl. Cup says #1 Mom. **CMV $20. MB.**

FLOWERS FOR A KISS FIGURINE 1993
1st in series of **"Carousel Wonderland Miniatures Collection"**. Each 3" high porcelain figurine is signed by artist Kathy Jeffers. Squirrels riding a rabbit. **CMV $10. MB.**

WAITING FOR OUR TURN FIGURINE 1993
2nd in series of 4 **"Carousel Wonderland Miniatures Collection"**. 3 3/4" high. **CMV $10. MB.**

BEST BUDDIES "SQUIRRELS CLOWNING AROUND" FIGURINES 1992
4th & last in series. Gray & brown porcelain squirrels. 2 3/4" high. **CMV $10 set. MB.**

BEST BUDDIES "KITTENS SHARING" 1992
2 1/2" high pair of porcelain kitten figurines. 1st is series. 4 sets total. **CMV $10. set MB.**

BEST BUDDIES DISPLAY STAND 1992
6 3/4" high - 10" wide wood shelves. Holds 4 sets. **CMV $15. MB.**

PASSING DOWN THE DREAM FIGURINE 1991
3 3/4" high porcelain. Choice of white or black men. **CMV $20 ea. MB.**

COUNTRY PURR-FECTION SUGAR & CREAMER SET 1991
4 1/2" high ceramic cats - marked Avon. **CMV $25. MB.**

COUNTRY PURR-FECTION SALT & PEPPER SET 1992
3" high ceramic kitten salt & pepper shakers. **CMV $17 set. MB.**

COUNTRY PURR-FECTION TEA POT 1992
11" high mother cat ceramic tea pot. **CMV $50. MB.**

BEST BUDDIES "PUPPIES PLAYING BALL" 1992
2 1/4" high porcelain puppies - 2nd in series. **CMV $10. set MB.**

BEST BUDDIES "MICE-SKATING" 1992
2 3/4" high porcelain mice figurines. 3rd in series. **CMV $10. set. MB.**

McCONNELLS CORNER GENERAL STORE 1982
5 1/2" ceramic box, roof lifts off. Dated "Christmas 1982". **CMV $24. MB.**

KWANZAA FIGURINE 1996
(Right) 7 1/2" high by 6 3/8" wide black Mother & Father ceramic figurine. **CMV $30. MB.**

COUNTRY VILLAGE CANISTER SET 1985
White pottery canisters by Platzgraff. Marked Avon on bottom. **CMV $50. set of 3 MB.**

SILENT NIGHT CRYSTAL CHURCH 1992
5" high lead crystal church. Gold tone base. Top lights up with batteries. **CMV $19. MB.**

CHRISTMAS THIMBLE 1983
Small white porcelain thimble with decal. 1983 Christmas in gold. **CMV $9. MB.**

AMERICAN HEIRLOOM PORCELAIN BOWL 1983-84
6" across, 4" high porcelain bowl. Plastic stand. Flower design on bowl. **CMV $17. MB.**

AMERICAN FASHION THIMBLES 1982-86
Hand painted porcelain ladies from 1890s to 1940s design. 8 different. **CMV $10 ea. MB.**, 1938 **CMV $20. MB.**
AMERICAN FASHION THIMBLE DISPLAY RACK 1983
12 1/2" long mahogany rack with 8 pegs. Can hang on wall or sit on shelf. **CMV $13. MB.**

BUTTERFLY FANTASY PORCELAIN TREASURE FAN 1980-81
Fan shaped porcelain box. Dated 1980 on bottom. **CMV $13. MB. Add $5. for backward printed bottom label.**
SWEET REMEMBRANCE 1982
4 1/4" porcelain box. Valentines Day 1982 on bottom. "A Token of Love" on inside with a gold foil wrapped chocolate. Short issue. **CMV $15. MB.**

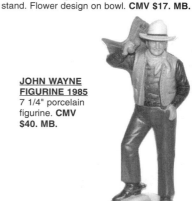

JOHN WAYNE FIGURINE 1985
7 1/4" porcelain figurine. **CMV $40. MB.**

CHRISTMAS THIMBLE 1982
(Left) White porcelain, dated 1982.
CHRISTMAS THIMBLE 1981
(Right) Issued in 1982, but dated 1981. **CMV $9. ea. MB.**

STATUE OF LIBERTY CENTENNIAL BOWL 1985
6" porcelain white bowl. Wood base. **CMV $20. MB.**

MEMORIES PORCELAIN MUSIC BOX 1983-84
White 4 1/4" long porcelain box with music box in lid. **CMV $27.50. MB.**

CHRISTMAS THIMBLE 1984
Porcelain - Dated Christmas 1984. **CMV $7. MB.**

DUCK SERIES 1983-84
6 different hand painted metal ducks. 4" long. 2" high. **CMV $13 ea. MB.**
DUCK DISPLAY RACK 1983-84
12 1/2" long two tier wood rack to display all six duck figurines. **CMV $25. MB.**

AMERICAN HEIRLOOM PORCELAIN BOWL 1981
6" across 4" high, white bowl. "Independence Day 1981" on bottom. Comes with black plastic base stand. **CMV $20. MB**

**BENJAMIN J. BEARINGTON FIGURINES
1983-84**
2" high pewter **"First Day Back"**, **"Hard At
Work"**, **"Report Card Day"**, **"Schools Out"**.
4 in a series. **CMV $10. ea. MB.**
"FATHER'S ARMS FIGURINE 1984
Wood base. Pewter figurine. **CMV $12. MB.**

ELVIS PRESLEY FIGURINE 1987
6 1/2" high hand painted porcelain. **CMV $40.
MB.**

**NATIVE AMERICAN DUCK FIGURINE'S
COLLECTION 1989**
6 different hand painted, hand cast plaster duck
figurines. Choice of **Wood Duck, Goldeneye
Duck, Widgeon Duck, Mallard Duck, Hooded
Merganser** (not shown) & **Blue Winged Teal**,
(now shown). All are 3" to 3 3/4" long. **CMV $13.
ea. MB.**
**NATIVE AMERICAN DUCK COLLECTION
SHELVES 1989**
Set of two 12" wood shelves to hold all six
ducks. **CMV $15. Set MB.**

SEASON'S TREASURES TEA POTS 1995
Small hand painted porcelain tea pots. 4 different - Peony, Tulip, Sunflower, and Rose. **CMV
$17. ea. MB.**

EAGLE - PRIDE OF AMERICA 1982-83
7 3/4" high porcelain eagle figurine. **CMV $30.
MB.**

**PRECIOUS MOMENTS
PORCELAIN 'BIRTHSTONE
BOX' 1997**
(Right) Made only for Avon. 12
different small 2 1/2" wide bisque
porcelain heart boxes for each
month of the year. **CMV $10.00
ea. MB.**

SUNNY COTTAGE LAND FIGURINES 1994
Set of 3 Hartford porcelain figurines sold separately. Left to right: **MANOR** - 3" wide, 2 1/2" high; **SHOPS** - 3" wide, 2 1/4" high; **BAKERY** - 2 3/4" wide, 2 3/4" high. **CMV $13. ea. MB.**

CAROUSEL COLLECTION"HOLD ON TIGHT, FIGURINE 1993
3" X 3" bisque porcelain. Squirrel and turkey figurine 3rd in Carousel collection. **CMV $10. MB.**

"CAROUSEL COLLECTION" HAVE A NICE RIDE FIGURINE 1993
2 3/4" X 3 3/8" bisque porcelain, rabbits riding a deer figurine. 4th and last in Carousel Collection. **CMV $10. MB.**

CAROUSEL WONDERLAND DISPLAY STAND 1993
13 1/2" long, 4 3/4" wide, 7" high wood stand. Holds 4 figurines. **CMV $17. MB.**

SANTA PORCELAIN FIGURINE 1994
"Father Christmas" 2nd in Series. 7" high porcelain, red and white figurine. Marked Avon. **CMV $30. MB.**

SANTA TOWN FIGURINES 1994
3 porcelain houses with 7 watt light inside. Electric cord on each. Reindeer Lodge, Elves Workshop, and Santa's House. **CMV $13. ea. MB.**

RIBBONS AND LACE PORCELAIN BOX 1994
2 1/4" high and 3" across porcelain box. Lace ribbon on top. **CMV $10. MB.**

MR & MRS SANTA CLAUS SALT & PEPPER SHAKERS 1995
2 3/4" high ceramic shakers . **CMV $10. pair MB.**

SANTA PORCELAIN FIGURINE 1993
5 3/4" high, red and white porcelain figurine. **CMV $35. MB.**

CHERISHED TEDDIES FIGURINE 1998
3 1/4" high Bear made of resin by Enesco only for Avon. Comes with adoption certificate. **CMV $20. MB.**

"SITTING CAT" CRYSTAL CATS COLLECTION 1994
1st in series lead crystal cat. 2 1/4" wide, 3" high. **CMV $15. MB.**

SANTA PORCELAIN FIGURINE 1995
7" high porcelain santa & girl is dated 1995. Choice of white or black santa & child. **CMV $25. ea. MB.**

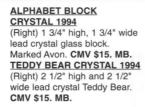

ALPHABET BLOCK CRYSTAL 1994
(Right) 1 3/4" high, 1 3/4" wide lead crystal glass block. Marked Avon. **CMV $15. MB.**
TEDDY BEAR CRYSTAL 1994
(Right) 2 1/2" high and 2 1/2" wide lead crystal Teddy Bear. **CMV $15. MB.**

CRYSTAL "CAT ON PILLOW" 1995
Lead crystal cat is 2 3/4" high X 2 1/4" wide. 3rd in series. **CMV $15. MB.**

BERRY SALT AND PEPPER SHAKERS 1994
2" high plastic shakers. Red or Blue berries. **CMV $5. set MB.**

"CAT IN BASKET" CRYSTAL CAT 1994
Lead crystal cat 2 3/4" high, 2 1/4" wide. **CMV $15. MB.**

CRYSTAL SLEIGH CENTERPIECE 1993
Lead crystal sleigh 6 3/4" wide, 3 1/2" deep, 4 3/4" high. **CMV $20. MB.**

SPRINGTIME BUNNY SALT AND PEPPER SHAKERS 1994
2 1/2" high ceramic rabbits. **CMV $10. set MB.**

PRECIOUS BABY TREASURES 1993
Lead crystal "Bootie", 2 1/2" long "Baby Carriage", 2 3/4" long. **CMV $15. ea. MB.**

SPRING MELODIES SALT & PEPPER SHAKERS 1995
2 plastic bird shakers in a wire basket. **CMV $7. set MB.**

M. J. HUMMEL CRYSTAL TRINKET BOX 1993
24% lead crystal box 4" X 4" round. **CMV $20. MB.**

HOLIDAY DOVE SALT & PEPPER SHAKERS 1993
White porcelain doves 2 1/2" high and 3" high. set. **CMV $13. set MB.**

MAGIC OF CHRISTMAS "SANTA ROCKER" 1993
7 1/4" high, 4 3/4" wide. Made of plastic, Santa rocks and talks. Battery operated. **CMV $25. MB.**

DAYS OF THE WEEK BEAR COLLECTIONS 1994
7 Hartford porcelain bears 2" to 3" high for each day of the week. **CMV $10. ea. MB.**

SANTA'S ELVES COLLECTION 1994
Hartford Porcelain figurines: Elf Wrapping Present; Elf with Rocking Horse; Elf with , 2 1/2" to 3" high ea. **CMV $7. ea. MB.**

COUNTRY QUARTET FIGURINES 1994
Hand painted porcelain and polyester resin: **Otis Owl** - 3 1/4" high; **Roscoe Raccoon** 3 1/2" high. 4 different figurines. **CMV $13. ea. MB.**

BANDSTAND WOOD STAND
8 3/4" high, 4 1/2" deep, 8 3/4" wide. **CMV $15. MB.**

BUNNY LUV COLLECTION 1984 - 94
(Right) All are white ceramic: Napkin Holder, 1990 **CMV $8.**; Trinket Dish 1985 **CMV $8.**; Bunny Picture Frame, 1988 **CMV $8.**; Bunny Country Planter, 1989, Blue flowers around planter. **CMV $10.** Bunny Dessert Plate 1994 7" basket weave plate. **CMV $10.**

PRECIOUS MOMENTS SALT & PEPPER SHAKERS 1998
"Seasoned with a Smile" 31/2" high porcelain . Girl sits on seperate bench shaker. **CMV $13. set MB**

SEASONS HARVEST MINI TEA POTS 1996
Small hand painted porcelain tea pots 3" to 4" high. Choice of **"EGGPLANT",** purple & green, **"RED PEPPER",** red & green, " **SQUASH",** yellow & green, & **"ASPARAGUS",** green & yellow. Dated on bottom of each. **CMV $17. ea. MB.**

COTTAGE COLLECTION SPICE JAR'S 1997
12 different small ceramic jars 3 1/2" high. Roof lids, stick on spice labels. **CMV $8. ea. MB. add $15.** for the off white wood **SPICE RACK** to hold all 12 jars.

BUNNY COLLECTION MUG 1993
3 1/2" high white & green basket weave design mug. **CMV $10. MB.**

BUNNY SUGAR & CREAMER SET 1992
Ceramic basket weave design. **CMV $20. MB.**

BUNNY CANDY DISH 1991
5 1/2" wide 2 1/2" high ceramic Bunny dish. **CMV $13. MB.**

BUNNY BUD VASE 1986
3 1/2" high porcelain. Comes empty. **CMV $9. MB.**

BUNNY LUV CERAMIC BOX 1982
Ceramic top & bottom. Rabbit on lid. Sold empty. **CMV $12. MB.**

EGYPTIAN ROYALTY FIGURINES 1997
"Pharaoh & Queen"
6 1/2" high, made of cold cast resin. Dated 1997. **CMV $20. ea. MB.**

ESSENCE OF MOTHERHOOD FIGURINE 1997
10" high cold cast resin black Mother & Child in white gown & hat. 4" base dated 1997. **CMV $30. MB.**

NEGRO LEAGUE BASEBALL FIGURINE'S 1997
"JOSH GIBSON" & **"SATCHEL PAIGE"** both are 6" high made of cold cast resin and dated 1997 on base. **CMV $20. ea. MB.**

CAROUSEL ANIMAL COLLECTION "LION" 1997
Hand painted porcelain Lion on metal pole and wood base. 5 1/4" high. Dated 1997 on bottom. 4th & last of this series. **CMV $20. MB.**

CAROUSEL ANIMAL COLLECTION "REINDEER" 1996
Hand painted porcelain deer figurine on metal pole & wood base. 5 1/2" high. 3rd in series. **CMV $20. MB.**

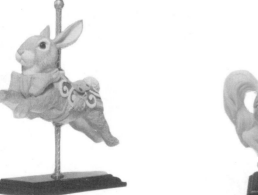

CAROUSEL ANIMAL COLLECTION "RABBIT" 1996
4 7/8" high porcelain Rabbit sits on wood base & metal poll. Ist in series of 4. **CMV $20. MB.**

CAROUSEL ANIMAL COLLECTION "HORSE" 1996
5" high hand painted porcelain Horse figurine mounted on metal poll and wood base. 2nd in series. **CMV $20. MB.**

BE 1ST TO KNOW,
BE INFORMED

If you want to be 1st to know when the next Bud Hastin Avon Collectors Encyclopedia will be for sale in the future, get on Bud's personal mailing list. Please tell us what your last Avon Book from Bud Hastin is. Please send SASE when requesting an answer to any question relating to Avon or Avon Books to Bud Hastin. Just PRINT your name and address and send it to:

BUD HASTIN
P.O. BOX11530
Ft. Lauderdale, Fl. 33339

Just say: "Put me on your next book list."Please state last book ordered. Buds E-mail address.
wwwavonman@pstcomputers.com

COLLECTORS
All containers are Priced Empty

BO means ....Bottle only (empty)

CMV means ....Current Market Value

MB means...Mint and Boxed

COLOGNE ROYAL 1972-74
1 oz. clear glass, gold cap. Came in Field Flowers, Roses Roses, Bird of Paradise, Sonnet, Charisma, Unforgettable, Somewhere. **CMV $4. MB..**
COURTING CARRIAGE 1973-74
1 oz. clear glass, gold cap. Came in Moonwind, Sonnet, Field Flowers or Flower Talk. **CMV $5. MB.**
PINEAPPLE PETITE 1972-74
1 oz. clear glass, gold cap. Came in Roses Roses, Charisma, Brocade or Regence. **CMV $4. MB.** Reissued in 1977 in Field Flowers & Unforgettable.

KEY NOTE PERFUME 1967
1/4 oz. glass key with gold plastic cap. 4A design on cap. Choice of Here's My Heart, To A Wild Rose. Somewhere, Topaze, Cotillion. Unforgettable, Rapture, Occur!. **CMV $20. MB, $12.** key only.
LADY BUG PERFUME 1975-76
1/8 oz. frosted glass, gold cap. Choice of Sonnet, Moonwind or Patchwork. **CMV $6. MB.**
SCENT WITH LOVE 1971-72
1/4 oz. frosted glass with gold pen cap, white and gold label around bottle. Came in Field Flowers, Moonwind, Bird of paradise, Charisma, Elusive, Moonwind. **CMV $12. MB.**

PRECIOUS TURTLE 1975-76
.66 oz. gold jar with plastic lid. Came in Patchwork, or Roses Roses Cream Sachet. **CMV $5. MB.**
TREASURE TURTLE 1971-73
1 oz. brown glass turtle with gold head. Holds Field Flowers, Hana Gasa, Bird of Paradise, Elusive, Charisma, Brocade, Unforgettable, Rapture, Occur!, Somewhere, Topaze, Cotillion, Here's My Heart and Persian Wood. **CMV $8. MB.**

TREASURE TURTLE 1977
1 oz. clear glass turtle with gold cap. Came in Sweet Honesty or Charisma cologne. Avon on bottom & 'R' for reissue on tail. **CMV $5. MB.**
EMERALD PRINCE FROG 1977-79
1 oz. green frosted paint over clear glass. Came in Sweet Honesty or Moonwind cologne. **CMV $5. MB.**

AUTUMN ASTER DECANTER 1978-80
(Left) .75 oz. clear glass, gold cap. Holds Topaze or Sun Blossoms cologne. **CMV $3. MB.**
DOGWOOD DEMI DECANTER 1978-80
(Right) .75 oz. flower shaped bottle, gold flower lid. Came in Apple Blossom, Moonwind or Topaze cologne. **CMV $3. MB.**

WHAT'S HOT AND WHAT'S NOT IN WOMEN'S FIGURINES

What's hot is any decanter or figurine that's made of glass or ceramic. It has to look like something. This is what collectors are after today. What's not hot is plain looking bottles of no particular shape. Almost all plastic bottles, wall tiles & wall decorations, plain tin can items, jars, fabric items such as sachet pillows etc., ceramic items not marked Avon on bottom & kitchen items that have no shape that would not appeal to most collectors.

Avon collecting is 30 years old as we know it and the Avon product line has expanded well beyond most people's ability to collect everything in their product line. There are thousands of products to collect. Choose the one's that appeal to most collectors & you should have a market when you decide to sell your collection in years to come.

This book has been researched to include all products that are hot with most collectors. Some new products not shown in this book fall in the category of new collectible. There are over 500,000 Avon Reps, we feel there are more than ample supplies to collectors. It will take several (Up to 25 or more) years for almost any new products to become scarce & start to rise in value due to supply & demand. Keep this in mind in buying new collectibles. Only the older products are true collectibles. This is why the CPC items, the first Avon products, are so scarce & have risen so high in price. We hope you find this information helpful in guiding your collecting.

Candy products from Avon are not in this book unless they come in a figurine type container. Boxes of candy will not be considered collectible as it easily melts & is dangerous when it gets old & could cause harm to children. We suggest you buy this type of product to use.

Most new items in this book 20 years old or less are listed at or near the original selling price from Avon Products.

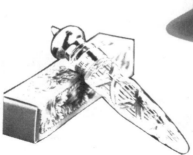

DREAM GARDEN 1972-73
1/2 oz. pink frosted glass with gold cap. Came in Moonwind, Bird of Paradise, Charisma, Elusive or Unforgettable perfume oil. **CMV $15. MB, $12. BO.**
SNOW MAN PETITE PERFUME 1973
.25 oz. textured glass with pink eyes, mouth & scarf. Gold cap. Came in Cotillion, Bird of Paradise, Field Flowers. **CMV $8. MB.**
PRECIOUS SWAN PERFUME 1974-76
1/8 oz. frosted glass with gold cap. Came in Field Flowers, Bird of Paradise or Charisma. **CMV $7. MB.**

ICICLE PERFUME 1967-68
1 dram, gold cap. Came in Here's My Heart, To A Wild Rose, Somewhere, Topaz, Cotillion, Unforgettable, Rapture, Occur!, Regence. with gold neck label. **CMV $7. MB.**

PRECIOUS SLIPPER 1973-74
.25 oz. frosted glass bottle with gold cap. Came in Sonnet or Moonwind. **CMV $7. MB.**
LOVE BIRD PERFUME 1969-70
1/4 oz. frosted bird with silver cap. 2 1/2" long. Came in Charisma, Elusive, Brocade, Regence, Unforgettable, Rapture, Occur!. **CMV $9. MB.**
SMALL WONDER PERFUME 1972-73
1/8 oz. frosted glass with gold cap. Holds Field Flowers, Bird of Paradise, Charisma. **CMV $7. MB.**

BOW TIE PERFUME 1970
1/8 oz. clear glass. Shape of bow with gold cap. Came in Pink Slipper Soap in Charisma & Cotillion. **CMV $4. mint.**

ONE DRAM PERFUME 1974-76
Clear glass with gold cap. Came in Bird of Paradise, Charisma or Field Flowers. Sonnet, Moonwind or Imperial Garden. **CMV $3. MB.**
STRAWBERRY FAIR PERFUME 1974-75
1/8 oz. red glass, silver cap. Came in Moonwind, Charisma or Sonnet. **CMV $6. MB.**

FRISKY FRIENDS 1981
3 different frosted 1 oz. glass cats. With blue cap, Honeysuckle, yellow cap has Roses Roses & pink cap has Hawaiian White Ginger. **CMV $6. MB each.**

HEAVENLY ANGEL 1981
(Left) .5 oz. blue glass angel, silver cap. Choice of Ariane, Candid, Timeless. Red box dated 1981. **CMV $4. MB.**
WINGED PRINCESS 1981
(Center) .5 oz. swan shaped iridescent glass, gold cap. Choice of Occur!, Charisma, Sweet Honesty. Box dated 1981. **CMV $4. MB**
LOVE CHIMES 1981-82
(Right) .5 oz. clear glass bell shape, gold cap. Choice of Roses Roses, Charisma, Moonwind, Sweet Honesty. **CMV $3. MB.**

SEWING NOTIONS 1975
1 oz. pink and white glass with silver cap. Holds Sweet Honesty, To A Wild Rose or Cotillion. **CMV $4. MB.**
CRYSTALIER COLOGNE 1975
2 oz. clear glass. Filled with Field Flowers, Bird of Paradise or Roses Roses Cologne. **CMV $4. MB.**
BABY OWL 1975-77
1 oz. clear glass, gold cap. Holds Sweet Honesty or Occur! Cologne. **CMV $4. MB.**
PERT PENGUIN 1975-76
1 oz. clear glass, gold cap. Holds Field Flowers or Cotillion Cologne. **CMV $4. MB.**

ROLLIN GREAT ROLLER SKATE 1980-81
2 oz. glass red top. Choice of Zany Cologne or Lover Boy Cologne. **CMV $5. MB.**

PETITE PIGLET 1972
2" long embossed clear glass with gold cap. Holds 1/4 oz. perfume in Field Flowers, Bird of Paradise, Elusive & Charisma. **CMV $9. MB.**
SNAIL PERFUME 1968-69
1/4 oz. gold cap, clear glass. Came in Charisma, Brocade, Regence, Unforgettable, Rapture & Occur!. **CMV $13.50 MB, $7. BO.**
PERFUME PETITE MOUSE 1970
Frosted glass with gold head and tail, holds 1/4 oz. perfume in Elusive, Charisma, Brocade, Regence, Unforgettable, Rapture & Occur!. **CMV $17.50 MB, $12. BO.**

HUGGABLE HOP-A-LONG 1982
1 oz. green glass frog. Plastic hat. Comes with 20 stick on decals. Choice of Sweet Honesty for girls or Light Musk for guys. **CMV $5. MB.**

SONG OF CHRISTMAS 1980
.75 oz. frosted glass. Red cap. Choice of Moonwind, Sweet Honesty or Bird of Paradise. **CMV $3. MB.**
CHRISTMAS SOLDIER 1980
.75 oz. clear glass, gold cap. Choice of Sportif, Sweet Honesty, Charisma or Moonwind. **CMV $5. MB.**
OWL MINIATURE 1980-81
.6 oz. clear glass, gold owl cap. Choice of Tasha, Ariane, Candid or Timeless. **CMV $4. MB.**

COLOGNE GO ROUND 1980
.5 oz. clear glass, gold cap. Choice of Roses Roses, Honeysuckle, Hawaiian White Ginger, Field Flowers. **CMV $3. MB.**
SEAHORSE MINIATURE 1980-81
.5 oz. clear glass, gold cap. Choice of Sweet Honesty, Charisma, Occur! or Moonwind. **CMV $4. MB.**
COLOGNE RONDELLE 1980
5 oz. clear glass, gold cap. Choice of Moonwind, Charisma, Topaze, Occur!, Sweet Honesty, Zany Sportif or Country Breeze. In special Christmas box. **CMV $1. MB.**

WOMEN'S DECANTERS & COLLECTIBLES

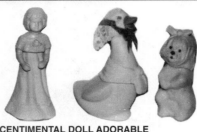

SCENTIMENTAL DOLL ADORABLE
ABIGAIL 1979-80
4.5 oz. clear glass painted beige. Beige plastic top. Comes in Regence or Sweet Honesty cologne. **CMV $10. MB.**
MRS. QUACKLESS 1979-80
2 oz. clear glass painted off white. Off white plastic top with white lace and green bonnet. Comes in Delicate Daisies Cologne. **CMV $7. MB.**
SWEET TOOTH TERRIER 1979-80
1 oz. white glass and white plastic top. Comes in Topaze or Cotillion Cologne. **CMV $6. MB.**

WEDDING FLOWER MAIDEN 1979-80
(Left) 1.75 oz. white painted over clear glass. Holds Unforgettable or Sweet Honesty cologne. **CMV $7. MB.**
GARDEN GIRL 1978-79
4 oz. pink painted over clear glass. Holds Charisma or Sweet Honesty cologne. **CMV $8. MB.**
ANGEL SONG DECANTER 1978-79
1 oz. frosted glass base with off white plastic top. Holds Here's My Heart or Charisma cologne. **CMV $6. MB.**

FASHION FIGURINE 1971-72
(Left) 4 oz. white plastic top & white painted bottom, over clear glass. 6" high. Came in Field Flowers, Elusive, Bird of Paradise, Brocade. **CMV $12. MB.**
VICTORIAN FASHION FIGURINE 1973-74
(Center) 4 oz. light green (some call it blue or aqua) painted over clear glass base with green plastic top. Came in Charisma, Field Flowers, Bird of Paradise Cologne. **CMV $30. MB.**
ELIZABETHAN FASHION FIGURINE 1972
(Right) 4 oz. pink painted glass bottom over clear glass with pink plastic top. 6" high. Came in Moonwind, Charisma, Field Flowers & Bird of Paradise Cologne. **CMV $20. MB.** Also came pink painted over white milk glass. Remove cap to see difference. **CMV $15.**

GARDEN GIRL 1975
4 oz. sprayed frosted glass with yellow plastic top. Holds Sweet Honesty, Somewhere, Cotillion or To A Wild **CMV $11. MB.**
FLOWER MAIDEN 1973-74
4 oz. yellow skirt painted over clear glass with white plastic top. Came in Unforgettable, Somewhere, Topaze, Cotillion. **CMV $9. MB.**
DEAR FRIENDS 1974
4 oz. pink painted with light pink plastic top. Came in Field Flowers, Bird of Paradise or Roses Roses Cologne. **CMV $13. MB.**

ANGEL SONG WITH MANDOLIN 1979-80
(Left) 1 oz. frosted over clear glass. White plastic top. Holds Moonwind or Unforgettable cologne. **CMV $5. MB.**
SKATER'S WALTZ 1979-80
(Center) 4 oz. blue flock base over clear glass. Light blue plastic top. Holds Charisma or Cotillion cologne. **CMV $9. MB.**
LITTLE JACK HORNER 1979-80
(Right) 1.5 oz. white glass painted white frosted. Came in Topaze or Roses Roses cologne. **CMV $7. MB.**

ON THE AVENUE 1978-79
2 oz. blue painted over clear glass. Pink plastic top with lavender hat. White detachable umbrella. Holds Topaze or Unforgettable cologne. **CMV $8. BO, $10. MB.**
PROUD GROOM 1978-80
2 oz. white painted over clear glass. Holds Sweet Honesty or Unforgettable Cologne. **CMV $9. MB.**

TUG-A-BRELLA 1979-80
2.5 oz. clear glass painted yellow, plastic top. Black plastic umbrella on wire. Holds Moonwind or Cotillion Cologne. **CMV $11. MB.**
GOOD FAIRY 1978-80
3 oz. clear glass painted blue. Blue plastic top. Plastic wand. Blue and pink fabric purse and wings. Holds Delicate Daisies cologne. **CMV $8. MB.**

SONG OF SPRING 1977
(Left) 1 oz. frosted glass with frosted plastic bird bath top. Blue plastic bird attachment. Came in Sweet Honesty or Topaze. **CMV $6. MB.**
FELINA FLUFFLES 1977-78
(Right) 2 oz. blue paint over clear glass, white plastic top, blue ribbon on head. Pink cheeks. Came in Pink & Pretty Cologne. **CMV $7. MB.**

FLY-A-BALLOON 1975-77
3 oz. glass sprayed blue with light blue top &
red plastic balloon. Holds Moonwind or Bird of
Paradise cologne. **CMV $8. MB.**
SKIP-A-ROPE 1977
4 oz. yellow sprayed glass with yellow plastic
top and white plastic rope. Holds Sweet
Honesty, Bird of Paradise or Roses Roses
cologne. **CMV $8. MB.**

PRETTY GIRL PINK 1974-75
(Left) 6 oz. glass sprayed pink base with light
pink top. Holds Unforgettable, Topaze, Occur!
or Somewhere cologne. **CMV $9. MB.**
LITTLE GIRL BLUE 1972-73
(Center) 3 oz. blue painted glass with blue
plastic cap. Came in Brocade, Unforgettable,
Somewhere or Cotillion. **CMV $9. MB.**
LITTLE KATE 1973-74
(Right) 3 oz. pastel orange painted glass with
orange plastic hat over cap. Came in Bird of
Paradise, Charisma, Unforgettable. **CMV $10.
MB.**

**18th CENTURY CLASSIC FIGURINE YOUNG
BOY 1974-75**
(Left) 4 oz. white sprayed glass with white
plastic head. Choice of Sonnet or Moonwind
cologne or foaming bath oil. **CMV $9. MB.**
**18th CENTURY CLASSIC FIGURINE YOUNG
GIRL 1974-75**
(Right) 4 oz. white sprayed glass with white
plastic head. Choice of Sonnet or Moonwind
cologne or foaming bath oil. **CMV $9. MB.**

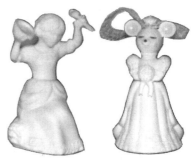

BETSY ROSS 1976
4 oz. white painted over clear glass. Came in
Sonnet or Topaze Cologne. Sold 2 campaigns
only. **CMV $7. MB.** Also came white painted
over white milk glass. Remove cap to see
color of bottle. **CMV $20. MB.** The regular
issue Betsy Ross bottle was one of the all time
biggest sellers in Avon history.
MAGIC PUMPKIN COACH 1976-77
1 oz. clear glass, gold cap. Comes in Bird of
Paradise or Occur! Cologne. **CMV $6. MB.**

SWEET DREAMS 1979-80
1.25 oz. blue frosted over clear glass. White
plastic boys head cap. Holds Zany or
Somewhere cologne. **CMV $6. MB.**

LITTLE MISS MUFFET 1978-80
(Left) 2 oz. white painted over milk glass.
Came in Sweet Honesty or Topaze. **CMV $7.
MB.**
CHURCH MOUSE BRIDE 1978-79
Plastic top with separate white veil. Came in
Delicate Daisies cologne. Base is white dull
paint over milk glass. **CMV $7. MB.**

CATCH-A-FISH 1976-78
3 oz. dark tan, painted over clear glass, light
tan plastic top, yellow hat & brown plastic
removable pole. Came in Field Flowers or
Sonnet cologne. **CMV $11. MB.**
ROLL-A-HOOP 1977-78
3.75 oz. dull pink painted over clear glass
base. Light pink plastic top, white plastic
hoop. Came in Field Flowers or Cotillion
cologne. **CMV $10. MB.**

AMERICAN BELLE 1976-78
(Left) 4 oz. yellow dull paint over clear glass,
yellow cap. Came in Cotillion or Sonnet
cologne. **CMV $8. MB.**
LITTLE BO PEEP DECANTER 1976-78
(Right) 2 oz. white dull paint over white milk
glass base, white plastic top & can. Came in
Sweet Honesty or Unforgettable cologne.
CMV $8. MB.

WOMEN'S DECANTERS & COLLECTIBLES

VICTORIAN LADY 1972-73
5 oz. white milk glass, white plastic cap. Came in Bird of Paradise, Unforgettable, Occur!, Charisma Foaming Bath Oil. **CMV $8. MB.**

SCOTTISH LASS 1975
(Left) 4 oz. blue with red, green & blue plaid skirt, blue plastic top. Holds Sweet Honesty, Bird of Paradise, Roses Roses or Cotillion cologne. **CMV $10. MB.**

SPANISH SENORITA 1975-76
(Center) 4 oz. red base with white designs and pink plastic top. Holds Moonwind, To A Wild Rose or Topaze cologne. **CMV $12. MB.**

ROARING TWENTIES FASHION FIGURINE 1972-74
(Right) 3 oz. purple painted over clear glass with plastic purple top. Came in Unforgettable, Topaze, Somewhere, Cotillion. **CMV $10. MB.**

DUTCH MAID 1977-79
(Left) 4 oz. blue painted base over clear glass, flower design & blue plastic top. Came in Sonnet or Moonwind cologne. **CMV $9. MB.**

MARY MARY 1977-79
(Center) 2 oz. frosted white over milk glass & white plastic top. Came in Sweet Honesty or Topaze. **CMV $9. MB.**

SKATERS WALTZ - RED 1977-78
(Right) 4 oz. red flock on clear glass & pink plastic tip. Came in Moonwind or Charisma cologne. **CMV $11. MB.**

BIRD OF PARADISE COLOGNE DECANTER 1970-72
8" high 5 oz. clear glass with gold head. **CMV $11. MB.**

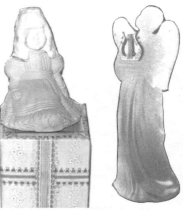

CLASSIC DECANTER 1969-70
(Left) 8 oz. white glass bottle with gold cap. 11" high, filled with Skin-So-Soft bath oil. **CMV $10. MB.**

SEA MAIDEN SKIN-SO-SOFT 1971-72
(Right) 6 oz. gold cap, clear glass, 10" high. **CMV $10. MB.**

PRECIOUS PRISCILLA 1982-83
(Left) 3 oz. pale pink paint over clear glass. Plastic head top. Holds Sweet Honesty or Moonwind. **CMV $10. MB.**

ANGEL'S MELODY DECANTER 1987
8" high angel. Holds 3 oz. of cologne. **CMV $10. MB.**

LIBRARY LAMP 1976--77
(Left) 4 oz. gold plated base over clear glass, gold cap. Came in Topaze & Charisma cologne. **CMV $10. MB.**

BRIDAL MOMENTS 1976-79
(Right) 5 oz. white paint over clear glass. White plastic top. Came in Sweet Honesty or Unforgettable cologne. **CMV $10. MB.**

FIRST PRAYER 1981-82
(Left) 1.5 oz. light bisque yellow painted bottom over clear glass. Light yellow top. Choice of Charisma, Occur!, Topaze cologne. 4" high. **CMV $7. MB.**

PRIMA BALLERINA 1981
(Center) Pink frosted glass over clear glass, 1 oz. Choice of Zany or Sweet Honesty. Bottle & box label dated 1981. **CMV $7. MB.**

NOSTALGIC GLOW 1981-82
(Right) 1 oz. clear glass lamp bottom, blue plastic shade top. Choice of Moonwind, Wild Jasmine or Topaze. **CMV $6. MB.**

DUTCH GIRL FIGURINE 1973-74
(Left) 3 oz. blue painted with light blue plastic top. Came in Unforgettable, Topaze or Somewhere. **CMV $11. MB.**

GAY NINETIES 1974
(Center) 3 oz. orange sprayed bottle with white top and orange hat. Holds Unforgettable, Topaze or Somewhere. **CMV $13. MB.**

SWEET DREAMS 1974
(Right) 3 oz. sprayed white bottom with blue top. Holds Pink & Pretty or Sweet Honesty cologne. **CMV $15. MB.**

SNOW BIRD 1973-74
1.5 oz. white milk glass, white plastic cap. Came in Patchwork, Moonwind, Sonnet Cream Sachet. **CMV $6. MB.**

ROBIN RED-BREAST 1974-75
2 oz. red frosted glass with silver plastic top. Holds Charisma, Roses Roses, Bird of Paradise. **CMV $6. MB.**

FLIGHT TO BEAUTY 1975
5 oz. glass jar with white frosted top. Holds Rich Moisture or Vita-Moist Cream or SSS Skin Softener. **CMV $4. MB.**

PARTRIDGE 1973-75
5 oz. white milk glass with white plastic lid. Came in Unforgettable, Topaze, Occur!, Somewhere. **CMV $6. MB.**

PIERROT COLOGNE 1982-83
(Left) 1.75 oz. bottle. Black & white. Choice of Charisma or Occur! **CMV $10. MB.**

PIERRETTE COLOGNE 1982-83
(Right) Same as Pierrot. **CMV $10. MB.**

CRYSTAL FACETS 1973-75
3 oz. clear glass. Choice of Roses Roses or Field Flowers. **CMV $4. MB.**

OWL FANCY 1974-76
4 oz. clear glass. Came in Raining Violets or Roses Roses. **CMV $4. MB.**

LITTLE DREAM GIRL 1980-81
(Left) 1.25 oz. aqua paint over clear glass. Cream color top. Choice of Sweet Honesty or Occur! cologne. **CMV $5. MB.**

BUNDLE OF LOVE 1980-81
(Center) .75 oz. light blue paint over clear glass. Sits on red plastic sled. Choice of Hello Sunshine cologne or Sure Winner Bracing Lotion. **CMV $5. MB.**

FLOWER MOUSE 1980-81
(Right) .75 oz. dull red paint over clear glass and white & yellow mouse cap. Choice of Cotillion or Zany cologne. **CMV $4. MB.**

LOVING TREATS BUTTERMINTS 1982
Flowered tin box filled with buttermint candy. Tin dated 1982. Comes in lavender box. **CMV $4. MB. empty.**

FOSTORIA CRYSTAL BUD VASE 1980
(Left) 6" high clear glass. Dated 1980 on bottom. Comes with white scented carnation. **CMV $13. MB.**

CRYSTAL SNOWFLAKE CHRISTMAS BELL 1980
(Center) 3.75 oz. clear glass. Bottom label dated 1980. Choice of Charisma, Topaze, Occur! or Cotillion cologne. **CMV $8. MB.**

MARCHING PROUD 1980-81
(Right) 8 1/2" high, 2 oz. blue base paint over clear glass. White top, red hat, cloth flag. Choice of Sweet Honesty or Topaze cologne. **CMV $12. MB.**

HOLIDAY TREATS CAN 1981
(Left) Green metal can made in England for Avon Christmas 1981. Full of Candy. **CMV $4. MB. Empty.**

SWEET SCENTIMENTS VALENTINE CANDY 1981
(Right) Metal pink & tan can full of candy. Bottom stamped "Avon Valentine's Day 1981" **CMV $4. MB empty.**

WOMEN'S DECANTERS & COLLECTIBLES

BEARING GIFTS LIP BALM 1981-82
(Left) Small fuzzy bear, head turns, holds red & green lip balm in red box. **CMV $5. MB.**

HEARTHSIDE 1976-77
(Left) .6 oz. bronze plated over clear glass. Came in Sweet Honesty or Occur!. **CMV $6. MB.**

GOLDEN ANGEL 1976-77
(Right) 1 oz. gold plated over clear glass. White angel head cap. Came in Sweet Honesty or Occur!. **CMV $6. MB**

SPRING DYNASTY VASE 1982-83
7" high glass vase with fragranced outer coating in blue, pink or green. **CMV $6. MB each color.**

CHRISTMAS SPARKLERS 1968-69
4 oz. bubble bath. Came in gold, green, blue and red with gold caps. 2 sides of bottle are indented. **CMV $12. MB, $8. BO. Mint.**

CHRISTMAS SPARKLER PURPLE 1968
4 oz. painted over clear glass, gold cap. **CMV $25 Mint. Sold only in West Coast Area.**

CHRISTMAS TREES 1968-70
4 oz. bubble bath. Came in red, green gold silver painted over clear glass. **CMV $12. MB. $8. BO. mint.**

DAPPER SNOWMAN 1978-79
(Left) 1 oz. white milk glass with black painted spots and black hat cap. Holds Moonwind or Sweet Honesty cologne. Brown, blue and red neck scarf. **CMV $4. MB.**

JOLLY SANTA 1978-79
(Right) 1 oz. clear glass, white painted beard. Red cap. Came in Here's My Heart or Topaze cologne. **CMV $3**

HOLIDAY HOSTESS COLLECTION
PLATTER 1981
11" clear glass, holly & berry decal. Plate does not say Avon. **CMV $15 MB.**

COMPOTE 1981
4" high clear glass, holly decoration. Avon on bottom. **CMV $12. MB.**

CANDLESTICKS 1981
3" high clear glass, holly decoration. Avon on bottom. Set of 2. **CMV $12. set MB.**

HEAVENLY ANGEL 1974-75
(Left) 2 oz. clear glass with white top. Holds Occur!, Unforgettable, Somewhere, Here's My Heart, or Sweet Honesty cologne. **CMV $7. MB.**

GOLDEN ANGEL BATH OIL 1968-69
(Right) 4 oz. gold bottle, gold paper wings. Gold & white cap. **CMV $12. MB.**

GARDEN FRESH DECANTER 1979-80
10 oz. clear glass. Yellow & gold pump & cap. Green box. **CMV $5. MB.**

CHRISTMAS TREE HOSTESS SET 1979
9" high ceramic green tree. Comes with Mountain Pine fragrance wax chips and rag Doll & Teddy Bear ceramic salt & pepper shakers. This was a very short issue at Xmas. 1979. **CMV $30. set MB.**

SPRING BOUQUET VASE 1981
6" glass vase with special plastic coated scented outside. Comes in red, green or amber. **CMV $6. each MB.**

YULE TREE 1974-79
(Left) 3 oz. green with plastic with green plastic top and gold star. Came in Sonnet, Moonwind or Field Flowers cologne. **CMV $6. MB.**

TOUCH OF CHRISTMAS 1975
(Center) 1 oz. green glass with red cap. Holds Unforgettable or Imperial Garden. **CMV $4. MB. Reissued 1979 in Zany & Here's My Heart. Same CMV.**

CRYSTAL TREE COLOGNE 1975
(Right) 3 oz. clear glass with gold plastic star cap. Holds Moonwind or Sonnet. **CMV $8. MB.**

HEAVENLY MUSIC 1978-80
(Left) 1 oz. clear glass, gold cap. Holds Charisma or Topaze cologne. **CMV $4. MB.**

LITTLE BURRO 1978-79
(Center) 1 oz. light gray glass. Straw hat with red flower. Holds Sweet Honesty or Charisma cologne. **CMV $5. MB.**

HONEY BEE 1978-80
(Right) 1.25 oz. amber coated over clear glass. Gold bee on lid. Holds Honeysuckle or Moonwind cologne. **CMV $4. MB.**

SNIFFY "SKUNK" 1978-80
1.25 oz. black glass, white trim. Holds Sweet Honesty or Topaze cologne. **CMV $6. MB.**

"CALCULATOR" IT ALL ADDS UP 1979-80
4 oz. black glass. Holds Deep Woods After Shave or Sweet Honesty Body Splash. **CMV $8. MB.**

CHRISTMAS COLOGNE 1969-70
3 oz. each. Unforgettable is silver & pink, Occur! is gold & blue, Somewhere is silver & green, Topaze is bronze and yellow. **CMV $8. BO, Mint. $11. MB.**

KANGAROO TWO 1978-79
8" red calico stuffed Kangaroo with Avon tag. Green neck ribbon. Came with .75 oz. frosted glass kangaroo bottle with gold head. Holds Topaze or Sweet Honesty cologne. **CMV $10. both MB, BO $4., Stuffed toy $5. mint.**

CHRISTMAS ORNAMENTS 1967
Round 4 oz. bubble bath. Came in gold, silver, red, green. Silver caps. **CMV $14. MB, $9. BO mint.**

FESTIVE FACETS DECANTER 1979-80
1 oz. with gold caps. Comes in Charisma "red glass", Sweet Honesty "green glass", and Here's My Heart in "blue glass". **CMV $6. MB.**

FAIRYTALE FROG 1976
1 oz. clear glass with gold frog cap. Choice of Sweet Honesty or Sonnet Cologne. **CMV $5. MB.**

LUCKY PENNY LIP GLOSS 1976-80
2" diameter copper colored. Contains 2 colors lip gloss. **CMV $2. MB, $1. no box.** Reissued in 1980 with R on bottom.

GOLDEN NOTES (CANARY) 1979-80
1.75 oz. clear glass coated light yellow, Yellow head. Came in Charisma or Moonwind cologne. **CMV $4. MB.**

CHURCH MOUSE GROOM 1979-80
.75 oz. white glass, white plastic top. Holds Delicate Daisies cologne. **CMV $6. MB.**

FUZZY BUNNY 1979-80
1 oz. clear glass coated with white flock. Pink ears, orange carrot. Holds Sweet Honesty or Honeysuckle cologne. **CMV $6. MB.**

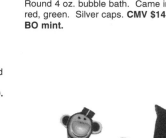

PRETTY PIGLET 1979-80
(Left) .75 oz. clear glass. Holds Roses Roses, pink cap; Honeysuckle, yellow cap; Hawaiian White Ginger, blue-green cap. Fabric flower around neck. **CMV $4. MB.**

MONKEY SHINES 1979-80
(Inside Left) 1 oz. clear glass painted light gray, brown eyes and ears. Red cap and neck strap. Holds Sonnet or Moonwind cologne. **CMV $6. MB.**

BON BON 1979-80
(Inside Right) .75 oz. dark amber glass. Pink and green top came with Sweet Honesty cologne or Cotillion with yellow and green top. **CMV $4. MB.**

GENTLE FOAL 1979-80
(Right) 1.5 oz. dark amber glass and plastic head. Comes in Charisma or Sun Blossoms cologne. **CMV $5. MB.**

WOMEN'S DECANTERS & COLLECTIBLES

MERRY MOUSE 1979-80
(Left) .75 oz. white milk glass bottle & head. Stick on holly leaf. Choice of Zany or Cotillion cologne. **CMV $6. MB.**
PRECIOUS CHICKADEE 1979-80
(Center) 1 oz. white glass. Red & white cap. Came in Here's My Heart or Sun Blossoms cologne. **CMV $5. MB.**
SNUG CUB 1979-80
(Right) 1 oz. milk glass. Green cap. Pink & green paint. Comes in Occur! or Sweet Honesty cologne. **CMV $5. MB.**

PERFUME CONCENTRE 1974-76
1 oz. clear glass with gold cap. Came in Imperial Garden, Moonwind, Sonnet, Charisma or Bird of Paradise. **CMV $4. MB.**
UNICORN 1974-75
2 oz. clear glass with gold cap. Came in Field Flowers, Charisma, Bird of Paradise or Brocade. **CMV $7. MB.**

TEDDY BEAR 1976-78
.75 oz. frosted glass, gold cap. Came in Sweet Honesty or Topaze. **CMV $5 MB.**
PRECIOUS DOE 1976-78
1/2 oz. frosted glass bottle. Came in Field Flowers or Sweet Honesty. **CMV $5. MB.**

ROCKING HORSE TREE ORNAMENT 1979-80
.75 oz. clear glass rocker shapes bottle with gold plastic rocking horse top. Bottom of horse says 1979. Holds Sweet Honesty or Moonwind cologne. **CMV $6. MB.**

LOVE SONG 1973-75
6 oz. frosted glass with gold cap. Holds Skin-So-Soft bath oil. **CMV $6. MB.**
BATH TREASURE SNAIL 1973-76
6 oz. clear glass with gold head. Holds Skin-So-Soft. **CMV $9. MB.**

ENCHANTED FROG CREAM SACHET 1973-76
(Left) 1.25 oz. cream colored milk glass with cream colored plastic lid. Came in Sonnet, Moonwind or Occur!. **CMV $5. MB.**
HANDY FROG 1975-76
(Right) 8 oz. white milk glass with red cap. **CMV $8. MB.**

HIGH-BUTTONED SHOE 1975-76
2 oz. clear glass with gold cap. Holds Occur! or Unforgettable cologne. **CMV $5. MB.**
GRACEFUL GIRAFFE 1976
1.5 oz. clear glass with plastic top. Holds Topaze or To A Wild Rose cologne. **CMV $6. MB.**

BABY HIPPO 1977-80
1 oz. frosted glass with silver head. Came in Sweet Honesty or Topaze cologne. **CMV $6. MB.**
LITTLE LAMB 1977-78
.75 oz. white milk glass, white head. Came in Sweet Honesty or Topaze cologne. **CMV $6. MB.**

SNOW BUNNY 1975-76
3 oz. clear glass with gold cap. Holds Moonwind, Charisma, Bird of Paradise or Sweet Honesty cologne. **CMV $6. MB.**
LA BELLE TELEPHONE 1974-76
1 oz. clear glass with gold top. Holds Moonwind, Sonnet or Charisma perfume concentre. **CMV $9. MB.**

GOOD LUCK ELEPHANT 1975-76
1.5 oz. frosted glass, gold cap. Holds Sonnet, Imperial Garden or Patchwork cologne. **CMV $6. MB.**
SWISS MOUSE 1974-75
3 oz. frosted glass with gold cap. Holds Roses Roses, Field Flowers or Bird of Paradise cologne. **CMV $7. MB.**

HUGGABLE HIPPO 1980
1.75 oz. white glass. Red hat. Holds Zany cologne or Light Musk After Shave. Comes with card of stick on decals. **CMV $5. MB.**

GREEN-BLUE-BROWN EYED SUSAN COMPACT 1980
3 different color centers with yellow flower rim. **CMV $2. each MB.**

COUNTRY KITCHEN 1973-75
6 oz. white milk glass with red plastic head. Holds moisturized hand lotion. **CMV $8. MB,**

BATH SEASONS 1967
3 oz. foaming oil. Each is white glass & top with orange design in Honeysuckle, green in Lily of the Valley. Lavender in Lilac, yellow in Jasmine. Matching ribbons on each. each. **CMV $10. MB. ea.**

VENETIAN PITCHER COLOGNE MIST 1973-75
3 oz. blue plastic coated bottle with silver plastic top. Came in Imperial Garden, Patchwork, Sonnet or Moonwind. **CMV $5. MB.**

COMPOTE DECANTER 1972-75
5 oz. white milk glass bottle, gold cap. Came in Moonwind, Field Flowers, Elusive or Brocade. **CMV $7. MB.**

BATH URN 1971-73
5 oz. white glass & cap with gold top plate. Foaming bath oil in Elusive & Charisma or bath foam in Lemon Velvet & Silk & Honey. 6" high. **CMV $7. MB.**

KOFFEE KLATCH 1971-74
5 oz. yellow paint over clear glass pot with gold top. Foaming Bath Oil in Field Flowers, Honeysuckle or Lilac. Also Lemon Velvet Bath Foam. **CMV $8. MB.**

FORGET ME NOT PORCELAIN BOX 1989
Heart shaped box and matching pin. **CMV $8. MB.**

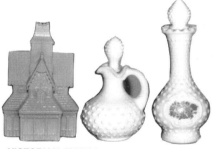

ROYAL COACH 1972-73
5 oz. white milk glass, gold cap. Holds Moonwind, Bird of Paradise, Charisma or Field Flowers foaming bath oil. **CMV $9. MB.**

SITTING PRETTY 1971-73
4 oz. white milk glass with gold cat cap. Came in Topaze, Rapture, Cotillion, Somewhere or Persian Wood. **CMV $9. MB.**

VICTORIAN MANOR 1972-73
(Left) 5 oz. white painted over clear glass with pink plastic roof. Holds Roses Roses, Bird of Paradise, Unforgettable, Cotillion. **CMV $9. MB.**

HOBNAIL DECANTER 1972-74
(Center) 5 oz. white opal glass. Came in Moonwind, Elusive, Roses Roses Bath Foam, Lemon Velvet Bath Foam. **CMV $6. MB.**

HOBNAIL BUD VASE 1973-74
(Right) 4 oz. white milk glass with red & yellow roses. Holds Charisma, Topaze, Roses Roses cologne. **CMV $6. MB** Also came 4.75 oz. size.

FRAGRANCE HOURS 1971-73
6 oz. ivory glass grandfathers clock, gold cap. Bird of Paradise, Field Flowers, Charisma or Elusive. **CMV $9. MB.**

EIFFEL TOWER 1970
3 oz., 9" high clear glass with gold cap. Came in Occur!, Rapture, Somewhere, Topaze, Cotillion or Unforgettable. **CMV $9. MB.**

BUTTERCUP CANDLESTICK 1974
(Left) 6 oz. white milk glass, yellow & white flowers. Holds Moonwind, Sonnet or Imperial Garden cologne. First issue has yellow band around neck. **CMV $9. MB.** Later issue was plain with no band on neck and yellow or brown decals. **CMV $8. MB.**

BUTTERCUP FLOWER HOLDER 1974
(Center) 5 oz. milk glass with plastic white top. Holds Moonwind, Imperial Garden or Sonnet. **CMV $6. MB.**

BUTTERCUP SALT SHAKER 1974
(Right) 1.5 oz. white milk glass with yellow & white flowers, yellow plastic cap. Came in Moonwind, Sonnet or Imperial Garden. **CMV $3. MB.**

DUTCH TREAT DEMI-CUPS 1971
3 oz. white glass filled with Cream Lotion in Honeysuckle, yellow cap; Blue lotus, blue cap; Hawaiian White Ginger, pink cap. **CMV $8. MB.** Also each came with white caps.

SALT SHAKERS 1968-70
3 oz. pink ribbon, pink flowers. Yellow ribbon & flowers in Hawaiian Ginger White, Honeysuckle & Lilac bath oil. **CMV $8. MB ea.**

SWEET SHOPPE PIN CUSHION 1972-74
(Left) 1 oz. white milk glass bottom with white plastic back with hot pink pin cushion seat. Came in Sonnet, Moonwind, Field Flowers, Roses Roses, Bird of Paradise or Charisma. **CMV $7. MB.**

FRAGRANCE TOUCH 1969-70
(Right) 3 oz. white milk glass. Cologne came in Elusive, Charisma, Brocade or Regence. **CMV $6. MB.**

BLUE DEMI-CUP 1968-70
(Left) 3 oz. white glass, blue cap & design, some came with gold top with blue lid. Came in Brocade, Topaze or Unforgettable. **CMV $8. MB.**

DEMI-CUP 1969-70
(Center Two) 3 oz. white milk glass. Charisma has red cap and design. Regence has green cap and design. **CMV $8. MB.**

TO A WILD ROSE DEMI-CUP 1969
(Right) 3 oz. white glass, red rose, pink cap. 6 1/2" high. Contains Foaming Bath Oil. **CMV $9. MB.**

VICTORIANA SOAP DISH 1978
Blue marbleized glass - white soap. May 1978 on bottom. **CMV $10. MB. with soap.**

VICTORIANA PITCHER & BOWL 1978
Blue marbleized glass bowl and 6 oz. pitcher. Holds bubble bath. May 1978 on bottom. **CMV $9. MB.**

ENCHANTED HOURS 1972-73
(Left) 5 oz. blue glass bottle with gold cap. Came in Roses Roses, Charisma, Unforgettable or Somewhere cologne. **CMV $9. MB,**

BEAUTIFUL AWAKENING 1973-74
(Right) 3 oz. gold painted over clear glass front paper clock face, gold cap. Came in Elusive, Roses Roses or Topaze. **CMV $7. MB.**

LEISURE HOURS 1970-72
5 oz. white milk glass bottle contains foaming bath oil in 6 fragrances. Gold cap. **CMV $9. MB.**

LEISURE HOURS MINIATURE 1974
1.5 oz. white milk glass bottle, gold cap. Holds Field Flowers, Bird of Paradise or Charisma cologne. **CMV $6. MB.**

KITTEN PETITE 1973-74
1.5 oz. amber glass ball with white plastic cat for cap. Came in Sonnet or Moonwind. **CMV $6. MB.**

MING CAT 1971
6 oz. white glass & head, blue trim & neck ribbon. Came in Moonwind, Bird of Paradise, Elusive, Charisma. **CMV $10. MB.**

KITTEN LITTLE 1972-76
3 1/2" high, white glass bottle holds 1 1/2 oz. cologne in Occur!, Topaze, Unforgettable, Somewhere, Cotillion. **CMV $6. MB.**

HEARTSCENT CREAM SACHET 1976-77
.66 oz. white glass bottom with white plastic top. Gold dove design. Came in Charisma, Occur! or Roses Roses. **CMV $4. MB.**
FOSTORIA COMPOTE 1975-76
12 Skin-So-Soft capsules. Clear glass with glass top. **CMV $6. MB.**

GRECIAN PITCHER 1972-76
6 1/2" high, 5 oz. white glass bottle & white stopper holds Skin-So-Soft. **CMV $8. MB.**
CORNUCOPIA 1971-76
6 oz. white glass, gold cap. 5 1/2" high. **CMV $8. MB.**

LOVABLE SEAL 1976-77
1 oz. frosted glass, gold cap. Came in Cotillion or Here's My Heart. **CMV $5. MB.**
LOVE BIRD 1978
1 1/2 oz. milk glass bottle with gold cap. Came in Charisma or Moonwind cologne. **CMV $5. MB.**

STYLISH LADY DECANTER 1982-83
8 oz. white glass pig with white and pink pump top. Choice of Country Orchard Liquid Cleanser or Moisturizer Hand Lotion. **CMV $9. MB.**

VICTORIANA PITCHER & BOWL 1971-72
6 oz. turquoise glass pitcher with Skin-So-Soft bath oil & turquoise glass bowl with Avon bottom. Some bowls have double Avon stamp on bottom. **CMV $11. MB, $9. no box, $12. with double stamp on bottom.**
VICTORIANA PITCHER & BOWL 1972-73
Same as above only came in Moonwind, Field Flowers Foaming Bath Oil. **CMV $8. no box, $11. MB.**
VICTORIANA POWDER SACHET 1972-74
1.5 oz. turquoise glass jar & lid. Came in Moonwind, Field Flowers. **CMV $8. MB.**
VICTORIANA DISH & SOAP 1972-73
Turquoise glass dish with white soap. **CMV $8. MB, dish only $3.**

SECRETAIRE 1972-75
7" high, pink paint over clear glass, gold cap. Holds 5 oz. of Foaming Bath Oil in Moonwind, Charisma, Brocade, Lilac & Lemon Velvet. **CMV $10. MB.**
ARMOIRE 1972-75
7" high, 5 oz. white glass bottle with gold cap. Choice of Field Flowers, Bird of Paradise, Elusive or Charisma bath oil. 1975 came in Field Flowers, Charisma & Bird of Paradise only. **CMV $8. MB.**

FRENCH TELEPHONE 1971
6 oz. white milk glass base with gold cap & trim. Holds Foaming Bath Oil. Center of receiver holds 1/4 oz. of perfume in frosted glass. Came in Moonwind, Bird of Paradise, Elusive or Charisma. **CMV $30. MB.**

CHRISTMAS BELLS 1979-80
1 oz. red glass. Silver cap. Holds Topaze or Sweet Honesty cologne. **CMV $3. MB.**
RED CARDINAL 1979-80
2 oz. clear glass painted red. Red cap. Holds Bird of Paradise or Charisma cologne. **CMV $6. MB.**

SILVER SWIRLS SALT SHAKER 1977-79
3 oz. silver plated over clear glass. Silver top. Came in Sweet Honesty or Topaze cologne. **CMV $4. MB.**
ISLAND PARAKEET 1977-78
1.5 oz. blue glass base & blue & yellow plastic top. Approx. 4 1/2" high. Came in Moonwind or Charisma Cologne. **CMV $6. MB.**

REGAL PEACOCK 1973-74
4 oz. blue glass with gold cap. Came in Patchwork, Sonnet or Moonwind. **CMV $10. MB.**

PRECIOUS HEARTS 1980
(Left) Heart embossed clear glass, 5 oz. gold tone cap. Comes in Here's My Heart, Unforgettable, Moonwind, Topaze or Sweet Honesty. **CMV $2. MB.**
FLUFFY CHICK 1980
(Center) 1 oz. clear glass yellow flock coated. Holds Hello Sunshine cologne. **CMV $4. MB.**
FLUTTERING FANCY 1980
(Right) 1 oz. clear glass with pink butterfly on yellow frosted plastic cap. Holds Sweet Honesty or Charisma cologne. **CMV $5. MB.**

SNOW OWL POWDER SACHET II 1979-80
(Left) 1.25 oz. frosted glass. Holds Moonwind or Timeless powder sachet. Blue Rhinestone eyes. Label in black lettering. **CMV $7. MB.**
CUTE COOKIE 1979-80
(Center) 1 oz. dark amber glass. Pink cap & point. Holds Hello Sunshine cologne. **CMV $3. MB.**
CHARMING CHIPMUNK 1979-80
(Right) 5 oz. clear glass painted frosted peach color. Holds Field Flowers or Sweet Honesty. **CMV $4. MB.**

FLAMINGO 1971-72
5 oz. clear bird shaped bottle with gold cap. 10" tall. Came in Bird of Paradise, Elusive, Charisma, Brocade. **CMV $7. MB.**
SWAN LAKE 1972-76
8" high, 3 oz. white glass bottle with white cap. Came in Bird of Paradise, Charisma & Elusive. Moonwind **CMV $8. MB.**
BATH URN (CRUET) 1963-64
8 oz. white glass top & bottle. Perfume bath oil in Somewhere, Topaze, Cotillion. Here's My Heart, Persian Wood, To A Wild Rose. **CMV $12. MB, $6. bottle with label.**

COUNTRY STORE COFFEE MILL 1972-76
5 oz. ivory milk glass, white plastic cap & plastic handles on side with gold rim. Came in Sonnet, Moonwind, Bird of Paradise, Charisma cologne. **CMV $10. MB.** Came in 2 different size boxes.
LITTLE DUTCH KETTLE 1972-73
5 oz. orange painted clear glass with gold cap. Came in Cotillion, Honeysuckle Foaming Bath Oil or Lemon Velvet Bath Foam. **CMV $7. MB.**

SILVER DOVE ORNAMENT 1976
1/2 oz. bottle with gold or silver cap. Came in silver metal bird holder marked Christmas '76 on both sides & Avon on inside. Came in Bird of Paradise or Occur! cologne. **CMV $6. MB.**

SONG BIRD 1971-72
1.5 oz. clear glass with gold base cap. Came in Unforgettable, Topaze, Occur!, Here's My Heart & Cotillion. **CMV $6. MB.**
BIRD OF HAPPINESS 1975-76
1.5 oz. light blue glass, gold cap. Holds Charisma, Topaze, Occur!, or Unforgettable cologne. **CMV $5. MB.**

DR. HOOT 1977-79
(Left) 4 oz. white milk glass owl with blue plastic cap and white, gold or green tassel. Came in Sweet Honesty or Wild Country. **CMV $7. MB.**
DR. HOOT 1975-76
4 oz. opal white glass, black cap, gold tassel. Holds Wild Country After Shave or Sweet Honesty cologne. **CMV $8. MB.**
PRECIOUS OWL 1972-74
(Center) 1 1/2 oz. white bottle with gold eyes. Came in Moonwind, Field Flowers, Charisma, Roses Roses. **CMV $5. MB.**
SNOW OWL 1976-77
(Right) 1.25 oz. frosted glass base and frosted plastic head with blue eyes. Came in Moonwind or Sonnet. Label in blue lettering. **CMV $5. MB.**

ROYAL SWAN 1971-72
1 oz. white glass, gold crown cap. Came in Elusive, Charisma, Bird of Paradise, Topaze, Unforgettable, Cotillion. **CMV $7. MB.**
ROYAL SWAN 1974
1 oz. blue glass with gold crown cap. Came in Unforgettable, Topaze, Cotillion, Here's My Heart. **CMV $8. MB.**

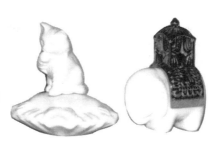

HEART STRINGS DECANTER 1983
.5 oz. red glass with gold cap. Choice of three fragrances. **CMV $3. MB.**

AUTUMN SCURRY "SQUIRREL" 1982-83
.5 oz. clear glass squirrel, gold cap. Choice of Moonwind, Topaze or Charisma cologne. **CMV $2. MB.**

BABY BASSETT DECANTER 1978-79
1.25 oz. amber glass and matching plastic head. Holds Topaze or Sweet Honesty Cologne. **CMV $3. MB.**

SITTING PRETTY 1976-77
1.5 oz. white milk glass base, white plastic top. Came in Charisma or Topaze. Pink ribbons painted on each corner. **CMV $8. MB.**

ROYAL ELEPHANT 1977-79
1/2 oz. white milk glass with gold snap on top. Came in Charisma or Topaze. **CMV $6. MB.**

CURIOUS KITTY 1979-80
2.5 oz. clear glass, yellow cat cap. Came in Sweet Honesty or Here's My Heart cologne. **CMV $6. MB.**

PEEK A MOUSE CHRISTMAS STOCKING 1978-79
1.25 oz. green glass with gold mouse cap. Holds Sweet Honesty or Unforgettable cologne. Came with red velvet stocking with gold trim. **CMV $6. MB.**

EMERALD ACCENT COLLECTION
DECANTER 1982-83
10" high, clear glass, green glass stopper. **CMV $15. MB.**

CORDIAL GLASSES
Set of two clear glasses with green glass stems, 4 1/2" high. **CMV $13. MB set.**

SERVING TRAY
11 1/2" long green glass tray. **CMV $15. MB.**

KITTEN LITTLE 1975-76
1.5 oz. black glass with black head. Holds Sweet Honesty, Bird of Paradise or Roses Roses. **CMV $6. MB.**

TABATHA 1975-76
3 oz. black glass and plastic. Holds Imperial Garden, Bird of Paradise or Cotillion cologne. **CMV $8. MB.**

MANSION LAMP 1975-76
6 oz. blue glass with white plastic top. Holds Bird of Paradise or Moonwind cologne. **CMV $10. MB.**

EMPIRE GREEN BUD VASE 1975
3 oz. green glass with silver base. Holds moonwind, Sonnet or Imperial Garden cologne. **CMV $6. MB.**

BUTTERFLY GARDEN BUD VASE 1975-76
6 oz. black glazed glass with gold stopper. Holds Roses Roses, Bird of Paradise or Topaze cologne. **CMV $6. MB.**

SEAGREEN BUD VASE 1972-73
5 oz. 9" high green glass bottle holds foaming bath oil in Field Flowers, Honeysuckle or Bird of Paradise. **CMV $6. MB.**

LADY SPANIEL 1974-76
1.5 oz. opal glass with plastic head. Holds Patchwork, Sonnet or Moonwind cologne. **CMV $6. MB.**

ROYAL SIAMESE CAT 1978-79
Light gray paint over clear glass. 4.5 oz. gray plastic head has blue glass jewel eyes. Came in Cotillion or Moonwind cologne. **CMV $8. MB.**

KITTEN'S HIDEAWAY 1974-76
1 oz. amber basket, white plastic kitten cap. Came in Field Flowers, Bird of Paradise or Charisma Cream Sachet. **CMV $6. MB.**

BLUE EYES 1975-76
1.5 oz. opal glass with blue rhinestone eyes. Available in Topaze or Sweet Honesty cologne. **CMV $7. MB.**

SEA TREASURE 1971-72
5 oz. clear glass coated iridescent sea shell shaped bottle, gold cap. Came in Field Flowers, Charisma, Honeysuckle, Lilac. 7" long. **CMV $10. MB.**

WOMEN'S DECANTERS & COLLECTIBLES

PRINCESS OF YORKSHIRE 1976-78
(Left) 1 oz. off white over milk glass. Came in Sweet Honesty or Topaze cologne. **CMV $5. MB.**

ROYAL PEKINESE 1974-75
(Center) 1.5 oz. white glass & white plastic head. Came in Unforgettable, Somewhere, Topaze. **CMV $7. MB.**

FUZZY BEAR 1977-79
(Right) Tan flock over clear glass base & head. Came in Sweet Honesty or Occur! **CMV $6.50 MB.**

TIFFANY LAMP 1972-74
5 oz. brown glass base with pink shade, pink and orange flowers, green leaves on lavender background. Came in Sonnet, Moonwind, Field Flowers, Roses Roses. **CMV $12. MB,** Also came in pink and yellow flowers on shade, also all white flowers. **CMV $13. MB.**

HEARTH LAMP 1973-76
8 oz. black glass with gold handle, has daisies around neck with yellow & white shade. Holds Roses Roses, Bird of Paradise or Elusive. **CMV $12. MB.**

CHIMNEY LAMP 1973-74
2 oz. clear glass bottom with white plastic shade with pink flowers. Holds Patchwork Sonnet or Moonwind. **CMV $6. MB.**

QUEEN OF SCOTS 1973-76
1 oz. white milk glass, white plastic head. Came in Sweet Honesty, Unforgettable, Somewhere, Cotillion, Here's My Heart. **CMV $6. MB.**

DACHSHUND 1973-74
1.5 oz. frosted glass, gold cap. Came in Unforgettable, Somewhere, Topaze, Cotillion. **CMV $7. MB.**

SEA SPIRIT 1973-76
5 oz. light green glass with green plastic tail over cap. Holds Elusive, Topaze or Cotillion. **CMV $7. MB.**

SONG OF THE SEA 1974-75
80 bath pearls, aqua colored glass with plastic head. Holds Moonwind, Sonnet or Imperial Garden. **CMV $8. MB.**

FLORAL BUD VASE 1973-75
5 oz. white milk glass. Holds Roses Roses, Lemon Velvet Bath Foam, Field Flowers or Honeysuckle Foaming Bath Oil. **CMV $6. MB.**

SUZETTE 1973-76
5 oz. cream colored milk glass with cream colored plastic head & a pink-lavender bow around neck. Holds Field Flowers, Bird of Paradise or Cotillion Foaming Bath Oil. **CMV $9. MB.**

DOLPHIN 1968-69
8 oz. frosted glass with gold tail cap. **CMV $11. MB**

BUTTERFLY 1972-73
1 1/2 oz. 3 1/2" high, gold cap with 2 prongs. Holds cologne in Occur!, Topaze, Unforgettable, Somewhere & Here's My Heart. **CMV $7. MB.** Reissued in 1976 in Field Flowers & Sweet Honesty. **Same CMV.**

DOLPHIN MINIATURE 1973-74
1.5 oz. clear glass, gold tail. Holds Charisma, Bird of Paradise or Field Flowers cologne. **CMV $5. MB.**

CRYSTAL POINT SALT SHAKER 1976-77
1.5 oz. blue glass. Holds Sonnet or Cotillion cologne. **CMV $4. MB.**

PARISIAN GARDEN 1974-75
(Left) .33 oz. white milk glass with gold cap. Came in Sonnet, moonwind or Charisma perfume. **CMV $5. MB.**

EVENING GLOW 1974-75
.33 oz. white milk glass with green flowers, white and gold plastic cap. Came in Moonwind, Sonnet or Charisma. **CMV $7. MB.**

FRAGRANCE SPLENDOR 1971-74
4 1/2" high clear glass bottle with gold cap & frosted plastic handle. Holds perfume oil in Bird of Paradise, Elusive, Occur!, Charisma or Unforgettable. **CMV $6. MB.**

BON BON "BLACK" 1973
1 oz. black milk glass with black plastic cap.
Holds Field Flowers, Bird of Paradise, Roses
Roses or Elusive. **CMV $7. MB.**
BON BON "WHITE" 1972-73
1 oz. white milk glass with white cap. Holds
Unforgettable, Topaze, Occur!, Cotillion or
Here's My Heart cologne. **CMV $7. MB.**

MING BLUE LAMP 1974-76
5 oz. blue glass lamp, white plastic shade with
gold tip. Holds Charisma, Bird of Paradise or
Field Flowers Foaming Bath Oil. **CMV $8. MB,**
CHARMLIGHT 1975-76
.88 oz. cream sachet in white shade and 2 oz.
cologne in pink base. Holds Imperial Garden,
Sonnet or Moonwind. **CMV $8. MB.**

SKIN-SO-SOFT DECANTER 1966
(Left) 10 oz. bottle with glass & cork stopper.
10" high. **CMV $12. MB.**
SKIN-SO-SOFT DECANTER 1967
(Right) 8 oz. bottle with glass & cork stopper.
11" high. **CMV $12. MB.**

SEA HORSE 1970-72
Clear glass 6 oz. container holds Skin-So-Soft,
gold cap. **CMV $9. MB.**
**SEA HORSE MINIATURE COLOGNE 1973-
76**
1.5 oz. clear glass, gold cap. Came in
Unforgettable, Here's My Heart, Cotillion.
CMV $6. MB.

AVONSHIRE DECANTER 1979
6 oz. clear glass painted blue and white.
Holds Charisma or Somewhere cologne. R on
bottom for Reissue and dated May, 1979. **CMV
$9. MB.**
AVONSHIRE BATH OIL DECANTER 1979
6 oz. clear glass painted blue and white.
Holds Skin-So-Soft. R on bottom for reissue
and dated May, 1979. **CMV $8. MB.**
AVONSHIRE HOSTESS SOAPS 1979
Blue box holds 3 white bars. **CMV $7. MB.**

PARLOR LAMP 1971-72
2 sections. Gold cap over 3 oz. cologne top
section in light amber iridescent glass. Yellow
frosted glass bottom with talc 6 1/2" high.
Holds Bird of Paradise, Elusive, Charisma,
Regence or Moonwind. **CMV $14. MB, $10.
BO.**
COURTING LAMP 1970-71
5 oz. blue glass base with white milk glass
shade & blue velvet ribbon. Holds Elusive,
Brocade, Charisma, Hana Gasa or Regence.
CMV $14. MB, $10. BO.

COUNTRY CHARM 1976-77
(Left) 4.8 oz. white milk glass, yellow stove
window. Green & white plastic top. Came in
Field Flowers or Sonnet. **CMV $10. MB.**
HURRICANE LAMP 1973-74
(Right) 6 oz. white milk glass bottom with clear
glass shade, gold cap. Holds Roses Roses,
Field Flowers, Bird of Paradise or Charisma
cologne. **CMV $13. MB.**

FLOWER FANCY 1979-80
1.25 oz. clear glass, gold flower cap. Holds
Field Flowers or Roses Roses. **CMV $4. MB.**
SPRING SONG 1979-80
1.5 oz. clear glass. Comes with plastic frosted
flower stopper. Came in Lily of the Valley or
Sweet Honesty cologne. **CMV $6. MB.**

SKIN-SO-SOFT DECANTER 1965-66

10. oz. bottle with gold painted glass stopper. 1st issue came with solid painted gold around center & later issue not solid band as pictured. **CMV solid band $13. MB, Not solid band $12. MB.**

CREAMERY DECANTER 1973-75

8 oz. yellow painted over clear glass with brown basket of blue & orange flowers. Holds Roses Roses, Field Flowers, Bird of Paradise hand & body cream lotion. **CMV $10. MB.**

LIQUID MILK BATH 1975-76

6 oz. frosted glass bottle with gold cap. Holds Imperial Garden, Sonnet or Moonwind. **CMV $5. MB.**

SKIN-SO-SOFT DECANTER 1964

(Left) 6 oz. gold crown top, came with gold neck tag. **CMV $12. MB, $6. BO with tag, mint.**

SKIN-SO-SOFT DECANTER 1962-63

(Right) 5 3/4 oz. gold neck string with white label, pink & white box. **CMV $12. MB, BO $5. mint with tag.**

COUNTRY STYLE COFFEE POT 1979-80

Came in special color of box. 10 oz. clear glass painted red or green, blue or yellow. Holds moisturized hand lotion. Comes with matching hand pump. **CMV $8. MB.**

OOPS COLOGNE DECANTER 1981

(Left) White glass, brown spots. Ice Cream bottle with tan plastic cone top. 1.5 oz. Sweet Honesty or Country Breeze. **CMV $6. MB.**

BIG SPENDER 1981-82

(Center) 1 oz. green glass, silver cap. Light Musk for men or Sweet Honesty cologne. **CMV $4. MB.**

ULTRA CRYSTAL COLOGNE 1981-82

(Right) Gray box holds 2 oz. clear glass & glass cap. Choice of Tasha, Foxfire, Timeless, Ariane. **CMV $3. MB.** See Soap Dish section & Candle section for other Ultra Crystal Collections.

HUDSON MANOR COLLECTION 1978-79
SALTCELLAR CANDLE & SPOON

Silver plated. Comes with glass lined candle. Bottom says HMC Avon Silver Plate on both pieces. Silver and white box. **CMV $19. MB.**

SILVER PLATED DISH AND SATIN SACHET

6" silver plated dish with red satin sachet pillow. Bottom of dish says Avon Silver Plate HMC, Italy. **CMV $15. MB.**

SILVER PLATED HOSTESS BELL

5 1/2" high silver plated bell. Avon Silver Plate HMC on bottom. **CMV $19. MB.**

SILVER PLATED BUD VASE AND SCENTED ROSE

8" high silver plated bud vase. Came with long stemmed fabric rose and 2 Roses Roses pellets. **CMV $15. MB.**

BATH SEASONS 1969

(Left) 3 oz. bath oil. Came in Charisma & Brocade. Black milk glass with silver cap & base. **CMV $6. MB.**

EMOLLIENT FRESHENER FOR AFTER BATH 1972-74

(Center) 6 oz. clear glass with gold cap, holds Sonnet, Charisma, Imperial Garden or Moonwind pearlescent liquid. **CMV $3. MB.**

AMBER CRUET 1973-75

(Right) 6 oz. light amber ribbed glass. Holds Field Flowers, Bird of Paradise or Charisma foaming bath oil. **CMV $5. MB.** 1975 Came only in Field Flowers & Bird of Paradise.

LADY SKATER TALC 1979-80

3.75 oz. gold top can. Red cap. Choice of Ariane or Sweet Honesty talc. **CMV $2. mint, no box issued.**

GENTLEMAN SKATER TALC 1979-80

3.75 oz. gold top can. Blue cap. Choice of Clint or Trazarra talc. **CMV $2. mint.** No box issued.

COUNTRY CREAMERY "MILK CAN" 1978-79

10 oz. white painted over clear glass. Holds moisturized hand lotion. **CMV $6. MB.**

HEARTS FROM THE HEART 1987
Heart shaped lead crystal dish & 8 pink heart shaped bath pearls. **CMV $8. MB.**

COLOGNE ELEGANTE 1973-74
3 oz. clear glass, gold cap with atomizer, also white plastic cap. Holds Imperial Garden, Patchwork, Sonnet or Moonwind. **CMV $4. MB.**

COURTING ROSE 1974
1.5 oz. red glass rose with gold cap & stem. Came in Moonwind, Sonnet or Imperial Garden. Later issue painted red over clear glass. **CMV $7. MB each.**

SWEET TREAT COLOGNE 1974-76
White & brown painted glass with red cap. Came in Pink & Pretty cologne. **CMV $4. MB.**

COURTING ROSE 1977
(Right) 1.5 oz. amber coated over clear glass rose bottle with gold top. Came in Roses Roses or Moonwind cologne. **CMV $6. MB,**

PYRAMID OF FRAGRANCE 1969
Top is 1/8 oz. perfume, gold cap. Center is 2 oz. cologne. Bottom is 2-3 oz. cream sachet in black glass. 6" high, came in Charisma, Brocade or Regence. **CMV $12.50 BO. mint. $20. MB.**

FASHION BOOT PIN CUSHION 1972-76
5 1/2" tall, blue milk glass with lavender bow & velvet cushion that fits over cap. Holds 4 oz. cologne in Roses Roses, Charisma, Sonnet or Moonwind **CMV $8. MB,**

PICTURE FRAME COLOGNE 1970-71
4 oz. gold paint on clear glass. Gold cap & gold plastic frame to hold bottle. Came in Elusive, Charisma, Brocade, Regence. **CMV $11. mint, $17. MB.**

ALADDIN'S LAMP 1971-73
(Left) 7 1/2" long, 6 oz. green glass bottle with gold cap. Holds foaming bath oil in Charisma, Bird of Paradise, Elusive, Occur! or Unforgettable. **CMV $10. MB.**

VENETIAN BLUE 1974-76
Frosted turquoise glass with turquoise plastic lid & gold tip. Holds 75 bath pearls. Came in Moonwind, Sonnet or Imperial Garden. **CMV $6. MB.**

DOVECOTE 1974-76
4 oz. clear glass with gold roof & 2 white doves. Holds Field Flowers, Bird of Paradise, Charisma or Roses Roses cologne. **CMV $4. MB.**

ROYAL APPLE COLOGNE 1972-73
(Left) 3 oz. frosted red glass with gold cap. Came in 4 fragrances. **CMV $7. MB.**

GARNET BUD VASE 1973-76
(Right) 3 oz. garnet colored translucent glass bottle & stopper. Came in Occur!, Somewhere, Topaze or To A Wild Rose cologne. **CMV $5. MB.**

ROYAL VASE 1970
(Left) 3 oz. blue cologne bottle in Elusive, Charisma, Brocade or Regence. **CMV $6. MB.**

RUBY BUD VASE 1970-71
(Right) 3 oz. red box holds ruby glass vase filled with Unforgettable, Rapture, Occur!, Somewhere, Topaze or Cotillion. **CMV $7. MB.**

WOMEN'S DECANTERS & COLLECTIBLES

LOVELY TOUCH DECANTER 1971
(Left) 12 oz. clear glass, gold cap with dispenser cap. Holds Vita Moist or Rich Moisture body lotion. **CMV $3. MB.**

LOVELY TOUCH DECANTER 1972-73
(Inside Left) 12 oz. clear glass with dispenser cap. Holds Vita Moist or Rich Moisture body lotion. **CMV $3. MB.**

CLASSIC BEAUTY 1972-76
(Inside Right) 10 oz. clear glass. Holds Bird of Paradise or Field Flowers hand & body cream. **CMV $3. MB.**

PINEAPPLE 1973-74
(Right) 10 oz. clear glass with green plastic leaves, dispenser top. Holds Moisturized Hand Lotion. **CMV $4. MB.**

BELL JAR 1973-75
(Left) 5 oz. clear glass with bouquet of pink & white flowers. Had gold cap & base with pink ribbon. Holds Field Flowers, Bird of Paradise, Charisma or Brocade cologne. **CMV $9. MB.** 1976 sold only in Field Flowers, Bird of Paradise & Charisma. **Same CMV.**

CRUET COLOGNE 1973-74
(Right) 8 oz. clear glass with glass stopper & flat dish. Holds Imperial Garden, Patchwork, Sonnet or Moonwind cologne. **CMV $13. MB.**

PERSIAN PITCHER 1974-76
(Left) 6 oz. blue glass. Holds Bird of Paradise, Charisma or Elusive foaming bath oil. **CMV $3. MB.**

COLOGNE ELEGANTE 1971-72
(Center) 4 oz. gold sprayed over clear glass & red rose on gold cap. 12" high. Came in Bird of Paradise, Hana Gasa, Elusive, Charisma, or Moonwind. **CMV $10. MB.**

EMERALD BUD VASE 1971
(Right) 3 oz. green glass & glass top, 9" high. Came in Topaze, Occur!, Unforgettable, Here's My Heart or To A Wild Rose. **CMV $4. MB.**

GRAPE BUD VASE 1973
(Left) 6 oz. grape frosted glass holds Skin-So-Soft. **CMV $5. MB.**

NILE BLUE BATH URN 1972-74
(Right) 6 oz. deep blue glass with gold trim. **CMV $5. MB.**

NILE GREEN BATH URN 1975
(Right) Same as above only green glass. **CMV $5. MB.**

CRYSTALIQUE COLOGNE 1975
(Left) 4 oz. clear glass with glass stopper. Holds Moonwind, Sonnet or Imperial Garden. **CMV $5. MB.**

BREATH FRESH APOTHECARY DECANTER 1974
(Center) 8 oz. clear glass with gold cap. Holds Breath Fresh Mouthwash. **CMV $3. MB.**

COUNTRY PUMP 1975
(Right) 10 oz. clear glass with plastic top. Holds Rich Moisture or Vita Moist body lotion. **CMV $4. MB.**

APOTHECARY 1973-74
(Left) 8 oz. Spicy After Shave in light brown glass with gold cap.

APOTHECARY 1973-76
(Center) 8 oz. Lemon Velvet Moisturized Friction Lotion in light yellow glass with gold cap. Also came in light green or blue-green glass.

APOTHECARY 1973
(Right) 8 oz. Breath Fresh in dark green with gold cap.
CMV $6. MB each.

SAPPHIRE SWIRL 1973-74
(Left) 5 oz. blue glass with gold cap. Holds Charisma or Bird of Paradise perfumed skin softener. **CMV $2. MB.**

PERIOD PIECE 1972-73
(Right) 5 oz. frosted glass. Came in Moonwind, Bird of Paradise, Charisma or Elusive. 1976 came with Charisma & Bird of Paradise. **CMV $7. MB.**

PETTI FLEUR COLOGNE 1969-70
(Left) 1 oz. gold cap. Shaped like flower. Came in Elusive, Brocade, Charisma or Regence. **CMV $8. MB.**

PURSE PETITE COLOGNE 1971
(Right) 1 1/2 oz. embossed bottle with gold trim and cap & chain. Elusive, Charisma, Bird of Paradise, Field Flowers or Hana Gasa. **CMV $10. MB.**

COUNTRY CHARM BUTTER CHURN 1973-74
(Left) 1.5 oz. clear glass, gold bands & cap. Came in Field Flowers, Elusive, Occur! or Somewhere cologne. **CMV $6. MB.**

GOLDEN THIMBLE 1972-74
(Right) 2 oz. clear glass with gold cap. Came in Bird of Paradise, Brocade, Charisma or Elusive cologne. **CMV $5. MB.**

COUNTRY JUG 1976-78
(Left) 10 oz. gray painted over clear glass. Blue & gray plastic pump. Came with almond scented hand lotion. **CMV $5. MB.**

SEA FANTASY BUD VASE 1978-79
(Right) 6 oz. bottle. Gold & white fish & seaweed design on both sides. Holds Skin-So-Soft bath oil, bubble bath & Smooth As Silk. **CMV $4. MB.**

DEW KISS DECANTER 1974-75
(Left) 4 oz. clear glass with pink lid. **CMV $2. MB.**

SEA LEGEND DECANTER 1975-76
(Right) 6 oz. clear glass with white cap. Holds Moonwind or Sonnet foaming bath oil or Roses Roses creamy bath foam. **CMV $4. MB.**

GOLDEN FLAMINGO 1975
(Left) 6 oz. clear glass with gold flamingo on front. Holds Bird of Paradise, Charisma or Field Flowers foaming bath oil. **CMV $4. MB.**

ATHENA BATH URN 1975-76
(Right) 6 oz. clear glass. Holds Field Flowers, Bird of Paradise foaming bath oil or Roses Roses cream bath foam. **CMV $4. MB.**

COUNTRY STYLE COFFEE POT 1975-76
(Left) 10 oz. yellow speckled paint over clear glass. Came with yellow & white pump top. Came with moisturized hand lotion. **CMV $7. MB.**

GOLDEN HARVEST 1977-80
(Right) 10 oz. ear of corn shaped clear & green glass bottle. Gold & plastic pump top. Came with Avon almond scented hand lotion. **CMV $6. MB.**

KEEPSAKE CREAM SACHET 1971-73
(Left) 6 1/2" high, gold lid on marbleized glass jar with flower in colors. Came in Moonwind. OSP $5. Bird of Paradise, Field Flowers, Elusive, Charisma. **CMV $7. MB.**

KEEPSAKE CREAM SACHET 1970-73
(Right) 5 1/2" high gold metal tree lid on .66 oz. frosted glass jar. Came in Bird of Paradise, Elusive, Charisma, Brocade or Regence. **CMV $8. MB.**

BAROQUE CREAM SACHET 1974
(Left) 2 oz. white milk glass with gold top & bottom. Came in Imperial Garden, Sonnet or Moonwind. **CMV $7. MB.**

COUNTRY STORE MINERAL SPRING BATH CRYSTALS 1973-75
(Right) 12 oz. clear glass with gold cap. Holds green Mineral Springs Bath Crystals. **CMV $7. MB.**

PORCELAIN FLORAL BOUQUET 1980
(Left) 4" high porcelain. Dated 1980 on bottom. **CMV $18. MB.**

ULTRA MIST ATOMIZER 1980-81
(Right) 1.5 oz. clear swirl glass bottle with gold top & atomizer bulb. Choice of Ariane, Timeless, Tasha or Candid. **CMV $2. MB.**

CRYSTALINE BOWL & FLOWERS 1982
Pink box holds 5" long glass bowl with plastic insert to hold artificial flowers. Comes with fragrance tablet. **CMV $18. MB.**

FLAVOR FRESH APOTHECARY 1977-80
6 oz. clear glass bottle & stopper. Holds mouthwash. **CMV $2. MB.**

LOOKING GLASS 1970-72
6 1/2" high, clear glass mirror. Frame holds 1 1/2 oz. cologne in Bird of Paradise, Elusive, Charisma, Brocade, Regence, Unforgettable, Rapture, Occur!, Somewhere, Topaze, Cotillion, Here's My Heart or To A Wild Rose. With gold handle cap. **CMV $13. MB.**

FOAMING BATH OIL DECANTER 1975
6 oz. clear glass with gold cap. Came in Cotillion, Field Flowers, Bird of Paradise, Charisma, Sonnet, Imperial Garden, Moonwind & Timeless. This sold C26 - 1975 only. Very short issue. **CMV $5. MB.** This is the same bottle as the 1972-74 Emollient Freshener for After Bath. Only label & box are changed.

HONEY BEAR BABY 1974-76
4 oz. yellow painted glass with blue plastic bear on lid. **CMV $4. MB.**

WINTER GARDEN 1975-76
(Left) 6 oz. clear glass with gold cap. Holds Here's My Heart, Topaze or Occur! cologne. **CMV $5. MB.**
REGENCY DECANTER 1974-75
(Right) 6 oz. clear glass filled with Skin-So-Soft bath oil. **CMV $5. MB.**

TREE MOUSE 1977-79
(Left) .66 oz. clear glass & clear plastic top. Gold mouse. Came in Sweet Honesty or Charisma. **CMV $4. MB,**
SILVER PEAR 1977
(Center) .66 oz. silver plated over clear glass. Silver top. Came in Sweet Honesty or Charisma. **CMV $4. MB.**
ENCHANTED APPLE 1976-78
(Right) .66 oz. gold plated over clear glass. Gold top. Came in Charisma or Sonnet. **CMV $4. MB.**

PEAR LUMIERE 1975-76
(Left) 2 oz. clear glass & plastic with gold leaf. Holds Roses Roses, Charisma or Bird of Paradise cologne. **CMV $5. MB.**
SONG OF LOVE 1975-76
(Right) 2 oz. clear glass, clear plastic top with white bird. Holds Bird of Paradise, Charisma or Sweet Honesty. 1976 issued with blue base, blue top in Moonwind & Here's My Heart. **CMV $3. MB.**

VICTORIAN SEWING BASKET 1974-76
(Left) 5 oz. white milk glass basket with lavender plastic, gold cord holds pink flower. Came in Roses Roses, Bird of Paradise or Charisma perfumed Skin-So-Soft. **CMV $6. MB.**
VANITY JAR 1975-76
(Right) 5 oz. clear glass with silver lid. Choice of Rich Moisture Cream or SSS skin conditioner. **CMV $1. MB.**

CASTLEFORD COLLECTION EMOLLIENT BATH PEARLS 1974-76
(Left) Holds 60 bath pearls. Clear glass. Came in Imperial Garden, Sonnet or Moonwind. **CMV $6. MB.**
CASTLEFORD COLLECTION COLOGNE GELEE 1975-76
(Right) 4 oz. glass holds Raining Violets, Roses Roses or Apple Blossoms cologne gelee. **CMV $6. MB.**

HUMPTY DUMPTY BANK 1982
Box holds ceramic bank made in Korea for Avon. Dated 1982. Sold empty. 5" high. **CMV $12. MB.**
CRYSTAL CLEAR HOSTESS DECANTER 1980-81
Clear glass jar & glass lid, Avon stainless spoon. Comes in 5.5 oz. Strawberry Bubble Bath Gelee. **CMV $6. MB.**

TEATIME POWDER SACHET 1974-75
1.25 oz. frosted white with gold cap. Holds Moonwind, Sonnet or Roses Roses. **CMV $7. MB.**

LIP TOPPING LIP GLOSS 1982-83
Tin box holds choice of Chocolate Fudge or Butterscotch. **CMV $1. each.**

SCENTIMENTS COLOGNE 1978-79
(Left) 2 oz. clear glass. Came with pink card on front to write your own message. Came in Sweet Honesty or Here's My Heart cologne. **CMV $4. MB.**
GOLDEN BAMBOO VASE 1978-79
(Right) 1 oz. yellow painted over clear glass, black cap, base. Came in Moonwind or Sweet Honesty cologne. **CMV $5. MB.**

VICTORIAN WASHSTAND 1973-74
(Left) 4 oz. buff painted with gray plastic simulated marble top with blue pitcher & bowl for cap. Came in Field Flowers, Bird of Paradise or Charisma foaming bath oil. **CMV $8. MB.**
REMEMBER WHEN SCHOOL DESK 1972-74
(Right) 4 oz. black glass with light brown plastic seat front & desk top, red apple for cap. Came in Rapture, Here's My Heart, Cotillion or Somewhere cologne. **CMV $8. MB.**

SILVER FAWN 1978-79
.5 oz. silver coated over clear glass. Choice of Sweet Honesty or Charisma cologne. SSP $2. **CMV $3. BO, $4. MB.**

FUNBURGER LIP GLOSS 1977-78
(Left) Came in Frostlight Rose & Frostlight Coral lip gloss. Brown plastic. **CMV $2. MB.**
CHRISTMAS SURPRISE 1976
(Center) 1 oz. green glass boot. Came in Sweet Honesty, Moonwind, Charisma or Topaze cologne. Red cap or silver cap. **CMV $3. MB,**
ORIENTAL PEONY VASE 1977
(Right) 1.5 oz. red paint over clear glass with gold design. Came in Sweet Honesty or Moonwind. **CMV $7. MB.**

AMERICAN HEIRLOOM SHIPS DECANTER 1981-82
(Left) 6 oz. clear glass, top. Choice of Wild Country After Shave or Sweet Honesty Body Splash. **CMV $9. MB.**
SOFT SWIRLS BATH DECANTER 1981-82
(Right) 8 oz. clear glass, frosted cap. Choice of Smooth As Silk bath oil or Skin-So-Soft. **CMV $8. MB.**

LAVENDER & LACE 1970-72
Lavender & white box holds 1.7 oz. white glass bottle of Lavender cologne with lavender ribbon. A lavender & white lace handkerchief came with it. **CMV $8. set MB. $3. BO. with ribbon.**

NATURE'S BEST WOODEN DISPLAY SPOON HOLDER 1981-82
Made of wood, 3 1/2" x 7". Does not say Avon. Comes in Avon box. **CMV $7. MB.**
NATURE'S BEST COLLECTOR'S SPOONS 1981-82
4 different stainless spoons with Avon on them. 5" long in flannel pouch. porcelain inlaid with fruit - strawberry, orange, plum, raspberry. **CMV $10. each MB.**

PURRFECT CAT 1987
1.5 oz. cologne. Black glass. **CMV $5 MB.**
COUNTRY CHICKEN 1987
9.5 oz. white ceramic bottle with pump. Holds hand lotion. **CMV $7. MB.**

MOM'S PRIDE AND JOY PICTURE FRAME 1983
6 1/2" x 2" clear glass MOM frame. **CMV $10. MB.**

ANNIVERSARY KEEPSAKE - MEN 1981-82
Replica of California Perfume Co. "Early Day Avon". Bay Rum After Shave. 3 oz. clear glass with glass top in plastic cork. **CMV $7. MB.**
ANNIVERSARY KEEPSAKE - WOMEN 1981-82
3 oz. clear glass CPC replica of 1908 design. Holds White Lilac cologne. Dated 1981. **CMV $7. MB.** Both came to Avon managers as a Demo empty and marked Not For Sale. **CMV $10. each.**

CALIFORNIA PERFUME CO. ANNIVERSARY KEEPSAKE COLOGNE 1975
(Left) Issued in honor of 89th Anniversary. 1.7 oz. bottle, pink ribbon & gold cap. Came in Charisma or Sweet Honesty cologne. Sold in 2 campaigns only. **CMV $5., $7. MB.** 1st issue Avon Presidents Club Reps received this bottle with 4A design under bottom label. Regular issue had Avon on bottom. **CMV for 4A design & "M" for Managers.** Given to Managers only. **CMV $15. MB.**
CPC ANNIVERSARY KEEPSAKE COLOGNE 1976
(Right) 1.7 oz. clear glass bottle, gold cap. Bottle is embossed on back side (Avon 90th Anniversary Keepsake). Came in Moonwind or Cotillion cologne. Sold 2 campaigns only. **CMV $7. MB.**

DINGO BOOT 1978-79
6 oz. camel tan plastic bottle and cap. Choice of Sweet Honesty Body Splash or Wild Country After Shave. **CMV $2. MB.**
VINTAGE YEAR "CHAMPAIN YEAR" 1978-79
2 oz. green glass, gold cap. 1979 embossed in bottom. Came in Sweet Honesty or Wild Country cologne. Green and gold box. **CMV $4. MB.**
ANNIVERSARY KEEPSAKE C.P.C. 1978-79
1.5 oz. clear glass. Old style C.P.C. label and design. Pink neck ribbon. Came in Trailing Arbutus, Sweet Honesty or Somewhere cologne. **CMV $5. MB.**

ANNIVERSARY KEEPSAKE EAU DE TOILETTE 1979
Large 8 oz. clear glass bottle, CPC embossed on back side. Avon 1979 on bottom. Gold cap. Pink and green box. Came in Trailing Arbutus cologne. Pink neck ribbon. **CMV $10. MB.**

ANNIVERSARY KEEPSAKE C.P.C. FLACON 1979
.75 oz. clear glass. Silver cap has 1979 on top. Came with Sweet Honesty or Trailing Arbutus cologne. **CMV $6. MB.**

COUNTRY TALC SHAKER 1977-79
3 oz. gray and blue speckled metal can shaker top. Came in Sweet Honesty or Charisma perfumed talc. **CMV $3. MB.**
CALIFORNIA PERFUME CO. ANNIVERSARY KEEPSAKE 1977-78
3.75. oz. blue can sold to public with Avon 1977 on the bottom. **CMV $2. MB.** Was also given to Avon Reps during 91st Anniversary with "Anniversary Celebration Avon 1977" on the bottom. **CMV $6. MB.** Came in Roses Roses or Trailing Arbutus Talc.

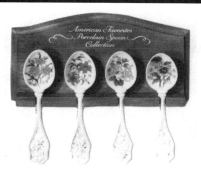

PIERRE DECANTER 1984
8 oz. white glass pig. Cloth apron on front. Holds Care Deeply Hand Lotion. CMV $10. MB.

AMERICAN FAVORITES PORCELAIN SPOONS 1989
Porcelain spoons on wood rack. Daffodil, Daylily, Rose, Pansy. CMV $10 ea. MB, Rack $5. MB.

COUNTRY GOOSE DECANTER 1988
4 3/4" high holds 1.75 oz. cologne. Ceramic goose head. Wicker hat, cotton dress. CMV $8. MB.

YOU'RE THE BERRIES CANDY JAR 1984
Clear glass 5" high fruit jar with berry cloth lid cover. Holds hard candy. CMV $6. MB.
COUNTRY CHARM LOTION PUMP 1985
10 oz. jug bottle with pump. CMV $5. MB.

MEADOW BLOSSOMS DECANTER 1987
1.75 oz. Frosted glass bottle, porcelain flower top. Holds cologne. CMV $8. MB.

PRETTY CAT DECANTER 1988
1.5 oz. white glass 4" high. Holds cologne. CMV $6. MB.

WRITE TOUCH MOUSE 1982-83
(Left) 1 oz. green glass and white plastic mouse with stick on decals. Choice of Sweet Honesty or Charisma cologne. CMV $6. MB.
FRAGRANCE NOTABLES 1982
(Center) .5 oz. clear glass with ribbon design. Red cap and box. Choice of Wild Jasmine, Occur!, Moonwind, Charisma, Topaze or Sweet Honesty cologne. CMV $2. MB.
CRYSTALLIQUE TREE 1982
(Right) .5 oz. clear glass tree bottle with bronze color cap. Choice of Foxfire, Timeless or Odyssey cologne. CMV $3. MB.

STATUE OF LIBERTY BRASS STAMP 1985
1886-1986 on wood base. CMV $10. MB.
HOSPITALITY SPOON SERIES 1985
Wood rack with 4 spoons - Italian Grapes, German Maiden, Scottish Thistle, American Pineapple. CMV $30. set MB with rack. or $6. ea. piece.

FRAGRANCE KEEPSAKE 1983
.5 oz. fan shaped clear glass, with rose red cap. Choice of Somewhere, Here's My Heart, Regence, Rapture, Persian Wood, Brocade, Cotillion. CMV $2. MB.
GINGERBREAD COTTAGE 1983-84
.5 oz. dark amber glass, pink cap. Choice of Sweet Honesty or Charisma cologne. 2" high. CMV $4. MB.

SNUG CUB DECANTER 1987
1 oz. white glass, red cap. Holds cologne.
CMV $4. MB.

GIFT OF LOVE CRYSTAL BOX 1988
1 1/4" high, 2 3/4" wide glass box. **CMV $10. MB.**

CRYSTAL CONFECTIONS JAR 1988
Lead crystal glass jar 5 3/4" high. **CMV $15. MB.**

McCONNELLS CORNER TOWN TREE 1982
8" high ceramic tree, green and white. Dated "Christmas 1982". **CMV $12. MB.**

SEA SHELL DECANTER 1990
2 oz. sea shell. Holds S.S.S. bath oil. **CMV $7. MB.**

ROMANTIC MEMORIES "HEART" CO-LOGNE SPLASH 1994
Box holds heart shaped .5 oz. cologne with gold caps. 5 fragrances. Sold 2 campaigns only. **CMV $4. ea. MB.**

DELICATE WINGS CRYSTAL BUTTERFLY BOX 1992
Lead crystal dish & lid. 4.5" x 3.25" x 1.25" size. Short issue. **CMV $10. MB.**

CRYSTAL TREASURE BOX 1990
2.75" square 1.75" high clear lead crystal box.
CMV $18. MB.

VINTAGE FRAGRANCE COLOGNE 1992
One time issue. .5 oz. cologne in special box. Choice of 8 old Avon fragrances. **CMV $2. MB.**

HEARTS & BOWS COLOGNE 1991
.5 oz. tie bag shaped clear glass. Red cap & heart box. Ladies cologne. **CMV $2.50 MB.**

PEPPERMINT GINGERBREAD TIN 1994
3 7/8" X 6" X 3 7/8" tin gingerbread house box holds 12 oz. peppermint candy. **CMV $4. empty.**

HOLIDAY MINI COLOGNE SPLASH 1993
Special Xmas boxes are short issue items. Choice of Men's Black & Red box or Women's Gold box, holds choice of .5 oz. cologne. Must be in Box shown. **CMV $2. ea MB.**

BE MY VALENTINE COLOGNE SPLASH 1995
Red box holds .5 oz. heart shaped bottle, gold cap. Choice of 9 fragrances. Sold 2 times only. Must be in box shown. **CMV $ 3. MB.**

ATLANTA 1996 "OLYMPIC" DECANTER
7 3/4" high 5 oz. frosted glass with gold flame cap. Holds Imari cologne. **CMV $20. MB.**

NATIVITY FIGURINES

NATIVITY ANGEL & STABLE 1985
White porcelain angel & plastic stable. set.
CMV $23. set MB.

HOLY FAMILY NATIVITY FIGURINES 1986
Porcelain figurines 2 1/2" to 3 3/4" high. **Mary, Joseph & Baby Jesus in manger. Set of 3.
CMV $47. set MB.**

O' HOLY NIGHT THREE KINGS SET 1989
(Left) Hand painted bisque porcelain. **Melchior & Balthasar** each 3 1/2" high. **Kasper** is 2 5/8" high. **CMV $15 ea. MB.**

NATIVITY WOOD STAND 1988
11" wide. **CMV $25. MB.**

NATIVITY COLLECTION 1980's-1990's
All are white bisque porcelain.. Sold each year since introduction at Christmas. Left to Right:

COW 1987
5 1/2" long. **CMV $20. MB.**
SHEEP 1983
4 " long. **CMV $16. MB.**
STANDING ANGEL 1987
6" high. **CMV $25. MB.**
WOMAN WITH WATER JAR 1990
6 3/4" high. **CMV $25. MB.**
SHEPHERD BOY 1983
4 3/4" high. **CMV $22. MB.**

GABRIEL 1992
7" high. **CMV $30. MB.**
THE INNKEEPER 1988
4 1/2" high. **CMV $25. MB.**
THE DONKEY 1984
3" high. **CMV $20. MB.**
THE CAMEL 1984
4 3/4" high. **CMV $28. MB.**
POOR MAN 1990
3 1/2" high. **CMV $25. MB.**

NATIVITY ORNAMENT COLLECTION 1985
All white porcelain. The Shepherd, The Holy Family, The Three Magi. **CMV $12. MB ea.**

NATIVITY COLLECTION 1980's-1990's

All are white bisque porcelain and are sold each year at Christmas from date of introduction thru 1994.

From left to right:

CHILDREN IN PRAYER 1991
4" high. **CMV $25. MB.**
THE SHEPHERD 1983
6 1/2" high. **CMV $22.50. MB.**
THE MAGI - 1982 "THREE WISE MEN"
Kaspar 7 1/2", Melchior 4 1/2", Balthasar 6 1/2". **CMV $25. ea. MB.**

THE CHERUB 1989
3" high. **CMV $20. MB.**
HOLY FAMILY 1981
Mary 4" high, **Joseph** 6" high, **Baby Jesus in Manger,** 2 1/2" long. Set of 3. **CMV $38.50. MB. set of 3.**

'O HOLY NIGHT NATIVITY COLLECTION 1989
Made of porcelain. Background - "CRECHE" 5 1/4" high. **CMV $15. MB.**
Baby Jesus 1 5/8" long, **Mary** 2 3/4" high, **Joseph** 3 1/2" high. Set of 3. **CMV $25. set MB.**

'O HOLY NIGHT NATIVITY SET - CAMEL SHEPHERD BOY & LAMB 1990
Both are bisque porcelain and dated on bottom. **CMV $13 ea. MB.**

BETHLEHEM NATIVITY COLLECTION 1993 THE MAGI
3 blue painted shiny porcelain figurines. 3rd in series "**Gaspar**" 6 1/2" high, "**Melchior**" 6 1/2" high, "**Balthasar**" 4 3/4" high. **CMV $35. ea. MB.**

NATIVITY COLLECTION - THE BLESSED FAMILY 1992
High glazed porcelain figurines. 1st in new series. **Baby Jesus** 2" high, **Mary** 4" high, and **Joseph** 6 3/4" high. Set of 3. **CMV $50. set. MB.**

NATIVITY "SHEPHERD WITH LAMB" 1993
19th in series, 6" high bisque porcelain. **CMV $25. MB.**

BETHLEHEM NATIVITY "CAMEL" 1994
5 1/2" long, 4" high porcelain camel with blue blanket in porcelain, dated 1994. **CMV $25. MB.**
BETHLEHEM NATIVITY "OXEN" 1994
4 3/4" long, 2 3/4" high porcelain oxen, dated 1994. **CMV $20. MB.**

HEAVENLY BLESSINGS NATIVITY COLLECTION 1986-89
All hand painted pastel porcelain figurines marked avon. **THE MAGI with BALTHASAR,** 3 1/2" high, **KASPAR,** 3 3/4", **MELCHOIR,** 2 1/2" high. **CMV $10. ea. MB.**
"LITTLE DRUMMER BOY" 3 1/4" high. **CMV $10. MB.**
"THE HOLY FAMILY"
JOSEPH, 3 1/4" high, **MARY,** 2 1/2" high, **BABY JESUS IN MANGER,** 2 1/4" long. Sold as set of 3. **CMV $25. set MB.**
DONKEY, 2 3/4" high. **CAMEL,** 3 1/4" high. **BOY ANGEL,** 2 1/2" high. **ANGEL,** 3" high. **SHEPHERD BOY,** 3 1/4" high. **SHEEP,** 1 3/4" high. **CMV $10. ea. MB.**

NATIVITY HEIRLOOM COLLECTION "HOLY FAMILY" 1996
Hand painted resin & dated 1996. **JOSEPH,** 43/4" high, **MARY,** 3 1/2" high, **BABY JESUS,** 1 1/4" high by 2 1/2" long. Sold as set of 3. **CMV $35. set MB.**

NATIVITY HEIRLOOM COLLECTION "MAGI" 1996
Melchior, 5" high, Gaspar, 4 1/8" high, Balthasar, 3 1/4" high. Sold as set of 3. **CMV $35. set MB.**

NATIVITY HEIRLOOM COLLECTION "ANGEL" 1996
Hand painted resin Angel is 5" high. Dated 1996 on bottom. **CMV $15. MB.**

NATIVITY HEIRLOOM COLLECTION "SHEPHERDS" 1996
Set is hand painted resin. Each is dated 1996. **"PRAYING SHEPHERD",** 4 3/4" high, **"BOY",** 4 1/4" high, & **"LAMB",** 1 1/2" high. Sold as set of 3. **CMV $35. set MB.**

HOLY FAMILY NATIVITY COLLECTION "My First Christmas"1995
Black or white family made of plastic. **BABY JESUS,** 2" long, **MARY & JOSEPH,** 3" high. Sold set of 3. **CMV $10. set MB.**

NATIVITY COLLECTION "MY FIRST STORY"1993-95
All are made of plastic and are 1 1/2" to 3" high. 3 different sets.
HOLY FAMILY in choice of white or black family. **BABY JESUS, MARY, JOSEPH.**
THE WISE MEN, 3 different men.
THE ANIMALS, COW, DONKEY, SHEEP.
CMV each set. $10. M.B.

All AVON Christmas Tree ornaments must be marked AVON and dated to be collectable. Avon has made a lot of tree ornaments but most are not marked AVON or dated.

MELVIN P. MERRYMOUSE KEEPSAKE ORNAMENT 1983
2 3/4" high Santa mouse on sleigh. Dated 1983. Plastic, 2nd in series. **CMV $8. MB.**

FOSTORIA ORNAMENTS 1985
Christmas village, Christmas tree or Angel ornament. **CMV $7. ea. MB.**

BABY'S FIRST CHRISTMAS ORNAMENT 1986
4" high white porcelain by Joan Walsh Anglund. **CMV $10.. MB.**

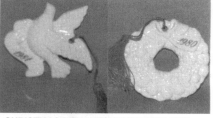

CHRISTMAS REMEMBRANCE DOVE 1981
Second in a series of tree ornaments from Avon. White ceramic dove, gold cord. **CMV $10. MB.**
CHRISTMAS REMEMBRANCE CERAMIC WREATH 1980
White ceramic, gold tassel. Dated 1980. 3" across. 1st in series. **CMV $10. MB.**

MELVIN P. MERRYMOUSE ORNAMENT 1982
Small plastic mouse Santa. Back of mirror says Avon Christmas, 1982. **CMV $10. MB.**

CHRISTMAS REMEMBRANCE ANGEL 1982
White ceramic angel, gold tassel. Comes in white felt bag. **CMV $10. MB.**

MERRY CHRISTMAS ORNAMENT CARD 1985
Xmas card holds 3" porcelain ornament. **CMV $8. MB.**

SNOWFLAKE ORNAMENT 1983 👉
(Left) White porcelain snowflake dated 1983. 2 1/2" wide on gold tassel. **CMV $10. MB.**
CAPTURED MOMENTS FRAME ORNAMENT 1983
(Right) Green & red plastic wreath. Slide a picture in center. 4" across. **CMV $5. MB.**

BABY'S FIRST CHRISTMAS ORNAMENT 1991
FIRST CHRISTMAS TOGETHER ORNAMENT 1991
Both ornaments are white bisque porcelain & dated 1991. **CMV $10. ea. MB.**

CHRISTMAS ORNAMENT 1987
Clear lead crystal dated 1987. Gold Tassel.
CMV $10. MB.

**"FATHER CHRISTMAS" TREE ORNAMENT
1993**
3 1/2" high pewter ornament in red felt pouch.
1st in series. **CMV $10.**

**"OUR FIRST CHRISTMAS TOGETHER"
ORNAMENT 1992**
3" bisque porcelain tree ornament. Dated 1992.
CMV $10. MB.
**"BABY'S FIRST CHRISTMAS" ORNAMENT
1992**
Bisque porcelain 3 3/4"high. Baby
carriage.Dated 1992. **CMV $10. MB.**

**"SANTA'S ARRIVAL" HOLIDAY PEWTER
ORNAMENT 1994**
3 1/2" high pewter Santa. Red bag. **CMV
$10. MB.**

**FIRST CHRISTMAS PORCELAIN ORNAMENT
1993**
2 kittens in porcelain, white and gold socks,
hanging tree ornament. Dated 1993. **CMV $10.
MB.**
BABY'S FIRST CHRISTMAS ORNAMENT 1993
3" white bisque porcelain with green ribbon.
Dated 1993. **CMV $10. MB.**

**CHRISTMAS ORNAMENT 1992 "DASHING
THROUGH THE SNOW"**
3 5/8" silver plate deer ornament. Dated 1992.
Red flannel pouch. **CMV $10. MB.**

SPARKLING ANGEL ORNAMENT 1990
Silver plate angel with gold 1990 star. 3 1/4"
high. **CMV $10. MB.**

"BABY'S FIRST CHRISTMAS" ORNAMENT 1994
4" high, 2 1/4" wide porcelain ornament. **CMV $10.
MB.**
**"OUR FIRST CHRISTMAS TOGETHER" ORNA-
MENT 1994**
4" high, 3 1/4" wide porcelain ornament. Each
ornament above is dated and marked Avon. **CMV
$10. MB.**

**BABY'S FIRST CHRISTMAS ORNAMENT
1996**
Bisque porcelain ornament dated 1996. 4
1/8" high by 2 3/8" wide. **CMV $10.00 MB.**

SEASON'S JOY ORNAMENTS 1997
White resin ornaments 4 1/2" high. Choice of
"Mother & Child", **"Angel"**, or **"Nativity"**.
CMV $8. ea. MB.

**"ST NICHOLAS" HOLIDAY PEWTER ORNAMENT
1995**
Red felt bag holds pewter Santa, dated 1995 and
marked Avon. 3" long, 2 3/4" high. **CMV $10.**
BABY'S FIRST CHRISTMAS ORNAMENT 1995
3 1/2" high pink, white & blue tree ornament. Dated
1995. **CMV $10. MB.**

SANTA ORNAMENT 1996
2 3/8" wide by 3 1/4" high pewter Santa
ornament. Dated 1996. **CMV $10. MB.**

SANTA PEWTER ORNAMENT 1997
4" wide Santa pewter ornament dated 1997. Comes
in a felt pouch. **CMV $8. MB.**

BABY'S FIRST CHRISTMAS ORNAMENT 1997
4" high porcelain bear ornament. Dated 1997. **CMV
$8. MB.**

**CHRISTMAS COMMEMORATIVE TREE
ORNAMENT 1995**
Brass oval 2 1/2" wide by 3" high. Says
"Christmas 1995". **CMV $15. MB.**

**BARBIE SUGAR PLUM FAIRY
PORCELAIN ORNAMENT 1997**
5 1/2" high porcelain Barbie ornament.
Fabric skirt. Comes with Avon certificate of
authenticity. **CMV $15. MB.**

**BABY'S FIRST CHRISTMAS ORNAMENT "LOVE
FROM ABOVE" 1989**
Quarter moon & baby porcelain ornament. Dated
1989. 3 1/2" high. **CMV $12. MB.**
PEACE DOVE CHRISTMAS ORNAMENT 1989
3 1/2" silver plate ornament with small dove in the
center. Dated 1989. **CMV $10. MB.**

**PRECIOUS MOMENTS PORCELAIN HOLY
FAMILY ORNAMENT 1997**
3 1/2" high Angel's ornament. **CMV $13. MB.**

**PRECIOUS MOMENTS PORCELAIN
BIRTHSTONE ANGEL ORNAMENT 1997**
3" high porcelain Angel has 12 different
birthstones for each month of the year.
Made only for Avon. **CMV $13. ea. MB.**

CHRISTMAS ORNAMENTS

PRECIOUS MOMENTS ORNAMENT "JOY TO THE WORLD" 1996
lst in new series porcelain Angel, dated 1996. Made only for Avon. **CMV $8. MB.**

AMERICAN HEIRLOOM PORCELAIN HEAD DOLL 1981
11" high fabric doll with porcelain head. Blue ribbon around waist. **CMV $16. MB.**

VICTORIAN COLLECTOR DOLL 1983-84
8" high 19th century doll with porcelain head, arms and legs. Comes with metal stand. Fancy box. **CMV $25. MB.**

RAPUNZEL FAIRY TALE DOLL 1986
(Left) 8" tall doll with porcelain head, feet & hands. Lavender dress, gold trim. Blonde hair. **CMV $25. MB.**

EARLY AMERICAN DOLL 1987
(Right) 18 1/2" doll with green skirt, white apron. **CMV $18. MB.**

AVON DOLLS WILL ONLY BE FEATURED WITH PORCELAIN HEAD, HANDS & FEET. NO STUFFED DOLLS.

LITTLE RED RIDING HOOD DOLL 1985
(Left) 8 1/4" high, porcelain face, hands & feet. Red cape on metal stand. **CMV $25. MB.**

CINDERELLA FAIRY TALE DOLL 1984
(Center) 9 1/4" high, porcelain face, hands & feet. Blue dress. Blonde hair. On Stand. **CMV $25. MB**

SNOW ANGEL TREE TOPPER DOLL 1986
10 1/2" high. Head & hands are porcelain. Blue lace dress. **CMV $12. MB.**

"FIRST DAY OF SCHOOL" TENDER MEMORIES DOLL 1995
14" high black or white doll. Red & white dress on metal stand. Dated 1995. **CMV $40.00 ea MB**

"LITTLE BO PEEP" STORYTIME DOLL COLLECTION 1996
lst in new series. 12" tall doll with mini white lamb. Pink & white dress. Choice of white or black doll. **CMV $30.00 ea. MB.**

GIRL SCOUT DOLL 1995
From "Tender Memories" series. 14" high girl scout dolls in green scout outfits. White or black doll. **CMV $40.00 ea. MB.**

ROARING TWENTIES DOLL 1989
8" high porcelain doll, black dress. Feather Boa on metal stand. **CMV $30. MB.**

SOUTHERN BELL PORCELAIN DOLL 1988
8 1/4" high, pink and blue dress, on metal stand. **CMV $30. MB.**

LUPITA MEXICAN INTERNATIONAL DOLL 1990
8" tall doll with porcelain head, feet and hands. On metal stand. **CMV $35. MB.**

FAIRY PRINCESS PORCELAIN DOLL 1989
8 1/2" high, blue dress on metal stand. **CMV $30. MB.**

COLLEEN FROM IRELAND DOLL 1990
1st in series porcelain doll 8" high on metal stand. **CMV $35. MB.**

MASSAKO INTERNATIONAL DOLL 1990
9" high Japanese doll on metal stand. Has porcelain head, hands and feet. **CMV $35. MB.**

VICTORIAN FASHION OF AMERICAN TIMES PORCELAIN DOLL 1987
8 3/4" high on metal stand. **CMV $25. MB.**

NIGERIAN ADAMA PORCELAIN DOLL 1990
8 1/2" high doll. Porcelain head, hands and feet. 4th in series, on metal stand. **CMV $35. MB.**

HOWDY PARTNER DOLL 1993
5th in Childhood Dreams collection. Cowboy doll has porcelain head, hands & feet. 10" high on metal stand. **CMV $40. MB.**

SKATING PARTY CHILDHOOD DREAMS DOLL 1991
3rd in series. 9" tall porcelain doll. Knit fabric clothes. **CMV $35. MB.**

TASIME SIOUX WOMAN DOLL 1991
Last of International Doll series. 9" high. Face, arms & legs are porcelain. Fabric body & clothes. Metal stand. **CMV $35. MB.**

"BALLET RECITAL" DOLL 1991
9 3/4" tall child has porcelain face, arms & legs. Pink satin ballet dress. Metal stand. 1st in a new series of Childhood Dreams. **CMV $35. MB.**

GRAND SLAMMERS DOLL 1991
2nd in Childhood Dreams Collection. 9 1/2" high, 1st male doll by AVON. Porcelain face, legs and arms. Wood bat, metal stand. **CMV $35. MB.**

"FIRST SCHOOL PLAY" TENDER MEMO-RIES "ANGEL" DOLL 1994
1st Doll in Tender Memories Collection. 14" tall doll with porcelain look vinyl head, hands and legs. Fabric body. Metal Stand, whit e and gold dress. **CMV $40. MB.**

HUGGY BEAN DOLL 1997
12" tall bright yellow dress & hat. **CMV $20.00 MB.**

"KITTY LOVE" DOLL 1993
4th in Childhood Dreams Doll Collection. Porcelain head, arms & legs. Fabric body, purple dress. Metal stand. 9 1/4" high doll. **CMV $40. MB.**

AFRICAN PRINCESS & PRINCE DOLL 1996
Each 14" high doll has yellow & redish brown dress & hats with metal display stand. Each is dated 1996. **CMV $30.00 ea. MB**

MENELIK AFRICAN PRINCE DOLL 1995
11 1/2" high doll. Orange clothes. **CMV $13. MB.**

"BATTER UP" TENDER MEMORIES DOLL 1995
14" tall Black or white doll. Procelain look vinyl head, hands and legs. Fabric body, blue, green and white uniforms. Dollw are num bered and marked AVON. Metal Stand. **CMV $40. ea. MB.**

SUNDAY BEST DOLL 1993
6th in Childhood Dreams Doll series. 9" high black doll. Porcelain arms, head and legs. On Metal Stand. **CMV $40. MB.**

BARBIE DOLL "SPRING PETALS" 1997
Made only for Avon. 11 1/2" tall with pink dress. Comes in Blonde, Brunette & African version. **CMV $40.00 MB.**

CHILDHOOD DREAMS "FAVORITE DOLLY" 1993
7th in series, 9 1/2" tall porcelain head, hands and legs. Red coat, black and white checkered dress. Metal Stand. **CMV $40. MB.**

NORTH AFRICAN INSPIRED DOLL 1997
14" high Moroccan doll on metal stand. Dated 1997. **CMV $40.00 MB.**

BARBIE DOLL "SPRING TEA PARTY" 1998
11 1/2" tall doll on plastic stand. Rainbow shaded polyester long dress. Choice of Blonde, Brunette or Black doll. **CMV $40.00 ea. MB**

"GRAND SLAMMER" CHILDHOOD DREAMS DOLL 1994
9 1/2" tall black baseball doll. Comes with ball and wooden bat. Porcelain head, arms and legs. Metal Stand. **CMV $40. MB .**
"BALLET RECITAL" CHILDHOOD DREAMS DOLL 1994
9 1/2" tall black ballet doll. Procelain head, arms and legs. Metal Stand. Pink lace dress. **CMV $40. MB.**

BARBIE DOLL 1996
Ist in a series made only for Avon. Comes in white or black dolls. Pink dress with yellow hat & waist ribbon. Yellow shoes. 11 1/2" tall **CMV $35.00 MB.**

BARBIE DOLL "WINTER RHAPSODY" 1997
2nd in winter series doll made only for Avon by Mattel. Pink & black dress, white fur on metal stand. Doll is 11 1/2" high. Choice of blonde, brunette or black doll. Comes in gold display box. **CMV $45.00 ea. MB**

BARBIE DOLL "WINTER VELVET" 1996
Made only for Avon. 11 1/2" tall doll with dark
blue velvet outer dress with silver brocade trim.
Blue high heels. Comes with necklace,
earrings & ring & brush for hair on display
stand. Choice of black or white doll. Short
issue. **All Barbie dolls from Avon must be in
the Avon box to be collectible as a avon
item.** CMV $40.00 ea. MB.

BUTTERFLY FANTASY PORCELAIN TREASURE EGG 1974-80

5 1/2" long white porcelain multi-colored butterfly decals. Sold empty. 1974 stamped on bottom. Sold 1974-75 then reissued 1978. The 1978 issue was a 1974 "R" for reissue on bottom and the big butterfly on top is much lighter than the 1974 issue. **CMV $25. MB for 1974 issue. CMV $15. MB for 1974 "R" issue.** 1979-80 issue has "R" 1979 on bottom, **CMV $15. MB.** Also came with bottom label upside down or backwards, **Add $6. CMV.**

FOUR SEASONS EGG SERIES 1984

4 different porcelain eggs - wood base. Winter, Spring, Summer, Autumn. **CMV $14. MB. ea.**

SUMMER'S ROSES PORCELAIN EGG 1988

3" high porcelain egg. 1" wood base. **CMV $15. MB.**

WINTER'S TREASURE PORCELAIN EGG 1987

3" high egg. 1" wood base. **CMV $15. MB.**

ORIENTAL EGG CHINESE PHEASANT 1975

(Left) 1 oz. white opal glass, black plastic base. Came in Imperial Garden, Charisma and Bird of Paradise cologne. **CMV $14. MB, $11. BO.**

ORIENTAL EGG PEACH ORCHARD 1974-75

(Right) 1 oz. white opal glass with green marbleized plastic base. Came in Imperial Garden, Sonnet or Moonwind or Patchwork perfume concentre. **CMV $14. MB.**

ORIENTAL EGG DELICATE BLOSSOMS 1975-76

(Center) 1 oz. light blue opal glass with blue-green plastic base. Came in Patchwork, Sonnet & Charisma cologne. **CMV $14. MB.**

AUTUMN'S COLOR PORCELAIN EGG 1987

3" high egg on wood base. **CMV $15. MB.**

SPRING BRILLIANCE EGG 1988

3" porcelain egg on wood base. **CMV $15. MB.**

SPRING FLOWERS BUTTERMINT EGG TIN 1995

6" long, 3 1/2" wide, 4" deep multi-color tin box holds 10 oz. of buttermint candy. **CMV $10. MB.**

ORIENTAL EGG - CHINESE PHEASANT 1975

Upside down label mistake made at factory. Upside down bottle only. **CMV $18.**

MAJESTIC CRYSTAL EGG 1993

24% lead crystal egg 3" high. With pewter stand. Total height 4.5" **CMV $30. MB.**

SEASON'S TREASURES EGG COLLECTION 1994
4 3/4" high Hartford Porcelain egg and base. Choice of 4 different eggs. Floral Bouquet, Seashells of Summer, Fruit Harvest and Birds of Joy. **CMV $17. ea. MB.**

IF YOU PAID MORE FOR ANY AVON COLLECTIBLE IN THIS BOOK IN THE LAST 2 YEARS & FEEL YOU PAID A FAIR PRICE. SEND THIS INFORMATION TO BUD HASTIN, PO BOX 9868, KANSAS CITY, MO. 64134 SO HE CAN CHANGE THE PRICE IN HIS NEXT BOOK. REMEMBER THAT AVON TIMES EACH MONTH REFLECTS THE AVERAGE GOING PRICE ON MOST AVONS. IF YOU DON'T GET AVON TIMES. YOU MAY PAY TO MUCH .

HUMMINGBIRD CRYSTAL

HUMMINGBIRD CRYSTAL CUP AND SAUCER SET 1994
CMV $25. set MB.

HUMMINGBIRD CRYSTAL BEVERAGE GLASSES 1994
7 3/4" high crystal glasses. Set of 2. Frosted base. **CMV $30. set MB.**

HUMMINGBIRD CRYSTAL SOUP/SALAD BOWL 1995
8 1/2" wide, 1 1/4" high crystal bowl. **CMV $23. MB.**

HUMMINGBIRD CRYSTAL HURRICANE LAMP 1982-84
This was sold by Avon with the name Gallery Original on base. **CMV $40. MB.**
HUMMINGBIRD CRYSTAL CANDLE HOLDERS 1984
Also sold by Gallery thru Avon. Set of 2. **CMV $30. set. MB.**

HUMMINGBIRD CRYSTAL DINNER PLATE 1993
10 1/2" lead crystal plate. **CMV $23. MB.**

HUMMINGBIRD CRYSTAL

HUMMINGBIRD CRYSTAL BELL 1985
Each piece is clear glass & etched frosted design.
CMV $12. MB.
HUMMINGBIRD CHAMPAGNE GLASSES 1985-94
9" high box of 2 glasses. **CMV $26. MB.**
HUMMINGBIRD CRYSTAL VASE 1986
7 1/2" high vase. **CMV $27. MB.**
HUMMINGBIRD CRYSTAL CAKE PLATE 1985
12" glass cake plate on 3" glass stand. (not shown).
CMV $50. MB.

HUMMINGBIRD CRYSTAL COLLECTIONS 1990S
PLATTER 1992
12.5" in diameter. **CMV $40. MB.**
DESSERT PLATES 1988
Set of 2. 7.75" diameter **CMV $25. Set. MB.**
WINE GLASS
Set of 2. 7.5" high. **CMV $28. MB.**

SALT & PEPPER SHAKER 1991
2.75" high. **CMV $20. Set MB.**
GOBLETS 1987
Set of 2. 8" high **CMV $28. Set MB..**
DESSERT BOWLS 1992
5.25" diameter. Set of 2. **CMV $28. Set. MB.**
PITCHER 1991
8" high. **CMV $35. MB.**
All are etched 24% lead crystal clear glass.

HUMMINGBIRD CRYSTAL CANDLE HOLDERS 1987
Set of 2 – 4 1/4" wide, 2 5/8" high. **CMV $20. MB.**

HUMMINGBIRD CRYSTAL BUD VASE 1990
9 1/2" high clear glass. **CMV $25. MB.**

HUMMINGBIRD ORNAMENT 1986
3 1/2" lead crystal ornament has "1986" on it.
CMV $12. MB.

HUMMINGBIRD CRYSTAL COVERED DISH 1989
Lead Crystal 5" wide dish. **CMV $30. MB**

HUMMINGBIRD CRYSTAL SERVING BOWL 1993
(Left) 24% lead crystal bowl is 8 3/8" across by 4.25" high. **CMV $35. MB.**

CAPE COD CHRISTMAS ORNAMENT 1990
3 1/4" wide red glass with plaid box. Back says "Christmas 1990. **CMV $12. MB.**

CAPE COD TALL BEVERAGE GLASS SET 1990
Set of 2 red glasses 5 1/2" tall. **CMV $20. Set. MB.**

CAPE COD TWO TIER SERVER 1987
9 3/4" high red glass server. Brass handle. **CMV $65. MB.**

CAPE COD COLLECTION 1984-88
All red glass.
CONDIMENT DISH 1985
 CMV $15. MB.
HURRICANE CANDLE HOLDER 1985
 CMV $25. MB.
COLLECTION FLOWER VASE 1985
8" tall. **CMV $15. MB.**
WATER PITCHER 1984
8 1/4" high. **CMV $40. MB.**

CAPE COD NAPKIN RINGS 1989
1 1/2" red glass napkin rings. Set of 4. **CMV $45.. MB. Set.**

CAPE COD CANDY DISH 1987
6" wide 3 1/2" high, red glass dish. **CMV $15. MB.**

CAPE COD FOOTED GLASS SET 1988
Set of 2 red glass 3 3/4" glasses. **CMV $15. MB. Set.**

CAPE COD FOOTED SAUCE BOAT 1988
8" long red glass. **CMV $25. MB.**

CAPE COD SERVING BOWL 1986
8 3/4" red glass bowl. **CMV $25. MB.**

CAPE COD HEART BOX 1989
4" wide red glass heart box. **CMV $15. MB.**

CAPE COD CUP & SAUCER 1990
Red glass cup 3 1/2" high and saucer 5 3/4" wide. **CMV $18. MB.**

CAPE COD 1876 COLLECTION
(all are ruby red glass)

1876 HOSTESS BELL 1979-80
6 1/2" high "Christmas 1979" on bottom. **CMV $15. MB.** Also came in clear glass coated red.

CAPE COD DESSERT PLATES 1980
Box of 2 red glass plates marked Avon. **CMV $15. MB.**

CAPE COD CRUET 1975-80
5 oz. red glass Holds Skin-So-Soft. **CMV $10.. MB.**

CAPE COD CANDLESTICK COLOGNE 1975-80
5 oz. red glass. Came in Charisma, patchwork or Bird of Paradise. **CMV $10. MB.**

CAPE COD WINE GOBLET 1976-82
Red glass candle. **CMV $8. MB.** Also issued to Reps. with Presidents Celebration 1976 embossed on bottom. **CMV $10. MB.**

DESSERT BOWL & GUEST SOAPS 1978-80
CMV $12. MB.

SALT SHAKER 1978-80
May 1978 on bottom. **CMV $5. MB.** Latter issue not dated on bottom.

CAPE COD WATER GOBLET 1976-80
Red glass candle. **CMV $12.. MB.**

CAPE COD WINE DECANTER 1977-80
16 oz. red glass holds bubble bath. **CMV $20. MB.**

SALT & PEPPER SHAKER SET 1984
CMV $20. MB.

CAPE COD SAUCER CHAMPAGNE GLASS SET 1991
Red glass 5 1/4" high. Set of 2. **CMV $20. set MB.**

CAPE COD WINE GLASS SET 1992
Red glass set of 2 is 5 1/4" high. 4.5 oz. size. **CMV $15. set MB.**

CAPE COD WINE GOBLET 1982
4 1/2" high red glass. **CMV $10. MB.**

CAPE COD SUGAR BOWL 1980-83
(LEFT) 3 1/2" high red glass. Comes with 3 sachet tablets. **CMV $10. MB.**

CAPE COD CREAMER CANDLE 1981-84
4" high ruby red glass. Holds candle, also came in 1983 without candle. **CMV $10. MB.**

CAPE COD DESSERT SERVER 1981-84
8" long, ruby red plastic handle. Stainless blade made by Regent Sheffield for Avon. **CMV $22. MB.**

CAPE COD PEDESTAL MUGS 1982-84
Box holds 2 ruby red glass mugs 5"high. **CMV $16. MB set.**

CAPE COD COVERED BUTTER DISH 1983-84
7" long red glass. **CMV $20. MB..**

CAPE COD CANDLE HOLDERS 1983-84
3 3/4" wide, 2 in a box. **CMV $15. MB.**

CAPE COD SERVING PLATTER 1986
Red glass, 10 3/4" x 13 1/2". **CMV $70.. MB.**

CAPE COD DESSERT BOWL 1982
5" diameter. **CMV $12.**

CAPE COD - SOUP/CEREAL BOWL 1991
Red glass 7 1/2" wide. **CMV $15. MB.**

CAPE COD PIE PLATE SERVER 1992
38th piece to Cape Cod collection. Ruby red glass pie plate 10 7/8" wide.. **CMV $30.**

CAPE COD PEDESTAL CAKE PLATE 1991
Red glass cake stand 3 1/4" high 10 3/4" diameter. **CMV $50. MB.**

BELLS

CAPE COD BREAD & BUTTER DISH SET 1992
5 3/4" ruby red glass butter dishes. This is the 37th item in the Cape Cod Collection since AVON started this series in 1975. set. **CMV $20.. set MB.**

"SOLOIST" CRYSTAL BELL 1994
2nd in series, 5" high lead crystal bell. Choirboy frosted handle. Signed M.I. Hummel and marked Avon. **CMV $25. MB.**

MARJOLEIN BASTIN MINI BIRD BELLS 1997
Mini 2 3/4" high bells made of hand painted resin. Choice of **CARDINAL** (Flower Pot), **SPARROW** (Birchbark Birdhouse), **REDBREAST** (Thatched Roof Birdhouse), or **BULLFINCE** (Watering Can). **CMV $10.00 ea. MB.**

BASKET OF LOVE CRYSTAL BELL 1994
4 3/4" high lead crystal bell. White, pink and green plastic basket handle dated 1994 and marked Avon. **CMV $20. MB.**

CHRISTMAS BELL "SOUNDS OF CHRISTMAS" 1995
4" high by 2 1/2" wide white, red & green porcelain bell . **CMV $17. MB**

"LOVE'S BEGINNINGS" PORCELAIN BELL 1995
4 1/2" high, 2 3/4" wide pink porcelain bell. Dated and marked Avon. **CMV $17. MB.**

PRECIOUS MOMENTS PORCELAIN BELL 1997
Made only for Avon. Dated 1997. 5" high white porcelain bell with pink top. **CMV $15. MB**

CHRISTMAS BELL 1986
White porcelain bell 5" high dated 1986. Gold
trim. **CMV $15. MB.**

EMERALD BELL 1978-79
3.75 oz. light green glass. Gold and green
plastic cap. Bottom has "Avon 1978"
embossed. Came in Sweet Honesty or Roses
Roses cologne. **CMV $10. MB.**

JOYOUS BELL 1978
Light blue frosted over clear glass. Silver cap.
Came in Charisma or Topaze cologne. In blue
& white box. **CMV $10. MB.**

CRYSTAL SONG BELL 1975-76
4 oz. red glass with frosted bow and handle.
Holds Timeless or Sonnet. **CMV $10. MB.**
CHRISTMAS BELLS 1974-75
1 oz. red painted glass with gold cap. Came
in Topaze, Occur!, Cotillion To A Wild Rose
or Sweet Honesty. **CMV $8. MB.**

FRAGRANCE BELL 1968-69
(Left) 1 oz. gold handle. Bell actually rings.
Came in Charisma, Brocade, Regence,
Unforgettable, Rapture, Occur!, Somewhere,
Topaze, Cotillion, Here's My Heart, To A Wild
Rose, Wishing. **CMV bell with tag $15., $20.
MB.**
FRAGRANCE BELL 1965-66
(Center) 4 oz. clear glass, plastic handle, neck
tag. Came in Rapture, Occur!, Somewhere,
Topaze, Cotillion, Here's My Heart, To A Wild
Rose, Wishing. **CMV bell with tag $15., $20.
MB.**
HOBNAIL BELL 1973-74
(Right) 2 oz. white milk glass with gold handle &
gold bell underneath. Holds Unforgettable,
Topaze, Here's My Heart, To A Wild Rose or
Sweet Honesty. **CMV $12. MB.**

MOONLIGHT GLOW ANNUAL BELL 1981-82
3 oz. glass bell, frosted top. Choice of
Moonwind or Topaze. **CMV $10. MB.**

TAPESTRY COLLECTION BELL 1981
5" high white porcelain bell. Dated 1981.
Dove on top of bell. **CMV $15. MB.**

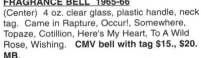

**HEAVENLY CHERUB HOSTESS BELL 1979-
80**
3.75 oz. clear glass painted frosted tan. Gold
plastic handle. 1979 embossed on bottom.
Comes in Topaze or Bird of Paradise cologne.
CMV $10. MB.

ROSEPOINT BELL 1978
(Left) 4 oz. clear glass, clear plastic top.
Came in Charisma or Roses Roses cologne.
CMV $10. MB.
HOSPITALITY BELL 1976-77
(Right) Silver top, 3.75 oz. blue glass bottom.
Came in Moonwind or Roses Roses cologne.
Avon 1976 stamped in bottom. **CMV $10. MB,**

TREASURED MOMENTS BELL 1984
Fostoria glass bell. 5" high. **CMV $11. MB.**

CHRISTMAS BELL 1987
4 3/4" high porcelain bell. **CMV $15. MB.**

CRYSTAL BUTTERFLY BELL 1990
Lead crystal bell 6 1/2" high butterfly decals.
CMV $15. MB.

CHRISTMAS BELL 1985
(Right) Wood handle, porcelain bell dated
Xmas 1985. **CMV $15. MB.**
AVON COUNTRY PORCELAIN BELL 1985
(Center) 3 1/4" high porcelain bell. **CMV $10.
MB.**
GOOD LUCK BELL 1983
(Left) 4 1/2" high porcelain elf on flower bell.
CMV $15. MB.

MOTHERS LOVE PORCELAIN BELL 1988
3" high porcelain bell. **CMV $10. MB.**

GIVING THANKS BELL 1990
4 1/2" high porcelain pumpkin bell. **CMV $15.
MB.**

BIRTHDAY BELL 1986
5 3/4" high clear lead crystal bells. Choice of
12 different flowers on bells. **CMV $12. MB.**
BUNNY BELL 1984
3" high ceramic rabbit bell. **CMV $10.. MB.**

**UNDER THE MISTLETOE CHRISTMAS
BELL 1989**
Porcelain bell 5 1/2" high. **CMV $20. MB.**

**CHRISTMAS BELL 1990 "WAITING FOR
SANTA"**
5 1/2" high porcelain bell. **CMV $20. MB.**

**CHRISTMAS BELL 1991 "GARLAND OF
GREETINGS"**
4 3/4" high red & green porcelain bell with
teddy bear handle. **CMV $20. MB.**

SPRING CHIMES PORCELAIN BELL 1991
6" pink porcelain bell and pink ribbons.**CMV $18. MB.**

HEARTS & FLOWERS CRYSTAL BELL 1992
4 1/2" high lead crystal bell with pink & white flowered handle. Dated 1992.**CMV $20. MB.**

FLORAL BOUQUET CRYSTAL BELL 1989
6" high lead crystal bell. **CMV $23. MB.**

LOVE CRYSTAL BELL 1991
4 1/4" high clear lead crystal, frosted Cupid top and red heart clapper. **CMV $17. MB.**

FLORAL FANTASY CRYSTAL BELL 1992
6" lead crystal bell. Stain glass design.**CMV $20. MB.**

HEART SONG CRYSTAL BELL 1988
4 3/4" high clear glass bell. Red heart top dated 1988. **CMV $13. MB.**

"AVON HEAVENLY NOTES" CHRISTMAS BELL 1992
5 1/2" high, blue porcelain bell with angel handle. Dated 1992. . **CMV $20. MB.**

HEARTS DELIGHT PORCELAIN BELL 1993
4 3/8" high porcelain bell in red & green strawberry shape. **CMV $17. MB.**

HARVEST BOUNTY CRYSTAL BELL 1988
6 1/2" lead crystal bell. Hand painted porcelain handle. **CMV $15. MB.**

PERFUME JEWEL GLACE 1965-66
Gold & white box contains gold locket. Came as pin or on a chain with solid perfume in Unforgettable, Rapture, Occur!, Somewhere, Topaze, Cotillion, Here's My Heart, To A Wild Rose and Wishing. **CMV $17. each MB.**

PERFUME GLACE NECKLACE 1966-67
Silver with black stone & gold with brown stone. Came in Unforgettable, Rapture, Somewhere, Cotillion, Topaze, To A Wild Rose, Here's My Heart, Wishing. **CMV $17. each MB.**

GOLDEN CHARMER LOCKET 1968-70
(Left) Gold locket holds perfume glace in Somewhere, Topaze, Cotillion, Here's My Heart, To A Wild Rose, Unforgettable, Rapture, Occur!, Brocade, & Regence. **CMV $14. MB.**
PILLBOX PERFUME GLACE 1967
(Top Right) Black & gold with red rose on top. Came in Occur!, Rapture, Unforgettable, Somewhere, Topaze, Cotillion, Here's My Heart, To A Wild Rose. **CMV $15. MB.**
DAISY PIN PERFUME GLACE 1969
(Bottom Right) White & gold pin Charisma, Brocade, Regence, Rapture, Occur!, Unforgettable, Somewhere, Topaze, Cotillion. **CMV $10. MB.**

OWL PIN PERFUME GLACE 1968-69
(Left) Gold metal pin with green eyes. Green & gold box. Came in Unforgettable, Brocade, Regence, Rapture, Occur!, Cotillion, Here's My Heart, To A Wild Rose. **CMV $12 MB.**
FLOWER BASKET PERFUME GLACE 1970-71
(Right) 1 1/2" x 1 1/4" gold tone. Choice of Bird of Paradise, Elusive, Charisma, Brocade, or Regence. **CMV $10 MB.**

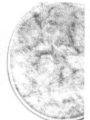

MEMORY BOOK PERFUME GLACE 1971-75
1 1/2" long gold book. Choice of Moonwind, Elusive, Brocade, Regence or Bird of Paradise perfume glace. **CMV $9. MB.**
BABY GRAND PIANO PERFUME GLACE 1971-72
2" wide gold piano. Came in same fragrances as Memory Book. **CMV $14. MB.**

RING OF PEARLS GLACE 1969-70
Perfume glace ring is gold with white pearls. Comes in Charisma, Regence & Brocade. **CMV $10. MB.**

PERFUME GLACE NECKLACE 1966-67
Special issue gold round box. Came with either silver with black stone or gold necklace with brown stone. **CMV $20. as shown.**

CAMEO RING & PIN 1970
Both are perfume glace. Comes in Elusive, Charisma, Brocade, Regence, & Bird of Paradise. **CMV $15 each MB.**

GOLDEN LEAF PIN 1969-70
Blue box contains gold leaf pin with pearl at stem. Perfume glace comes in Elusive, Charisma, Brocade, Regence, Unforgettable, Rapture, Occur!, Topaze, Somewhere, & Cotillion. Same pin also issued with out glace. **CMV $11. MB.**

MANDOLIN PERFUME GLACE 1971-72
2 1/2" long gold mandolin Choice of Moonwind, Elusive, Charisma, Brocade, Regence, or Bird of Paradise perfume glace. **CMV $14. MB.**
TORTOISE PERFUME GLACE 1971-75
2 1/2" long gold turtle with turquoise back. Came in same fragrances as Mandolin. **CMV $10. MB.**

DO NOT COLLECT METAL PLATES

FREEDOM PLATE 1974-77
9" ceramic plate, blue trim with gold edge. Blue printing on back. Made by Wedgewood, England for Avon. **CMV $20. MB.**

SCHOOL IS A NEW BEGINNING PLATE 1986
5" porcelain plate. **CMV $8 MB.**

TENDERNESS PLATE 1974-75
9 1/4" Ironstone plate. Blue & white with gold edge. Made in Spain for Avon by Pontesa. The plate sold to public with word "Pontesa" on the back side in blue letters. This was also awarded to Avon Reps. Plate was also sold with no inscription on back. No. 1 (Regular issue)-all blue lettering on back of plate, No. 2 (Reps Award)- all blue lettering including Pontesa logo. No. 3 (Reps Award)- all blue lettering on back of plate except the Pontesa logo which is red. **CMV $20 MB. regular issue, $25 Rep plate MB.**

GENTLE MOMENTS PLATE 1975-77
8 3/4 ceramic plate. Green letters on back. Made by Wedgewood, England. **CMV $20. MB.**

CHILDRENS PERSONAL TOUCH PLATE 1982-83
7 5/8 ceramic plate. **CMV $12 MB.**

BETSY ROSS PLATE 1973-77
White with colored scene, gold trim and lettering. 9" plate. **CMV $20. MB.**

AMERICAN PORTRAITS PLATE COLLECTIONS 1985
Set of six 4 1/2" porcelain plates. Choice of The East, The West, The Rockies, The Southwest, The Midwest, The South. **CMV $8. each MB.**

BABY KEEPSAKE SPOON & BOWL SET 1984
6 1/4 porcelain bowl & 5" spoon. **CMV $14. MB.**

CHRISTMAS LIGHTS DESSERT PLATE 1985
7" white ceramic plate with X-mas light design. **CMV $7 MB.**

CARDINAL NORTH AMERICAN SONG BIRD PLATE 1974-76
10" ceramic plate. Gold & green letters on back. **CMV $20. MB.**

CLASSIC WEDDING PLATE 1986
9" bisque porcelain plate with 2 Doves on face. Gold trim. **CMV $15 MB.**

FOUR SEASONS CALENDAR PLATE 1987
9" porcelain plate. **CMV $15 MB.**

BAKED WITH LOVE PLATE 1982-83
9" porcelain plate dated 1982 **CMV $20. MB.**

CUPIDS MESSAGE PORCELAIN DISH 1984
White heart shaped dish with Angel Love in red letters. red box. **CMV $10 MB.**

SWEET DREAMS KEEPSAKE PLATE 1983
7 5/8" porcelain plate. **CMV $15 MB.**

EASTER PLATE "ALL DRESSED UP" 1994
5" porcelain plate says Easter 1994, rabbit family on fron side. **CMV $10. MB.**

BOUQUET OF LOVE PLATE 1987
7" white porcelain Bisque plate. **CMV $10. MB.**

SINGIN IN THE RAIN PLATE 1986
8" porcelain plate. Both came with or without wood base music box. **CMV $18 MB. Add $5 for music box base.**
EASTER PARADE PLATE 1986
8" porcelain plate came with wood base music stand, plays Easter Parade. **CMV $18. MB. Add $5. for music box base.**

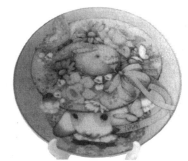

EASTER PLATE 1995 "MY EASTER BONNET"
5" porcelain plate dated 1995. **CMV $10. MB.**

JESUS FEEDS THE MULTITUDE PLATE 1993
(Right) 8 3/8" blue porcelain plate. 3rd in series. **CMV $25. MB.**

ABIGAIL ADAMS PLATE 1985
9" porcelain plate. Wood stand. **CMV $20. MB.**
CHORUS LINE PLATE 1986
8" porcelain plate. Wood music box stand. **CMV $20. MB.**

MOMENTS OF VICTORY SPORTS PLATES 1985
Set of 4 different 7" porcelain plates Football, Basketball, Hockey, or Baseball. **CMV $8. each MB.**

KEEPSAKE BABY PLATE 1992
5" sleeping baby plate with white or black child. Plastic display stand. **CMV $10. ea. MB.**

HOLY FAMILY PLATE 1991
8 1/2" blue and white porcelain, nativity scene plate. **CMV $22.50. MB.**

"BLESS THE LITTLE CHILDREN" PLATE
1992
8 1/2" blue porcelain plate with date on back.
CMV $22.50. MB.

EASTER PARADE PLATE 1993
5" porcelain plate, "Easter 1993". Plastic stand.
CMV $10. MB.

EASTER PLATE "COLORFUL MOMENTS"
1992
5" porcelain plate with Rabbits coloring eggs.
2nd in Easter Plate. Plastic Stand. **CMV $10.**
MB.

EASTER PLATE "SPRINGTIME STROLL"
1991
5" porcelain plate with rabbit family strolling.
CMV $10. MB.

"THE LAST SUPPER" PLATE 1994
8 1/4" Blue and white porcelain plate. Dated
1994. **CMV $25. MB.**

MARTIN LUTHER KING JR. PLATE 1995
5" porcelain plate, comes with plastic stand.
CMV $10. MB.

EASTER PLATE 1996 "EASTER BOUQUET"
5" porcelain plate. Dated 1996.**CMV $13. MB.**

SISTERS IN SPIRIT PLATE 1996
8" blue, red & yellow porcelain african plate.
CMV $20. MB.

CUP & SAUCER - AVON BLOSSOMS OF THE MONTH SERIES 1991
Porcelain flowered cup & 5 1/2" saucer. 12 different for 1991. Jan.- Carnation; Feb.- Violet; Mar. - Jonquil; April - Sweet Pea; May - Lily of the Valley; June - Rose; July - Larkspur; Aug. - Gladiola; Sept. - Aster; Oct. - Calendula; Nov. - Chrysanthemum; Dec. - Narcissus. Marked Avon and dated on each. **CMV $20. ea. MB.**

M.I. HUMMEL "ANGEL PLATE" 1996
8 1/2" lead crystal angel plate dated 1996.
CMV$30.00 MB

AFRICAN ANCESTRY LAST SUPPER PLATE 1997
8" porcelain plate dated 1997. Plastic stand.
CMV $20. MB.

EUROPEAN TRADITION CUP & SAUCER COLLECTION 1984-85
FRANCE
2 1/2" cup & 4 1/2" saucer. Pink & white porcelain.
GERMANY
Yellow & white porcelain.
NETHERLANDS
Blue & white porcelain.
FLORENCE
Blue & white porcelain. **CMV $15. ea. MB.**

JOYOUS OCCASIONS ANNIVERSARY PLATE 1995
8 1/4" porcelain plate with flowers. Says "Happy Anniversary" on front. **CMV $20. MB**

OLYMPIC WOMAN PLATE 1996
5" blue plate with red & white letters for Atlanta Olympics. Dated 1996. **CMV $13. MB.**
TEAM USA "OLYMPIC" PLATE 1996
5" blue & white porcelain plate. Dated 1996. **CMV $13. MB.**

PLATES MISCELLANEOUS & EASTER PLATES

12 DAYS OF CHRISTMAS COLLECTIONS 1985
All white porcelain.
CANDLE HOLDERS CMV $11. pair MB.
DESSERT PLATES
Set of 4. **CMV $20. Set. MB.**
MUGS
set of 4 **CMV $16. Set MB.**

CUP & SAUCER - "PINK ROSES"1974
(Left) White china with pink flowers & green leaves with gold trim. Made by Stoke-on Trent, England. **CMV $12. MB** Also came with double printed letters on bottom. **CMV $20.00 MB**
CUP & SAUCER - BLUE BLOSSOMS 1974
(Right) White china with blue & pink flowers & 22K gold rim. Made in England. **CMV $12. MB.**

DO NOT COLLECT METAL PLATES

CHRISTMAS ON THE FARM 1973 CHRISTMAS PLATE
9" ceramic plate. White with colored scene, turquoise border, gold edge and lettering. **CMV $55. MB.**

CHRISTMAS "BETSY ROSS" PLATE 1973
Factory mistake 1973 Christmas plate has inscription on back for Betsy Ross plate. Very Rare. **CMV $100.**

COUNTRY CHURCH 1974 CHRISTMAS PLATE
9" ceramic plate. Second in a series of Christmas plates by Avon. Made by Wedgewood, England. Blue writing on back. Blue & white front, gold edge. **CMV $35. MB.** Rare issue came without Christmas 1974 on front of plate. **CMV $75 MB.**

SKATERS ON THE POND 1975 CHRISTMAS PLATE
8 3/4 ceramic green & white plate. Green letters on the back. Made by Wedgewood, England for Avon. This plate was not sold till 1976 Christmas selling season. **CMV $20. MB. Some have 1976 on back Add $10.**

BRINGING HOME THE TREE 1976 CHRISTMAS PLATE
9" blue ceramic plate, gold edge. Blue printing on back. Made by Wedgewood, England for Avon. **CMV $20. MB. Some have 1975 on back Add $10.**

"CAROLLERS IN THE SNOW" 1977 CHRISTMAS PLATE
8 3/4 ceramic blue & white plate, gold edge. Blue letters on back. Made by Wedgewood, England for Avon. **CMV $20. MB.**

"TRIMMING THE TREE" 1978 CHRISTMAS PLATE
(6th edition) 8 5/8 ceramic plate. Turquoise rim with gold edge trim. Made for Avon by Enoch Wedgewood in England. **CMV $20. MB.**

DASHING THROUGH THE SNOW 1979 CHRISTMAS PLATE
8 3/4 blue and white ceramic plate with gold trim. Christmas 1979 on front. Back of plate says Made for Avon Products by Enoch Wedgewood in England. **CMV $20. MB.**

CHRISTMAS PLATE 1983
"Enjoying the night before Christmas". 9" porcelain plate. **CMV $20 MB.**

SHARING THE CHRISTMAS SPIRIT 1981 CHRISTMAS PLATE
(Left) 9" porcelain plate has 2 kids carrying Christmas tree, Christmas 1981 on front. **CMV $20. MB.** Rare issue came with no Christmas 1981 on front. **CMV $75.**

CHRISTMAS PLATES

MINIATURE CHRISTMAS PLATES 1989
(Right) 1st issued in 1989 are the 1978, 1979, 1980 Christmas plates in 3" size. **CMV $10. ea. MB**

CHRISTMAS PLATE TEST 1976
8 3/4 test plate. Does not say Avon. Christmas 1976 on front 6 times in gold. Was never sold by Avon. Came from factory. Has blue border. **CMV $75.**

CHRISTMAS PLATE - 15 YEAR 1978
Same plate as 15 year anniversary plate inscribed on back. We have no info on this or where it came from. Write Bud Hastin if you know what this plate is for. **CMV $50.**

CHRISTMAS PLATE "KEEPING THE CHRISTMAS TRADITION" 1982
9" ceramic plate, back says Christmas Memories, 1982. Comes in green & gold box. **CMV $25. MB.**

CHRISTMAS PLATE 1994 "THE WONDER OF CHRISTMAS"
8 1/4" porcelain plate. Date 1994. **CMV $25. MB.**

CHRISTMAS PLATE 1993 "SPECIAL CHRISTMAS DELIVERY"
8" porcelain plate. Santa and reindeer. **CMV $25. MB.**

CHRISTMAS PLATE 1990 "Bringing Christmas Home"
8" porcelain plate. Christmas 1990 on front. **CMV $25. MB**

CHRISTMAS PLATE 1985
"A Child's Christmas" 7 3/4 white bisque porcelain. **CMV $15. MB.**

CHRISTMAS PLATE 1984
(Right) 9" porcelain decal plate. Last in this series. **CMV $25. MB.**

CHRISTMAS PLATE 1989
"Together for Christmas" bears on plate. 8" wide.porcelain plate. **CMV $25. MB**

CHRISTMAS PLATE 1988
"Home for the Holidays" 8" porcelain plate. **CMV $25. MB**

CHRISTMAS PLATE 1987
Magic that Santa Brings. 8" porcelain plate. **CMV $25. MB**

CHRISTMAS PLATE 1986 - "A Child's Christmas"
8" porcelain plate with snowman and 2 kids. **CMV $25. MB**

CHRISTMAS PLATE 1995 "TRIMMING THE TREE"
8 1/4" porcelain blue plate dated 1995. **CMV $25. MB**

COUNTRY CHRISTMAS PLATE 1980
9" ceramic 1980 Christmas plate. **CMV $25. MB**

CHRISTMAS PLATE 1996 "SANTA'S LOVING TOUCH"
8 1/4" porcelain plate dated 1996. Stand not included. **CMV $25. MB.**

CHRISTMAS PLATE 1992 "SHARING CHRISTMAS WITH FRIENDS"
8" porcelain plate. Animals decorating Christmas tree. **CMV $25. MB.**

CHRISTMAS PLATE 1997 " HEAVENLY DREAMS"
8 1/4" porcelain plate dated 1997. Choice of white or black angel plate. **CMV $20. MB.**

CHRISTMAS PLATE 1991 "PERFECT HARMONY"
8" porcelain plate. **CMV $25. MB.**

MOTHER'S DAY PLATES

MOTHERS DAY PLATE "CHERISHED MOMENTS" 1981
5" porcelain plate dated 1981,with stand. **CMV $10. MB.**

MOTHER'S DAY PLATE 1986
5" porcelain plate called "A New Tooth" Comes in White or Black Mother & child. **CMV $25. MB.**

MOTHER'S DAY PLATE 1990
"A Message from the Heart" 5" porcelain plate, with stand. **CMV $10. MB**

MOTHER'S DAY PLATE 1982
5" size plate. Little Things Mean A Lot inscribed on face. Comes in yellow box & plastic plate stand. **CMV $10 MB**, Same plate given to presidents Club Reps. Label on back reads "January 1982 Presidents Club Luncheon". **CMV $15 MB.**

MOTHER'S DAY PLATE 1987
"A Mother In Love" 5" porcelain plate. **CMV $7 MB.**

MOTHER'S DAY PLATE 1991
"Love Makes all Things Grow". 5" porcelain plate with plastic stand. **CMV $10. MB.**

MOTHER'S DAY PLATES 1983-84
5" ceramic plates. Both dated on back. **CMV $10. each MB.**

MOTHERS DAY PLATE 1988
"A mother's works isnever done." 5" ceramic. .Choice of black or white child. **CMV $10. ea. MB**

MOTHER'S DAY PLATE 1992
Titles "How Do You Wrap Love". 5" porcelain plate, dated 1992. **CMV $10. MB.**

MOTHER'S DAY SPECIAL MEMORIES PLATES 1985
5" porcelain plate, choice of white or black body and child. **CMV $10. each MB.**

MOTHERS DAY PLATE 1989
Titles Loving is Caring, 5" plate with stand. **CMV $10. MB**

MOTHER'S DAY PLATE "RECIPE FOR LOVE" 1993
5" porcelain plate. Plastic stand. **CMV $10. MB.**

MOTHERS DAY PLATE 1995 "A MOTHERS LOVE"
8 1/4" porcelain plate with choice of black or white Mother & Child. **CMV $20. MB.**

MOTHER'S DAY PLATE "LOVE ON PARADE" 1994
5" porcelain plate. Dated 1994. **CMV $10. MB.**

MOTHERS DAY PLATE 1998 "SPECIAL MOMENTS"
5" porcelain plate with choice of black or white mother & daughter. Dated 1998. Comes with white plastic stand. **CMV $11. MB.**

MOTHERS DAY PLATE 1996 " LOVE, IT'S A GIFT"
5" porcelain plate has Mama Bear & 2 babies on front. Comes with plastic stand. **CMV$13. MB.**

MOTHERS DAY PLATE 1997 "TENDER MOMENTS"
5" porcelain plate designed by Helene Leveillee & dated 1997. Choice of white or black mother & child. **CMV $10. MB.**

CANDLES

Whats hot & whats not? Candles are very popular in Avon Collecting. Most popular are all glass figurine type candles. They are selling faster & at better prices then the non figurine type candles. All wax Figurine candles are popular but are hard to keep clean & in mint condition. We will no longer picture wax taper candle or tin can candles. Keep these thoughts in mind when buying & collecting candles. Candle refills & wax chips are no longer considered collectable. There is little resale interest to most collectors in these items.

COLLECTORS

All candles are priced full & Mint..

CO means......................................Candle Only
BO means ....Bottle Only (empty)
CMV means..................Current Market Value
MB means..............................Mint and Boxed

FLORAL FRAGRANCE CANDLE 1971-75
(Left) Metal gold leaf stand & pink or yellow flower candle. **CMV $12 MB.**
WATER LILY FRAGRANCE CANDLE 1972-73
(Right) Green lily pad base with white plastic petals with yellow center candle. **CMV $8 CO, $10 MB.**

REVOLUTIONARY SOLDIER SMOKERS CANDLE 1979-80
Clear, or dark amber glass, clear harder to find, 2 different. Red & gold box. **CMV $8.. MB.**
FOSTORIA CRYSTAL POOL FLOATING CANDLE 1979-80
6" clear crystal dish, green & white flower candle. **CMV $13. MB.**

OVALIQUE PERFUME CANDLEHOLDER 1974-75
(Left) 4" high, clear gloss, choice of Sonnet, Moonwind, Patchwork, Roses Roses, Charisma, Bird of Paradise, Bayberry, Frankincense & Myrrh or Wassail. **CMV $10 MB.**
FACETS OF LIGHT FRAGRANCE CANDLETTE 1975-76
(Center) 4" high, clear glass. Came with Bayberry candle but any refill candlette will fit. **CMV $8. MB.**
GOLDEN PINE CONE FRAGRANCE CANDLETTE 1974-75
(Right) Gold toned glass. Choice of Bayberry only. **CMV $8 MB.**

CRYSTALLITE COLOGNE CANDLE 1970-71
(Left) Clear glass bottle with gold cap holds 4 oz. cologne in Unforgettable, Rapture, Occur!, Somewhere, Topaze, & Cotillion. **CMV $10. MB.**
CANDLESTICK COLOGNE 1972-75
(Right) 5 oz. silver painted over clear glass with silver cap. Came in Moonwind, Field Flowers, Bird of Paradise, Roses Roses. **CMV $12 MB. $8. BO.** 1975 came only in Imperial Garden, Moonwind, or Sonnett.

WASHINGTON GOBLET FOSTORIA CANDLEHOLDER 1975-77
Blue glass by Fostoria. Came with Frankincense & Myrrh or Floral Medley candle. **CMV $14 MB.**
MARTHA WASHINGTON GOBLET 1976-77
Blue glass Fostoria candleholder. **CMV $14. MB.**

DANISH MODERN CANDLE 1970
(Left) Stainless steel candleholder with red candle. **CMV $10 with candle. MB.**
FLAMING TULIP FRAGRANCE CANDLE 1973
(Right) Red candle in Floral Medley fragrance. Gold holder. **CMV $10. MB.**

JOYOUS MESSAGE CANDLES 1985
3 elf candles 1 1/2 high. **CMV $3 MB.**

TURTLE CANDLE 1972
(Left) White glass turtle candle with green glass shell top. **CMV $12 MB.**
MUSHROOM CANDLE 1972
(Right) White glass candle with pink glass mushroom top. **CMV $11 MB.**

COLOGNE & CANDLELIGHT 1975-76
(Left) 2 oz. clear glass with gold cap and clear plastic collar. Hold Imperial Gardens, Roses Roses, or Charisma. **CMV $6. MB.**

CANDLESTICK COLOGNE 1970-71
(Right) 4 oz. red glass bottle, gold cap. Holds Elusive, Charisma, Brocade, Regence, Bird of Paradise. **CMV $8 MB.** Also came in smoked red glass. Appears much darker than red glass issue. It looks smokey red. **CMV $15 MB.**

REGENCY CANDLESTICK COLOGNE 1973-74
(Left) 4 oz. clear glass. Came in Bird of Paradise, Charisma, Elusive, or Roses Roses. **CMV $11. MB. $8 BO.**

OPALIQUE CANDLESTICK COLOGNE 1976-77
(Right) 5 oz. swirl glass & cap. Came in Charisma or Sweet Honesty. **CMV $10. MB, $8. BO.**

FOSTORIA CANDLELIGHT BASKET CANDLEHOLDER 1975
(Left) Clear glass, gold handle. Choice of Sonnet, Moonwind, Patchwork, Charisma, Roses Roses, Bird of Paradise, Wassail, Frankincense, & Myrrh or Bayberry candle refill. **CMV $12. MB. $10. CO.**

FOSTORIA SALT CELLAR CANDLE 1969-70 & 1981
(Right) Clear glass with small silver spoon. **CMV $10 MB, $7 candle only.** Reissued in 1981 with "R" on bottom of foot for reissue. **CMV $10 MB.**

CANDLESTICK COLOGNE 1966
3 oz. silver coated over clear glass. Silver cap. Came in Occur!, Rapture, Unforgettable. **CMV $15. ea. mint, $25. ea. MB.**

CRYSTAL GLOW PERFUMED CANDLE-HOLDER 1972-73
(Left) Clear glass. Came in Moonwind, Bird of Paradise, Elusive, Charisma, Brocade, Regence, Wassail, Bayberry, Frankincense, Myrrh, Roses Roses. **CMV $12 MB.**

FOSTORIA PERFUMED CANDLEHOLDER 1973
(Right) Clear glass. Came with Patchwork, Sonnet, Moonwind, Roses Roses, Charisma, Bird of Paradise, Bayberry, Wassail, Frankincense, & Myrrh candles. **CMV $8, $10 MB.**

TULIP CLEARFIRE TRANSPARENT CANDLE 1980-82
(Left) Clear glass. 4" high. **CMV $8. MB.**

SPARKLING SWIRL CLEARFIRE CANDLE 1980-82
(Center) Clear glass 5 1/8" high. **CMV $11. MB.**

SHERBERT DESSERT CANDLE 1980-82
(Right) 5" high clear glass. Comes with red, yellow or pink candle. **CMV $8 MB.**

FLORAL MEDLEY PERFUMED CANDLES 1971-72
Box holds yellow & purple frosted glass candleholders. **CMV $10 MB.**

CHESAPEAKE COLLECTION JIGGER CANDLE 1981
Amber glass dog head candle, candle in bottom. **CMV $12 MB.**

HEARTS & FLOWERS FRAGRANCE CANDLE 1973-74
(Left) White milk glass with red green & pink design. Came in Floral Medley fragrance. **CMV $10 MB.**

POTPOURRI FRAGRANCE CANDLE 1972-73
(Right) White milk glass, came with Potpourri candle. **CMV $10. MB.**

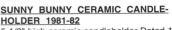

HEART & DIAMOND FOSTORIA LOVING CUP PERFUMED CANDLEHOLDER 1978
(Left) Approx. 7" high claer Fostoria glass. Came with floral Medley perfumed candle. Embossed with "Avon 1978" on it's base. Refillable. **CMV $15. MB. glass only $10.**

MOUNT VERNON SAUCE PITCHER 1977-79
(Right) Approx. 5 1/2" high. Blue Fostoria glass. Came with Floral Medley perfumed candle. Refillable. Avon on bottom. **CMV $16 MB. pitcher only $12.**

SUNNY BUNNY CERAMIC CANDLE-HOLDER 1981-82
5 1/2" high ceramic candleholder Dated 1981 . **CMV $15 MB.**

HEART & DIAMOND CANDLESTICK 1978-79
7" high heart embossed Fostoria clear glass candle. Avon 1979 on bottom. Comes with long red candle for one end or turn it over and insert the small glass candleholder on other end. Comes in red box. **CMV $13 MB.**

CHINA TEA POT CANDLE 1972-73
White china with blue flower design or without decal. Thousands came from factory, not sold by Avon, with or without decals, some decals were on front, some on back. The factory rejects **CMV $9 each.** Came from Avon with Roses Roses, Moonwind, Bird of Paradise, Elusive, Charisma, Brocade, Regence, Wassail, Bayberry, Frankincense & Myrrh candles. **CMV $15 MB.**

WHITE MILK GLASS CANDLE 1964-66
(Left) **CMV $12, $17. MB.**

AMBER GLASS CANDLE 1965-66
(Center) Amber Paint over clear glass. **CMV $20 MB, $15 candle only.**

RED GLASS CANDLE 1965-66
(Right) Red paint over clear glass **CMV $15. $20 MB,** Dark red 1968 glass candle, not painted **CMV $50.**

KITCHEN CROCK FRAGRANCE CAN-DLETTE 1974-75
(Left) Yellow crock with red, yellow & blue flowers with cork cap. Came in Meadow Morn fragrance. **CMV $8 MB.**

WASSAIL BOWL CANDLE 1969-70
(Right) Silver paint over red glass with silver spoon. **CMV $18 MB.**

REGENCE CANDLE 1967
(Left) Gold paint over clear glass with green paper band. Lid makes base for bottom. **CMV $25. MB. $20 CO MINT**

REGENCE CANDLE 1968-69
(Right) Green glass candleholder with gold handle & base. **CMV $20 candle only, $25 MB.**

CHRISTMAS CHARMER CANDLESTICK 1981
Small white, red & green girl, plastic candle holder. Remove top sleeve to fit small bottle of cologne with red cap. Choice of Zany or Charisma. .33 oz. cologne, red box. **CMV $7. set MB.**

FROSTED GLASS CANDLE 1967
(Left) Gold band around edge. lid makes stand for base. OSP $5 **CMV $20 MB, $15 CO.**

WHITE & GOLD CANDLE 1966-67
(Right) White glass top & bottom with gold band. Top makes stand for base. **CMV $15. $20. MB.**

CRYSTAL CANDLEIER 1969-70
(Left) 7" high, clear glass with blue crystals inside, gold handle on glass lid. **CMV $15 MB. $12 CO.**

GOLD & WHITE CANDLE 1969-70
(Right) Painted gold & white over clear glass, lid makes stand for base. **CMV $15. $20 MB.**

FIRST CHRISTMAS CANDLE 1967-72
All shiny gold, red inside. 1967 had label on bottom and no Avon. 1972 Reissue had Avon on bottom & no label. **CMV $10. CO. $15. MB.**

M.I. HUMMEL CRYSTAL CANDLESTICKS 1995
set of 2 frosted lead crystal angels 3 1/2" high. Does not come with taper candles. **CMV $30.00 Set MB.**

ULTRA CRYSTAL CANDLE 1981-82
(Left) 2 1/2" high clear glass. Gray box. **CMV $10. MB.**

ULTRA SHIMMER CANDLE 1981-82
(RIght) 2 1/2" high clear glass octagonal shaped. Gold box. **CMV $9. MB.**

NESTING DOVE CANDLE 1970
White base glass & lid with dove on top. **CMV $15 MB.**

HOBNAIL PATIO CANDLE 1973
(Right) White milk base clear glass top. Came with Sonnet, Moonwind, Roses Roses, Bird of Paradise, Charisma, Wassail, Bayberry, and Frankincense & Myrrh candles. **CMV $12 MB.**

BERRY CANDLE 1997
3 1/2" high by 3" wide berry wax candles in metal buckets. Choice of **Blackberry, Strawberry, or Blueberry. CMV $8. ea. MB.**

HOT CHOCO-LITE CANDLE 1981-82
(Left) Beige or white color wax cup with brown chocolate smelling candle. **CMV $7. MB.**

PITKIN HAT CANDLE 1981-82
(Right) Blue swirled glass hat holds candle. Comes in green box. **CMV $8. MB.**

BRIGHT CHIPMUNK CANDLETTE 1978-79
Clear glass candleholder. Refillable. **CMV $9. MB.**

FRESH AROMA SMOKERS CANDLE 1978-79
Non refillable brown wax like pipe with black plastic and chrome top. Bottom cardboard label. **CMV $8. MB.**

GOLDEN APPLE CANDLE 1968-69
Shiny gold over clear glass. **CMV $18 mint, $25 MB.**

SILVER APPLE CANDLE 1968
Factory test sample same as gold apple only in shiny silver over clear glass. Was not filled. **CMV $90 on silver top & bottom, Silver bottom with gold top CMV $55 mint.**

HOLIDAY DOVE CANDLE HOLDERS 1993
White porcelain doves 4 1/2" long, 2 3/4" high. Candles come separate. Set of 2. **CMV $15. set MB.**

CUPID CANDLE HOLDER 1995
3 1/4" high, white glazed porcelain cupid candle with red votive candle. **CMV $7. MB.**

PERSONALLY YOURS FRAGRANCE CANDLE 1980-82
(Left) Clear glass with refillable candle. Comes with sheet of stick on gold letters. **CMV $12. MB.**

STAR BRIGHT FRAGRANCE CANDLE 1980-81
(Right) Icy clear glass holds refillable candle. **CMV $8. MB.**

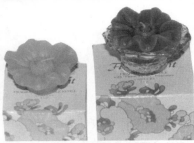

FLORAL LIGHT CANDLE REFILL 1980-81
(Left) Comes in lavender, green or yellow. Flower shaped. **CMV $4. MB.**
FLORAL LIGHT FRAGRANCE CANDLE 1980-81
(Right) Clear glass flower shaped base holds flower shaped refill candle. **CMV $7. MB.**

SNUG 'N COZY "CAT" FRAGRANCE CANDLE 1980-82
Clear glass cat candleholder. **CMV $10. MB.**

GLISTENING TREE CLEARFIRE CANDLE 1981-82
4 1/2" high clear ribbed glass tree shaped candle. **CMV $10. MB.**
LOVE LIGHT CLEARFIRE CANDLE 1982
Clear ribbed glass heart shape candle. **CMV $10. MB.**

BUNNY PATCH CANDLE 1988
6" tall wax rabbit candle. **CMV $5. MB.**

SHIMMERING PEACOCK CANDLE 1979-80
(Left) Box holds clear glass peacock. **CMV $11. MB.**

CHRISTMAS TEDDY CANDLE 1988
3" high bear candle. **CMV $5. MB**

CATNIP FRAGRANCE CANDLE 1975-76
4" high yellow plastic. Floral Medley fragrance. **CMV $7. MB.**
DYNAMITE FRAGRANCE CANDLETTE 1975-76
Red & white. **CMV $8. MB.**

NATURAL HOME SCENTS TOWNHOUSE CANDLE 1988
4-3/4" high ceramic candle town house. **CMV $18. MB.**

NORTH POLE PALS CANDLES 1988
Reindeer, Penguin & Polar Bear candles also used as tree ornaments. **CMV $4 ea. MB.**

PLUM PUDDING CANDLE 1978-79
(Left) 4" high brown, green & white candle. Bottom label. **CMV $6. MB.**
WINTER LIGHTS CANDLETTE 1978-79
(Right) Clear glass square candleholder. Holds glass candlette. Avon on bottom of both. **CMV $10. MB.**

GEM GLOW CANDLE 1981-82
(Left) Clear glass multi-faceted. Comes with green, amber or red filled candle. **CMV $10. MB.**

MRS. SNOWLIGHT CANDLE 1979-81
(Left) White, red & green wax candle. **CMV $7. MB.**

WINTER WONDERLAND CENTERPIECE CANDLE 1979-80
(Right) White wax base, green wax trees, red & white wax house. Center holds glass candlette. **CMV $15. MB.**

ENCHANTED MUSHROOM FRAGRANCE CANDLE 1975
(Left) White wax shell / yellow cover. Meadow Morn fragrance. **CMV $6. MB.**

SLEIGH LIGHT FRAGRANCE CANDLE 1975-76
(Right) 4" high, red & green. Bayberry scented. **CMV $7. MB..**

HOLIDAY CANDLE DISH & WREATH 1980
Clear glass candleholder, red candle and holly wreath. **CMV $9. MB.**

BLACK-EYED SUSAN FRAGRANCE CANDLE 1975-76
Yellow with brown center. Wild Flowers fragrance. **CMV $8. MB.**

GRAPEFRUIT FRAGRANCE CANDLE 1974-76
Yellow with red center. Has grapefruit fragrance. **CMV $7. MB.**

CRYSTALGLOW CLEARFIRE CANDLE 1980
(Left) Clear glass. Avon on bottom under candle. **CMV $10. MB.**

BUNNY BRIGHT CERAMIC CANDLE 1980
(Right) White ceramic with pink & green trim. "1980 Avon" on bottom. **CMV $12. MB.**

GINGERBREAD HOUSE FRAGRANCE CANDLE 1977-79
Brown & white candle. Came in Frankincense & Myrrh fragrance. **CMV $9. MB, $5. no box.**

GLOW OF CHRISTMAS CANDLE 1980
White wax with red center refillable candle. **CMV $10. MB.**

CAROLLING TRIO CANDLES 1981-82
Comes in separate boxes. **Melodic Mouse** candle, **Howling Hound** candle, **Crooning Cat** candle. **CMV $5. each MB.**

HARVEST TIME FRAGRANCE CANDLE 1980-81
(Left)Tan wax candle, 6" high. **CMV $8. MB.**

ROMANTIC LIGHTS SCENTED CANDLE 1994
2 3/4" X 3 1/4" lead crystal scented candle. 4 fragrance. **CMV $13. ea. MB.**

MR. SNOWLIGHT CANDLE 1981
5 1/2" high white wax, green trim. **CMV $7. MB.**

LOTUS BLOSSOM PERFUMED CANDLE-HOLDER 1974-75
(Left) Black glass with green & white design. Available with candle fragrance: Bayberry, Frankincense & Myrrh, Wassail, Sonnet, Moonwind, Roses Roses, Bird of Paradise or Charisma. **CMV $15. $20.. MB.**
DYNASTY PERFUMED CANDLE 1971-72
(Right) 6" high, white glass jar & lid. **CMV $15. $20. MB.**

AMERICAN HEIRLOOM CANDLESTICK & CANDLE 1982-84
Pewter metal candlestick & 6" red candle. **CMV $10. MB.**

TERRA COTTA BIRD CANDLETTE 1976-77
Reddish brown clay bird candleholder. Avon on bottom. **CMV $8. MB.**

GARDEN BOUNTY CANDLE 1979-80
(Left) Beige & pink cart, red candle. **CMV $8. MB.**
COUNTRY SPICE CANDLE 1979-80
(Center) Light blue green glass jar & lid. Wire bale. Comes with candle inside. **CMV $9. MB.**
FLOWER FROST COLLECTION WATER GOBLET CANDLETTE 1979-80
(Right) Frosted glass goblet holds glass candle insert. **CMV $11. MB.**

TOCCARA SPECIAL EDITION CANDLE 1982-83
(Left) Clear cut glass Fostoria candle. Blue box. **CMV $13. MB.**
HARVEST GLOW CANDLE 1982-83
(Right) Clear glass pumpkin shaped candle and lid. **CMV $13. MB.**

DOVE IN FLIGHT CANDLETTE 1977-78
Clear glass dove candleholder. Came in Meadow Morn fragrance candlette. Refillable. **CMV $10. MB.**
BUNNY CERAMIC PLANTER CANDLE-HOLDER 1977-79
3 different rabbits. One made in Brazil and recesses on bottom; one flat bottom made in U.S. and lighter in weight; 1978 issue same flat bottom only different type letters on bottom. Came with Floral Medley or Roses Roses perfumed candle. **CMV $12. MB each, rabbit only $10. each.**

BUNNY CERAMIC PLANTER CANDLE 1979-80
Made of ceramic in Brazil for Avon. Green, pink & yellow flowers. Brown eyes, pink inner ears. Comes with Floral Medley or Spiced Garden candle. **CMV $15. MB.**
TENDER BLOSSOM CANDLE 1977-80
Light pink wax base with dark pink inner candle. **CMV $7. MB.**

SNUGGLY MOUSE CANDLEHOLDER 1983
Ceramic mouse holder base 4 1/4" wide. Comes with 6" red candle. **CMV $10. MB.**

CORAL GLOW CANDLE 1983-84
Clear glass Conch shell design candle. **CMV $12. MB.**

COUNTRY JAM CANDLES 1985
2" high clear glass. Cloth covers over lid. Comes in Mint, Black Raspberry, Strawberry and Orange. **CMV $4. each MB.**

SOFT ROSE FLOATING CANDLES 1985
Box holds white, pink & red flower candle. **CMV $6. MB.**

SPICE CUPBOARD CANDLE 1982
1 1/2" high clear glass refillable candle. **CMV $5. MB.**

GLISTENING STAR CRYSTAL CANDLE HOLDERS 1993
2' X 2" lead crystal. Set of 2. **CMV $8. set. MB.**

SPARKLING TURTLE CANDLETTE 1978-79
4 1/2" long clear glass turtle. **CMV $9. MB.**

FIREPLACE FRIENDS CANDLE HOLDER 1988
3 1/2" high fire place has candle holder on back side. **CMV $10. MB**

CHRISTMAS TRADITIONS GLASSWARE HURRICANE CANDLE 1995
7 5/8" high glass candle holder comes with 4" white candle. **CMV $20. MB.**

TRICK OR TREAT TRIO CANDLE SET 1995
(RIGHT) 3 Halloween wax candles 2 3/4" high. **CMV $4. set of 3 MB.**

HOLIDAY FLOATING CANDLES 1983
Box of 2 candles in choice of Red Poinsettia flowers or green & red wreath, 2 1/2" wide. **CMV $5. set MB.**

YEAR TO YEAR BIRTHDAY CANDLE 1983-84
4 1/2" ceramic clown candle holder with yellow candle, 1-2-3-4 on sides. **CMV $10. MB.**

HO HO GLOW "SANTA" CANDLE 1982-83
5" ceramic red, white & black Santa candle. **CMV $16. MB.**

THREE WEE TEDDY CANDLES 1987
Three 1 1/2" high bear candles on 1 wick. Cut separate. **CMV $4 set or $1 ea. Mint**

GLITTER & GLOW HOLIDAY CANDLE'S 1989
Red or gold metallic candles. **CMV $5. MB.**

SUMMER LIGHTS INDOOR-OUTDOOR CANDLE 1984
(Left) 2 1/4" high green glass. **CMV $5. MB.**
CLEARFIRE TULIP CUP CANDLE 1986
(RIght) Clear glass. 4" high. **CMV $8. MB.**

CHRISTMAS FUN CANDLE GIFT SET 1985
Green horse, white doll, red soldier candles.
CMV $4. set MB.

SHIMMERING GLASS CONVERTIBLE CANDLEHOLDER 1985
2 3/4" high clear glass. Holds big candle on 1 side, flip it over to holds taper candle. **CMV $7. MB.**

SPARKLING JEWEL STACKABLE CANDLES 1984
Green or blue glass. **CMV $7. MB each.**

EASTER CANDLES 1997
4 3/4" high wax candles with choice of
Bunny, Lamb, Duck. CMV $5. ea.MB.

GLISTENING GLOW CANDLE 1986
Clear glass candle. **CMV $8. MB.**
GINGERBREAD HOUSE CANDLE 1986
Ceramic house holds glass cup candle. **CMV $16. MB.**

PERSONAL CREATION CANDLE 1985
GLISTENING CREATING CANDLE 1985
(Right & Center) Both glass candles the same. Different boxes & candle mix. **CMV $6. each MB.**
AUTUMN IMPRESSIONS CANDLE 1984
(Left) 2 1/4" high clear glass. **CMV $4. MB.**

TRINKET BOX "SEA SHELL" CANDLE 1987
Small ceramic 3 1/2" pearlized sea shell. **CMV $7. MB.**

JOLLY SANTA CANDLE 1986
5 1/2" high Santa candle. **CMV $5. MB.**

NATURE'S FRIEND CANDLE HOLDER 1988
Hand painted ceramic squirrel holds scented candle. **CMV $12. MB.**

ANNIVERSARY TAPER CANDLE HOLDER 1985
Small porcelain doves & flowers. **CMV $11. MB.**
PORCELAIN ANGELS CANDLE HOLDER 1985
5" high white porcelain. Empty. **CMV $13. MB.**

AVON COUNTRY FRESH CANDLE 1985
Chicken egg candle with blue or red base. **CMV $3. MB.**

DOVE CANDLE HOLDERS 1986
2 white bisque porcelain candle holders. **CMV $9 MB.**
BUNNY TAPER CANDLE HOLDERS 1987
2 small ceramic rabbit candle holders. **CMV $10. MB.**

EXCHANGING GIFTS CANDLE 1987
Mr. & Mrs. Santa candle. **CMV $4. MB.**

FIRESIDE FRIENDS CANDLE HOLDER 1992
3" high ceramic candle holder & candle. **CMV $12. MB.**

GLOWING MESSAGE CANDLE 1984
1" high each. Flower - Star - Apple. **CMV $3.50 MB each.**

CRYSTAL CANDLE 1987
Clear pressed cut crystal glass. Pear shaped or Apple shapped. **CMV $8 ea. MB**

ST. NICK'S STARLIT JOURNEY GLASS CANDLEHOLDER 1991
5" x 5" frosted glass candleholders comes with 2 white bayberry tealight candles. **CMV $15. MB.**

GLOWING ANGEL CRYSTAL CANDLE-STICKS 1992
Set of 2 lead cut crystal angel candle holders, 7" high. **CMV $30. set MB.**

CHILDREN'S DECANTERS & TOYS

ICE CREAM LIP POMADE 1974-76
.13 oz. white plastic bottom with light pink,
dark pink, or red top for Cherry, Strawberry or
Tutti-Frutti flavors. **CMV $4. MB.**

ICE CREAM CONE LIP POMADE 1974-76
Yellow cone with different color tops for Cherry,
Strawberry, Tutti-Frutti, Mint, Chocolate. **CMV
$3. BO, $4. MB.**

SUNNY SHINE UP 1978-79
White plastic base with yellow screw on egg
lid. **CMV $2. MB.**

BY THE JUG 1974-75
All 3 - 10 oz. beige plastic. Strawberry Bath
Foam, Astringent, Balsam Shampoo. Brown
caps look like corks. No boxes issued. **CMV
$1. each.**

ALLSTAR LEAGUE "BASEBALL BAT" 1987
9 1/2"long tan plastic bottle. Holds shampoo.
CMV $2. MB.

TOOL KIT SCREWDRIVER 1986
6 3/4" yellow plastic. Holds 3.5 oz. Bubble
bath. **CMV $2. MB.**

TOOL KIT WRENCH 1986
6 1/2" green plastic. Holds 3.5 oz. Non Tear
Shampoo. **CMV $2. MB.**

E.T. ZIPPER PULL 1984
2" plastic. **CMV $1.**

BABY BEAR FLOATING DECANTER 1987
6oz. yellow & blue plastic. Holds shampoo.
CMV $4. MB.

**SUN SOUNDS TANNING LOTION DECANT-
ER 1987**
6oz. blue plastic. **CMV $4. MB.**

SPACE MISSION DECANTER 1988
10 3/4" long space ship in blue & yellow
plastic. Holds liquid soap & shampoo. **CMV
$4.MB**

LIP POP COLA'S 1973-74
.13 oz. plastic tube with plastic top. Came in
Cherry (light red case), Cola (brown case),
Strawberry (pink case) lip pomade. Strawberry
& Cherry also came solid red plastic **(rare
CMV $7.) others CMV $3. BO, $4. MB.**

SNOOPY'S SKI TEAM 1974-75
7 oz. white plastic bottle, red skis, yellow
"Woodstock". Holds bubble bath. **CMV $5.
MB.**

WOODSTOCK BRUSH & COMB 1975-78
Yellow plastic brush, green comb. **CMV $2.
MB.**

SNOOPY MUG 1969-72
5 oz. white glass, 5 inches high. Came 2
ways, red or blue top. Blue top is more rare.
Also came with oval or round decal. **CMV $7.
red top MB, $9. blue top MB.**

PERRY THE PENGUIN 1966-67
Black and white penguin soap dish and white
plastic soap dish.**CMV Set $12. MB.**

SNOOPY SOAP DISH 1968-76
White bar of Avon soap sets in black and white
plastic soap dish. **CMV $6. MB, Snoopy only
$2.**

434

CHILDREN'S TOYS & COLLECTIBLES

Children's toys and collectibles continue to be popular with many collectors. Almost all children's toys are plastic which are about the only plastic items in the book truly collectible. <u>All children's items must be in new mint condition.</u> If they are not, I suggest you do not buy them. Be sure to read <u>What's Hot and What's Not</u> in the introduction section of this book.

SNOOPY COME HOME SOAP DISH AND SOAP 1973-74
6" long, brown raft with white sail, has 3 oz. brown soap. **CMV $6. MB.**

SNOOPY & DOG HOUSE 1969-72
8 oz. white plastic dog and red plastic 3" high dog house, holds Non Tear Shampoo. **CMV $3., $5. MB.**
LINUS 1968-74
Red, white and green plastic 4 oz. tube of Gel Bubble Bath with red, white and black plastic Linus, plastic holder. **CMV $5. MB, $3. Linus & tube only.**

SIX SHOOTER 1962-63
6 oz. gray plastic and white gun with No Tears Shampoo. **CMV $18. BO mint, $24. MB.**

BO BO THE ELEPHANT 1973-74
6 oz. pink plastic with squeeze head. Filled with baby shampoo. **CMV $3. BO, $5. MB.**
SNOOPY'S SNOW FLYER 1973
10 oz. red, white and black. Holds bubble bath. **CMV $5. MB, $3. BO.**

CHARLIE BROWN 1968-72
4 oz. red, white and black plastic bottle of Non Tear Shampoo. **CMV $5. MB, $3. BO.**
LUCY 1970-72
4 oz. red, white and black plastic bottle holds bubble bath. **CMV $5. MB, $3. BO.**

SNOOPY COMB & BRUSH SET 1971-75
5 1/2" long black and brush and white comb. **CMV $5. MB.**

LUCY MUG 1969-70
5 oz. white glass, yellow top and label. White cap, Non Tear Shampoo. **CMV $8.**
CHARLIE BROWN MUG 1969-70
5 oz. white glass, blue top and label. White cap, bubble bath. **CMV $8.**

SNOOPY THE FLYING ACE 1969
4 oz. 6" high white plastic with blue hat, yellow glasses, holds bubble bath. **CMV $2., $5. MB.**
JUMPIN' JIMMINY 1969-73
8 oz. 6" high, green, red and yellow pull toy with yellow cap. Holds bubble bath. **CMV $5. MB, $3. BO.**

CLEAN AS A WHISTLE 1960-61
8 oz. red & white plastic bottle, real whistle cap. Came in bubble bath. **CMV $15. MB, $10. BO**
E.T. FLOWERS FIGURINE 1984
2 1/2" high hand painted porcelain. **CMV $5. MB.**

CHARLIE BROWN COMB & BRUSH 1972
4 1/2" long, red, black and white with white comb. **CMV $5. MB.**

GRID KID BRUSH & COMB 1973-74
4 1/2" long, red, black and white with white comb. **CMV $5. MB.**

LITTLE RED RIDING HOOD 1968
4 oz. yellow plastic bottle, red cap. Holds bubble bath. **CMV $2. BO, $6. with glasses MB.**

WOLF 1968
4 oz. yellow and blue plastic bottle, green cap, holds Non Tear Shampoo. **CMV $2. BO, $6. MB with white fang teeth.**

BUBBLE BUNNY 1964-65
Pink and white rabbit puppet with 6 oz. tube of bubble bath gel. **CMV $5. puppet only, $11. MB.**

SNOOPY'S BUBBLE TUB 1971-72
5" long, 12 oz. blue and white plastic tub, bottle holds bubble bath. **CMV $4. BO. $7. MB.**

PEANUTS PALS SHAMPOO 1971-72
6 oz. plastic, white, red, and black bottle with yellow cap. 6" high. **CMV $6. MB. $3. BO.**

MR. MANY MOODS 1965-66
6 oz. white plastic bottle with blue and yellow hat, red nose and mouth, black eyes. Holds shampoo. **CMV $8., $10. MB.**

MR. PRESTO CHANGO 1968
6 oz. yellow plastic bottle with red hat, black eyes and pink lips. Holds No Tear Shampoo. **CMV $6., $8. MB.**

BUGLE 1965
6 oz. blue plastic bugle with yellow cap. Holds Tot 'N Tyke Shampoo. **CMV $10. BO, $15. MB.**

FIFE 1965
6 oz. yellow plastic bottle with red cap. Came in hand lotion or hair trainer. **CMV $10. BO, $15. MB.**

THREE LITTLE PIGS 1967-68
3 oz. each, 4 1/2" high. Blue pigs, yellow hat holds bubble bath, yellow pig, green hat holds baby shampoo, and pink pig with pink hat holds baby lotion. **CMV $6. BO. each, $9. MB.**

GOOD HABIT RABBIT 1967
3 oz., 4 1/2" high. White plastic rabbit, green hat and orange carrot. Came in Tot 'N Tyke Shampoo. **CMV $8., $12. MB.**

THREE BEARS 1966-67
4 3/4" high each. 3 oz. each. White plastic bottles with blue caps. **Papa Bear** holds baby oil. **CMV $10. BO, $14. MB. Mama Bear** holds baby lotion, **Baby Bear** holds shampoo. **CMV $8. BO, $12. MB each.**

A WINNER 1960-62
4 oz. maroon plastic boxing gloves with white caps. Tied togehter with white plastic cord. Hand Guard and Hair Guard. **CMV $20. MB, $7. each bottle.**

SPACE AGE 1968-69
4 oz. silver and yellow plastic rocket holds liquid hair trainer. **CMV $3., $5. MB.**
BO BO THE ELEPHANT 1970
5 oz. light or dark pink plastic bottle of Non Tear Shampoo. **CMV $3. BO, $5. MB.**
RED STREAK BOAT 1972-73
5 oz. red plastic boat, white cap. Holds bubble bath. **CMV $5. MB, $3. BO.**

SPINNING TOP 1966-67
4 oz. red and white top holds bubble bath, yellow top spinner. **CMV $10. MB, $6. BO.**

LITTLE CHAMP 1967-68
1/2 oz. each with white caps. Blue boxing glove holds Non Tear Shampoo, yellow glove holds Hair Trainer. **CMV $17. MB. Each glove $5.**

WHISTLE TOTS 1966-67
6 3/4" high, 4 oz. white plastic bottle with whistle cap. Red cap **Fireman** holds Tot 'N Tyke Shampoo. Blue cap **Policeman** holds Hair Trainer and green **Clown** holds bubble bath. **CMV $7. BO mint, $10. MB. each.**

SCHOOL DAYS 1966-67
8 oz. red and white plastic ruler holds Non Tear Shampoo. Yellow cap. **CMV $7., $10. MB.**
MILK BATH 1968-69
6 oz. pink plastic milk can holds powdered bubble bath. **CMV $3. BO, $5. MB.**

CUCKOO CLOCK 1965-66
10 oz. red, white and blue plastic clock holds bubble bath. **CMV $8., $10. MB.**
WRIST WASH BUBBLE BATH 1969-70
2 oz. orange plastic clock with blue cap. **CMV $6. MB, $4. BO.**

RING 'EM UP CLEAN 1970-72
8 oz. orange plastic bottle with red or white cap holds Non Tear Shampoo. **CMV $3., $5. MB.**
SAFE SAM 1965
8 oz. red and black plastic safe holds bubble bath. **CMV $8., $11. MB.**

GLOBE BANK 1966-67
10 oz. blue plastic globe holds bubble bath. Black base. Bank has 5 different colored sets of stick on countries. North America came in orange, blue, tan, pink or yellow. **CMV $16. MB, $10. BO.**
MAD HATTER 1970
6 oz. bronze plastic with pink hat and clock. Came in bubble bath. **CMV $4. BO, $6. MB.**

CONCERTINA 1970-72
8 oz. blue and yellow plastic squeeze bottle. Holds bubble bath. Musical cap with pink strap. **CMV $8. MB, $6. BO.**
CONCERTINA 1962-65
8 oz. red and yellow plastic squeeze bottle with musical cap. Holds bubble bath. **CMV $12., $15. MB.**

MR. LION 1967
4 oz. white plastic bottle with red bubble pipe over white cap. Holds bubble bath. **CMV $6. BO, $8. MB.**

TIN MAN 1967
4 oz. white plastic bottle with blue bubble pipe over white cap. Holds Non Tear Shampoo. **CMV $6. BO, $8. MB.**

STRAW MAN 1967
4 oz. white plastic bottle with yellow bubble pipe over white cap. Holds hand lotion. **CMV $6. BO, $8. MB.**

AVONVILLE SLUGGER 1961-62
6 oz. tan plastic bat holds shampoo. **CMV $12. BO, $17. MB.**

SURE WINNER SLUGGER DECANTER 1973
6 oz. yellow plastic bat. Holds Sure Winner Bracing Lotion or Liquid Hair Trainer or Avon Spicy After Shave. **CMV $4. mint, no box issued.**

LAND HO 1961-62
(Left) 8 oz. blue & white plastic telescope holds Hair Trainer. CMV $17. MB, $12. BO mint.

NAUGHTY-LESS 1961-62
(Right) 8 oz. red & white submarine with whtie & blue cap. Holds bubble bath. **CMV $15. BO mint, $20. MB.**

FIRST MATE SHAMPOO 1963-64
8 oz. blue and white plastic sailor with white hat. **CMV $15. MB, $11. BO.**

CAPTAIN'S BUBBLE BATH 1963-64
8 oz. white, yellow and black plastic bottle with blue hat. **CMV $15. MB, $11. BO.**

BIRD HOUSE 1969
7" high orange plastic bottom with tan roof. Holds 8 oz. of Powdered Bubble Bath. **CMV $7. BO, $9. MB.**

TOPSY TURVEY CLOWN 1965 ONLY
10 oz. red, white and yellow plastic clown. Blue hat, black feet. Holds bubble bath. **CMV $16. MB, $12. BO mint.**

AQUA CAR 1964-65
(Left) 8 oz. red & white plastic bottle of bubble bath. **CMV $10., $15. MB.**

S.S. SUDS 1970-71
(Right) 8 oz. blue & white plastic boat holds No Tear Shampoo. **CMV $5., $7. MB.**

SANTA'S HELPER 1967-68
Red and white sponge with 6 oz. tube of Gel Bubble Bath. **CMV $8. MB.**

ONE TWO LACE MY SHOE 1968-69
8 oz. bubble bath. Pink plastic shoe with orange tie on and yellow cap. Green or yellow roof. **CMV $6. BO, $9. MB.**

TIC TOC TURTLE 1968-69
8 oz. 5 1/2" high. Green turtle, yellow clock face with pink hands. Bubble bath. **CMV $6. BO, $9. MB.**

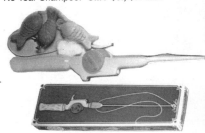

TUB CATCH 1968-69
2 ft. long yellow rod & reel holds 6 oz. bubble bath. Pink, green & blue plastic fish. **CMV $9. MB.**

LITTLE MISSY ROLLING PIN 1966-67
12" long, 8 oz. pink plastic center with orange ends. Holds Non Tear Shampoo. **CMV $9. BO mint, $13. MB.**

BIRD FEEDER 1967-68
11" high, black and white plastic center with red base and yellow top. Holds 7 1/2 oz. powdered bubble bath. **CMV $8. BO, $12. MB.**

PACKY THE ELEPHANT 1964-65
3 oz. each. Each has white hat. Blue holds baby oil, yellow holds baby shampoo, baby lotion in red. **CMV red & blue $10. BO each, $15. MB, Yellow $15. BO, $20. MB.**

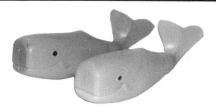

SMILEY THE WHALE 1967-68
(Left) 9" blue plastic whale holds 9 oz. bubble bath. **CMV $6. BO, $9. MB.**
WHITEY THE WHALE 1959-62
(Right) 8 oz. white plastic whale holds bubble bath. **CMV $15. MB, $10. BO.**

SANTA'S CHIMNEY 1964-65
Red & white box holds 5 oz. of powdered bubble bath. Top of box makes a puzzle game. **CMV $20. MB.**

TOOFIE TWOSOME 1963-64
This is the 1st issue of the Toofie series. 3 1/2 oz. green & blue tube & green cap. Choice of red, yellow, blue or green toothbrush. **CMV $8. MB.**

EASTER DEC A DOO 1968-69
(Left) 8 oz. pink & yellow plastic egg holds bubble bath. Came with stick on decorations. **CMV $6. MB, $4. BO.**
HUMPTY DUMPTY 1963-65
(Right) 8 oz. plastic bottle of bubble bath. Blue bottom, white top, black belt. **CMV $9. MB, $5. BO.**

LIL FOLKS TIME 1961-64
(Left) 8 oz. yellow & white plastic clock with yellow cap & red time hands, holds bubble bath. **CMV $8. BO, $11. MB.**
TIC TOC TIGER 1967-69
(Right) 8 oz. orange & white plastic clock with yellow cap & hands, holds bubble bath. **CMV $6. BO, $9. MB.**

TOOFIE TOOTHPASTE 1967-68
3 1/2 oz. white tube with racoon & pink cap & toothbrush, pink & white box. **CMV $6. MB,**

MARY NON TEAR SHAMPOO 1968-69
(Left) 3 oz. pink plastic bottle. **CMV$8. MB.**
LITTLE LAMB BABY LOTION 1968-69
(Center) 3 oz. white plastic lamb with blue cap. **CMV $7. MB.**
LITTLE RED SCHOOLHOUSE 1968-69
(Right) 3 oz. red plastic school with yellow cap. Contains bubble bath. **CMV $8. MB.**

LITTLE HELPER IRON 1962-64
(Left) 8 oz. blue plastic iron with white handle. Holds bubble bath. **CMV $13. mint, $17. MB.**
WATERING CAN 1962-64
(Right) 8 oz. yellow plastic bottle holds bubble bath. Blue cap. **CMV $13. mint, $17. MB.**

TOOFIE TOOTHPASTE 1969-70
3 1/2 oz. blue & green tube with pink cap & toothbrush in blue & green box. **CMV $5. MB, $2. BO.**

CHIEF SCRUBBEM 1969-70
(Left) 4 oz. red & yellow plastic Indian holds liquid soap. **CMV $6. MB.**
SCRUB MUG 1968-69
(Right) 6 oz. blue plastic mug with blue brush lid. Holds liquid soap. **CMV $6. MB.**

LIL TOM TURTLES 1961-63
3 oz. plastic turtles. Each has white hat. Yellow holds baby shampoo,, blue has baby oil & baby lotion in red. **CMV $15. MB.ea.**

PADDLE 'N' BALL SET 1966-67
6 oz. tan plastic paddle with red cap. Holds shampoo. Rubber ball hooked to paddle. 8" long by 4 1/2" wide. **CMV $15. MB.**

TOY SOLDIERS 1964
4 oz. each. Red, white & blue plastic bottles, black caps. Came in Hair Trainer, shampoo, hand lotion, bubble bath. **CMV $12. MB. ea,**

MICKEY MOUSE 1969-71
(Left) 4 1/2 oz. red pants, black & white palstic Mickey with yellow feet. Holds bubble bath. **CMV $5. BO, $7. MB.**
PLUTO 1970-71
(Right) 4 oz. yellow & black plastic dog with red collar. Holds Non Tear shampoo. **CMV $5. BO, $7. MB.**

JET PLANE 1965 ONLY
3 oz. red, white & blue plastic tube with white plastic wings came in gel bubble bath, children's gel shampoo or Hair Tainer. **CMV $10. mint, $15. MB.**

TOPSY TURVEY 1970-72
(Left) 4 oz. green plastic bottle with white cap holds bubble bath. **CMV $2. MB, $1. BO.**
BALL & CUP 1972-73
(Right) 4 oz. blue bottom with green cup & ball. Holds shampoo. **CMV $4. MB, $2. BO.**

TUB TALK TELEPHONE 1969
(Blue) 6 oz. blue plastic telephone with yellow cap & holder. Holds No Tear Shampoo. **CMV $7., $9. MB.**

VERY OWN TELEPHONE 1964-65
(Red) 6 oz. red plastic telephone & base. Holds Baby Shampoo. **CMV $9. BO, $13. MB.**

TUB TALK TELEPHONE 1967-68
(Yellow) 6 oz. yellow telephone with red cap & holder. Holds Tot 'N' Tyke shampoo. **CMV $8. BO, $11. MB.**

FRILLY DUCK 1960-62
(Left) 3 oz. yellow plastic duck with blue cap. Came in baby oil, baby lotion & Tot 'N' Tyke shampoo. **CMV $10., $13. MB.**

PIG IN A POKE 1960-62
(Right) 8 oz. pink plastic pig holds bubble bath. Came in pink bag. **CMV $9. BO, $14. BO with bag, $18. MB.**

BUNNY FLUFF PUFF 1979-80
(Left) 3.5 oz. yellow plastic with fluff tail & pink eyes & ears. Holds children's talc. SSP $6. **CMV $3.50 MB.**

RED STREAK CAR 1979-80
(Right) 7 oz. red plastic with blue & silver stick on decals. Holds bubble bath for children. SSP $4. **CMV $3. MB.**

TOOTHBRUSH DUO (CHILDREN'S) 1979
(right) Red & pink box holds 1 red & 1 white toothbrush for kids. **CMV $1. MB.**

PINK PANTHER TOOTHBRUSH HOLDER 1979
(left) Pink plastic holder. Yellow & red toothbrushes. Blue & pink box. **CMV $3. MB.**

BARNEY BEAVER TOOTHBRUSHES & HOLDER 1973
(Left) 4" high, brown plastic with white & blue. Has pink & blue toothbrushes. Comes with a sticker to put on wall. **CMV $4. MB.**

'I LOVE TOOFIE' TOOTHBRUSHES & HOLDER 1973
(Right) 5" high, white & pink, holds red & blue toothbrushes. Comes with sticker to put on wall. **CMV $4. MB.**

BABY SHOE PIN CUSHION 1973-74
(Left) 7 oz. whie plastic with pink pin cushion & blue bow. Filled with baby lotion. **CMV $5. MB.**

SUNNY BUNNY BABY POMANDER 1973-76
(Center) Wax figurine with nursery fresh fragrance. **CMV $6. MB.**

SAFETY PIN DECANTER 1973-74
(Right) 8 oz. yellow plastic filled with baby lotion. **CMV $5. MB.**

TENNIS ANYONE? 1975-76
(Left) 5 oz. gray & black plastic. Holds Sweet Honesty after bath freshener or Avon Spicy after shave. **CMV $3. MB.**

SLUGGER BRUSH 1974-75
(Right) 7" long brown & black plastic. **CMV $3. MB.**

ON THE RUN "JOGGING SHOE" 1978-79
(Left) 6 oz. blue plastic with white stripes. Holds Wild Country after shave or Sweet Honesty body splash. **CMV $4. MB.**

CONAIR "HAIR DRYER" 1978-79
(Right) 6 oz. off-white plastic. Blue letters and cap. Holds Naturally Gentle shampoo. **CMV $4. MB.**

ACCUSING ALLIGATOR 1978-79
(Left) 6 oz. green, yellow & tan plastic. Holds bubble bath. **CMV $6. MB.**

SUPERMAN BUBBLE BATH 1978-79
(Right) 8 oz. blue, red & gray plastic. Holds bubble bath. Box came with 2 red and yellow plastic cut out capes. **CMV $8. MB.**

HANG TEN SKATEBOARD DECANTER 1978-79
(Left) 5.5 oz. yellow plastic with top stick on decal. Holds bubble bath for children. **CMV $3. MB.**

KARROT TAN DECANTER 1978-79
(Center) 4 oz. orange plastic with green leaf top. Holds Bronze Glory tanning lotion. **CMV $4. BO, no box issued.**

HEAVY HITTER DECANTER 1978-79
(Right) 4 oz. dark blue plastic. White letters. holds non tear shampoo. **CMV $3. MB.**

TOOFIE THE TIGER 1966-67
(Left) 3 1/2 oz. green & orange tube, green cap, toothbrush. **CMV $6. MB.**
TOOFIE ON GUARD 1968-69
(Right) 3 1/2 oz. red, white, & blue tube, blue cap. Avon toothbrush. **CMV $5. MB.**

MR. ROBOTTLE 1971-72
8" high plastic bottle with blue body and red legs and arms. Silver and yellow cap. Holds bubble bath. Came with white plastic wrench to put together. **CMV $7. MB.**

SPACE PATROLLER DECANTER 1979-80
(Left) 8 oz. gray plastic, black cap & stick on decals. **CMV $3. MB.**
SPIDERMAN TOOTHBRUSH & HOLDER 1979-80
(Right) Red & blue plastic. Yellow & green Avon toothbrushes. **CMV $2.50 MB.**

BATMOBILE 1978-79
(Left) 6 oz. blue & silver plastic with stick on decals. Came in bubble bath for children. **CMV $5. MB.**
LIP POP POMADE "PEPSI" 1978-79
(Right) Dark amber plastic. Gray cap. Looks like Pepsi Cola bottle. **CMV $3. MB.**

FREDDY THE FROG MUG 1970
5 oz. white glass mug with red or orange top and white cap. Holds bubble bath. **CMV $9. MB.**
GAYLORD GATOR MUG 1970-72
5 oz. white glass mug with yellow top and white cap. Holds non tear shampoo. **CMV $9. MB.**

SPOTTY TO THE RESCUE TOOTHBRUSH HOLDER 1976-77
Red, white & black plastic toothbrush holder holds 2 Avon toothbrushes. **CMV $3. MB.**

GRID KID LIQUID HAIR TRAINER 1974-75
(Left) 8 oz. red, black & white plastic. **CMV $3. MB.**
ARCH E. BEAR BRUSH & COMB 1975-76
(Right) Red, white & blue brush with white comb. **CMV $3. MB.**

JACKKNIFE COMB & BRUSH 1974-76
(Left) Blue & silver plastic comb. Cub Scout gold label on top. **CMV $3. MB.**
ICE CREAM COMB 1977-78
(Center) Orange plastic comb with pink & brown ice cream & red cherry on top. **CMV $2. MB.**
REGGIE RACCOON HAIRBRUSH & COMB 1977
(Right) 6 1/4" long. Brown, white, pink & black brush & white comb. **CMV $2. MB.**

GIRAFFABATH BATH BRUSH 1977-79
(Left) Orange & beige plastic. Blue eyes. **CMV $3.50 MB.**
BATMAN STYLING BRUSH 1977-78
(Center) Blue, gray & black plastic brush. **CMV $5. MB.**
SUPERMAN STYLING BRUSH 1977
(Right) Red & blue plastic brush. **CMV $5. MB.**

WALLY WALRUS TOOTHBRUSH HOLDER & TOOTHBRUSH 1977-78
Adhesive back holder sticks to wall. Came with 2 child sized Avon toothbrushes in red & white. Plastic holder is blue & red with white hat & trim. **CMV $2. MB.**

HOT DOG! BRUSH & COMB 1975-76
(Left) Yellow & red plastic comb. **CMV $3. MB.**

SUNANA BRONZE GLORY TANNING LOTION 1974-76
(Right) 6 oz. yellow plastic banana. **CMV $3. BO, no box issued.**

TED E. BEAR TOOTHBRUSH HOLDER 1974-75
Box holds tan, pink & white plastic holder & pink & white Avon toothbrushes. **CMV $3. MB.**

TOOFIE THE CLOWN 1978
Orange, yellow & white plastic toothbrush holder. Blue & pink toothbrushes. **CMV $2. MB.**

PRECIOUS LAMB BABY LOTION 1975-76
6 oz. white plastic lamb with blue bow. Holds baby lotion. **CMV $4. MB.**

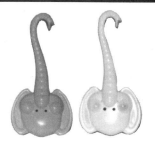

SCRUBBO THE ELEPHANT BATH BRUSH 1975
White plastic, pink ears & cheeks. **CMV $2. MB.** 1976 issue was all pink plastic. Each is 8" long. **CMV $2. MB.**

SCHOOL DAYS RULER COMB 1976-79
Box holds yellow plastic 6" ruler comb. **CMV $2. MB.**

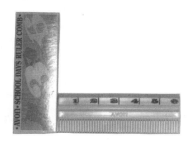

TOOFIE TOOTHPASTE 1971-73
(Left) 3 1/2 oz. yellow & orange tube & box. **CMV $2., $3. MB.**

TOOFIE TOOTHBRUSH DUO 1973-74
(Right) Pak of 2, green worm & yellow bird. **CMV $2. MB.**

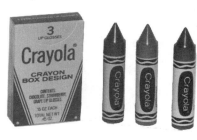

CRAYOLA LIP GLOSS SET 1980-81
Crayola box holds 3 plastic crayon shaped Avon lip gloss in chocolate, grape and strawberry. **CMV $2. MB.**

LOVING LION DECANTER 1978-79
(Left) 8 oz. plastic purple, yellow, pink & orange. Holds Non Tear Shampoo. **CMV $5 MB.**

THREE RING CIRCUS CHILDREN'S TALC 1978-79
(Center) 5 oz., 2 sections of center turn around. **CMV $2. MB.**

OCTOPUS TOOTHBRUSH HOLDER 1978-79
(Right) Purple & orange plastic toothbrush holder. Comes with orange & white Avon toothbrushes. **CMV $2. MB.**

MOST VALUABLE GORILLA 1979-80
(Left) 4 oz. orange & blue plastic stick on front & back decals in any letter. Holds bubble bath for children. **CMV $3. MB.**

WILLIE WEATHERMAN 1979-80
(Center) 6 oz. tan plastic, pink cap. Blue umbrella changes color with the weather. Holds Non Tear Shampoo. **CMV $3. MB.**

IMP THE CHIMP BATH BRUSH 1980
(Right) Brown plastic, yellow, black & pink trim. 10" long. **CMV $4. MB.**

TOOFIE TIGER TOOTHBRUSHES & HOLDER 1976
(Left) Yellow, black, white & pink. Has 1 pink & 1 white toothbrush. **CMV $3. MB.**

TOOFIE TOOTHBRUSH DUO 1971-73
(Center) One yellow giraffe, 1 pink rabbit brush. **CMV $2. MB.**

TORTOISE 'N' HARE TOOTHBRUSH DUO 1975-76
(Right) Green tortoise & yellow hare. **CMV $2. MB.**

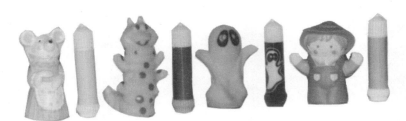

BRONTOSAURUS BUBBLE BATH 1975-76
(Left) 10 oz. blue gray plastic. **CMV $3. BO, $5. MB.**

LOVABLE LEO 1974-76
(Right) 10 oz. yellow plastic, pink cap. Children's shampoo. **CMV $3. MB.**

MILLICENT MOUSE DEMI STICK 1977-78
(Left) Came with Pink & Pretty fragrance demi stick. Colors are pink & white. **CMV $5. MB.**

GLOW WORM 1977-79
(Inside Left) Came with Care Deeply lip balm. White rubber top with purple spots. Demi stick is blue & green. **CMV $5 .MB.**

GILROY THE GHOST 1977-78
(Inside Right) Came with Care Deeply lip balm. White & black rubber top with black, green & white demi stick. **CMV $5. MB.**

HUCK L. BERRY 1977-78
(Right) Came with Care Deeply lip balm. Blue, yellow & white rubber top with yellow & white demi stick. **CMV $5. MB.**

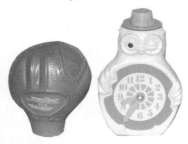

SURE WINNER CATCHER'S MITT 1974-75
(Left) 6 oz. brown plastic with brown cap. Holds Avon liquid hair trainer. **CMV $3. MB.**

WINKIE BLINK CLOCK BUBBLE BATH 1975-76
(Right) 8 oz. yellow with blue clock hands & blue cap. **CMV $4. MB.**

KISS 'N' MAKEUP LIP GLOSS COMPACT 1977-79
(Top) Came with Frostlight Peach & Frostlight Pink lip gloss. Red plastic container. **CMV $1.**

LOVE LOCKET GLACE 1972
(Bottom) **CMV $6. MB, $4. BO.**

ROBOT BANK 1985
Blue, yellow & orange plastic bank. **CMV $3. MB.**

BABY ELEPHANT PUMP 1985
8 oz. blue plastic, holds baby lotion. **CMV $2. MB.**

MUPPET BABIES - MISS PIGGY & KERMIT1985
4 oz. each plastic, rubber finger puppet tops. Non Tear Shampoo & Bubble Bath. **CMV $1. each MB.**

TURN A WORD BUBBLE BATH 1972-74
8 oz. pink plastic bottle with white cap & green lettered sides. **CMV $3. MB.**

CLANCY THE CLOWN SOAP HOLDER & SOAP 1973-74
Orange, pink and white clown holds green and white, pink and orange 3 oz. soap. **CMV $8. MB.**

JACK IN A BOX GLACE 1976
(Left) White plastic with pink & green trim. **CMV $3. MB.**

CHICK A PEEK GLACE 1977
(Right) Yellow plastic back & chick with purple egg. **CMV $3. MB.**

TOOFIE TRAIN 1974-75
Red plastic train, yellow plastic cup. Red & blue toofie toothbrushes & yellow with red cap Toofie toothpaste. **CMV $5., $7. MB.**

RAPID RABBIT PIN PAL 1974-75
(Left) White plastic with pink & green. Feet swing. Filled with perfumed glace. **CMV $2., $3. MB.**
MYRTLE TURTLE PIN PAL 1974
(Right) Green plastic with pink & green. Filled with perfumed glace. **CMV $2., $3. MB.**

CHILDREN'S FUN JEWELRY
LUV-A-DUCKY 1973
(Top Left) Yellow & orange. **CMV $3. $5. MB.**
PANDY BEAR PIN 1973
(Bottom Left) Black & white. **CMV $3. $5. MB.**
FLY-A-KITE 1973
(Center) Red, white and blue. **CMV $3. $5. MB.**

FUZZY BUG 1973-74
(Top Right) Blue with green fur. **CMV $3. $5. MB.**
PERKEY PARROT 1973
(Bottom Right) Red & green. **CMV $3. $5. MB.**

ON THE FARM BANK 1985
(Center) Stick on stickers & packets of bubble bath inside. **CMV $3.**
CHRISTMAS TOYLAND CANDY 1984
(Left) 8 1/4" high tin can full of candy. **CMV $2. can only.**
PLUSH LAMB BANK 1984
(Right) 8" long, 6" high. Fabric covered plastic bank. **CMV $8. MB.**

ROTO-BOAT FLOATING SOAP DISH & SOAP 1973-75
9" long blue & white boat with red rudder holds 3 oz. blue soap. **CMV $8. MB.** Reissued with "R" on bottom.

BOBBIN' ROBIN PIN 1975-76
(Top Left) White cage, red bird (bird movable). **CMV $3. MB.**
MINUTE MOUSE PIN 1974-75
(Bottom Left) White with blue clock, orange hands & numbers. **CMV $3. MB.**
PEDAL PUSHER PIN 1975-76
(Top Center) Blue elephant with green jacket & pink bike. **CMV $3. MB.**

LICKETY STICK MOUSE PIN 1974-76
(Bottom Center) White plastic with green hat & pink striped stick. **CMV $3. MB.**
MAGIC RABBIT PIN 1975-76
(Top Right) White & pink rabbit with gray hat. **CMV $3. MB.**
COTTON TAIL GLACE 1976-78
(Bottom Right) Yellow & pink with white tail. **CMV $3. MB.**

BUMBLEY BEE PINS 1973-74
Yellow with black stripes. One with big stripes & 1 narrow stripes. **CMV $4., $6. MB.**

GREAT CATCH, CHARLIE BROWN, SOAP HOLDER & SOAP 1975-76
(Left) Red, white, black & brown plastic. **CMV $8. MB.**

QUACK & DOODLE FLOATING SOAP DISH & SOAP 1974-75
(Right) Yellow rubber with yellow soap. **CMV $7. MB.**

RING AROUND ROSIE 1966-67
Pink rubber elephant sticks on wall with blue bar of Avon soap. **CMV $15. MB, soap only $6., elephant only $4.**

CLEAN SHOT 1970-72
Orange net holds orange basketball sponge & 1 bar of Clean Shot soap. **CMV $8. MB. set.**

FUNNY BUNNY 1973-74
(Top Left) Pink & white. **CMV $4.**

CALICO CAT 1973
(Top Center) Red with white dots. Also came red & no dots.**CMV $4.**

CALICO CAT 1974-75
(Repeat Top Center) Blue with white dots. Also came blue with no dots on bottom half. **CMV $3. each.**

BLOUSE MOUSE 1972
(Top Right) Green & pink. Also came green with white trim. **CMV $4.**

BLUE MOO 1974
(Middle Left) Blue & pink. **CMV $3.**

SNIFFY PIN PAL 1972-75
(Middle Center) Black, white & pink. **CMV $3.**

ELPHIE THE ELEPHANT 1973
(Middle Right) Yellow & pink. **CMV $4.**

GINGERBREAD PIN PAL 1973
(Bottom Center) Brown & pink. Also came brown & white. **CMV $5. pink, $6. white.**
Add $1. ea. MB.

PUPPY LOVE PIN PAL GLACE 1975
(Top Left) Beige dog with black ears & pink pillow. **CMV $4. MB.**

WEE WILLY WINTER PIN PAL GLACE 1974-75
(Top Center) White snowman with pink hat, scarf & mittens. **CMV $4. MB.**

SUNNY FRESH ORANGE GLACE NECKLACE 1974-75
(Top Right) Orange & yellow with green cord. **CMV $4. MB.**

PETER PATCHES PIN PAL GLACE 1975-76
(Bottom Left) Yellow with red & blue trim. **CMV $4. MB.**

CHICKEN LITTLE PIN PAL GLACE 1975
(Bottom Inside Left) Yellow chicken with pink flower & green leaf. **CMV $4.**

WILLIE THE WORM PIN PAL GLACE 1974-75
(Bottom Inside Right) Red apple, green worm. **CMV $4. MB.**

ROCK-A-ROO PIN PAL GLACE 1975-77
(Bottom Right) Pink with dark pink rocking pouch. **CMV $3. MB.**

WASH AWEIGH SOAP & DISH 1966-67
Green plastic boat dish & yellow anchor soap on a rope. **CMV boat $6., anchor soap $9., set $20. MB.**

REGGIE RACOON HAIR BRUSH AND COMB 1973
6 1/2" long, tan and black with tan comb. **CMV $4. MB.**

REGINALD G. RACOON III 1970-71
Black, brown and white rubber soap dish and 3 oz. pink vest soap. **CMV $10. set MB.**
RANDY PANDY SOAP DISH 1972-74
Black, white & pink rubber soap dish & 3 oz. white soap. **CMV $10. set MB.**

FREDDIE THE FROG 1969-70
(Left) Green rubber frog soap dish & green vest soap. Pink lips & pink band around hat. **CMV frog only $3., with soap $10. MB.**
FREDDIE THE FROG 1965-66
(Right) Green rubber frog with yellow hat & eyes, pink lips, green soap. **CMV frog only $5., with soap $10. MB.**

GAYLORD GATER 1967-69
10" long green and yellow rubber soap dish with yellow soap. **CMV gater only $2., $10. set MB.**
TOPSY TURTLE FLOATING SOAP DISH & SOAP 1973-74
7" long green rubber soap dish with 3 oz. pink soap. **CMV $8. MB.** Reissued 1979. Some came light green body and dark green head. Also came matching body and head.

BARNEY BEAVER SOAP DISH & SOAP 1971-72
10 1/2" long, brown soap dish and brown vest soap. **CMV $10. MB.**

FIRST DOWN 1965-67
Large box holds real junior size football & 6 oz. brown football soap on a rope. **CMV Soap $10. MB, ball $15. $30. for set MB.** .

PADDLEWOG FROG FLOATING SOAP DISH & SOAP 1975-76
Green plastic with pink propeller and yellow soap. **CMV $8. MB.**

SOAP BOAT, FLOATING SOAP DISH AND SOAP 1973-74
7 1/2" long blue and red boat with white sail and white soap. **CMV $10. MB.**

CHILDREN'S DECANTERS & TOYS

PINK PEARL SCRUB AWAY NAIL BRUSH AND SOAP 1977-78
3 oz. soap, pink brush shaped like pink pearl eraser. CMV $8. MB.

FUN IN SPACE SOAPS 1986
Box holds yellow & blue soaps. CMV $4. MB.
SUDSVILLE TRUCK & SOAP 1986
Box holds yellow, blue & red plastic dump truck & bar of yellow Sudsville soap. CMV $7. MB.

TERRIBLE TUBBLES FLOATING SOAP DISH AND SOAP 1977-78
(Left) Blue plastic dish with 3 oz. soap. CMV $7. MB.
RANDY PANDY SOAP DISH AND SOAP 1976-77
(Right) Black, light blue and red rubber soap dish and 3 oz. blue and white soap. CMV (Panda only) $2. Set $7. MB.

MOON FLIGHT GAME 1970-72
4 oz. white Space Capsule holds Non Tear Shampoo. Comes with black game sheet. CMV $6. set MB.

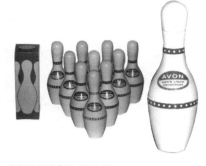

BOWLING PIN 1960-62
4 oz. white plastic trimmed in red. Came in Vigorate, Liquid Deodorant, Hand Guard, Hair Trainer, After Shaving Lotion, After Shower for Men, Liquid Hair Lotion, Shampoo, Cream Hair Lotion & Electric Pre-Shave. **CMV 10 different $10. each BO, $15. MB, Vigorate $15. BO, $20. MB.**

KANGA WINKS 1971-72
7" high yellow and orange plastic bottle with pink hat, holds 8 oz. of bubble bath. Box also holds black and white plastic target and package of 16 plastic chips for tiddlywinks. CMV $8. set MB.

CHOO-CHOO TRAIN 1971-72
Soap coach is 4" long plastic soap dish with yellow bar of soap. CMV $6. MB with soap, $3. soap coach only. **Caboose** is pink plastic bottle, 3" long with Non Tear Shampoo. CMV $4. MB **Puffer Chugger** is 3" long green plastic bottle with yellow cap and nose. Holds bubble bath. CMV $4. MB

SOMERSAULTS PRODUCTS 1985-86
TABINA & HERBY DERBY
2 oz. plastic cologne green & yellow & yellow & pink. CMV $2. each.
MINI DOLLS
Mini plastic - Zippy, Herby Derby, Charley Barley, Miss Pear & Tallulah. CMV $2. each MB.

SPLASH DOWN BUBBLE BATH 1970-71
8 oz. white plastic bottle with red cap and yellow base ring. Came with 3 plastic toss rings. CMV $5. MB.

HICKORY DICKORY CLOCK 1971-72
5 1/2" high, 8 oz. yellow plastic cheese clock with orange face and pink hands, purple mouse cap. Contains Non Tear Shampoo. CMV $6. MB.

POP-A-DUCK GAME 1978
6 oz. blue plastic with red-orange cap. Came with 3 green balls. Pink, orange and yellow ducks and red-orange ball holder. Bottle holds bubble bath for children. CMV $4. MB.

ROCKABYE PONY DECANTER 1975-76
6 oz. yellow plastic, holds Clearly Gentle Baby Lotion. **CMV $4. MB.**
JACK-IN-THE-BOX 1975-76
4 oz. yellow and pink plastic, holds baby cream. **CMV $4. MB.**

POP A DUCK 1971-72
6 oz. blue plastic bottle holds bubble bath. 3 plastic ducks and ball. **CMV $5. complete set MB.**

LOOP-A-MOOSE GAME AND SOAP 1972-75
7" high brown plastic moose, yellow antlers. has green, pink and yellow rings to toss. Comes with 3 oz. yellow soap. **CMV $4. MB.**

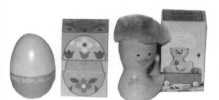

EASTER DEC-A-DOO FOR CHILDREN 1978
(Left) 8 oz. plastic yellow base, pink top. Came with stick on decals. This is different from 68-69 issue. Old one does not say for children on label. Holds bubble bath. **CMV $3. MB.**
DUSTER D. DUCKLING FLUFF PUFF 1978-82
3.5 oz. yellow plastic and fluff top. Holds Delicate Daisies or Sweet Pickles perfumed talc. **CMV $3. MB.**

MAZE GAME 1971-72
6 oz. green plastic bottle, white cap. holds Non Tear Shampoo. **CMV $5. MB.**
HUGGY BEAR 1971-72
8 oz. brown plastic bottle with lace-up vest, holds bubble bath. **CMV $5. MB.**

SCHROEDER 1970-72
6 oz. red, white, black and yellow plastic bottle holds bubble bath, in piano shaped box. **CMV $4., $9. MB in piano box.**
LINUS 1970-72
4 oz. red, white and black plastic bottle holds Non Tear Shampoo. **CMV $6. MB.**

LITTLE WIGGLY GAME & BUBBLE BATH 1973
8 oz. green with pink legs, red and yellow hoops. Holds bubble bath. **CMV $3. MB.**

TYRANNOSAURUS REX 1976-78
4 oz. green plastic bottle, green rubber head. holds bubble bath for children. **CMV $3. MB.**
TUB SUB 1978-79
6 oz. yellow plastic, 10" long. Holds bubble bath for children. **CMV $3. MB.**

CUSTOM CAR 1976-78
7 oz. blue plastic bottle with red tire cap. Filled with bubble bath for children. **CMV $3. MB.**
TRICERATOPS 1977-78
8 1/2 oz. green plastic bottle. Came with bubble bath for children. **CMV $3. MB.**

CHILDREN'S DECANTERS & TOYS

ARISTOCAT 1971-72
4 oz. gray cat with pink collar holds Non Tear Shampoo. **CMV $5. MB.**

CLUCK A DOO 1971
8 oz. yellow bottle, pink hat. Came with stick on decals. holds bubble bath. **CMV $5. MB.**

SUNBONNET SUE DEMI STICK 1975-77
.19 oz. red and white plastic. Pink & Pretty fragrance. **CMV $3. MB.**

NUTSHELL COLOR MAGIC LIPSTICK 1974-75
Peanut shaped case came in Pink Sorcery (blue lipstick) or Peach Sorcery (green lipstick). **CMV $3. MB.**

SCHOOL DAYS PENCIL LIP POMADE 1975-76
.13 oz. red, white and yellow plastic. Choice of strawberry, cherry or tutti-frutti. **CMV $3. MB.**

SWEET LIPS LIP GLOSS COOKIE 1975-76
Brown plastic with 2 shades of lip gloss. **CMV $3. MB.**

BED OF NAILS COMB 1978-79
5 1/2" comb, tan, white and red. **CMV $2. MB.**

WONDER WOMAN MIRROR 1978-79
7 1/2" long plastic mirror. **CMV $2. MB.**

SWEET PICKLES ZANY ZEBRA HAIR BRUSH 1978-79
White, black, pink and green plastic. **CMV $2. MB.**

TASTI MINT LIP GLOSS COMPACT 1978-79
Green and silver plastic. **CMV $2. MB.**

COMBSICLE 1979-80
Popsicle box holds brown and beige Avon comb. **CMV $1. MB.**

CHOCOLATE CHIPLICK COMPACT 1979-80
Tan and brown plastic, holds lip gloss. **CMV $2. MB.**

POWER DRILL 1979-80
5 oz. yellow plastic with silver plastic drill cap. Holds Wild Country or Electric Pre Shave. **CMV $4. MB.**

TUGGABLE TEDDY TOOTHBRUSH HOLDER 1980-81
Tan and blue plastic. Pink and green Avon toothbrushes. Orange ring on gold cord. **CMV $5. MB.**

SMILEY SNAIL TOOTHBRUSH HOLDER 1980-81
Yellow and green plastic. Orange and blue Avon toothbrushes. **CMV $6. MB.**

TONKA TRUCK AND SOAP GIFT SET 1993
Yellow and black plastic and metal truck 4 1/2" long. Comes with Red soap. **CMV $5. set MB.**

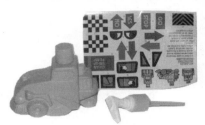

CLEAN-'EM-UP-PUMP 1981-82
8 oz. yellow plastic with white and yellow pump dispenser. Comes with card of stick on decals. Come in Liquid Cleanser. **CMV $3. MB.**

TED E. BEAR BABY LOTION DISPENSER 1981-82
10 oz. plastic in choice of pink or blue bear. Comes with matching pump dispenser. **CMV $2. MB.**

SPONGIE THE CLOWN 1981
6 oz. plastic bottle with green cap and comes with orange sponge for top. **CMV $3. MB.**

MAJOR LEAGUE MITT DECANTER 1993
6 oz. plastic baseball glove. Blue cap. Non-tear shampoo. Card of 28 team stickers for glove. **CMV $6. MB.**

MARIA MAKEOVER BATH DECANTER 1982
6 oz. plastic face bottle and sheet of stick-on decals. Choice of Non Tear Shampoo or Children's Liquid Cleanser. **CMV $2. MB.**

CHILDREN'S DECANTERS & TOYS

E.T. & ELLIOTT DECAL SOAP 1983
3 oz. blue bar with decal of E.T. on face. Back of bar says "I'll be right there". **CMV $5. MB.**
E.T. BATH DECANTER 1983-84
7 oz. blue plastic with tan plastic head. Holds Bubble Bath. **CMV $6. MB.**
E.T. MUG 1983-84
4 1/2" high white porcelain mug with E.T. for the handle. **CMV $15. MB.**

ORANGATAN 1976
6 oz. orange shaped and colored plastic bottle. Holds suntan lotion. **CMV $2., no box issued.**

SPOTLIGHT MIKE DECANTER 1991
9" long plastic mike holds 3 oz. of liquid cleanser. Blue & yellow plastic, red rope. **CMV $4. MB.**

WABBIT CAR 1983
5 oz. blue plastic car & white rabbit cap. Choice of Children's Bubble Bath or Non-Tear Shampoo. Comes with sheet of stick on decals to decorate. **CMV $6. MB.**

I.M. CLEAN II "ROBOT" 1980-81
Blue plastic robot with pump dispenser. Comes with card of stick-on decals. holds 8 oz. of Liquid Cleanser. **CMV $4. MB.**
TUB TUG 1980-81
5 oz. plastic. Comes in yellow and green cap with Non Tear Shampoo, red and lavender cap with bubble bath, and blue and red cap with Liquid Cleanser. **CMV $1. each. No boxes.**

SUPER SHOE 1974-76
6 oz. white plastic shoe with blue plastic toe section cap. holds Sure Winner Liquid Hair Trainer or Sure Winner Bracing Lotion. **CMV $3. MB.**
JUST FOR KICKS 1974-75
7 oz. black & white plastic shoe with black plastic cap. Holds Avon Spicy or Avon Sure Winner Bracing Lotion. **CMV $4. MB.**

E.T. & GERTIE DECAL SOAP 1984
3 oz. pink bar. **CMV $6. MB.**

THE PENGUIN 1993
4 oz. plastic with finger puppet. Liquid Cleanser.
CAT WOMAN 1993
4 oz. Bubble Bath, plastic. Finger puppet.
BATMAN 1993
4 oz. plastic holds non-tear shampoo. Finger puppet. **CMV $3. ea. MB.**

BUBBA LEE BUNNY 1982-83
6 oz. white plastic rabbit, yellow cap. Choice of Bubble Bath or Non-Tear Shampoo. **CMV $5. MB.**

TWEETHOUSE PAPER CUP TOOTHBRUSH HOLDER 1982-83
White plastic cup holder with stick on decals & 2 child toothbrushes. **CMV $4. MB.**

PLAY PUPS TOOTHBRUSH HOLDER 1981-82
Blue and orange shoe, brown ears, holds green and pink Avon toothbrushes. Dated 1981 on back. **CMV $3. MB.**
CLEAN FLIGHT DECANTER 1982
6 oz. plastic sea plane shaped. Choice of Non Tear Shampoo in yellow plastic with blue cap or Liquid CLeanser in orange with yellow cap. **CMV $3. No box issued.**

MIGHTY MORPHIC POWER RANGERS FIN-GER PUPPETS 1994
4 oz. plastic bottles, Red, Body Cleanser. **CMV $2. ea. MB.**

TWEETY BATH MITT AND BUBBLE BATH 1994
Yellow Tweety Mitt and Sylvester tube of Bubble bath. **CMV $3 set MB.**

IF YOU PAID MORE FOR ANY AVON COLLECTIBLE IN THIS BOOK IN THE LAST 2 YEARS & FEEL YOU PAID A FAIR PRICE. SEND THIS INFORMATION TO BUD HASTIN, PO BOX 9868, KANSAS CITY, MO. 64134 SO HE CAN CHANGE THE PRICE IN HIS NEXT BOOK. REMEMBER THAT AVON TIMES EACH MONTH REFLECTS THE AVERAGE GOING PRICE ON MOST AVONS. IF YOU DON'T GET AVON TIMES. YOU MAY PAY TO MUCH .

WARNING

KEEP ALL SOAPS OUT OF SUNLITE AS THEY FADE QUICKLY. ALL SOAPS MUST BE MINT & BOXED FOR FULL VALUE. DAMAGED SOAPS HAVE NO VALUE.

CHILDREN'S SOAPS

"OLD 99" SOAP 1958
Yellow train engine soap. **CMV $65. MB.**

CIRCUS WAGON SOAP SET 1957-58
Pink, yellow, black & white circus wagon box contains 1 blue elephant, 1 pink monkey, 1 yellow lion soaps. **CMV $75. MB.**

POOL PADDLERS SOAP 1959
Pond display box holds green frog, yellow fish & blue turtle soap. **CMV $45. MB.**

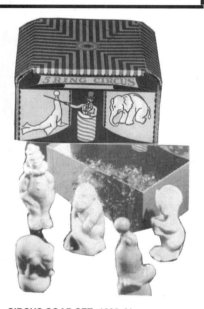

CIRCUS SOAP SET 1939-41
5 ring circus on box holds 5 figural soaps. This set is Avon's first figurals. Soaps are clown, elephant, monkey, seal & horse. **CMV $325. MB.** Very rare.

FORWARD PASS 1958
7 1/2 oz. brown football soap on a white rope on side of soap. **CMV $45. MB.**

FIRE ENGINE SOAP 1957
Red box contains red fire truck soap. **CMV $70. MB.**

BO PEEP SOAP 1953-54
Blue & green box holds 3 white sheep soaps. **CMV $75. MB.**

BEST FRIEND SOAP 1956
Blue & white box holds blue dog soap. **CMV $60. MB.**

KIDDIE KENNEL SOAP 1955
Blue & yellow box holds blue, yellow & pink dog soaps. **CMV $150.00 MB.**

AWAY IN THE MANGER SOAP SET 1955

Box holds 4 bars of pink, blue, white & yellow soap. 2 different scenes as shown. Remove panel on bottom picture to show inner panel as shown on top picture. CMV $80. each set, MB.

SANTA'S HELPER SOAP 1956

(Left) Box holds 3 green, yellow & red Santa & 2 helpers soaps. CMV $120. MB.

SANTA'S HELPER SOAP 1955

(Right) Box holds green, red & yellow soap. Red Santa soap much larger than 1956 set. CMV $110. MB.

HIGH SCORE 1959

Green net box holds brown basketball soap on a rope. CMV $15. soap only mint, $30. MB.

CASEY JONES JR. 1956-57

Red, white & blue box holds red engine soap, yellow passenger car & red carboose. CMV $65. MB.

THREE LITTLE BEARS SOAP SET 1954

3 brown bear soaps. CMV $80. MB.

FRILLY DUCK SOAP 1960

Box contains yellow & blue soap 5 3/4 oz. CMV $30. MB.

AVONLITE SOAP ON A ROPE 1960-61

Green bowling ball shaped soap in green box. Brochure says "Bowl 'em Over", soap says "Avon Lite". CMV $35. MB, soap only $20. mint.

LI'L FOLKS TIME SOAP ON A ROPE 1961-62

Red box holds yellow clock soap on a rope. CMV $35. MB.

A HIT! SOAP ON A ROPE 1961-62

Box holds white baseball soap on a rope. CMV $30. MB.

SHERIFF'S BADGE SOAP 1962-63

Box holds yellow soap on a rope with embossed sheriff's badge. CMV $35. MB.

HANSEL & GRETAL SOAP 1965
Blue & pink soap in a box.   **CMV $35. MB.**

"WATCH THE BIRDIE" SOAP 1962-64
White molded camera soap on a rope. **CMV $40. MB.**

LIFE PRESERVER SOAP 1963-64
White life preserver soap on a rope.**CMV $35. MB.**

LIL TOM TURTLE SOAP 1962-63
Box holds green turtle soap with white hat. **CMV $35. MB.**

LITTLE SHAVER SOAP 1966-67
(Left) Yellow shaver soap on a rope. **CMV $25. MB.**
TEXAS SHERIFF SOAP 1958
(Right) Box holds 2 blue pistol soaps & silver sheriff's badge. Box comes with band around outside of box as shown at top. **CMV $65. MB.**

PACKY THE ELEPHANT SOAP 1964-65
Green box holds pink elephant with white hat. **CMV $30. MB.**

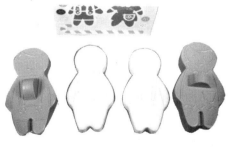

GINGERBREAD SOAP TWINS 1965
Pink, white & brown box holds 2 blue plastic gingerbread cookie cutters with 2 yellow bars of gingerbread soap. **CMV $30.**

SPEEDY THE SNAIL 1966
Green snail soap on a rope.**CMV $30.**

GOLDILOCKS SOAP 1966-67
5 oz. yellow soap.   **CMV $25. MB.**

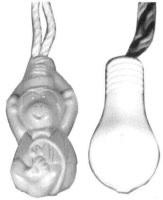

MR. MONKEY SOAP ON A ROPE 1965
(Left) Brown monkey soap.. **CMV $25. MB.**
LIGHT BULB SOAP ON A ROPE 1967
(Right) Yellow soap on black, orange & yellow rope. **CMV $25. MB.**

YO YO SOAP SET 1966-67
Pink & red wood Yo Yo & pink soap. **CMV $25.
MB, Yo Yo only $6.**

TUB RACERS SOAP 1969
Green box holds red, yellow & green racer
soap. **CMV $15. MB.**

SUNNY THE SUNFISH SOAP 1966
Yellow fish soap on a rope. **CMV $25. MB.**

MIGHTY MITT SOAP ON A ROPE 1969-72
Brown soap. **CMV $15. MB.**

BUNNY'S DREAM SOAP ON A ROPE 1967
Box holds orange carrot soap on a green rope.
CMV $20. MB.

**SEA BISCUIT - THE SEA HORSE SOAP ON
A ROPE 1964-66**
Box holds green soap on a rope. Sea Horse.
CMV $25. MB.

YANKEE DOODLE SHOWER SOAP 1969-70
White drum shaped soap on a rope. **CMV
$15. MB.**

**EASTER QUACKER SOAP ON A ROPE
1968**
Yellow soap. **CMV $18. MB.**

MODELING SOAP 1969-70
Pink 6 oz. soap in blue & pink box. **CMV $7.
MB.**

CHICK-A-DEE SOAP 1966-67
Yellow soap on a rope. **CMV $20. MB.**

RUFF, TUFF & MUFF SOAP SET 1968-69
Blue, pink & yellow dog soaps. **CMV $12. MB.**

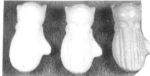

MITTENS KITTENS SOAP 1969-70
Pink, green & yellow soap. Blue box. **CMV $12. MB.**

TUBBY TIGERS SOAP SET 1974-75
3 orange soaps in orange & green box. **CMV $6. MB.**

SCRUB TUG SOAP 1971
4" long plastic boat scrub brush holds 2 oz. yellow boat soap. **CMV brush & soap $8. MB, brush only $1.**

PIG IN A TUB SOAP 1973-75
3" long yellow scrub brush holds 2 oz. pink pig soap. **CMV $6. MB.** Reissued 1979.

M.C.P. SOAP 1977-79
Tan color Male Chauvinist Pig soap. Came in Deep Woods scent. **CMV $8. MB.**

BUTTON BUTTON GUEST SOAPS 1977-79
Cardboard spool container holds 5 blue button shaped soaps. **CMV $8. MB.**

FOOTBALL HELMET SOAP ON A ROPE 1974-75
(Left) Yellow soap, white cord. **CMV $7. MB.**

WILBUR THE WHALE SOAP ON A ROPE. 1974-75
(Right) 5 oz. blue soap with white rope. **CMV $7. MB.**

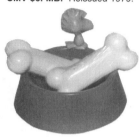

SNOOPY'S PAL SOAP DISH & SOAPS 1973-74
4 1/2" diameter red plastic dish says "Snoopy" on front with yellow bird. Comes with two 2 oz. white bone shaped soaps. **CMV $10 MB.**

FIRST DOWN SOAP 1970-71
Box holds brown 5 oz. football soap on a rope. This soap is different from older one. Rope is on end of football. **CMV $10. MB.**

PERCY PELICAN SOAP ON A ROPE 1972-73
5 oz. yellow soap on white rope. **CMV $10. MB.**

PETUNIA PIGLET SOAP ON A ROPE 1973-74
5 oz. pink soap on white rope. **CMV $10. MB.**

HOOTY & TOOTY TUGBOAT SOAPS 1973-75
2 oz. yellow & orange tugboat shaped soaps. **CMV $8. MB.**

TWEETSTERS SOAPS 1971
Yellow box holds 3 pink bird soaps. **CMV $12. MB.**

PEEP A BOO SOAP ON A ROPE 1970
Yellow chick soap on pink or white rope. **CMV $12. MB.**

EASTER BONNET SOAP ON A ROPE 1970
Yellow soap. **CMV $12. MB.**

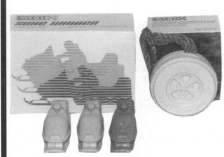

SURE WINNER SOAPS 1973-75
(Left) 3 snowmobile soaps in blue, red & yellow. **CMV $7. MB.**
SURE WINNER SHOWER SOAP 1972-73
White with blue cord. **CMV $8. MB.**

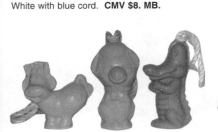

BLUE MOO SOAP ON A ROPE 1972
(Left) 5 oz. blue cow soap on a rope. **CMV $10. MB.**
HONEY LAMB SOAP ON A ROPE 1971-72
(Center) 5" high yellow soap on blue rope. **CMV $10. MB.**
AL E. GATOR SOAP ON A ROPE 1971-72
5" high green soap on white rope. **CMV $10. MB.**

HOOPER THE HOUND SOAP HOLDER & SOAP 1974
White & black plastic head with pink, green & yellow hoops. Has yellow soap. **CMV $8. MB.**

HAPPY HIPPOS NAIL BRUSH & SOAP 1973-74
3" Long pink nail brush with yellow soap. **CMV $8. MB.**

FURRY, PURRY & SCURRY SOAPS 1978-79
Red box with white dots holds 3 kitten shaped soaps in yellow, blue & green. **CMV $6. MB.**

TUBBO THE HIPPO SOAP DISH & SOAP 1978-80
(Left) Blue box holds light green plastic hippo soap dish & 3 oz. pink embossed wrapped bar of hippo soap. **CMV $6. MB, soap dish only $1, soap only wrapped $1.50.**
ALKA SELTZER SOAPS 1978-79
Blue, white & red box holds 2 white embossed bars. **CMV $7. MB.**

SAFE COMBINATION BANK SOAPS 1978-79
Black & gold tin bank comes with 2 yellow bars of soap embossed "Avon, 99.9 mint". Bottom of bank says "Made in England, exclusively for Avon". **CMV $10. MB.**

HYDROJET SCRUB BRUSH & SOAP 1972-73
Red plastic jet with yellow soap. **CMV $8. MB.**

TREE TOTS SOAP 1970-72
Red & green box holds 3 squirrel soaps. **CMV $10. MB.**

ARISTOCAT KITTENS SOAP 1971
Box holds white, brown & blue kitten soaps. **CMV $10. MB.**

TUB RACERS 1970-72
Three speed boat soaps in red, blue & yellow. **CMV $10. MB.**

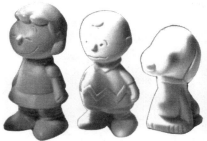

PEANUTS GANG SOAP 1970-72
Red Lucy, yellow Charlie, white Snoopy soaps. **CMV $12. MB.**

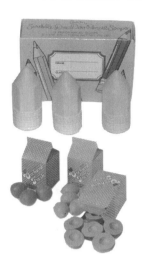

THREE MICE SOAPS 1971-72
Box holds green, white & pink mice soaps.
CMV $10. MB.

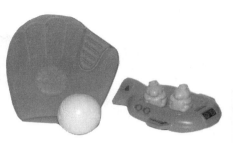

ALL STAR BASE BALL MITT & SOAP 1987
7" orange sponge mitt & white baseball soap.
No box. **CMV $5. MB.**
SEA SUB & CREW SOAPS 1987
Orange plastic boat holds 2 small sea creature
soaps. **CMV $6. MB.**

SCRIBBLE DEE DOO PENCIL SOAPS 1980-81
(Top) 3 pencil shaped yellow soaps.**CMV $7. MB.**
ORCHARD FRESH GUEST SOAPS 1980-81
(Bottom) Choice of orange, lemon or peach
shaped soaps. 6 bars in each box. **CMV $7. each kind.**

DARLING DUCKLINGS SOAP 1983
Box holds 3 yellow duck soaps. **CMV $5. MB.**

EGGOSAURS SOAPS 1986
Yellow & blue shells hold soaps. Comes with
20 pg. mini book. **CMV $5. MB.**

GOOD HABIT RABBIT SCRUB BRUSH & SOAP 1975
(Left) Pink plastic with white bristles. **CMV $8. MB.**
GAYLORD GATOR SCRUB BRUSH & SOAP 1974-75
(Right) Green plastic with white bristles. **CMV $8. MB.**

BUBBLE BLAZER SOAP 1982-83
(Left) Box holds 4 oz. yellow space gun bar.
CMV $5. MB.
PARTY LINE SOAP ON A ROPE 1982-83
(Right) Box holds 5 oz. yellow telephone bar
on white rope. **CMV $5. MB.**
TRAIN SOAP 1982-83
(Bottom) 5 3/4" long blue train soap breaks
into 3 cars. Must be all together or of no
value. **CMV $5. MB.**

STORY BOOK SOAPS 1984
Book shaped soaps. **Pinnochio, Hansel &
Gretel or Cinderella.CMV $4. MB. ea.**

GRIDIRON SCRUB BRUSH & SOAP 1976-77
Brown plastic with yellow soap **CMV $8. MB.**

BATH TUB BUGGIES SOAP SET 1986
Box holds blue, red or yellow truck soaps.
CMV $4. MB.

BUMBEE BABEE TOY & SOAP 1987
Bumble Bee wind up tub toy & matching soap.
CMV $5. MB

BONNIE & BENNY BUFFLE & SOAP 1990
Plastic water squirters and 3oz. bar of Soap
for each. **CMV $4. MB each set.**

SWEET PEA SOAPS 1986
(Top) different soaps, 2 oz. each. **Mud puppy,
Goldie Purrsha, Sea Star, and Starfish. CMV
$2 ea. MB.**
DUCKS ON PARADE 1987
Box holds 3 small yellow duck soaps. **CMV $3.
MB.**
SOUNDS OF CHRISTMAS SOAPS 1986
3 different small bars. **Drum, Horn or Harp**
soap. **CMV $2 ea. MB.**

MICKEY & MINNIE HOLLYWOOD SOAP 1989
Micky, blue & Minnie, yellow. Box of 2. **CMV $3.
MB**

SNOOPY & WOODSTOCK SOAP 1990
White Snoopy & yellow Woodstock soap.
CMV $2. MB

**CHRISTMAS FRIENDS ORNAMENT SOAPS
1988**
Red Santa, Blue Penquin, Green Elf soaps.
CMV $2. ea. MB

ANIMAL SOAPS 1985
Choice of Elephant, Hippo or Lion. **CMV $2.
MB.**
EASTER FUN BATH CUBES 1985
Box holds 6 Easter cubes. **CMV $3. MB.**
SOMERSAULTS SOAP & MINI BOOKS 1985
Each box has different colored soaps. **CMV
$3. MB.**

SAY CHEESE SOAP SET 1990
3oz. pink mouse bar snaps apart. **CMV $2.
MB**

PUMPKIN PALS SOAP SET 1989
Orange Box holds 3 black cat soaps. **CMV $3.
MB**

**BILLY ROCKET & SKY BLAZERS CO-
LOGNE GIFT SET 1987**
Box holds soap & 2oz. cologne. **CMV $4.00
MB**

SOAP PETS 1987
Ruffy the puppy in blue, **Squeaky the mouse**
in lavender, **Fluffy the kitten** in orange. **CMV
$2. each MB**

MICKEY & FRIENDS SOAP 1990
5 different soaps. Mickey, Pluto, Minnie, Gofy,
Donald. 1oz. ea. **CMV $2. ea. MB**

UR2B CLEAN ROBOT SOAP 1988
Orange & lavender robot soaps. . **CMV $3.**
ea. MB

GARFIELD SOAP 1990
Orange cat soap. **CMV $2.50 MB**

GOOFY GOBLINS CRAYON SOAP 1991
Choice of **Ghost**-yellow, **Witch**-purple,
Pumpkin-orange. **CMV $1. ea. MB.**

TINY TEDDY BEAR SOAPS 1988
3 yellow bear soaps. **CMV $2. MB**

FISH N' FUN FINGER PAINT SOAP 1989
Red, yellow & blue fish soap in matching
plastic boxes. **CMV $6. Set MB**

ARCTIC ANTIC SOAPS 1991
1 oz. bars are Seal-green, Penguin-red, or
Polar Bear-blue. Boxed separately. ea. **CMV
$1. ea. MB.**

NEW KITTY TRIO SOAPS 1987
3-kitten soaps 1oz. ea. **CMV $2.00 MB**

BABY BUNNY SOAPS 1989
3 green bunny soaps. **CMV $2.50 MB**

KING FOR A DAY SOAP 1991
3 oz. Lion bar marked "Dad is King".
CMV $2.50. MB.

COTTAGE FRIENDS SOAPS 1991
1 oz. size Bunny-lavender, Goose-yellow. **CMV
$1. ea. MB.**

HEART TO HEART SOAP 1991
Heart shaped pink-lavender or peach shaped
soap. 1 to a box. **CMV $1. ea. MB.**

CHILDHOOD RHYME SOAPS 1991
1 oz. bars - Mary Had a Little Lamb, Little Jack
Horner, Cat & the Fiddle, Humpty Dumpty, and
Little Boy Blue. . **CMV $1. ea. MB.**

SUDS OF THE SEASONS SOAPS 1992
1 oz. soap bars. **"Betty Bell"**-red, **"Timmy Twinkles"**-yellow, and **"Douglas Fir"**-green. **CMV $1. ea. MB.**

SONG BIRD SOAP 1993
Pink, blue or purple. Sold separately. ea. **CMV $1. ea. MB.**

GARFIELD SOAP RAFT AND SOAP 1992
Inflatable Garfield soap dish.   **CMV $7.**
GARFIELD SOAP 1992
Sold separately from raft.   **CMV $2. MB.**

JUNGLE LOVE SOAPS 1992
1 oz. ea. Cupid Monkey, Cupid Lion and Cupid Elephant.   **CMV $2. ea. MB.**

SAMMY THE FROG FLOAT 1991
Green frog soap and green lily pad plastic float base. **CMV $4. MB.**

THREE BEARS SOAP SET 1992
4" high x 5 1/2" wide wicker sofa holds 3 shades of 3 brown bear soaps. **CMV $8. MB.**

TINY TOON CARTOON SOAPS 1992
5 different pop-up soap boxes, holds 1 oz. bar soap in Buster Bunny, Babs Bunny, Plucky Duck, Hamton and Dizzy David. ea. **CMV $2. ea. MB.**

BUBBLY SOAP 1991
3.5 oz. Champagne bottle shaped pink soap. **CMV $2. MB.**

NEW YEAR'S GREETING SOAP 1993
1994 Gold 3 oz. Soap. **CMV $2. MB.**

ARIEL SOAP DISH 1991
Red, white and green 6 1/2" x 5" plastic soap dish. Sold Separately. **CMV $6. MB.**
FLOUNDER SOAP 1991
2 oz. yellow fish soap made to go with Ariel Soap Dish. Sold separately. **CMV $ 2. MB.**

SEA STRIPED SOAP 1991
Fish designed box holds Fish, Starfish and Sea Horse striped soaps. **CMV $2. MB.**

7 DWARF SOAPS 1994
7 different 1 oz. soaps. **CMV $1.50 ea. MB.**

GOBLIN SOAPS 1994
1 oz. soaps in Pumpkin, Ghost, Cat. **CMV $1. ea. MB.**

CHRISTMAS CHARACTER SOAPS 1994
1 oz. bars. Choice of Mrs. Claus-yellow, Rudolf-blue, Santa-red. **CMV $1. ea. MB.**

CHRISTMAS CHARACTERS CRAYON SOAPS 1993
1 oz. Red **Santa** or Green **Elf** soaps. **CMV $1. ea. MB.**

SEA FRIEND'S STRIPED SOAPS 1995
1 oz. bars of Frog, Turtle or Crab. **CMV $1.50 ea. MB.**

EASTER PET SOAP'S 1994
Lamb-pink, duck-yellow, rabbit-purple. 1 oz. bars each. **CMV $1. ea. MB.**

BABY SAURUS SOAP'S 1993
1 oz. bars, choice of "Stegly"-blue, "Prosey"-yellow, "Rexie"-Green. **CMV $1. ea. MB.**

MICKEY'S STUFF FOR KID'S SOAPS 1996
2 oz. bars. Choice of **MICKEY MOUSE** - "orange", **MINNIE MOUSE** - "red", **DONALD DUCK** - "Yellow" , or **GOOFY** - "green". **CMV $1.50 ea. MB.**

MICKIE & MINNIE MOUSE SOAP DISH AND SOAP 1995
7" long - 6 1/4" wide plastic soap dish, Mickie-blue, Minnie-pink. Mickie and Minnie shaped soaps sold separately. **C MV $5. ea. Dish. CMV $1.50 ea. Soap**

ZZY'S OLYMPIC GAMES SOAP 1996
2 oz. oval bars of Izzy. Choice of Red, White, or Blue soap. **CMV $1.50 ea. MB.**

MIGHTY MORPHIN POWER RANGER 1995
1 oz. bars. Choice of red, yellow, pink, blue, and black. **CMV $1.ea. MB.**

BASKETBALL SOAP ON A ROPE 1996
5 oz. bar in Triumph - white bar, green rope, Wild Country - orange bar - blue rope, Black Suede - yellow bar - black rope. **CMV $5. ea. MB.**

MUPPET TREASURE ISLAND SOAP ON A ROPE 1996
(LEFT) 3 oz. bars. Pink bar is "Miss Piggy", Light green bar is "Kermit" **CMV $4. ea. MB.**

SOAP - CHILDREN'S

HOLIDAY ORNAMENT SOAPS 1997
Three 1 oz. bar in choice of **SANTA** - "red",
REINDEER - "green", **SNOWMAN** - "blue". **CMV
$1.50 ea. MB.**

EASTER SOAPS 1996
1 oz. bars each in choice of **CHICK** - yellow,
BUNNY - red, **LAMB** - blue. **CMV $1.50 ea. MB.**

BASEBALL SOAP ON A ROPE 1996
Box holds 5 oz. white baseball soap in choice of
triumph - red rope, trailblazer - white rope, wild
country - blue rope. **CMV $5.50 ea. MB**.

FOOTBALL SOAP ON A ROPE 1995
5 oz. bars in triumph, trailblazer, wild country, or
black suede. **CMV $5. ea. MB.**

BATH FLOWERS SOAP & SPONGE 1965-66
Pink and white floral box contains 1 bar To A Wild Rose soap pink, green and white sponge. **CMV $12. MB.**

MINNIE THE MOO SOAP & SPONGE 1965-66
White foam cow with yellow ears and black eyes. Soap is in green wrapper. **CMV $14. MB.**

MISTERJAW BATH MITT & SOAP 1978
Blue sponge mitt 9" long with fish design bar of soap. **CMV $7. MB.**

CHARLIE BROWN BATH MITT & SOAP 1969-71
Red and white sponge with white bar of Snoopy embossed soap. **CMV $10. MB.**

POLLY PARROT PUPPET SPONGE & SOAP 1969-70
Green and orange sponge with bar of soap. **CMV $12. MB.**

CEDRIC SEA SERPENT SPONGE AND SOAP 1973
(Left) 9 1/2" long, green and pink sponge, white soap. **CMV $10. MB.**
CEDRIC SEA SERPENT SPONGE AND SOAP 1974-75
(Right) 9 1/2" long, purple and pink sponge. **CMV $10. MB.**

SPONGAROO SOAP & SPONGE 1966-67
Brown kangaroo sponge is 15" x 5 3/4". White kangaroo soap. **CMV $15., soap only $7. mint.**

SPIDERMAN SPONGE & SOAP 1980
Blue and red sponge. Red wrapped soap. **CMV $6. MB.**

YAKETY YAK TAXI SOAP AND SPONGE 1978-79
Box holds yellow taxi and bar of wrapped Sweet Pickles soap. **CMV $7. MB.**

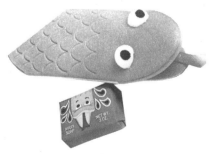

CLARENCE THE SEA SERPENT 1968-69
Orange and yellow sponge with bar of serpent soap in blue and yellow wrapper. **CMV $12. MB.**

OSCAR OCTOPUS & SOAP 1980-81
Yellow and orange with blue and green trim sponge. Green, red and purple rings, 1 bar of Oscar Octopus soap. **CMV $7. MB.**

SOAPS WITH SPONGES

BABY KERMIT & MISS PIGGY SPONGE & SOAP 1986
3 1/2" high sponge with soap inside, doubles in side when wet. Kermit in green & Piggy in red. **CMV $3. MB.**

GOOD HABIT RABBIT BATH MITT & SOAP 1974
White and pink foam mitt with yellow carrot soap. **CMV $7 MB.**

PINK PANTHER SPONGE MITT AND SOAP 1977-80
Pink mitt, yellow eyes. Blue, green and pink wrapped soap. **CMV $8. MB.**

LITTLE PRO SOAP 1966
White baseball soap and brown sponge. **CMV $14. MB.**

MONKEY SHINES 1969
Brown and pink sponge and bar of soap. **CMV $9 MB.**

LITTLE LEAGUER SOAP AND SPONGE 1972
Tan sponge mitt and white baseball soap. Sponge is different from Little Pro soap and sponge in 1966. **CMV $10 MB.**

NEST EGG SOAP & SPONGE 1967-68
Box holds yellow nest sponge and pink soap. **CMV $12. MB.**

HUBIE THE HIPPO SOAP & SPONGE 1970-71
Turquoise and red sponge with Hippo wrapped soap. **CMV $10 MB.**

BATH BLOSSOM SPONGE AND SOAP 1979-80
(Left) Box holds yellow, green and blue sponge and yellow soap. **CMV $6 MB.**
SWEET PICKLES WORRIED WALRUS SOAP AND SPONGE 1979-80
(Center) Purple, green and brown sponge. Comes with wrapped bar of Sweet Pickles childrens bath soap. **CMV $5. MB.**
FEARLESS FISH SPONGE AND SOAP 1979-80
(Right) Green fish sponge and Sweet Pickles wrapped soap with fish on a scooter. **CMV $4 MB.**

BATH BLOSSOMS 1969
Pink and yellow sponge with pink soap. **CMV $10 MB.**

SOAPY THE WHALE BATH MITT AND SOAP 1973-74
8 1/2" long blue and red sponge mitt with blue soap. **CMV $7 MB.**

SOAPS - MEN'S

GO TO NEXT PAGE.

CHEERY CHIRPERS KITCHEN SOAP & SPONGE 1990
Yellow chicken sponge, white chick soap.
CMV $4. MB

BATH TIME BASKETBALL & SOAP SET 1989
Orange sponge basketball & purple slam dunk soap. **CMV $7. MB**

NO NEW SOAPS WITH SPONGES WILL BE PUT IN THIS BOOK AS THE SPONGES DRY OUT AND DETERIORATE & CRUMBLE AFTER ABOUT 20 OR MORE YEARS. THESE ITEMS WILL BE VERY RARE & MUST BE IN MINT SHAPE AS THEY AGE FOR (CMV) CURRENT MARKET VALUE.

MOST VALUABLE SOAP SET 1963-64
Yellow box holds 3 yellow bars. CMV $30.
MB.

SHAVING SOAP 1949-57
Two bars in green & red box. CMV $32.50
MB.

CPC SHAVING SOAP 1908
White bar embossed. Came in yellow box.
CMV $60 MB.

CARRIAGE SHOWER SOAP 1960-62
Red, white and black box contains 6 oz. cake
embossed Stage Coach soap on red or white
rope. CMV $35. MB.

LONESOME PINE SOAP 1966-67
Green & gold box holds woodgrained soap cut
in half. CMV $25. MB.

BATH SOAP FOR MEN 1966-67
Two white soaps with red buttons, silver &
white box. CMV $25 MB.

SHAVING SOAP 1930-36
White bar. CMV $35. MB.
STYPTIC PENCIL 1930
 CMV $10. MB.

OATMEAL SOAP 1961-63
Two brown bars, 2 different boxes. "A spicy
fragrance." CMV $30. MB, deluxe box $35.
MB.

**SHAMPOO SHOWER SOAP FOR MEN
1972-73**
5 oz. bar on red & black rope. Also came with
white rope. Red & black box. CMV $8. MB.

SHAVING SOAP 1936-49
Two bars in maroon box, white soap. CMV
$42.50 MB.

OATMEAL SOAP FOR MEN SPICY 1963-64
Embossed stage coach on brown bar of soap.
CMV $10 in wrapping.

MODEL 'A' 1928 SOAP SET 1975
Two 3 oz. white bars of soap with dark & light
blue wrapper & box. CMV $8. MB.

GOLF BALL SOAPS 1975
Three white soaps in yellow & green box.
Spicy scented **CMV $7 MB.**

ON DUTY 24 SOAP 1977-84
Deodorant soap. **CMV $1. each. 3 different labels.**
MUSK FOR MEN 1983-84
Shower soap on rope. **CMV $3. MB.**

ROYAL HEARTS SOAP 1978-79
(Left) King & Queen box holds 2 white bars with king & queen of hearts soaps. **CMV $7. MB.**
SUITABLY GIFTED SOAP 1978-79
(Right) Blue box holds blue bar that is shaped like a shirt and tie. **CMV $7. MB.**

BUFFALO NICKEL 1913 SOAP DISH & SOAP 1978-79
5" nickel plated Buffalo Nickel metal soap dish & light gray or off white color soap. **CMV $10 MB.**

BARBER SHOP DUET MUSTACHE COMB & SOAP SET 1978-79
Box holds white bar man's face soap & small brown plastic mustache comb. **CMV $6. MB set.**

FARMERS ALMANAC THERMOMETER & SOAPS 1979-80
Box holds tin top with plastic bottom with 2 bars of Farmers Almanac soap. Comes with copy of Avon 1980 Farmers Almanac. **CMV $12 MB complete, CMV Farmers Almanac only $1.**

LUCKY SHOEHORSE SOAP DISH & SOAP 1979-80
(Left) Brown box holds amber glass horseshoe soapdish & soap. **CMV $10. MB.**
PERPETUAL CALENDAR CONTAINER & SOAP 1979-80
(Right) Yellow box holds Avon tin can calendar & white bar of soap. Bottom of can says Made in England for Avon. **CMV $8. MB.**

WEEKEND SOAP ON A ROPE 1979-80
Tan soap on green rope. **CMV $3. MB.**

ANCIENT MARINER BOX & SOAP 1982-83
Tin box with bar compass design soap. **CMV $6. MB.**

THATS MY DAD DECAL SOAPS 1983
(Left) Choice of 3 different decal soaps. "We love you dad" or "You taught me all the important things Dad" or "You're always there when I need you Dad" **CMV $3 each bar MB.**
GRANDFATHERS & GRANDMOTHERS ARE SPECIAL SOAPS 1983
(Right) Metal can holds choice of black or white grandfather or black or white grandmother. **CMV $6. MB.**

HUDDLES SOAP ON A ROPE & CARDS 1984
Box holds brown football marked Huddles & deck of NFL football team playing cards. **CMV $5. MB.**
DAD SOAP ON A ROPE 1985
Yellow bar. **CMV $4. MB.**

SOAPS - MEN'S

AURES SOAP ON A ROPE 1986
AMERICAN CLASSIC SOAP ON A ROPE
1987
Both boxed single bar on rope. **CMV $4. MB.**

MEN'S SOAPS 1984
Cool soap, Cordovan, Wild Country, Musk for Men. **CMV $1. Each.**
DADS LUCKY DEAL DECAL SOAP &
CARDS 1984
Bar of dog soap & deck of cards. **CMV $7. MB.**

GENTLEMEN'S QUARTER GIFT SET 1989
Box holds black suede soap & sponge. **CMV $7. MB**

SPORTING DUCK SOAP 1990
3oz. brown duck bar. **CMV $2. MB**

WILDERNESS BOX SOAP 1988
Wood box 3 1/4" wide with deer lid & soap. **CMV $9. MB**

SHOWER SOAP ON A ROPE 1992
5 oz. bar, choice of Black Suede, Wild Country Musk, Wild Country, Everafter for Men, Cavalier, Musk for Men, Undeniable for Men, and Triumph. **CMV $4.50 ea. MB.**

LEMONOL TOILET SOAP 1931-36
Yellow soap wrapped in blue and silver paper. Came in box of 3. **CMV $45. MB. Box of 12 bars CMV $65. MB.**

LEMONOL SOAP 1921-33
Box of 12 cakes. **CMV $100 MB.**

LEMONOL TOILET SOAP 1923-31
Box of 3 bars. **CMV $80 MB.**

LEMONOL SOAP 1941-58
Yellow and green lemon box holds 3 flat bars with round edges and flat on bottom. **CMV $35 MB.**

LEMONOL TOILET SOAP 1936-41
Three yellow bars in turquoise and white box and wrapping. **CMV $40. MB. Box of 12 bars CMV $60 MB.** Add $3 per bar for CPC label mint.

LEMONOL SOAP 1958-66
Yellow and green box holds 3 yellow bars with flat edges. Box comes lift off, (older) and flip up as shown. **CMV $30. MB.**

LEMONOL SOAP 1966-67
Blue and yellow box holds six 2 1/2" yellow bars. **CMV $30. MB.**

HOSTESS BOUQUET SOAP 1959-61
Pink and yellow box holds bars **CMV $25. MB.**

GIFT BOWS SOAP 1962-64
Box holds 6 bow tie soaps. **CMV $30. MB.**

HOSTESS SOAP SAMPLER 1964-65
Floral box holds 12 cakes of soap. **CMV $30. MB.**

FACIAL SOAP 1945-55
Box holds 2 bars. **CMV $25. MB.**

FACIAL SOAP 1955-61
Turquoise box holds 2 bars. **CMV $20. MB.**

WHIPPED CREAM SOAP 1968
Green, blue, pink and yellow soap. **CMV $15. MB.**

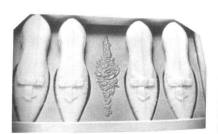

LADY SLIPPERS SOAP 1965-66
4 shoe soaps in box. **CMV $35. MB.**

SOAPS - WOMEN'S

CHERUB SOAP SET 1966-67
Blue box holds 2 pink angel soaps.
CMV $30. MB.

PINE CONE GIFT SOAPS 1970-73
Box contains blue, yellow and green pine
scented soaps. **CMV $10. MB.**

SOAP TREASURE 1963
Gold and white box holds 5 bars of perfumed
soap in choice of Lilac, Lily of the Valley,
Floral, Lemonol, Cotillion, Here's My Heart,
Rose Geranium, To A Wild Rose, Royal
Jasmine, Persian Wood, Somewhere, Royal
PIne, and Topaze Set. Came with 2 different
kinds of soap as shown. **CMV $25. MB each
set.**

PARTRIDGE & PEAR SOAPS 1968-70
Two green pears and white partridge. **CMV
$12. MB.**

SLIPPER SOAP & PERFUME 1970-71
1/8 oz. bow tie perfume sits in light pink slipper
soap in Cotillion, and dark pink soap in
Charisma. **CMV $20. MB. soap and
perfume only mint.**

BAY BERRY SOAP 1967
Blue and gold box holds 3 wrapped bars in
plastic holder. **CMV $25. set Soap only $5.
each.**

FRUIT BOUQUET SOAP 1969
Orange, lavender, and green soap. **CMV $12.
MB.**

SPRING TULIPS SOAP 1970-73
Blue and pink box holds 6 green white and
pink soaps. **CMV $20. MB.**

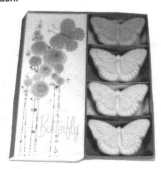

BUTTERFLY SOAP 1966-67
4 bars in box. **CMV $30. MB.**

DECORATOR SOAPS 1969
Pink box holds 3 egg shaped soaps in green,
pink and blue. **CMV $12. MB.**

CUP CAKE SOAP 1972-73
Green, pink and orange soap. 2 oz. each.
CMV $10. MB.

472

GRADE AVON HOSTESS SOAPS 1971-72
Plastic carton holds 2 blue and 2 pink egg shaped soaps. **CMV $8. MB.**

HIDDEN TREASURE SOAP 1972-75
Two 3 oz. turquoise soaps with pearl colored and shaped 1/8 oz. bottle of perfume. Came in Bird of Paradise only. **CMV $12. MB.**

LACERY HOSTESS BATH SOAP 1972-73
Cream colored with foil center design. Box gold and pink. **CMV $6. MB.**

HOSTESS BOUQUET GUEST SOAP 1972-73
3 pink bars shaped like flower bouquet tied with green ribbon. Came in pink and blue boquet box. **CMV $10. MB.**

FRAGRANCE & FRILLS SOAP 1972-75
4 lavendar soaps in lavender plastic box. In center a 1/8 oz. bottle of Dazzling perfume in Field Flowers or Bird of Paradise. **CMV $15. MB.**

MELON BALL GUEST SOAP 1973
1 oz. honey dew and cantaloupe colored balls inside cantaloupe shaped plastic container. **CMV $8 MB.**

SOAP SAVERS 1973
9 oz. total of green soaps in spearmint fragrance. **CMV $10. MB.**

SOAP FOR ALL SEASONS 1973
1.5 oz. each, 4 soaps, yellow, green, blue and orange. **CMV $8 MB.**

RECIPE TREASURES 1974-75
5 orange scented soaps in yellow and orange decorative metal file box. **CMV $10. MB.**
COUNTRY KITCHEN SOAPDISH AND SOAP 1974-75
Red plastic scooped dish contains 5 green apple fragranced soaps. **CMV $10. MB.**

1876 WINTERSCAPES HOSTESS SOAPS 1976
Two Currier and Ives scenes soaps. Came in Special Occasion fragrance. **CMV $10. MB.**

PETIT FOURS GUEST SOAPS 1975-76
Eight 1 oz. soaps, 3 pink hearts, 2 yellow squares. 3 rounds. **CMV $10. MB.**
BAYBERRY WREATHS GIFT SOAPS 1975
3 Bayberry scented in Christmas box. **CMV $8. MB.**

ANGEL LACE SOAPS 1975-76
3 blue soaps in blue and white box. **CMV $10. MB.**

TOUCH OF LOVE SOAPS 1975
3 white soaps in lavender box. Spring lavender fragrance. **CMV $8. MB.**

PICK A BERRY STRAWBERRY SOAPS & CONTAINER 1975-76
4 1/2" high red plastic with 6 strawberry scented soaps. **CMV $10. MB.**

LITTLE CHOIR BOYS HOSTESS SOAPS 1976
Box holds 3 pink soaps. Came in light or dark pink. **CM $8. MB.**

TAPESTRY HOSTESS SOAPS 1981
Box holds 2 decorator bars. **CMV $6. MB.**

TIDINGS OF LOVE SOAPS 1976
3 pink soaps in pink and white box. **CMV $8. MB.**

PARTRIDGE 'N PEAR HOSTESS SOAP 1974-75
3 yellow soaps in festive Christmas box. **CMV $10. MB.**

GOLDEN BEAUTIES HOSTESS SOAP 1974-76
2 oz. each, 3 cakes yellow soap. **CMV $8. MB.**

MERRY ELFKINS GUEST SOAPS 1977
Box holds 3 green soaps. **CMV $7. MB.**

BLUE TRANQUILITY REFRESHING SOAP 1978-80
5 oz. blue embossed bar on white rope. Blue box. **CMV $4. MB.**

BOUQUET OF PANSIES SOAP 1976-77
Blue box holds 2 flower decorated special occasion white soaps. **CMV $8. MB.**

TENDER BLOSSOMS GUEST TOWELS & SOAPS 1977-78
Came with 12 paper hand towels and 3 special occasion fragranced soaps. **CMV $7. MB.**

WINTER FROLICS HOSTESS SOAPS 1977-78
Came with 2 Festive Fragrance scented soaps with long lasting decals. 3 oz. each. **CMV $8. MB.**

PERFUMED SOAP CHRISTMAS WRAP 1979-80
Single fragrance bar in red. Tempo or Ariane, bronze Candid, Blue Emprise or Unspoken. **CMV $2. MB.**

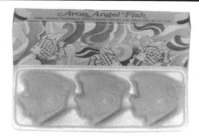

ANGEL FISH HOSTESS SOAPS 1978
Box holds 3 blue fish soaps. **CMV $6. MB.**

TREASURE BASKET GUEST SOAPS 1978-79
Silver basket holds 2 yellow and 2 pink tulip soaps. **CMV $10. MB.**

COUNTRY GARDEN SOAPS 1978-80
Box holds 2 Avon bar flower soaps with 2 different flower decals. **CMV $5. MB.**

CHRISTMAS CAROLLERS SOAPS 1978-79
Box holds 2 turquoise color carollers. **CMV $5. MB.**

SUMMER BUTTERFLIES HOSTESS SOAPS 1977-78
Two scented soaps with long lasting decals. 3 oz. each. **CMV $7. MB.**

BALLET PICTURE SOAPS 1978-80
White plastic box and lid holds 2 blue picture decal bars of soap. **CMV $8. MB.**

A TOKEN OF LOVE HOSTESS SOAPS 1978
All three pieces are special occasion fragranced soaps. Light pink outside dark pink inside soap. **CMV $8. MB.**

LITTLE ANGELS HOSTESS SOAPS 1980-81
Blue box holds 3 blue angel soaps. **CMV $6. MB.**

COMPLEXION BAR 1966-70
4 oz. bar. **CMV $4. MB.**

BUBBLY BEAR SOAP-IN-SOAP 1980-81
Blue box holds small ribbon box of blue soap with small white bear soap inside. **CMV $7. MB.**
CALIFORNIA PERFUME CO. 1980 ANNIVERSARY SOAPS 1980-81
1980 CPC box holds two Violet bars. **CMV $6. MB.**

CLEAR SKIN SOAP 1960-63
Brown bar in gray and white box. **CMV $4.**
CLEAR SKIN SOAP 1964-69
Brown bar in gray and white wrapper. **CMV $3.**

PERFUMED SOAPS & PERFUMED DEODORANT SOAPS 1961-64
1 bar of each in Lemonol, Persian Wood, Somewhere, Facial, Floral, Royal Pink, Royal Jasmine, Here's My Heart, Cotillion, To A Wild Rose, Topaze and Rose Geranium. **CMV $4. each mint.**

FEELIN' FRESH SOAP 1978-83
Regular issue bar on left. **CMV $1.** Introductory trial size bar on right, short issue. **CMV $3.**

475

SOAPS - WOMEN'S

PERFUMED SOAP HOLIDAY WRAPPING 1977
Came in Charisma and Touch of Roses in red poinsettia wrap. Sonnet and Field Flowers in green and Moonwind and Bird of Paradise in blue. **CMV $3. each.**

ARIANE PERFUMED SOAPS 1978
Red box holds 3 white soaps. **CMV $8. MB.**

PERFUMED DEODORANT SOAP 1963-67
CMV $4. mint.

FRESH AS NATURE SOAP 1982-83
3 different bars in Aloe Vera, Wheat Germ and Glycerine, Witch Hazel and Lyme. **CMV $2. each MB.**

SOFT MUSK SOAP 1982-84
Single 3 oz. bar. **CMV $1. mint.**

SCENTED SOAPS 1971-73
3 oz. bars in matching soap and wrapping. Mint, Pine Tar, Almond, Camomile, Papaya, Avacado. **CMV $4. MB.**

CANDID PERFUMED SOAPS 1977-78
Open end box, 3 cakes each. 3 oz. white bars. **CMV $5. MB.**

FIVE GUEST SOAPS 1983
Flower design box holds 5 small bars in Timeless, Candid, Ariane, Tasha, Foxfire, Odyssey or Soft Musk. **CMV $5. MB.**

CREAM SOAPS 1981-83
1 pink, yellow or blue wrapped bar. **CMV $1.** .
HEARTS & LACE SPECIAL OCCASION SOAP 1981
Pink flower wrapped bar. **CMV $1. mint.**

EMPRISE PERFUMED SOAPS 1977-78
Open end box holds 3 beige color bars. **CMV $5. MB.**

FLORAL BOXED SOAPS 1983
(Left) Box has different flower design for each fragrance. 4 flowered bars. Choice of Wild Jasmine "gold", Hawaiian White Ginger "white", Honeysuckle "yellow" or Roses Roses "pink". **CMV $4. MB.**
FLORAL GUEST SOAP 1983
(Right) Single 1 oz. bar in box. Different color soap for each fragrance. Choice of Roses Roses, Wild Jasmine, Hawaiian White Ginger. **CMV $2. MB.**

CHRISTMAS WISHES DECAL SOAPS 1983
3 different boxed bars. Choice of Happiness in pink, Togetherness in green & Sharing in tan color soap. **CMV $2. each MB.**

TIMELESS SOAP 1975-78
3 cakes amber soap in amber, gold & yellow box. **CMV $7.**
TIMELESS PERFUMED SOAP 1976-78
3 oz. bar. **CMV $1.**

A MOTHER'S JOY SOAP SET 1983
Blue box holds 2 white mother & child soaps. **CMV $4. MB.**

SWEET HONESTY PERFUMED SOAPS 1978
Boxed 3 cakes, 3 oz. each. **CMV $7. MB.**
SWEET HONESTY SOAP 1982-83
Single bar. **CMV $1/**
SEA GARDEN PERFUMED BATH SOAP 1970-73
6 oz. blue bar with blue box. **CMV $4. MB.**

FLORAL BATH CUBES 1984
Box of 6 wrapped cubes. **CMV $3. MB.**
LIGHT ACCENT SOAP 1984
Single bar, choice of Tea Garden, Willow, Amber Mist. **CMV $1. each.**
VALENTINE SOAP SET 1986
Pink box holds 3 pink heart soaps. **CMV $4. MB.**

COUNTRY CHRISTMAS DECAL SOAPS 1982
Box holds 2 bars. **CMV $5. MB.**

LETTER PERFECT GUEST SOAP 1984
Single bar with choice of pesonal letter on soap. **CMV $2. MB.**
ULTRA GUEST SOAPS 1984
Silver box holds choice of 5 small bars in 7 fragrances. **CMV $6. MB.**
WATER LILY BATH CUBES 1985
Blue box holds 6 soap cubes. **CMV $5. MB.**

TIS THE SEASON SOAPS 1985
Small bars of **Mistletoe, Poinsettia or Holly. CMV $2. each MB.**
SPRING GARDEN GLYCERINE SOAPS 1985
White, pink or yellow bars. **CMV $2. each MB.**
FIVE GUEST SOAPS 1984
Flowered box has 5 small bars in choice of 7 fragrances. **CMV $6. MB.**

SKIN-SO-SOFT SOAP 1965-74
3 oz. bar. **CMV $1. mint.**
WINTER GLOW SOAP 1981
Green & white. **CMV $1.**

RICH MOISTURE BATH BAR SOAP 1972-82
Single 5 oz. bar, turquoise & white wrapper. **CMV $1. mint.**

GARDEN FRESH SOAPS 1985
Box holds 3 peach shaped soaps or box of 6 strawberry soaps. **CMV $5. each MB.**

ENCHANTED LAND SOAP SET 1984
(Right) Box holds 2 white bars with fairy decals. **CMV $5. MB.**

CALIFORNIA PERFUME CO. SOAP 1984
(Left) Small bars, choice of Violet, Apple Blossom or Lilac. **CMV $2. each MB.**

GIFTS OF THE SEA SOAP SET 1988
Box holds 4 pink shell soaps. **CMV $4. MB**

IMARI LUXURY PERFUMED SOAPS 1986
Maroon & gold box holds 2 bars. **CMV $4.50 MB.**

FIFTH AVENUE SCULPTURED SOAPS 1986
Black, white & purple box holds 2 lavender bars. **CMV $4.50 MB.**

TRANQUIL MOMENTS SOAP 1986
SILK TAFFETA SOAP 1986
Single bars each. **CMV $1. each.**

CHRISTMAS BERRIES SOAP SET 1988
Holly box holds 2 holly decal bars. **CMV $5. MB**

PEACEFUL TIDINGS SOAP & BATH CUBE SET 1985
Blue box has soap bar & 2 bath cubes **CMV $5. MB.**

COLONIAL ACCENT SOAP & SACHET 1985
Box holds decorator bar soap & 3 packets of sachet. **CMV $5. MB.**

HOLIDAY FRIENDS SOAP 1987
Choice of **Santa** - red soap, **Teddy** - green or **Mr. Snowman** in white. **CMV $1. ea. MB**

FRIENDSHIP GARDEN SOAPS 1988
Flower embossed bars in yellow, green & violet. **CMV $2. ea. MB**

FERAUD SOAP 1985-87
5 oz. bar. Silver, black wrapper. **CMV $1.**
SOFT MUSK SOAP 1982-85
TOCCARA SOAP 1981-85
CLEAR SKIN SOAP 1984-86
PEARLS & LACE SOAP 1984-87
All single bars. **CMV $1. each.**

JOLLY REINDEER SOAP 1987
Box holds 5" long soap that can break apart. Must be in 1 piece to be mint. **CMV $5. MB**

COUNTRY CHRISTMAS SOAPS 1988
Choice of green, pink or yellow bars. **CMV $2. ea. MB**

CITRUS SCENTS SOAP SET 1989
Box holds 3 fruit slice bars. **CMV $4. MB**

TENDER LOVE SOAP SET 1989
Box holds 2 white swan soaps. **CMV $4. MB**

PASTEL 'N PRETTY SOAPS 1992
Box holds 3 ribbon embossed egg soaps.
CMV $4.

SCENTIMENTAL SOAPS 1989
Box holds 3 pink heart bars. **CMV $4. MB**

GLISTENING HOLIDAY SOAPS 1990
1oz. bar in Angel, Dove or Bell. **CMV $2. ea.
MB**

LUXURY FRAGRANCE SOAPS 1991
Box holds 3 - 1 oz. bars in choice of Imari,
Splendour, Everafter or Beguiling. set. **CMV
$4. ea. MB.**

CHRISTMAS COUPLES MINI SOAP 1989
Choice of Snowman, Reindeer, & Santa Claus.
CMV $2. ea. MB

GEM SOAPS 1990
Box holds 4 Gem-like bars. **CMV $3. MB**

ANGELIC SPLENDOR SOAP SET 1994
Box holds 8 white cherub head soaps 1oz. ea.
CMV $7. MB.

PEACH ORCHARD SOAP SET 1989
3 bars peach soaps in box. **CMV $3. MB**

ASPIRIN SOAP 1990
4oz. white bar inscribed ASPIRIN. **CMV $2.
MB**

HEARTS FOR YOU SOAP SET 1995
Red box holds 5 heart shaped soaps. **CMV $5.
set. MB.**

ELVES AT PLAY SOAP 1994
Choice of **Elf** on "**Sled**", "**Skates**", or "**Jumping in Tree**". White, red or green soaps. **CMV $1.50 ea. MB.**

C'EST MOI LUXURY SOAPS 1995
Box holds 3 white soaps. **CMV $15. set. MB.**

LAHANA TROPICAL SOAPS 1993
Box holds 2 blue flower embossed soaps. **CMV $4. MB.**

HONEY AND ALMOND SOAP SET 1994
Box holds 3 bars, 2 oz. ea. **CMV $6. set. MB.**

CHRISTMAS CLASSICS MINI SOAPS 1993
Box holds 3, 1 oz. bars in pearlized colors of green, red, and gold. **CMV $3. set. MB.**

BUBBLE BATH SOAP ON A ROPE 1993
5 oz. bar, choice of 5 pink, blue, gold, green and lavender. **CMV $4. MB.**

SPARKLING ORNAMENT SOAP 1996
1 oz. bars in choice of **STAR** - yellow, **OCTAGON** - green, **TEARDROP** - pinkish red. **CMV $1.50 ea. MB.**

DOZEN ROSES FOR MOM SOAP SET 1994
Pink box holds 12 rose embossed soaps. **CMV $9. set. MB.**

SWEET SCENT SOAP 1995
Heart design box hold choice of 3 heart shaped soaps embossed "True Love", "Sweet Heart", and "Hugs & Kisses". **CMV $1. ea. MB.**

FLORAL BASKET SOAP SET 1994
Box holds 3, 1 oz. basket bars in pearlized pink, yellow and purple. Sold 2 times only. **CMV $3. set. MB.**

CHERUB SOAP 1997
3 heart shaped soaps .75 oz. ea. Choice of pink, cream or lavender. **CMV $1. ea. MB.**

BUBBLE BATH SOAP ON A ROPE 1995
Box holds 5 oz. soap on a rope in herbal green, soft pink, gentle blue, delicate lavender, warm gold. **CMV $4. ea. MB.**

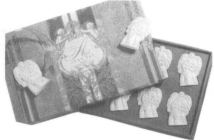

ANGEL SOAPS 1997
2 oz. angel bars. Choice of vanilla soft musk, odyssey, night magic evening musk & soft musk.
CMV $1.50 ea. MB. ANGEL SOAPS 1997
2 oz. angel bars. Choice of vanilla soft musk, odyssey, night magic evening musk & soft musk.
CMV $1.50 ea. MB.

ANGEL SOAP SET 1996
Box holds 8 angel shaped white pearlized soaps.
CMV $8. set MB.

ELEGANT DOVE SOAP SET 1995
Box holds 2 dove shaped soaps. **CMV $3. MB.**

SOAP ON A RIBBON 1995
Shower soap for women in choice of lahina, sweet honesty, soft musk, contrast, & night magic. **CMV $4. ea. MB.**

SOAP IN A SOAP 1997
3 oz. bars in choice of **Snowflake** - blue, **Wreath** - green, or **Cherub** - red. **CMV $4. ea. MB**

MOTHERS DAY SOAP IN A SOAP 1997
Flower soap inside transparent outer soap. Choice of **Rose** - pink, **Dahlia** - blue, **Sunflower** - yellow. **CMV $4. ea. MB.**

NATURALS GLYCERIN CUBE SOAP 1996
3.5 oz. square bars. Choice of Raspberry, Peach or Pear. **CMV $4. ea. MB**

SOAP DISHES & SOAP SETS

ULTRA CRYSTAL SOAP DISH & SOAP 1981-82
(Left) 5" long clear glass soap dish and bar of cream color soap. **CMV $10. MB.**

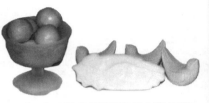

FLOWER FROST SHERBERT GLASS AND SOAPS 1979-80
Frosted glass holds 6 yellow Avon balls of soap. **CMV $11. MB.**

BIRD IN HAND SOAP DISH AND SOAPS 1978-80
5 1/2" long white glass hand soap dish with 3 small blue bird soaps. **CMV $8. MB.**

MOUNT VERNON PLATE & SOAPS 1979-80
9" long blue glass plate. Has Mount Vernon, George and Martha Washington on front. Came with 2 white George and Martha bars of soap. **CMV $11. MB.**

AVON SOAP JAR 1965-66
Pink ribbon on clear glass jar and lid. Came with 12 cakes of soap. **CMV $25. MB, jar only with ribbon and no soap $6., jar and soap with ribbons mint $16.**

HOSTESS FANCY SOAP DISH & SOAP 1975-76
8" wide clear glass with 5 pink soaps. **CMV $10. MB.**

BUTTERFLY FANTASY DISHES & SOAPS 1979-80
Two 4" porcelain with butterfly design. 1 pink butterfly soap. **CMV $12. MB.**

SITTIN' KITTENS SOAP DISH AND SOAPS 1973-75
White milk glass dish with 3 kitten soaps in gold colored, yellow and orange. **CMV $10. MB.**

DOLPHIN SOAP DISH AND HOSTESS SOAPS 1970-71
Silver and aqua plastic soap dish holds 4 blue soaps. **CMV $12. MB.**

FLOWER FROST COLLECTION CRESCENT PLATE & GUEST SOAPS 1979-80
Frosted glass soap dish holds 3 yellow flower soap bars. **CMV $14. MB.**

NESTING HEN SOAP DISH & SOAP 1973
White milk glass hen with beige painted nest. Holds 4 yellow egg soap, 2 oz. each. **CMV $15. MB.**

BICENTENNIAL PLATE & SOAP 1975-76
Clear glass plate with blue soaps embossed with the face of George & Martha Washington on each. Some have Avon on bottom and some don't. **CMV $10. MB.**

WINGS OF BEAUTY SOAP DISH & SOAP
1975-76
White milk glass dish with 2 pink soaps. **CMV**
$10. MB.
NUTTY SOAP DISH & SOAPS 1974-76
Plastic dish with 2 peanut scented soaps.
CMV $8. MB.

BIRDS OF FLIGHT CERAMIC BOX &
SOAP 1980-81
Embossed ducks on lid and sides. Bar of duck
soap inside. Made in Brazil. **CMV $23. MB.**

GIFTS OF THE SEA SOAPS & BASKET
1987
6 1/2" wide wicker basket holds 4 pink sea
shell soaps. **CMV $6. MB.**
SEA TREASURE SOAPS 1986
Black & gold trim tin box holds 4 pink sea shell
soaps. **CMV $6. MB.**

TOUCH OF BEAUTY 1969-70
White milk glass hand holds 4 small bars of
pink soap. **CMV $15. MB.**

COUNTRY PEACHES SOAP JAR &
SOAPS 1977-79
Replica of a 19th century mason jar. Holds 6
yellow peach seed soaps. Blue glass jar with
wire bail. Avon on bottom. **CMV $10. MB.,**
Jar only $3.

FOSTORIA EGG SOAP DISH & SOAP
1977
Blue soap came in Spring Lilacs fragrance.
Egg dish about 4 1/2" long clear glass. Avon
on bottom. **CMV $15. MB. Egg dish only**
$5. 1st issue had "Mother's Day 1977" on
bottom. **CMV $18. MB.**

LOVE NEST SOAPS 1978
Light green glass holds 3 yellow bird soaps in
Special Occasion fragrance. **CMV $10. MB.**

"HEART AND DIAMOND" SOAP DISH &
SOAP 1977
Fostoria clear glass soap dish. Came with red
heart shaped Special Occasion fragranced
soap. Avon on dish. **CMV $10. MB.**

SKIN-SO-SOFT DISH & SOAP 1965
Blue & white plastic soap dish with white bar of
SSS soap. **CMV $10. MB.**

FOSTORIA HEART VASE & SOAPS 1985
(Right) 5" high heart shape vase with 5 pink
heart soaps. **CMV $8. MB.**
CITRUS FRESH SOAPS 1984
(Left) Glass jar holds 5 lemon soaps. **CMV $9.**
MB.

HOLIDAY CACHEPOT SOAPS 1985
(Right) Metal can holds 5 red apple soaps.
CMV $7. MB.
WATER LILY SOAP DISH & SOAPS 1985
(Left) Blue glass dish. 3 white flower soaps.
CMV $8. MB.

BUTTER DISH & HOSTESS SOAPS 1973-
74
Clear glass with 2 yellow 3 oz. butter soaps.
CMV $12. MB.

SOAP DISHES & SOAP SETS

NATURE BOUNTIFUL CERAMIC PLATE & SOAPS 1976-78
Wedgewood ceramic plate made in England, edged in 22K gold. Two soaps decorated with pears decals. Avon stamped on plate. **CMV $20. MB. Plate only $10.**

DECORATOR SOAP DISH & SOAPS 1971-73
7" long frosted glass dish on gold stand. Came with 2 pink soaps. **CMV $12. MB.**

FLOWER BASKET SOAP DISH & SOAP 1972-74
Clear glass dish with gold handle. Came with 5 cakes of soap (2 yellow, 3 pink) 1 oz. each. Hostess Fragrance. **CMV $12. MB.** Also came with double stamp on bottom, add $4.

CRYSTALUCENT COVERED BUTTER DISH & SOAP 1975-76
7" long clear glass with 2 yellow soaps. **CMV $14. MB.**

SUNNY LEMON SOAP DISH & SOAP 1975-76
8 1/2" long clear glass with 3 lemon scented yellow soaps. **CMV $9. MB.**

GIFT OF THE SEA SOAP DISH & SOAPS 1972-73
Iridescent white glass dish looks like a shell. 6 cakes, 1 oz. each, pink soap. 2 each of 3 different shells. **CMV $10. MB.**

LOVE NEST SOAP DISH & SOAPS 1973-75
White dish with green plastic lining, holds 2 aqua and 1 blue bird soap. **CMV $8. MB.**

STRAWBERRY PORCELAIN PLATE & GUEST SOAPS 1978-79
7 1/2" plate made in Brazil for Avon. Comes with 6 red strawberry soaps **CMV $15. MB. $8 plate only.**

LOVEBIRDS SOAP DISH & SOAPS 1974
White milk glass dish with two 4 oz. pink soaps. **CMV $10. MB.**

BEAUTY BUDS SOAP DISH & SOAP 1974-76
6" long white milk glass with 4 yellow soaps. **CMV $10. MB.**

HOSTESS BLOSSOMS FLOWER ARRANGER SOAP DISH & SOAP 1975-76
4 1/2" high white milk glass, plastic top and light green soap. **CMV $10. MB.**

SHIMMERING SEA SOAP GIFT SET 1990
Sea shell glass bowl holds 3 pearlized sea shell soaps. **CMV $10. MB**

OWL SOAP DISH 1971-73
5 1/2" long white glass soap dish with 2 owl eyes in bottom of dish. Holds 2 yellow bars of owl soap. **CMV $12. MB.**

HEAVENLY SOAP SET 1970
White glass dish and 2 pink soaps. **CMV $14. MB.**

HEARTS OF HEARTS BASKET SOAPS 1988
Red wicker basket holds five 1oz. red heart soaps. **CMV $8.50 MB**

We will no longer picture soap sets in open straw baskets as there is no way to protect the soaps and the straw will not hold up for a long period of time for future value.

LAHANA SOAP DISH GIFT SET 1992
Box holds 1.7 oz. Cologne Spray and 2 blue bars of flower design soaps in flower design ceramic dish. **CMV $13.50. MB.**

WINTER IN WOODLAND HILLS SOAP GIFT SET 1992
Etched glass bowl 5 5/8" wide holds pine scent potpourri and three 1 oz. pine cone soaps. **CMV $10. MB.**

SURROUNDINGS FRAGRANT HOME SOAP SET 1998
White bisque porcelain soap dish 5 1/2" long, 3 3/4" wide & 1 3/4" deep. Holds 3 lavender scented glycerin soaps 1 oz. each. **CMV $15. set MB.**

LOVE CHERUB SOAP DISH SET 1996
White ceramic dish is 4 1/2" long by 4 1/4" high. Pink heart shaped soap. **CMV $8. set MB.**

SOAPS CPC

All Soaps Must Be Mint For CMV.

<u>OSP</u> MEANS ORIGINAL SELLING PRICE.

JAPAN TOILET SOAP 1905
Box of 3 cakes. OSP 25c. **CMV $110. MB.**

ALMOND BOUQUET TOILET SOAP 1925
Yellow, green & pink wrapping around 3 bars of soap. Soap is embossed. OSP 30c. **CMV $90. MB.**

ALMOND MEAL TOILET SOAP 1905
Box of 3 cakes. OSP 25c. **CMV $110. MB.**

PEROXIDE TOILET SOAP 1915
Box of 3 cakes. OSP 50c. **CMV $95. MB.**

SAVONA BOUQUET SOAP 1896
Maroon colored box & wrapping. Two bars. OSP 50c. **CMV $110. MB.**

SAVONA BOUQUET SOAP SAMPLES 1936
(Left) **CMV $15. each.**
SAVONA BOUQUET TOILET SOAP SAMPLES 1929
(Right) **CMV $15. each.**

SAVONA BOUQUET TOILET SOAP 1932-36
Box of 6 bars. OSP 50c. **CMV $70. MB.**

ALMOND, BUTTERMILK & CUCUMBER SOAP 1906
Yellow, pink & green box & wrapping holds 3 bars soap. OSP 40c. **CMV $100. MB.**

CASTILE IMPORTED SOAP 1923-25
Box holds 2 silver wrapped bars. OSP 60c. **CMV $60. MB.** Same box also came with 1 large bar. OSP 33c. **CMV $75. MB.**

VEGETABLE OIL SOAP 1936-38
Three light orange colored bars wrapped in turquoise & white paper & box. OSP 46c. **CMV $45. MB.**

VEGETABLE OIL SOAP 1931-36
Box of 3 bars. OSP 45c. **CMV $50. MB.**

CPC IMPORTED CASTILE SOAP 1908
5 oz. cake. First came out about 1893. OSP 25c. **CMV $60. MB.**

CASTILE IMPORTED SOAP 1931-36
Box holds 2 silver wrapped bars. OSP 60c.
CMV $45. MB.

CASTILE SOAP 1925
One bar of soap. OSP 33c. **CMV $50. MB.**

A.B.C. SOAP 1915
Six bars in yellow box with pink flowers on
box. OSP 40c. **CMV $110. MB.**

CASTILE SOAP 1936-43
Two white bars wrapped in silver paper &
turquoise box. OSP 62c. **CMV $45. MB.**

STARCH DRESSING SAMPLE 1911
1" size box holds 3 samples. **CMV $60. MB.**

SAVONA BOUQUET TOILET SOAP 1936-43
Turquoise & white box holds 6 square bars.
OSP 72c. 1936-39 has cpc label on soap &
box. **CMV $75. MB.** 1940-43 Avon label only
on soap and box. **CMV $65. MB.**

EASY CLEANER 1925
Box of two 1/2 lb. cakes. OSP 33c. **CMV $75.
MB.**
NAPTHA LAUNDRY CRYSTALS 1925
Two different box labels. One box has blue
letters & 1 box has green letters. Thirteen
white crystals in box, with instruction sheet.
OSP 33c. **CMV $60. MB.**
STARCH DRESSING 1925
25 tablets in box. Each tablet is marked CPC
& has instruction sheet in box. OSP 33c.
CMV $60. MB.

OSP means Original
Selling Price.
CMV means Current
Market Value.

CPC STARCH DRESSING 1911
(Right) Paper box holds 25 blue tablets. OSP
25¢. **CMV $65. MB.**
CPC NAPTHA LAUNDRY CRYSTALS 1915
(Left) White tablets, paper box. OSP 25¢.
CMV $65. MB.

**STARCH DRESSING DIRECTIONS SHEET
1911**
Came in box of Starch Dressing. Printed on
both sides. **CMV $5. mint.**

487

DR. ZABRISKIE'S SOAP

DR. ZABRISKIE'S CUTANEOUS SOAP 1936-56
Green bar in turquoise box. OSP 33¢. **CMV $25. MB.** Add $5. for CPC label on box.

DR. ZABRISKIE'S SOAP 1915
Brown or green bar embossed, came in blue box. OSP 25¢. **CMV $60. MB.**

DR. ZABRISKIE'S CUTANEOUS SOAP 1956-62
Turquoise box holds 1 green bar. OSP 43¢. **CMV $20. MB.**

DR. ZABRISKIE'S CUTANEOUS SOAP 1940-47
3 oz. green bar and box with Ichthynat. OSP 33¢. **CMV $25. MB.**

DR. ZABRISKIE'S CUTANEOUS SOAP 1920
Green cake & box. OSP 24¢. **CMV $50. MB.**

DR. ZABRISKIE'S CUTANEOUS SOAP 1931-33
(Right) Gray box holds 1 bar. OSP 31¢. **CMV $30. MB.**
DR. ZABRISKIE'S SOAP 1933-36
Gray box holds 1 bar. CPC & Avon on box & soap. Two different labels on boxes. OSP 33¢. **CMV $30. MB.**

DR. ZABRISKIE'S CUTANEOUS SOAP 1895
One bar in box. OSP 25¢. **CMV $85. MB.**

ALBEE FIGURINE AWARD 1986
Fine porcelain. Special designed for Avon 100 Anniversary. **CMV $75. MB.**

(Left to Right)
ALBEE AWARD NO. 1 1978
Porcelain figurine 8 1/2" high in honor of the 1st Avon lady of 1,886, Mrs. P.F.E. Albee. Given to top Reps. in sales in each district. Pink umbrella is also porcelain. **CMV $125.00 MB.**
ALBEE AWARD NO. 2 1979
Hand painted porcelain figurine of the 1st Avon Rep. of 1886. 2nd in a series. Given to President's Club Reps. for outstanding sales. Colors are blue and pink. **CMV $100.00 MB.**
ALBEE AWARD NO. 3 1980
3rd in the Albee series. Given to President's Club Reps. only. **CMV $90. MB.**
ALBEE AWARD NO. 4 1981
4th in the Albee series. Given to President's Club Reps. only. **CMV $65. MB.**

ALBEE FIGURINE AWARD 1984
Hand painted porcelain. Given to P.C. Reps. **CMV $60. MB.**

ALBEE FIGURINE AWARD 1983
Purple dress lady given to all Presidents Club reps for top sales. **CMV $60. MB.**

ALBEE AWARD 1982
5th in a series. Given to President's Club members for sales of $7,000 in 1 year. **CMV $50.00 MB..**

WOMEN OF ACHIEVEMENT AWARD 1961
(Left) Painted ceramic figure of 1886 sales lady. One given in each district for highest sales. Came with stained walnut base & gold plaque inscribed "Avon Woman of Achievement Award". Printed on bottom of figure "Imported Expressly for Avon Products, Inc. Made in West Germany". **CMV $300.,**
WOMEN OF ACHIEVEMENT AWARD 1969
(Right) White ceramic figure much the same as 1961 model. Base is tall & of white wood with gold trim. Printed on bottom of figure "Imported Expressly for Avon Products, Inc. Made in Western Germany Dresden Art". Brass plaque on base (not shown) says "Presented to. . .for Outstanding Contribution to the Better Way". **CMV $275.**

ALBEE AWARDS GOLD & SILVER 1985
Gold tone Albee given 2 in each district. **CMV $50.**

SILVER TONE ALBEE
4 given in each district. Both have black bases & came in red felt bags. **CMV $40.**

ALBEE AWARD - 1987 GOLD & SILVER
Gold tone Albee only 2 given in each district. Comes with "PC 1987 Sales Excellence" plaque across base **CMV $50.**

SILVER TONE ALBEE
Only 4 given in each district. **CMV $60.**

ALBEE FIGURINE AWARD 1988
Hand painted porcelain figurine 11" high with detachable umbrella. Lavender and white dress. **CMV $75. MB.**

ALBEE AWARDS - GOLD & SILVER 1986
Same as 1985 Albee's only base has "Avon 100 1886-1986" to match the gold tone or silver tone. **CMV $50. gold, $40 silver MB.**

ALBEE AWARD 1987
Porcelain figurine given to Presidents Club Reps. Green dress. **CMV $60. MB.**

ALBEE FIGURINE AWARD 1990
(left) 1990 yellow & white porcelain figurine. Given for $8500.00 in Sales. **CMV $100.00 MB**

ALBEE FIGURINE AWARD 1991
(right) Orange color porcelain figurine. **CMV $100.00 MB**

ALBEE DOME AWARDS 1990'S
Large glass dome on left is 12" high. 8" wood base and felt lining. Fits most Albee award figurines. Dome is inscribed Mrs. P.F.E. Albee on top of each dome. **CMV $75.** Dome & base only.

SMALL DOME
(Center) Is 11" high and 5 1/2" base. **CMV $50.** Dome & base only.

LARGE DOME
(Right) 12" high glass dome and wood base is made for full size Albee figurines only. **CMV $75.** Dome & base only.

ALBEE FIGURINE AWARD 1985
Hand painted porcelain. **CMV $60. MB.**

ALBEE AWARD 1989
Rose pink or maroon color coat dress with detached cart. Given to Star Presidents Club Avon Reps. **CMV $100.00 MB**

ALBEE & LADY DOLL AWARDS

MRS ALBEE "Spring Magic Splendor" AWARD PLATE 1990
7" porcelain plate. 1st is series of 4. Given for $50.00 sales increase. **CMV $20. MB**

ALBEE FIGURINE AWARD GOLD & SILVER 1989-90-91
Metal figurines given to reps in silver for recruiting & gold for total sales. Both have blue base in red bags. **CMV Silver $40.00, CMV Gold $50.00**

STAIN GLASS ALBEE AWARD 1988
Blue glass, silver trim Albee given at Presidents Celebration only 2 given in each division. Not marked Avon - plain box. **CMV $45.**

MRS ALBEE "Summer's Soft Whisper" AWARD PLATE 1990
7" porcelain plate. 2nd in series of 4. Given for $50.00 sales increase. **CMV $20. MB**

ALBEE AWARD 1987-88
1st in District in sales volume & sales increase is gold tone. **CMV $50.00**
2nd thru 5th in sales in District in volume & sales increase is silver tone. **CMV $40.**

SSTARR DOLL AWARD 1989
Only 12 dolls given in U.S. 17 inch porcelain doll face, hands & feet. White satin dress, pink roses, blue ribbons. Given at Night of Avon Stars National Celebration. **CMV $400.00 in Avon Box.**

MRS ALBEE "Autumn's Bright Blaze" AWARD PLATE 1990
7" porcelain plate. Given to Presidents Club Reps for top sales. 3rd in series of 4. **CMV $35.00 MB.**

ALBEE FIGURINE AWARD 1992
Blue and white dress lady sitting on purple and white striped love seat. Hand painted porcelain figurines 8" high - 6" wide. **CMV $100. MB.**

MRS ALBEE "Majesty of Winter" AWARD PLATE 1990
7" porcelain plate 4th in series of 4. Given for top sales. **CMV $35.00 MB.**

ALBEE FIGURINE MUSIC BOX AWARD 1991
Porcelain figurine lady in white dress sitting next to table with small lamp and Xmas tree that lights up. Battery power turning base. Music box plays "Let It Snow". Plastic picture window background is 12" high from the base. Given to 1 representative in a drawing at each President's Celebration Meeting 1991. **CMV $300. MB.**

1993 ALBEE MINIATURES AWARDS
3" high porcelain replicas of the full size Mr. Albee Awards 1983 thru 1990. 9 different mini's. The 1982 Mini Albee not pictured was offered in Atlanta Branch and the 1987 Albee was also not offered nation wide. Given to Avon Reps. for sales increase from year before. 1982 and 1987 Albee's offered for $100.00 sales increase. **CMV (All years) $35. ea.** You could win a 6 compartment shadow box to hold the Mini's. **CMV $25.**

SMALL TREASURES ALBEE MINIATURES 1982
Pink box holds mini Albee figurines of number 2,3 & 4 Albee Awards. Given to Avon reps for 5th Step sales goal. **CMV $35 MB set.**

FIGURINE AWARD 1973
Awarded to each representative in district with greatest total sales increase. Made by Hummel, numbered & says "Made for Avon" on bottom. "Figurine 8" sits on white marble base with glass dome. **CMV $200.00**

LLADRO PORCELAIN LADY DIVISION MANAGER AWARD 1975
12 1/2" lady figurine made by Lladro in Spain. Comes with detachable porcelain umbrella. Given to division managers only. Dose not say Avon. Same figurine can also be purchased in fine stores. **CMV not eatablished**

ALBEE JEWELRY BOX AWARD 1989
Wood box with Mrs. Albee etched in glass top. Not marked Avon. **CMV $25.00**

ALBEE DOLL AWARD 1988
16" doll with porcelain face, hands & legs. Dress is same as 1988 Albee Award figurine. Made by EFFANBEE. Not marked Avon. 2 given in each division. **CMV $250.00 in Avon Marked Box.**

FIRST LADY PORCELAIN FIGURINE 1976
Blue, white & pink porcelain made in Spain. Given to President's Club members only for outstanding sales in 90th Anniversary celebration. **CMV $45 MB.**

ALBEE WATCH AWARD 1990
Gold tone watch with brown strap & picture of 1990 Albee on face. **CMV $25.00**

ALBEE & LADY DOLL AWARDS

ALBEE RING AWARD 1982
Gold plated sterling silver. Given to Reps for meeting sales goals. **CMV $20. MB.**

ALBEE CHRISTMAS ORNAMENT 1989
Clear glass ornament with 1989 Albee etched on glass. Dated Avon 1989. Given to Reps. **CMV $10. MB.**

ALBEE LAMP AWARD 1988-93
29 1/2" high lamp with blue and purple Mrs. Albee design on front. **CMV $135.**
ALBEE PLAQUE AWARD 1988-93
(Left) 10" high oval porcelain plaque on brass stand. Mrs. Albee design. **CMV $40.**
ALBEE PLATE AWARD 1988-93
(Right) 9" porcelain Mrs. Albee plate. Brass stand. **CMV $40.**
All awards are dated 1988 but were given out 1988 thru 1993.

MRS. ALBEE AWARD 1994
Porcelain figurine 10" high. Pink dress, white jacket with black and white stripes. Given to top selling Reps. **CMV $100.00 MB.**

MRS. ALBEE GOLD AND SILVER FIGURINE AWARD 1991- 92
Metal, gold tone statue on black plastic base. Plaque says 1992 District Award. #1 for Total Sales. **CMV $50. Gold.** Silver tone Statue Given for #2 in Total Sales. **CMV $40. Silver**

MRS. ALBEE MINI AWARD #10, 1993
Small blue, white and peach porcelain figurine. Comes on lead crystal dish with mirror bottom. Both marked Avon. **CMV $35. MB.**

MRS. ALBEE FIGURINE AWARD 1995
Porcelain figurine, white dress, green jacket. Avon on Bottom. Given to all President's Club Reps. **CMV $100.00 MB.**

MRS ALBEE FIGURINE AWARD 1993
Peach & white dress & hat. Porcelain figurine. Blue door background. **CMV $100.00 MB.**

ALBEE TRIBUTE UMBRELLA AWARD 1995
Hand painted Mrs Albee Umbrella. Wood handle says "Tribute 1995". 1 to a district given to Reps. **CMV $85.00 Mint.**

MRS ALBEE FIGURINE AWARD 1996
Given to reps for selling $8700.00 or more in 1 year. Hand painted porcelain figurine is blue, white, & lavender dress, pink purse. **CMV $100.00 MB**.

MRS ALBEE FIGURINE AWARD 1998
Fine hand painted porcelain figurine dated 1998. Blue & white dress. Given to reps for $9400.00 in sales in 1 year. Bird bath on side. **CMV $100.00 MB.**

MRS P.F.E. ALBEE BARBIE DOLL 1997
lst in a series of Barbie Dolls sold only to Presidents Club avon reps. They could order only 3 dolls at $60.00 ea. Vinyl doll stands 11 1/2" tall & includes stand. She has a purple dress & ivory trim & purple hat. Comes in nice California Perfume decorated box. **CMV $80.00 MB.**

MRS ALBEE FIGURINE AWARD 1997
Hand painted porcelain figurine with red dress & hat. Given to reps for $9100.00 in sales. Dated 1997. **CMV $100.00 MB**

MRS ALBEE BRIDE MUSICAL FIGURINE AWARD 1998
13" high bisque porcelain bride figurine sits on white musical base. Will come with brass plaque of each winner on front of base. Given to reps for $800. to $1,000. total sales increase over 4 campaigns. **CMV $250.00 MB.**

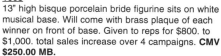

MRS ALBEE THROW AWARD 1995-96
(LEFT) Teal green cotton throw. One to a distric given to top rep in sales. **CMV $50.00 Mint.**

MRS ALBEE ORNAMENT AWARD 1997
4 different Albee glass tree ornaments. Given to reps for sales increase. Each is dated. **CMV $20.00 ea. MB.**

MRS ALBEE THROW AWARD 1994-95
Blue Ist issue & pink second issue cotton throw given to reps at Presidents Club luncheon. **CMV $50.00 ea. Mint.**

The Albee's are the #1 collectible in Avon Collecting as of 1999. Most of the Albee doll figurines will bring full book value.

AWARDS & REPRESENTATIVES GIFTS

What's Hot & What's Not in Awards

Avon Representative Awards continue to be one of the hottest areas of Avon Collecting. California Perfume products are the single best collectible followed closely by Avon Rep Awards in the Avon Collection.

What's Hot in Awards Albee Figurine Awards is the #1 best collectible in Avon Collecting. All jewelry type awards that are marked Avon or the Avon symbols on them. Most all glass awards, figurines, clocks, watches, ceramic items such as cups, dishes, plates, etc. Metal trays, plates, boxes. Anything with sterling silver or real gold in it. Paper weights, lucite items, perfume bottles, pen & pencil sets, buttons. Sets in boxes, key chains, stuffed toys marked Avon, radios, telephones & Avon umbrellas. **All of the above must be marked Avon on the Award. It it's not marked Avon, don't buy it.** These are the main items most award collectors are looking for & pay a fair price for.

What's Not Hot

Plaques - picture frames or pictures, trophies, cloth material items, clothes, bags, anything that is too big or hard to display. Paper items, purses, sets of silverware, display banners, guide books, portfolios. Only things that are very old "1940s" or older of this type award will bring a fair price. Most collectors do not want these items as they don't display well. T-shirts and jackets with Avon logos are popular items and an exception to collecting clothes. **All of the above items should be bought with caution.** I have a lot of this type of collectibles in this book but **some may be removed in future issues due to low collector interest.**

MANAGERS DIAMOND RING 1968
1/4 carat art carved 58 faceted diamond set in a gold 4A design mounting. Given to managers for achievement of sales goals for several quarters. **CMV $500. mint**

PRESIDENT'S CLUB RING "LADY'S" 1978
(Left) Gold plated sterling 4A ring with red simulated ruby. Stone comes in several different shades. Given to all female Presien'ts Club Reps. **CMV $25. MB.**
MANAGERS 4A RING 1978
(Right) Silver 4A ring with high grade ruby stone given to 4 managers in Atanta branch for best planning.
CMV price not etablished.

MANAGERS DIAMOND 4A PIN 1961
4A diamond pin with diamond crown guard. Given to managers reaching a special quota in 1961. **CMV $125.**

CPC I.D. PIN 1900
Brass I.D. pin given to early day Reps. to show they worked for the CPC company. This is the 1st I.D. pin ever given by the CPC. **CMV $125.00**

MANAGERS DIAMOND PIN 1961
Gold 4A pin same as Representatives except has an "M" made of 11 diamonds. **CMV $100. MB.**

DIAMOND 4A PIN 1961-76
Larger than other 4A pins; set with diamond. Given for selling $3,000. at customer price in an 18 campaign period. In 1974-76 you had to sell $4,500. in 13 campaigns. **CMV $35. MB.**

SAPPHIRE 4A PIN 1963-76
Set with a genuine sapphire. Awarded for reaching $2,000. in customer sales price in a 9 campaigne period. In 1974-76 you had to sell $,500. in 13 campaigns. **CMV $20. MB.**

PEARL 4A PIN 1963-70
10 kt. gold in a 4A design with a pearl in center. Awarded for reaching $1,000 in customer price sales in a 9 campaign period. 5/8" diameter. **CMV $15. MB**

RUBY 4A PIN 1973-76
10 kt. gold with ruby in center. Awarded for selling $2,500. in customer price sales in 6 month period to become eligible for President's Club Membership. **CMV $10.**

CPC IDENTIFICATION PIN 1910-25
Given to all Representatives to identify them as official company Representatives. Says CPC 1886 on face. also came with blue enamel center. **CMV $90. mint.**

CPC IDENTIFICATION HONOR PIN 1910-15
Given to Representatives for selling $250. in merchandise. **CMV $90. mint. Both pins are brass.**

QUEENS AWARD PIN 1964
Gold colored metal 11/4" across. Given to each member of the winning team during the 78th Anniversary for top sales. **CMV $20.**

IDENTIFICATION PIN 1938-45
Silver with aqua enamel. Given to all Representatives for identification. "Avon Products, Inc., Avon" on face of pin. **CMV $30 mint.**

HONOR I.D. PIN "GOLD" 1938-45
Gold plated with aqua enamel Given for $250. in sales. "Avon Products, Inc., Avon Honor" on face of pin. **CMV $35. mint.**

CIRCLE OF EXCELLENCE RING 1971
Same as pin only ring. **CMV $275. mint.**

CIRCLE OF EXCELLENCE PIN 1969
4A gold pin circled with pearls and diamonds in center. Managers only pin has a logo on back and can also be worn as a pendant. **CMV $200.**

CPC AVON I.D. PIN 1929-38
(Top) Given to all Reps to show they work for Avon and the CPC. Silver pin with blue enamel. "California Perfume Co., Inc., "Avon" on face of pin. This pin is larger in size than the 1938-45 I.D. pins. This pin came in two different ways. The A and V on Avon is close together on one and wide apart on the others. **CMV $45.**

I.D.HONOR AWARD PIN 1929-38
(Bottom) Gold tone with dark blue enamel. Given to Reps for $250. in sales. "CPC - AVON - HONOR" on face of pin. **CMV $55. mint.**

JEWELED PIN - DIAMOND 1956-61
Same as pearl jeweled pin except has five diamonds instead of pearls. Came with black and gold star guard also containing five diamonds. This was the top award and was given after attaining the 4 diamond star guard. A minimum of $25,000 in sales were required for this award. **CMV $175. mint.**

CITY MANAGERS I.D. PIN & PEARL GUARD 1945-61
Given to all City Managers. Pin has 5 pearls. Guard is set with 11seed pearls. **CMV $75. mint.**

JEWELED PIN PEARL - HIGHEST HONOR CASE 1945-61
10K gold with black enamel background. 5 oriental pearls are set in the A. Came in black highest award case. Given for sales of $1000. **CMV $30. pin, $40 in case.**

IDENTIFICATION PIN 1945-51
Gold pin with black background. "A" has scroll design rather than jewels. Edges are plain, no writing. Given to Representatives for $1,000. in sales. **CMV $20.**

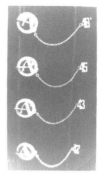

I.D. HONOR PIN & CASE "SILVER" 1938-45
(Left) Silver with aqua enamel. Given to all Representatives for identification. "Avon Products, Inc., Avon Honor on face of pin. **CMV $30.**

FIELD MANAGER'S I.D. PIN & GUARD 1945-61
(Right) Same design as the jeweled pin but has no printing. The "M" guard is smooth gold. **CMV $55.**

JEWEL PIN NUMERAL GUARDS 1945-56
Smooth gold numerals given for additional sales in multiples of $1,000. starting with No. 2. There was no No. 1. These are made to attach to the jewel pin. Highest numeral known is 115. The higher the number the more valuable. **CMV $8. on numbers 2 to 10, $12. on 11 to 20, $14. on 21 to 30, $18. on 31 to 40, $20. on 41 to 75, $25. each on 76**

GOLDEN ACHIEVEMENT AWARD 1971-76
Bracelet & 1st charm awarded for $5,500. total sales in 6 month period. Each succeeding charm awarded for $5,500. within each subsequent 6 month period. First charm - 2 joined 4A design with green stone. Second charm - Avon Rose with red stone. Third charm - The First Lady with a genuine topaze. Fourth charm - The "World of Avon" set with a genuine aquamarine. Fifth charm - "The Doorknocker" with a genuine amethyst. Sixth charm - jeweled "A" with a genuine sapphire. Seventh charm - the "Key" with a genuine garnet. Eighth charm - Great Oak. (Above order of charms correct) **CMV $20. each charm. Charm No. 8 $30.**

50th ANNIVERSARY PIN 1936
Red circle with gold feather. Given to every representative who made a house to house sales trip of her area. **CMV $40. mint.**

HEART DIAMOND A PIN 1977
14k gold heart shape pin with 12 small diamonds. Can also be used as a pendant on chain. Came in gray felt box with white outer box. Only 1 given in each division for top Rep. Rare. **CMV $400. mint**

JEWELED PIN - HIGHEST HONOR - "PEARL" 1945-61
10K gold with black enamel background, 5 oriental pearls are set in the A. Given for sales of $1,000. **CMV $30.**

STAR GUARDS 1956-61
Raised star on round gold metal pin. Given for each $5,000. in sales in any 12 month period. Four guards could be won, each had an additional diamond. Made to wear with the jeweled pin. **CMV $15. one diamond. Add $10 for each additional diamond.**

CHARM BRACELET AWARD 1969
22 kt. gold finish, double-link bracelet with safety chain & 5 charms. Each charm given for progressively higher sales. **CMV $5. ea. charm, plus bracelet.**

A PIN AWARD 1976-78
Given to Reps. for selling $1,500. in Avon in a 13 campaign period. **Came in blue lined box, CMV $5. MB. Red lined box, CMV $4. MB**

MANAGERS CHARM BRACELET 1963-65
One charm was given each quarter for 3 years making a total of 12 charms possible. These were won by attaining certain sales increases which increased with each quarter making the later charms very difficult to get. For this reason past the eighth quarter are very hard to find. The bracelet charms are 10 kt. gold. Only four bracelets were won with all 12 charms. A total of 6191 individual charms were given to 1445 managers. The last four charms are like the one pictured in center of bracelet. No. 9 has Rubys, No. 10 Sapphire, No. 11, Emerald & No. 12 Diamond. Each one had 4 stones. **CMV 1st 8 charms $45. each., plus bracelet No. 9 & 10 $60. each, No. 11, 12, $75. ea., CMV all 12 charms $800. mint.**

AWARDS & REPRESENTATIVES GIFTS

CHARM BRACELET - SILVER 1959
Only 2 districts won in each branch. This was a test bracelet & very few were given for sales achievement. **CMV $200. mint with all 6 charms.**

PRESIDENT'S CLUB RING FOR MEN 1978
Gold plated sterling silver 4A ring with ruby stone. Given to male Avon Reps. for selling $6000 worth of Avon in 1 year period. Came in plain blue velvet ring box. **CMV $100. MB.**

SMOKY QUARTZ RING - MANAGERS 1978
Smoky quartz stone, 14K gold mounting marked Avon. Given to managers in C26-78 for best activity event in Atlanta branch. **CMV $40.**

PRESIDENT'S CELEBRATION STAR AWARD 1977
Sterling silver star & chain with small diamond made by Tiffany. Was given to winning district manager in division. **CMV $35.**

GOLDEN CIRCLE CHARM BRACELET AWARD 1965
22 kt. gold finish double-link bracelet with safety chain and 5 gold charms. Each charm given for progressively higher sales. **CMV $7. each charm, plus bracelet $7. Came in an Avon box.**

PRESIDENT'S CELEBRATION DIAMOND RING AWARD 1977
14K gold ring with 8 small diamond in center. Given to managers in Pasadena branch for largest increase in sales. Only 20 rings given in this branch. Does not say Avon. **CMV $100.**

MANAGERS ACHIEVEMENT AWARD PIN & CHARM BRACELET 1974
1 given to top sales manager in each division. Brush sterling silver with blue sapphire in center of Avon Door Knocker. **CMV $70., $75. MB each.**

DIVISION MANAGERS ACHIEVEMENT CUFF LINKS AWARD 1974
Same as awards pin on left, only are cuff links. Given to male Division Managers. **CMV $85. set. Mint.**

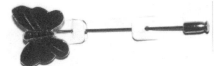

BUTTERFLY PIN AWARD 1981
Gold tone enameled stick pin given to Reps. Does not say Avon. **CMV $5.**

CIRCLE OF EXCELLENCE CHARM BRACELET 1972-79
10K gold bracelet & gold charm with 3 diamonds & 4A design. Black & gold Avon box. Green inside. Given to managers only. **CMV $300. MB. Also came charm with 4 diamonds last charm. CMV $350. MB.**

COTILLION PERFUME AWARD 1957
Black and gold box. Given to managers. **CMV $30. MB. Rare.**

SILVER DOOR KNOCKER PIN 1964
Given to all managers in conjunction with the door knocker award program. **CMV $25., $30 MB.**

GOLD DOOR KNOCKER PIN 1964-83
Came on green or white cards. **CMV $3 on card. CMV pin only $2. Also came in bue box with white sleeve. Same CMV.**

DON'T KNOCK ME DOORKNOCKER NECKLACE AWARD 1981
Gold tone door knocker with simulated diamond. Given to Reps. Comes in "Jo Anne Jewels" box. Made only for Avon. **CMV $15. MB.**

DOOR KNOCKER EARRINGS 1966
Gold tone earring. Avon Calling on them. **CMV $20 pr. MB.**

PRESIDENT'S CLUB PIN AWARD 1980-81
Gold tone pin given to President's Club Members only. Comes in Blue Avon box. Given in 1980 & 1981. **CMV $7.50. MB.**

IDENTIFICATION PIN AUSTRALIA 1980
Gold toned door knocker pin. **CMV $10.**
AVON REPRESENTATIVE STICK PIN 1980
Blue & gold. (Says Avon Representative) **CMV $20.**

HEART STICK PIN AWARD 1978
Sterling silver heart pin made by Tiffany & Co. with Avon products slip. Given to managers only, during President's Celebration. Does not say Avon. Must be in box with Tiffany & Co. Avon card. **CMV $15. MB.**

APPLE STICK PIN 1977
Red apple with 4A design 1977 & P.C. for President's Club on green Leaf. Pin is gold tone color. Given to winning team in each district for highest sales. **CMV $15.**
LIVE-LOVE-LAUGH DIAMOND PIN AWARD 1978
14K gold with 2 point diamond. Given to Avon managers for reaching appointment goal for August conference. **CMV $30. MB.**

DOOR KNOCKER DIAMOND PIN 1981
Gold with small diamond. Given to managers. Came in Tan box. **CMV $40. MB.**

ACORN STICK PIN AWARD 1979
Sterling silver acorn pin from Tiffany & Co. given to managers. Came with small card with great oak & Tiffany card for Avon products. **CMV $15. MB.**

PRESIDENT'S CELEBRATION "A" PIN AWARD 1978
White box holds "A" sterling silver pin given to President's Club Reps. only. **CMV $7.50 MB.**

EMPLOYEES GIFT KEY CHAIN 1971
Blue box with gray flannel bag holds gold horseshoe with Avon on one side and You're in Demand on back side of charm. **CMV $15. MB.** horeshoe with Avon on one side and You're in Demand on back side of charm. **CMV $20. MB.**

AN OPEN LETTER TO ALL AVON REPS.

Do you want to increase the number of Avon collectors in the world? This would greatly increase your sales, too, you know! Try to find out your customer's various interests and those of her children and husband, too! For example:

Mrs. Smith loves animals - bring every animal decanter or figurine to her attention as they appear on the market. Sell her the first one and she'll likely buy more, or all, that come! Mr. Smith is a sports fan! Point out what a smart collection he could have on a neat shelf in his den. Young Johnny would love the majestic elephant, or that dinosaur decanter and teenager Sue really "digs" the "Fried Egg" or "Hamburger" compacts.

All these people have a good chance of ending up being a collector! So what does that really mean? Well it means that your collectibles may maintain their value and the market will grow steadily. Avon Reps. will have good steady sales. Collectors will have a wider and wider circle of ever growing and interested folk to swap and shop with.

Show your own collection to friends, help to stir the interest of others. Believe me, it will pay off in the end!!

Most important of all, don't forget to carry a copy of Hastin's Avon Collectors Encyclopedia to show your customers. "By showing this book to your customers, you can help create new collectors and you will profit 10 fold, as collectors will buy many more Avon products from you. Be sure to point out information on the **Avon Times** - Avon Club which they can enjoy right from their own living room. **Tell them about the free advertising to thousands of members to buy, sell or trade Avons. Remember, if you help educate your customers on Avon Collecting you will profit greatly in larger future sales.**

For more information on the Avon Times, write or send $24.00 for 1 full year subscription in U.S. or $26.00 U.S. Funds in Canada to: Avon Times, Box 9868, Kansas City, Missouri 64134. Send a SASE when requesting information.

PRESIDENT'S CELEBRATION MEN'S AWARD KEY CHAIN 1980
Sterling silver with oak tree on one side & inscribed on other. Given to men Reps. only for top sales. **CMV $100. MB.**

5 YEAR SERVICE AWARD KEY RING 1970'S
Sterling silver - 4A design on front comes in Blue felt Tiffany bag & box. **CMV $25.**

SALES ACHIEVEMENT KEY CHAIN 1976-77
Silver tone key chain. 4A emblem on front & back market "Avon Sales Achievement Award C/23/76, C/9/77." In special Sales Achievement Award Avon box. **CMV $11. MB.**

ANNIVERSARY CAMPAIGN KEY CHAIN 1968
(Left) Silver charm and key chain. **CMV $15**
CIRCLE OF EXCELLENCE KEY CHAIN 1972
(Right) Silver charm and chain with 4A design on one side and Mexico 1972. This was given by Mexico Avon branch to Circle of Excellence Award winning managers for the year 1971. Trip was made in 1972 for approximately 185 winning managers. **CMV $40. mint.**

ANNIVERSARY CAMPAIGN HONOR AWARD KEY CHAIN 1968
White Avon box holds gold & silver double key ring. Made by Swank. **CMV $15 MB.**

BOCA OR BUST MANAGERS KEY CHAIN 1975
Silver 4A design, **CMV $15. MB.**

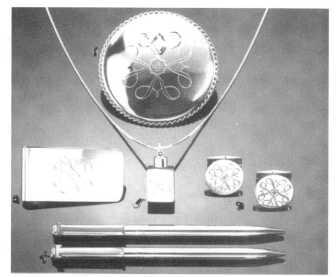

10 YEAR SERVICE AWARDS 1980
5 different gifts. All of sterling silver. All marked with 4A design. Each comes in Tiffany & Co. box. Given to Avon managers & all Avon Employees for 10 years service. They had their choice of Pen & Pencil set with T clips, 3 inch purse mirror, Cuff Links 7/8" diameter, & Small 1 1/4" high silver flask that opens, on sterling silver chain 23 1/2" long. **CMV each item or set $40 MB, Flask $60, Pen set $50 MB.**

4A KEY RING AWARD 1973-75
Gold lucite key ring in green or red lined box. **CMV $10. MB each.**

DISTINGUISHED MANAGEMENT AWARD 1967
Sterling silver key chain with raised 4A design set in brushed finish area. Given to top manager in each division. **CMV $35. MB, $27.50 chain only.**

"KEY CHAIN" DISTRICT MANAGER SAFE DRIVER AWARD 1978

Large brass key chain has "4A" on one side & "Avon District Manager Safe Driver Award 1978" on other side. Came in white & green box. 4A on box lid. Came also with Avon card shown. **CMV $10. MB.**

KEY CHAIN "THANKS AMERICA" AWARD 1979

Team leader white box holds silver tone heart key chain "Thanks America for making us number one" Back side says "Avon loves team leaders." **CMV $10 MB.**

LUCKY 7 PIN 1964

Gold tone pin with simulated pearl in center. Given to each representative who sent in a certain size order. **CMV $10., $13. MB.**

GOOD LUCK BRACELET 1966

Gold double link bracelet with gold charm. Good luck four leaf clover on the front. Back is plain. Not marked Avon.
CMV $12., $15. MB.

AWARD BRACELET 1953

1953 on back of sterling silver heart shaped charm. **CMV $40 MB**

AVON ATTENDANCE CHARM 1969-70

1969 AD on one round charm & 1970 Heart shape AD on the other. Both gold tone & chain. **CMV $17 ea.**

FIGURE 8 CHARM BRACELET 1951

Sterling silver bracelet with 2 skates attached. Given to representatives for interviewing 120 Avon customers during the figure 8 campaign 3-1951. Made only for Avon. **CMV $50.**

MANAGERS BRACELET 1956

Bracelet given to top selling city & district managers during President's campaign 1956. **CMV $100 MB.**

BELL BRACELET AWARD 1961

Silver bracelet & bell that rings. Avon not on bell. **CMV $30.**

BELL AWARDS 1964

Gold bell earrings. Christmas sales award. Gold bell charm bracelet. **CMV $20.** Christmas sales award. **CMV $30.**

DREAM CHARM MANAGERS NECKLACE 1979

Gold tone necklace & 3 charms of orchid, butterfly & sea shell. Given to Avon managers at 1979 Dream Conference. Does not say Avon on charms. Came in maroon satin bag with pink tie string. **CMV $25. mint in bag.**

TLC NECKLACE AWARD 1977

Given to Team Leaders. 14K gold. **CMV $25.**

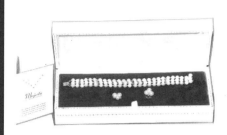

MANAGERS CHRISTMAS GIFT 1961
Pearl bracelet with small diamonds & matching earrings. Given to Avon managers at Chritmas 1961. Does not say Avon. Made by Majestic. **CMV $300. MB.**

MANAGERS GIFT DIAMOND LOOP 1977
Diamond Loop necklace given to managers in special gold bar type box, on introduction of Avons new 14K gold filled jewelry. **CMV $40. MB as pictured.**

SUNNY STAR AWARD NECKLACE 1975
Given to managers on introduction to Sunny Star necklace. This is the same one that sold only it has Aug. 1975 engraved on it. It can easily be duplicated so a price above the cost from Avon should not be paid. Brass star & chain. **CMV $10. MB.**

PRESIDENTS CELEBRATION AWARD 1974
14 kt. gold necklace with 3 point diamond. Given to 10 top representatives in each of the 81 winning districts for outstanding sales during this presidents celebration. **CMV $60. MB.**

SMILE PENDANT AWARD 1978
Red and gold pendant, given to all Avon Team Leaders. Back side says Avon, Team Leader, March 1978. **CMV $10. MB.** Also given to District Managers with D.M. on back. **CMV $15.** Both came in red box with Avon sleeve. Smile Pendant also given to Division managers at conference. Back says "N.Y. March, 78, Avon". Red box comes with plain white sleeve. **CMV $30. MB.**

PRESIDENT'S CELEBRATION DIAMOND HEART LOCKET AWARD 1979
Given to top 20 Reps. in each district during President's Celebration. Inscribed on back "President's Club 1979" **CMV $20. MB.** Same given to district managers only has DM Inscribed on back also. **CMV $30. MB.**

FIRST AVON LADY PENDANT AWARD 1975
Siver toned with scroll 'A' design around glass insert. On the presentation card it starts "Congratulations! We're happy to present you with this exclusive award. Designed especially for you. It's symbolic of the personal service upon which Avon was founded and which has guided us throughout the years" **CMV $15., $20. MB.**

HONOR AWARD CAMEO PERFUME GLACE NECKLACE 1966
Blue & white set trimmed in gold. **CMV $12., $17.50 MB.**

CHRISTMAS GIFT - REPS. 1979
Sterling silver goldtone chain with 10K gold charm with 2 small diamonds. Came in black felt box. Back is marked District managers 1979 **CMV $50.**, Team Leaders 1979 **CMV $35.**

AWARDS & REPRESENTATIVES GIFTS

VALENTINE HEART PENDANT AWARD 1978

14K gold heart. Does not say Avon. Only 2500 were given to Reps. at sales meetings. Must have C3-78 brochure with heart to prove it's from Avon. **CMV $15. with brochure.**

EARRINGS - TEAM LEADER CHRISTMAS GIFT 1978

10K solid gold with small diamond chip. Given to team leaders at Christmas, 1978. Came in Avon box. **CMV $40. MB.**

TEAM LEADER TEDDY BEAR AWARD 1982

Sterling silver bear with movable arms & sterling silver chain. From Tiffany. Approx. 1/2 inch high. Marked T.L. on back of bear. **CMV $30. MB.**

SILVER CIRCLE CELEBRATIONNECKLACE AWARD, ENGLAND 1982

Blue box holds clear crystal pendant on sterling silver chain. Marked Avon. Given to Silver Circle Reps **CMV $40. MB.,** Also shown with silver Circle Celebration Banquet Menu **CMV $5.**

ACORN NECKLACE AWARD 1980

Sterling Silver acorn Pendant & necklace. Comes with great oak card & Tiffany Box in velvet pouch. Given to managers only. **CMV $40. MB with card.**

"YOU'RE PRECIOUS TO US" PENDANT MANAGERS GIFT 1978

14K gold filled with real pearl & small diamond. Gold box says "You're Precious to Us" on lid. Given to Avon managers. Must be in box as described. Came with card signed by S.M. Kent. **CMV $50. MB.**

HEART NO. 1 PENDANT AWARD 1979

14K gold heart with small diamond given to 1 top Rep. in each division. In Avon blue velvet box. **CMV $90. MB**

85th ANNIVERSARY AWARD JEWELRY 1971

22 Kt. gold plated sterling silver necklace, ring & earrings. Each shaped like a rose with diamond in center. Necklace was for representatives not in the presidents club, and the earrings for the presidents club members only. Two diamond rings were given in each district by a drawing. One was given to a presidents club member the other to a non-member. Ring also available in prize catalog for 2400 points. **CMV necklace $35., $40. MB. Ring $80., $85. MB. Earrings $35., $40. MB.**

85th ANNIVERSARY PINS 1971

22 Kt. gold plated sterling silver pin with diamond. Small pin for representative not in president club, representatives only. Given for meeting sales goal in C-12-71. **CMV small pin $15., $20. MB. Large pin $20., $25. MB.**

CUSTOMER'S COUNT "AVON" PIN AWARD 1998

Gold tone pin & simulated diamond given to all Reps for a $50.00 order in lst three sales periods of 1998. **CMV $5. MB.**

RISING STAR PIN AWARD 1991

Gold tone with 3 rhinestones & detachable silver tone star pin. Can be used as a lapel or tie pin. Given to Reps for $4500.00 in total sales. **CMV $5. MB.**

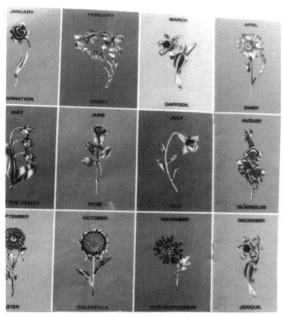

"G" CLEF MANAGERS PIN 1968
Gold in color. Awarded to managers. **CMV $15. pin only, $20. MB.**

MOONWIND AWARD PIN 1971
Sterling silver pin given to Reps. for meeting sales goals. **CMV $22.50.**

AWARD PIN 1965
White plastic on blue background with silver or gold frame. **CMV $25. in box., $15. pin only.**

81st ANNIVERSARY PINS 1967
Sterling silver pins came in 12 different flowers. Representatives who met their personal prize goal for this anniversary campaign had their choice of one of these 12 flowers. Carnation, Violet, Daffodil, Daisy, Lily of the Valley, Rose, Lily, Gladiolus, Aster, Calendula. Chrysanthemum and Jonquil. **CMV Rose $15., $25. MB. Calendula $30., $40. MB. All others $20., $30. MB.**

SALES ACHIEVEMENT AWARD 1969
Large gold Charisma design pin came in black Avon box. **CMV $20. MB.**

SHELL SALES LEADER AWARD 1979
Sterling silver shell comes in Tiffany felt bag & box. Given to managers. **CMV $125.00 MB.**

15 YEAR SERVICE AWARDS 1980's
All are marked Avon or has 4A design. Each comes from Tiffany & design. Each comes from Tiffany & Co. Given for 15 years service at Avon. Choice of:
STERLING SILVER PERPETUAL CALENDAR
6" wide, 4 1/4" high. **CMV $50.**
CRYSTAL DECANTER WITH STERLING SILVER TAG
11" high. **CMV $50.**
STERLING SILVER SALT & PEPPER SET
2 1/4" high. **CMV $50 set.**
STERLING SILVER PIN BOX
3" diameter. **CMV $50.**

ANNIVERSARY AWARD ROSE PIN 1968
Victory luncheon July 9, 1968. Gold rose pin with ruby stone in Avon box**CMV $27.50 MB only.**

SHELL JEWELRY 1968
(Left) Given for recommending someone as a representative. For each name representatives could choose either the pin or earrings. For 2 or more names you got the set. **CMV $12. Set.**

NEARNESS MANAGERS PIN 1955
(Right) Gold shell pin with pearl. **CMV $35.**

KEY PIN AWARD 1962
(Top) Gold key, surprise gift for activity. **CMV $10.**

AWARD EARRINGS 1961
(Bottom) Gold star design. Avon is not on them. **CMV $15. MB pair.**

CLOVER TIME PIN 1951
Given to representatives for calling on 120 customers in one campaign. Made by Coro. Pin is outlined with imitation seed pearls & dotted with aquamarine stones for color. Does not say avon. Came with certificate from Avon in Coro box. **CMV $40. MB.**

AWARD PIN 1944 Only
Hand made sterling silver pin with roses & lilies, given to Reps. for selling $300. to $400. during Christmas campaign. **CMV $60. MB.**

MANAGERS AWARD PIN 1943
Gold plated lapel pin with hand set stones, cost Avon $25. in 1943. Only 2 were given to the 2 top selling managers in U.S. during loyalty campaign, March 2-22, 1943. **CMV $125.00**

VICTORY PIN AWARD 1942
Sterling silver wing pin with red, white and blue center. Given to Reps. during Acres of Diamonds campaign 1942 for getting new customers. **CMV $70., $80 MB.**

BOW PIN AWARD 1944
Lapel pin is gold plate with center stone of synthetic aquamarine. Given to Reps. for selling over $300. in 1 campaign. **CMV $30, $45 MB.**

BOWKNOT AWARD PIN 1942
Gold pin with sequins shaped like bow. Given to representatives for selling $100. to $150. in one campaign. **CMV $50 MB.**

5 YEAR SERVICE PIN 1970
For Avon plant employees, not Reps. Gold circle with 4A emblem & blue stone. **CMV $30. MB., $25. pin only.**

RED ROBIN PIN 1955
Sterling silver pins made by Cora Company. does not say Avon on it. Given in pairs for getting 12 new customers. **CMV $30. MB.**

EIFFEL TOWER MANAGERS PIN 1979
Small gold tone tie tack type pin given to managers on Paris trip. Does not say Avon. In plain blue box. Pin is 1 1/8" high. **CMV $15.**

TOP FIFTY PIN AWARD 1977
Gold tone pin has top 50 & 4A design with red backgound. Given to top 50 Reps. in division for sales. **CMV $16.**

TOP FIFTY PIN AWARD 1978
Same as 1977 pin only has red rose with green leaves. **CMV $12.50**

SHOOTING STAR PIN - MANAGERS 1980
Gold tone pin in brown box with outer sleeve. Given to managers. **CMV $15. MB.** Also came as tie tack for men. **CMV $25. MB.**

ROYAL RIBBON TAC PIN AWARD 1980
Sterling silver with yellow, red, white, or blue enamel. Given to managers for recruiting new Reps. **CMV Yellow $5., Red $10., White $15., Blue $20., MB each.**

FLAG PIN AWARD 1979
Gold tone red, white and blue enamel lapel pin. Given to Circle of Excellence winners in Paris trip. Came in red velvet Avon ring box. **CMV $25. MB.**

MANAGERS PANELIST PIN 1976
Gold tone name pin. Marked "Nat. District Managers Panelist" **CMV $10.** Given each year.

TELEPHONE TIE TAC AWARD 1981
Gold tone telephone Tie Tac. Given to Reps. **CMV $10.**

AVON'S BEST PIN AWARD 1982
Small brass pin says "Avon's Best, Morton Grove." With 4A design. Given to managers for Atlanta conference. **CMV $10.**

UNICORN PIN AWARD 1981
Brass unicorn lapel pin given to managers at August conference 1981. Back inscribed Conference 81. Avon box says For Display Only - not for resale, **CMV $15. MB.** Same pin given to Team Leaders, **CMV with TL on back $10.** Pin also sold to public only plain no marking on back, **No CMV.** Also came with SC on back, **CMV $20. MB.**

AVON NO. 1 PIN - HOLLAND 1979
Gold tone pin given to Zone Avon Managers in Holland. **CMV $50.**

25 YEAR SERVICE AWARD PIN 1970
1/10 yellow 10K gold 4A pin with 25 on it. Was for 25 years service. Was never issued. Very Rare. **CMV $100.**

AVON PIN - DIVISION MANAGER 1979
Gold tone pin with red enamel filled heart shaped O given to division managers only. **CMV $15. MB, in red box.**

AVON PIN - REPS 1979
Gold tone pin same as above only does not have red heart. **CMV $5. MB, in white box.**

AVON PIN - DISTRICT MANAGERS 1979
Same gold tone pin as reps. above only DM inscribed on back. **CMV $15. MB, in white box.**

RESIDENTS CLUB PIN AWARD 1995
Gold tone pin with small stone marked PC. Given to Reps for $8600. in sales. **CMV $10.00 MB.**

HONOR SOCIETY PIN AWARD 1995
Gold tone pin with blue stone and marked HS. Given to Reps for $16,200. in sales. **CMV $15.00 MB.**

ROSE CIRCLE PIN AWARD 1995
Gold tone pin with red stone marked RC. Given to Reps for $30,500. in sales. **CMV $20.00 MB.**

DAVID H. McCONNELL CLUB PIN AWARD 1995
Gold tone pin with DHM and small stone. Given to Reps for $51,000. in sales. **CMV $25.00 MB**

AWARDS & REPRESENTATIVES GIFTS

C OF E PIN 1980
Small pin says C of E 1980. **CMV $10.**
C OF E WINNERS PIN 1979
Blue Enamel on gold tone pin. **CMV $10.**
SELL A THON TIE TAC 1981
Red, white & blue tie tac pin. Given to all Reps. at sales meeting. **CMV $2.**
CABLE CAR STICK PIN 1980
Gold tone, sterling silver cable car stick pin given t o Avon managers on trip to San Francisco. Does not say Avon. **CMV $15.**

1500 PIN 1963
(Top) Given to reps. for $1,500. in sales in one campaign. **CMV $20.**
TEAM CAPTAIN PIN 1969-70
(Bottom) Torch pin says T C -69-70. **CMV $20.**

MONEY CLIP TEAM LEADER AWARD 1969
Green & white lined black & brass box holds 12K gold filled money clip with solid 10K gold emblem with 2 small diamonds on top. Awarded to male team leaders. Rare. "Team Leader 1979" on back. **CMV $75. MB.** Also given to male managers with D.M. on back. **CMV $75. MB.**

AVON STAR PIN
(left) **CMV $60.** If you have any information on what year or what this pin was given for, please write Bud Hastin and tell him.
SERVICE AWARD 1938
(Right) Bronze medallion hangs from aqua colored bar with Avon in gold. Given to representatives for outstanding improvement in sales. **CMV $50. mint.**

MONEY CLIP 1963
(Left) 10K gold fIled. Back says Pathways of Achievement 1963. 4A design on front and initials. **CMV $75. MB.**
MONEY CLIP 1969
(Center) Black and gold box holds 10K gold filled 4A design on front with initials. Back says Management Conference Atlanta, Georgia November 1969. **CMV $75 MB.**
MONEY CLIP 1960
(Right) 10K gold filled. Small 4A design on face and initials. Nothing on back. **CMV $75.**

MEDALLION OF HONOR 1945
Made of solid gold, it is 7/8 inches long & 1 3/8 inches wide. Woman on the front is raised. Back side is engraved to person & date. Came with award scroll. Medal can be worn on a ribbon or brooch. This medal was given to women only in 1945 during World War II both military & civilian for service to their country above and beyond the call of duty. Very few medals were given out. **CMV medal $500., Scroll $50.**

STAR REPRESENTATIVE GOLD MEDALLION 1937-45
10kt. gold filled medal, given to representatives for selling $1,000. worth of Avon in any 12 month period. **CMV $50., $60. in Black Highest Award box shown.**

STAR REPRESENATIVE GOLD MEDALLION 1931-37
10 kt. gold filled medal. Given to representatives for selling $1,000. worth of Avon in any 12 month period. **CMV $150., $165. MB.**

GOLD STAR REPRESENTATIVE MEDAL - CPC 1930-31
Highest honor given to Representatives that achieved the goal of $1000. in sales from January to January. If goal reached second year a second gold star is engraved, and so on. Made of gold. **CMV $275. MB.**

ANNIVERSARY PRINCESS BRACELET 1960
Awarded for increased sales. Bracelet with diamond. Bracelet with emerald, Bracelet with ruby or topaze. 14K gold. **CMV $260. each MB.**

LOYAL SERVICE AWARD - 15 YEAR 1970's
Solid 10K gold. 4A emblem on front. Avon 15 years loyal service on back. Given to employees of Avon. Came on 10K gold wrist chain. **CMV $150.**

4A TIE CLIP SERVICE AWARD 1970's
Gold tone with 4A design. Given to Avon employees. **CMV $25.**

KEY RING 5 YEAR SERVICE AWARD 1978
1/10 10K gold 4A symbol key ring given to Avon plant employees for 5 years service. Started in 1978. **CMV $17.50. MB.**

SWEATER GUARD AWARD 1968
6" gold chain with 4A design clips on each end. Given as general managers honor award to each representative of the winning team in each district. **CMV $25., $30. MB**

SERVICE AWARD CHARM 1962
22 kt. gold finish slightly larger than a quarter, given to all representatives who sold 50 or more customers during campaign 6. **CMV $10.**

PRESIDENTS COURT CHARM 1969
22 kt. gold finish charm. Given to all representatives of the team in each district. **CMV $10.**

4A BLUE ENAMEL PIN 1978
Gold tone & blue enamel pin. Comes in Avon box. No information on what it's for. **CMV $12. MB.**

AWARDS & REPRESENTATIVES GIFTS

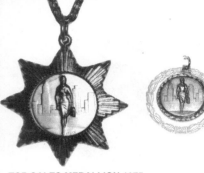

TIE TAC AWARD 1969
Small 1/10 10K gold tie tac given to Avon Male Executive with blue sapphire in center. Came in Avon Box. **CMV $50 MB.**

TOP SALES MEDALLION 1975
Gold colored metal medallion. Avon lady carrying case. Italy at bottom of foot. No Avon on it. Given to Avon Reps. for top sales and touring Springdale plant. 2 different designs. One star & one round. **CMV $17, $22.50 MB each.**

TOUR GUIDE JACKET GUARDS 1966
Silver color aluminum with 4A design. Used by Avon plant tour guides. **CMV $32.50.**

15 YEAR SERVICE CUFF LINKS 1970's
4A design on face and Avon 15 years Loyal Service on back with persons initials. Given to Avon male executives after 15 years service with Avon. Made of solid 10K gold. **CMV $300. pair mint.** Also came 30 year service. Same cuff links. **Same CMV.**

DEDICATED TO SERVICE AWARD 1962
1886-1962 4A deisgn - gold tone. **CMV $10.**
GREAT OAK NO. 1 MEDALLION AWARD 1980
Small medal - Avon Oak Tree on one side, Pasadena No. 1 - 1980 4A deisgn on other side. **CMV $12.**
CIRCLE OF EXCELLENCE PIN 1970'S
Brass - 4A design and C of E Managers only. **CMV $15.**

4A DOUBLE STICK PIN AWARD 1960'S - 1970'S
10K gold double 4A stick pin. We have no information on what it is. Please contact Bud Hastin if you know. Comes in Avon box. **CMV $75. MB.**

RETIREMENT PIN 1967
Gold disk with raised 4A design hanging from a golden bow. Given to retiring representatives with 10 years or more of service. **CMV $50.**

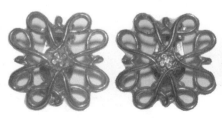

DISTINGUISHED MANAGEMENT AWARD EARRINGS 1965-68
4A design clip-on earrings. **CMV $35. pair MB.**

4A MENS CUFF LINKS 1966
Silver links with 4A design. Given to plant & office employees only. **CMV $35. pr.**

TOUR GUIDE JACKET GUARDS 1973
Gold metal with pressed flower in center of 4A. Used by Avon plant tour guides. **CMV $25.**

PRESIDENT'S CLUB LADY'S PINS 1979-80
Gold colored 4A pin - 79 in middle is 1st of an annual 4A year pin given to President's Club Reps. for meeting sales goal for that year. **CMV $5. each year.**

PRESIDENT'S CLUB MEN'S TIE TAC 1980-81
Small gold tone 4A - 81 on face. Given to male President's Club members.
CMV $15., $20. MB.

PRESIDENT'S CLUB MEN'S PIN AWARD 1979-80
Gold tone 4A design & 79 on one & 80 on the other. Given to all male President's Club members. Smaller than lady's pin. CMV $15, $20. MB.

AVON HAWAIIAN HOLIDAY CHARM AWARD 1965
14K gold given to 7 avon managers in Hawaii in 1965. Each manager had their initials put on back. CMV $150.00

CHARM "DAY TO REMEMBER" AWARD 1976
Small gold tone charm marked "A Day to Remember - C21-76" Came in blue Avon box. CMV $15. MB.

PRESIDENT'S CELEBRATION GREAT OAK MANAGER CHARM AWARD 1980
Sterling silver cut out great oak tree charm. Comes with oak tree card in Avon box. Given to top managers in each district. CMV $100. MB. 1 top manager in each division won a cut out silver oak charm with sapphire around edge. CMV $150. MB. 1 top manager in each branch won same charm only with Ruby's around edge. CMV $200. MB. The top manager in the U.S. won same cut out oak charm with a diamond. Very Rare. CMV not established.

DISTRICT MANAGERS CHARM BRACELET 1980
Sterling silver chain & heart shaped charm says "DM 1980". Came in Tiffany & Co. Box. Given to District Managers at September conference. CMV $75.

PRESIDENT'S CELEBRATION NECKLACE 1980
Gold tone charm with Great Oak on one side & The President's Celebration 1980 on other side. Given to top Reps. in each district. CMV $10. MB. Same charm in silver tone given to 10 top winning district Reps. CMV $15. MB.

SALES LEADERSHIP AWARD 1980
Gold tone & black face. Says "Outstanding Sales Leadership" 5th Qtr. 1979-80 Avon. Came with red neck velvet ribbon. CMV $40.

PRESIDENT'S CELEBRATION SALES ACHIEVEMENT MEDAL 1981
(Left) Dated Dec. 11, 1981 on back side. Only 1 given to each branch. Put on red, white and blue ribbon. CMV $150.
PRESIDENT'S CAMPAIGN KEY CHAIN 1976
(Right) Chrome & white with red letters. Given to President's Club Reps. CMV $10.

CIRCLE OF EXCELLENCE PIN 1987
Small pin C of E 1987 4A design. CMV $10.

ALBEE KEY CHAIN 1987
Blue & gold tone. For sponsorship of new Reps. CMV $15.
SPONSORSHIP PIN 1986
Gold tone pin for sponsorship. CMV $10.

90th ANNIVERSARY BICENTENNIAL PENDANT AWARD 1976
Brass coin & chain given to Reps. for selling $285. worth of Avon in 2 campaigns. Front & back view shown. **CMV $15. MB.**

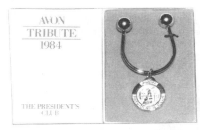

INTERNATIONAL RUNNING CIRCUIT MEDALION & NECKLACE 1978-82
Silver tone medalion given to winners in each city in each age group for running in Avon races. Came in black & gold box. Rare.**CMV $125.00 MB.**

PRESIDENT'S CLUB ACHIEVEMENT PINS AWARD 1984-85-86
Brass pin with stones for sales increase. 4 steps, 1 stone, 2 stones, 3 stones, 4 stones. 1984 - Red Stones - 1985 - Pearl - 1986 - Blue Stones. **CMV $10. 1 stone., CMV $15. 2 stones., CMV $20. 3 stones., CMV $25. 4 stones.**

PERFECT ATTENDANCE PIN 1979-82
Gold tone pin given to Avon Branch employee for perfect attendance at work for a 1 year period. Marked with each year record. **CMV $25.**

PRESIDENT'S CLUB KEY RING AWARD 1984
Gray box says Avon Tribute 1984. Gold tone with Albee charm. **CMV $15.**

BLUE HEART AVON AWARD PIN 1986
Silver tone pin with blue heart stone. Given to Reps in Newark branch for 3 orders.**CMV $10. MB.**

GOLD FEVER AWARD 1985
Small walnut plaque imprinted in wood says "Avon Gold Fever Additions Achievement Sept. 1985" with winners name on brass plaque. 1 oz. 999 fine pure gold "Avon 4A Pasadena" gold coin. Coin is loose but must be with plaque. **CMV $50. plus current value of 1 oz. of gold.**

ROYAL AVON PIN 1985
Blue, white & green enamel lapel pin. Given to Managers. **CMV $10.00**
AVON 86 ROSE PIN 1986
Gold tone Rose-Avon 86 lapel pin given to Avon Reps. **CMV $5.**
GOLD DIGGER PIN 1987
Small gold tone pick ax. Not marked Avon. Given for signing new avon Reps.**CMV $5.**

I LOVE AVON PIN AWARD 1985
Gold tone - red heart. **CMV $5.**
LIBERTY PIN AWARD 1985
Avon on front. **CMV $5.**

"CLOCK" AVON QUARTZ AWARD 1988
Clear lucite with red front clock, Mirror back. **CMV $15.00**
INDEX ALARM CLOCK & CALCULATOR AWARD 1990
Black case, red letters. **CMV $20.00**
AVON HOWARD MILLER CLOCK AWARD 1989
Maroone case, brass Avon front. **CMV $10.00**

AVON 5000 PIN 1985
(Left) Red, black & gold pin says Avon 5000. Given to Reps for top sales. **CMV $15.**
THOUSANDAIR CLUB 5000 PIN 1986
(Center) White & gold and red pin with "TC 1886-1986 $5,000.00" on face. **CMV $15.**
THOUSANDAIRE CLUB PIN 1986
(Right) White, gold & red pin 1886-1986. **CMV $10.**

4A STICK PIN AWARD 1980
1" 4A design in silver tone, gold outer trim. **CMV $10.**

AVON PIN AWARD 1987
Gold tone Avon pin. **CMV $15.**
PRESIDENT'S CLUB PIN AWARD 1987
Gold tone with hanging rose. **CMV $25.**
ALBEE AVON 100 PIN - ENGLAND 1986
Gold tone. Blue enamel. **CMV $65.**

PRESIDENT'S CLUB PIN "MENS" 1984
Brush gold tone stick pin or tie tac. Given to male Reps for meeting sales goals. 4A design on each. **1st goal 1 red ruby. CMV $35., 2 Rubys $50., 3 Rubys $75., 4 Rubys $100., All MB. In black velvet box. Maroon liner.**

SPONSORSHIP MEDALLION AWARD 1985
Gold tone pendant on white ribbon. **CMV $10.**
CIRCLE OF EXCELLENCE MEDALLION AWARD 1981
Gold tone 4A design, 1981 on back. Red ribbon. **CMV $10.**

GREAT OAK CUFF LINK AWARD 1983
Sterling Silver - not marked Avon. Plain black box. Given to male Div. Managers. **CMV $100.**
GREAT OAK COIN AWARD 1981
Sterling Silver coin says Kansas City #1 - 1981 with great oak tree. Given to Managers in Tiffany bag & box. **CMV $40.**

HONOR SOCIETY PIN 1987
HS on gold tone pin.
Level 1 - Has a Ruby. **CMV $15.**
Level 2 - Has a Sapphire. **CMV $20.**
Level 3 - Has a Diamond. **CMV $25.**
PRESIDENT'S CLUB PIN 1987
Gold tone pin with "PC" on face.
Level 1 - Has a Pearl. **CMV $10.**
Level 2 - Has a Topaz. **CMV $15.**

CHARM BRACELET AWARD 1980
Sterling silver charm & heart pendant. Both dated 1980 & "S.C." for Sales Coordinator & "TL" for Team Leader.
Comes in blue bag & blue Tiffany box, with white bow ribbon. **CMV "SC" $90. MB., CMV "TL" $40. MB.**

5 YEAR HEART KEY RING AWARD 1980s
In Tiffany box. Sterling silver. For 5 year Avon service. **CMV $15.**
OAK TREE ATLANTA BRANCH PENDANT 1976
(Right) Gray pewter on neck chain. **CMV $15.**

GROUP SALES LEADER I.D. PIN 1984
Gold tone stick pin comes in red velvet box. Pin says GSL - Avon. Comes with outer sleeve with Lang all over it. **CMV $15. MB.**

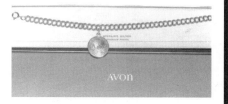

AVON SALES ACHIEVEMENT AWARD BRACELET 1975
Given for sales. Avon on one side and sales achievement on the other. Sterling. **CMV $15., $20. MB.**

GROUP SALES LEADER PIN AWARD 1983
Gold tone - 4A design. **CMV $8.**
MORTON GROVE 25 YEAR PIN 1981
Silver tone pin - not sterling. **CMV $8.**

#1 DIAMOND HEART PENDANT AWARD 1979
Given to top Manager for top sales. 7 diamond on gold heart & chain. **CMV $50.**
#1 PENDANT AWARD 1976
Given for top sales in Morton Grove Branch. Gold tone pendant. **CMV $15.**

HAPPY ANNIVERSARY NECKLACE 1964
For 38 years as a representative. October 1964. **CMV $35.**

TEAM LEADER PIN 1974
(Right) Gold raised letters & rim. Given to team leaders. **CMV $4., $6. MB.**
TEAM LEADER PIN 1975
(Left) Gold with indented letters. Given to team leaders. **CMV $4., $6. MB.**

SALES ACHIEVEMENT AWARD PENDANT 1977
1" gold pendant with 18" chain. Says 1977 Avon Sales Achievement Award & 4A design on other side. Came in white Avon box. Given to top 10% of sales Reps. in each division. **CMV $15. MB.** Same pendant slightly larger - came in blue box. **CMV $20. MB.**

FIELD OPERATIONS AWARD 1968
Solid brass, Avon 4A emblem on front. Field operations seminar on back. Given to managers in Pasadena branch in Better Way program. **CMV $55.**
GOLF LEAGUE CHARM 1960
1960 on back. Front has Avon League with 4A design & golfer. Solid brass. Given to Avon plant employees, Pasadena branch, for playing golf tournament. **CMV $40.**

SALES ACHIEVEMENT AWARD 1979
Solid bronze with Oak Tree on front with "District Manager Quarterly Sales Achievement Award - Avon" 4A symbol on back. Given to managers only. **CMV $50.**

RUNNING CIRCUIT AVON MEDAL 1980
2 1/4" medal has red, white and blue ribbon & medal says "Avon International Running Circuit." Given to people who ran in Avon Running Circuit. **CMV $25.**

STAR PRESIDENTS CLUB PIN AWARD 1991
Gold tone pin marked "PC" **CMV $10. MB.**
STAR HONOR SOCIETY PIN AWARD 1991
Gold tone pin marked "HS". Comes in 4 different levels of sales. $16,000. - $30,000. - $50,000. - $75,000. **CMV $10. - $15. - $20. - $25. MB. each.**

PRESIDENT'S CLUB MEN'S POCKET WATCH AWARD 1981
Gold tone Swiss made 17 jewel watch. Avon on face of watch, metal face cover. Given to male President's Club members. **CMV $100 MB.**

PRESIDENT'S SALES CHALLENGE AWARD WATCH 1982
Black face, Avon Quartz & small diamond on 12 on face. Gold tone case. Black lizard strap. 1 top rep in each district won. Came in Avon gray felt case & outer sleeve. **CMV $100 MB & sleeve.**
Same watch only gold face watch & no diamond & black lizard look leather strap in tan felt Avon case & outer sleeve. 20 given in each district to Presidents Club reps only. **CMV $30 MB sleeve.**

CLOCK 20 YEAR AWARD 1978
(left) Small brass Tiffany & Co. Quartz clock. Top engraved "Avon 20 years & winners initials". Given to Avon managers for 20 years service. CMV $75.

CLOCK AUGUST CONFERENCE AWARD 1978
(right) Brass Relice 400 electronic clock. Given to managers for going to August Conference 1978, bottom engraved. CMV $50.

HOLIDAY BEAR 1993
10" high white stuffed teddy bear. Red cap and shirt. Says "Happy Holiday's AVON". Sold only to reps CMV $10.

HOLIDAY SWEATSHIRT 1993
White cotton sweatshirt with Santa and Bears on front in red. Sold to reps. CMV $17.

HOLIDAY MUG 1993
White coffee mug with Santa and Bears on one side, "Happy Holiday's AVON" on other side. Sold only to Reps. CMV $4. MB.

CIRCLE OF EXCELLENCE AWARD CLOCK 1982
Clear lucite digital clock with engraved name of winning Avon manager. Is not marked Avon. CMV $50.

PRESIDENTS CLUB CARD CASE AWARD 1982
Silver plated card case in Tiffany box & felt bag. Engraved on case "Presidents Club & 4A design". CMV $20 MB.

NEWARK FIRST AWARD CLOCK 1973
Alfry electric clock, black face, white painted over brass. Back side says "Newark First 1973" plus owners initials. Given to district supervisors. CMV $40.

HONOR SOCIETY CLOCK 1986
Small Lucite quartz clock given for selling $15,000 in Avon. CMV $20.

CIRCLE OF EXCELLENCE HOUR GLASS AWARD 1981
Tall brass hour glass C of E. 1981 on top. CMV $50.

40th AVON ANNIVERSARY CLOCK AWARD 1981
Hamilton Quartz clock, glass dome, Avon 40th name plate on base for 40 years of service. CMV $100.

CUSTOMER SERVICE AWARD CLOCK 1980
(left) Brass Tiffany & Co. clock given to Avon managers. Engraved on top "Avon Customer Service Award Conference 1980". Comes in Tiffany box & felt bag. CMV $75.

MILLION DOLLAR INCREASE AWARD CLOCK 1981
(right) Gold tone round Seth Thomas alarm clock. Given to managers for 1 million dollar increase in sales. Engraved on back side "Our First Million $ Increase". CMV $65.

CLOCK - FIELD OPERATION SEMINAR 1970
(Left) Brass Relide 7 jewel clock. CMV $50.

CLOCK - SUMMER SHAPE UP AWARD 1970
(Right) Brass Linder clock - top inscribed "Summer Shape Up Award." CMV $75.

SELLATHON CLOCK AWARD 1981
Mirrow Clock. CMV $20.

CLOCK SPEEDWAY DIVISION AWARD 1978
For outstanding sales. **CMV $35.**
SALES CLUB AWARD 1977
$100,000 sales increase plaque. Atlanta
Branch. **CMV $15.**

HEAT CLOCK AWARD 1981
(Left) Clear lucite - red face - Avon on front.
CMV $20.
CLOCK PICTURE FRAME AWARD 1983
(Right) Clear lucite, purple & red clock face.
Avon on front. **CMV $25.**

CLOCK "WE'RE HOT" AWARD 1982
White plastic Isis quartz battery clock. **CMV
$75.**
CLOCK "AVON" AWARD 1982
White plastic Isis electric clock. Face is red &
marked Avon. **CMV $75.**

**25 YEAR WATCH BAUME & MERCIER
AWARD**
Gold case watch. Given for 25 year Avon
service. Back inscribed "Avon - 25 years."
CMV $75. plus value of used watch.

**MEN'S PRESIDENTS SALES
CHALLENGE WATCH AWARD 1982**
(Left) Gold tone case & face marked Avon.
Black strap. Avon box. **CMV $100. MB.**
WINNING IS BEAUTIFUL WATCH AWARD
(Right) Ladies quartz watch. Avon on face &
on box. **CMV $25. MB.**

**1974 PRESIDENT'S CLUB MEMBERS
WATCH**
Awarded to club members. Gold watch &
hands with black strap. Box blue & white.
CMV $30. MB.

**PRESIDENT'S CLUB 1981 WATCH
WOMEN'S 1980**
(left) gold tone 17 jewel watch on chain. Back
says "President's Club 81". **CMV $30. MB.**
**PRESIDENT'S CLUB 1981 MEN'S WATCH
1980**
(right) gold tone pocket watch on chain given
to male President's Club Reps. Inscribed on
back "President's Club 1981". **CMV $100 MB.**
No face cover, **CMV $100 MB.**

COLOR UP WATCH AWARD 1979
Le Jour Time Co. watch in gold tone case,
white strap. Back side says "For the most
colorful time of your life". Came in white box,
sleeve & blue felt wrap. Given to Reps for
customers served. **CMV $25 MB.**

PENDANT WATCH AWARD 1970
Gold tone watch on neck chain given to 6
Reps. in each district for top sales. Made by
Sheffield. Also sold in stores. 9,000 watches
given by Avon. **CMV $20.**

**DIVISION MANAGERS AWARD
CLOCK 1969**
Sterling silver Seth Thomas electric
clock. 4" square face, bottom says,
"Divisional Managers Tribute
1969".**CMV $100.00 mint.**

Color never looked so good!

MARY RAMCZYK
1978
NAT. DISTRICT MANAGER PANELIST

AVON MANAGERS ACHIEVEMENT CLOCK 1968
Box with 4A design & outer Avon sleeve. Clock set in top of brushed gold hour glass inscribed on bottom "1968 Avon Managers Achievement". **CMV $75 clock only., $100 MB with outer sleeve.**

TEAM LEADER WATCH 1977
Given to all Avon team leaders for Christmas 1977. 2 different. (left) for women, (right) for men. The cases are different and the difference in size of winding stem. Very few of the mens watches given. **CMV for womens $40 MB., CMV for mens $100 MB.**
MANAGERS WATCH 1977
Avon watch same as team leader watch only face says Avon in place of Team Leader & 4A symbol that rotates instead of Avon. Came in male & female size watch as above. **CMV $75 MB.**

OUTSTANDING SALES MANAGEMENT CLOCK AWARD 1977
Relide 15 jewel Swiss solid brass clock. Inscribed on top "In Recognition of Outstanding Sales Management - Third Quarter 1977". Given to No. 1 Avon manager in each division. **CMV $100.00**

WATCH STICK PIN, MANAGERS 1979
(left) Gold tone 4A design on face. Given to managers. **CMV $75.**
FIELD SUPPORT PENDANT AWARD 1978
(right) 1/20 12K gold filled. Back is dated "1978 Field Support Manager". Given to managers. **CMV $30.**
NAT. DISTRICT MANAGER PANELIST PIN 1978
(bottom) Gold tone. Given to managers. **CMV $10.**

PRESIDENT'S CELEBRATION CLOCK AWARD 1974
Solid brass clock with "President's Celebration 1974" on face. Clock made by Relide, 15 jewels. Given to Avon managers. Came in plain box & pink felt bag. **CMV $75. mint.**

LIBERTY CLOCK AWARD 1977
Given to managers for 1 million dollar sales increase. Gold tone clock by Bulova. Inside slide clock cover says "To a Million Dollar Baby (name of manager) Division $1,000,000 Sales Increase 1977". Came in Bulova Americana Collection. **CMV $75.**

PRESIDENT'S CELEBRATION AWARD CLOCK 1976
Gold plastic & metal Westclock. 4 red roses on face. Was not made only for Avon. **CMV $12.**

ANTIQUE CAR GLASSES 1971
Eight different glasses picturing Stanley Steamer, Silver Duesenberg, Gold Cadillac, Sterling Six, Electric Charger, Packard Roadster, Touring T & Straight Eight. Selling 10 Avon cars won a set of 4 glasses. Selling 15 Avon cars won a set of 8 glasses. **CMV set of 4 $12, set of 8 $27.50 MB.**
ANTIQUE CAR PITCHER 1971
Reps. won this by having one person they recommended a representative appointed. Also available in prize catalog for 1,400 points. 2 different pitchers. Rare one has silver Duesenberg & Stanley Steamer on it. **CMV $35, $40 MB.** Most of them have Straight Eight & Packard Roadster decal on it. **CMV $25, $30. MB.**

HOURS FOR EXCELLENCE CLOCK AWARD 1977
Gold label on top of Bulova travel alarm. Does not say Avon. Given to Reps. **CMV $15 MB.**

DIARY CLOCK 1968
Made by Seth Thomas. Gold, back opens & says "Avon Award", **CMV $40.**

ROSE ANNIVERSARY PITCHER AWARD 1980
9" tall clear glass with engraved rose. Given to Reps. for selling $800 in C14-15 1980. **CMV $25 MB.**

ROSE ANNIVERSARY GOBLETS AWARD 1980
6 1/2" high with engraved rose. Set of 4 for selling $400 in C14-15 1980. **CMV $15 set of 4.**

KEY CHAIN SERVICE AWARD 10 YEARS 1970's
Gold tone key chain with blue stone in center of 4A design. Comes in Avon white & green lined box. Given to managers. **CMV $15 MB.**

20 YEAR SERVICE AWARDS 1980's
Given for 20 years service. All are marked Avon or has 4A emblem on it. All from Tiffany. Choice of:
STERLING SILVER PICTURE FRAME
9" high x 7" wide. **CMV $100.**
QUARTZ POLISHED BRASS CLOCK
2 1/2" square. **CMV $75.**
CRYSTAL CANDLESTICKS - TALL
9 1/4" high, 4 1/8" wide baase. **CMV $75 set.**
CRYSTAL CANDLESTICKS - SHORT
4 1/2" high x 4 1/8" wide base. **CMV $75 set.**

PRESIDENTS COUNCIL PICTURE ALBUM AWARD 1995.
Silver plated cover says "New Orleans 95". Blue velvet book. **CMV $50.00 Mint**

PIN "WATCH US GROW" AWARD 1981
(left) Gren & white tie tac type pin . Says "Newark - Watch us Grow". Given to managers. **CMV $5.**
NEWARK NO. 1 1982 PENDANT AWARD 1982
(right) Gold tone 1/2" size pendant. Given to managers No. 1 in sales. Brown box. **CMV $15 MB.**

HOP SKIP & JUMP MEDAL AWARD 1982
Gold tone medal with 4A design on one side & Hop, Skip & Jump Order Count Growth 1982 on back. Hangs on blue & yellow ribbon. **CMV $25.**

20 YEAR SERVICE AWARDS 1980's
Given for 20 years service. All are marked Avon or has 4A design. All come from Tiffany & Co. Choice of:
CRYSTAL PITCHER
5 3/4" high. **CMV $60.**
CRYSTAL VASE
7 1/2" wide. **CMV $60.**
CRYSTAL TULIP WINE GLASSES
Set of 6, 8" high. **CMV $75 set.**

HEART PRESIDENTS SALES CHALLENGE AWARD 1982
Small clear crystal heart on gold tone ribbon pin. Maroon velvet Avon box & outer sleeve. **CMV $10 MB with sleeve.**

ROSE STICK PIN AWARD 1981
Small Sterling silver rose. No markings in Tiffany & Co. turquoise box. Given to Avon reps for recruiting & sales goals. **CMV $20 MB**

20 YEAR SERVICE CLOCK AWARD 1980's
7" wide x 4 1/2" high Tiffany brass clock. Avon on top. Given for 30 years service at Avon. **CMV $75.**

30 YEAR SERVICE PEARL NECKLACE AWARD 1980's
17" long cultured pearl necklace with 14K gold Avon marked clasp. Given for 30 years service. Comes in blue holder from Tiffany. **CMV $75 mint.**

PENDANT - PRESIDENTS CELEBRATION 1980
Sterling silver chain & pendant with 25 blue sapphires around edge. Oak tree in center. Back says "The Presidents Celebration 1980 Avon". Given to 250 top managers in US, 1 per division. **CMV $150.**

CIRCLE OF EXCELLENCE TRINKET BOX 1982
Small leaded glass box with Rose embossed on lid. Comes with 4A brass coin. Back says "Roman Holiday C of E 1982". Only given to Pasadena Branch managers. **CMV $35 box & coin.**

PRESIDENTS CLUB PIN AWARD 1981
Gold tone pin with 81 in center of 4A design cut out. **CMV $5 MB.**

DOOR KNOCKER TIE TAC AWARD 1970's
10K gold. Given to male executives at Avon. **CMV $60.**

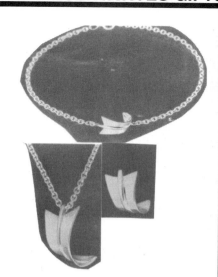

PRESIDENTS SALES COMPETITION JEWELRY AWARDS 1983
3 levels, all Sterling Silver made by Tiffany.
BRACELET
Given 10 to a district. **CMV $25 MB.**
PENDANT NECKLACE
Given 2 to a district. **CMV $35 MB.**
LAPEL PIN
Given to each rep in top sales group who met individual sales goals. **CMV $15 MB.**
Each comes in Tiffany box & Avon card.

PRESIDENT'S CLUB HOLIDAY PLATE GIFT SET 1994
Avon Box holds 4 arcoroc clear glass plates with sleigh ride and evergreen tree scene. **CMV $15. Set MB.**

PRESIDENT'S CLUB PIN AWARD 1993-94
Gold Tone "A" pin with "P.C." on it. For 1st year President's Club Reps. **CMV $10. MB.**

"DAVID H. MCCONNELL CLUB" AWARD PIN 1993-94
Gold-tone "A" pin with "D.M." on it. Given to Reps for $50,000 in sales in 12 months. **CMV $25. MB.**

AVON HONOR'S SALES AWARD 1994
Lucite top with black base and mirror. Given to Reps for top sales in district. **CMV $50.**

HONOR SOCIETY AWARD PIN 1993-94
Gold-tone "A" pin with "H.S." on it. Given to Reps who had $16,000 in sales in 12 months. **CMV $15. MB.**

PRESIDENT'S COUNCIL DIAMOND AWARD PIN 1993-94
14K gold "A" pin with small diamond onn side. Given to Reps for $75,000 in sales in 12 months. **CMV $60. MB.**

PRESIDENT'S INNER CIRCLE AWARD PIN 1993-94
14K gold square pin with cut out "A" and 3 small diamonds. Says "Inner Circle" on bottom. Given to Reps for $200,000 in sales in 12 months. **CMV $125.00 MB.**

ROSE CIRCLE AWARD PIN 1993-94
Gold-tone "A" pin with "R.C." on it. Given to Reps who had $30,000 in sales in 12 months. **CMV $20. MB.**

TREE ORNAMENT FOR REPS. 1994
Metal Avon Rep tree ornament. Given to Avon Reps. **CMV $5.**

SPIRIT OF AVON AWARD PLATE 1990'S
8" glass plate, frosted trim. Given in "Star Tribute" sales program to top Reps. **CMV $30.**

STAR TRIBUTE AWARD FRAME 1990
6 3/4" high, 5 1/8" wide picture frame, gold ribbon and PC on frame. Given to top sales Reps. **CMV $20.**

REP AWARD PINS 1998
Each given to Avon Reps for reaching higher level sales goals each year. Antique looking pins with blue cameo like center stone.
PRESIDENTS CLUB PIN.
Marked "PC" **CMV $10. MB.**
HONOR SOCIETY PIN
Marked "HS". **CMV $15. MB.**
ROSE CIRCLE PIN
Marked "RC". **CMV $20. MB.**
D.H. McCONNELL PIN
Marked "DHM". **CMV $25. MB.**

TIE TAC MEN'S PRESIDENTS CLUB AWARD 1981-82
Gold tone 4A design Tie Tac given to men's Presidents Club. Comes in Avon box with 2 different backs as shown. **CMV $20 MB.**

FASHION HISTORY GLASSES AWARD 1980
Set of 6, 12 oz. glasses marked 1890's, 1920's, 1940's, 1950's, 1960's & 1970's. Given as set to Avon reps for signing up new Avon reps. **CMV $20 set.**

TEST DIVISION HEART PENDANT AWARD 1981
(left) Sterling silver & gold heart pendant & silver chain. Given to managers only in Tiffany & Co. box. **CMV $150 MB.**

ANNIE PENDANT MANAGERS 1982
(right) 14K gold filled pendant & chain. Back marked "I love you" & marked DM on side. Given to district managers. Came in gray Avon box with special card from Avon. **CMV $60 MB.**

PRESIDENTS CLUB VANITY BOX AWARD 1995
Silver plate top on glass box. "PC" on front & back side. Given to Reps. **CMV $50.MB.**

PRECIOUS MOMENTS CHRISTMAS MOUSE 1980
(Right) Given to Avon Reps. for signing up 2 new Avon Reps. **CMV $55 MB.**

COLLECTORS CORNER FIGURINE AWARD 1982
Cherished Moments Collection mouse figurine. Given to 25 Reps. for top sales in Campaign 8, 1982 in each district. **CMV $25 MB.**

PRECIOUS MOMENTS AWARD 1980
Rabbit figurine marked on bottom "President's Club Luncheon 1980". Given to Reps. at President's Club Luncheon only. **CMV $20 MB.**

GOING AVON CALLING AWARD 1982
Yellow ceramic car with rabbit in pink, green base. Given to reps for Recommendation prize. **CMV $50 MB.**

COME RAIN OR SHINE AWARD 1983
Ceramic Cherished Moments Rabbit with screw on ceramic umbrella. Given to reps for sales goals. 1st of 3 levels. **CMV $25 MB.**

TOP HAT AWARD 1991
3 7/8" high, 5" x 51/2" base, Black ceramic top hat. "Avon 1991" embossed on top. "You're the top. Tribute 1991" on black ribbon band around hat. Given for top sales. **CMV $15.**

PRECIOUS MOMENTS AWARD SET 1980
(Left) Set of 3 rabbit figurines given to Reps. for top sales. No. 1 is "**Ready for an Avon Day**". **CMV $25.**
No. 2 is "**My first call**". **CMV $35.**
No. 3 is "**Which shade do you prefer**". **CMV $60.**
Set of 3 CMV $110. Made in Japan only for Avon.

SMALL TREASURE CHERISHED MOMENTS MINI'S AWARD 1982
Pink box holds 3 mini rabbit ceramic figurines. Given to reps for Step 4 sales goals. **CMV $15 MB set.**

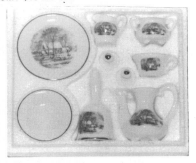

SMALL TREASURES CURRIER & IVES MINIS AWARDS 1982
Pink box holds mini ceramic Tea Set. Given to reps for Step 2 of sales goal. Made in Japan. **CMV $15 MB set.**

SMALL TREASURE MINI ROSE AWARD 1982
Pink box holds small green leaf & pink ceramic rose. "The Avon Rose" on base, made in Taiwan. Given to reps for Step 1 of sales goal. **CMV $5 MB.**

PRESIDENT'S AWARD PERFUME 1963
(Right)Clear glass with stopper, silver 4A tag & string. Given to national winners in each division for President's Campaign, 1963. Box silver & white base with clear plastic lid. Bottom label on bottle says "Occur! Perfume Avon Products, Inc. N.Y., N.Y. contains 1 fl. oz.". **CMV $200.00 bottle only., $250.00 MB with label & tag.** Also came in 1/2 oz. size with gold neck 4A tag. Please write Bud Hastin if you know when and what the 1/2 oz. size was given for.

WE DID IT TOGETHER AWARD 1985
2 rabbit ceramic figurine in Cherished Moments Award series to Reps. **CMV $25. MB.**

OCTOBER 8 AWARD 1951
1 dram Forever Spring Perfume, smooth gold cap & bottle. Given to each representative sending an order in campaign 12, 1951. **CMV $40 MB.**

PERFUME - CIRCLE OF EXCELLENCE 1978
1 oz. glass stopper bottle, made in France. Paper neck tag says "Made Exclusively For You. Circle of Excellence 1978". **CMV $100.00 mint.**

REPRESENTATIVE CHRISTMAS GIFT 1975
Clear glass in blue box. Reproduction of Trailing Arbutus Powder Sachet. **CMV $10. MB.**

CHRISTMAS GIFT PERFUME 1963
Given to Avon sales ladies for Christmas. The bottle at left is same as the one sealed in gold plastic container with green tassel & red ribbon. 4-10 oz. Christmas gift given to all representatives submitting an order in Dec. 1963. **CMV $40 complete., Bottle only $15.**

GOLDEN SLIPPER AWARD 1959
All gold metal slipper with red stone in toe & clear plastic heel. 1/2 oz. glass stoppered perfume bottle fits in slipper toe . No Avon name on shoe but has paper label on bottom of bottle saying "73rd Anniversary. Avon Products, Inc." Given to each representative in the winning group of each branch for top sales. **CMV $100 slipper & bottle with label., $150 MB.**

AVON 100 THOUSANDAIRE CLUB PIN 1986
Red, white & gold lapel pin. Came with numbers to hang below. Marked 1886-1986. **CMV $10. No numbers.**
AVON 100 THOUSANDAIRE CLUB PIN 1985
Same pin only blue border design. **CMV $10.**

TASHA TEAM LEADER COLOGNE AWARD 1979
1.8 oz. spray cologne. Says "Team Leader 1979" in gold letters on front. Came in gold wrapped box with maroon color ribbon. **CMV $10 MB.**
TASHA "GO AHEAD AND DREAM" MANAGERS GIFT
Same bottle as above only "Go Ahead & Dream" in gold letters on face of bottle for managers at Christmas Conference. **CMV $20. MB.**

MANAGERS GIFT PERFUME 1950
(Left) 1/2 oz. glass stoppered bottle in plastic case. Given to managers to help introduce To A Wild Rose. Paper label on bottom reads "Perfume Avon Products, Inc., Distributor, New York, Montreal, Vol. 1/2 oz.". Came with neck tassel. **CMV $250 mint, in plastic case.**
PRESIDENT'S AWARD CELEBRATION PERFUME 1955
(Right) 1/2 oz. perfume, glass stopper. Given to the winning team members for top sales. **CMV $75 BO mint., $100 MB.**

GREAT OAK CARD CASE AWARD 1987
(TOP) Brass. **CMV $5.**
HONOR SOCIETY CARD CASE AWARD 1985
(BOTTOM) Brass card case. **CMV $10.**

AVON 100 AWARD PINS 1986
Small gold tone on left with black letters. **CMV $7.** Small silver tone with black letters. **CMV $7.**
TRENDSETTER PIN AWARD 1984
Gold tone pin. **CMV $10.**

PURSE OF GOLD AWARD 1948
Cardboard tube contained 8 samples of Golden Promise. CMV in packages shown. Given to each representative sending in an order at the close of campaign 3. **CMV $30.**

AVON 100 WATCH AWARD 1986
Black face quartz watch with Avon 100 on face - brown leather grain strap. Given to managers in Newark Branch. **CMV $65.**
AVON 100 PRESIDENT'S CLUB PIN 1986
Gold tone pin. Given to Reps. in black velvet Avon box. **CMV $15. MB.**
HONOR SOCIETY PIN 1986-87
Same as President's Club only came with Honor Society on bottom. **CMV $15.**

G.S.L. #1 PIN 1983
Red Pin. **CMV $10.**
AVON 100 TRENDSETTER PIN 1986
Blue, white & gold. **CMV $15.**
NIGHT MAGIC PIN 1987
CMV $2.
THOUSANDAIRE CLUB PIN 1985
Blue & white enamel. CMV with numbers up to 4. **CMV $10. Add $5 for each number up to 4.**
PEACH TREE PIN 1985
CMV $15.
AVON $1000 CLUB PIN 1986
CMV $10.
AVON LOVES ORDERS HEART PIN 1981
CMV $10.

AVON 100 GLASSES 1986
Set of 4 drinking glasses. Embossed Avon 100. **CMV $15. Set.**

AVON 100 MANAGERS COMPACT AWARD 1986
Gold tone. Inscribed on back "Avon Centennial 1986 Dist. Sales Managers Conference." **CMV $25.**

AVON 100 CALCULATOR 1986
Gold tone face Avon 1886 - 1986. Given to Managers. **CMV $10.**
AVON 100 BELL 1986
Clear glass bell, 5 3/4" high. Avon 100 embossed. **CMV $25.**

AVON 100 DESK CADDY 1986
Clear plastic with Avon 100 1886 - 1986 or caddy - white pen & note paper. Given to Managers. **CMV $15.**

AVON 100 BINOCULARS AWARD 1986
7 x 35 Binolux - Black. Given to Reps. Case says Avon 100. **CMV $75.**
AVON 100 TOTE BAG AWARD 1986
White canvas bag trimmed in blue & red. Given to people on trip to New York for 100 year celebration. **CMV $25.**
AVON 100 COFFEE CUP AWARD 1986
Blue ceramic cup. Avon 100 1886 - 1986 in gold letters. Given to representatives. **CMV $8.**

CENTENNIAL ARCH WATCH 1986
Enamelled arch stand with Avon face quartz pocket watch. Can be hung on chain around neck. Given to 10 top reps in each division for 100th anniversary. Comes in Avon 100 pink box & white Avon sleeve. **CMV $60.**

AVON 100 ALBEE MIRROR 1986
13" x 17" gold tone frame mirror. 1886 - 1986 & 1st Avon Rep embossed on mirror. Given to managers at August Conference & also given for sponsorship. **CMV $45.**

AVON 100 COFFEE MUG PASADENA 1986
White glass cup. Avon 100 on front. **CMV $10.**
AVON 100 PASADENA #1 AWARD 1986
Wood base, clear lucite Avon 100 plaque. **CMV $15.**

AVON 100 LEMONADE SET 1986
White plastic pitcher & 4 plastic Avon 100 glasses. **CMV $20.**

WORLD SALES LEADER RING AWARD 1984
(Left) 14K gold ring marked "Avon Division Sales Manager 1984" and Globe of the world. Very Rare. **CMV $300.**
"AVON 100" CENTENNIAL SALES LEADER RING AWARD 1986
(Right) All of above inscribed on 14K ring. Very rare. **CMV $300.**

AVON 100 CLOCK AWARD 1986
Clear lucite clock. Black face & letters. Given to Managers. **CMV $35.**

AVON 100 LIBERTY APRON 1986
Small red apron. White design from N.Y. Liberty Weekend. **CMV $25.**

AVON 100 HEAD BAND 1986
White head band. 100 years of beauty. **CMV $5.**

AVON 100 YEARS BAG CLOSER 1986
White plastic strip bag fastener. **CMV $1.**

AVON 100 CUP 1986
Plastic coffee cup. Look how good we look now. **CMV $1.**

AVON 100 LIBERTY WEEKEND T-SHIRT 1986
White T-shirt with collar. Given to workers on 4th of July Celebration in N.Y. **CMV $15.**

CENTENNIAL JEWELRY CASE AWARD 1986
8 3/4" square brass box. Given to Reps. **CMV $25.**

AVON NAME PLATE 1986
Gray & white plastic cork board. **CMV $2.**

100 YEAR ZIP LOCK FOR BAGS 1986
White & red letters. **CMV $1.**

PENS 1986
2 different. Both white, 1 Parker, 1 Shaffer. **CMV $15. ea.**

AVON 100 LICENSE PLATE 1986
1886 - 1986

AVON LICENSE PLATE 1986
White & red letters. **CMV both $2.**

I LOVE AVON LICENSE PLATE FRAME
White frame given to Reps. **CMV $5.**

CENTENNIAL JEWELRY COLLECTION AWARDS 1986
All gold tone & rhinestones. Given to Reps.
Pin **CMV $10.**
Earrings **CMV $15.**
Bracelet **CMV $15.**
Necklace **CMV $20.**

AVON 100 PLATE AWARD 1986
White porcelain plate. Back says C26 - 1985 Limited Edition. Pasadena Branch only. **CMV $25.**

CHECK BOOK COVER 1986
White plastic 1886 - 1986. Given to Avon Reps. **CMV $3.**

AVON 100 T-SHIRT AWARD 1986
White shirt, black letters, red trim. **CMV $10.**

NEWARK AVON FAMILY T-SHIRT AWARD 1987
White shirt, red design for Newark branch employees. **CMV $10.**

PRESIDENTS CLUB BIRTHDAY GIFT 1986
Chrome picture from "Avon 100" & note from James Preston Avon President. **CMV $8.**

MEDAL - 4A PENDANT AWARD 1980
Silver tone & black 4A design about 2 1/2" on red, white & blue neck ribbon. Given to managers only. Back says "You are a winner 1980" & name. **CMV $20.**

AVON 100 ROSE KEY CHAIN PENDANT 1986

Pink or gray Avon 100 box & sleeve has gold tone key chain & chain to use as necklace. Back says "Avon 1886-1986". Given to top 10 Reps. **CMV $15.**

"AVON 100" PILL BOX AWARD 1986

Small chrome box "Avon 100" on lid. Given at Presidents Club luncheon. **CMV $10.**

AVON 100 GOLD PIN AWARD 1986

14K gold. Small diamond. Given to Division Managers. **CMV $75.**

LIBERTY DIVISION PIN 1986

Blue & gold tone lapel pin. Status of liberty on face. Given to reps. **CMV $10.**

AVON 100 AWARD PINS 1986

Left is Newark branch Managers pins 14K gold. Has hook on back to wear as necklace. Back says Newark 1886-1986 14 K. **CMV $75. MB.**
Center is Newark branch. Gold tone. Larger in size. Very thin. **CMV $10.**
Right is Morton Grove Pin. Thicker gold tone. Design is different on all 3. **CMV $10.**

AWARD PINS MISC. 1986

AVON 2000 PIN
Black, white & gold. **CMV $10.**
AVON 100 PIN LARGE
1886-1986 - Black, red & gold. **CMV $10.**
AVON MEMBER PIN
Blue, black & gold. **CMV $10.**
AVON PIN
Black, red & gold. **CMV $10.**
AVON 100 PIN
Small black, red & gold. **CMV $10.**
AVON 100 PIN
Blue, white & red. **CMV $10.**
I LOVE AVON PIN
Black, red & gold. **CMV $10.**

AVON RAINBOW PIN 1986

CMV $15.
AVON BEAUTY ADVISOR PIN 1970s
CMV $15.
ARROW, APPLE PIN 1986
Red apple, white cross stick pin. **CMV $15.**
1-2 PIN 1970s
Gold tone. **CMV $25.**

AVON100 DIVISION SALES MEDALLIONS 1986

Gold tone, siver tone & bronze tone medallions. Each say PC-Avon 100. Given in each division, 1 gold, 4 silver & 5 bronze. **CMV $75. gold CMV $60. silverCMV $40. bronze**

PAPERWEIGHT CHRISTMAS IS FOR CHILDREN 1986

Avon - 1986 embossed clear glass. Given to Managers only at 6 places in U.S. **CMV $50.**

PAPERWEIGHT - GREAT OAK - AWARD 1981

Clear glass Avon, Kansas City #1-1981 etched on bottom. **CMV $50.**

GIVE N GAIN PRIZE 1970

10 3/4" high, 4" in diameter. A rose, butterfly and lady bug are etched in glass. Given to Avon ladies as prize. This was also sold in stores to public. Came in plain box with Avon stamped on it. Made by Abilities. **CMV $20 MB.**

RENAULT CAR GLASS 1971

(Right) Some sets came with this Renault car in set. Rare. **CMV $15.**

AVON 100 MIRROR 1986

Red plastic holder & Avon printed on mirror. **CMV $2.**

AVON 100 MATCHES 1986

Silver box. **CMV $1.**

RECOGNITION AWARD PIN 1974
About 1" size gold tone. Given to branch employees, rare. **CMV $35.**

REPRESENTATIVE OF THE MONTH PIN 1983-84
(Right) gold tone pin given to reps each month for meeting goals for the month. 2 in each district. Passed on to new rep each month. **CMV $10.**

45TH ANNIVERSARY VASE AWARD 1970'S
9 3/4" high x 4" across. Atlantis engraved "45th Avon Anniversary". Given for 45 years of Avon service. **CMV $200.**

PRESIDENTS DAY BOWL "LARGE" AWARD 1964
12 1/4" Oneida silver plate bowl. Center of bowl engraved with big 4A design & says "Presidents Day 1964 - Low Net." **CMV $45.**

PRESIDENTS DAY BOWL "SMALL" AWARD 1964
9 1/8" Oneida bowl as above. Center says "Presidents Day 1964 - Closest to Pin", 4A design. **CMV $40.**

SUBTLE REFLECTIONS HEART FLOWER VASE & FLOWERS 1982
Small heart shape lucite vase & silk flowers with Avon tag. Given to Presidents Club reps. Does not say Avon. **CMV $8.**

GOLDEN BELL COLLECTION AWARDS 1983
4 small brass bells given for meeting sales goals for C23, C24, C25, 1983. 1st bell has 4A design on top. 2nd bell has Acorn on top, 3rd bell has Avon door knocker. 4th bell was given if all 3 bells were won in all 3 campaigns as a bonus. 4th bell has a rose on top. **CMV 1st bell $10, 2nd bell $10, 3rd bell $15, 4th bell $20. MB. Add $5. to set if in plain boxes. For managers.**

CIRCLE OF EXCELLENCE CUP AWARD 1976
(left)Polished pewter cup says "C of E 1976" engraved on side. Given to Circle managers only. **CMV $25.**

VALENTINE ATOMIZER AWARD 1980
Small clear crystal bottle, chrome top & red squeeze bulb. Given to team leaders & district manager. TL on bottom & DM. **CMV $10, TL bottle MB. CMV $20, DM bottle MB.**

ROSE ANNIVERSARY LUNCHEON PLATES AWARD 1980
Set of 4 clear glass 8" plates with engraved rose in center. Given to Reps. for selling $600 in C14-15 1980. **CMV $20 set of 4 plates.**

AVON LADY STEMWARE GLASSES AWARDS 1975
C-20 1975. Set of 6, 10 oz. & 6, 6 oz. glasses with 1st Avon Lady design. 1 set given to all Reps. in the winning district for top sales. **CMV set $50. MB.**

GREAT AMERICAN SELLATHON CHAMPAGNE GLASS 1981
Given to team leaders and managers. December 1981 on trip to Hawaii. **CMV $15.**

AWARDS & REPRESENTATIVES GIFTS

INITIAL GLASS AWARD 1970
Campaign 12 & 13, 1970. Reps. won the glasses and President's Club members won the goblets with initial of their choice for reaching sales of their choice or reaching sales goals in each campaign. The coasters were won by both for reaching sales goals both campaigns. **CMV on coasters $2, glasses $2, goblets $3 each.**

1st DIVISION GLASS AWARD 1977
Lead crystal champagne glass given to No. 1 division Avon managers. **CMV $30.**
WINE GLASS FOR MANAGERS 1975
Yellow painted letters say "Avon Espana 1975". Came in 1975 Osborne Cream Sherry. Managers Gift Set on trip to Spain. **CMV $37.50.**

PASADENA BRANCH WINE GLASS 1974
No. 1 in sales. 429 given. "19 Avon 74 Pasadena Branch" on glasses. **CMV $15.**
CIRCLE OF EXCELLENCE GLASS 1974
Pasadena Branch No. 1 in sales C of E. Made by Fostoria, very thin glass. Only 30 given to managers. "C of E 1974" on side of glass. **CMV $25.** Same glass also came in 1973 & 1975. **Same CMV.**

ULTRA CRYSTAL EVENT GLASS AWARD 1981
Tiffany & Co. box holds 2 engraved glasses. Given to Reps. who met sales goal by drawing for winner at sales meeting. **CMV $50 set MB.**

CIRCLE OF EXCELLENCE WINE GLASS 1979
Given to managers. Glass embossed "C of E 1979". Came in sets of 2 glasses. **CMV $25 each glass.**
CIRCLE OF EXCELLENCE CHAMPAGNE GLASS 1980
"C of E 1980" embossed on glass. Given to managers only in sets of 2 glasses. **CMV $25 each glass.**

TEAM ACHIEVEMENT AWARD 1977
Goblet given in 1st and 3rd quarters to top team in each district. Came in white embossed Avon box. **CMV $10. each quarter. MB.**

SALES ACHIEVEMENT AWARD 1979
Small gold tone trophy with wood base. Says "Avon Sales Achievement Award." **CMV $10.**
HONOR SOCIETY GOBLET 1987
Clear glass with black 4A design. Given to top reps. **CMV $15.**

GOLD PANNER TROPHY 1981
Metal gold panner. Plaque says "Sierra Division Achievement Break the Bank" 4A - 1981. Given to managers. **CMV $50.**

$100,000 TROPHY AWARD 1982
Glass dome holds $100,000 of chopped up U.S. money. Says $100,000 on dome. Wood base. Brass plaque from Avon 4A design given to 1 manager in Pasadena Branch. **CMV $50.**

PICTURE FRAME RETIREMENT 1970s - 1980s
Sterling silver picture frame 8 x 10. Given to managers for retirement. Not marked Avon. Came with letters from Avon. **CMV $75.**

TRIBUTE VASE 1987
8" high clear glass vase. Embossed "Tribute 1987." Given to P.C. Reps only. **CMV $10.**
PRESIDENTS CLUB SILVER BASKET 1987
5 1/2" high silver plated basket. Has "PC Avon Presidents Club" tag attached. Given only to P.C. Reps only. **CMV $15.**

NEWARK #1 CRYSTAL BOX AWARD 1985-86
Lead crystal box with Newark with a heart 1985-1986 #1 embossed on glass lid. Given to managers in blue box. **CMV $25.**

AVON 100 CHAMPAGNE AWARD 1986
1886-1986 Avon 100 label. Given to Honor Society Reps. **CMV $25.**

FOSTERIA COIN GLASS BUD VASE AWARD 1970s
8" high in Avon box. **CMV $30. MB**
FOSTERIA COIN GLASSES SALT & PEPPER SHAKER AWARDS 1970s
Came with Avon literature. **CMV $15. set.**

CHRISTMAS GIFT TO REPS 1986
Lead crystal dish from France given to all reps at Christmas in green box. **CMV $10. MB** Given to Presidents Club Members in red P.C. box. **CMV $15. MB**

ALL YOU CAN BE CANDY DISH AWARD 1984
Clear glass full of candy. Given to managers 1984. **CMV $15.**

PRESIDENTS SALES CHALLENGE FLOWER AWARD 1983
Glass & brass box holds orchid. Label on top. Given to Reps for trip to Hawaii. **CMV $45.**
CIRCLE OF EXCELLENCE WINE AWARD 1981
Bottle of Abbey Chenin Blanc wine. Special black & gold label for Circle of Excellence 1981. **CMV $40. unopened.**

COMBOURG CRYSTAL AWARDS 1985
Each given to P.C. Reps for sales goals. Crystal made in France not just for Avon.
CMV Decanter $25.
Set of 6 Champagne Glasses $20.
Set of 6 Wine Glasses $20.
Crystal & Chrome Ice Bucket $20.

REPRESENTATIVE X-MAS GIFT 1983
(Left) 3" ceramic box with dove on top. Bottom says "Holiday Greetings Avon 1983". Given to all avon Reps. **CMV $10. MB.**
REPRESENTATIVE X-MAS GIFT 1984
Heavy clear glass vase with snowflakes etching. Bottom says "Happy Holidays Avon 1984." Came in nice silver box & outter sleeve. **CMV $20. MB.**

AVON "THROUGH THE YEARS" THROW AWARD 1998
Large fabric throw with all the Avon & CPC logo's. Given to Reps for recruiting 5 new Avon Reps. **CMV $75.00 Mint.**

FRONT PAGE TUMBLERS 1971
14 oz. tumblers with Reps. name printed on "front page" of glass. Given for having a person reccommended as a Rep. appointed. **CMV $25 set of 8 MB.**

YOU MAKE ME SMILE GLASSES AWARDS 1978
Set of 6 glasses made only for Avon given to Avon Reps. for signing up a new Avon lady. **CMV $12 set MB.**

CERAMIC SAC AWARD 1986
White ceramic bag. Given to reps in U.S. & Canada. **CMV $20.**

SALES EXCELLENCE AWARD 1983
Lead crystal glass box. Inscribed "Sales Excellence Award 1983 Avon President's Sales Competition." **CMV $50.**

SPIRIT OF '76 CROCK SET AWARDS 1974
(Left) Multipurpose Pitcher - earned for $150 in sales. **CMV $7 MB.**
(Center) Bean Pot Casserole - earned for $200 in sales. **CMV $14 MB.**
(Right) Goodies Jar - earned for $300 in sales. **CMV $18 MB.**

AVON 100 CERAMIC BOX 1986
White porcelain. Avon 100 front & back. 4A on top in red. **CMV $35.**

CRYSTAL SALAD BOWL AWARD 1956
7 1/2" cut glass with silverplate edge. Comes with serving fork & spoon & card from Avon. Given to Reps. during 70th Anniversary Celebration in 1956. Made by Fina. **CMV $55 complete.**

SUGAR & CREAMER AWARD 1952
Sterling silver base and glass tops. Given to Avon Reps. in 1952. White and silver stiped box. Made by Fina. **CMV $55 set MB.**

CANDY DISH SET AWARD 1952
Sterling silver base by Fina. Glass screw on tops. Given to Avon Reps. in 1952. Came in plain white box. **CMV $55.**

PEOPLE WHO LIKE PEOPLE PRIZE PROGRAM AWARDS 1972
3rd level prize is a set of 8 10 oz. crystal and silver glasses. Won by Reps. for meeting 3rd level sales goals. Was not made only for Avon. **CMV $25 set MB.**

CRYSTAL CANDLE HOLDERS 1980
10" high clear crystal. Given to Reps. for 30 years continuous service. Base is inscribed "30th Avon Anniversary". **CMV $100.00 pair.**

MILLION DOLLAR INCREASE GOBLET 1978
(Left) Silver plated goblet given to all managers in top division for 1 million dollar increase in sales. **CMV $25.**

PORT O'CALL CANDY DISH & BAR 1977
(Right) China dish by IImoges - France & bar of French candy given to managers for meeting appointment goal. Box has gold label "Meet me at the lamp post, Port O'Call Pasadena". **CMV $10 MB.**

SMALL TREASURES FRAGRANCE BOTTLES IN MINIATURE AWARDS 1982
Pink box holds 3 mini size CPC reproductions with gold caps. Given to reps for Step 3 of sales goals. **CMV $15 MB.**

TOWNHOUSE CANNISTER & COOKIE JAR SET AWARDS 1983
Given to reps for sales quota. 1st level, small, **CMV $10.**, 2nd level, **CMV $20.**, 3rd level, **CMV $30.**. 4th level, Cookie Jar (right) **CMV $50, or CMV $90 entire set.**

JOLLY SANTA AWARDS 1986
All white & red ceramic.
Level 1 - Candy jar 7 1/2" high. **CMV $10.**
Level 2 - Set of 4 Santa mugs. **CMV $15.**
Level 3 - Santa Plate. **CMV $20.**

REPRESENTATIVE CHRISTMAS GIFT 1982
Small 4" porcelain dish made by Royal Worcester for Avon. Given to all Avon reps at Christmas 1982. Comes in green box with Avon card. **CMV $10 MB.**

ASH TRAY (AVON) 1982
Used at Avon plants. **CMV $2.50.**

REP AWARD PINS 1997
PRESIDENT CLUB PIN
Marked "PC" **CMV $10. MB.**
HONOR SOCIETY PIN
Marked "HS". **CMV $15. MB.**
ROSE CIRCLE PIN
Marked "RC" **CMV $20. MB.**
D.H. McCONNELL PIN
Marked "DHM". **CMV $25. MB.**
All above are gold tone and ladies face in center.

PRESIDENTS CLUB PIN AWARD 1996-97
Gold tone pin marked "PC". Given to Reps for sales of $8700. **CMV$10. MB.**
HONOR SOCIETY PIN AWARD 1996-97
Gold tone pin marked "HS" Given to Reps for sales of $16,500. **CMV $15. MB.**
ROSE CIRCLE PIN AWARD 1996-97
Given to Reps for sales of $31.000. or more. Gold tone pin marked "RC" **CMV $20. MB.**
DAVID H. McCONNELL PIN AWARD 1996-97
Gold tone pin marked "DM" given to Reps for sales of $52,000. or more. **CMV $25. MB.**

AWARDS & REPRESENTATIVES GIFTS

CHRISTMAS GLASSES & TRAY AWARD 1985
Set of 6 12 oz. glasses with red & green X-mas tree design. **CMV $20.00 MB set.** Matching white ceramic 2 tier serving tray with brass handle. **CMV $15.00 MB.**

SPRINGDALE FOUNDERS CLUB COFFEE CUP AWARD 1979
(top) White glass cup given to all Plant employees who had worked from 1965 to 1979. Red letters. **CMV $10.**

COLOR UP AMERICA PEN 1979
(bottom) White, black & silver pen on brown leather neck cord. Given to managers. **CMV $10.**

GOBLET-CIRCLE OF EXCELLENCE AWARD 1975
(left) 7 1/2" high sterling silver goblet. Given to C of E managers who went to Madrid, Spain 1975. Base says "Circle of Excellence, Madrid, 1975" **CMV $60.**

TEAM LEADER MUG AWARD 1976
(right) White glass mug. **CMV $10.**

OSBORNE CREAM SHERRY MANAGERS GIFT SET 1975
Wine cask on box lid. Box holds 2 wine glasses with "Avon Espana 1975" painted in yellow, bottle of Osborne Cream Sherry with special label "Especially bottled for the 1974 members of the Circle of Excellence". This set was given to each manager on their C of E trip to Madrid, Spain. Only 200 sets given out. **CMV $130 set mint full.**

PROSPECT COFFEE JAR & CUP AWARD 1977
Clear glass jar with green painted design on front says "1886-Avon 1977". Filled with coffee beans. **CMV $20 jar only.** Coffee cup-came with jar in white box as set. Has Avon district manager 1977 on cup & other writings. **CMV $10 cup only.** Both given to Avon managers only.

CIRCLE OF EXCELLENCE MUG AWARD 1978
Avon C of E District No. 1978 in red letters. Given to Reps. In winning districts. **CMV $10.**

MERRY CHRISTMAS MUG 1977
Short glass mug with green lettering on front. **CMV $8.**

CIRCLE OF EXCELLENCE MUG 1970'S
Pewter mug inscribed C of E Avon on front. **CMV $25.**

ACHIEVEMENT AWARD MUG 1978
"1st Quarter 1978" on white ceramic mug given to team getting most new Avon ladies to sign up. **CMV $10.**

QUEEN ELIZABETH CUP & SAUCER 1953
Avon 67th Anniversary celebration coincided with Queen Elizabeth Coronation. Awarded at a banquet for top organization. **CMV $80 mint.**

CURRIER & IVES SUGAR & CREAMER AWARD 1982
(Right) Set given to Avon Reps. for signing up 1 new Avon Rep. **CMV $10 set.**

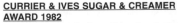

AWARD COMPACT 1966
(left) Sterling silver compact. Engraved on back "National Champion, President's Campaign, 1966". CMV $17.

AVON SUGAR BOWL CLUB 1960
(right) Awarded to sales ladies for getting new customers. CMV $50.

MIKASA CHINA SET 1972
Candle holders & sugar/creamer set for reaching first prize goal, CMV $5 each MB. Beverage server for reaching second goal, CMV $10 MB. Eight cups & saucers for reaching third goal (to be won by President's Club members only), CMV $4. For each cup & saucer set. **These items must be in Avon boxes with card or outlook as this set was not made just for Avon.**

PLATE AWARD "CPC" 1930's
China plate about 9" has 2 deer on face, gold trim - "CPC Avon" on back. No information. CMV $100.

CURRIER & IVES 5 PIECES PLACE SETTING AWARD 1981-82
Each set has dinner plate, salad plate, cup & saucer, and soup bowl. Given to Avon Reps. for signing up 1 new Avon Rep. CMV $25 set of 5 pieces.

CURRIER & IVES 5 PIECES PLACE SETTING AWARD 1977-81
Same set only marked 1977-81 on bottom of each piece in set. Only 300 sets got out in Newark Branch. CMV with 77-81 bottom date $100.00 MB set.

5 YEAR ANNIVERSARY PLATE 1980's
8 1/2" porcelain plate, "The Great Oak" for 5 year service to Avon. 1st issued 1987. CMV $10 MB.

10 YEAR ANNIVERSARY PLATE 1987
8 1/2" porcelain plate. "The California Perfume Co." for 10 years service to Avon. 4 different plates issued starting in 1987. CMV $15. MB.

FOSTORIA SUGAR & CREAM SET AWARD 1970
From Fostoria glass, box says "Avon Cosmetics". Given to Reps for sales achievement. Design is from the Henry Ford Collection. CMV $30 MB only.

15 YEAR ANNIVERSARY PLATE 1980's
8 1/2" porcelain plate. "The Avon Rose" on plate. Given for 15 years service. 1st issued 1987. CMV $30 MB.

CURRIER & IVES TEA SET 1977-78
Set consists of plate, tea pot, sugar bowl & creamer. Avon Products, Inc. on bottom of each piece. Awarded to Avon Reps. for Distinguished Sales Achievement 1977. Plate -1st step, CMV $6.50. Sugar bowl & creamer-2nd step, CMV $12.00. Tea pot-3rd step, CMV $17.50. Cup & saucer-4th step, Saucer 1st issue marked 1977 on bottom, 1978 issue has no date, Add $2 each piece for 1977 date. CMV $35 set of 4. Add $10 if writing on bottom is printed backwards for each piece.

CURRIER & IVES COLLECTION AWARD 1977-78
Made only for Avon & stamped on bottom. Given to Avon. Reps. for meeting sales goals.
1st step - Dinner bell, CMV $6.50 MB
2nd step - Butter dish, CMV $12.00 MB
3rd step - Water pitcher 6 1/2" high. CMV $17.50 MB
4th step - Cake plate 9 1/2" diam. CMV $32.50 MB
Add $10 each piece for bottom writing printed backwards.

20 YEAR ANNIVERSARY PLATE 1980's
8 1/2" porcelain plate. "The 1st Avon Representative" on plate. Given for 20 years service. !st issued 1987. CMV $40 MB.

SPIRIT AVON AWARD PLATE 1986
7 1/4" clear glass plate. White lettering. 1 to a district. **CMV $35.**

25 YEAR SERVICE PLATE AWARD 1985 UP
8" Sterling Silver Plate. Inscribed "In Grateful Appreciation of Twenty Five Years of Loyal Service to Avon Customers. James Preston - President Avon Division." **CMV $75 in Tiffany bag & box.**

POSSET POT AWARD 1976
(left) 9" high stoneware. Bottom reads "Made in Brazil exclusively for Avon Products, Inc.". **CMV $25.**

PITCHER & BOWL RECOMMENDATION PRIZE 1975-77
(right) Given for recommending someone, if appointed as a Rep. Has Avon on bottom of both pieces. **CMV $50 set.**

DECORATORS CHOICE PITCHER AND BOWL PRIZE 1977
Ceramic pitcher 10" high & bowl 15 1/4" across. Made only for Avon. Given to Reps. for signing up 1 new Avon Rep. **CMV $50.**

If Avon Awards or prizes do not say Avon or a Avon trademark to identify it on the item, You should not buy it as most collectors do not want them. They must be marked Avon to be collectible.

DISTINGUISHED MANAGEMENT AWARD 1967
Glass plate with 4A design on bottom. Came in white box lined in red velvet. **CMV $45 plate only. $55 MB.**

BICENTENNIAL PLATES 1976
Blue & white. Given to Reps. that sent in order for campaign 1, 2, 3 totaling $100 or more. (left) Independence Hall. (right) Liberty Bell. Made in England. Has Inscription on back. **CMV $20 Independence Hall; $30 Liberty Bell.**

RECOMMENDATION GIFT SNACK SET 1973
Fostoria lead crystal dish & bowl. Came in set of 4 each. Given to Avon. Reps. for signing up new Avon ladies. **CMV $15 each setting. $60 for all 8 pieces.**

TENDERNESS COMMEMORATIVE PLATE 1974
9" diameter ceramic plate, pastel blue and greens. Awarded to Reps. for sending in orders for campaign 1, 2, and 3,, 1974. **Inscription on back in blue letters "Tenderness Commemorative Plate Special Edition, awarded to Reps. in January, 1974".** Plate is made by Pontessa Ironstone of Spain. Award plate has Pontessa in blue letters. Plate also sold with no inscription on back **CMV $22 MB.** Red letter plate only.

77TH ANNIVERSARY QUEEN AWARD 1963
Awarded to 10 Reps. in each district that had greatest dollar increase in sales, were crowned Queen & also received Fostoria Crystal serving dish with Avon 4A in bottom. Tiara not marked Avon. Came with Avon Queen certificate - 2 different certificates were given. Also came with 1963 Queen Ribbon. 11 1/4" bowl. **CMV bowl only $50. CMV Tiara with ceritficate & ribbon $50. CMV complete set MB $100.**

CHRISTMAS BELLS-MANAGERS GIFT 1971
Red strap with 5 bells given to Avon managers at Christmas. Came with card with bells on it & "For you from Avon". Must have Avon card. **CMV $15 MB.**

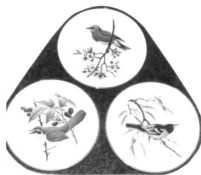

BIRD PLATE AWARDS 1975
Campaign 10, 1975. Available to Reps. for meeting product goals; serving specified number of customers and meeting goals at suggested customer prices. Bluebird was lowest goal, Yellow Breasted Chat second and Baltimore Oriole last. If total goals attained, Rep. received all three plates. **CMV Bluebird, $20 MB, Yellow Breasted Chat $20 MB, Baltimore Oriole $30 MB.**

WILD FLOWERS AWARD PLATES 1976-78
Each is 8 3/4". Southern Wild Flower plate for $195 in sales. Southern & Eastern given for $245 in sales & Southern, Eastern, Nothern & Western flower plates for $330 in sales. C-11, 1976. **CMV Southern $10 MB. Eastern $15 MB. All 4 plates MB $60 set. Northern & Western $20 each MB.** These same plates were reissued by Geni Products, a division of Avon in March, 1978, as awards to their sales reps.

HONOR SOCIETY CUP & SAUCER AWARD 1996
White porcelain cup & saucer with flower design sits on wood base with dated 1996 brass plaque. Given to Reps for sales of $16,200. in 1 year. **CMV $35. MB.**

HONOR SOCIETY CUP & SAUCER AWARD 1994
Porcelain cup & saucer sits on wood base with brass plaque. **CMV $35. MB.**

FOSTORIA COIN PLATE AWARD 1970
Does not say Avon. Must be in Avon box. **CMV $25 MB.**

LENOX CHINA PRESIDENT'S CLUB BOWL AWARD 1979
White box with gold trim & burgundy inside holds 4A inscribed china bowl. Bottom inscribed "For Avon's Very Best" given to all President's Club members for 1980. Box has Avon outer sleeve. **CMV $40 MB, bowl only $30.**

FOSTORIA LEAD CRYSTAL PLATES AWARD 1978
Given for top sales. 1st four plates won by Reps: Jeweled A, 1st Rep., Door Knocker, great oak tree. **CMV $30 set of 4 or $7 each.** President's Club Reps. & District Managers could win 1st 4 plus 4 more: 4A Avon Key, World of Avon Globe, Avon Rose Last. President's Club set had P.C. marked on Rose plate & D.M. marked Jeweled a plate for managers set. **CMV $100 D.M. set of 8, CMV $75 P.C. set of 8.**

COIN GLASS 1961-72
(Left) Coin glass in Avon boxes only are collectable. The same pieces are available in local stores with both 1886 and 1887 at low prices so get the box. Many pieces available at many different prices starting at **$10 up to $100 in Avon box.** 1st issue 1961.

CHRISTMAS GIFT PLATE 1971
(Top Left) Sent to Reps. at Christmas. Clear glass with frosted First Avon Lady.
CMV $17 MB. $12 no box.

CHRISTMAS GIFT PLATE 1972
(Top Right) Sent to every Rep. at Christmas. Clear glass frosted rose.
CMV $15 MB. $10 no box.

CHRISTMAS GIFT PLATE 1973
(Bottom Left) Sent to Reps. who had been with company less than 2 years. Clear glass frosted 4A. **CMV $15 MB. $10 no box.**

CHRISTMAS GIFT PLATE 1974
(Bottom Right) Sent to Reps. at Christmas. Clear glass with frosted Door Knocker.
CMV $12 MB. $8 no box.

REPRESENTATIVES SERVICE AWARD PLATES 1979-86
Awarded for years of service. 1st issued in 1973 and some design changes in 1979. 1st 5 are white porcelain with decals. All are the same CMV as 1973 to 79 plates except the 25 year plate which is silver tone only and **CMV $40. CMV complete set $140 MB.**
1979-86 plates have pink rose borders.

FRAGRANCE JAR AWARD 1924
American Beauty fragrance jar hand painted design in blue & gold. Pink & green flowers on lid. Pink ribbon. Given to Reps. for top sales. **CMV $350.**

REPRESENTATIVES AWARD PLATES 1973-79
Awarded for years of service. First 5, white with colored decals. Two years-Doorknockers **CMV $10.** Five years-Oak Tree with pink or brown acorns, **CMV $15. 5 year "Factory Mistake Plate" marked as normal 5th Anniversary plate on back but same as 10th year plate on front. Rare.**
Add $25 to 5 year plate. Ten years-California Perfume Co. **CMV $20.** Fifteen years-Rose **CMV $25.** Twenty years-First Avon Lady **CMV $30.** Twenty-five years-Sterling silver with message from Avon President. **CMV $100.** All Prices are mint & boxed. **CMV complete set $200 MB.**

NATIONAL CHAMPION AWARD 1966
Glass bowl with 4A design on bottom. **CMV $50 MB.**

GRAVY BOAT AWARD 1930'S
CPC Avon on bottom. Given to Reps. for sales award in 1930's. Blue & green flowers on both sides. Gold trim. **CMV $75.**

COVERED DISH AWARD 1930'S
White ceramic bowl & lid. Gold trim with green & pink flowers. Bottom is stamped CPCo. Avon under glazing. Given to Avon Reps. for sales. **CMV $110.00 mint.**

GREAT SCENT EVENT TRAY AWARD 1980
9 1/2"x 17 3/4" gold tone mirror tray given to 15 Reps. In each district for selling the most Ultra colognes. Does not say Avon on tray. Came with & must have Great Scent Event card from division manager. **CMV$20 with card.**

CAKE STAND AWARD 1978
(Front) Given to top 50 Reps. in state. "Avon Division Top 50" inscribed in center. Silver plated. **CMV $25.**
IMPERIAL DIVISION AWARD TRAY 1979
(Back) Silver plated, inscribed "Avon Imperial Division Top 50, 1979 #29". **CMV $25.**

50 YEAR SERVICE PLATE 1976
Gold plated plate given to the late Mrs. Bessie O'Neal on July 27, 1976, by David Mitchell, President of Avon Products, for 50 continous years as an Avon lady. A letter from Avon & Mr. Mitchell came with the plate. The plate is 1 of a kind & priceless. The plate is made by Dirilyte. No value established.

SILVER SERVER AWARD 1977
(top) 11 3/4"x 18 3/4" silver plated tray & cover. Marked Avon Wm. Rogers on bottom. No information on why it was given to Reps. **CMV $45 mint.**
SILVER CREAMER AWARD 1950'S
(bottom) Avon Wm. Rogers on bottom. Silverplate creamer. **No information on this as Avon award CMV $35.**

SILVER SERVICE AWARD TRAY 1957
Silver tray 13 1/2" long, "Avon-Wm. Rogers" on bottom. Awarded to Avon ladies in Anniversary Campaign. **CMV $30.**

HIGHEST SALES AWARD BOWL 1976
Silver plated fruit bowl was awarded to 10 different Reps. for highest sales in their category. Each bowl is engraved different from the other. The one is engraved with "4A" design. "Highest Percentage Increase Christmas 1976". **CMV $25, $30 MB.** Not awarded in all branches.

PRESIDENT'S CELEBRATION AWARD BOWL 1977
Over 40,000 were given as awards. 6 7/8" silver plated bowl given to Avon Reps. in 2 winning districts in each division for top sales. Inscription in center of bowl "President's Celebration 1977"; on bottom of bowl, "Awarded exclusively to Avon Reps." F.B. Rogers. Came in white box as shown. Red silk rose also given at same time with name tag. **CMV Rose only with tag, $5. CMV bowl $25 MB.** Bowl did not come with rose.

PRESIDENT'S AWARD SILVER BOWLS 1962
3 sizes silver bowls. 4A emblem and writing on outside. **CMV (left to right) $27.50, $32.50, $37.50.**

75TH ANNIVERSARY SALES CHAMPION SILVER TRAY 1961
Awarded to the top Avon district managers for best sales in campaign 9 & 10, 1961. **CMV $40.**

SILVER SERVER AWARD 1963
12 5/16" x 2" given to the top 4 established Reps. In each district for sale improvement over the previous year. 4A design engraved in the bottom. Small 9" servers were given to 3 newer Reps. for highest sale & 3 for outstanding sales ability. **CMV 9" $40. 12" $45.**

ACHIEVEMENT AWARD SILVER TRAY 1961
4A design in center of silver tray. **CMV $35.**

PRESIDENT'S CELEBRATION TRAY AWARD 1978
12" silverplated tray marked "Awarded Exclusively to Avon Reps." on back side. Given to 1 winning team Rep. In each division. **CMV $35 MB.**

DIVISION SALES WINNER TRAY AWARD 1975
17 3/4" long 13" wide silver tray. Inscribed in center 'Awarded to (name of manager) President's Program Best Wishes, David S. Mitchell'. Given to top district managers in sales. Came in blue felt bag & white box. **CMV $150 MB in bag.**

EL CAMINO DIVISION SUGAR & CREAMER SET AWARD 1977
Silverplated creamer & sugar bowl. Tray is engraved "Top 10 Sales-El Camino Division Campaigns 10-22, 1977". Made by Sheridan. **CMV $35 set mint.**

SILVER SERVER 1964
9" diameter. Same as 1963 server except no 12" bowls given and all are gold lined on the inside. **CMV $40.**

SILVER TRAY 1965
9 7/8" x 1" given to each Rep. from the winning group in each branch during the General Manager's Campaign, engraved "Honor Award-General Manager's Campaign 1965". **CMV $35.**

88TH ANNIVERSARY AWARD BOWL 1974
6" across and 3" high silverplated by Oneida. Paul Revere Silver. Given to top 5 sales Reps. in each district. **CMV $20.** Same bowl given to top 5 President's Club Sales Reps. and their award bowl says "President's Club" over 4A ensigna. **CMV $20.**

SALES EXCELLENCE AWARD 1977
Paul Revere, Jostens Pewter 5" bowl C26-76-C9-77. Awarded to top sales Reps. **CMV $20 MB.**

SILVER AWARD BOWL 1969
Silverplate bowl by Fina. Has 4A symbol and Avon in center of bowl. 2 3/4" high and 5" wide at top. Awarded to Avon Reps. **CMV $20.**

CHINA BELL REP. GIFT 1973
Christmas present to all Reps. that had been with Avon over 2 years. White China with pink roses. **CMV $10 MB.**

CHRISTMAS ORNAMENTS MUSICAL GIFT SET 1974

Given to Reps. for getting new Reps. Red & gold bell & green & gold ball. Both have music boxes inside. Made by Heinz Deichett, West Germany. Both came in red box as set. **CMV $30 each no box, $75 set MB.**

MANAGERS CHRISTMAS GIFT 1979

Blown glass in green leaves & red holly with red velvet ribbon. 2 pieces. Holly leaves ornament & candle holder. Given to managers for Christmas 1979. Does not say Avon. **CMV $15 set.**

REPRESENTATIVE AWARD BOWL 1956

Sterling silver Paul Revere Bowl was given to each Rep. in the top selling district in each division during President's Campaign 1956. **CMV $45.**

THE GREAT AMERICAN SELLATHON CHRISTMAS TREE AWARD 1981

Approximately 600 given out at Hawaiian President's Celebration in Hawaii. Has bottom Avon label & green & white gift box. **CMV $45.**

REPRESENTATIVE CHRISTMAS GIFT 1979

Ceramic tile picture frame made in Japan. Box says "Happy Holidays Avon 1979". Given to all Avon Reps. at Christmas. **CMV $10 MB.**

COMPOTE TALL 1960'S

Fostoria coin glass award. Must be in Avon box. Given to Reps for sales award. **CMV $45.**

MANAGERS CHRISTMAS TREE GIFT 1977

(Left) Hand blown glass Christmas tree in clear, green, red & yellow. Given to Avon managers at Christmas 1977. Does not say Avon. **CMV $25.**

MANAGERS CHRISTMAS TREE GIFT 1978

(Right) Brass Christmas tree ornament signed by "Bi Jan" on back. Given to Avon managers at Christmas 1978. Came in green box. **CMV $20 MB.**

FLOWER BASKET AWARD 1981

Small white ceramic flower basket. **CMV $25.**

91ST ANNIVERSARY COIN GLASS AWARD 1977

Footed compote on right won by Reps. for selling $270 in C8-9-1977. **CMV $7 MB.** Centerpiece bowl and footed compote won for selling $540 in C8-9-1977. **CMV $12 MB.** Centerpiece bowl. A pair of candle holders won by President's Club members only with P.C. embossed on bottom. This coin glass was made only for Avon, using Avon emblems in coins and 1886-1977 and the name Avon. Came with card on each piece from Avon and in Avon box. **CMV$17 candle holders, MB.** District managers received a full set of Coin Glass with D.M. embossed in center of each piece. **CMV $75 MB for complete D.M. set.**

"PICTURE FRAME" DREAM AWARD SEPTEMBER CONFERENCE 1979

Ceramic picture frame. White, pink & green flowers with white doves. Center is pink, says "Hold fast to your dreams, For if you do . . .Tomorrow you'll see More dreams can come true". **CMV $15.**

APPLE PAPER WEIGHT AWARD 1978
Given to divisional managers for top sales. Clear crystal glass apple is engraved "You Made New York Smile", Avon, March 1978, on front side. **CMV $100.**

HEART TREASURE BOX AWARD 1976
Top sales teams in 252 winning districts won ceramic heart shaped box given in President's Celebration of 1976. Bottom says "Avon President's Celebration 1976". Made in Spain **CMV $20 MB.**

CAKE PLATE FOSTORIA COIN GLASS AWARD 1960'S
Fostoria glass cake plate given to Reps. for sales award. Comes in Avon box. Same piece was sold in local stores. Must be in Avon box as shown. **CMV $75 MB.**

PRESIDENT'S CELEBRATION HEART AWARD 1979
Lucite heart marked "You're our number one- Avon 1979 President's Celebration". Made in Taiwan. Comes in white Avon box. **CMV $15 MB. MANAGER'S HEART "YOU'RE NO. 1"**
(Right) Clear lucite, has smaller hole on top & heart is about 1/2" smaller. Came in red velvet bag. This one was given to managers only. **CMV $20 mint in bag.**

HEART PORCELAIN BOX AWARD 1980
Given to managers. Came in Tiffany & Co. box. Small porcelain heart box says "Bernardaud Limoges Made in France. Does not say Avon. **CMV $25 in box with card.**

TEAM LEADER BELL AWARD 1980
Fostoria bell inscribed "Avon Team Leader Recruit A Thon 1980". Only 1 in each district given. **CMV $30.**

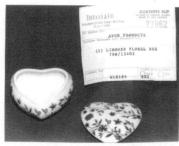

LIMOGES FLORAL HEART BOX AWARD 1979
Small heart shaped ceramic box made by Limoge of France. Given to Avon managers. Must have Tiffany & Co. card as shown for Avon Products. 2 different designs as shown. **CMV $25 with card.**

LIMOGES FLORAL BOX AWARD 1980
Small white ceramic heart box with blue painted flowers. Given to managers. Does not say Avon. Must have Tiffany card for Avon Products. Was not made only for Avon. **CMV $25 MB with card.**

78TH ANNIVERSARY FOSTORIA AWARD SET 1964
Box marked Avon Cosmetics holds Fostoria salt & pepper, cruet & glass holding tray. Given to Reps. **CMV $45 in Avon box.**

MERRY MOODS OF CHRISTMAS ORNAMENT 1960'S
Dark blue ornament for managers only. Other side says "Avon Presents" with 4A design. **CMV $35 mint.**

CANDLESTICK AWARDS 1952

Sterling silver candlesticks 2 1/2" tall and 2 3/4" wide at the base. They were given to Reps. for calling on 120 customers during the 66th Avon Anniversary campaign, 1952. Came in nice gift box. The candlesticks were not made just for Avon. Must be in box with Avon card as shown. **CMV $60 MB.**

50TH ANNIVERSARY AWARD LAMP 1936

Made only for Avon "Lalique reproduction" lamp. 22" high, 19" wide shade. Frosted carved glass base. Pink ribbon on shade, clear beads around edge of shade. White painted base. Given only to 50 Reps. for top sales in nation. **CMV $300.**

SILVER FLOWER BASKET AUGUST CONFERENCE AWARD 1978

Sterling silver basket made by Cartier, hand made. "August Conference 1978" on top of handle. Yellow silk flowers, green leaves. Given to managers only. **CMV $100 mint.**

ROSE PERFUME LAMP AWARD 1926

Pink rose colored frosted glass, rose shaped electric lamp with antique green metal base. Top of rose has a small indentation to put perfume to scent the air when lamp was burning. Lamp 4 5/8" across, rose 5" high. Given to only 8 Reps. for top sales. **CMV $200.**

TEAM LEADER JEWELRY BOX 1980

Silver tone box with blue felt interior. Mirror inside tray says "Team Leader-President's Celebration 1980". **CMV $20 mint.**

CIRCLE OF EXCELLENCE STEUBEN VASE AWARD 1970

9" high Steuben Vase, sits on Black wood base. Brass name plate says "Circle of Excellence Repeat Member-1970" plus name of winner. Comes in Steuben felt bag & box. Given to top C. of E. Managers only. **CMV $500.00 MB. (NOTE)** This vase alone sells in 1998 for $540.00.

NATIONAL DISTRICT SALES MANAGER PANEL AWARD 1980

Silverplated card case. Given to top managers only. Made by Reed & Barton. In box & blue bag. **CMV $50.00 MB.**

GREAT OAK LAMP AWARD 1980

Electric light in wood base with solid hunk of clear glass with great oak engraved. Given to district managers at yearly conference. **CMV $75 mint.**

CARTIER CRYSTAL BELL AWARD 1968

Crystal bell in Cartier bag & box. Signed Val Lambert. Is not marked Avon. Given to one Rep. per district for most recommendations. **CMV $65 MB, Bell only $50.**

PRESIDENT'S CELEBRATION SILVER CHEST 1974

Silverplated, red lined. Embossed rose on lid. **CMV $47.50 MB.**

WE DID IT TOGETHER TRAY 1983
7 1/4" x 12" silver plated server tray. Given to Managers. **CMV $25.**

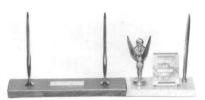

$1,000,000 DESK SET AWARD 1978
(Left) Wood base. Brass plaque. **CMV $50.**
DESK SET NATIONAL G.M. CHAMPIONS AWARD 1973
(Right) Marble base. **CMV $20.**

TOP RECRUITER PEN AWARD 1979
(Left) Sterling silver pen set. Engraved "Top Recruiter May 1979". **CMV $100.**
CIRCLE OF EXCELLENCE 8 YEAR PEN AWARD 1980
(Center) Engraved sterling silver pen set. **CMV $125.**
AVON TENNIS PAPER WEIGHT 1982
(Right) Heavy sterling silver paper weight engraved "1982 Avon Tennis". All are made by Tiffany & Co. **CMV $150.**

OPPORTUNITY UNLIMITED MUG AWARD 1981
Brass mug inscribed on side. **CMV $20.**
OPPORTUNITY UNLIMITED GLASS AWARD 1981
Champagne glass inscribed on side. **CMV $10.**

WINTER RECRUITING EVENT AWARD BOWL 1977
8" International silver plate. Side inscribed name - Gateway Division Winner 1977 - Winter Recruiting Event. **CMV $20.**
GATEWAY APPOINTMENT GOBLET AWARD 1975
Poole silver plate. Inscribed on side. **CMV 20.**

PAPER WEIGHT AWARD 1983
Square lucite with gold 4A center. Marked The Answer is Avon. **CMV $20.**
PAPER WEIGHT AWARD NEWARK 1983
Small round lucite, with 1979 Susan B. Anthony Dollar inside. **CMV $15.**

PAPER WEIGHT LOS ANGELES -1983
(Left) Clear & red lucite marked "Road to the Gold." **CMV $25.**
PAPER WEIGHT - SAN FRANCISCO 1982
(Center) Small clear lucite. Gold inner base. **CMV $30.**
PAPER WEIGHT - LONDON 1980
(Right) Clear & red lucite. Avon Marathon. **CMV $35.**

OAK TREE PAPER WEIGHT AWARD 1978
(Left) Lucite case holds oak tree coin with 4A design. Atlanta #1 - 1978. **CMV $20.**
READ LISTEN FOLLOW UP PLAQUE 1981
(Right) 4A design on sign. **CMV $10.**

VISION AWARD 1985
Clear lucite paper weight. Says "Avon Our Vision is Clear 1985". **CMV $15.**

MANAGER'S CONFERENCE CORSAGE 1960'S
Green & gold with red holly has Avon 7 dollar bill attached. Bill says "United States of Avon". Given to managers. **CMV $22.**

JEWELRY BOX AWARD 1968
10" long x 5" wide brocade & brass music box. Red lined. Given to Reps. for top sales. Does not say Avon. **CMV $60 mint.**

WOMEN'S INTERNATIONAL AVON "RUNNING" MARATHON AWARD 1979
Gold tone medallion in clear lucite with red background. Came on marble base with 22/9/79 plaque. **CMV $50.**
INTERNATIONAL WOMEN'S CHAMPIONSHIP MARATHON AWARD 1978 ATLANTA
Same as above only silver tone medallion with black background. **CMV $50.**

ARIANE NECKLACE & BOUQUET 1977
Wood basket & plastic flowers holds sterling silver necklace with August Conference 1977 on side. Given to Avon managers at August Conference Banquet. Necklace holds sample vial of Ariane perfume. **CMV $65 mint.**

HUDSON MANOR BUD VASE GIFT 1978
Avon silverplated bud vase & red rose in silver box. Bottom says "Team Leader, August 1978". Made in Italy. Same as regular issue only regular issue does not say Team Leader 1978 on bottom. **CMV $20.**
MANAGERS BUD VASE GIFT 1978
Same as above only says "August Conference 1978" on bottom instead of Team Leader. **CMV $30 MB.**

MANAGER'S FLOWER BASKET 1979
Basket of silk flowers with Avon tag to managers. In Avon box. **CMV $15 MB with tag.**
TEAM LEADER FLOWER BASKET 1979
Same flower basket only different box and different tag given to team leaders. **CMV $10 MB.**

SOUNDS OF SEASONS MUSIC BOX 1966
Given to managers only. Box holds green & gold Christmas Tree Pin, gold Key & Bell. Came from Cartier in New York. **CMV Music box only $65.00, Complete set $85 MB.**

SALES LEADERSHIP AWARD 1980
Large clear glass emerald diamond shaped paper weight. Engraved "Avon Sales Leadership Award Conference 1980". Tiffany & Co. on bottom. Comes in Tiffany box. Given to mangers only. **CMV $100 MB.**

OAK TREE PAPER WEIGHT AWARD 1980
Clear lucite with siver tone 4A design & oak tree. "Pasadena No. 1 - 1980" inscribed inside. Given to managers. **CMV $25.**

NO. 1 PAPER WEIGHT AWARD - CANADA
Chrome-plated No. 1, gold tone plaque says "You're Number One With Us". Given to Avon managers in Canada. **CMV $30.**

95th ANNIVERSARY CELEBRATION AWARD MUG 1981
(Left) White - Red letters. **CMV $10.**
WE'RE HOT MUG AWARD 1984
(Right) White mug - red & black letters. **CMV $10.**

PRESIDENT'S CLUB CUP 1986
Pinkish orange coffee cup. "Avon President's Club 86" on side in blue letters. **CMV $5.**
PEN "LOOK HOW GOOD YOU LOOK NOW" 1987
White pen. **CMV $2.**
PHYLLIS DAVIS ACHIEVEMENT AWARD 1985
Clear lucite 3" square with black background. C-26-85. **CMV $25.**

LIBERTY DIVISION PAPER WEIGHT 1978
Clear lucite has 4A design. "Liberty Division - Two Million Dollar Increase 1978". Given to top managers. **CMV $15.**
CIRCLE OF EXCELLENCE PINS 1979
(lower left) Small blue & gold tone pin says "C of E Winners 1979". Given to top managers. **CMV $10.**

AWARDS & REPRESENTATIVES GIFTS

OUTSTANDING IN FIELD CUP AWARD 1981
Ceramic cup with cow on other side. **CMV $10.**

CUSTOMER SERVICE AWARD MEASURING CUP 1982
By Fire King - Avon inscribed. **CMV $10.**

COFFEE CUP AWARDS 1984
Left to right.
WHITE GLASS - red letters, gold trim. **CMV $5.**
WHITE MUG - Avon in red letters all over. **CMV $5.**
SAY YES TO AVON MUG - White plastic, red letters. **CMV $5.**

TELEPHONE HONOR SOCIETY AWARD 1986
Red telephone given for $50,000 in sales. Engraved on top "PC Avon Honor Society". Comes in Unisonic box. **CMV $75.**

WE LOVE YOU MUG AWARD 1986
White ceramic cup. **CMV $5.**

AVON MARATHON AWARD, OTTAWA 1981
Clear lucite with white back. Dated 23 August 1981. Given in women's running circuit. **CMV $35.**

WONDER MUG AWARD 1987
White plastic mug. **CMV $5 MB.**

AVON TELEPHONE 1986 AWARD
White phone, wall or desk mount. Avon in black letters - red slash. Given to reps. **CMV $25.**

#1 TREND SETTERS WALL TILE AWARD - 1985
White tile given in Morton Grove branch. **CMV $25.**

HOLIDAY GREETINGS GLASS AWARD 1971
Clear glass, red letters. **CMV $12.**

GOBLET 1971
Ruby coated glass says Lena - Avon 1971. **CMV $10.**

P.C. X-MAS PREVIEW CUP 1985
White plastic, red letters. **CMV $2.**

CHRISTMAS ORNAMENT AWARD 1984
White plastic, green letters. Teddy bear on back side. **CMV $5.**

P.C. COFFEE CUP GIFT 1987
Ceramic coffee cup given to President's Club members on birthdays. White, blue, orange & pink. Has ceramic lid. **CMV $6. MB.**

TELEPHONE AWARD 1986
Red wall mount or can sit on table. Says Avon in white letters. Given to reps. **CMV $20.**

SALES ACHIEVEMENT MUG 1977
White coffee cup, pink rose. Back says "Avon Sales Achievement Highest Percentage Increase Third Quarter 1977". **CMV $10.**

TELEPHONE PRESIDENT'S CLUB AWARD 1983
Red plastic Touch Tone, given to top sales reps only. Made by Webcor. Outer sleeve says "Avon Calling" & Avon Calling on telephone. **CMV $25.**

SHAWNEE DOOR KNOCKER IN LUCITE AWARD 1970's
Gold tone door knocker sealed in lucite - has Shawnee in blue. **CMV $20.**

DIVISION COMPETITION AWARD 1973
Clear lucite paper weight given in Springdale branch. **CMV $10.**

HEAT THERMOMETER AWARD 1981
Clear lucite, black letters & trim given to managers in 4 test areas only. **CMV $25.**

REP. CHRISTMAS GIFT BOWL 1978
Fostoria bowl with 4A design & 1978 on bottom. Given to all Avon Reps. for Christmas 1979. Box shown with red ribbon & gold tag & white & gold plastic bell given to managers. **CMV $10 Reps. MB, CMV $15 managers with ribbon.**

VALENTINE TEAM LEADER GIFT 1979
3 1/2" across crystal heart shaped glass dish given to all team leaders for Valentine's. **CMV $12.50 MB.**

CIRCLE OF EXCELLENCE CRYSTAL VASE 1980
Given to managers on trip to Spain. Box has "Avon Vase Soliflor". Was not made only for Avon. **CMV $40 in Avon box.**

SEASONS GREETINGS AVON REPS. 1977
5 1/2" high vase marked on bottom has 4A symbol. Given to all Avon Reps. at Christmas 1977 in special box. **CMV $10. MB.**

DIVISION MANAGER'S TROPHY 1966
Large pewter trophy given to winning manager in each division. **CMV $80.**

PRESIDENT'S CUP AWARD 1949
Sterling silver trophy engraved with top selling team in city & district in each division during President's Campaign during the late 40's & early 50's. Given to managers. **CMV $200 mint.**

JUBILEE ANNIVERSARY QUEEN AWARD 1977
Small wood base, gold top for division manager. **CMV $10.**

HOOSIER CUSTOMER SERVICE TROPHY 1975-76
(Left) Given to managers for most customers served. **CMV $22.50.**

PRESIDENT'S CELEBRATION TROPHY 1978
(Right) Marble base. **CMV $15.**

TRAVELING TROPHY 1972
Gold 4A with first Avon Lady over emblem on walnut base with engraved plate Team Honor Award. **CMV $20.**

35th ANNIVERSARY AWARD 1980's
Silver plate pitcher engraved on front. Given to Reps. for 35 years service as an Avon Rep. Comes with Avon card. In Avon box from Tiffany & Co. Engraved on side of pitcher "35th Avon Anniversary". **CMV $100 MB.**

ADDITION'S AWARD 1978
Black & clear plastic picture cube for recruiting new Reps. **CMV $25 MB.**

OBELISK COMMUNITY SERVICE AWARD 1979
8 1/4" clear lucite. 1 given to managers in each division. Has 4A design & message of Ralph Waldo Emerson in center. Came in 2 sizes - 1 is 2" shorter. **CMV $35 ea.**

PRESIDENT'S CLUB TROPHY 1977
Gold tone top. **CMV $8.**

PRESIDENT'S CELEBRATION TROPHY 1978
Given to Reps. for best increase over sales goal. Came with certificate. Marble with wood base. **CMV $20.**

KANSAS CITY BRANCH TROPHY 1969
"Number One" national sales increase. **CMV $17.**

LOVING CUP TROPHY 1961
Gold cup on white base. **CMV $20.**

BUD VASE AWARD 1954
(Left) 8" tall sterling silver vase awarded to each Rep. in winning district during President's Campaign. **CMV $45.**

PRESIDENT'S TROPHY 1954-56
(Right) 13 5/8" high, sterling silver trophy was given to top selling city & district managers in each division during President's Campaign each year. Trophy sits on black base. **CMV $125.**

ROYAL RIBBON TEAM LEADER AWARD TROPHY 1982
Wood base & silver toned cup. 1 given per district. **CMV $15.**

TOP SALES TROPHY 1966
(Left) Small 5" high gold trophy, wood base. C-11-13-1966. **CMV $15.**

ACHIEVEMENT AWARD TROPHY 1954
(Right) Avon in raised letters on the base of the metal figure. Given to top Reps. in each district. **CMV $20.**

PRESIDENT'S CELEBRATION TROPHY 1977
Inscribed to Top Selling Rep. for President's Celebration. **CMV $20.**

AVON CALLING PEN 1976
(Left) 14K gold filled. Made by Cross. In grey bag and red leather pen holder with rose design in gold. Pen is 5 1/4" long. Given to Reps. for recommendation prize. **CMV $20 MB.**

TOP 6 TEAM LEADER TROPHY 1977
(Right) Given for Top 6 Sales in Anniversary Celebration 1977. White marble base, gold statue. Blue plaque. **CMV $10.**

3 YEAR WINNER TROPHY 1971
Small wood base, brass plaque that says
"Avon 3 Year Winner".Given to Reps.**CMV**
$15.

DIVISIONAL SALES CAMPAIGN AWARD
1954-56
Only 20 black plaques with solid sterling silver
rose, were given each year to managers in top
selling district in each of the 20 divisions in
U.S. **CMV $200.**

BEST SUPPORTING PERFORMANCE
TROPHY 1965
(Left) This type trophy should not get too high
in price as you can still buy the trophies &
have brass name plate put on them.
CMV $15.
ACHIEVEMENT AWARD TROPHY 1958-59
(Right) This type has Avon in raised letters
on the base of the metal figure. These cannot
be purchased & should be worth more.
CMV $25.

KEY TO SUCCESS TROPHY AWARD 1978
Trophy floated to each winning manager in
division till final winning manager won & kept
it. **CMV $60.**

PRESIDENT'S TROPHY 1959-60
Sterling silver trophy given to managers in top
selling district in each division. Given late 50's
to early 60's. Trophy is inscribed with winning
team & year. **CMV $150.**

ANNIVERSARY QUEEN TROPHY 1978
Marble Base, Given to top Rep. in each
division for top sales. **CMV $15.**
QUEEN'S TIARA 1978
Came with Queen's Trophy. Is not marked
Avon. **No price established.**

STAR SPANGLED MANAGER PLAQUE 1970
"Avon-Star Spangled Manager Summer 1970"
on face plate. **CMV $14.**

NATIONAL DISTRICT PANEL PLAQUE 1974
Picture frame plaque-Sara Fleming. Gold &
brown. **CMV $15.**

DISTINGUISHED SALES MANAGEMENT
PLAQUE AWARD 1977
Solid walnut base holds white ceramic tile
center plaque & brass name tag on bottom.
Given to top 10 managers in each division.
CMV $30.

PRESIDENT'S CELEBRATION PLAQUE
1977
(right) Engraved wood plaque with Cape Cod
Water Goblet attached. Given to team leaders
with highest sales. **CMV $15. mint.**

AWARDS & REPRESENTATIVES GIFTS

OUTSTANDING MANAGERS PLAQUE 1971
Wood base with gold plaque. Outstanding managers first quarter. **CMV $15.**

TEAM LEADER PLAQUE AWARD 1979
Given to team leaders in C of E winning division. **CMV $30.**

MILLION DOLLAR CLUB PLAQUE PASADENA BRANCH 1978
Walnut base with red front & gold trim. Presented to district managers for outstanding sales increase. **CMV $50.**

PRESIDENT'S CELEBRATION GREAT OAK PLAQUE AWARD 1980
Scrimshaw great oak on white plastic center, wood frame. Comes with Avon card also with or without brass inscription plate on face. Given to managers only. **CMV $35.**

BLUE RIBBON SOCIETY AWARD 1981
Wood & brass plaque. **CMV $15.**

MILLION DOLLAR SELECT GROUP AWARD 1977
(Left) Plaque with bag of money on front from Sovereign Divison. **CMV $75.**
OUTSTANDING ACHIEVEMENT AWARD 1975
(Right) Blue velvet on wood plaque, metal wreath with red, white & blue ribbon with 4A pendant with green stone in center. **CMV $100.**

AWARD PLAQUE 1971
Presented in campaign 1-26, 1971 for increased sales. **CMV $10.**

TOP 10 DIVISION TROPHY 1977
4 1/2" high 4A design inside lucite top on wood base & brass plaque. Given to top 10 sales Reps. in each division. Came in plain white box. **CMV $40.**

HONORABLE MENTION PLAQUE 1960'S
Green pearlessence plastic base with wood and brass plaque. **CMV $15.**

PICTURE GLASS FRAME PRIZE 1943
Etched glass frame holds 8x10 size picture. Given to Reps. for selling over $75 during campaign. **CMV $150.**

20 YEAR SILVER PICTURE FRAME AWARD 1981
Sterling silver picture frame from Tiffany & Co. given to Avon Reps. for 20 years service. Bottom of frame engraved "Avon 20 Years", & the initial of person winning frame. Comes in Tiffany felt bag. **CMV $100.**

CIRCLE OF EXCELLENCE HEART PICTURE FRAME 1981
Silver tone small picture frame with C of E card. Given to C of E managers. **CMV $25.**

MANAGERS DIPLOMA 1963
Certificate given to new Avon managers during the 1960's. Did not come in frame. **CMV $10.**

TEAM LEADER PICTURE FRAME AWARD 1978
Chrome picture frame marked on top of frame "Made Exclusively for Avon Team Leaders". Given for meeting sales goals. **CMV $10 mint.**

ACHIEVEMENT AWARD 1950
(left) Pink & white with gold. Given for high sales during 64th Anniversary Celebration. This was celebrating new packaging & redesign of Cotillion. This matches packaging for this era. Approx. 10 x 14 inches. **CMV $25.**

PAUL GREGORY PLAQUE 1964
Silver plaque on black wood. Given to each manager in the winning division. **CMV $35.**

PAUL GREGORY PLAQUE 1965-67
Black & silver plaque given to winning division of Avon's Paul Gregory Trophy. **CMV $30.**

DIVISION CHAMPION PLAQUE 1965
Given for highest sales during general managers campaign 1965. **CMV $30.**

WHITE HOUSE PICTURE FRAME AWARD 1986
100th year signed by Ronald Reagan. **CMV $10.**

PICTURE FRAME "CERAMIC" AWARD 1984
Blue box holds small white ceramic picture frame with blue, green & yellow flowers. Given to Reps. for Sales Quota. **CMV $8.**

CHRISTMAS CONFERENCE AWARD 1985
2" deep wood frame with brass inscribed plaque with rose & 4A design & dated 1985. Given to managers only. **CMV $35.**

MANAGERS PICTURE FRAME AWARD 1986
Small oval brass tone frame with 4A design. Given at August conference. **CMV $15.**

THIS IS FOR YOU PEN & NOTE PAD AWARD 1984
White Avon Box holds note pads. **CMV $7.** White Avon light pen. **CMV $10., $20. for set MB.**

I LOVE NEW YORK GIFTS 1985
Note pad - blue plastic, apple rubber stamp & button. **CMV $5. all.**

SAN FRANCISCO RECORD 1980
Circle of Excellence envelope with Tony Bennet record. "I Left My Heart in San Francisco." **CMV $5.**

STICK WITH IT SOAP HOLDER 1973
Rubber soap holder given to Reps. Rare. **CMV $3.**

CARDS - PASADENA #1 1980s
Deck of cards. **CMV $8.**

CARDS - NEW YORK - LAS VEGAS - AWARD 1980
Deck of cards. **CMV $10.**

ICE SCRAPER AWARD 1984
White plastic - says "You're #1 with me - Avon" **CMV $1.**

FLASHLIGHT AWARD 1985
White plastic. Avon marked. Given to Reps. **CMV $8.**

KEY CHAIN AWARD 1983
Tan leather. Metal Avon tag. Given to Reps. **CMV $5.**

(Left to Right)

CIRCLE OF EXCELLENCE AWARDS 1977
NEW YORK - BERMUDA TRAVEL ITINERARY
Beige plastic cover & itinerary inside. **CMV $5.**

CANDY CUP
White plastic with gold covering. Rhinestone on front. **CMV $7.**

NAME TAG
White & blue plastic. **CMV $5.**

ORDER BOOK COVERS 1980s
Misc. order book covers used by Avon Reps. **CMV $1. to $5 each.**

AVON 100 BOOK MARK 1986
(left) Pocono Division leather book mark. Given to Reps. **CMV $5.**

SMALL TREASURE CABINET AWARD 1982
Small wood cabinet made in Brazil for small treasure figurines. **CMV $10.**

JEWELRY BOX MALE AWARD 1981
Fine wood box made by Buxton given to Male District Managers or Male Team Leaders. Brass label on front is only difference in both boxes. Same box can be bought in stores. Must have brass Avon name plate. District Managers **CMV $90,** Team Leaders **CMV $75**

CIRCLE OF EXCELLENCE BUTTON 1979
2 1/4" brown & white button. **CMV $2.**

CALCULATOR 1986
Pocket calculator, in Avon box. Brass & green face. **CMV $15.**

"YO YO AVON" 1986
White Avon yo yo. **CMV $5.**

LEFT- CALCULATOR AWARD 1983
Red canvas holds small Novus solar calculator. **CMV $20.**

CALCULATOR AWARD 1982
Black vinyl with 4A holds Casio battery calculator. **CMV $15.**

DIRECTOR CHAIR AWARD 1985
White fold up chair, red canvas. 5 given in each district. **CMV $35.**

BLAZER JACKETS 1982-83
Blue blazer with 4A brass buttons & gold 4A ensignia or jacket for Reps. **CMV $75.**
Also came for Managers with M in center of 4A ensignia. **CMV $100.**

AVON MENU SCARF 1976
White silk scarf with Circle of Excellence dinner menu in L.A. Calif. 1976 printed in blue letters. **CMV $25.**

DOOR MAT AWARD 1980s
Red door mat, white letters. Black rubber back. Bottom mat is 2" smaller and is red with black letters. **CMV $15. ea.**

BASEBALL HAT 1978
White & black Avon cap. **CMV $5.**

INCENTIVE AWARDS 1985
Stocking hat, mittens & neck scarf. White knit with red letters. Given to Reps. **CMV $25 set.**

PRESIDENT'S DAY FRISBEE BAG AWARD 1984
White nylon zipper bag given to Reps. **CMV $20.**

PRESIDENT'S CLUB SCARF X-MAS GIFT 1985
White silk scarf with red & gold P.C. design in red box. **CMV $5.**
PRESIDENT'S CLUB BIRTHDAY PICTURE FRAME GIFT 1985
Red front paper frame with floral back. **CMV $5.**

FUN SHIRT AWARD 1985
White sweat shirt. Red & blue design. Given to Reps. **CMV $10.**

SANTA'S SACK BY AVON 1986
(left) Red canvas bag. White letters. Given to Reps. **CMV $5.**

SWITCH TO AVON TOTE BAG AWARD 1987
Beige canvas bag. Orange letters. Also came larger in size from Newark branch. **CMV $5.**
T-SHIRT AVON SUNSET AWARD
Light blue shirt - yellow sun. **CMV $10.**

T-SHIRTS AWARDS MISC. 1970s - 80s
ROSE BOWL SWEATSHIRT 84
Red - **CMV $20.**
FUTURES CIRCUIT TENNIS
Red t-shirt.
AVON CHAMIONSHIP TENNIS
Red t-shirt.
AVON T-SHIRT
Blue shirt.
AVON T-SHIRT CANADA
White with Avon on both sleeves.
CMV $10. all T-shirts.

CHRISTMAS IS FOR CHILDREN APRON 1986
White apron - green & red design. Given to workers only at 6 parties in U.S. **CMV $20.**

T SHIRTS AWARDS MISC. 1970s-1980s
AVON WOMENS RUN - GREEN
AVON RUNNING CANADA - WHITE & RED
AVON MARATHON INT. WOMEN'S
CHAMPIONSHIP - RED & WHITE
AVON INTERNATIONAL MARATHON
TRAINNG 1983
White - red design - 2 girls running. L.A.
AVON RUNNING
White - red letters.
CMV $10. each.

CUSTOMER SERVING APRON 1987
Red apron, white letters & trim. Given to Reps. **CMV $5.**

APRON AWARD 1979
Fruit on apron with red or yellow border & straps. Given at representatives meetings. **CMV $8. ea.**

T-SHIRT AWARDS 1985-86
I'M SO EXCITED
Avon on back. White - red trim. **CMV $10.**
AVON BELT
Red canvas - white letters. **CMV $5.**
AVON - SAME FAMILY - NEW ADDRESS
Red sweatshirt. **CMV $10.**
NIGHT SHIRT - AVON
Red - white letters. **CMV $10.**
"I SURVIVED THE AVON BRANCH CLOSING KANSAS CITY 1985"
Yellow shirt. **CMV $10.**

APRON AWARDS 1986
"AVON" CMV $5.
"I LOVE AVON" CMV $5.
"I LOVE SUMMER WITH AVON" CMV $7.
All are white - red & black letters & trim.

WE'RE HOT T-SHIRT & SWEATSHIRT & BUTTON 1984
Red T-Shirt & Sweatshirt & We're Hot button. Given to Reps. **CMV button $2., T-Shirt $10., Sweatshirt $12.**

T-SHIRT AWARD - "WE CAN DO IT TOGETHER" 1984
Red T-shirt given to Reps. **CMV $10.**
YOU'RE HOT - HOT PAD AWARD 1982
Red & white glove hot pad. Given to Reps. **CMV $3.**

CIRCLE OF EXCELLENCE BEACH ROBE & BAG 1977
White terry cloth robe trimmed in light blue with C of E on pocket. White canvas bag C of E 1977. **CMV $15. Bag., $35. Robe.**

SPORTS BAG AWARDS - 1980s
AVON SPORTS
Silver & black bag. Avon sports red patch on both sides. **CMV $30.**
GIRL SCOUT AVON BAG
Silver & black bag. Girl Scouts Leadership today & tomorrow on back side. Avon on other. **CMV $30.**
AVON CHAMPIONSHIPS OF WASHINGTON TENNIS RACKET COVER
White, red trim. **CMV $25.**
AVON CORPORATE PRESIDENT'S DAY 1984
Frisbee shape blue & white bag unzips to make tote bag. **CMV $25.**

TOTE BAGS 1985 - 1986
AVON HAWAII
White. **CMV $12.**
AVON
White. **CMV $5.**
AVON LIFE
Red. **CMV $12.**
HAT AVON
White Avon Hat. **CMV $5**

TOTE BAG "AVON SPORTS" 1982
White canvas, red & lavender letters. Given to staff members of Avon Running Circuit. **CMV $15.**

TOTE BAG "HAWAIIAN" 1983
Turquoise canvas bag given to Top Reps on 1983 Hawaiian trip. **CMV $15.**

AVON RUNNING BAG 1983
White canvas bag with red & fushia color lettering. **CMV $20.**

ROSE PARADE AVON SEAT CUSHION 1984
(left) Reddish orange plastic - white letters. Only 150 made & given to people at Rose Bowl game 1984. **CMV $50.**

LICENSE PLATE FRAME AWARD 1980s
White plastic, marked Avon. **CMV $2.**
MANAGER'S TAMBORINE 1970's
Wood frame, skin marked Avon. Made in China. **CMV $30.**

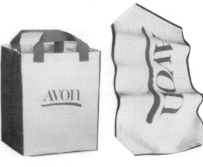

TOTE BAG 1987
Canvas bag with red handle & letters. **CMV $10.**

BEACH TOWEL 1987
29" x 60 " white beach towel. Red letters. **CMV $15.**

HORIZONS CLOTHES BAG GIFT 1977
Given to Avon managers. White plastic bag. **CMV $15.**

TIME OF YOUR LIFE BAG AWARD 1978
Beige canvas bag with red letters given to Reps. on trip to New York. **CMV $10.**

CIRCLE OF EXCELLENCE LOVE CAMERA 1985
Coke can size love container with top & side C of E labels. Holds small black & red love plastic camera in felt bag. Given to Managers for Hawaii trip. **CMV $15. MB.**

TRAVEL BAG - CIRCLE OF EXCELLENCE 1978
White leatherette bag given to 250 district managers. **CMV $50.**

ENVIRA VISOR HAT - AUSTRALIA 1980
Light pink visor hat given to Reps. at the introduction of Envira in Australia. **CMV $10.**

EMPRISE T-SHIRT 1977
Black t-shirt given to Avon managers to introduce Emprise line. **CMV $15.**

SELLATHON VISOR CAP 1981
(Left) Blue or red. **CMV $5.**

AVON TENNIS VISOR CAP 1981
(Right) White cap. **CMV $5.**

COLOR UP AMERICA NECK TIE 1979
(Top left) Given to male managers only. **CMV $10.**

COLOR UP FLAG
(Center) **CMV $2.**

COLOR UP HAT
(Bottom) **CMV $4.**

PYRAMID PAPERWEIGHT AWARD 1981
(right) Clear lucite with gold 4A design on bottom & 2 sides on top. Given to district managers only. **CMV $50.**

H-E-A-T BAG AWARD 1981
Canvas bag. **CMV $10.**

H-E-A-T HAT
White hat. **CMV $8.**

YOU MAKE ME SMILE LUGGAGE TAG 1978
White plastic. **CMV $3.**
AVON CHAMPIONSHIP TENNIS HAT 1978
White hat, red letters. **CMV $7.**

PRESIDENT'S CELEBRATION BANNER 1974
Small dark blue felt banner about 18" long, yellow letters & cord. Used by managers. **CMV $15.**

PRESIDENT'S AWARD PENNANT 1951-52
Royal blue pennant with gold trim & letters. Given to top selling city & district division managers during early 50's. **CMV $45.**

OUR BANNER YEAR 1966
Used during district sales meetings. **CMV $20.** There are many different banners of this type. **CMV will range $15 to $20 on most.**

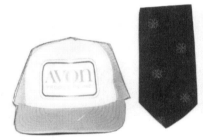

BASEBALL CAP 1978
Blue & white Avon Products Inc. hat. Used by plant employees. **CMV $12.50**
NECKTIE - AVON 4A 1970's
Used by Avon management. Tie has 4A design & is dark blue. Made of Dacron Polyester. **CMV $12.50.**

PRESIDENT'S AWARD BANNER 1961
Small banner given to top sales team in each division. Each winning division had their name on banner. **CMV $25.**

AVON CHRISTMAS TABLE CLOTH 1977
4x4 ft. blue satin, white letters, used at Christmas dinner 1977 for Avon Reps. in Atlanta branch. **CMV $15.**

MOISTURE SECRET MANAGERS GIFT SET 1975
Pink box holds pink plastic jars of creme gel 4oz., enriched freshened 5oz., and night concentrate 3 oz. C-8-75. **CMV $15 set MB.**

GREAT AMERICAN SELLATHON AWARDS 1981
Given to Avon Reps. for meeting top sales goals in C18-81.
T-Shirt, **CMV $5.**
Calculator, **CMV $20.**
Coffee Mugs, set of 2, **CMV $10.**
Drinking glasses, set of 4, **CMV $12.**
Hot Plate, **CMV $20.**
Telephone, antique, **CMV $75.**
Travel beach bag, **CMV $15.**
Clock, **CMV $35.**
Directors chair, **CMV $35.**
Umbrella, **CMV $25.**
Poncho in bag, **CMV $10.**
All are red, white & blue decoration.

KEY CHAIN "RECORD BREAKER" 1979
Yellow, green, white or pink plastic. Has 4A design & says "I'm an Avon Record Breaker". Given to reps for getting new reps. **CMV $5.**

MATCHES-PRESIDENT'S CELEBRATION 1979
Blue foil top box. **CMV $2**
LUGGAGE TAG 1970'S
White plastic with gold 4A emblem & The Better Way. **CMV $5.**

WHAT'S COOKING RECIPE BOX 1975
Given to Reps. for drawing their name at sales meetings. Avon on the bottom. **CMV $5.**
NAME TAGS LATE 1970'S
3 different stick on name tags used by Reps. **CMV .50¢ each.**

AVON SMILE SALES PROMOTION ITEMS 1978
Are all red and white.
Silk Scarf, **$6**
Ballons, 2 different, **.25¢ each**
Hat-paper, **$1**
The Smile Lips, red paperlips, **.50¢**
Record, Avon Smile, red small record, **$2.**

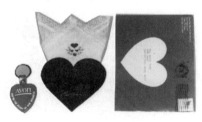

VALENTINE-PRESIDENT'S CLUB 1980
Given to President's Club Reps. Red valentine and white, red and green lace hankercheif, **CMV $5 mint in envelope.**
KEY CHAIN HEART 1978
Red plastic heart given to managers. **CMV $2.**

TEDDY BEAR CANDLE AWARD 1980
Small plastic bear candle holder. Given to Avon Team Leaders. Neck tag says "From Avon with Love". Red candle. **CMV $15.**

DISTINGUISHED MANAGEMENT AWARD LUGGAGE TAG 1966
Plastic name tag for luggage on white strap. **CMV $7.50.**
POCKET ADDRESS MEMORANDUM 1966
2"x3" white w/gold lettering. **CMV $8.**

TRAVEL SURVIVAL KIT 1982
(Top) Given to managers March, 1982. **CMV $7.**
AVON CALLING KEYCHAIN AWARD 1980
(Bottom) Clear lucite with blue letters. Given to Avon Reps. **CMV $5.**

MOISTURE SECRET PRESIDENT'S CLUB GIFT 1975
Sent to President's Club members to introduce Moisture Secret. **CMV $6. MB.**
I KNOW A SECRET PIN 1975
For President's Club members. Pink pin. **CMV $1., $2. on card.**

TEDDY BEAR TEAM LEADER GIFT 1981

White ceramic heart shaped box. Given to Team Leaders for 1981 year end party. Can also be bought in Hallmark stores. Does not say Avon . **CMV $10 MB**

POLLY PROSPECTING BIRD AWARD 1977

Stuffed toy by Possem Trot. Tag has Avon Products on it. Given to Avon managers for recruiting new reps. Came with 2 large cards as shown. **CMV $25 with Avon tag. Add $1 each card. Came in Avon mailer tube & letter. CMV $35 MB all.**

AWARD BANK 1980

Black & gold tin bank. Given to Avon managers in Springdale branch. Special hold label on front says "Fifth National Bank & Trust Co. Springdale Branch. Assets 367 Managers, R. Manning President". Bottom marked "Made in England for Avon". **CMV $30.**

TEDDY AWARD 1979

Black base with plaque. Brown top & bear has red shirt with Avon in white. Given to one Team Leader for recommendation support in each district. **CMV $35.**

TEDDY BEAR COOKIE JAR AWARD 1979

Tan & red ceramic bear cookie jar. Given to Team Leaders at Christmas. **CMV $25.**

SALES AWARD SACHET 1962

Cream sachet in blue glass with blue, gold & white lid. Gold metal stand. **$12 jar only, $15 in box.**

CABLE CAR MUSIC BOX AWARD 1981

Only 100 given to Circle of Excellence Managers at San Francisco C of E meeting. Was not made for Avon. **CMV $35.**

TED. E. BEAR TEAM LEADER GIFT 1978

Tan teddy bear with red shirt was given to all team leaders at end of year party Nov. 1978. Fold out Teddy Bear card was on each table at party. **CMV $4 card, CMV $25 bear mint.**

MONTE CARLO BRASS BOX AWARD 1981

Brass box with burgundy velvet lining. Lid inscribed Casino Monte Carlo. Given to Avon managers eligible to win a free trip to Monte Carlo. **CMV $40.**

TEMPO MANAGERS GIFT 1978

(Left) .33 oz. splash cologne. Given to district sales managers at August Conference 1978. Came with red felt belt. **CMV $15 in bag.**

TEMPO SPRAY ATOMIZER GIFT 1978

(Right) Given to avon Reps. for advanced orders of Tempo fragrance. Silver color container red letters. "Tempo Fall 1978" printed on bottom of case. Came in beige velvet bag, red pull string in special issue box. **CMV $10 MB.**

PRESIDENT'S CAMPAIGN COMPACT AWARD 1966

Case marked sterling silver & back marked "Branch Champions President's Campaign 1966". Came in white & gold Avon box in felt bag. **CMV $35 in silver case MB.**

AWARDS & REPRESENTATIVES GIFTS

**ANNIVERSARY HONOR AWARD PURSE
1966**
Red leatherette purse given to Reps. for high
sales. 4A design on snap & Avon Anniversary
Honor Award in gold letters on purse. Came in
Avon box. **CMV $15 purse only, $20 MB.**

SURPRISE GIFT 1960
Silver and Gold box contained one Deluxe
Lipstick. Given as a Christmas Gift to all
representatives. **CMV $22.50 MB.**

CIRCLE OF EXCELLENCE TOTE BAG 1976
Tan & brown tote bag with C of E on front.
Given to Avon managers on Hawaii C of E
front. Given to Avon managers on Hawaii C of
E trip. **CMV $16.**

AWARD PURSE 1960'S
Avon marked box holds beige vinyl clutch
purse trimmed in brass. Made by St. Thomas.
Given to Reps. during President's Campaign.
Purse does not say Avon. **CMV $9 mint in
Avon box.**

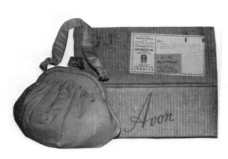

PURSE AWARD 1951
Egg shell off white purse with clear plastic
closure. Given to Avon Reps. for best sales.
Came in Avon box. Purse not marked Avon.
Must be in Avon box. **CMV $27.50 MB.**

TRENDSETTER CARRY ALL BAG 1975
Made of tan burlap & brown leatherette. Given
to managers only. **CMV $45.**

**CIRCLE OF EXCELLENCE TOTEBAG
1972**
About 18" across, black plastic. For trip to
Mexico. Aztec calendar design. Given to C of
E managers on Mexico trip. **CMV $30.**

FOAMING BATH OIL SAMPLE GIFT 1975
Given to President's Club members. 1/2 oz.
bottle, white cap. President's CLub label on
bottom. Came in introductory envelope. **CMV
$3.50 in envelope.**

CIRCLE OF EXCELLENCE BAG 1981
White canvas bag, red line around bottom.
Given to managers in San Francisco C of E
trip. **CMV $15 mint.**
CIRCLE OF EXCELLENCE MAP 1981
Map of San Fraancisco given to C of E
managers on trip. **CMV $3.**

**ANNIVERSARY CAMPAIGN AWARD PURSE
1961**
Same purse with deluxe lipstick & compact as
Champagne Mood Set. In Avon award box.
CMV $20 MB.

GREAT OAK BAG AWARD 1980
Canvas bag. **CMV $10.**

PRESIDENT'S CAMPAIGN AWARD PURSE 1965
Bone beige coin & bill purse with 4A design on flap. Given to each Rep. in 2 top sales teams in each branch for greatest sales increase over year before period. **CMV $15.**

CIRCLE OF EXCELLENCE TOTEBAG 1979
Khaki color bag. Says "Circle of Excellence". Given to top 250 managers. **CMV $15.**

PRESIDENT'S SERVICE AWARD PURSE 1963
Given to all Reps. who called on 35 or more customers during President's Campaign 1963. Egg shell color vinyl coin purse with 4A design on snap. Box says "Avon Fashion First". **CMV $20 MB.**

PURSE - AVON PLANT TOUR GUIDE 1970
Gray plastic purse with heavy silver chain. 4A silver button on purse. Used by tour guides at Avon Plants. **CMV $20.**

TOTE BAG 1977
White canvas with black nylon straps. Came from Avon in New York. Was not issued to Reps. in U.S. **CMV $25.**

SWEET PICKLES BAG GIFT 1978
Green canvas bag given to district managers on introduction of Sweet Pickle products. **CMV $12.50 bag only.**

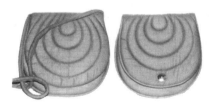

TASHA STOWAWAY BAG 1980
Purple shoulder bag given to Reps. Avon tag inside. Pink inside bag. **CMV $15.** Managers also got the same bag without the brass snap on the outside. Same color inside as outside. **CMV $20.**

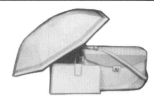

SALES MATES PRIZES PRESIDENT'S CLUB 1978
All are tan & beige in color, covered with "A" design. Umbrella, Beauty Showcase handbag and jewelry demonstrator given to President's Club Reps. for selling $975 worth of Avon in C4-5-6 1978.
Umbrella, CMV $20.
Jewelry Demo Case, CMV $7
Handbag, CMV $7.

TASHA UMBRELLA "I'M NUMBER ONE" 1980
Tan silk umbrella given Reps. on Flight to Fantasy Trip to Monte Carlo. **CMV $75.**

LIBERTY WEEKEND UMBRELLA 1986
Red & white umbrella. Marked Avon Liberty Weekend. **Rare** N.Y. Liberty Celebration. **CMV $150.00**

APRIL SHOWERS UMBRELLA GIFT 1976
(Left) Beige canvas, wood handle. Avon in blue letters. Given as recommendation prize. **CMV $27.50.**

AWARDS & REPRESENTATIVES GIFTS

ADVERTISING UMBRELLA 1977
White Avon box holds brown plastic handle umbrella. Has the names of Avon & magazines & TV shows Avon advertises on. Given to district managers. **CMV $30 MB.**

PRESIDENT'S CELEBRATION UMBRELLA 1977
Marked New York. Given to winning teams. **CMV $35.**

UMBRELLA & BAG AWARD 1980
Tan & brown Avon bag comes with Avon umbrella. Given to Reps. for selling $425 of products in C16-17 1980. **CMV $18.**

DEVOTEE TREASURE BOX AWARD 1986
Brass & glass box mirror bottom. Given to Reps. in black box. **CMV $25 MB.**

AVON TENNIS UMBRELLA 1980
Only 50 silver nylon with fine wood handle umbrellas were given to press & promoters of Avon tennis matches. Comes in matching silver pouch. Rare. **CMV $125.**

AVON TENNIS CLOTHES BAG 1980
Red & white patch on silver & black nylon travel bag. Comes in small carrying pouch. Given to players of Avon tennis matches. **CMV $50. Rare.**

AVON TENNIS WRISTS BANDS 1980
Pair of white cotton wrist bands used by players in Avon tennis matches. **CMV $4.**
AVON TENNIS HAND TOWEL 1980
White cotton, used by Avon tennis players. **CMV $10.**

EMPLOYEE GIFT 1939
Blue box with Avon's Suffern Plant on box. Holds Tulip label and gold cap of Cotillion Toilet water. CPC label & Cotillion powder sachet. Rare. **CMV $125 MB.**

CHRISTMAS CAROL CANDLE SET 1959
Red velvet box with green lining holds 4 red & white angel candles with blue eyes & blond hair. Candles made by Gurley Novelty Co., label on bottom. Outside of box says "An Avon Christmas Carol". Given to Avon managers at Christmas 1959. **CMV $130 MB.**

UMBRELLA LIPSTICK AWARD 1981
White nylon, black & red trim, red plastic handle. Given to Team Leaders. **CMV $25.**

58th ANNIVERSARY GIFT BOX 1944
Holds heart shaped sachet pillow. Given to all Reps. on Avon's 58th anniversary. **CMV $100 MB.**

DESK SET ACHIEVEMENT AWARD 1979
Black plastic note pad & pen. Given to district managers for sales achievement. **CMV $5 with pen.**

ANNIVERSARY ALBUM AWARDS SET 1942
Book type box opens to show 2 satin pillowettes with 56th Anniversary on back of each. One is blue & one pink. Given during Anniversary campaign. **CMV $125.**

56th ANNIVERSARY AWARD 1942
Satin Sachet pillows given to each Rep. who worked her territory for 56 hours during the Anniversary Campaign. Came 2 to a box, in blue & pink. **CMV $30 mint.**

BETSY ROSS RED GIFT SET 1941
Set given to employees of Avon's Suffern Plant as Anniversary campaign gift. Rare. Came with handwritten gift card. **CMV $100.00 MB.**

DOOR BELL - DOOR KNOCKER AWARDS 1979
Redwood box with brass Avon Calling door knocker on front, door bell on back side. Given to 5 managers in each division. **CMV $75.**

MANAGER DESK SET AWARD 1972
Has 4A emblem, marble base, 14K gold plated pen. Set made by Cross. **CMV $60, $75 MB.**

AVON CALLING DOOR BELL 1950's
(Left) Used at Avon meetings. Has button on back to ring door bell. **CMV $85. mint.**
PERFUME CREME ROLLETTE CHRISTMAS GIFT 1962
(Right) .33 oz. gold cap, 4A embossed bottle & box. Given to Reps. at Christmas 1962. Came in Here's My Heart, Persian Wood, To A Wild Rose, Topaze, Somewhere, Cotillion. **CMV $12. in box shown.**

INKWELL & PEN SET AWARD 1977
Blue & gold display box holds wood base with old glass ink well & 3 feather quill pens & plastic bottle of ink. Avon card about pen set. Avon brass plaque on base. Given for recruiting new Reps. **CMV $45 MB.**

88th ANNIVERSARY DESK SET 1974
White marble base. Black pen. Turquoise & silver 4A says "Avon 88th Anniversary". Given to Reps. for selling $125 worth of Avon. **CMV $10, $15 MB.**

REPRESENTATIVE GIFT CIGARETTE CASE 1961
Siver colored metal case. 4A design & Christmas 1961 on lid. **CMV $47.50.** Also given to managers in gold tone case. **CMV $70.**

DESK VALET - CPC AWARD 1922
Solid bronze. Marked CPC 1922. Awarded to CPC Reps. **CMV $100.00**

TOCCARA PINS 1981
3 different pins. Same design on face, edges are different. **CMV $10 each.**

TOCCARA NECKLACE AWARD 1981
Toccara design on one side & Avon Toccara 1981 K.C. on back. Sterling Silver pendant & chain in Tiffany bag & box. Given to Division Managers. **CMV $100.00 MB.**

STEAK KNIFE & CARVING SET 1972
C-12, 1972. In Avon box. **CMV $20 each set MB with sleeve.**

WINNING TEAM DESK SET AWARD 1976
Given for best sales team in district in 1976. White marble base, silver color pen. **CMV $8.**

IMARI 1ST EDITION COLOGNE AWARD 1985
1.2 oz. spray cologne marked First Edition 1985 on bottle. Given only to Reps. **CMV $15.**

SPOON - PRESIDENT'S CLUB AWARD 1979
(Left) Silver plated serving spoon marked "Avon President's Club 1979". Came in Avon box. **CMV $10 MB.**
CAKE SERVER AWARD 1978
(Right) Silver plated serving spatula. "Avon 92nd Anniversary - President's Club 1978" on spoon. Given to all President's Club members. Special box & card. **CMV $10. MB.**

LETTER OPENER MANAGER AWARD 1975
Red & black box holds wood handle letter opener. Brass Avon lady insignia & K.C. No. 1, 1975 on hand. **CMV $20 MB.**

PRESIDENTS CLUB FRUIT JARS AWARD 1988
Set of 3 glass jars marked Avon Presidents Club on side. **CMV $20.00 Set**

50th ANNIVERSARY SPOON - 1936
Gold spoon engraved "Compliments Mr. & Mrs. D. H. McConnell - Anniversary 50". The gold on these spoons does not stay very well so many are found silver. **Spoon in box gold CMV $100 mint., Silver spoon only CMV $50., Spoon with gold CMV $75. mint.**

CIRCLE OF EXCELLENCE LETTER OPENER 1976
Given in Indiana only to C of E Reps. Only 25 were given. Brass plaque & door knocker pin is embedded in black plastic handle. **CMV $40.**

DOLLAR INCREASE CLOCK AWARD 1978
(left) Dark amber lucite clock stand with pen set & 4A. **CMV $20.00**

CPC SPOON "STERLING SILVER" 1915
Sold as souvenir at the CPC exhibit at the Panama-Pacific International Exposition. Front reads "Palace of Liberal Arts - Panama-Pacific Exposition Tower of Jewels". Back of spoon reads "CPC 1915 Court of Four Seasons". **CMV $100 with card shown, $75 spoon only.** Was also given to Reps. for selling 12 CPC talcum powders, 1 free for each 12 talcs.

WINDBREAKER 1980
Blue jacket, red & white trim. Sold to Avon employees in Springdale branch for $15. Modeled by Dwight Young. **CMV $15.**

CANDID BLAZER & TIE 1977
Off white blazer with CA on left pocket. Given to division managers only. Came in both male & female sizes. Tie is Candid color with CA on it. Very few of these blazers around. Modeled by Dwight Young. **Blazer CMV $75., Tie CMV $10.**

AVON AWARD SPOONS 1969
6 silver plated demitasse spoons. Each engraved with a design signifying a different fragrance: Occur, Rapture, Unforgettable, Regence, Brocade & Charisma. Each spoon was given in this order for progressively higher sales. A seventh spoon was given to each Rep. in the winning district of each branch. It was engraved "1886-1969" and had a picture of the 1886 Sales Lady. **CMV $45 set MB with sleeve or $5 each spoon. 7th spoon $12.50 in silver envelope.**

AVON RUNNING RAIN COAT 1981
Shown front & back side. Given to people helping in Avon Running Tournament. Red plastic. Modeled by Vera Young. **CMV $10.**

BLAZER JACKET 1977
Blue blazer with 4A design buttons. Inside label says "Made exclusively for the Avon Representative by Family Fashions". Sold to Avon Reps. Red Avon sewn on patch for pocket. **CMV $35.**

SILVERWARE AWARD 1938
Made only for Avon. Each piece marked on back Simeon L. & George H. Rogers Co. Ltd. X-tra. Given for meeting sale goal during Avon's 50th Anniversary. 55 piece set. **CMV set in box. $125.00 mint.**

CPC SILVERWARE 1920-30's
Used in CPC fatories for employee eating areas. CPC stamped on back of knife, fork & spoons. **CMV $5 each piece.**

IF YOU PAID MORE FOR ANY AVON COLLECTIBLE IN THIS BOOK IN THE LAST 2 YEARS & FEEL YOU PAID A FAIR PRICE. SEND THIS INFORMATION TO BUD HASTIN, PO BOX 9868, KANSAS CITY, MO. 64134 SO HE CAN CHANGE THE PRICE IN HIS NEXT BOOK. REMEMBER THAT AVON TIMES EACH MONTH REFLECTS THE AVERAGE GOING PRICE ON MOST AVONS. IF YOU DON'T GET AVON TIMES. YOU MAY PAY TO MUCH .

AWARDS & REPRESENTATIVES GIFTS

MANAGERS CHRISTMAS GIFT 1980
Red & white scarf and mittens given at
Christmas time. **CMV $30 set.**

TOCCARA AWARDS 1981
(Sweater) Dark navy blue with Avon tag.
Given for 1st level sales achievement. **CMV
$10.**
(Caftan) Lavender & white with Avon Toccara
label. Given to 2nd level sales achievement.
Came in shiny silver plastic Toccara bag.
CMV $25 in bag.

AVON SMILE HAT 1978
White hat given to Avon collectors at Houston,
Texas, 1978 National Association of Avon Club
Convention by Avon Products. **CMV $15.**

CIRCLE OF EXCELLENCE TOWEL 1979
Given to top 250 managers. **CMV $20.**

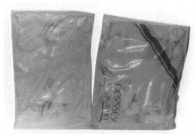

CIRCLE OF EXCELLENCE AWARDS 1979
Each item given to managers on C of E trip to
Paris 1979.
TRAVEL ALARM CLOCK
(right) Plaque on top says "Circle of Excellence
1979". **CMV $25.**
TOTE BAG Dark navy blue. Circle of
Excellence on front. **CMV $15.**
CIRCLE OF EXCELLENCE YEAR BOOK
Blue & gold cover shows all C of E winners.
CMV $10.
FRAGRANCE & FASHION BINDER
White plastic. **CMV $25 with contents.**

ODYSSEY AWARDS 1980
(Bathrobe) Pink bathrobe given to Reps. for
meeting 2nd level sales goals. **CMV $25 in
Avon bag.**
(Nightgown) Pink nightgown matches
bathrobe. Given to Reps. for meeting 1st level
sales goals. **CMV $15 MB.**

**I'M GOING TO MONTE CARLO MAGNET
1981**
(Center) Given to managers. White, red &
gold. **CMV $4.**
VALENTINE SUCKER 1981
(Left) Red heart shaped sucker with red tag.
Given to Avon managers. **CMV $10.**
NUMBER ONE SCARF AWARD
(Right) Given to team leaders. **CMV $4.**

TOCCARA PILLOW AWARD 1981
Dark blue satin pillow with Avon card. Given
to managers at August Conference. **CMV $15
with Avon card.**

AVON REP. CHRISTMAS GIFT 1981
(left)Red box says "Happy Holidays Avon 1981".
Tapestry design address book. Managers book
says "District Manager" on front. **CMV $15 MB.**
Reps. same except plain on front. **CMV $10
MB.**
HOSTESS APRON
Cotton tapestry design apron given to team
leaders who met requirements. **CMV $15.**

RECOMMENDATION CASIO PRIZE 1980
Casio LC 315 calculator in 4A design black
case. **CMV $20.**

AVONS BEST BANNER 1982
(Top) Red & white banner. **CMV $5.**
AVONS BEST SCARF 1982
(Bottom) From Morton Grove branch. Red & white scarf given to managers at Atlanta Conference. **CMV $15.**

CIRCLE OF EXCELLENCE BEACH TOWEL 1976
White & brown towel given to managers on C of E Hawaii trip. **CMV $20 mint.**

T-SHIRT - AVON RUNNING 1979
Red t-shirt given to each runner in Avon marathon race. **CMV $10.**

SYMPHONY SCARF 1952
Blue background with pink rose & parts of letters in French. Pure silk. Purchased from store in New York & awarded for selling 36 products in the Prelude to Spring campaign. **CMV $30 mint.**

PRESIDENTS CAMPAIGN GLACE AWARD 1967
Managers is in script writing with white lined box. **CMV $22.50 MB. $18.50 compact only.**
Representatives is in block writing on Presidents Campaign with blue felt lined box. **CMV $10. $12 MB.** Both came in Hawaiian White Ginger box.

FOUNDERS CAMPAIGN ACHIEVEMENT AWARD SCARF 1941
Blue & white folder holds blue border, white pink & green silk scarf. Shows 1st CPC factory & 1st Avon lady with "The doorway to loveliness" marked under her. Given to reps in 1941. Very rare. **CMV $75 in folder mint, $50 scarf only mint.**

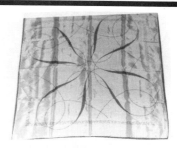

SILK SCARF AWARD 1970
Beige & brown silk scarf. 4A design. Given to Avon reps. **CMV $20.**

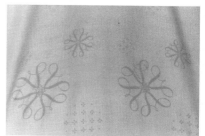

AVON CURTAINS 1960's
Used to decorate offices & Avon plant **CMV $35.**

64TH ANNIVERSARY SCARF 1950
Silk scarf was made only for Avon. Given to representatives for selling 64 pieces of Avon in campaign 9, 1950. Silk scarf has blue border, white center with sketches in turquoise & rose. Some words on scarf say "Long, long ago"; "A thing of beauty is a joy forever"; "The doorway to loveliness". **CMV $50.**

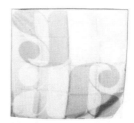

AVON SCARF 1972
All silk pink, orange & white scarf with 4 big "A" on it. Avon in corner. Made in Italy. Came in silver box. **CMV $12. mint.**

AWARDS & REPRESENTATIVES GIFTS

CANDID SCARF GIFT 1976
Silk scarf designed by S.M. Kent in Candid folder. Given to Avon President's Club members. **CMV $7.**

CIRCLE OF EXCELLENCE STATIONERY ROME 1983
2 boxes given to all managers on trip to Rome in 1983. **CMV $25 MB set.**

AVON APRON 1948
Aqua in color with white center. Avon in center & pictures of Avon products of 1948. Given to Managers only for sales demo. **CMV $50 mint.**

TASHA AWARDS 1980
Monte Carlo scarf, **CMV $20.**
Tasha picture of the late Princess Grace of Monte Carlo with Tasha card. **CMV $20.**
Tasha matches - box & book matches, **CMV $1 each.**
Items were won by reps on Avon trip to Monte Carlo.

GREAT AMERICAN SELLATHON PRIZES 1981
Name tag, **CMV $1.**
Luggage tag, **CMV $2.**
Menu Presidents Celebration, **CMV $2.**
Portfolio, **CMV $2.**

WALL PLAQUE 1960's
Used at sales meetings. Blue & gold cardboard. **CMV $25.**

4A QUILT 1971
Reversible, ruffled edged, cotton filled comforter in gold, avocado or blue. Given for having a person recommended a a representative appointed. **CMV $150 mint.**
4A QUILT 1969
Pink quilt with white 4A design. **CMV $150 mint.**

4A WALL PLAQUE 1960's
Used at sales meetings. Large size. **CMV $25.**

ORDER BOOK & CALCULATOR 1983
Red Avon box has red Avon order book cover with order book, calculator & calendar. 5 reps in each district won them. **CMV $17.50 MB.**

TOTE BAG (WHO COULD SELL AVON) 1983
Beige canvas hand bag, red letters. Given to reps. **CMV $5.**

JAM GIFT SET AWARD 1980
Set of 16 small jars of jam with front label "Especially for You from Avon". Given to managers. Was not made only for Avon. **CMV $10. MB.**

AFTER CONFERENCE MINTS 1979
Pink box of fifty 1979 Susan B. Anthony dollar coins with card for Avon managers for Outstanding Recuiting. **CMV $125.00 MB with all 1979 coins mint.**

VALENTINE GIFT TO REPRESENTATIVES 1976
Whitman Sampler went to all reps. with Avon card. **CMV $3 with card only.**

VALENTINE CANDY 1978
Red and gold heart box. Holds 4 1/2 oz. of chocolates by Bartons. Back of box says "This candy heart selected by Avon and packaged especially for you. Given to Avon reps. **CMV $5 box only., $10 MB full.**

GENERAL MANAGERS HONOR AWARD 1960
(Top) Order book cover in blue. **CMV $8 mint**
HONOR AWARD ORDER BOOK COVER 1959
(Bottom) Red plastic with gold trim, also had gold pen. **CMV $10.**

ORDER BOOK COVERS 1980-81
Blue plastic. Avon pen inside. Given to all new Avon reps. Gold Avon stamped on face. **CMV $2.** Also came wtih Avon stamped upside down. **CMV $5.**

TREND SETTERS ORDER BOOK AWARD 1976
(Left) Yellow plastic with 4A design and Avon Trend Setters on front. Given to Avon Trend Setters Reps. **CMV $5.**
TEAM LEADER MIRROR GIFT 1977
(Right) Mirror in red plastic, holder with white star and letters. Given to Avon Team Leaders at Avon luncheon, Dec. 1977. **CMV $4.**

ACHIEVEMENT AWARD ORDER BOOK COVER 1960'S
(Left) Light blue cover. **CMV $7.**

ORDER BOOK COVER 1973
Blue and green design matches delivery bag. Has turqoise and gold pen. Earned for prize points. **CMV $5.**

75 YEAR HONOR AWARD ORDER BOOK 1961
Red with gold letters. **CMV $8 mint.**

PRESIDENT'S CLUB ORDER BOOK COVER 1960
CMV $7.

PRESIDENTS HONOR AWARD ORDER BOOK COVER 1977
Blue plastic with gold trim. **CMV $8.**
REGENCE ORDER BOOK HONOR AWARD 1966
Green plastic with gold trim to match Regence packaging. **CMV $3.**

ALBEE STATIONERY NOTES 1980
Box of 1st Avon lady notes with outer sleeve given to President's Club Reps. **CMV $5 MB.**

LADY DESK FOLIO 1971
Pink cover holds calendar to be used as a plan guide for sending orders and making appointments. Given for sending a $75 or larger order in. c1-71 **CMV $7.**

CHRISTMAS GIFT FOR AVON REPS. 1980
Ceramic base & green note pad holder signed by William Chaney, Avon President. Given to all Avon Sales Reps. at Christmas 1980. **CMV $10 MB.**

IF YOU LOVE TO LAUGH, GO TO THE BACK PAGE FOR INFO ON BUD HASTIN'S NEW JOKE BOOK AND HOW TO GET IT. LAUGH MORE AND LIVE LONGER.

A Must For All Avon Representatives and Collectors

SUBSCRIBE TO

AVON TIMES

WORLD'S LARGEST AVON CLUB & COLLECTORS' MAGAZINE SINCE 1971

DWIGHT and VERA YOUNG Publisher - Owners

ONLY
$24.00 *per year*

Canadian Members - $26 per year U.S. Money Orders Only!

- YOU GET -

*12 BIG ISSUES OF AVON TIMES
(First Class Mail) 16 pages each month mailed directly to yourdoor.

*BOTTLE SHOW LISTINGS

***3 FREE ADS
(a $22.50 value)**

Buy direct and save $.
*DIRECT COMMUNICATIONS
with THOUSANDS of collectors to buy-sell-or trade Avons free.

SEND SUBSCRIPTIONS TO:
AVON TIMES
**P. O. Box 9868
Kansas City, MO 64134**
Send $3.00 for Sample Copy.

PRESIDENTIAL WINNERS AWARD 1957
Blue felt booklet given to winning district Avon representatives upon touring district Avon plant. **CMV $30.**

MANAGER-REPRESENTATIVE INTRODUCTION BOOK 1952
Turqoise & silver booklet. Used by managers to train new Avon Reps. **CMV $10.**

CIRCLE OF EXCELLENCE PASSPORT HOLDERS 1969-80
Given each year. Each marked Circle of Excellence. Given to top managers only for annual C of E trip. Different color each year. **CMV $5 each.**

MANAGERS SALES MEETING NOTE BOOK 1961
Campaign 15,16,17,18 sales meeting plans. Inside front cover says "# so & so of a limited edition for the Management Staff Only". Cover is red satin 12"x20", comes in white box. For you from Avon on cover. **CMV $75 mint.**

NOTE PAD TRENDSETTERS 1976
Clear plastic, Avon on top holder. Trendsetter note pads. Given to managers only. **CMV $20.**

AUGUST CONFERNCE PICTURE HOLDER 1978
Tan cover. Given to managers at August conference. **CMV $15.**

CPC SALES MANAGERS GIFT 1909 -1912
4" x 4" size, pressed crystal glass jar with Rogers Silver Plate lid. Given to each Rep. selling $50 in sales in December 1909 & 1912. The silver lid has an embossed floral design. **CMV $200 mint.**

NICE KRISPIES BOX 1980
Small size cereal box given to team leaders. **CMV $10. mint.**

TEAM LEADER CARDS 1978
4 different cards given to team leaders, with bears on them. **CMV $1 each.**

71ST ANNIVERSARY CAKE 1957
A real cake with 71 on top with Avon card given to managers. Made by Schraffts. **CMV $50.**

AVON DUNCE CAPS 1964-65
Came in several different colors of plastic. Used at sales meetings. 4A design on top and bottom. **CMV $10 each.**

PARIS PICTURE GIFT 1978
French print scene by Bernard Picture Co. given to each manager with French printed Avon circle of excellence card & ribbon. **CMV $7.50. Must have Avon card as shown.**

McCONNELL FAMILY REUNION COASTERS 1980
Package of 4 white Fiesta Coasters. Center says "James McConnell Family Reunion 1980". Were given at 1st family reunion of David McConnell ancestors since 1948. **Very rare. CMV $50.00 Mint**

AWARDS & REPRESENTATIVES GIFTS

CARD CASES AWARDS 1970'S
President's Club. Pink & turqoise; vinyl, **CMV $2.50.** Top one Foreign, **CMV $5.**

BROCADE HONOR AWARD ORDER BOOK COVER 1967
Given to Reps. for calling on customers during introduction of Brocade. Came with Avon pen also. **CMV $5.,** With pen **$8.**

PRESIDENTS CELEBRATION ORDER BOOK COVER 1977
Red plastic. **CMV $3.**
PERSONAL POCKET DIARY 1976
Blue plastic cover with Avon pocket diary and calendar inside. **CMV $3.**

WACKY MONEY BAG 1980
Silver tone bag with red tie string & red $ design. Used at sales meetings. Does not say Avon. **CMV $15.**

PORTFOLIO & CALCULATOR 1984
Red canvas zipper portfolio with small NSC calculator & 1984 calendar & note pad & Avon red pen inside. Given to Reps. **CMV $30.** Calculator also given by itself in red canvas folder. **CMV $15.**

COOK BOOK FOR TEAM LEADERS 1978
Red cover 96 page book given to Team Leaders July 1978. **CMV $10 mint.**

TEDDY BEAR AWARD PLAQUE 1980
Certificate in black frame. Given for high sales. **CMV $10.**
TEDDY BEAR RECRUITING AWARD PLAQUE 1980
Ceritficate in black frame. Given for recommendation. **CMV $10.**

AVONOPOLY 1978
Game used by managers at Avon Rep. sales meeting C12-78. Also came with Avon play money of 25 & 50 green notes. **CMV set $12.**

TASHA FLIGHT TO FANTASY VASE 1980
White porcelain vase given to Reps. on Monte Carlo trip. **CMV $40.**
TASHA PASSPORT HOLDER 1980
Given to Reps. on Monte Carlo trip, held luggage tag & misc. Tasha paper items, program, etc. **CMV $20 for all.**

PRESIDENT'S CLUB THANK YOU NOTES 1979
White box with outer sleeve. Both has "President's Club, Avon's Very Best" on lid. Holds 25 thank you notes. Given to President's Club Reps. only. **CMV $5 MB complete set.**

PICTURE ALBUM AWARD 1966
White Avon box holds large and small picture album and picture frame in brown and gold. Cover says "For you, from Avon". **CMV $45 MB.**

PLACE MAT AWARD 1966
Plastic place mat showing Avon Daily Need Products. Given to Reps. for meeting sales. **CMV $5.**

TENNIS OFFICIAL BUTTON - 1977
Red futures circuit Avon official button. **CMV $5.**

AVON FUTURES SPONSOR 1980 BUTTON
White - red letters. **CMV $5.**

ROSE PARADE FLOAT DECORATOR BUTTONS
1982 white, 1984 gold. **CMV $10.**

PRESIDENT'S DAY CORPORATE MEDALLION 1983
3" brass medallion with red, white & blue ribbon. **CMV $20.**

AVON QUEEN CERTIFICATE 1964-65
78th & 79th Anniversary Award Certificates. One red and others blue border. Given to top selling Reps. only. **CMV $10 each.**

PASADENA BRANCH DEDICATION BOOKLET 1947
Gold spiral bound booklet given at opening of Pasadena Branch, Sept. 22-27, 1947. Front says "**Avon Serves the Golden West**". **CMV $25.**

BUTTONS
GOING FOR THE GOLD BUTTON 1984
TENNIS CHAMPION SPONSOR 1982
GOOD BYE CHARLIE 1984
100 YEARS BEAUTIFUL AVON
CMV $2. each button.

MANAGERS INTRODUCTION BOOK 1945
Blue cover, 28 page book, used by Avon Managers to sign up new Avon Reps. 11" x 14" size. Came with clear plastic cover. **CMV $35 mint.**

BEAUTY & FRAGRANCE CALENDAR 1978
Punch out calendar given to special good customers in C24-77 by Avon Reps. Made only for Avon. **CMV $5.** Only given in certain ^tates for test marketing.

AVON 100 CUSTOMER SERVICE PIN 1986
Gold & black pin.
AVON 100 YEARS OF BEAUTY PIN 1986
White & black.
WHO'S THE BOSS PIN 1985
Red & white.
WHO COULD SELL AVON PIN 1985
Tan & black.
CMV $2. each.

AVON CHRISTMAS CARD 1976
Green & gold Christmas card. Inside says "From your Avon Representative". Box of 75 cards given to Avon Reps. for recommendation of new Avon lady. **CMV $20 box of 75 mint, .25¢ each card mint.**

MUSIC BOX TEAM AWARD 1978
Red painted wood music box made in Japan only for Avon. Brass plate on lid says "You Made Avon Smile". Given to winning team for selling most lipsticks. **CMV $20.**

AWARDS & REPRESENTATIVES GIFTS

BUTTONS 1983-85
Misc. buttons given to Avon Reps.
CMV $1., $2. each.

BUTTONS 1983-85
Misc. buttons given to Avon Reps.
CMV $1., $2. each.

BUTTONS 1981-85
Misc buttons given to Avon Reps. CMV $1.,
$2. each.

AVON AWARDS MISC. - 1985-86
ROSE PARADE BUTTON
THE SMILE STARTS HERE BUTTON
LOOK HOW GOOD YOU LOOK KEY CHAIN
AVON ICE SCRAPER
WE THINK YOU'RE BEAUTIFUL MIRROR.
CMV $2. each.

BOWLING AVON PATCHES 1981-82
Cloth patches from Baltimore & St. Louis Avon
Bowling Tournaments. CMV $20. ea.
**AVON TENNIS CHAMPIONSHIPS BADGES
1981**
1 red & 1 yellow badge. CMV $20. ea.
AVON DOUBLE PEN AWARD
White & black & white & blue double pen.
CMV $10.

CUSTOMERS SERVICE FILE 1969
Turquoise paper box holds file envelopes for
Avon lady sales. CMV $5.

FILE BOX 1961
Turquoise cardboard file box with 4A design on
lid. CMV $6 mint.

JUNE 15 BUTTON PIN 1971
Bright green to remind customers June 15 was
Father's Day. CMV $3.
HELLO 1970 BUTTON PIN 1970
Black background with red, yellow & blue
letters & numbers. Given to all representatives
to tell the world she welcomes successful
seventies. CMV $3.

**EARLY TEAM LEADER RIBBON BADGE
1970's**
Yellow badge and ribbon used by Team
Leaders at sales meetings. CMV $5.
I GOT IT PIN 1978
Gray and white pin given to Reps. at Avon
sales meetings. Measures 2 1/4". CMV $1.

ZANY BUTTON 1979
Given to Avon Reps. on introduction of Zany
Products. CMV $1.
TEAM LEADER BUTTON 1979
Given to Avon Reps. CMV $1.

I'M THE HEART PIN 1974
Given to Reps. as being the heart of Avon.
CMV $2.

HI, I'M BUTTON 1981
(left) Says "I'm going to make you feel
beautiful". CMV $2.

BUTTON - PINS 1978
1978 Top Horizon 50 pin. **CMV $2.**
1976 Say Yes Yes To No No's. **CMV $1.**
1978 The Smile Starts Here. **CMV $1.**

4A NAME PIN 1960
Used by Avon Reps. at meetings. 2 1/2" in diameter. **CMV $3.**
COLOR WORKS MAKEUP BUTTONS 1977
Given to Reps. for sales meeting attendance. **CMV $1.**

AVON CARDS AWARD 1980
(right) Silver faced playing cards say 1980 - Avon New York - Las Vegas. Given to Division Managers at Las Vegas conference for Pasadena Branch **CMV $15 MB.**
FRISBEE - AVON 1980
(left) White plastic, blue and red letters. **CMV $10.**

AVON 91st BUTTON & RIBBON 1977
(left) Red and white button. **CMV $1. button, CMV $2. button & ribbon.**
LUGGAGE TAG 1977
(right) Round white plastic, back side says "The Magic of Avon". **CMV $2.**
"ASK ME ABOUT THE LOVE OF MY LIFE" BUTTON 1979
(top right) White & red letter button. **CMV $1.**

TEAM LEADER BOOK MARK 1974
Gold & red Book Mark. For Avon Reps. use. **CMV $8.**

FACE POWDER GOLD KEY 1936
9 1/2" long key is gold on one side with large tulip A & Avon. Back side holds silver face powder sample. CMV label. Given to Reps. only. **CMV $25 mint as shown.**

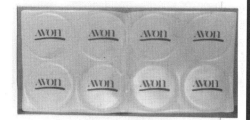

AVON COASTERS 1981
Plastic sheet of 8 white plastic coasters. Had to be cut out. Given to managers. **CMV $5 for sheet of 8.**

ROYAL RIBBON AWARDS 1980
Given to Reps. for sales achievements. Yellow or red ribbon. **CMV $2.** White & blue given with certificate. **CMV $5 each with certificate.** Some dated 1980 and some not.

CONFERENCE PIN MANAGERS 1946-47
On gold braided rope. **CMV $50 mint.**

FRISBEES - GIFT TO REPS. 1976
(left) White plastic with red letters. **CMV $6.**
White with red & green letters. **CMV $8.**

AWARDS & REPRESENTATIVES GIFTS

RECORD-HAPPY BIRTHDAY 1980
It's a most unusual day on cover. Given to President's Club Reps. on their birthday. **CMV $5 mint.**

FLIGHT TO FANTASY RECORD 1979
(left) Given to Reps. in C20-79 to introduce Fantasy fragrance. **CMV $3 record and cover mint.**

BON APPETIT COOK BOOK 1979
(right) Given to managers on Circle of Excellence trip to Paris. Avon on front, **CMV $5.**

TEAM LEADER & MANAGERS CHRISTMAS GIFT 1981
Wood case jewelry music box with mirror inside says "Avon Team Leader 1981". **CMV $65.**
Same thing given to Avon managers only says **"Managers 1981". CMV $85.**

CASTINET AWARD 1975
Given to Circle of Excellence managers only on trip to Spain. Comes with Circle of Excellence orange award card as shown. **CMV $25 MB with card.**

AVON RECORDS 1970's
Christmas Records, given to Reps. at Christmas. **CMV $3.**
Campaign 21, 1974 Sales Meeting record. **CMV $3.**

AVON CHRISTMAS RECORD 1970
33 1/3 RPM record in blue holder with letter from Avon President Fred Fusse. **CMV $5.**

DOOR KNOCKER RING DISPLAY BOX AWARD 1979
Black ring box with gold tone door knocker on cover. Given to Avon managers. **CMV $30 mint.**

TRAINING RECORDS-FILM STRIPS
(left) Used by managers to show new products at sales meetings. Box came with record and 1 film strip for each record. Have been used for many years by Avon. Many different varieties. **Record only CMV $2., $5 set MB.**

RECOMMENDATION PRIZE 1976
Blue plastic case holds 2 order books and an Avon book calculator made by Arizona. Warranty card says "Made for Avon". Given to Reps. for getting 2 new Avon Reps. **CMV $25 mint in working order.**

ROOSTER AWARD 1968
Rooster shape leather covered green glass bottom on wood base. Brass plaque says "Rooster Highest Percent Increase, 4A design & all 7 Avon branches". Given to district supervisor. **CMV $45.**

CURRIER & IVES COASTERS 1977
Pack of 6 given to Team Leaders at Christmas. Also given to Reps. for recommendation prize. Marked Avon. **CMV $5 pack of 6.**

ROSE PARADE JACKETS AWARD 1981-83
Avon Products issued 100 Rose Parade jackets in red to people working with Avon float in '81-'83 parade, rare. Same inscription on front. **CMV $100 each.**

GATEWAY SPRING COMPETITION AWARD 1977
Lucite man on plastic base & nameplate. Given to managers in Morton Grove branch. **CMV $35.**

PARKER PEN AWARD SET 1982
2 gold tone Parker pens. Says Avon on side. Given to managers. **CMV $35 MB.**

MUSK FOR MEN TRAVEL KIT AWARD 1983
Travel kit bag & 2.8 oz. Musk Cologne for men. Comes with Avon letter to reps for meeting sales goals. Bag does not say Avon. **CMV $15 MB with letter.**

RAIN GEAR UMBRELLA AWARD 1983
Tan umbrella. Avon tags. Umbrealla, **CMV $25.**

DISTRICT AWARD TROPHIES 1998
Green marble base with gold tone Mrs Albee faced top. All look the same. Different plaques. **"LEADERSHIP", "RECRUITING", "SALES", "SALES INCREASE", "BEST NEW PERFORMER", "CUSTOMER SERVICE EXCELLENCE", & "SPIRIT OF AVON". CMV $50.00 each trophy MB.**

C OF E SALES GROWING BUTTON 1983
Yellow button. **CMV $2.**
PASADENA NO. 1 BUTTON 1982
White button with red , white & blue ribbon. **CMV $2.**

AWARDS & REPRESENTATIVES GIFTS

FOOT HILL DIVISION HIGHEST DOLLAR SALES INCREASE AWARD PLAQUE 1982
Wood base plaque given to managers only. **CMV $40.**

JEWELRY BOX PRESIDENTS SALES COMPETITION AWARD 1983
Black lacquer music box made only for Avon. Bottom says "President Sales Competition 1983". 8"x 4 3/4" size. Given for sales goals. Comes with Avon card. **CMV $25.**

KEY CHAIN NEW YORK AWARD 1982
I Love Avon's New York on front. Given to group sales leaders at Leadership Circle Celebration in N.Y. **CMV $15.**

JEWELRY BOX AWARD 1965
White box has 2 lids, blue inside, 4A design & says "Bleding Corticelli" inside lid. Given to managers. **CMV $15 box only mint.**

DIRECTOR'S CHAIR AWARD 1980
White folding chair with green seat & back. Back says "You never looked so good". Given to reps for signing up new Avon reps. **CMV $30.**

NECKTIE 1980'S
Blue necktie with "Avon" in red, white & blue design. Label says "Neatwear Tie London, The Club Tie Specialist". Given to Avon Executives. **CMV $25.**

FEEL LIKE A STAR BUTTON 1981
3" blue & white button. **CMV $2.**

CALCULATOR-COLOR UP AMERICA AWARD 1979
(Left) Avon color never looked so good on face of calculator. Came in Avon leatherette case & matching box. Given to Reps. for sales awards. **CMV $22.50 MB.**
COME COLOR WITH US ANNOUNCEMENT 1979
(Right) Inside has crayola & invitation to meeting. **CMV $2.**

AVON BEAR SMALL TEDDY AWARD 1979
About 6" high brown bear. Made in Korea, given to managers. **CMV $50.**

BEAR PRIDE OF NEWARK AWARD 1982
Small 6" bear hobo name tag with gold tone chain & pendant around neck. Says "Thanks for making us No.1 & 4A design" on 1 side & "District managers are the pride of Newark" on the other side. Bear must have Avon pendant. **CMV $30.**

AVON'S SPRING FEVER 1968
Green felt board with 6 tin painted flowers pins. Managers gave a pin to each representative for recommending a new Avon representative. **$35 complete card mint. Each pin $4.**

PRESIDENT'S CLUB APRON 1978
Beige & red canvas apron says "I'd rather be selling Avon." Given to all President's Club Reps. Modeled by Grace Powers. **CMV $10.**

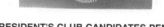

AVON TENNIS BALLPOINT PEN 1980
Gold tone pen says "Avon Tennis" & has tennis racket on side. Given to Avon tennis match players. Comes in tan suede Avon tennis pouch. **CMV $20 mint.**

REPRESENTATIVE CHRISTMAS CARD GIFT 1976
White Avon embossed box holds hand screened fold-out glass Christmas card given to all Reps. in 1976. **CMV $10 MB.**

YOU'RE THE HEART OF AVON AWARD 1986
Calculator, black & silver color. Given to managers. **CMV $35.**

PRESIDENT'S CLUB CANDIDATES PEN SET AWARD 1980
Red & gold Avon box holds gold tone pen & pencil set. Inscribed on side of pens, "President's Club Candidate". **CMV $25 MB.**

KEY CASE AWARD 1967
Blue case with gold 4A emblem. Given to Reps. for reaching sales goal in campaign 12. **CMV $10.**

KEY CASE FLASHLIGHT 1970
Red key case with flashlight inside. Not marked Avon. Made only for Avon. Given to Reps. for meeting sales goals. **CMV $5., $8 MB.**

DIVISION MANAGERS TRIBUTE PEN 1969
Silver pen with 4A on clip. Came in blue flannel sleeve & white box. **CMV $35 MB.**

PEN FOR LEADERSHIP AWARD 1969
Silver, black top with olive leaf on top. Garland Pen. Given to Avon Reps. **CMV $15 MB.**

FORUM MONEY PEN AWARD 1977
Clear plastic pen full of chopped up money. **CMV $10.**

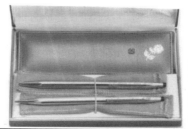

15 YEAR PEN SET AWARD 1976
(left) 2 Cross 14K gold filled pens engraved "Avon 15 Years" & person's initials. Both pens are in gray felt bags & pink leather pen holder with gold. 4A pen with red ruby in center & gold rose embossed. **CMV $75 MB.**

STERLING CLOCK PEN AWARD 1979
Sterling silver pen with digital clock & calendar inside. Inscribed "Number 1 in $ Inc.", plus name of division. Given to managers only. **CMV $50 MB.**

TEDDY BEAR PEN AWARD 1979
Cross chrome pen with small bear marked TL for Team Leader. Avon bear sleeve fits over box. **CMV $27.50 MB.**

PRESIDENT'S CLUB PEN AWARD 1979
Parker 75 silver & gold pen. Inscribed on side, "President's Club 1979". Comes in blue felt Parker case. **CMV $20.**
DIVISION MANAGER'S PEN & PENCIL SET AWARD 1969
Sterling silver pens. 4A emblem on pens. Came in blue brocade Cross pen box. Given to managers only. **CMV $50 set MB, each pen only $20.**

AWARD PENCIL 1950
Deluxe Eversharp, gold color. Given to Reps. for writing 50 or more orders in campaign 2, 1950. 5 inches long with "Avon Woman of Achievement on pencil. **CMV $40 pencil only, $50 MB.**

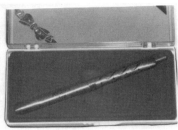

TOP REPRESENTATIVE PEN GIFT 1975
Brass & black design ball point pen. Small size. Came in red velvet lined, plastic display box & gold sleeve. Given for meeting sales goals. **CMV $10 MB as shown., Pen only $5.**

AVON PEN AWARD 1940'S
Yellow & black plastic, "Avon "on clip. Fountain pen on one end, lead pencil on other end. No information. **CMV $40.**

AVON PENS 1970'S
Blue & silver "Diamond Quarter 1977". **CMV $2.**
Red pen says "Get Write to the Point-Sell Avon". **CMV $2.**

RAIN HAT 1972
Plastic rain hat in pink & white case. Given at Beauty Salons only. **CMV $2.**
DING-DONG AVON CALLING PEN 1974
Given at Christmas. Black & white pen. **CMV $3.**

AVON BRASS MOLD STAMP 1936-53
2" brass mold stamp in reverse says "Avon Products Inc". "Tulip A" in center-New York-Montreal. **Rare, CMV $150.00**

RADIO AWARD 1985
White, plastic battery powered Blue face. AM-FM in blue sleeve Avon Box. Given to Reps. **CMV $35 MB.**

CHRISTMAS MAGIC PENCIL 1960'S
White pencils from Avon. **CMV $1 each.**

CIGARETTE HOLDER AWARD 1934
Made of solid ivory in velvet lined custom made blue & gold box marked "Avon" inside lid. Green & silver center band. **CMV $75 MB.**

WORLD OF CHRISTMAS-FLOWER PEN AWARD 1970
Small white pen with red, yellow & green holly flower on cap. Given to Avon Reps. **CMV $3.50 mint.**

84TH ANNIVERSARY FLOWER PENS 1970
Given for sending in an order C-12 84th anniversary. White barrel with red printing with yellow, pink, red, orange or white rose. **CMV $2 each, $3 in cellophane wrapper with card.**

SUGAR 'N SPICE CANDY JAR AWARD 1980
(left) Glass jar full of red candy drops. Yellow neck label. Red Avon sleeve fits over white box. Given to President's Club members. **CMV $6 MB.**

ULTRA WEAR DEMONSTRATOR 1980
(right) Box holds clear plastic box with steel ball to test Ultra Enamel to customers. Given to Avon Reps. in C10-80. **CMV $5 MB.**

UNSPOKEN PERFUME VIAL 1975
Blue box holds small 1-5/8" vial Unspoken perfume. Given to Managers only. Outside sleeve on box. **CMV $10 box.**

WESTERN CHOICE (STEER HORNS) "MANAGERS" 1967
Managers received the steer horns in a special box with "Avon" embossed all over the box. Was used to show at meetings on introduction of Steer Horns. Rare in this box. **CMV $45 MB as shown.**

ZANY RADIO 1979
Orange and pink Zany bottle shaped AM radio made in Hong Kong for Avon Products. Given to Avon customers in a drawing. Came in pink bag and certificate. **CMV $25 MB, $20 mint in bag complete, radio only $15.**

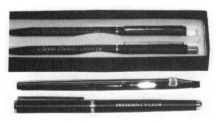

TOPAZE JEWELRY AWARDS 1960
Awarded for sales of Topaze products. 12 carat gold filled with imported Topaze stones. Necklace **CMV $40, $50 MB,** Bracelet **CMV $60, $70 MB,** Earrings **CMV $30, $40 MB.**

RADIO AWARD 1980
Red and white plastic AM-FM Avon radio given 1 to each district manager to give at a drawing. Made by ISIS, in box. **CMV $60 MB.**

CHRISTMAS CUP 1969
White glass mug. Avon on bottom. Given to district managers for Christmas. **CMV $30.**

HONOR SOCIETY PEN SET AWARD 1990
Box holds 2 black & gold tone pens with Avon Honor Society on side of each pen. **CMV $25.00 MB**

PRESIDENTS CLUB PEN AWARD 1990
Chrome pen with PC on it. **CMV $10.00**

PRESIDENTS CLUB PEN 1989
On bottom is black & gold with Presidents Club on side. **CMV $10.00**

PRESIDENT'S CELEBRATION CANDLE HOLDERS 1980
Blue candles in clear glass base. "Avon" on bottom label. Given to all Reps. at banquet. **CMV $10 pair.**

CIRCLE OF EXCELLENCE PEN SET AWARD 1990
(left) Grey box holds 3 black Quill pens with C of E on top of each pen. **CMV $35.00**

REGENCE EARRINGS AWARDS 1966
Gold with truqoise settings. Customer service award campaign 14-18, 1966. Has green velvet box. **CMV $60 in box.**

REGENCE NECKLACE AWARDS 1966
Crown performance award. Gold with turqoise setting & gold crown set in center, can also be worn as a pin. Has green velvet box. **CMV $50 MB.**

TIMELESS ULTRA COLOGNE MIST FOR PRESIDENT'S CLUB ONLY 1974
2 oz. size, gold cap. 1st issue to Avon President's Club members only, had 4A design on bottom under label. Regular issue had Avon on bottom. Box also came with special card saying it was collectors edition, fall 1974. **CMV $6 MB shown.**

SALES EXCELLENCE AWARD CUP 1977
6 1/2" high pewter cup. "4A design, Avon Sales Excellence Award 1977" on side of cup. Given to top 2% of sales Reps. in each division. Same cup also in 1979, only dates are different. **CMV $15 MB.**

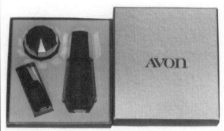

TIMELESS MANAGERS GIFT SET 1975
Gold box holds perfume rollette, cologne mist & creme perfume. Given to Avon Mnagers only at introduction of Timeless. **CMV $35 MB.**

RAPTURE PIN 1964
Silver gray in color. **CMV $7. Pin only, $10. on Avon card pictured.**

ROSES ROSES AWARDS 1972
ROSES ROSES HOT PLATE 1972
6" square, white Corning Ware with pink and green rose. Given for selling Mist of Roses Cologne. **CMV $12 MB.**

ROSES ROSES GOBLET 1972
Gold trimmed goblet with bouquet of pink artificial roses. Came with card of congratulations. Given for selling Mist of Roses Cologne. **CMV $15 MB.**

ROSES ROSES CLOCK 1972
3" clock by Hamilton, 4 small roses on front. Given for selling Mist of Roses Cologne. **CMV $18 MB.**

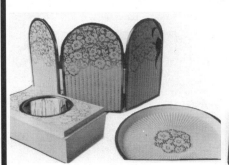

RAPTURE AWARD BOWL 1965
Fostoria glass bowl with Rapture doves etched in bottom. Given to each Representatives in the winning district during the 79th Anniversary campaign. **CMV $35, $40. MB**

SONNET AWARDS 1972
(all earned for selling Cologne Mist)
VANITY TRAY
10" white plastic, gold trim. **CMV $10.**
VANITY BOX
White plastic, gold tirm. **CMV $18. MB.**
THREE PANEL MIRROR
White and gold. **CMV $24. MB.**

MOONWIND ORDER BOOK COVERS 1971
Dark blue with silver trim. President's Club cover earned for entry into President's Club. Honor Award earned for sales goal. Each came with pen. Honor cover with pen, **CMV $4,** President's cover with pen, **CMV $6**

ROSES ROSES ORDER BOOK AND PEN 1972
Redesigned size is larger than older Order Books, pink with darker pink rose and green leaves. Given to all President Club members. **CMV $5 mint.**

PATCHWORK COOKIE JAR AWARD 1972
Level 2. Earned for selling cologne mists. White glass with orange, green, red & yellow. **CMV $15 MB $20.**

IMPERIAL GARDEN TEA SET 1973
White Bone China with Imperial Garden design. Given to one Representative in each district when her recommendation name was drawn at the Christmas Party. **CMV $175.00 MB.**

PATCHWORK CANNISTER AWARD 1972
Level 3. Earned for selling cologne mists. White glass 3 piece cannister set with Patchwork decals. **CMV $25 set MB.**

PATCHWORK BINGO CARD 1973
9 1/2" paper bingo card used by Reps at meetings. **CMV $2.**

IMPERIAL GARDENS AWARDS 1973
Earned for selling certain numbered Cologne Mists for each level.
Level 1 BUD VASE
White china with orange and gold trim. **CMV $8 MB.**
Level 2 TRAY
White plastic with orange and gold trim. **CMV $10, $15 MB.**
Level 3 GINGER JAR
White china with orange and gold trim. **CMV $25 MB.**

PATCHWORK COOKER AWARD 1972
Patchwork design. Level 4. Earned for selling cologne mists. **CMV $30, MB $35.**

HANA GASA JEWELRY AWARDS 1970
Enameled pin and clip on earrings are deep red and purple. Given when someone a Representative recommended was appointed as a Representative. **CMV $15 set.**

PATCHWORK REFRIGERATOR AWARD 1972
Level 1. Earned by selling cologne mists. White plastic with orange, green, red & yellow patchwork decals. **CMV $10 set, $12 MB.**

FIELD FLOWERS ORDER BOOK COVER & PEN 1971
(right) President's Club. One was given for being eligible for membership. Honor award was earned for sales goal. Cover on left- Canadian President's Club Honor Award. Each came with Avon pen. **CMV $5 each with pen.**

HANA GASA UMBRELLA 1970
Bamboo painted in Hana Gasa colors. Used at sales meetings at introduction of Hana Gasa. Came in Avon box. Very rare. **CMV $100 in box.**

EMPRISE PURSE AWARD 1977
Black satin purse with jewel snap. Has gold carrying chain inside. Purse does not say Avon on it. Given to Reps for top sales of Emprise products. Came in clear plastic bag marked Avon. Designed by S.M. Kent. **CMV $10 MB.**

CANDID SALES LEADER TROPHY 1977
Wood base with brass plaque with bottle of Candid cologne mist glued in base. Given to 1 Rep in each district who sold the most Candid cologne mists on its introduction. **CMV $12.50.**

EMPRISE NECKLACE GIFT 1977
Gold double E necklace given to Avon Team Leaders to introduce the new fragrance. T.L. on back side and it came in an Avon box. **CMV $10.** District Managers also got one marked D.M. on back and in D.M. Avon box. **CMV $15 MB.** Was also given to Division Managers. **CMV $15 MB.** Emprise money clip for male Reps. **CMV $15 MB.**

CHARISMA JEWELRY AWARD 1968
Red & gold necklace, bracelet & earrings. Given for meeting or exceeding a prize goal. **CMV $37.50 set MB, $12 each MB.**
CHARISMA ORDER BOOK COVER 1968
(Back) Introducing Charisma. Came with red pen. **CMV $5, With pen $6.**

ELUSIVE PINK & GOLD SCARF AWARDS 1969
Given to Avon sales ladies on first Elusive sales campaign. White box has 4A design & signed by S.M. Kent, designer. **CMV $7.50 MB.**

KEY CHAIN YOU NEVER LOOKED SO GOOD 1982
White plastic, black letters. Never issued to reps. **CMV $5.**

MERRI RAT AWARD 1982
(left) White stuffed rat with pink ears & feet, red hat has wood sign around neck "To the best from your N.Y. Buddy". Given to Avon managers just for the hell of it. **CMV $20.**
TEDDY BEAR SWITCH TO AVON 1982
(right) Small brown & white stuffed bear. Red Avon banner, made by Ruso. Given to winning team in each district. **CMV $7.50.**

PICTURE YOURSELF MIRROR 1970
Two sided mirror with antiqued gold. Awarded for selling 7 body lotions during campaign 7. **CMV $7., $9 MB.**

KEY CASE AWARD 1971
Blue case with large 4A design. **CMV $10.**

CANDID BAG FOR MANAGERS 1976
Maroon and white canvas bag. Back side says
Avon, New York, London, Paris. **CMV $10.00**

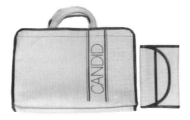

CANDID TOTE BAG 1977
Light colored canvas bag given to Reps for
going to C-10 sales meeting. **CMV $3.00**
They could also win a Candid matching purse
organizer. **CMV $3.00**

BIRD OF PARADISE ROBE 1970
Blue terry cloth robe given to Reps for selling
24 Bird of Paradise 3 oz. cologne mists in C-
19-1970. Came in S-M-L sizes. Bird of
Paradise on pocket. **CMV $35.**

**BIRD OF PARADISE ORDER BOOK
COVERS**
(Left) Canadian. Presidents Club earned for
eligibility into Presidents Club. Honor Award
earned for sales goal. Each came with pen in
matching design. **CMV $5 each with pen.**
**BIRD OF PARADISE ORDER BOOK COVER
1970**
Blue & turquoise, awarded for qualifying for
Presidents Club, has matching pen. **CMV
$7.50.**
BIRD OF PARADISE SCARF 1970
Awarded for selling cologne mists. Blue and
turquoise silk. **CMV $10.**

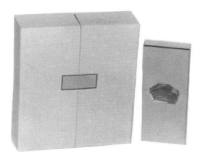

**AVON 100 DEVOTEE PERFUME AWARD
1986**
.33 oz. glass stopper perfume given to
Managers. Same as public issue only
inscribed on bottom of gold tone container
"100 years of Beauty 1886 Avon 1986". **CMV
$15 MB.**

**BIRD OF PARADISE AWARD JEWELRY
1970**
Gold pin, bracelet and earrings with turquoise
stones. **CMV pin $12, bracelet and earrings
$20 MB.**

ARIANE ADDRESS BOOK 1977
Red velvet booklet with note pad and address
book. Chrome pen has no markings. Given to
team leaders. **CMV $6.**
ARIANE "INCH" NECKLACE 1977
Silver container holds small vial of Ariane
cologne. 3 different ones, came in red velvet
bag, 1 for Avon Reps with black pull cord on
bag. **CMV $10 in bag.** 1 for President's Club
members with PC on back of necklace and
silver pull cord, **CMV $15 in bag.** 1 for
Managers, sterling silver, back side says
"August Conference", has red pull cord, **CMV
$50 in bag.**

MOONWIND TRAY 1971
(Top Left) Blue glass tray trimmed in silver
emblem of Diana in center. Given for selling
10 Moonwind cologne mists during C18-19.
CMV $22, MB $25.
MOONWIND JEWELRY BOX 1971
(Bottom Left) Blue & silver. Emblem of Diana
on top in silver. Given for selling 20 Moonwind
cologne mists in C18-19. **CMV $25, 30 MB.**
MOONWIND ROBE 1971
(Right) Blue, zipper front with silvery trim.
Zipper pull is emblem of Diana. Given to
President's Club representatives for selling 35
Moonwind cologne mists. **CMV $30.00.
$45.00 MB.**

AWARDS & REPRESENTATIVES GIFTS

STAR PC TRIBUTE PLATE AWARD 1989
5" Blue & silver porcelain plate. Marked PC Star Tribute 89. **CMV $5.00.**

PC TRIBUTE PLATE AWARD 1988
6" chrome plate marked PC Tribute 1988. **CMV $5.00**

C OF E IMARI BOWL 1987
Porcelain bowl given to Avon managers on 1987 Japan C of E. trip. Not marked Avon. Must have C of E. Avon Card. **CMV $75.00 MB with card.**

MOOSE AWARD PLATE 1930'S
White ceramic plate with green edging trim with 2 moose in brown on face. Back of plate is marked CPC Avon. **CMV $150.00 Mint**

PRESIDENTS CAMPAIGN BRACELET AWARD 1976
Chrome chain & red letters on heart pendant. **CMV $10.00**

ACAPULCO CHARM BRACELET AWARD 1990
Sterling silver sombrero charm. Marked Avon on back. **CMV $25.00 MB**

STARS SYSTEM PIN 1989
(left) silver tone star & blue inlay given for $4500.00 in Sales. **CMV $3.00 MB**

TRIPLE CROWN NECKLACE 1988
(center) 14k gold pendant with 3 crowns on it & chain. Given to managers. **CMV $40.00 MB**

PRESIDENTS CLUB MANS TIE TAC AWARD 1988
(right) gold tone tie tac with small red stone. **CMV $15. MB.**

PRESIDENTS CLUB PIN 1988
Gold tone pin - "PC 88". 4 levels.

#1 Pearl	**CMV $10.00**
#2 Cintron "Topaz color"	**CMV $15.00**
#3 Ruby	**CMV $20.00**
#4 Sapphire	**CMV $25.00**

SPONSORSHIP LAPEL PIN MEN'S AWARD 1986-88
Gold filled pins given to male Avon Reps for signing up new Avon Reps.

1 Sapphire	**CMV $35.00 MB**
2 Ruby	**CMV $60.00 MB**
3 Emerald	**CMV $85.00 MB**
4 Diamond	**CMV $110.00 MB**

HONOR SOCIETY AWARD PINS 1988-89
Gold tone pins "HS 88" or "HS 89". With:

Ruby	**CMV $20.00**
Sapphire	**CMV $25.00**
1 Diamond	**CMV $30.00**
2 Diamond	**CMV $35.00**
3 Diamond	**CMV $40.00**

ROSEBUD PEARL NECKLACE AWARD 1990
20" strand of pearls with 14k gold rose clasp. Given to Reps for 45 years service. Made only for Avon. Does not say Avon. **CMV $300.00 MB**

HONOR SOCIETY KEY CHAIN AWARD 1988
(bottom right) Gold tone key ring with H-S in red letters under clear Lucite. Given to top Reps. Came in Maroon box. **CMV $8.00**
SPONSORSHIP CHARM AWARDS 1986-88
Gold filled charms with colored stones.
Step 1-Lapel Pin ....**CMV $10.00**
Step 2-Sapphire ....**CMV $25.00**
Step 3-Ruby ....**CMV $50.00**
Step 4-Emerald ....**CMV $75.00**
Step 5-Diamond ....**CMV $100.00**

ROSEBUD PEARL BRACELET AWARD 1990
Double strand pearl bracelet with 14k gold rose clasp. Given to Reps for 40 years service. Not marked Avon. Made only for Avon. **CMV $250.00 MB**

SIGNATURE COLLECTION AVON PIN 1990
Gold tone pin for Avon Peps. Has simulated Diamonds & Rubies. **CMV $8.00**
EXCELLENCE ROSE PIN AWARD 1990
1" gold tone pin. Red enamel rose. Excellence on edge. Does not say Avon. **CMV $7.50**

PRESIDENTS CLUB STAR PIN AWARDS 1989-90
Gold tone pin with gold star....**CMV $10.00**
Blue & white star charm ......**CMV $15.00**
Red star ....**CMV $15.00**
Green star ....**CMV $20.00**
Blue star ....**CMV $25.00**
White star ....**CMV $35.00**
Star charm with pearl ....**CMV $20.00**
Gold star in circle charm ......**CMV $15.00**

DISTRICT ACHIEVEMENT AWARDS 1989
Blue Lucite stand holds one quarter oz. sterling silver Avon coin. 4 Steps - Volume, Customers, Recruiting, Sales Increase. **CMV $12.50 ea.**
Also came in gold over silver "Best of the Best" in same 4 Steps above. **CMV $25.00**

HONOR SOCIETY QUARTZ CLOCK PICTURE FRAME AWARD 1987
Brass & maroon frame. **CMV $15.00**
COLOR WHEEL WATCH AWARD 1988
Color Watch - Avon on back. Gray strap. Given for sales incentive. Came in Avon Plastic box. **CMV $30.00 MB.**

ROSEBUD PIN 30 YEAR SERVICE AWARD 1990
(Left) 14k gold rose pin with diamond chip center. Given to Avon Reps for 30 years service. Made only for Avon. Not marked Avon. **CMV $100.00 MB**
ROSEBUD EARRINGS 35 YEARS SERVICE AWARD 1990
14k gold rose earrings with diamond chip. Given for 35 years service. Does not say Avon. Made only for Avon. **CMV $125.00 MB**

CIRCLE OF EXCELLENCE PIN 1988
(Bottom) 4A red & white or blue & white pin. **CMV $3.**
WHISTLE KEY CHAIN AWARD 1989
(Top) Brass whistle key chain says Avon in red letter. **CMV $6.**

CLOCK CIRCLE OF EXCELLENCE AWARD 1988
Gold & brass tone Seth Thomas clock. Has "1988 Circle of Excellence District" on face. Comes in white box marked Circle of Excellence. **CMV $125.00 MB**

AWARDS & REPRESENTATIVES GIFTS

KISS WATCH AWARD 1990
Gold tone watch, Avon & red lips on face. Given to Reps. **CMV $50.00 MB**
HUNDRED YEAR MANAGERS WATCH AWARD 1986
Back says **"1886-1986 Avon"** gold tone band & case has 3 diamond type stones & says Quartz. **CMV $100.00**

PEARL BRACELET WATCH AWARD 1990
Gold tone watch made in China. Pearl face marked "Avon 1990". Given for top sales. **CMV $35.00**

PRESIDENTS CLUB HEART BOX AWARD 1990
White satin lining says Avon PC 1990. Chrome heart box with gold ribbon on lid. **CMV $15.**
PRESIDENTS CLUB PEN AWARD 1990
Black & gold Chromatic pen. Says PC Presidents Club. **CMV $3.**

TOWNHOUSE CANISTER AWARD SET 1989
5 ceramic canisters. Not marked Avon but lady on second canister has bag marked Avon. **CMV $10.00 ea., $25.00 for large one on right.**

KOALA BEAR 1993
10" stuffed Koala with AVON Logo T. Shirt. Sold only to AVON Reps. **CMV $10.**

PRESIDENTS CLUB CHRISTMAS GIFT 1987
White porcelain box with Music box in lid. Pink rose on lid. **CMV $15.00 MB.**

RING THE BELL AWARD 1949
Metal inscribed bell given to reps in 1949 for sales goal. **CMV $75.00**

WATCH INCENTIVE AWARD 1989
Gold tone case Avon on Face. Made in Clina. Brown Strap. **CMV $25.00**
WATCH PSST AWARD 1989
Quartz gold tone watch. PSST on face. Beige leather skin strap. **CMV $50.00**

MESMERIZE AWARDS 1992
(Left) All are blue and gold. Given to Avon Reps. for selling "Mesmerize" cologne.
TREASURE CHEST
(Top) **CMV $25.**
TREASURE JEWELRY BOX
(Bottom) **CMV $30.**
MESMERIZE FLACON PENDANT
Pendant is on 30" blue cord and blue tassel. **CMV $15.**

STAR AWARDS 1989
(left) Small Tribute chrome picture frame.
CMV $3.00
STAR PAPER WEIGHT
(center) Sstarr Tribute PC 89 on clear glass
paper weight. **CMV $5.00**
STERLING STAR PIN
(right) Comes in blue box. Sterling silver pin
marked on back side (National Star Event
3/19/90). **CMV $75.00 MB**

**STAR BEST OF BEST PAPERWEIGHT
AWARD 1989**
Glass paperweight given to top Manager in
each division. 1ea. given for Best Percent
increase, Best $ Dollar increase & Best Sales
increase. **CMV $50.00 MB**

**DIAMOND JUBILEE PAPERWEIGHT AWARD
1986**
Clear glass marked C-12-15-1986. In grey box
& Diamond card. **CMV $30.00 MB**

STAR CLOCK AWARD 1989
(Left) 2 3/4" high clear Lucite quartz clock says
Avon. **CMV $10.00**

**SUPPORT PROGRAM DESK SET CLOCK
AWARD 1986**
Black plastic set says Avon 1986. **CMV
$20.00**

SUPPORT PROGRAM AWARD 1986
Small maroon & gold trim picture frame &
clock. Given to group sales leaders. **CMV $5.**

**STARS OF CHRISTMAS RECORD AWARD
1988**
Framed Platinum tone record in silver & blue
frame. **CMV $40.00**

SALES EXCELLENCE AWARD 1988
Wood plaque with brass Avon lady design,
came with brass stand. #1 Division is gold.
CMV $100.00
#2 thru 5 is silver tone. **CMV $75.00**

**AVON CALLING AMERICA PHONE AWARD
1990**
Blue, white & red telephone given to Reps.
CMV $40.00 MB

**MANAGERS CHRISTMAS GIFT SPOON
1977**
Small silver spoon has Christmas tree &
Rejoice 1977 inscribed. Came in red & white
felt boot bag. **CMV $15.00**

PRESIDENTS CLUB BIRTHDAY GIFT 1989
Small white porcelain picture frame with pink &
green flower decoration. Comes in Avon green
PC box. **CMV $10.00 MB**
PRESIDENTS CLUB CHRISTMAS GIFT 1988
Gold tone metal trivet. Came in green & red
PC Avon box. **CMV $10.00 MB**

AVON TENNIS BALL KEY CHAIN AWARD 1986
Small yellow, red & white tennis ball. **CMV $2.**

WHEEL OF FORTUNE CLOCK 1990
Wall clock. White plastic with glass face, says Avon. **CMV $25.00**

HONOR SOCIETY POCKET MIRROR AWARD 1987
Brass inscribed small pocket mirror given to Reps. Came in Red felt sleeve & white box with flower & yellow ribbon. **CMV $10.00 MB**

CALCULATOR AWARD 1987
Small white mini calculator given to Reps. Red design on face. **CMV $5.**

PEN & KEY CHAIN SET AWARD 1989
White pen & key chain. **CMV $2. set MB**

C OF E AWARDS 1987
(left) Wood paddle, hand painted Yukata. Must have C of E Avon card. **CMV $20.00**

C OF E CHOPSTICKS
(right) Set of 2 hand painted chopsticks. Must have C of E Avon card. **CMV $5.00 MB**
Both items given to C of E Avon Managers on 1987 Japan trip.

SUNGLASS AWARD 1990
Avon marked sunglasses in red Avon case. Given for recruitment. **CMV $20.**

CHRISTMAS GIFT TO AVON REPS 1987
Avon note pads in green book box. Red pen. **CMV $3.00**
Matching address book was also given to Reps. **CMV $3.**

PANDA BEAR AWARD 1990
9" tall panda bear with red Avon shirt given for recruitment. **CMV $20.00**

FRAGRANCE 50 CLUB FIFTH AVENUE BOWL AWARD 1986
Clear glass bowl with blue lettering given to Reps on Intro of Fifth Avenue products. **CMV $20.**

CUP & SAUCER 1980'S
4A marked ceramic dinnerware use in Avon Plant cafeterias. **CMV $3. ea. piece.**

CERAMIC JAR AWARD 1988
Off white ceramic Jar with gold 4A on front. **CMV $15.**

GLASS PEN SET 1986
Beveled edge glass base with chrome and black pen. Says "AVON AVANT: DIVISION #1 USA 1986" **CMV $25.**

PRESIDENT'S RECOGNITION SALES VOLUME AWARD 1995-96
(Left) Wood base, glass & brass award given to Reps. in each district for best sales volume increase. **CMV $50.**

PRESIDENT'S RECOGNITION BEST NEW PERFORMER AWARD
(Right) Wood base & glass & brass award. Given to new President's Club Reps. in each district for Highest Total Sales. **CMV $50.**

MISSION GARDEN PERFUME AWARD 1923
8" tall cut glass bottle with sterling silver trim, glass stopper. Given to Reps for top sales. **Very rare. CMV $250.00 mint**

HONOR SOCIETY CUP & SAUCER AWARD 1997
White porcelain cup & saucer with red & gold trim. Sits on wood base & dated 1997 on brass plaque. Given to Reps for $17,200. in sales in 1 year. **CMV $35. MB.**

HONOR SOCIETY CUP AND SAUCER AWARD 1995
Wood base with brass "1995 Honor Society" holds blue, gold and white cup and saucer. Given to Reps. for $16,200. in sales. **CMV $35. MB**

PRESIDENTS CUP AWARD 1932
8 1/2" tall silver plate, gold lined. Given to only twenty Reps. in U.S. Engraved on side-winners name, from D.H. McConnell, President California Perfume Co., Inc., July 18, 1932. **CMV $300.00 mint.**

HONOR SOCIETY CUP & SAUCER AWARD 1998
Blue & white porcelain cup & saucer sits on wood base with brass plaque dated 1998. Given to Reps for $17,900. in sales in 1 year. **CMV $35. MB.**

ELEPHANT CRYSTAL JAR AWARD 1928
6" long and 4" high, wrinkled glass to look like skin. Came filled with Vernafleur Bath Salts. Glass top of elephant lifts off. Given to 36 Reps. for highest sales. **<u>This will be considered the 1st decanter Avon ever issued.</u> Very rare. CMV $300.00 mint**

PERFUME ATOMIZER AWARD 1927
Peacock blue opaque crystal bottle with embossed gold top. Silk net over bulb. Given to six Reps. In each district for top sales of gift sets in December, 1927. **CMV $125.00 BO mint, $165.00 MB.**

HONOR SOCIETY CUP & SAUCER AWARD 1991 & 1992
1991 was the first year this award was given. Mrs Albee cup & saucer on wood base and brass plaque dated 1991 & 1992. Each year different. **CMV $35. MB. each year**

HONOR SOCIETY CUP & SAUCER AWARD 1993
This award was not given in 1993

AWARDS & REPRESENTATIVES GIFTS

CRYSTAL STAR TROPHY AWARD 1991
Fine crystal glass Star given to Top 5 National Leaders in Best "TOTAL SALES", "SALES INCREASE", & "RECRUITING". **CMV $250.00 MB. each Trophy**

NATIONAL PRESIDENTS TROPHY AWARD 1990's
Clear lucite trophy was given to top Reps in the nation for "SALES", "SALES INCREASE", "RECRUITING", & "LEADERSHIP". They are given each year & dated 1995-96 - 1996-97 - 1997-98 - 1998-99. **CMV $100.00 MB. each trophy for each year.**

STAR TROPHY BRANCH AWARD 1991
Fine crystal glass trophy given to top Reps in each branch for Best in "TOTAL SALES", "SALES INCREASE", & "RECRUITING". **CMV $75.00 each trophy MB.**

PRESIDENTS RECOGNITION PROGRAM AWARD 1996-97
Glass & brass on marble base trophy given to top 5 Reps in each district for "TOP SALES", "SALES INCREASE", "RECRUITING", & "LEADERSHIP". **CMV $50.00 MB. each Trophy**

RESIDENTS RECOGNITION PROGRAM TROPHY AWARD 1997-98
Mrs Albee etched in glass with brass & marble base. 5 of each given in each district for "TOP SALES", "SALES INCREASE", "RECRUITING" & LEADERSHIP". **CMV $50.00 MB. each Trophy.**

BEST NEW PERFORMER TROPHY AWARD 1991
Star Tribute lucite trophy given to top sales Rep in each district. **CMV $50.00 MB.**

NAAC CONVENTION BOTTLE & BELL 1988 SAN DIEGO, CA.
5 1/2" high porcelain, brown & tan dress. 800 made with brown trim on hat. **CMV $18.00**
100 CLUB SAMPLES
Made with blue trim on hat. **CMV $25.00**
400 BELLS
Made with dress color reversed. **CMV $22.00**

NAAC MRS. ALBEE COMMEMORATIVE BOTTLE & BELL 1988
1200 made of porcelain 5 1/2" high. Black hand bag. **CMV $18.00**
100 CLUB SAMPLES
Made with brown hand bag. **CMV $35.00**
400 BELLS
Were made with dress color reversed. **CMV $22.00**

NATIONAL ASSOCIATION AVON COLLECTOR'S AVON CLUB BOTTLES & NAAC COLLECTABLES.

SOLD ONLY TO MEMBERS OF NAAC CLUBS

NAAC and club bottle offers not affilliated with Avon Products, Inc.

CLUB BOTTLES-PLATES-CONVENTION BOTTLES-BELLS

What are they? Where did you get them? Club bottles were made for Avon collectors and sold thru any of the more than 100 Avon Collectors Clubs throughout the United States and Canada. These clubs are all members of the National Association of Avon collectors (N.A.A.C.). Club bottles or plates were sold for a period of 60 days only and only the amount sold in that time were made. At the end of the sale period, the order was placed with the factory. Each bottle is numbered with the quantity made. All club bottles are hand painted porcelain of the finest quality. If you do not have an Avon Club in your area belonging to the N.A.A.C. we invite you to join the Avon Times. $24.00 yearly membership ($26.00 for Canada, U.S. funds money orders only from Canada).

Send to:

AVON TIMES
Box 9868
Kansas City, Missouri 64134

Phone 816-537-8223 9am to 5pm

All N.A.A.C. Avon club & convention bottles & bells 1972 to 1986 were designed, created & manufactured by Bud Hastin. Bud has created over 100 different hand painted porcelain bottles & figurines. They have become very collectable over the years. All are very limited editions.

NAAC CONVENTION BOTTLE & BELL 1988 - INDIANAPOLIS
5 1/2" high, all are yellow dress, green trim. Indianapolis Avon Convention 700 made. Brown hair, yellow fan. **CMV $18.00**
100 CLUB SAMPLES
Made with red fan. **CMV $35.00**
100 CONVENTION DELEGATE BOTTLES
Made with blonde hair. **CMV $35.00**
CONVENTION BELL
Is reverse color dress, with green fan. 400 made. **CMV $22.00**

2nd NAAC McCONNELL CLUB BOTTLE 1973
2nd annual Club Botle issued by the NAAC Clubs in honor of Mr. & Mrs. D. H. McConnell, founders of Avon. Registration certificate goes with the bottle. 5,604 bottles were sold & numbered. **CMV $50.**

1st ANNUAL NAAC AVON CLUB BOTTLE 1st AVON LADY 1972

7" high, hand painted porcelain bottle. Made for Avon Club members only belonging to the National Association of Avon Collectors. 1st NAAC Club bottle issued. Made in image of first CPC saleslady. Each bottle is numbered. Released in June 1972. **Total issue was 2,870.** Bottle made and issued by National Association of Avon Collectors. **CMV $200. 18 made with red hair & green purse. CMV $600. for a redhead.** No registration certificates were issued with the '72 Club Bottle. **4 bottles had blue lettering on bottle.** All others had black letters. **CMV blue letter bottom $700.** 1972 factory sample of 1st lady sold by mistake. Same as above only no lettering on bottom & neck is flush where cork fits top of bottle. No raised lip for cork as regular production was. Bottle has letter from Bud Hastin as 1 of a kind sample. **CMV $500.**

NAAC MINI McCONNELL & CPC FACTORY 1978

(Left) Miniature size figurines of the 1886 CPC Factory and Mr. & Mrs. McConnell the founders of Avon. Issued by the National Association of Avon Clubs. **Only 1,200 sets** were sold. Original set came with McConnell & factory 2nd from right. Factory was too large so issued a second smaller factory on left. 1,200 small factories made. **CMV set with 1 factory & McConnell $35. CMV with both factories in center $55.**

NAAC CPC FACTORY CLUB BOTTLE 1974

(Right) 3rd annual club bottle issued by the NAAC Clubs in honor of the 1st California Perfume Co. Factory in 1886. Came with a registration card. **4,691 bottles were made,** the mold was broken at 3rd annual NAAC Convention June 22, 1974 in Kansas City. **CMV $30.**

5th ANNUAL NAAC AVON CLUB BOTTLE 1976

(Left) In the image of the 1896 CPC Avon lady. Blue dress, black bag, and blue feather in hat. Black hair. **5,622 were made.** Came with registration card and numbered on the bottom. **CMV $25.**

BLOND AVON LADY 1976

(Right) Of the **5,622 regular issue** 1896 lady, **120 had blond hair. CMV $175. on blond, rare.**

4th ANNUAL NAAC CLUB BOTTLE 1975

The modern day Avon Lady is the 1975 Club bottle from the NAAC. Blue hand painted porcelain. Each bottle is numbered on bottom & came with registration card. **6,232 were made. CMV $20. CMV Club Sample Bottle $50.**

NAAC CLUB BOTTLE 1906 AVON LADY 1977

6th annual club bottle issued by the National Association of Avon Clubs. Made of porcelain and hand painted in the image of the 1906 Avon lady. She stands 7 1/2" high with yellow dress, brown hat and carrying the CPC Avon sales case of the period. Only **5,517 were made & sold.** Came with NAAC registration certificate and is numbered on the bottom. **CMV $25. MB. 100 sample bottles** were given to each NAAC Club and are the same only they are numbered and marked club sample on bottom. **CMV $50. sample bottle.**

NAAC CLUB BOTTLE 1978

7th annual club bottle made in the image of the 1916 CPC Avon lady. She stands 7 1/2" high with a rust colored hat and coat. Brown hair. Only **5,022 were made.** The bottle is numbered on the bottom and comes with a registration certificate. Made of hand painted porcelain. **CMV $25. Club Sample** was marked on bottom of **125 club bottles** given to each club in the NAAC. Sample bottles are same as regular issue only marked club sample. **CMV $50.**

NAAC CLUB BOTTLE 1936 AVON LADY 1980
(Left) 9th annual club bottle. Purple dress, black bag. 7 1/2" high. 4,479 were made & sold & numbered on the bottom as total sold. Did not come with certificate. Bottom cork. . **CMV $25.** Same bottle came with blue bag & marked club sample on bottom. 155 club samples were made & given to to NAAC clubs. **CMV $50. blue bag club sample.**

NAAC CLUB BOTTLE 1946 AVON LADY 1981
(Right) 10th annual club bottle. Only 3,589 sold and made. Green dress, black bag, cork in bottom. **CMV $25.** 140 sample club bottles made and marked club sample on bottom. **CMV $50.**

NAAC 1st CONVENTION BOTTLE 1980
Sold only to NAAC club members. 1st in an annual series of NAAC Convention bottles to commemorate the annual NAAC Convention held in Spokane, Washington in 1980. 7 1/2" high, lavender dress of 1890s style. Hand painted porcelain. This bottle is the only one in the series that the cork is in the head, and 7 1/2" size. All rest are 5 1/2" size starting in 1981. The rest of the series will have a cork in the bottom to present a prettier bottle. Only 3,593 were made & sold. **CMV $25.**

NAAC CLUB BOTTLE 1984 AVON REPRESENTATIVE 1984
13th annual club bottle 7 1/2" high, hand painted porcelain. Gray pants suit, pink blouse, red hair. Brown bag says Avon. Bottom cork. Choice of a white or black representative. 1,133 white rep bottles were made. 1,070 black reps made. **CMV $25. MB each.**

NAAC CLUB BOTTLE "MR. AVON" 1985
7 1/2" high porcelain bottle. 14th & last in club bottle series. Only 1,800 made. **CMV $25. MB.** 100 club sample bottles made. **CMV $50.**

NAAC CLUB BOTTLE 1926 AVON LADY 1979
8th annual club bottle. Purple & black. Brown hat & shoes. 4,749 were made & numbered on bottom. Came with certificate that says 4,725. Actual count is 4,749. **CMV $25.** 150 club samples were issued to NAAC Clubs. Bottom is marked club sample. **CMV sample $50.**

NAAC CLUB BOTTLE 1956 AVON LADY 1982
(Left) 11th annual club bottle for NAAC club members. 7 1/2" high, red dress, bottom cork. Only 3,000 made & sold. **CMV $25.** 150 club sample 1956 lady bottles made & marked on bottom. **CMV $50. for club sample.**

NAAC CLUB BOTTLE 1966 AVON LADY 1983
(Right) 12th annual club bottle. 7 1/2" high, hand painted porcelain bottle made only for the National Association of Avon Collectors in the image of dress of the 1966 Avon lady. She wears a black & white striped dress. Blue bag. 2,350 made, bottom cork. **CMV $25.** A new club bottle is issued each year to NAAC members only. 100 club samples made. **CMV $50.**

7th NAAC CONVENTION BOTTLE & BELL 1986
5 1/2" high porcelain bottle. Black dress, red hair on 100 club samples. **CMV $50.** Regular issue has red dress, black trim. Only 1,800 made. **CMV $25.**

7th NAAC CONVENTION BELL 1986
Same as regular issue bottle only bell with dress colors reversed. Only 500 made by Bud Hastin. **CMV $30.**

NAAC CONVENTION BOTTLE & BELL 1987
5 1/2" high porcelain bottle. 8th in series. 750 made for Chicago Avon Collector Convention. Hand painted porcelain, light blue, dark blue trim. **CMV $25.**
CONVENTION BELL
Same only dress color reversed. Only 300 made. **CMV $30.**

NAAC 2nd CONVENTION BOTTLE 1981
Long Beach, CA Convention. 5 1/2" high hand painted porcelain bottle. Yellow & green dress of the 1800s style. Second in a series of 11 bottles of the 1800s style. Only 3,128 were made & sold to NAAC club members. **CMV $25.**
CONVENTION CLUB SAMPLE 1981
140 club sample bottles were made for NAAC clubs. Each marked club sample on bottom & numbered 140 edition. **CMV $50. club sample.**
5th NAAC CONVENTION BELL 1981
Same as bottle only has green dress. 500 made & sold in 1984. **CMV $25.**

NAAC 4th CONVENTION BOTTLE 1983
5 1/2" high, bottom cork. Rust & brown color hand painted porcelain. 4th in a series of Avon ladies of the 1800s to commemorate the NAAC Avon Collectors Convention in Wilmington, DE in June 1983. Only 1,875 made. Total number sold marked on bottom. **CMV $25.** 150 club samples made & marked club sample. 1 of 150 on bottom. **CMV $50.**
2nd NAAC CONVENTION BELL 1983
Same as 1983 Convention bottle only dress colors are reversed and bottom is open as bell. Bottom label, only 500 made. **CMV $25.** Bells created and sold by Bud Hastin.

NAAC 1st CONVENTION BOTTLE RE-ISSUE 1982
Same as 1980 bottle only is 5 1/2" high to match rest of series in size. Only 1,775 reissue bottles made. Reissued bottles sold in 1982. Cork in bottom. **CMV $25.** 150 club sample bottles were made & marked in the bottom of the 5 1/2" size. **CMV $50.**
4th NAAC CONVENTION BELL 1980
(Left) 5 1/2" high porcelain bell same as bottle only dress colors reversed. Issued in 1984. Only 500 made by Bud Hastin. **CMV $25.**
6th NAAC CONVENTION BOTTLE & BELL 1985
(Right) Seattle, WA. Avon Convention. 5 1/2" porcelain bottle. Pink dress with dark pink trim. 1,800 made. **CMV $25.**
NAAC CONVENTION BELL 1985
Is same as bottle only dress color reversed. Only 500 bells made & sold by Bud Hastin. **CMV $25.** 15 bells were painted same as convention bottle by mistake & came in bottle boxes. Some have no inside labels. Rare. **CMV $125.**

NAAC 3rd CONVENTION BOTTLE 1982
(Left) 3rd in a series of 1800s style dress. Blue dress, pink bag & hat rim, blond hair. 5 1/2" high porcelain. Only 2,205 bottles were made & sold to NAAC convention was held in Las Vegas, Nevada. **CMV $25. mint.** No club samples were made.
NAAC CONVENTION BELL 1982
(Right) 1st issue - only 500 bells made in the same shape as the 1982 convention bottles. Only the dress colors are reversed. Pink dress & blue trim. You had to attend the 11th Annual NAAC Convention in Las Vegas, June 22-27-1982 to get a bell. **CMV $35.**

NAAC 5th CONVENTION BOTTLE 1984
5 1/2" high porcelain bottle, bottom cork. Brown dress, yellow and black umbrella. 1,650 made. 5th in a series of 11 convention bottles to be sold thru NAAC clubs of the Avon ladies of the 1890s for NAAC Avon Collectors 13th Annual Convention in Kansas City, MO June 1984. **CMV $25.** 100 NAAC Club Samples made and marked Club Sample on bottom. 1 of 100. **CMV $50. club samples.**
3rd NAAC CONVENTION BELL 1984
Same as 1984 NAAC Convention bottle only dress & umbrella colors reversed & bottom is open as bell. Bottom label. Only 500 made for Kansas City, NAAC Convention. Bells created & sold by Bud Hastin. **CMV $25.**

NAAC PLATE 1983
9" porcelain plate of the 1946 Avon Lady on face. Only 1,125 made. Label on back. **CMV $35.**

NAAC BOARD MEMBER PLATE 1983
Same as regular issue only back has special label marked "NAAC Board Member Sample". Only 7 made with each board member's name on back. **CMV $100.00**

NAAC CONVENTION PLATE 1975
Only 250 made for 4th annual NAAC Convention, Anaheim, Calif. **CMV $25.**

NAAC 6 YEAR PLATE 1977
1886 Avon lady on plate. Made by AVON Products for the National Association of Avon Clubs. A beautiful china plate. Total of 5,000 were made with 1,500 gold rimmed, and numbered. **CMV $35. MB.** 3,500 were silver rimmed and not numbered. **CMV $30. 7 plates marked board member. CMV $100.00 MB.**

NAAC PLATE 1974
1st in an annual series of plates. Clear crystal thumb print plate with blue & red background. Only 790 plates were made. **CMV $40.** Factory sample plate had decal instead of painted logo. **CMV $100.00**

NAAC BOARD MEMBER PLATE 1974
Same as regular issue only have Board Member on plate. **CMV $100.00**

NAAC SAMPLE PLATE 1975
(Left) Sample plate never issued to general public. 84 were made and sent to each Avon Collectors Club in NAAC, numbered on the back. **CMV $50. each.**

2nd ANNUAL NAAC PLATE 1975
(Right) General issue plate Mr. & Mrs. McConnell founders of Avon in center, gold 2 inch band around edge. **CMV $35. MB.**

PLATE - NAAC BOARD MEMBER 1975
(Left) 2" wide gold edge marked board member. Only 7 were issued, This was a general issue plate. **CMV $100.**

PLATE - NAAC BOARD MEMBER 1975
(Right) White plate with small gold edge marked board member. **Only 7 were made.** This plate was never issued to public. **CMV $100.00 MB.**

3rd ANNUAL NAAC 5 YEAR AVON COLLECTORS PLATE 1976
9 3/8" porcelain plate showing the 1st 4 NAAC club bottles. 1755 were made. OSP $13.95. **CMV $35.**

NAAC PLATE 1984
Limited edition 9" porcelain plate 1956 Avon Lady. 8th in series. **CMV $35.**

NAAC PLATE 1985
9th in series. 9" plate of 1966 Avon Lady. Limited edition. **CMV $35.**

NAAC ROSE BOWL PLATE 1987
9" porcelain plate. 1st in a series of Avon Floats in the annual Rose Bowl Parade. Floats in the annual Rose Bowl Parade. Less than 2,000 made. No NAAC plate was made in 1986. **CMV $35.**

NAAC 7 YEAR PLATE 1978
Made by Avon Products for the National Association of Avon Clubs. A beautiful china plate with a decal of the 1906 Avon Sales Lady. Only 5,000 were made. 2,310 were gold rimmed plates. **CMV $35. MB.** 2,690 are silver rimmed plates. **CMV $35. MB. 7 made for board members. CMV $100.00 MB.** Rare issue plate with backward printing on back. **CMV $60. MB.**

NAAC PLATE 1926 AVON LADY 1981
Limited edition of 2,000. Gold rim. Marked on back. **CMV $35. MB.**
NAAC BOARD MEMBER PLATE 1981
Same plate as above only back is marked 1981 board member sample. **Only 7 were made this way for NAAC board of directors. CMV $100. MB.**

NAAC CUP PLATES 1984-86
Sold at Annual Avon Convention. 1st issue 1984 in Kansas City. Light yellow glass. 2nd issue 1985 - Seattle, Wa. Green glass. 3rd issue 1986 - Nashville, Tn. Red glass. All under 500 issued. **CMV $15. each.**

NAAC PLATE 1896 AVON LADY 1979
Limited edition of 5,000. Made by Avon Products exclusively for the NAAC. Came with gold edge & numbered back. **CMV $35 MB.** Silver edge and no number. **CMV $25 MB.** Sold only by NAAC clubs. **7 plates made - marked board members. CMV $100.00**

NAAC PLATE 1916 AVON LADY 1980
Limited edition of 4,000. Came with gold edge & number on the back. 2.060 made. **CMV $35. Or silver edge, 1,940 made & no number $35. MB.** Made by Avon Products exclusively for the NAAC. **7 plates made marked board members. CMV $100.00**

NAAC PLATE 1982
Only 2,000 made and numbered. 6th in a series of the 1936 Avon lady. **CMV $35.**

NAAC CONVENTION GOBLETS 1976-83
Different color goblet sold each year at NAAC Convention. 1st year, red, 1976, 276 made. **CMV $60.** 1977, blue, 560 made. **CMV $30.** 1978, smoke, 560 made. **CMV $20.** 1979, clear, 576 made. **CMV $15.** 1980, purple, 576 made. **CMV $15.** 1978-83 a special marked goblet given to each NAAC delegate. **CMV $25.** Less than 100 delegate goblets made each year. Special marked goblets were made for each 7 NAAC board members. **CMV for board member goblets $100. each year.** 1981 - 684 goblets made. **CMV $15.** 1982 - 700 made. **CMV $15.** 1983 - 322 made. **CMV $25. 1983 is last year goblets made.**

NAAC CONVENTION BANQUET MIRROR 1974

(Left) Yellow and black, mirror on back. Convention held in Kansas City, Mo. June 22, 1974. **CMV $15.**

NAAC CONVENTION BANQUET MIRROR 1975

(Right) Blue and black, mirror on back. Convention held in Anaheim, Calif. June 21, 1975. **CMV $10.** Both were given to each person attending the annual NAAC Avon Convention Banquet.

NAAC CONVENTION BANQUET MIRROR 1976

(Left) 5th annual Avon collectors convention mirror in white with blue letters. Held in Cincinnati, Ohio, June 25-27, 1976. Mirror on back. **CMV $10.**

NAAC CONVENTION BANQUET MIRROR 1977

(Right) 6th annual Avon collectors convention mirror in blue with yellow letters. Mirror on back. Hollywood, Florida, June, 1977. **CMV $10.**

NAAC NASHVILE CONVENTION MIRROR 1986

Only 400 made. Red buttons with white letters. Mirror back. 15th Annual. **CMV $10.**

NAAC CHICAGO CONVENTION MIRROR 1987

400 made. White button, red letters, blue design. Given at 16th NAAC Convention banquet. **CMV $10.**

NAAC CONVENTION MIRROR & BUTTON 1984-85

1984 - yellow - Kansas City, Mo. Convention. 1985 - green - Seattle, Wa. Convention. Both less than 350 issued. **CMV mirror $10. each. CMV buttons $3.**

NAAC CONVENTION BANQUET MIRROR 1983

Only 500 small mirrors for the 12th annual Avon Collectors Convention in Wilmington, De, 1983. **CMV $10.**

NAAC CONVENTION BANQUET MIRROR 1978

(Left) Purple with mirror on back. Given to over 500 who attended the Avon Collectors Convention Banquet in Houston, Texas, June 1978. **CMV $10.**

NAAC CONVENTION BANQUET MIRROR 1979

(Right) White & red, mirror on back. Given to over 500 people attending the annual Avon Collectors Convention Banquet in St. Louis, Mo, June 1979. **CMV $10.**

BUD HASTIN CLUB BOTTLE 1974

Issued by the Gold Coast Avon Club in honor of Mr. Bud Hastin for his contribution to the field of Avon collecting. 1st in an annual series. Only 2,340 bottles were made. Bottle is 8 1/2" high, white pants, maroon coat, black turtle neck shirt, black shoes. **Few were made with white shirt. Rare. CMV black shirt $25. CMV white shirt $75.**

NAAC CONVENTION BANQUET MIRROR 1980-82

Only 500 of each made for annual NAAC Convention Banquet. 1980 - Spokane, Washington, 1981 - Queen Mary, Long Beach, Ca. 1982. - Las Vegas, Nevada. **CMV $10. ea.**

NAAC CONVENTION MIRROR 1972

Only 300 made. given at banquet, also some were made with pins instead of mirrors. These were dealers badges. **CMV $25. each.**

NAAC KEY CHAIN 1983

Red & white with black pen insert. Given to Delaware convention attendees from Avon Products. Only 500 made. **CMV $5. each.**

PRESIDENTS GOLD SET 1980
Set of six different U.S. Presidents Bust, with antique brush gold finish. Only 250 sets made & issued by Bud Hastin Avon Club. OSP $70. set. **CMV $100. MB set.**

OSP MEANS ORIGINAL SELLING PRICE. CMV MEANS CURRENT MARKET VALUE.

AVON ENCYCLOPEDIA COVER SHEET REJECTS 1976
30,000 covers for the 1976 Avon Encyclopedia were printed with the word Encyclopedia spelled encyclapedia. The covers were never used but about 200 sheets were given to collectors with 4 covers and backs printed on a sheet. These sheets are rare. The rest of the covers were destroyed. **CMV $15. each sheet.**

AVON LADY MINI SET NO. 2 1977
1,265 sets of 11 miniature Avon ladies of the 1886-1900 period. Issued by the Bud Hastin National Avon Club (now called Avon Times) in 1977. Set came in special display box. Came with numbered registration certificate. Sold only to Bud Hastin's National Avon Club members. OSP $60. set. **CMV $125. MB.**

BICENTENNIAL MINI AVON LADY SET NO. 1 1976
10 exact replicas in 3" high miniature figurines of the larger NAAC Club bottles. Issued by the Bud Hastin National Avon Club (now called Avon Times). 1775 sets were made and came with a numbered registration certificate. OSP $60. for set of 10. **CMV $125.00 MB.**

CLINT GOLD COAST CLUB BOTTLE 1977
7-5/8" tall. Blue pants, shirt, jacket. Black shoes, brown hair. 1,264 made & numbered on the bottom. Came with registration card. 4th Annual Club bottle. **CMV $25.**

PRESIDENTS 1978
A set of 6 3" high bust figurines of the 1st five presidents of the United States, plus Lincoln. Only 1,050 sets made. Hand painted porcelain and came with a numbered registration card. Issued by and Sold only to members of the Bud Hastin National Avon Club, now called Avon Times. . OSP for set of 6 $40. **CMV $85.00 MB.**
PRESIDENTS ALL WHITE 1978
Same set as painted presidents above only all white porcelain. Only 150 sets made. OSP $40. **CMV $125.00 MB.**

MINI REDHEAD SET 1977

965 sets of Something Old - Something New made. Issued by Bud Hastin's National Avon Club with registration card. 3 1/2" high, 1886 Avon lady on left has green purse and red hair. 1975 Avon lady on right has red hair & Avon Calling is misspelled on base of figurine.Sold as set only. **CMV $25. set.**

BUD HASTIN NATIONAL AVON CLUB BOTTLE 1976

2nd issue. Hand painted porcelain made in the image of Mr. Dale Robinson, past director of National Association of Avon Clubs. 1,000 bottles made & numbered. **CMV $30.**

BUD HASTIN NATIONAL AVON CLUB BOTTLE 1974

1st issue club bottle by Bud Hastin Avon Club (now called Avon Times) is a 3-piece Avon Family Scene. 3 separate bottles showing the Man, Child & Woman Avon Collectors. 1,091 sets sold. Sold in sets only. **CMV $100.00**

MID AMERICA NAAC CONVENTION PLATE 1972

(Left) Clear glass with frosted lettering, 134 were made for the 1st annual NAAC Convention in Kansas City, Kansas, June 1972. This plate was not made until 1975. **CMV $20.**

CENTRAL VALLEY NAAC CONVENTION PLATE 1973

(Right) Clear glass, frosted lettering. 124 were made and sold for 2nd annual NAAC Convention at Sacramento, Calif. This plate was not made until 1975. **CMV $20.**

WORLD WIDE JO OLSEN AVON CLUB BOTTLE 1975

(Left) Light blue dress, black hair. 1,102 bottles sold. Made in the image of Jo Olsen for her contribution to Avon collecting. **CMV $25.**

GOLD COAST RON PRICE CLUB BOTTLE 1975

(Right) Green suit, brown hair and shoes. Holding book "Testing 1-2-3". 1,096 bottles sold. Made in the image of Mr. Ron Price for his contribution to the field of Avon collecting. Mr. Ron Price was a member of the Board of Directors of the NAAC. Mr. Price passed away in 1977. **CMV $25.**

AVON ENCYCLOPEDIA HARD BOUND COLLECTORS EDITION 1974-75

Only 1,000 special limited collectors editions were printed. Blue hard bound cover with gold stamped letters on front. Each is signed and numbered by Bud Hastin. **CMV $32.50 mint.**

AVON ENCYCLOPEDIA HARD BOUND 2nd COLLECTORS EDITION 1976-77

Only 500 special limited collectors editions were printed. Maroon hard bound cover with gold stamped letters on front. Each book is numbered and signed by Bud Hastin. **CMV $30. mint. 6 hard bounds were found with all pages upside down. Each was signed by Bud Hastin as 1 of 6 rare upside down books. Very rare. CMV $40.**

AVON ENCYCLOPEDIA HARD BOUND 3rd COLLECTORS EDITION 1979

Only 350 special limited hard bound covers with gold letters on front. Each book was signed and numbered by Bud Hastin.**CMV $30.**

NAAC CONVENTION DELEGATE PLATE 1977

White china plate with the date & place of 6 NAAC Annual Conventions. Given to each NAAC Club delegate attending the convention "85 plates". **CMV $25.** 7 board member plates were made the same only marked Board Member. **CMV $100.**

GOLD COAST MINIS 1976

A set of 3 miniature figurines 3 1/2" high in the image of Bud Hastin, Jo Olsen and Ron Price. 914 sets were sold. **CMV $30. per set.**

NAAC AVON CLUB BOTTLES

NAAC CONVENTION PLATES 1975-83
Made by Mid-America Avon Club as the official NAAC Convention souvenir plate each year. Very low issue on each. All are etched clear glass & signed by the artist.each. 1975 Orange County, CA - 1977 Hollywood, FL - 1978 Houston, TX - 1979 St. Louis, MO - 1980 Spokane, WA - 1981 Long Beach, CA - 1982 Las Vegas, NV - 1983 Wilmington, DE - **CMV $20. each.**

MID-AMERICAN NAAC CONVENTION PLATE 1974
(Left) Crystal plate with frosted inscription made in honor of the 3rd NAAC Convention by Mid-America Club. 225 were made.**CMV $20.**
QUEEN CITY NAAC CONVENTION PLATE 1976
(Right) Clear glass with frosted letters**CMV $20.**

BETSY ROSS MOLD 1976
(Left) Very rare steel mold given to Avon Collectors at 1976 NAAC Convention. Mold was cut into 5 pieces. Must have a letter from Avon Products stating it is 1 of a kind. **CMV $300.00 with letter.**
ANNIVERSARY KEEPSAKE MOLD BASE 1976
(Right) Steel base of Avons anniversary keepsake mold given to National Association of Avon Clubs by Avon Products and auctioned off to Avon collectors. The numbers (17) and 5,215 on bottom. **CMV $300.00**

CALIFORNIA PERFUME ANNIVERSARY KEEPSAKE MOLD 1975
This is the actual steel mold Avon used to make the 1975 Anniversary bottle. Mr. Art Goodwin from Avon Products, Inc. New York presented this mold cut into 5 separate pieces to the National Association of Avon Clubs at the 4th annual NAAC Convention banquet at Anaheim, Calif. June 19, 1975. The mold was auctioned off bringing several hudreds of dollars on each piece. This is the 1st time an Avon mold has been destroyed & given to the general public. Very rare. **CMV $300. each piece.**

ST. LOUIE BLUE PERFUME 1979
Small glass bottle, white cap. Special perfume made & given by Mid-America Avon Club & NAAC at NAAC Convention in St. Louis, June 1979. 231 bottles with registration card & envelope. **CMV $20. mint & about 120 bottles only given without envelope & card. CMV $10. BO.**

BETSY ROSS NAAC CONVENTION SOUVENIR 1976
Given by Avon Products to all collectors touring Avon plant in Springdale, Ohio, June 24, 1976. Special NAAC label on bottom. **CMV $17.50 with special label.**

THE KING II "FOR MEN" 1975
(Left) Special label reads "Souvenir, June 19, 1975 NAAC Tour Monrovia Avon Plant". Given to each male taking the Avon plant tour at NAAC Convention, Monrovia, California. Only 150 bottles have this label. **CMV $17.50.**
SKIP-A-ROPE "FOR LADIES" 1975
(Right) Same special label given to all ladies on same tour. **CMV $17.50.**

ALL ANNUAL NAAC NATIONAL CONVENTION MIRRORS FROM 1995 FORWARD HAVE A CMV OF $10.00 EACH. ALL ARE LOW ISSUE, LESS THEN 300.

NAAC CONVENTION MIRROR 1988-89-90
88 - San Diego, CA
89 - Indianapolis, IN
90 - Canton, OH
CMV $10.00 each.

NAAC AVON CHESS BOARD 1975-76
21 1/2" square plastic chess board made for the Avon chess pieces. Silver & brown checker top with black rim border & back. NAAC logo in center, silver over black. **105 were made for sample to each NAAC club with center gold logo over black. CMV Club Sample with center gold logo. $200.00 MB.** 1,500 are numbered & last 1,000 are not numbered on back. **Regular issue silver logo with number $100.00. MB., Black border no number $65. MB. Also came Brown border with large black logo in center. CMV $50. MB.** Last one to be issued had brown border & small logos in center, brown back. **CMV $50.**
NAAC BOARD MEMBER CHEST BOARD
7 chess boards were made with White Boarder. **CMV $300.00 ea.**

NAAC COLLECTABLES PLAYING CARDS 1978
CMV $4.
CONVENTION TRAY 1984
Glass tray given by Avon Products to NAAC Convention. Marked "Avon Welcomes NAAC to Kansas City, Mo. Convention, June 19-24, 1984". **CMV $10.**
CONVENTION CARD HOLDER 1985
Brass business card holder given by Avon Products to NAAC Convention in Seattle, Washington, marked "Avon Welcomes NAAC Convention, July 1-7, 1985. **CMV $10.**
NAAC CHRISTMAS ORNAMENT 1985
1st in series. Clear glass center, brass chain rim. Marked "NAAC 1985". **CMV $10.**

CONVENTION DELEGATES RIBBON 1973
(Left) Red ribbon with a red rosette was given to all delegates. Gold printing reads "Official Delegate National Association Avon Clubs Convention Sacramento, California, June 22, 1973". **CMV $8.**
CONVENTION BOARD MEMBER RIBBON 1973
(Not Shown) Same as the delegate ribbon only in blue instead of red. Board Member replaced the Official Delegate on the ribbon. **CMV $15.**
CONVENTION NATIONAL CHAIRMAN RIBBON 1973
(Right) Same as the Delegate ribbon only in maroon instead of red. Only one of these ribbons was made. It is owned by Mr. Bud Hastin. No value established.
NAAC CONVENTION SOUVENIR BADGE 1972
(Center) Round, light blue background with first CPC Lady in center. Has pin back. **CMV $10.**
NOTE: Each ribbon & badge above was issued each year in a different color with the city & date from 1971 up to present date. All have same CMV as shown.

NAAC CONVENTION MIRROR 1994
Rochester, N.Y., June 19-26, 1994. 23rd Annual Avon Collector Convention on Front , mirror on back. Less than 300 made. **CMV $10.**

QUICK REFERENCE INDEX

AN AID TO FINDING CATEGORIES QUICKLY

ALL OTHER SECTIONS OF BOOK
IN ALPHABETICAL ORDER

᳊ THE "QUICK REFERENCE INDEX" COVERS THE HEADINGS OR CATAGORIES ON EACH SECTION OF THIS BOOK.

THE "GENERAL INDEX" COVERS THE REST OF THE BOOK BY ITEM NAME WITH THE EXCEPTION OF AWARDS.

᳊ THE "AWARDS INDEX" BEGINS ON PAGE 489 AND COVERS "MRS ALBEE & AVON LADY DOLLS", "AWARDS & REPRESENTATIVES GIFTS".

General Index

GENERAL INDEX

GENERAL INDEX

BEST PLACE TO SELL OR BUY AVON COLLECTIBLES

IF YOU ARE LOOKING FOR THE BEST PLACE TO BUY OR SELL AVON COLLECTIBLES, I CAN ONLY RECOMMEND 4 AVENUES THAT GET RESULTS.

AVON TIMES
PO BOX 9868
KANSAS CITY, MO. 64134
PHONE 816-537-8223 9 TO 5 WEEKDAYS CENTRAL TIME ZONE.

AVON TIMES SINCE 1971 HAS PROVEN TO BE THE #1 PLACE TO ADVERTISE AVON COLLECTIBLES. THE PRICE IS LOW AND THEIR MONTHLY NEWS PAPER GOES DIRECT TO ALL THE HARD CORE AVON COLLECTORS IN THE U.S. AND CANADA. WHY WASTE YOUR TIME PAYING HIGH PRICES FOR LOCAL NEWSPAPER ADS THAT USUALLY GET POOR RESULTS. AVON TIMES WILL LET YOU ADVERTISE FREE TO BUY ANY AVON COLLECTIBLE. ALL OTHER ADS ARE ONLY 15c PER WORD. OR BETTER YET SEND $24.00 FOR A YEARS SUBSCRIPTION AND GET 3 FREE ADS. $26.00 IN CANADA. US. FUNDS ONLY.

(NOTE) BUD HASTIN DOES NOT OWN AVON TIMES, THEY ONLY SHARE THE SAME PO BOX IN KANSAS CITY. PLEASE KEEP ALL ORDERS FOR BUDS BOOKS AND AVON TIMES SEPARATED. YOU CAN SEND THEM IN THE SAME ENVELOPE TO SAVE POSTAGE.

IF YOU ARE ON THE INTERNET YOU CAN TYPE IN (AVON COLLECTING) ON MOST SEARCH ENGINES AND FIND SEVERAL SPOTS ON AVON COLLECTING. A GOOD ONE IS **WWW.ANGELFIRE.COM/BIZ/TYPIST/AVON1.HTML**
THIS IS A EXCELLENT SITE RUN BY RHONDA SCHRIVER. HER E-MAIL ADDRESS IS alkmom@msn.com

IF YOU HAVE A LARGE COLLECTION AND YOU DON'T HAVE TIME OR WANT TO MESS WITH SELLING IT. CONTACT YOUR TAX ADVISOR FOR INFORMATION ON **DONATING IT TO A CHARITY AND DEDUCT THE GIFT ON YOUR INCOME TAX.** YOU WILL NEED MY CURRENT AVON COLLECTORS ENCYCLOPEDIA TO VERIFY THE CURRENT MARKET VALUE AND MAKE A COMPLETE LIST AND GET A RECEIPT FROM THE CHARITY YOU GIVE IT TO. **REMEMBER, YOU MUST FIRST ASK YOUR TAX ADVISOR FOR YOUR OWN PERSONAL SITUATION.**

IF YOU WANT TO JOIN A LOCAL AVON CLUB NEAR YOU OR START A LOCAL AVON CLUB, CONTACT CONNIE CLARK, PRESIDENT OF THE NATIONAL ASSOCIATION AVON COLLECTORS,(NAAC) PO BOX, 7006, KANSAS CITY, MO. 64113. SEND A SASE FOR A ANSWER. THIS IS A NON PROFIT ORGANIZATION.

Awards Index

Awards Index

Awards Index

Awards Index

Awards Index

CONTRIBUTORS

THIS BOOK WAS A MAJOR JOB FOR ME. NEEDLESS TO SAY, NOBODY CAN UNDERTAKE A JOB THIS SIZE WITHOUT INPUT FROM OTHERS IN THE FIELD. I PERSONALLY WANT TO THANK NOT ONLY THE PEOPLE LISTED BELOW, BUT ALL THE PEOPLE WHO HAVE CONTRIBUTED TO THIS BOOK OVER THE LAST 29 YEARS.

SANDRA HASTIN, MY WIFE. CUT THE BACKGROUND OFF ALL THE PICTURES. TYPED NAME LIST FOR MAILING LIST.

DWIGHT & VERA YOUNG, KANSAS CITY, MO. PRICING & ADVISOR THROUGHOUT THE ENTIRE BOOK. ALWAYS MY #1 ADVISORS WHO'S HELP AND FRIEND SHIP I VALUE VERY MUCH.

CONNIE DARES, AVON MANAGER AND **VIRGIE HODGES** AVON REP WHO IS OVER 80 YEARS OLD AND STILL SELLING AVON. BOTH WHO SUPPLY ME WITH AVON BROCHURES FOR RESEARCH & ADVISORS. **FT. LAUDERDALE, FL.**

JUNE HERDT, OAKLEY, KS. ADVISOR.

GEORGE GASPAR, JOLIET, ILL. ADVISOR, ALWAYS A BIG HELP TO ANYONE IN AVON COLLECTING.

GRACE POWERS, ATLANTA, GA. AVON REP. & ADVISOR.

WANDA LLOYD, ST. LOUIS, MO. ADVISER

BRUNO VECELLIO, PINE CITY, NY. ADVISOR

A SPECIAL THANKS GOES TO AVON PRODUCTS INC. FOR ALL THE LITERATURE THEY HAVE PRINTED SINCE 1886, WHERE MOST OF ALL THE DATES AND PRICES CAME FROM SINCE MY FIRST BOOK ON AVON COLLECTING IN 1969.

MY BIGGEST THANK YOU GOES TO CHRISTIE PECK, WHO HAD THE PATIENCE TO TEACH ME QUARK XPRESS WHICH IS THE SOFTWARE PROGRAM THIS BOOK WAS FORMATTED IN USING POWER MACINTOSH COMPUTER. CHRISTIE, THANK YOU FOR HELPING ME OUT NO MATTER WHAT TIME OF DAY OR NIGHT I CALLED YOU FOR HELP SEVEN DAYS A WEEK.

I PERSONALLY SPENT OVER 1400 HOURS WORKING ON THIS BOOK ENTERING ALL THE INFORMATION AND CHANGES INTO THE COMPUTER OVER A PERIOD OF 7 MONTHS. ANOTHER 840 MAN HOURS WERE SPENT BY A TEAM OF 3 PEOPLE SCANNING EVERY PICTURE (5600) INTO THE COMPUTER. I HOPE YOU FIND THIS 100% NEW BOOK, WORTH THE TIME AND EXPENSE TO MAKE THIS THE BEST BOOK ON AVON COLLECTING I HAVE EVER PUT MY NAME ON. THANK YOU, THE AVON COLLECTORS AND AVON REPRESENTATIVES, FOR YOUR SUPPORT FOR THE LAST 29 YEARS. THE FIRST PRINTING OF THIS 15TH EDITION MAKES 763,000 BOOKS I HAVE SOLD ON AVON COLLECTING.

SINCERELY,

BUD HASTIN, AUTHOR, PUBLISHER

Aunt Nell's Bathroom Jokes
and Funny Short Stories
"Laugh More & Live Longer"

Aunt Nelle Gumm is my wife's Great Aunt who lives in a senior citizens home in california. She is 86 years young. She is always calling us and telling some very funny jokes. She never learned to drive so she rides the local bus to go shopping, etc. She has stayed in touch with people. Something the rest of us can't say we have always done. Aunt Nell is the most likeable person you will ever meet. She never has a bad word to say about anybody. She only passes on her good nature and good cheer. Many people have sent her jokes in return with her sharing her jokes. In short, she just likes to make people laugh and keep them in a good mood. Aunt Nells slogan is "Laugh More & Live Longer."

Aunt Nell says If you want to lose weight, just read my jokes and you will laugh your butt off. And she adds that a smaller butt is what a lot of us would love to have. She says lots of laughter is the secret to a long and healthy life.

Many of Aunt Nells jokes are "G" rated to a little spicy. (Warning) She takes the jokes as she gets them and some of them are for "Adults Only". They are combined into the same book. Her jokes she has gathered are just that, "Jokes" and not ment to offend any one. As she says, If we can't laugh at ourselves, we would be a miserable bunch of people.

Aunt Nells first joke book (Volume 1) will be 160 pages. Small enough to take anywhere to share the humor. You will be the life of the party. This book is only available from Bud Hastin. It will not be sold in book stores at this time. (All type in this book is this size,) so our seniors can read it better.
This very funny Joke Book makes a great gift for Birthdays, Christmas, Father or Mothers day or just to say here is some humor to make your days brighter. DON'T FORGET YOUR LOVED ONES IN NURSEING HOMES. THEY NEED LAUGHTER IN THEIR LIVES.

- -

ORDER FROM;--- BUD HASTIN, PO BOX 9868, Kansas City, Mo. 64134
PLEASE PRINT

(NAME) _____

(ADDRESS)_____

(CITY)_____(STATE)_____(ZIP)_____

PLEASE SEND ME_____AUNT NELLS JOKE BOOKS I have enclosed Money Order _____Personal check _____

Book Cost
1 book $8.95 P.P., 2 books $16.00 P.P., 3 books $22.00 P.P., 4 books $27.00 P.P., 5 books $31.00 P.P., 6 books $35.00 P.P., 7 books $39. P.P., 8 books $45.00 P.P., 9 books $48.00 P.P., 10 books & up $5.00 each post paid. Contact Bud Hastin for large volume price.**Dealers invited to sell this book. This book is sure to entertain at a price all can afford. ALL AVON & JOKE BOOKS SHIPPED FROM Kansas City, Mo.**

15th Edition
AVON & CPC *Collector's Encyclopedia* <u>ORDER FORM</u>

All books sent FOURTH CLASS MAIL. Allow 3 weeks for delivery. Order Avon books only from Bud Hastin at his Kansas City, Mo. Address. No Avon Books are shipped from his Florida Home address.

Money Orders, Your order is filled immediatley. Personal Checks - Order is held till check has cleared your bank.

<u>All Avon book orders of 10 or more are shipped in boxes of 10 books. All orders over 10 are shipped in 2 or more boxes.</u>

- -

<u>DO NOT MIX ORDERS WITH AVON TIMES.</u>

<u>BUD HASTIN DOES NOT OWN AVON TIMES. THEY ONLY SHARE THE SAME PO BOX 9868, IN KANSAS CITY, MO. MAKE ALL CHECKS FOR AVON OR JOKE BOOKS PAYABLE TO BUD HASTIN.</u>

- -

Sorry - No COD's. No Credit Cards Accepted

Volume Discount Price U.S. ONLY	
BOOK COST	Postage & Handling
1-3 $24.95 ea. +P&H	1 Book $4.25
4-6 $20.00 ea. +P&H	2 Books $6.75
7-9 $18.00 ea. +P&H	3 Books $8.50
10 & up $16. ea +P&H	**Each Additional Book**
add .75c up to 10 books for P & H. Start over for each 10 books.	

U.S.A.	Canada
Book $24.95	Book $24.95
P&H 4.25	P&H 4.50
Total price $29.20	Total Price $29.45
U.S. Funds-Money Orders Only From Canada	

Please Send Me_____15th Edition Avon Books. I have enclosed Money Order_____
Personal Check_____Area Code/Phone number_____

Please Print (NAME)_____

(ADDRESS) _____

(CITY) _____ (STATE)_____ (Zip)_____

Give a new Avon Book to your Avon Rep for a gift. Don't forget your collector friends. Tell Your local library about this all new book.

ORDER FROM

**BUD HASTIN
P.O. Box 9868
Kansas City, MO 64134**

Phone 816-537-8223 10am to 4pm central time zone.

Aunt Nell's Bathroom Jokes
and Funny Short Stories
"Laugh More & Live Longer"

Aunt Nelle Gumm is my wife's Great Aunt who lives in a senior citizans home in california. She is 86 years young. She is always calling us and telling some very funny jokes. She never learned to drive so she rides the local bus to go shopping, etc. She has stayed in touch with people. Something the rest of us can't say we have always done. Aunt Nell is the most likeable person you will ever meet. She never has a bad word to say about anybody. She only passes on her good nature and good cheer. Many people have sent her jokes in return with her sharing her jokes. In short, she just likes to make people laugh and keep them in a good mood. Aunt Nells slogan is "Laugh More & Live Longer."

Aunt Nell says If you want to lose weight, just read my jokes and you will laugh your butt off. And she adds that a smaller butt is what a lot of us would love to have. She says lots of laughter is the secret to a long and healthy life.

Many of Aunt Nells jokes are "G" rated to a little spicy. (Warning) She takes the jokes as she gets them and some of them are for "Adults Only." They are combined into the same book. Her jokes she has gathered are just that, "Jokes" and not ment to offend any one. As she says, If we can't laugh at ourselves, we would be a miserable bunch of people.

Aunt Nells first joke book (Volume 1) will be 160 pages. Small enough to take anywhere to share the humor. You will be the life of the party. This book is only available from Bud Hastin. It will not be sold in book stores at this time. (All type in this book is this size.) so our seniors can read it better.

This very funny Joke Book makes a great gift for Birthdays, Christmas, Father or Mothers day or just to say here is some humor to make your days brighter. DON'T FORGET YOUR LOVED ONES IN NURSEING HOMES. THEY NEED LAUGHTER IN THEIR LIVES.

- -

ORDER FROM;--- BUD HASTIN, PO BOX 9868, Kansas City, Mo. 64134
PLEASE PRINT

(NAME) _____

(ADDRESS)_____

(CITY)_____(STATE)_____(ZIP)_____

PLEASE SEND ME _____ AUNT NELLS JOKE BOOKS I have enclosed Money
Order _____Personal check _____

Book Cost
1 book $8.95 P.P., 2 books $16.00 P.P., 3 books $22.00 P.P., 4 books $27.00 P.P., 5 books $31.00 P.P., 6 books $35.00 P.P., 7 books $39. P.P., 8 books $45.00 P.P., 9 books $48.00 P.P., 10 books & up $5.00 each post paid. Contact Bud Hastin for large volume price. **Dealers invited to sell this book. This book is sure to entertain at a price all can afford. ALL AVON & JOKE BOOKS SHIPPED FROM Kansas City, Mo.**

15th Edition
AVON & CPC *Collector's Encyclopedia* ORDER FORM

All books sent FOURTH CLASS MAIL. Allow 3 weeks for delivery. Order Avon books only from Bud Hastin at his Kansas City, Mo. Address. No Avon Books are shipped from his Florida Home address.

Money Orders, Your order is filled immediatley. Personal Checks - Order is held till check has cleared your bank.

All Avon book orders of 10 or more are shipped in boxes of 10 books. All orders over 10 are shipped in 2 or more boxes.

- -

DO NOT MIX ORDERS WITH AVON TIMES.

BUD HASTIN DOES NOT OWN AVON TIMES. THEY ONLY SHARE THE SAME PO BOX 9868, IN KANSAS CITY, MO. MAKE ALL CHECKS FOR AVON OR JOKE BOOKS PAYABLE TO BUD HASTIN.

- -

Sorry - No COD's. No Credit Cards Accepted

Volume Discount Price U.S. ONLY		
BOOK COST	**Postage & Handling**	
1-3 $24.95 ea. +P&H	1 Book	$4.25
4-6 $20.00 ea. +P&H	2 Books	$6.75
7-9 $18.00 ea. +P&H	3 Books	$8.50
10 & up $16. ea +P&H	Each Additional Book	
add .75c up to 10 books for P & H. Start over for each 10 books.		

U.S.A.		Canada	
Book	$24.95	Book	$24.95
P&H	4.25	P&H	4.50
Total price $29.20		Total Price $29.45	

U.S. Funds-Money Orders Only From Canada

Please Send Me_____15th Edition Avon Books. I have enclosed Money Order_____

Personal Check_____Area Code/Phone number_____

Please Print (NAME)_____

(ADDRESS) _____

(CITY) _____ (STATE)_____ (Zip)_____

Give a new Avon Book to your Avon Rep for a gift. Don't forget your collector friends. Tell Your local library about this all new book.

ORDER FROM

**BUD HASTIN
P.O. Box 9868
Kansas City, MO 64134**

Phone 816-537-8223 10am to 4pm central time zone.

Aunt Nell's Bathroom Jokes
and Funny Short Stories
"Laugh More & Live Longer"

Aunt Nelle Gumm is my wife's Great Aunt who lives in a senior citizens home in california. She is 86 years young. She is always calling us and telling some very funny jokes. She never learned to drive so she rides the local bus to go shopping, etc. She has stayed in touch with people. Something the rest of us can't say we have always done. Aunt Nell is the most likeable person you will ever meet. She never has a bad word to say about anybody. She only passes on her good nature and good cheer. Many people have sent her jokes in return with her sharing her jokes. In short, she just likes to make people laugh and keep them in a good mood. Aunt Nells slogan is "Laugh More & Live Longer."

Aunt Nell says If you want to lose weight, just read my jokes and you will laugh your butt off. And she adds that a smaller butt is what a lot of us would love to have. She says lots of laughter is the secret to a long and healthy life.

Many of Aunt Nells jokes are "G" rated to a little spicy. (Warning) She takes the jokes as she gets them and some of them are for "Adults Only." They are combined into the same book. Her jokes she has gathered are just that, "Jokes" and not ment to offend any one. As she says, If we can't laugh at ourselves, we would be a miserable bunch of people.

Aunt Nells first joke book (Volume 1) will be 160 pages. Small enough to take anywhere to share the humor. You will be the life of the party. This book is only available from Bud Hastin. It will not be sold in book stores at this time. (All type in this book is this size.) so our seniors can read it better.

This very funny Joke Book makes a great gift for Birthdays, Christmas, Father or Mothers day or just to say here is some humor to make your days brighter. DON'T FORGET YOUR LOVED ONES IN NURSEING HOMES. THEY NEED LAUGHTER IN THEIR LIVES.

- -

ORDER FROM;--- BUD HASTIN, PO BOX 9868, Kansas City, Mo. 64134
PLEASE PRINT

(NAME) _____

(ADDRESS)_____

(CITY)_____(STATE)_____(ZIP)_____

PLEASE SEND ME _____ AUNT NELLS JOKE BOOKS I have enclosed Money
Order _____Personal check _____

Book Cost
1 book $8.95 P.P., 2 books $16.00 P.P., 3 books $22.00 P.P., 4 books $27.00 P.P., 5 books $31.00 P.P., 6 books $35.00 P.P., 7 books $39. P.P., 8 books $45.00 P.P., 9 books $48.00 P.P., 10 books & up $5.00 each post paid. Contact Bud Hastin for large volume price. **Dealers invited to sell this book. This book is sure to entertain at a price all can afford. ALL AVON & JOKE BOOKS SHIPPED FROM Kansas City, Mo.**

15th Edition
AVON & CPC *Collector's Encyclopedia* <u>ORDER FORM</u>

All books sent FOURTH CLASS MAIL. Allow 3 weeks for delivery. Order Avon books only from Bud
  Hastin at his Kansas City, Mo. Address. No Avon Books are shipped from his Florida Home address.
Money Orders, Your order is filled immediatley. Personal Checks - Order is held till check has cleared
  your bank.

<u>All Avon book orders of 10 or more are shipped in boxes of 10 books. All orders over 10 are shipped
  in 2 or more boxes.</u>

- -

DO NOT MIX ORDERS WITH AVON TIMES.

BUD HASTIN DOES NOT OWN AVON TIMES. THEY ONLY SHARE THE SAME PO BOX
  9868, IN KANSAS CITY, MO. <u>MAKE ALL CHECKS FOR AVON OR JOKE BOOKS
  PAYABLE TO BUD HASTIN.</u>

- -

Sorry - No COD's No Credit Cards Accepted

Volume Discount Price U.S. ONLY	
BOOK COST	Postage & Handling
1-3 $24.95 ea. +P&H	1 Book $4.25
4-6 $20.00 ea. +P&H	2 Books $6.75
7-9 $18.00 ea. +P&H	3 Books $8.50
10 & up $16. ea +P&H	Each Additional Book
add .75c up to 10 books for P & H. Start over for each 10 books.	

U.S.A.	Canada
Book $24.95	Book $24.95
P&H 4.25	P&H 4.50
Total price $29.20	Total Price $29.45
U.S. Funds-Money Orders Only From Canada	

Please Send Me_____15th Edition Avon Books. I have enclosed Money Order_____
Personal Check_____Area Code/Phone number_____

<u>**Please Print**</u> (NAME)_____

(ADDRESS) _____

(CITY) _____(STATE)_____(Zip)_____

Give a new Avon Book to your avon lady for a gift. Don't forget your collector friends. Tell Your local library about this all new book.	**<u>ORDER FROM</u>** **BUD HASTIN** **P.O. Box 9868** **Kansas City, MO 64134**

Phone 816-537-8223 10am to 4pm central time zone.

Aunt Nell's Bathroom Jokes
and Funny Short Stories
"Laugh More & Live Longer"

Aunt Nelle Gumm is my wife's Great Aunt who lives in a senior citizans home in california. She is 86 years young. She is always calling us and telling some very funny jokes. She never learned to drive so she rides the local bus to go shopping, etc. She has stayed in touch with people. Something the rest of us can't say we have always done. Aunt Nell is the most likeable person you will ever meet. She never has a bad word to say about anybody. She only passes on her good nature and good cheer. Many people have sent her jokes in return with her sharing her jokes. In short, she just likes to make people laugh and keep them in a good mood. Aunt Nells slogan is "Laugh More & Live Longer."

Aunt Nell says If you want to lose weight, just read my jokes and you will laugh your butt off. And she adds that a smaller butt is what a lot of us would love to have. She says lots of laughter is the secret to a long and healthy life.

Many of Aunt Nells jokes are "G" rated to a little spicy. (Warning) She takes the jokes as she gets them and some of them are for "Adults Only." They are combined into the same book. Her jokes she has gathered are just that, "Jokes" and not ment to offend any one. As she says, If we can't laugh at ourselves, we would be a miserable bunch of people.

Aunt Nells first joke book (Volume 1) will be 160 pages. Small enough to take anywhere to share the humor. You will be the life of the party. This book is only available from Bud Hastin. It will not be sold in book stores at this time. **(All type in this book is this size,)** so our seniors can read it better.

This very funny Joke Book makes a great gift for Birthdays, Christmas, Father or Mothers day or just to say here is some humor to make your days brighter. DON'T FORGET YOUR LOVED ONES IN NURSEING HOMES. THEY NEED LAUGHTER IN THEIR LIVES.

- -

ORDER FROM;--- BUD HASTIN, PO BOX 9868, Kansas City, Mo. 64134
PLEASE PRINT

(NAME) _____

(ADDRESS)_____

(CITY)_____(STATE)_____(ZIP)_____

PLEASE SEND ME _____ AUNT NELLS JOKE BOOKS I have enclosed Money

Order _____Personal check _____

Book Cost
1 book $8.95 P.P., 2 books $16.00 P.P., 3 books $22.00 P.P., 4 books $27.00 P.P., 5 books $31.00 P.P., 6 books $35.00 P.P., 7 books $39. P.P., 8 books $45.00 P.P., 9 books $48.00 P.P., 10 books & up $5.00 each post paid. Contact Bud Hastin for large volume price. **Dealers invited to sell this book. This book is sure to entertain at a price all can afford. ALL AVON & JOKE BOOKS SHIPPED FROM Kansas City, Mo.**

15th Edition
AVON & CPC *Collector's Encyclopedia* <u>ORDER FORM</u>

All books sent FOURTH CLASS MAIL. Allow 3 weeks for delivery. Order Avon books only from Bud Hastin at his Kansas City, Mo. Address. No Avon Books are shipped from his Florida Home address. Money Orders, Your order is filled immediatley. Personal Checks - Order is held till check has cleared your bank.

<u>All Avon book orders of 10 or more are shipped in boxes of 10 books. All orders over 10 are shipped in 2 or more boxes.</u>

DO NOT MIX ORDERS WITH AVON TIMES.

BUD HASTIN DOES NOT OWN AVON TIMES. THEY ONLY SHARE THE SAME PO BOX 9868, IN KANSAS CITY, MO. <u>MAKE ALL CHECKS FOR AVON OR JOKE BOOKS PAYABLE TO BUD HASTIN.</u>

Sorry - No COD's. No Credit Cards Accepted

Volume Discount Price U.S. ONLY	
BOOK COST	Postage & Handling
1-3 $24.95 ea. +P&H	1 Book $4.25
4-6 $20.00 ea. +P&H	2 Books $6.75
7-9 $18.00 ea. +P&H	3 Books $8.50
10 & up $16. ea +P&H	Each Additional Book
add .75c up to 10 books for P & H. Start over for each 10 books.	

U.S.A.	Canada
Book $24.95	Book $24.95
P&H 4.25	P&H 4.50
Total price $29.20	Total Price $29.45
U.S. Funds-Money Orders Only From Canada	

Please Send Me_____15th Edition Avon Books. I have enclosed Money Order_____
Personal Check_____Area Code/Phone number_____

<u>**Please Print**</u> (NAME)_____

(ADDRESS) _____

(CITY) _____(STATE)_____(Zip)_____

Give a new Avon Book to your avon lady for a gift. Don't forget your collector friends. Tell Your local library about this all new book.

ORDER FROM

BUD HASTIN
P.O. Box 9868
Kansas City, MO 64134

Phone 816-537-8223 10am to 4pm central time zone.

Aunt Nell's Bathroom Jokes and Funny Short Stories
"Laugh More & Live Longer"

Aunt Nelle Gumm is my wife's Great Aunt who lives in a senior citizens home in california. She is 86 years young. She is always calling us and telling some very funny jokes. She never learned to drive so she rides the local bus to go shopping, etc. She has stayed in touch with people. Something the rest of us can't say we have always done. Aunt Nell is the most likeable person you will ever meet. She never has a bad word to say about anybody. She only passes on her good nature and good cheer. Many people have sent her jokes in return with her sharing her jokes. In short, she just likes to make people laugh and keep them in a good mood. Aunt Nells slogan is "Laugh More & Live Longer."

Aunt Nell says If you want to lose weight, just read my jokes and you will laugh your butt off. And she adds that a smaller butt is what a lot of us would love to have. She says lots of laughter is the secret to a long and healthy life.

Many of Aunt Nells jokes are "G" rated to a little spicy. (Warning) She takes the jokes as she gets them and some of them are for "Adults Only." They are combined into the same book. Her jokes she has gathered are just that, "Jokes" and not ment to offend any one. As she says, If we can't laugh at ourselves, we would be a miserable bunch of people.

Aunt Nells first joke book (Volume 1) will be 160 pages. Small enough to take anywhere to share the humor. You will be the life of the party. This book is only available from Bud Hastin. It will not be sold in book stores at this time. (All type in this book is this size,) so our seniors can read it better.

This very funny Joke Book makes a great gift for Birthdays, Christmas, Father or Mothers day or just to say here is some humor to make your days brighter. DON'T FORGET YOUR LOVED ONES IN NURSEING HOMES. THEY NEED LAUGHTER IN THEIR LIVES.

- -

ORDER FROM;--- BUD HASTIN, PO BOX 9868, Kansas City, Mo. 64134
PLEASE PRINT

(NAME) _____

(ADDRESS)_____

(CITY)_____(STATE)_____(ZIP)_____

PLEASE SEND ME _____ AUNT NELLS JOKE BOOKS I have enclosed Money
Order _____Personal check _____

Book Cost
1 book $8.95 P.P., 2 books $16.00 P.P., 3 books $22.00 P.P., 4 books $27.00 P.P., 5 books $31.00 P.P., 6 books $35.00 P.P., 7 books $39. P.P., 8 books $45.00 P.P., 9 books $48.00 P.P., 10 books & up $5.00 each post paid. Contact Bud Hastin for large volume price. **Dealers invited to sell this book. This book is sure to entertain at a price all can afford.**